EMPOWERMENT SERIES

HUMAN BEHAVIOR IN THE MACRO SOCIAL ENVIRONMENT

An Empowerment Approach to Understanding Communities, Organizations, and Groups

FIFTH EDITION

Karen K. Kirst-Ashman

University of Wisconsin – Whitewater Professor Emerita

Grafton H. Hull, Jr.

University of Utah – Professor Emeritus

Australia • Brazil • Mexico • Singapore • United Kingdom • United States

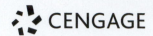

Human Behavior in the Macro Social Environment: An Empowerment Approach to Understanding Communities, Organizations, and Groups, **Fifth Edition**
Karen K. Kirst-Ashman and Grafton H. Hull, Jr.

Product Director: Marta Lee-Perriard

Product Manager: Julie Martinez

Content Developer: Alexander Hancock

Product Assistant: Allison Balchunas

Marketing Manager: Zina Craft

Photo and Text Researcher: Lumina Datamatics LTD.

Art Director: Vernon Boes

Production Management and Composition: MPS Limited

Text Designer: Lisa Delgado

Cover Designer: Lisa Delgado

Cover Image: Daniel Truta/EyeEm/ Getty Images

For product information and technology assistance, contact us at **Cengage Customer & Sales Support, 1-800-354-9706** or **support.cengage.com.**

For permission to use material from this text or product, submit all requests online at **www.cengage.com/permissions.**

Library of Congress Control Number: 2017962368

Student Edition:
ISBN: 978-1-305-38950-2
Loose-leaf Edition:
ISBN: 978-1-337-56858-6

Cengage
20 Channel Center Street
Boston, MA 02210
USA

Cengage is a leading provider of customized learning solutions with employees residing in nearly 40 different countries and sales in more than 125 countries around the world. Find your local representative at **www.cengage.com.**

Cengage products are represented in Canada by Nelson Education, Ltd.

To learn more about Cengage platforms and services, visit **www.cengage.com.** To register or access your online learning solution or purchase materials for your course, visit **www.cengagebrain.com.**

Printed in the United States of America
Print Number: 01   Print Year: 2018

To Susan and Jim Spielman, and Gary and Linda Kirst—with much love

To Patrick, Tatiana, Gregory, Ilsa, Marcus, and Michael Hull and Savannah

and Jonah Hurn, grandchildren all.

About the Authors

Karen K. Kirst-Ashman, BSW, MSSW, PhD, has been a full professor and was a former chairperson in the Social Work Department at the University of Wisconsin–Whitewater, where she taught for 28 years. She is certified as a Licensed Clinical Social Worker in the state of Wisconsin. She earned her BSW and MSSW at the University of Wisconsin–Madison, and her PhD in Social Work at the University of Illinois at Urbana–Champaign. She has worked as a practitioner and administrator in child welfare and mental health agencies. She received the University of Wisconsin–Whitewater's Excellence in Teaching Award in 1986 and the University Outstanding Teaching Award in 2007. She has been a member of the board of directors of the Council on Social Work Education (CSWE) in addition to being an accreditation site visitor. She is also a current member of CSWE, the Association of Baccalaureate Social Work Program Directors (BPD), and the National Association of Social Workers (NASW). She has served on the Editorial Board of *Affilia: Journal of Women and Social Work*, and as a consulting editor for many social work journals, including the *Journal of Social Work Education*. She is the author of numerous publications, articles, and reviews concerning social work and women's issues. Other books she has authored or coauthored include: *Introduction to Social Work and Social Welfare: Critical Thinking Perspectives* (5th ed.); *Understanding Human Behavior and the Social Environment* (10th ed.); *Understanding Generalist Practice* (8th ed.); *The Macro Skills Workbook* (2nd ed.); and *Generalist Practice with Organizations and Communities* (7th ed.).

Grafton H. Hull, Jr. BS, MSW, Ed. D. After graduating with his MSW for Florida State University, Dr. Hull worked at Central State Hospital in Milledgeville, Georgia, followed by two years as a captain in the U.S. Army, providing social work services to individuals, families, and groups at Fort Knox, Kentucky. Following military service, he served as foster care coordinator and later as foster care supervisor, and juvenile probation supervisor for Manitowoc County Department of Social Services in Wisconsin.

Dr. Hull has taught at Fort Knox Community College, Morningside College, the University of Wisconsin–Whitewater, the University of Wisconsin–Eau Claire, Missouri State University, Indiana University Northwest, and the University of Utah. He has been a faculty member, department chair, program director, director of a school of social work, and special assistant to the senior vice president for accreditation. He has taught BSW, MSW, and PhD courses in social work.

Professional activities include serving as president of the Association of Baccalaureate Social Work Program Directors (BPD); as site visitor, nominations committee member, accreditation commissioner, and board member of the Council on Social Work Education; and as president of the Wisconsin Council on Social Work Education and Missouri Consortium of Social Work Education Programs. He also served as a board member of the Indiana Association for Social Work Education, and the Institute for the Advancement of Social Work Research.

Dr. Hull has been a consultant to over 50 social work programs in the United States and Canada and has served as a member of the editorial board or consulting editor for the *Journal of Social Work Education*, *Journal of Baccalaureate Social Work*, *Journal of Teaching in Social Work, Advances in Social Work*, and *Areté*. He also served as editor-in-chief of the *Journal of Baccalaureate Social Work*.

His scholarship includes nine books in social work coauthored with esteemed colleagues, multiple book chapters, and more than two dozen publications in social work journals. He was a founder and principal in the Baccalaureate Educational Assessment Project (Now SWEAP). Dr. Hull's honors include the Mary Shields McPhee Memorial Award for Faculty Excellence in Research (Utah), Significant Lifetime Achievement Award (BPD), Social Work Educator of the Year (Wisconsin CSWE), President's Medal of Honor (BPD), and multiple certifications of appreciation and achievement for community and professional service. His biography is included in *Who's Who in America* and *Who's Who in the World*.

Brief Contents

Contents

6 Social Service Organizational Settings, Goals, and Environmental Contexts   169

10 Assessment of Geographic Communities and Empowerment   347

11 Neighborhood Empowerment 396

Preface

Focusing on empowerment and stressing critical thinking, this book explores human behavior in task groups, organizations, and communities. The intent is to provide a sound knowledge base for understanding how the macro social environment works and make it easier for students to apply theory in subsequent practice courses. Theories and major concepts concerning communities, organizations, and groups are explained. A strengths perspective, empowerment, and resiliency are underlying themes throughout the book. Applications of how macro systems operate and impact human behavior are examined. Critical thinking questions are posed throughout to stimulate students' understanding of content and exploration of issues. Professional ethics are accentuated throughout in *Focus on Ethics* segments. Human diversity is consistently emphasized and highlighted. Content reflects the Council on Social Work Education's (CSWE) 2015 Educational Policy and Accreditation Standards (EPAS) requirements for accreditation. A chapter on social justice and the global community stresses the need to advocate for social and economic justice and human rights at the international and global levels.

Numerous case examples are presented of how communities, organizations, and groups can enhance people's optimal health, well-being, and quality of life. These include how macro systems affect the lives and behavior of people of color, women, lesbian, gay, bisexual, transgender, and questioning (LGBTQ) people, people in spiritual communities, older adults, and people with intellectual and other developmental disabilities.

A major concern in social work education today is the strong tendency for students to veer away from thinking about how communities and organizations affect human behavior. Instead, students are frequently drawn to the perceived psychological drama and intensity of more clinically oriented practice with individuals, families, and treatment groups. This book relates content about the macro social environment directly to generalist social work practice. Applications of content to practice settings are integrated throughout. Students should clearly understand why a macro focus is a necessity in practice, in addition to their acquisition of micro and mezzo skills.

This book is especially written for undergraduate and graduate courses in human behavior and the social environment (HBSE) that incorporate content on communities, organizations, and task groups. It can be used independently to teach HBSE from a macro perspective, or in conjunction with other textbooks that include content on biological, social, cultural, psychological, and spiritual development throughout the life course. The intent here is to emphasize the dynamic interaction among systems in the macro social environment and provide breadth and depth of insight into the functioning of communities, organizations, and task groups.

A major thrust of this text is to present the material in a readable, interesting fashion. It uses numerous case applications and jargon-free language so that the reader can readily grasp theory and concepts. The three adjectives the author hopes best describe this text are *relevant*, *practical*, and *readable*. The macro social environment and the social forces acting upon it are clearly defined. Theory and major concepts are presented in a straightforward and thought-provoking manner. Applications to actual macro practice situations are emphasized throughout, as is the importance of client system empowerment. Concepts that students can readily understand, such as power, leadership, and interpersonal dynamics in macro settings, are stressed to enhance students' ability to grasp their relevance and practical significance.

In summary, the overall intent is to provide a dynamic, interesting, and relevant social work perspective on human behavior in the macro social environment. The authors strive to enhance students' understanding of social work values, develop their ability to empathize with people's situations and conditions in the macro environment, critically think about issues, and help them focus on the need for macro change in local, organizational, neighborhood, community, international (involving designated nations), and global (involving the entire world) contexts. Students should be able to relate these values and this knowledge to how social workers make assessments in real practice situations. They should have a glimpse into the vivid and fascinating macro environment in which social workers practice.

The Relationship between Content and EPAS Competencies and Practice Behaviors

It has been established that this book is oriented to following CSWE's Educational Policy and Accreditation Standards (EPAS).[1,2] The entire book addresses EPAS guidelines for content regarding human behavior and the social environment, as follows:

> *Educational Policy 6a, 7b, 8b, and 9b* each involve "applying knowledge of human behavior and the social environment, person-in-environment, and other multidisciplinary theoretical frameworks in interventions with clients and constituencies" to the steps in the planned change model of Engagement, Assessment, Intervention, and Evaluation and this book helps ensure that students have the requisite knowledge to demonstrate these competency components. Moreover, the EPAS notes that "social workers understand theories of human behavior and the social environment, and critically evaluate and apply this knowledge" throughout our work with all size systems.

The EPAS (2015) also requires that students demonstrate a wide range of competencies that encompass the ability to "demonstrate ethical and professional behavior, engage diversity and difference in practice, advance human rights and

---

[1]Please note that this content addresses standards posed in the EPAS. In no way does it claim to verify compliance with standards. Only the Council on Social Work Education Commission on Accreditation can make those determinations.

[2]Council on Social Work Education (CSWE). (2015). *Educational policy and accreditation standards (EPAS)*. Alexandria, VA: Author.

social, economic, and environmental justice, engage in practice-informed research and research-informed practice, engage in policy practice," and engage, assess, intervene, and evaluate their practice with individuals, families, groups, organizations, and communities. Content on all of these topics is presented in this text.

Altogether, the EPAS has identified 31 component behaviors that operationalize 9 core competencies, which are critical for professional practice. These competencies are reflected in the content just summarized. (See **http://www.cswe.org/** for access to the full EPAS document.) Accredited programs must demonstrate that they are teaching students to be proficient in these competencies and their associated component behaviors. Students require knowledge to develop skills and become competent. The intent here is to indicate what chapter content and knowledge coincides with the development of specific competencies and component behaviors. (This ultimately is intended to assist in a social work program's accreditation process.)

EP 1

To establish the linkage between EPAS competencies/component behaviors and chapter content, **"helping hands" icons** of two hands embracing a sun are located next to content throughout the book. Each icon is labeled with the competencies and component behaviors related to the content. For example, an icon might be labeled EP (Educational Policy) 1, which is the competency "Demonstrate ethical and professional behavior" (CSWE, 2015). (See the icon on the left-hand side of this paragraph.)

The EPAS document uses bullets to identify the component behaviors related to competencies. For clarity, we have alphabetized in lowercase the component behaviors under each competency to replace the bullets. For example, EP 2 has three bullets, and for convenience sake we have labeled them EP 2a, 2b, and 2c in this book. These bullets are considered collectively and have been alphabetized from EP 1a to EP 9d. Whenever we address the competencies and component behaviors, an appropriate icon will appear on the page.

For all icons, **Competency Notes** are provided at the end of each chapter. These Competency Notes, which follow the competencies' order in the EPAS, explain the relationship between chapter content and CSWE competencies and component behaviors. The notes also list page numbers where icons are located in the book, and this content is discussed.

A summary chart of the icons' locations in all chapters and their respective competencies and component behaviors is placed in the inside front covers of the book.

Changes and New Additions

The book continues to link content to EPAS competencies and component behaviors using the most recent CSWE 2015 Educational Policy and Accreditation Standards (EPAS). Overall, content has been updated to reflect changes at the national governmental level and key information on state and local actions affecting human behavior. Material on environmental justice has been added. Chapter openings have been changed by placing revised Learning Objectives at the beginning of the chapter. As needed, portions have been revised to increase clarity and provide additional examples of concepts. Callouts have been added in each chapter to identify content relevant to chapter learning objectives. Specific content has then been added in the following respective chapters:

Chapter 1

- Addition of brief case examples of typical situations social worker may encounter that reflect macro issues in human behavior

Chapter 2

- Addition of definition for environmental justice
- Addition of example of oppression from the 2016 presidential campaign

Chapter 3

- Addition of example of the importance of group cohesion from the 2016 presidential campaign
- Update of the usefulness of cognitive restructuring for specific problems

Chapter 4

- New example on how barriers to successful teamwork must be addressed
- Expanded list of characteristics of effective teams

Chapter 5

- Additional examples of proprietary or for-profit agencies
- Example of organizational culture becoming a problem

Chapter 6

- New examples of mission statements for social services agency
- More discussion of faith-based social services
- Discussion of NIMBY within the context of social service organizations in a community
- New definition of managed care
- Comparison of US health care system with those of other nations
- More discussion of managed care trends in the United States

Chapter 7

- Discussion and example of a climate of trust and openness issue
- Expanded list of worker's expectations for supervisors
- Discussion of environmental justice in a new Highlight

Chapter 8

- Additional material on the benefits of diversity in an organization
- Updated statistics on discrepancies in pay for women in the workplace
- New example of TQM in social services

Chapter 9

- New examples of potential community change activities for social workers
- New examples of situations with blurred boundaries within communities and the concept of sanctuary cities

- Additional perspectives on spirituality and spiritual communities
- Updated information on population characteristics and trends in rural areas

Chapter 10

- Additional examples of the power of youth
- New examples of using the Internet for social change
- Additional information on asset mapping and environmental influences on communities

Chapter 11

- Expanded list of empowerment activities that can be undertaken by neighborhood residents
- Examples of situations where neighborhood groups can assist other residents
- New examples of services provided by neighborhood centers in urban centers
- New examples of neighborhood community building projects

Chapter 12

- Additional examples of empowerment projects undertaken by racial and ethnic groups
- Example of intersectionality of race and religion in debate over immigration
- Discussion of Black Lives Matter and police violence
- Reorganization of chapter to first identify populations-at-risk and then discuss new empowerment examples
- More examples of current discrimination against LGBTQ community members
- Updated information on people with developmental disabilities and physical impairments

Chapter 13

- New examples of globalization and the interconnectedness of the world
- Examples of how actions in one country impact economic conditions in others
- Introduction of iatrogenic effects concept
- Discussion of definitions of poverty
- More discussion of immigration and immigration rates to the United States
- Discussion of sustainability in a global society

As was just described, "Helping Hands" icons are incorporated throughout the book that link content with EPAS competencies and component behaviors. "At a Glance" boxes are included periodically to summarize theories and other more complicated issues. Content has been thoroughly updated throughout and intermittently reorganized to enhance clarity.

Chapter Learning Objectives

Also note that each chapter in the book begins with learning objectives. These are reiterated at the end of each chapter with a summary of relevant content. Exam questions available in the supplementary resources are linked to the attainment of specific chapter learning objectives. The intent is to assist in demonstrating and articulating the acquisition of knowledge and attainment of competencies identified in accreditation standards.

Supplement Package

Note that the supplements include the Practice Behaviors Workbook, which contains dozens of classroom exercises related to the book's content. These exercises are intended to enhance students' knowledge base of human behavior in the macro social environment. Most of the exercise objectives are intended to comply with required competencies cited in the CSWE Educational Policy and Accreditation Standards (2015). (Please note that in no way do these exercises claim to *verify* compliance with EPAS standards. Only the Council on Social Work Education Commission on Accreditation can make those determinations.) Rather, the exercises are designed to help provide potential means of measuring various competencies related to human behavior and the social environment.

MindTap

MindTap®, a digital teaching and learning solution, helps students be more successful and confident in the course—and in their work with clients. MindTap guides students through the course by combining the complete textbook with interactive multimedia, activities, assessments, and learning tools. Readings and activities engage students in learning core concepts, practicing needed skills, reflecting on their attitudes and opinions, and applying what they learn. Videos of client sessions illustrate skills and concepts in action, while case studies ask students to make decisions and think critically about the types of situations they'll encounter on the job. Helper Studio activities put students in the role of the helper, allowing them to build and practice skills in a nonthreatening environment by responding via video to a virtual client. Instructors can rearrange and add content to personalize their MindTap course, and easily track students' progress with real-time analytics. And, MindTap integrates seamlessly with any learning management system.

Online Instructor's Manual and Test Bank

The online instructor's manual contains a variety of resources to aid instructors in preparing and presenting text material in a manner that meets their personal preferences and course needs. It presents chapter-by-chapter suggestions and resources to enhance and facilitate learning. The manual includes an introduction, chapter outlines/objectives, chapter strategies, supplementary readings, and a test bank featuring multiple-choice, matching, and essay questions.

PowerPoint® Slides

These vibrant Microsoft PowerPoint® lecture slides for each chapter assist you with your lecture by providing concept coverage using images, figures, and tables directly from the textbook!

Online Curriculum Quick Guide

The Instructor's Online Curriculum Quick Guide correlates the core text and accompanying Practice Behaviors Workbook to the EPAS 2015 requirements. The Quick Guide is designed to assist faculty and their social work departments in monitoring the implementation of the EPAS 2015 competencies and component behaviors. The Quick Guide details where in the text content is located on the 41 practice behaviors and provides a table that identifies where the Dynamic Case Exercises align with those practice behaviors.

Acknowledgments

Karen Kirst-Ashman wishes to express her heartfelt appreciation to Nick Ashman, who cooked for and supported her throughout the writing process. Special thanks and appreciation go to Susan Spielman, who carefully and conscientiously edited and significantly improved the content of this book.

Grafton H. Hull Jr. would like to thank his wife, Jannah Mather, for her support and patience in revising this edition of the text and to Dr. Dena Ned, University of Utah College of Social Work, for her helpful suggestions in Chapter 12. The authors also express special gratitude to Julie Martinez, product manager; Alexander Hancock, associate content developer; and Ali Balchunas, product assistant, for their creativity, enthusiastic help, and thoughtful support. Thanks also to Karen Thomson and Sandra Wenham, who did excellent work while assisting her. Many thanks to Rita Jaramillo, senior content project manager, for her careful oversight of the production process.

The author would also like to thank the following reviewers of the fifth edition of this book for their help and input.

Lorraine Marais
Hawaii Pacific University

Kelly Reath
East Tennessee State University

Karen Martin
Eastern Kentucky University

Pam Clary
Missouri Western State University

Dory Quinn
Pittsburg State University

1 | Introduction to Human Behavior in the Macro Social Environment

Social workers can address important social issues in the macro social environment.

LEARNING OBJECTIVES

After reading this chapter you should be able to...

1-1 Define and explain the macro social environment.

1-2 Describe the ecosystems theory as a useful conceptual framework for understanding the macro social environment, and discuss relevant concepts derived from systems theory and the ecological perspective.

1-3 Discuss people's involvement with multiple systems in the macro social environment.

1-4 Describe generalist practice and explain the relationship between some of its major concepts and the macro social environment.

1-5 Define critical thinking and discuss its use in generalist practice.

1-6 Discuss critical thinking questions that will be raised throughout the book.

1-7 Identify differences between historical approaches to social work practice in the macro social environment and contemporary macro practice.

A social worker employed by a large public social services department hears increasing numbers of complaints from clients about drug houses popping up in their residential neighborhoods. The worker identifies clients and other concerned citizens in the communities and organizes a community meeting. She then assists community residents in formulating a plan to band together, identify drug house locations, and establish a procedure to report such houses to the authorities.

- *The main tasks of a foster care unit are to assess potential foster parent applicants, monitor placement, and manage cases as they move in and out of foster care, and train foster parents in parenting and behavior management skills. The unit social workers hold biweekly meetings where they discuss how to improve agency service provision. The workers take turns organizing the meetings and running the discussions.*

- *A social worker employed by a neighborhood center determines that the professionals working with various adolescent clients within the community are not communicating with each other. For example, school social workers have no established procedure for conveying information to protective services workers, who in turn do not communicate readily with probation and parole workers. This is despite the fact that most of these professionals are working with many of the same clients. The neighborhood-center social worker decides to pull together representatives from the various involved agencies and establish more clearly defined communication channels.*

- *A social worker employed by a large private family-services agency specializes in international adoptions, especially those involving countries in the former Soviet Union. He discovers that many adoptive children are experiencing health problems resulting from early nutritional deprivation. The worker feels that the problem goes beyond one or two cases, and reflects a serious pattern. No referral process is in place to automatically assess adoptive children and refer them to needed resources, including designated medical specialists. The worker begins to establish a systematic process for assessment and referral.*

- *A school social worker notices that during the past two years, all of the students expelled from the school were African American when less than one-half of the school population is composed of African American students. She also notices a similar disproportionate pattern with other disciplinary actions meted out by the school system. He considers the most effective way of addressing this problem and eliminating what appears to be racial discrimination.*

- *A social worker at a public assistance agency is terribly troubled by the conditions of the agency's waiting room for clients and by the tedious process required for clients' intakes. She explores the issue, develops a proposed plan for improvement, and makes an appointment to speak with the agency's executive director about it.*

- *A local charitable funding organization decides to cut off its funding contribution to a Planned Parenthood agency that has three satellite clinics in addition to its larger, centrally located main clinic.[1] The result would be a severe*

---

[1] **Planned Parenthood** agencies assist people in making decisions about pregnancy and promote birth control and contraception.

cutback in services, including the closure of at least two of its satellite clinics. Many clients would find it difficult if not impossible to receive adequate services. A social work counselor at one of the clinics, with the support of her supervisor, gathers facts to support her argument that funding is necessary and arranges a meeting with the funding organization's leaders to discuss the cuts and try to persuade these leaders to change their minds.

- *A juvenile probation officer is distressed by a proposed legislative action to delete a vocational training program for juvenile offenders because of its expense. He talks to other workers and administrators in his state agency, and gathers facts and statistics that support the program's cost-effectiveness. He then begins calling and writing involved legislators and sets up a meeting with the chairperson of the legislative committee that recommended the program's deletion. Additionally, he contacts other concerned social workers and encourages them to participate in similar activities.*

- *A group of community residents approach a social worker about starting a Neighborhood Watch program.[2] The worker provides them with both encouragement and some information about how to go about it.*

- *The city is proposing to create a landfill within a few blocks of a low-income neighborhood, and the residents are concerned about the impact on their quality of life and the safety of their children. A social worker notes that the proposal is yet another example of poorer areas being further blighted by government and business decisions and decides to help the residents fight city hall.*

None of the vignettes just described involves direct service to clients. Yet, all are examples of social workers undertaking necessary activities as part of their daily role in providing effective service. Each scenario describes how social workers can help people within the context of larger macro environments, namely, organizations and communities. Generalist social work is much more than working with individual clients and families. It also is working in and with larger systems to pursue social, economic, and environmental justice.

People do not function in a void. They interact dynamically on many levels, assuming structured behavior patterns and having active involvement in various interpersonal relationships. Mary Beth is a sister, a mother, an aunt, a member of Mothers Against Drunk Driving (MADD), a Republican, a member of St. Mary and St. Antonious Coptic Orthodox Church, and a dentist, all at the same time. Understanding everything about human behavior, with all its complexity, is a vast task.

The Council on Social Work Education (CSWE) that accredits social work programs requires that students "apply knowledge of human behavior and the social environment, person-in-environment, and other multidisciplinary theoretical frameworks in interventions with clients and constituencies." This is an acknowledgment that people live in many social systems and that these systems can promote or block people from attaining and maintaining health and overall well-being.

---

[2] **Neighborhood Watch** programs involve neighborhood residents coming together and making a commitment to prevent crime in their neighborhood. They devise a system for observing any suspicious behavior, especially on the part of strangers, and for alerting the proper authorities in order to deter crime. Members also usually educate new people moving into the neighborhood about the program and publicize that the program exists via window decals and signs.

The intent is to provide a foundation so that social workers can practice and intervene with systems of all sizes. Thus, social workers must understand multiple theories and frameworks to assess individuals, groups, families, organizations, and communities.

Social workers practice *in agency organizational settings* to help clients *who live in communities*. The work environments of social work practitioners provide the structure and resources allowing them to help clients. A healthy organizational work environment permits social workers to function effectively and get things done for clients. An unhealthy work environment (e.g., one with few resources, poor morale, or policies not supportive of clients) interferes with social workers' performance and their potential to assist clients. Clients, in turn, live in communities that enjoy various degrees of prosperity and offer their citizens diverse levels of resources, support, and safety. Social workers must understand and negotiate the mazes of these macro environments in order to do their jobs effectively.

This book focuses on understanding human behavior in the *macro* social environment. How do communities, organizations, and groups serve as the background for human behavior? How do individuals and macro systems reciprocally influence each other? How do these organizations and communities operate to keep themselves and society going? What are the internal environments of communities, organizations, and the groups within them like? Exactly how and why do the answers to these questions affect how social workers can do their jobs?

Several terms reflect the meaning of *macro*, including large scale; affecting many people; emphasis on social, political, and economic forces; and a focus on community and organizations. In addition, we all live in a global community where actions occurring elsewhere can have profound implications across the world. For example, a war occurring in the Middle East forces people to become refugees because their homeland is destroyed by one or both sides in the dispute. These refugees become a challenge to the humanitarian values of other nations wanting to provide services, supplies, and a safe environment. If the other countries offer asylum or admittance to the refugees it will likely result in increased financial cost and may spark prejudice and discrimination within their own citizens. Failing to help creates a situation where more people are injured or killed trying to survive in refugee camps while the war further destroys the country.

Another example of how the global community produces challenges is through global warming. Most environmental scientists see global warming as a problem that is caused by, or contributed to, by human action. Protecting Earth from our continued influence on the environment is not just a problem for a specific portion of the planet, although poorer countries will be hurt the most. If predictions hold true, the rise of water levels from melting glaciers and related changes will result in communities across the globe being submerged under seawater. These include over 60 million residents of China, 20 million in India, 12 million in the United States, and 18 million in Japan (World Economic Forum, 2015). Other effects of global warming include droughts, more storms, rising temperatures, and an increase in wildfires, flooding, and landslides in unlikely places. Social workers must be aware of the kinds of difficulties that environmental issues can produce for the most vulnerable people, not just the clients we serve. We are all in the boat together.

It is social workers' responsibility to seek changes in the macro social environment that improve services, increase resources for clients and citizens, and change policies to implement improvements. This contrasts with a *micro* perspective, which emphasizes the actions and personal issues of individual clients. Micro practice skills focus on interventions with individuals that help them solve their problems. However, even individual problems may be caused or exacerbated by conditions in other systems such as the family, organization or community.

Communities, organizations, and the task groups functioning within them are important in understanding human behavior because they consist of individuals. Comprehending the nuances of behavior involves not only the psychological makeup of individuals and the interpersonal dynamics of intimate relationships, but also the interaction of these individuals with all the macro systems with which they're in contact.

In This Book

Note that "helping hands" icons are placed throughout the chapter to highlight information and skills important for attaining the nine core competencies and component behaviors designated by the CSWE Educational Policy and Accreditation Standards (EPAS). *Competencies* are basic capabilities involving social work knowledge, skills, and values that can be demonstrated and measured by component behaviors. Competencies reflect more general expectations for proficient social workers. *Component behaviors*, by contrast, are measurable actions that demonstrate the application of social work knowledge, skills, and values for effective social work practice. These behaviors are more specific and are used to operationalize and measure competency.

Students require knowledge to develop skills and become competent. The intent here is to specify what chapter content and knowledge coincides with the development of specific competencies and component behaviors. (This ultimately is intended to assist in a social work program's accreditation process.)

Throughout each chapter, icons call attention to the location of EPAS-related content. Each icon identifies what competency or component behavior is relevant by specifying the designated Educational Policy (EP) reference number beneath it. "Competency Notes" are provided at the end of each chapter that describe how EPAS competencies and component behaviors are related to designated content in the chapter. You might observe that the EPAS document lists component behaviors as bulleted items under each of the nine core competencies. To clarify the "competency notes" at the end of each chapter, the bulleted component behaviors have been alphabetized under each competency. Component behaviors are alphabetized both under the icons placed throughout the book and in the "competency notes" cited in each chapter.

The EPAS competencies and component behaviors are summarized in the inside cover of this book. The chart also indicates in which chapters icons for specific competencies and component behaviors are located throughout the book. In addition, the book includes several items designed to assist learning by providing examples, questions, scenarios, and summaries of materials. These include Highlights, At a Glance, Focus on Ethics, and Critical Thinking Questions.

What Is the Macro Social Environment? LO 1-1

EP 6a, 7b, 8b, 9b

The **social environment** is the sum total of social and cultural conditions, circumstances, and human interactions that encompass human beings. The *macro* social environment, for our purposes, is the configuration of communities, organizations, and groups within the latter that are products of social, economic, and political forces and social institutions. The following breaks down the definition of the macro social environment into various facets and explains what each means.

Communities

The macro social environment involves communities, organizations, and groups and how these systems affect people. A **community** is "a number of people who have something in common that connects them in some way and that distinguishes them from others" (Homan, 2016, p. 10). The concept of community with which you're probably most familiar involves geographic areas. People in geographic communities, of course, share the common variable of location. A geographic community has a huge impact on its residents' quality of life, accessible resources, available role models, and life opportunities. For example, consider the geographic community you come from. How has that community affected you, and how your life has progressed? How would you describe that community? Critical Thinking Questions 1-1 encourages you to think about the types of variables that characterize and differentiate geographical communities. (A subsequent section of this chapter will discuss the concept of critical thinking more thoroughly.)

In addition to geographic areas based on location, communities may also involve groups of people who have similar interests or who identify with each other. For example, people with degrees in social work who practice in the field are part of the professional social work community. There are communities involving scuba divers, hikers, bikers, Corvette clubs, Christmas ornament collectors, community theater groups, and any number of other groups of people who share something in common. Some communities are based on sexual orientation. Spiritual or religious communities include people who believe in the same doctrine and/or belong to the same religious denomination. Ethnic, racial, and cultural communities include people who have a similar background based on those variables. Later chapters discuss various aspects of communities, including theories, community empowerment, and neighborhood empowerment.

Organizations

Another facet of the macro social environment concerns organizations. Various organizations exist within the community context. **Organizations** are "(1) social entities that (2) are goal directed, (3) are designed as deliberately structured and coordinated activity systems, and (4) are linked to the external environment" (Daft, 2016, p. 13). In other words, organizations are structured groups of people who come together to work toward some mutual goal and perform established work activities that are divided among various units. Organizations have a clearly defined membership in terms of knowing who is in and who is out.

Think of the organizations around you. They all are clearly defined entities made up of people with structured roles that pursue designated purposes or goals.

**EP 1b,
7a, 8**

Critical Thinking Questions 1-1

How would you describe the geographic community you come from? Think about the following aspects (that represent only some of the variables characterizing such communities) (Kirst-Ashman & Hull, 2018):

- *Rural or urban setting*. Would you characterize your home community as being in the country, a small town, a medium-sized city, a major metropolis, or a suburb of a bigger city?

- *Population density*. How many people live in your community of origin? Would you describe the area as being spread out, crowded, or something between the two?

- *General standard of living*. How would you describe the social class of people living in the community? Poor? Middle class? Fairly well-to-do? Wealthy?

- *Housing*. What are the residents' homes like? Do most residents own their own property, or do they rent houses or apartments? How would you describe the quality of the homes? Older? Newer? Run down? Well kept? Are dwellings bunched together and cramped, or do homes have spacious yards? Does adequate affordable housing exist to meet community residents' needs?

- *Available resources*. To what extent are hospitals, parks, police and fire protection, garbage collection, and shopping readily available? Are there services and resources accessible for people in need, including shelters for battered women, crisis intervention hotlines, food pantries, counseling, and other social services?

- *Spiritual opportunities*. Are there churches and religious organizations in the community? How many? To what extent do community residents pursue spiritual involvement?

- *Education*. How would you characterize the educational system in your home community? Is it generally considered "good," "effective," "poor," or "substandard"? How does it compare with educational systems in neighboring communities? How would you describe the education you received there?

- *Other factors*. What other aspects of your home community are important to you, and why?

- *Summary impression*. When you think of your home community, what words first come to mind? How would you describe it to a complete stranger? What would you emphasize? Was it a generally happy, pleasant place? Or was it hostile, dangerous, and impoverished?

There are many examples of organizations. Businesses are organizations that have goals of production, or sales and profit. Each person working for the business has a structured role[3] and responsibilities (e.g., as employee, supervisor, or manager). The schools you attended are a type of organization aimed at providing young

---

[3] A *role* is a culturally expected behavior pattern for a person having a specified status or being involved in a designated social relationship.

people with education. Students, teachers, and administrators all had defined roles and expectations. Churches, mosques, and synagogues are organizations seeking to serve their members' spiritual needs. Your college or university is also a type of organization with the ultimate goal of providing you with an advanced education. Later chapters explore different facets of organizations and how they can operate to benefit or detract from clients', citizens', and employees' best interests, health, and well-being.

Organizations Providing Social Services   Especially relevant to social work are organizations that provide social services. **Social services** include the work that social work practitioners and other helping professionals perform in organizations for the benefit of clients. Goals include improving people's physical and mental health, enhancing their quality of life, increasing autonomy and independence, supporting and strengthening families, and helping people and larger systems improve their functioning in the macro social environment.

That is quite a mouthful. In essence, social services include the wide range of activities that social workers perform in their goal of helping people solve problems and improve their personal well-being. Social services can be provided to people from all economic levels and include resources and activities, such as counseling, child protection, residential treatment for emotional and behavioral problems, provision of financial resources, sheltered employment and assistance for people with disabilities, daycare, and employment coaching, among many other services.

A **social agency**, or **social services agency**, is an organization providing social services that typically employs a range of professionals, including social workers, office staff, paraprofessionals (persons trained to assist professionals), and sometimes volunteers. Social agencies generally serve some designated client population experiencing some defined need. Services are provided according to a prescribed set of policies regarding how the agency staff should accomplish their service provision goals.

Groups

A **group** is at least two individuals gathered together because of some common bond, to meet members' social and emotional needs, or to fulfill some mutual purpose. Our concern with groups involves their significance in the context of communities and organizations. Communities and organizations are made up of groups, which in turn are composed of individuals. Chapters 3 and 4 will describe various types of groups and focus on the operation of task groups in the macro social environment.

Figure 1-1 depicts the complexity of the macro social environment. Groups, organizations, and communities are made up of individuals like you. The large outer circle reflects the geographic community in which someone like you might live. You are portrayed in the bolded circle near the center of the large community circle. Also depicted are numerous organizations within the community. Each organization is also made up of various groups (e.g., task groups, departments, units, or levels of management). The macro environment also has numerous other groups of people who are not necessarily members of organizations. These might include friendship groups, recreational groups, study groups, neighborhood groups, and any other type of group configuration you might think of. In any community, you obviously will not

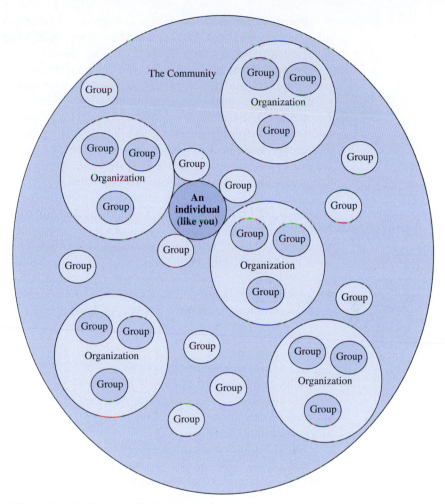

Figure 1-1 The Macro Social Environment

be involved with all groups and organizations. You probably won't even be aware of some of them. The groups and organization circles that touch the bolded circle representing you reflect those groups and organizations with which you are involved—perhaps including organizations like the college you attend and groups like your closest circle of friends. The point is that the macro social environment is a complex matrix of these various components. People don't function in a vacuum. They are integrally involved with others around them.

Social, Economic, and Political Forces

EP 3a, 5

Social forces are values and beliefs held by people in the social environment that are strong enough to influence their activities, including how government is structured or restricted. Key words here are *values* and *beliefs*. For example, social forces fuel the debate between anti-abortion and right-to-choice factions over the abortion issue.

Economic forces are the resources that are available, how they are distributed, and how they are spent. The key word here is *resources*. They involve how taxes are spent at the national level and how salaries are distributed to an agency's workers.

Political forces are the current governmental structures, the laws to which people are subject, and the overall distribution of power among the population. Political forces are reflected in laws and public policies. Here the key word is *government*. Elected politicians make decisions about what rules should govern public behavior and how to distribute resources. An example is the public welfare grant program Temporary Assistance to Needy Families (TANF), which was established by political forces. The program, discussed more thoroughly in a later chapter, structures how needy children and their families are treated.

The interplay of social, economic, and political forces is complex and often controversial. Ordinary citizens and political decision makers express huge variations in opinions over what is right and what is wrong, over what should be done and what should not be done. For instance, what should be done to address health care, the national debt, and economic opportunities? Disputes over what the various levels of government should provide and who should pay for services or benefits are common. These questions arise from our values and beliefs (social forces), available resources (economic forces), and legal decisions (political forces).

Social Institutions

Social forces converge over time to form social institutions. A **social institution** is an established and valued practice or means of operation in a society resulting in the development of a formalized system to carry out its purpose. Examples of social institutions are families, the military, religion, education, social welfare systems, and government. See Figure 1-2.

Social institutions establish expectations and requirements for expected behavior, and govern these through policies and laws. Communities provide the macro environments for social institutions to be upheld. Organizations carry out policies

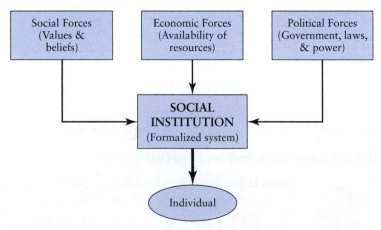

Figure 1-2 Individual Social, Economic, and Political Forces Result in Formalized Social Institutions That Affect Individuals

At a Glance **1-1**

Important Aspects of the Macro Social Environment

Social environment: The sum total of social and cultural conditions, circumstances, and human interactions that encompass human beings.

Community: "A number of people who have something in common that connects them in some way and that distinguishes them from others" (Homan, 2016, p. 10).

Organization: A "(1) social entity that (2) is goal-directed, (3) is designed as a deliberately structured and coordinated activity system, and (4) is linked to the external environment" (Daft, 2016, p. 13).

Social services: The work that social work practitioners and other helping professionals perform in organizations for the benefit of clients.

Social (or social services) agency: An organization providing social services that typically employs a range of professionals, including social workers, office staff, paraprofessionals (persons trained to assist professionals), and sometimes volunteers.

Group: At least two individuals gathered together because of some common bond, to meet members' social and emotional needs, or to fulfill some mutual purpose.

Social forces: Values and beliefs held by people in the social environment that are strong enough to influence people's activities, including how government is structured or restricted.

Economic forces: Resources that are available, how they are distributed, and how they are spent.

Political forces: Current governmental structures, the laws to which people are subject, and the overall distribution of power among the population.

Social institution: An established and valued practice or means of operation in a society resulting in the development of a formalized system to carry out its purpose.

and distribute services social institutions deem necessary. Decision-making groups and administrators in organizations and communities implement policies and distribute services based on social institutions.

For example, consider public education in the United States. The right of all US citizens to receive public education until age 18 is a social institution. Individual schools are organizations that comply with this concept. Individual communities make decisions regarding how schools will accomplish their educational goals. Community residents determine whether new schools will be built or old ones will suffice. They decide what content will be taught to students in family life education courses and whether or not to offer music or art.

Intricate interconnections exist among social forces, social institutions, communities, organizations, and groups carrying out public directives. Sometimes, forces and institutions are not clearly distinguishable from each other. All are collectively intertwined to make up the macro social environment.

Note that the macro social environment may include macro systems of various dimensions depending on your focus of attention. It may include small groups within organizations, as well as neighborhoods, towns, cities, large metropolitan areas, counties, states, nations, and the global macro social environment.

A Theoretical Framework for Understanding the Macro Social Environment and Social Work Practice: Ecosystems Theory LO 1-2

Theoretical or conceptual perspectives provide symbolic representations or pictures for how to view the world—in this case, the macro world of communities, organizations, and groups. Because the environment is so important in the analysis and understanding of human behavior, theoretical and conceptual perspectives must be clearly defined. Social work focuses on the interactions between individuals and various systems in the environment. Both systems theory terminology and the terminology used to refer to the social environment (based in the ecological perspective) are critically important in the conceptualization of social work practice. Thus, the following sections will explore the foundation theory upon which this book is based—namely, ecosystems theory.

Ecosystems Theory and the Macro Social Environment

EP 6

Ecosystems theory (ecological systems theory) provides one significant means of conceptualizing and understanding human behavior (Pittenger, Huit, & Hansen, 2016; Poulin, 2010). It often serves as a conceptual framework to help social workers comprehend people's interaction with various systems in the macro social environment.

The heart of the ecosystems perspective is the person-in-environment concept, which views individuals and their environments as an interrelated whole. We recognize that human beings are systems with multiple components. These components include biological, emotional, psychological, and cognitive factors. We are continually engaging in interactions with our environments, which include our families, friends and peers, and larger social institutions such as employers, schools, and community.

As indicated earlier, ecosystems theory draws its major concepts from two other major theoretical frameworks—systems theory and the ecological perspective. Systems theory provides a very broad perspective that can be applied to living and nonliving configurations of entities. (Note that the term *social systems theory* is often used when systems theory concepts are applied to groups of people and human interaction.) The ecological perspective focuses more specifically on living creatures' interaction with and relationship to their environment. However, many concepts characterizing systems theory and the ecological perspective provide a useful means of analyzing and understanding human behavior within the context of the encompassing macro environment. The following sections discuss these concepts.

Ecosystems Theory: Basic Terms Taken from Systems Theory

It has been established that a number of terms based in systems theory are extremely important in understanding ecosystems theory and its relationship to social work practice. They include *system, boundaries, subsystem, homeostasis, role, relationship, input, output, feedback, interface, differentiation, entropy, negative entropy,* and *equifinality*.

System   A **system** is a set of elements that are orderly, interrelated, and a functional whole. An individual person is a system with biological, psychological, and social qualities and characteristics. Examples of systems are Sheboygan, WI; a large urban department of social services; a tiny two-person, part-time counseling center in a town of 2,356 residents; Washington, DC; Buzzard, Saskatchewan; and a local chapter of Gamblers Anonymous.

Boundaries **Boundaries** are borders or margins that separate one entity (e.g., a system) from another. For instance, your skin provides a boundary between you as an independent, living system and the external environment. Boundaries determine who is a member of a system and who is not. If you haven't paid your dues to the National Association of Bungee Jumpers, Kiwanis, or your social work student club, you are not a member of that system. You are not within that particular system's boundaries. You are either in it or not.

Subsystem A **subsystem** is a secondary or subordinate system. It may be thought of as a smaller system within a larger system. The social work program, for example, is a subsystem of your college or university. Similarly, each member of the Green Bay Packers football organization from president to ticket taker is a subsystem of the overall organization.

Homeostasis **Homeostasis** is the tendency for a system to maintain a relatively stable, constant state of balance. If something disturbs the homeostatic balance, that system will strive to return to its prior stable state. Members of the group Neighborhood Warriors on Trash maintain homeostasis as long as they can relate well enough to stay together and pick up garbage, their designated purpose. The system, in this case, the group, must maintain some kind of homeostasis to function.

Homeostasis, however, does not mean that all group members will like each other or even talk to each other. Harry, for example, can't stand Izod, whom he feels bullies other group members by telling them the best way to organize trash collection. However, Harry feels the group and its purpose are important enough to continue his support and involvement. He simply ignores Izod. Homeostasis merely means maintaining the status quo. Sometimes, that status quo can be ineffective, inefficient, or seriously problematic.

Another example is a community that strives to maintain its homeostasis despite having corrupt political leaders. Community members may hesitate to depose their leaders because potential replacements scare residents even more. At least the residents already know about the leaders they have. The unknown is scary even though it might be better—because it also might be worse.

Roles A **role** is a culturally expected behavior pattern for a person having a specified status or involvement in a designated social relationship. In other words, each individual involved in a system assumes a role within that system. For instance, you assume the role of student in class. Expectations include performing required work, receiving grades the instructor assigns, and working toward your degree. If you hold a job, you assume the role of employee with whatever work expectations that job role involves. In a community, the mayor assumes a role with the decision-making responsibilities required in such a position.

Relationships A **relationship** is the dynamic interpersonal connection between two or more persons or systems that involves how they think about, feel about, and behave toward each other. For example, a social worker may have a professional relationship with her agency supervisor. Ideally, their communication and interaction maximizes the worker's effectiveness.

Relationships may exist between systems of any size. Workers within an agency have relationships with each other. Likewise, one agency or organization has a relationship with another. A local church may establish a relationship with a community Boys' Club. Together they could recruit and train volunteers, share activity space, and cosponsor community activities for the community's male youth.

Input   **Input** is the energy, information, or communication flow received from other systems. You receive input from instructors regarding class assignments. Elected officials receive input from constituents when they vote on whether or not to support a referendum that allows building a new grade school. As an employee, you receive input in the form of a paycheck, not necessarily a big enough paycheck, but it is still input. Other examples include a person who breaks both arms after falling with her new 800-pound hog motorcycle who will require substantial input by others to help her take care of daily personal tasks. Still another example of input is information received from the Atlanta Centers for Disease Control about new annual flu epidemic mutations.

Output   **Output**, on the other hand, is what happens to *input* after it's gone through and been processed by some system. It is a form of energy going out of a person's life or taking something away from it. For instance, a Moose Lodge may "adopt a highway" and take responsibility for cleaning up two miles of a local road. Another form of output is paying money to purchase a red 2016 Toyota Corolla coupe. Yet another form of output is the progress made with a client. Pablo, a worker, can expend time and energy, use his knowledge and skills, and work with a client, Astrid, to achieve the goal of finding employment. The intervention's output is Astrid's employment and her level of satisfaction with it.

At times these terms are confusing. For example, in the case above, Pablo provides Astrid with his input (time, energy, knowledge, skill, and expertise). Astrid then, hopefully, has output (seeking and finding a job). However, if we focus on Pablo instead of Astrid, we can apply the terms differently. On the one hand, Pablo's *input* includes his salary, ongoing skill development, and help from supervisors. Pablo's *output*, on the other hand, is the time, energy, knowledge, skill, and expertise he exercises to achieve intervention goals. How terms are applied and used depends on which individual, subsystem, or element of the systems involved is the focus of attention. One person's input is another's output.

A related issue critically significant in social work practice is whether the output is worth all the input. Are treatment results worth how much the treatment costs? Does a community program to fight crime (that requires significant financial input) have adequate results (output) to justify how much it costs? If 10 officers are hired to implement the program, how successful must the program be? Is it successful if crime is cut by 10 percent? Or 30 percent? What about 2 percent?

Many times, it's difficult to measure input and output in equal units. If money is the only measurement of inputs and outputs, it makes it easier. If a stockbroker invests more (input) than he earns (output), he is losing money and better change his investment strategy. In social services, it is often difficult to measure the value of a service or the extent it adds to peoples' quality of life. For example, is a hospice program geared to enhancing the comfort of terminally ill people worth the expense? The input in terms of financial resources for treatment, care, housing, and medicine can be substantial. However, the value of such care to a dying person (the output) may be priceless.

The bottom line concerns whether the community or agency is using its resources efficiently and effectively. Or, can those resources be put to a better use by providing some other more effective and efficient service?

Negative and Positive Feedback   **Feedback** is a special form of input where a system receives information about that system's own performance. As a result of **negative feedback**, the system can choose to correct any deviations or mistakes and return to a more homeostatic state.

For example, Natasha, a community resident, might give negative feedback to Boris, another, about how Boris's small children regularly run out into a busy street while playing and riding bikes. Natasha thinks it is very dangerous for Boris's children, so she gives Boris feedback about the problem. Hopefully, Boris will use this negative feedback to correct the problem.

Positive feedback, also valuable, is the informational input a system receives about what it is doing correctly in order to maintain itself and thrive. Receiving a significant pay raise resulting from an excellent job-performance review provides positive feedback to a worker that she is doing a good job. Likewise, an agency receiving a specific federal grant gets positive feedback that it has developed a plan worthy of such funding.

Interface   An **interface** is the point where two systems (including individuals, families, groups, organizations, or communities) come into contact with each other, interact, or communicate. An interface may be the interaction and communication between an agency supervisor and her supervisee. It may also be your communication with an instructor regarding expectations for some class assignment. A board of directors may be the interface between a community and a residential treatment center for adolescents with serious emotional and behavioral problems. Such a board is usually composed of influential community volunteers who oversee agency policies, goals, and how effectively the agency is generally run.

During an assessment of a client system's strengths, needs, and problems, the interface must be clearly in focus in order to target the appropriate interactions for change. For example, a young single mother of three is homeless and desperately needs services. The interface between her and the macro systems providing human services includes those services for which she might be eligible. The interface also involves her interactions with social workers helping to provide those services.

Differentiation   **Differentiation** is a system's tendency to move from a simpler to a more complex existence. As you grow older, get wiser, have more varied experiences, meet increasing numbers of people, and assume more responsibilities in general, your life gets more complicated. You experience differentiation. Likewise, as a social agency grows over time, it will likely develop more detailed policies and programs. A women's center might start out with one support group for battered women run by one volunteer. If that support group is a success, years later it may expand and differentiate into an entire program where eight groups addressing other issues commonly experienced by women are run by paid program staff and supervised by a director. Similarly, as laws and clarifications to laws proliferate in the legal system, that system differentiates and becomes more complex.

Entropy   **Entropy** is the natural tendency of a system to progress toward disorganization, depletion, and death. The idea is that nothing lasts forever. People age and eventually die. After early periods of growth and differentiation, agencies grow old, often obsolete, and disappear. As history moves on, older agencies and systems are eventually replaced by new ones.

Negative Entropy   **Negative entropy** is the process of a system toward growth and development. In effect, it is the opposite of entropy. Individuals develop physically, intellectually, and emotionally as they grow. Social service agencies grow and develop new programs and clientele. A sheltered workshop that provides supervised training and vocational guidance for people with intellectual disabilities begins in one small building with 20 clients. Negative entropy characterizes the agency as it grows to serve over 100 clients and adds new programs. These might include an information and referral helpline, a volunteer program called Special Friends that is similar to Big Brothers/Big Sisters programs, and a wide range of supervised recreational activities.

Equifinality   **Equifinality** is the notion that there are many different means to achieve the same end. It is important not to get locked into only one way of thinking. In any particular situation, alternatives do exist. Some may be better

At a Glance **1-2**

Major Concepts in Systems Theory

Ecosystems theory (ecological systems theory): A conceptual framework to help social workers comprehend people's interaction with various systems in the macro social environment.

System: A set of elements that are orderly, interrelated, and a functional whole.

Boundaries: Borders or margins that separate one entity from another.

Subsystem: A secondary or subordinate system.

Homeostasis: The tendency for a system to maintain a relatively stable, constant state of balance.

Role: A culturally expected behavior pattern for a person having a specified status or being involved in a designated social relationship.

Relationship: The dynamic connection between two or more persons or systems that involves how they think about, feel about, and behave toward each other.

Input: The energy, information, or communication flow received from other systems.

Output: What happens to input after it has gone through and been processed by some system.

Negative feedback: A special form of input where a system receives information about that system's own performance.

Positive feedback: The informational input a system receives about what it is doing correctly in order to maintain itself and thrive.

Interface: The point where two systems (including individuals, families, groups, organizations, or communities) encounter each other, interact, or communicate.

Differentiation: A system's tendency to move from a simpler to a more complex existence.

Entropy: The natural tendency of a system to progress toward disorganization, depletion, and death.

Negative entropy: The process of a system toward growth and development.

Equifinality: The notion that there are many different means to achieve the same end.

than others, but, nonetheless, there are alternatives. For example, a community might need funding to start up a new community center for holding community meetings and housing social and recreational events. The end goal is establishment of a place to conduct community activities. However, there are many ways to attain this goal. A citizen group might apply for grants from public and private sources, the community might undertake a massive fundraising campaign on the center's behalf, or residents might work with county and state leaders to solicit support.

Ecosystems Theory: Basic Terms Taken from the Ecological Perspective

It has been established that ecosystems theory incorporates basic ecological concepts in addition to those proposed by systems theory. The ecological perspective emphasizes the dynamic interactions between people and their environment. Gitterman (2014) explains that many of the problems faced by people "are outcomes of complex ecological chains that include attributes of the individual's genetic, biopsychosocial makeup; the structures of the family, social networks, community school, workplace, religious organizations, and health systems; recreational resources; general culture and subculture; (and) social class" (p. 20). He also notes that the way a government is structured can also play a role in this complexity. As you can see, people exist within multiple environments, including the physical, cultural, and social, while influenced by and influencing those who comprise their world.

We have established that concepts from both systems theories and the ecological perspective provide useful means for social workers to view the world. Both approaches focus on systems within the environment and how these systems interact with and affect people, resulting in ecosystems theory.

Some would say that subtle differences exist between the approaches and the terms inherent in each. Schriver (2011) explains:

> The ecological perspective . . . explicitly defines the environment as including physical (nonhuman) elements. Social systems [theories] . . . are less explicit about the place and role of nonhuman elements in the environment. Some would also argue that social systems and ecological approaches differ in their conceptualizations of boundaries and exchange across boundaries that occur in human interactions. Recognizing these areas of disagreement, we will consider these two perspectives similar enough to be treated together here. (pp. 113–114)

Hence, we will conceptualize this as ecosystems theory.

The following concepts derived from the ecological perspective are important facets of ecosystems theory: *social environment; transactions; energy; input; output; interface; adaptation; person-in-environment fit; stress, stressors, and coping; relatedness; habitat; niche; and personal characteristics including, competence, self-esteem,* and *self-direction.* As noted, input, output, and interface are terms used in both approaches. See Highlight 1-1 for brief comparison of terms. To avoid redundancy, please refer to the earlier descriptions of these terms within the context of social systems theory.

| Highlight **1-1** |

Comparison of Some of the Major Concepts in Systems Theory and the Ecological Perspective

Major Concepts in Systems Theory	Similar Concepts in Both	Major Concepts in the Ecological Perspective
System	Input	Social environment
Boundaries	Output	Energy
Subsystem	Interface	Adaptation
Homeostasis		Person-in-environment fit
Roles		Stress, stressors, and coping
Relationships		Relatedness
Negative feedback		Habitat
Positive feedback		Niche
Differentiation		Personal characteristics
Entropy		Competence
Negative entropy		Self-esteem
Equifinality		Self-direction

The Social Environment   The *social environment* involves the conditions, circumstances, and human interactions that encompass human beings. Persons are dependent upon effective interactions with this environment in order to survive and thrive. The social environment includes the actual physical setting that society provides. This involves the type of home a person lives in, the type of work that's done, the amount of money that's available, and the laws and social rules by which people live. The social environment also includes all the individuals, groups, organizations, and systems with which a person comes into contact. Families, friends, work groups, organizations, communities, and governments are all involved.

The **macro social environment** extends beyond the individual's interaction with immediate friends, relatives, and other individuals. We have established that it is the configuration of communities, organizations, and groups within the latter that are products of social, economic, and political forces and social institutions.

People communicate and interact with others in their environments. Each of these interactions or types of interactions are referred to as *transactions*. Transactions are active and dynamic. That is, something is communicated or exchanged.

They may be positive or negative. A positive transaction may be the revelation that you won the lottery. Another positive transaction might be that you are named state social worker of the year. A negative transaction, on the other hand, might be receiving news that your house burned down or was ruined in an earthquake, destroying almost all of your personal possessions. Another negative transaction is a huge fight with your significant other in which you discover your partner is having an affair.

Energy   **Energy** is the natural power of active involvement between people and their environments. Energy can take the form of *input* or *output*. Use of these latter terms in the ecological perspective resembles that in systems theory. The *interface* is also similar to the same term in systems theory. Namely, it is the exact point where the interaction between an individual and the environment takes place.

Adaptation   **Adaptation** is the capacity to adjust to surrounding environmental conditions. It implies an ongoing process of change. A person must adapt to new conditions and circumstances in order to continue functioning effectively. An individual diagnosed with severe rheumatoid arthritis must adapt to new, less difficult levels of physical activity. The individual must also adapt to the process of taking required medications and performing the appropriate exercises to maximize comfort, endurance, and agility. Another example is a family whose primary breadwinner is laid off from a high-paying management job after a serious dip in the economy. Family members must adapt to a less costly lifestyle until input returns to its former level when the breadwinner gets a new job.

In addition, larger systems must adapt to their environments. Decisions that companies make to move their factories to countries with lower labor costs are often justified by claims that labor costs in the United States are too high. They then move to locations with few if any minimum wage laws, health care expectations, and laws protecting the environment.

Environments also adapt and react to people. Consider the destruction of Brazil's rainforest to supply lumber and provide farmland. Many questions have been raised concerning the potential effects of this damage and the extinction of plant and animal life. Questions even have been asked about the impacts on global weather as oxygen-producing plants are destroyed. Plants, animals, and humans must all adapt to new conditions, positive or not, if they are to survive.

Person-in-Environment Fit   **Person-in-environment fit** is the extent to which a person or group has the resources to survive and flourish within the environment. Factors such as individual or group needs, abilities, behaviors, and capacities all have a bearing on the fit. When the fit is good, physical, social, and cultural needs are met. Sometimes, person-in-environment fit is amazingly good. Other times, it is exceedingly poor. Many variables are involved in how an environment meets individual and groups' needs.

The person-in-environment fit would likely be poor for a person using a wheelchair whose home is a third-story apartment without elevators or ramps. Likewise, Nassir is a Muslim person of color who is just beginning to learn English and lives in a neighborhood composed almost exclusively of Roman Catholic White people. The extent to which Nassir suffers neighbors' discrimination and rejection because of his differences negatively affects his person-in-environment fit. On the other hand, the extent to which neighbors accept and appreciate his differences enhances that fit.

Stress, Stressors, and Coping   Because they are so interrelated, stress, stressors, and coping will be addressed here together. A **stressor** is any situation or event that places a demand on the individual resulting in some degree of physiological and/ or emotional tension, in other words, stress. **Stress**, then, is the resulting physiological and/or emotional tension produced by a stressor that affects a person's internal balance. Stressors include any of a wide range of variables and circumstances: traumatic events such as sudden deaths or discovery of fatal disease; potentially troublesome life transitions such as adolescence or old age; and other changes in living patterns such as divorce. Even positive events such as getting a job, moving to a new home, or falling in love can be stressors. Adapting to new circumstances, regardless of what they are, can cause stress.

Coping is an adaptation to stress that people use to reduce the stressor in some fashion. The effort may be focused on (1) changing the environmental that is producing the stressor, (2) changing their own reactions to the stressor, (3) changing how they interact with the stressor, or (4) combining one or more of the other three approaches. For example, a parent must cope with the worry and distress caused by a sick child. That parent must decrease the extent of distress by curbing his or her worry (targeting personal reactions), make certain the child immediately gets the necessary treatment available in the medical environment (targeting the environment), or advocate with medical personnel and the insurance company to provide needed medical services (targeting the interaction between the family and the environment). That parent might also cope by pursuing a combination of these goals at the same time.

From a macro perspective, an example concerns an agency that must cope with new strict government regulations about service provision. Agency administration might work to accept and adjust to these regulations (targeting agency staff's own reactions), persuade government officials that these regulations really don't apply (targeting the environment), or establish a compromise with government officials to relax regulations so they aren't as stringent (targeting the agency's interaction with the governmental environment). Agency administration may also pursue all three of these tactics.

One other macro example involves a community that must cope with state and federal funding cuts. Community administrators and residents must learn to live with the cuts (targeting their own reactions), fight with state and federal government to abolish the funding cuts (targeting the environment), or work toward some compromise to decrease the cuts (targeting interaction with the state and national environment). As in the earlier illustrations portraying a parent and an agency, the community might also pursue a number of coping strategies.

Social workers help people cope with problems and issues. Assessing both people's coping skills (whether they are part of a group, organization, or community) and the potential for change in the macro environment is a critical aspect of preparing for generalist intervention.

Relatedness   **Relatedness** is the ability to connect to other people, groups or organizations. People need to feel they connect to and have support from others. Attachments may be made both to formal and informal resources and networks.

Formal service networks include service agencies or other institutions (e.g., the college or university you attend); *informal networks* include your friends, co-workers, neighbors, or those with whom you share a religious or spiritual belief system.

Think of your first day of class as a first-year student and all the unknowns you had to face. To what extent did you feel a sense of relatedness to the college environment? To what extent has your sense of relatedness changed from then until now? How many more people do you know now? How many friends have you made? With how many instructors' expectations have you learned to cope? To what extent do you feel a relatedness with the college or university?

Similarly, residents may experience various degrees of relatedness with their community. They may know most of the neighbors, be a member of a neighborhood association, and participate regularly in community events. On the other hand, residents may know no neighbors, lack involvement in any community activities, and feel isolated and alone. Whether an individual is a member of a group, an employee in an organization, or a neighborhood resident, that person must experience a positive sense of relatedness in order to achieve good person-in-environment fit. Assessing people's relatedness in their immediate social environment provides social workers with important clues for how to help clients get their needs met. A client's relatedness can pose many strengths upon which to draw in solving problems. Supportive people in the environment can be called on to provide emotional, financial, housing, babysitting, and daycare support. If they have substantial support systems, how can these systems be used to the best advantage? If social support is sadly lacking, how can it be improved? Later, we will discuss further how groups, organizations, and communities can serve to enhance or detract from people's sense of relatedness and their overall well-being.

Habitat and Niche   **Habitats** are the specific settings in which we live and work. A habitat is sometimes referred to as one's territory. It can be any place that we consider our place. This includes our home, regardless of type, the schools, employers, churches, social agencies and organizations, health care facilities, and recreational amenities that exist. Ideally, habitats provide for the healthy growth and functioning of people. Conversely, some habitats do not do this, and people may feel alienated and hopeless.

A **niche** is a specific social position that a person holds within the habitat's social structure (Payne, 2014). An individual's niche can be positive and supportive, or negative and isolating. Each society defines what it considers an ideal niche. Different historical eras also have had different definitions. Unfortunately, not all children or adults experience positive healthy niches, sometimes because the environment cannot (or chooses not to) provide it.

In other words, for example, an extremely poor person of a race discriminated against by the ruling majority might experience a niche that is characterized by deprivation and suffering. Conceptualizing the social environment in this manner helps generalist practitioners identify people in need and look carefully at the social conditions contributing to these needs.

Highlight 1-2

Personal Characteristics Affecting Human Interaction in the Social Environment

At least three basic concepts inherent in the ecological approach reflect personal characteristics. **Competence** involves people's understanding or belief in their own skills to handle life challenges or to get assistance from others when needed. An inherent assumption is that people will seek to change their environment if necessary to survive. People should have opportunities throughout life to effectively manipulate, improve, and thrive in their environment. The implication is that social workers should nurture people's natural tendency to work and succeed in their environment. This applies to people from all walks of life. For example, impoverished people living in a border shantytown require opportunities to improve their living conditions. In addition to food and clothing, needs include financial resources for building materials, skilled help regarding how to improve dwellings, and education to establish a higher standard of living.

Self-esteem involves the degree to which individuals feel they are inherently worthwhile and important. Each individual deserves to feel important and to have self-esteem, regardless of their job positions or salaries.

Self-direction involves people's feeling or belief that they have a degree of control over their lives and hold themselves accountable for their own behaviors. This concept is almost synonymous with self-determination, a core concept in social work values. People have the right to make their own decisions and control their own behavior within their environment if their actions don't harm others. Thus, practitioners must vigilantly assess the extent to which people's involvement in groups, organizations, and communities allows them to demonstrate self-direction.

At a Glance 1-3

Major Concepts in the Ecological Perspective

Macro social environment: The configuration of communities, organizations, and groups within the social environment that are products of social, economic, and political forces and social institutions.

Energy: The natural power of active involvement between people and their environments.

Adaptation: The capacity to adjust to surrounding environmental conditions.

Person-in-environment fit: The extent to which a person or group has the resources to survive and flourish within their environment.

Stressor: Any situation or event that places a demand on the individual resulting in some degree of physiological and/or emotional tension—in other words, stress.

Stress: The resulting physiological and/or emotional tension produced by a stressor that affects a person's internal balance.

Coping: A form of adaptation to stress that is employed to reduce the stressor in some fashion. The effort may be focused on (1) changing the

environmental that is producing the stressor, (2) changing their own reactions to the stressor, (3) changing how they interact with the stressor, or (4) combining one or more of the other three approaches.

Relatedness: The ability to connect to other people, groups, or organizations.

Habitat: The specific settings in which we live and work.

Niche: A specific social position that a person holds within the habitat's social structure (Payne, 2014).

Competence: People's understanding or belief in their own skills to handle life challenges or to get assistance from others when needed.

Self-esteem: The degree to which individuals feel they are inherently worthwhile and important.

Self-direction: People's feeling or belief that they have a degree of control over their lives and hold themselves accountable for their own behaviors.

All of the terms discussed thus far that are taken from the ecological perspective involve the essence of dynamic interactions between and among people. Highlight 1-2 cites three personal characteristics that also affect human interaction in the social environment.

People's Involvement with Multiple Systems in the Social Environment LO 1-3

EP 6a, 7b, 8b, 9b

We have established that people are constantly and dynamically involved in inter-actions with other systems in the social environment. There is constant activity, communication, and change. Understanding human behavior seeks to answer the question, "What is it in any particular situation that causes a problem or creates a need?" Ecosystems theory provides a perspective for social workers to assess and understand many aspects of a situation by looking at the various systems involved.

Several useful terms for conceptualizing interaction include *target of change, micro system, mezzo system, macro system, client system,* and *macro client system.*

Generalist social work practitioners work on the behalf of individuals, families, groups, organizations, and communities. Any of these systems may be a **target of change** (or *target system*), the system that social workers need to change or influ-ence in order to accomplish goals. It is helpful to think of different systems as mi-cro, mezzo, or macro systems.

A **micro system** is an individual. We have established that a system is a set of elements that are orderly, interrelated, and a functional whole. In a broad sense, this definition applies to individual persons. Hence, a person is also a type of system, for our purposes, a *micro system*. Individual systems entail all the many aspects of per-sonality, emotion, beliefs, behavior, interests, goals, strengths, and weaknesses that make a person unique. Targeting a micro system for change involves working with an individual, identifying issues and strengths, and enhancing that person's functioning. Figure 1-3 illustrates the complexity of an individual micro system. A **mezzo system** refers to any small group. Figure 1-4 reflects how individuals make up mezzo sys-tems. In the macro environment, groups include those involved with organizations or communities. A **macro system** is any system larger than a small group. This book, of course, focuses on larger systems, particularly organizations and communities.

Macro settings are made up of individuals and groups of individuals. Thus, so-cial workers must use their skills in developing relationships, interviewing, and prob-lem solving with individuals and groups who are responsible for making decisions

Figure 1-3 An Individual Micro System

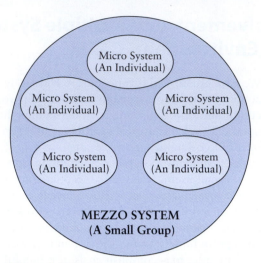

Figure 1-4 Micro Systems Make Up Mezzo Systems

about communities' and organizations' policies and activities. Workers can undertake projects, seek policy changes, and develop programs within the macro context. (Note that the explanation of specific skills for effecting macro-level change is beyond the scope of this book and is saved for future practice classes.) Figure 1-5

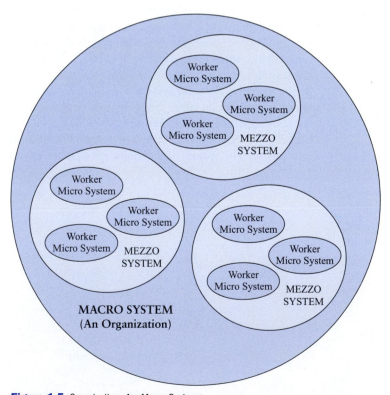

Figure 1-5 Organizations Are Macro Systems

depicts an organizational macro system that is made up of various groups and units (mezzo systems) that, in turn, are made up of individual workers (micro systems). Figure 1-6 illustrates a community macro system that is a complex, interconnected array of various smaller macro systems and groups (e.g., neighborhoods, businesses, social service agencies, schools, and churches).

The **client system** is any individual, family, group, organization, or community that will ultimately benefit from social work intervention. Figure 1-7 portrays how social workers, client systems, and macro systems operate within the social environment. A client system may be micro, mezzo, or macro. The client system and the social worker work together for change, reflected by their close contact or interface. Arrows leading from the social worker/client system to the organization and community macro systems depict how social workers and clients work together with these macro systems in the social environment on the behalf of clients. The two-way arrow between the organization and community macro systems reflects how organizations and communities are integrally involved with each other.

Macro client systems include communities, organizations, and larger groups of clientele who have similar issues and problems and are potential beneficiaries of positive change. The concept of macro intervention concerns agency or social change that affects larger numbers of people than an individual client or family. For example, a social worker might work with a community to establish a *food bank*

Figure 1-6 Community Macro Systems

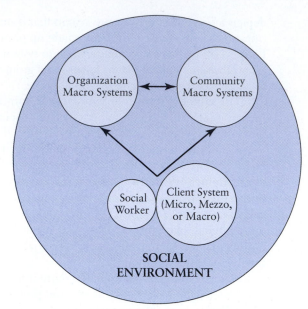

Figure 1-7 Social Workers Help Clients Negotiate the Social Environment

(a program where surplus food is collected from restaurants, cafeterias, grocery stores, individuals, and anywhere else it might be available, and redistributed to places such as soup kitchens serving people in need). A practitioner might also work with a social services organization to create a new position for an interpreter to serve as translator for a large population of Syrian refugee clients who recently emigrated from the Middle East. Likewise, a social worker might be part of a larger group determined to clean up a blighted neighborhood or prevent a landfill from being located adjacent to a neighborhood.

The next section describes generalist social work practice in the macro social environment. Using the terminology concerning the various systems explained here helps us to understand the dynamics of how social workers view the world and their work.

At a Glance 1-4

Concepts Concerning Social Work Practice with Multiple Systems in the Macro Social Environment

Target of change: The system that social workers need to change or influence in order to accomplish goals.

Micro system: An individual.

Mezzo system: A small group.

Macro system: Any system larger than a small group.

Client system: Any individual, family, group, organization, or community who will ultimately benefit from social work intervention.

Macro client system: Communities, organizations, and larger groups of clientele who have similar issues and problems and are potential beneficiaries of positive change.

The Macro Social Environment and Generalist Social Work Practice LO 1-4

Social workers help people in need by using a wide range of methods. They counsel individuals, work with families, run various types of groups, help clients in their communities, and strive to improve the organizations in which they practice. It is the ethical responsibility of professional social workers to address problems and issues in the macro social environment and to initiate and implement positive change (National Association of Social Workers [NASW], 2008). To do all this requires acquisition of a significant range of skills. Regardless of who their clients are or what their goals might be, social workers must follow an orderly process to get things done that stresses professional core values. This perspective is referred to as generalist practice.

Generalist practice is conducted in the context of the macro social environment. To understand the significance of this environment, it is necessary to know what social workers actually do in it. Therefore, we will spend some time here describing and examining generalist practice.

Describing Generalist Practice

EP 1c, 2, 6, 7c

Generalist practice is the application of an extensive and diverse knowledge base, professional values, and a wide range of skills to promote human well-being for individuals, families, groups, organizations, and communities. Thus, social work does not only focus on work with individuals and families, but also with groups, organizations, and communities. The following 10 concepts also characterize generalist practice:

1. The establishment of goals that target systems of any size for positive change.
2. Performance of work within an organizational structure.
3. Use of a structured planned change process going through seven steps: engagement, assessment, planning, implementation, evaluation, termination, and follow-up.
4. Assumption of a wide range of professional roles.
5. Application of critical thinking skills.
6. Incorporation of research-informed practice.
7. Adherence to professional values and the application of professional ethics (discussed more thoroughly in Chapter 2 and addressed elsewhere in the book).
8. Understanding of human diversity and how diverse factors affect people's quality of life (examined in Chapter 2, addressed elsewhere in the book, and stressed in Chapter 12).
9. Emphasis on client empowerment, strengths, and resilience (introduced in Chapter 2, addressed elsewhere in the book, and emphasized in Chapter 12).
10. Advocacy for human rights, and the pursuit of social and economic justice (discussed in Chapter 2, addressed elsewhere in the book, and highlighted in Chapter 13).

This chapter discusses the first six of these generalist practice concepts. As indicated above, later chapters will elaborate upon the remaining four concepts, all of which involve professional social work values.

Note that the terms *social worker, worker, generalist social worker, generalist practitioner,* and *practitioner* will be used interchangeably throughout this book to refer to professionals undertaking generalist social work practice.

Describing Generalist Practice: Goals Targeting Systems of Any Size for Change

EP 5b, 6, 8d

One relevant concept involved in generalist practice involves *targeting systems of any size for change*. It has been stressed that generalist practitioners work with and on the behalf of client systems of all sizes. Similarly, generalist practitioners may target any of these systems, including a macro system, as the system to influence in order to change and improve it. This is unlike many other helping professions that focus on working with and changing individuals and families. At the community macro level, a generalist practitioner might help a group of neighborhood residents develop a plan for identifying and getting rid of drug houses or start a summer recreation program for youth. The practitioner may help people register to vote so that their voices are heard when selecting those who will represent them at the local, state, or national levels. At the organizational macro level, a social worker might advocate on clients' behalf with administrators to change a restrictive policy. Similarly, an agency worker might lead a task group to develop a training program for teaching workers new skills to work with involuntary or angry clients.

Describing Generalist Practice: Work within an Organizational Structure

EP 1c, 1e

Generalist social workers typically practice within the context of an organizational structure. **Organizational structure** is the manner in which an organization systematically arranges workers into groups (or departments) and then coordinates these various groups' activities and interactions. Social workers are employed by social service agencies. Each such organization has its own organizational structure involving job descriptions and responsibilities, policies, or rules that govern workers' activities, departments addressing various aspects of agency functioning, communication systems, and a management hierarchy. (Later chapters will discuss these variables and many others characterizing organizations in greater depth.) Social workers should attend to their prescribed professional role, demonstrate professional behavior, and use supervision appropriately to the venues in which they practice.

As agencies are integral parts of larger communities in the macro social environment, workers must understand how social service organizations and communities function both together and independently. Practitioners must know how organizational and community systems work in order to improve how they provide resources and services.

Describing Generalist Practice: Use of a Seven-Step Planned Change Process

EP 6, 8, 8e, 9

The procedure of following a structured planned change process is yet another concept inherent in generalist practice. In the context of social work, **planned change** is the process of developing and implementing a strategy for improving or altering some aspect of the human condition. This may involve helping change a client's behavior, improving the quality of life of a neighborhood or community, addressing a particular problematic condition or social problem, or working to achieve circumstances that enhance overall well-being.

Another term often used to describe the helping process is **problem solving**, which refers to the steps followed to resolve some difficulty. Essentially, problem solving involves the same process as planned change. However, social work's emphasis on client strengths may be at odds with the more negative connotations of the word *problem*. The term *change* may have more positive implications despite the fact that most social work intervention deals with problem situations. Therefore, the term *planned change* will be used here.

Regardless of the size of system with which generalist practitioners work, they follow a basic seven-step process to solve a problem or pursue a positive change. This planned change process is portrayed in Figure 1-8 and is described as follows (Kirst-Ashman & Hull, 2018a):

Step 1. *Engagement* is the process of establishing a positive professional relationship between the worker and the client. It may include greeting the client, portraying appropriate verbal and nonverbal behavior, listening to the client's issues, discussing agency services, and identifying client expectations (Kirst-Ashman & Hull, 2018b).

An example of engagement in an organization is a worker approaching the administration with a new idea about how to distribute information to clients about the agency's services. A community example is a social worker attending a meeting at a senior citizen's center, introducing herself, and presenting some ideas about developing recreational activities.

Step 2. *Assessment* is the identification of the type and extent of needs presented by the client, along with strengths and resources available to address the needs or concerns. Concerns can arise from intrapersonal issues, interpersonal challenges, lack of resources, or problems in the environment. The goal is to formulate a plan of service that is responsive to the situation. From the perspective of this book, assessment is the most significant step in the planned change process. This book's purpose is to provide information that will help you understand what's going on in the organization where you work, other organizations with which you have contact, and the community, society, and world in which all the organizations function. It should provide information for how you should think about proceeding to make and undertake effective plans.

Step 3. *Planning* is the process of identifying goals, rationally considering various ways to implement them, and establishing specific steps to achieve them. Because this and the following steps involve learning skills that are taught in practice courses, they will only be briefly mentioned here.

Step 4. *Intervention* is the actual doing or implementation of the plan. It concerns applying the skills you will learn in practice classes to achieve goals.

Step 5. *Evaluation* is the appraisal of the effectiveness of the plan and its implementation. How well did the plan work? To what extent were goals achieved?

Step 6. *Termination* is the ending of the social worker–client system relationship. Virtually all relationships come to an end. Clients move. Workers get different jobs. Goals are attained and there's no longer any need for worker—client contact.

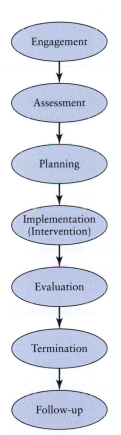

Figure 1-8 The Planned Change Process in Generalist Practice

Step 7. *Follow-up* is the retrieval of information about a client's functioning after the intervention has been terminated. Follow-up may provide information about the intervention's effectiveness after the fact, or it may be useful to determine if new needs have emerged.

Describing Generalist Practice: A Wide Range of Professional Roles

EP 1c

Another concept important in understanding generalist practice involves the adoption of a wide range of professional roles. Such roles when working with macro systems include the following (Kirst-Ashman & Hull, 2018a, pp. 20–24):

- **Advocate**: One who steps forward on behalf of the client system in order to promote fair and equitable treatment or gain needed resources.
- **Mediator**: One who resolves arguments or disagreements among micro, mezzo, or macro systems by assuming a neutral role.
- **Integrator/Coordinator**: One who oversees the process of assembling different elements to form a cohesive whole, product, or process (e.g., a new agency policy) and subsequently watches over its functioning to make sure it's effective.
- **Manager**: One who assumes some level of administrative responsibility for a social services agency or other organizational system.
- **Educator**: One who gives information and teaches skills to other systems.
- **Analyst/Evaluator**: One who determines the effectiveness of a program or agency for an organization or community.
- **Broker**: One who links a system of any size (individuals, families, groups, organizations, or communities) with community resources and services.
- **Facilitator**: One who guides a group experience.
- **Initiator**: One who calls attention to an issue or problem.
- **Negotiator**: One who acts to settle disputes and/or resolve disagreements, acting on the behalf of one of the parties involved.
- **Mobilizer**: One who identifies and convenes community people and resources and makes them responsive to unmet community needs.

Describing Generalist Practice: Application of Critical Thinking Skills   LO 1-5

EP 8, 8a

Critical thinking is yet another important concept involved in understanding generalist practice. **Critical thinking** is the careful scrutiny and analysis of:

- what is stated as true,
- what appears to be true,
- the answer to a question,
- the solution to a problem, or
- one's opinion concerning an issue.

Critical thinking concentrates on "the process of reasoning" (Gambrill & Gibbs, 2009, p. 4). It stresses *how* individuals think about the truth inherent in a statement or *how* they analyze an issue to formulate their own conclusions. As Gambrill (2013) so aptly states, "Critical thinkers question what others take for granted" (p. 111). This is an essential concept when trying to understand what's going on in the macro environment in which you practice as a social worker.

Critical thinking focuses on the questioning of beliefs, statements, assumptions, lines of reasoning, actions, and experiences. For instance, you read a "fact" in a book or hear about it from a friend or an instructor. Critical thinking focuses on *not* taking this "fact" at face value. Rather, it entails assuming the following Triple A approach to seriously examine and evaluate its validity (Kirst-Ashman, 2017):

1. *Ask* questions.
2. *Assess* the established facts and issues involved.
3. *Assert* a concluding opinion.

First, *ask* questions. For example, a friend and fellow student might tell you, "I think Muslim's are all a danger to the United States." To what extent is this statement true? To find out, first you could *ask* questions about what the statement is really saying. What does "all" mean? Does your friend lump all Muslim's together or recognize radical differences in religious beliefs within the Muslim religion? Does it make a difference whether a person has expressed animosity toward any other group? What kind of danger is your friend fearing? What experiences has your friend had to come to such a conclusion?

Second, *assess* the established facts and issues involved by seeking out information to answer the questions. Can this kind of a blanket statement really be true of every member of a particular religious group? What evidence is available to support or refute the person's contention?

Third, *assert* a concluding opinion. To what extent do you agree with your friend's statement? Is it a rational or reasoned opinion? How would you respond to your friend's assertion?

Critical thinking can be applied to virtually any belief, statement, assumption, line of reasoning, action, or experience proposed as being true. Consider the following statements that someone might maintain as "facts":

- Rich people are arrogant.
- Politicians are crooks.
- It is physically impossible for pigs to look up into the sky.
- Rats and horses can't vomit.
- A duck's quack doesn't echo, and no one knows why.[4]

These statements are silly (although some may be true), but the point is that critical thinking can be applied to an infinite array of thoughts and ideas. As specified in the Triple A approach, for each of the statements above: (1) what questions would you *ask*; (2) how would you *assess* the established facts and issues involved; and (3) what concluding opinion would you finally *assert*?

In addition to evaluating the accuracy of "facts," critical thinking can be used to answer questions, solve problems, or establish opinions about issues. Instead of being presented with a proposed "fact" to be scrutinized for its validity, you might be asked to answer some question. It might concern your opinion about an issue, assumption, or action. It might involve clarifying your values or evaluating your own way of thinking (Gambrill & Gibbs, 2009). Examples include:

---

[4] The last three statements were received in an e-mail from Keith McClory.

- Should murderers receive the death penalty?
- Should schools allow prayer or support events related to religious celebrations?
- Should the government pay college tuition for all students who qualify?
- Should abortion be legalized? If so, under what circumstances?
- What is the best way to eliminate poverty in this nation?

Consider answering the last question. It could be posed as a term paper question in one of your courses. First, what questions about it would you *ask*? What are the reasons for poverty in a relatively rich industrialized country? What social welfare programs are currently available to address poverty? To what extent are they effective? What roles do issues such as generational poverty, the opioid epidemic, and personal responsibility play in determining whether a program will be successful? What innovative new ideas for programs might be tried? Where might funding for such programs be found? How much money would it take to eliminate poverty, and who would pay for it?

Second, what facts and issues would you seek to address and *assess*? You probably would first seek to define poverty—what makes a person or family considered "poor"? What income level or lack of income is involved? You then might research statistics, costs, and studies concerning the effectiveness of various programs intended to reduce poverty. You might also investigate innovative ideas. Perhaps there are proposals for programs that you feel look promising. You might explore what various programs cost and how they are funded. Note that these suggestions only scratch the surface of how you might examine the issue.

Third, *assert* your opinion or conclusion. To what extent do you think it is possible to eliminate poverty? What kinds of resources and programs do you think it would take? What do you feel citizens and their government should do about poverty?

Types of Distorted Thinking   Critical thinking enhances self-awareness and the ability to detect various modes of distorted thinking that can trick people into assuming truth (Gambrill & Gibbs, 2009). The following are among the many traps to avoid by using critical thinking (Ruscio, 2006, pp. 6–10):

- *Outward appearance of science*. A supposed "fact" may superficially be cited in the context of scientific proof. How many times have you seen some well-groomed man wearing a doctor's lab coat appear in a television commercial state that this weight-loss supplement's effectiveness has been scientifically proven many times over? What questions might you ask about this? What tests were run to prove this effectiveness? Was the supplement taken by people who also were implementing other weight-loss approaches, including exercise and diet restrictions? Is the professional-looking person on TV telling the truth or being paid to read from a script? A related issue involves dietary supplements of all kinds that are supposed to do miraculous things for your health. Current federal standards allow "for anyone to sell almost any drug to the public, as long as he or she refers to the drug as a dietary supplement and does not make specific health claims about its effects . . .. Unproven remedies . . . are now officially tolerated under the guise of dietary supplements . . .. Vague wording and the sheer number of people who routinely violate . . . [legislative] provisions . . . have resulted in insufficient enforcement of even these weak standards" (Ruscio, 2006, p. 65). Hence, we really don't know the extent to which various supplements are helpful or harmful.

- *Absence of skeptical peer review.* Has the fact been evaluated by credible professionals who support its validity? An almost infinite number of websites addresses almost any topic you could think of and claims almost any "fact" to be true. A scary thing is that it's very difficult to tell which sites have well-established validity and which do not. Usually, websites ending in *.edu* or *.gov* enhance credibility because they're supposed to be initiated by formal educational or governmental organizations. But, how do you know for sure?

- *Reliance on personal experience and testimonials.* A woman enthusiastically proclaims, "This exercise equipment gave me awesome abs and made me look 20 years younger!" Because an approach worked for one person doesn't mean it will work for all. Perhaps that woman worked out with the equipment three hours a day for the past year. How has diet and stress management contributed to her youthful appearance? How old is she anyway, and can she prove it? Is she telling the truth? What scientific evidence is available to document the effectiveness of the equipment?

- *Wishful thinking (p. 43). Hoping that something is so can provide a powerful* incentive to believe in it. For example, consider the idea, "Putting magnets on your head can cure headaches." It would be nice to find an automatic cure for headaches that did not involve imbibing some substance. However, Ruscio (2006) explains:

> What about the alleged healing power of magnets as they interact with our bodies? The suggestion for how a magnetic field might be useful in curing disease is that it increases the flow of blood (which contains iron) to a targeted area, thereby bringing extra nutrients and carrying away the waste products of our metabolism. This theory, too, is directly contradicted by known facts. Blood, as with other bodily tissue and fluids, consists primarily of water. Thus, the fact that water is slightly repelled by a magnetic field is especially relevant. Why? Because the primary constituent of the human body—including not only our blood but also, as in most forms of life, all of our tissues and fluids—is water. We are therefore weakly repelled by magnetic fields. In principle, a strong enough magnet could be used to levitate a person, as has been done with drops of water, flowers, grasshoppers, and frogs. The small amounts of iron in our blood's hemoglobin do not exist in sufficiently dense quantities to offset the repulsive effect of the much larger amount of water. Therefore, to the extent that magnets have *any* influence on our blood—and this influence is minimal—they will drive blood *away* from the targeted areas. (pp. 82–83)

- *The "ancient wisdom" fallacy (p. 59).* "That must be the right way to do it because we've always done it that way." Ruscio (2006) points out that this type of argument can have dangerous consequences, because "if beliefs are granted truth owing merely to their age, this would provide justification for

EP 8a

> ### Critical Thinking Questions **1-2**
>
> What do you think about critical thinking? Do you use it often? If so, to what extent have you found it useful?

      sexism, racism, anti-Semitism, and a host of other repellent notions that have been widely held throughout human history" (p. 59).

- *The popularity fallacy* (p. 59). "Everybody else is doing it, so it must be right." I once had a classmate, age 26 no less, who said in an election year that he was going to vote for the current president because that president had already been elected, and all those people who voted for him surely couldn't be wrong. I stared at him in total disbelief. How could he be so naïve? How could he not think for himself? And, at his age? He obviously believed in the popularity fallacy.

Critical Thinking Questions in This Book   LO 1-6

Because of the importance of critical thinking in social work and in generalist practice, as well as in understanding macro systems and the social environment, a wide range of critical thinking questions will be posed throughout this book (such as Critical Thinking Questions 1-2).

Describing Generalist Practice: Incorporation of Research-Informed Practice

EP 4a, 4c, 9b

One other important concept involved in generalist practice involves the use of research. Social work students must demonstrate competency in *practice-informed research* and *research-informed practice*. This means social workers should use the approaches and interventions in their practice that research has determined are effective. Social workers should employ "Use and translate research evidence to inform and improve practice, policy, and service delivery" (CSWE, 2015, EP 4c). Social workers might also have opportunities to participate in *practice-based research*. This research, which closely involves the everyday work of practitioners, focuses on collecting data and providing results directly related to the processes of social work practice. Highlight 1-3 introduces a concept related to research-informed practice—evidence-based practice.

Why Research Is Important   Knowledge of social work research is important for two basic reasons. First, it can help social workers become more effective in their direct practice by choosing interventions that have been proven successful, thereby getting better and clearer results. Framing social work interventions so they can be evaluated through research provides information about which specific techniques work best with which problems. Evaluation of practice throughout the intervention process can help determine whether a worker is really helping a client.

      Second, accumulated research helps build a foundation for planning effective interventions. Knowledge of what has worked best in the past provides guidelines

---

Highlight **1-3**

Evidence-Based Practice

Another term frequently used in social work, which has a meaning similar to research-informed practice, is *evidence-based practice*. This is "the conscientious, explicit, and judicious use of current best evidence in making decisions about the care of clients" (Gambrill, 2000, p. 46; Race, 2008). Gambrill (2000) explains:

It involves integrating individual practice expertise with the best available external evidence from systematic research as well as considering the values and expectations of clients. External research findings related to problems are drawn on if they are available

and they apply to a client's situation. Involving clients as informed participants in a collaborative helping relationship is a hallmark of evidence-based practice. Clients are fully informed about the risks and benefits of recommended services as well as alternatives (including the alternative of doing nothing). . . . The term *evidence-based practice* is preferable to the term empirical practice. The latter term now seems to be applied to material that has been published, whether or not it is evidence-based. Such use represents an appeal to authority (not evidence). (pp. 46–47)

---

for approaches and techniques to be used in the present and in the future. Research establishes the basis for the development of programs and policies that affect many people. Such knowledge can also be used to generate new theories and ideas to further enhance the effectiveness of social work practice.

An Overview of Macro Practice

This book focuses on generalist practice with macro systems in the macro social environment. Macro practice is generalist social work practice intending to affect change in large systems, including communities and organizations. This closing section of this chapter's content provides a brief overview of historical and current macro practice. These sections intend to provide a context for subsequent chapters that go into much greater detail about practice in and with groups, organizations, and communities in the macro social environment.

The History of Generalist Practice with and within Communities   LO 1-7

EP 1, 1c

Historically, *community organization* has been the term used to refer to macro practice in social work. The methods and directions of social work practice have changed and evolved, just as the economic and social realities of the times have drastically changed. However, reviewing the historical perspective on community practice helps us to understand the significance of community assessment and work today.

Past major methods of community organization engaged in by social workers have included social action, social planning, and locality development (Rothman, 2001). **Social action** is coordinated effort to advocate for change in a social institution to benefit a specific population (e.g., homeless people), solve a social problem, enhance people's well-being, or correct unfairness (e.g., racism) (Kirst-Ashman & Hull, 2018b). (*Racism* is the belief that people of different races are inherently different and that some races are superior to others.) Social action applies macro-practice skills to advocate for people in local, state, national, and global communities. Frequently, social action can be used to remedy imbalances of power.

Social planning involves "a technical process of problem-solving with regard to substantive social problems, such as delinquency, housing, and mental health" (Rothman, 2001, p. 31). The emphasis here is to call in experts or consultants to work, usually with designated community leaders, to solve specific problems. People in the general community would have little, if any, participation or input into the problem-solving process. For example, a city might call in an urban renewal expert to recommend what should be done with a deteriorating area in the community.

Locality development emphasizes "community change . . . pursued optimally through broad participation of a wide spectrum of people at the local community level in determining goals and taking . . . action" (Rothman, 2001, p. 29). The idea is to involve as many people as possible within the community in a democratic manner to define their goals and help themselves. Locality development fits extremely well with social work values. Individual dignity, participation, and free choice are emphasized.

Contemporary Macro Practice

EP 1, 7

Today, macro practice is still a major thrust of generalist social work. The basic concept of community is just as important as ever. However, Rothman (2008) proposes a newer outlook more appropriate to current macro practice that calls for "multi modes of intervention" (p. 11). Two new ideas predominate.

One major initiative is that the traditional three community organization methods should be brought up to date to reflect a modification in focus. First, social advocacy should replace social action (p. 12). "**Social advocacy** deems the application of pressure as the best course of action to take against people or institutions that may have [brought about] . . . the problem or that stand in the way of its solution—which frequently involves promoting equity or social justice. When interests clash in this way, conflict is a given" (p. 12). Advocacy becomes the focus of attention.

"Planning and policy practice" then replace the traditional social planning approach (p. 12). Planning continues to involve "proposing and enacting particular solutions" (p. 12). **Policy practice** entails "efforts to change policies in legislative, agency, and community settings by establishing new policies, improving existing ones, or defeating the policy initiatives of other people" (Jansson, 2014, p. 1). Changing policy often becomes an objective.

"Community capacity development" is substituted for locality development (Rothman, 2007, p. 12). "**Community capacity development** assumes that change is best accomplished when the people affected by problems are empowered with the knowledge and skills needed to understand their problems, and then work cooperatively together to overcome them. Thus there is a premium on consensus as a tactic and on social solidarity [unity including diverse community groups that is based on mutual interests, support, and goals] as [a means] . . . and outcome" (Rothman, 2008, p. 12). Here community *capacity* (the potential use of the community's inherent strengths, resources, citizen participation, and leadership) is stressed.

The second primary initiative posed for contemporary macro practice involves the flexibility of mixing various aspects of these three approaches to get things done. Rothman (2008) reflects that macro practice is often a complex process that requires emphasizing various aspects of these three approaches depending on the situation. For example, planning and policy practice may require varying degrees of social advocacy. **Advocacy**, of course, involves stepping forward on behalf of the client system in order to promote fair and equitable treatment or gain needed resources. **Policy advocacy** is "policy practice that aims to help relatively powerless groups, such as women, children, poor people, African Americans, Asian Americans, Latinos, Native Americans, gay men and lesbians, and people with disabilities improve their resources and opportunities" (Jansson, 2012, p. 1).

Another example of a more flexible combination of methods involves community capacity development with an emphasis on planning. Traditionally, capacity development relied on seeking ideas from community residents about what problems needed attention and what thoughts they had about possible solutions. Current approaches to capacity development usually begin with a clear proposal to improve the economic health, and residents are encouraged to take actions that helps achieve this goal. Steps taken include improving access to affordable housing, developing alternative financing options for borrowers, and helping increase employment opportunities.

At a Glance **1-5**

Generalist practice: The application of an extensive and diverse knowledge base, professional values, and a wide range of skills to promote human well-being for individuals, families, groups, organizations, and communities.

Organizational structure: The manner in which an organization systematically arranges workers into groups (or departments) and then coordinates these various groups' activities and interactions.

Planned change: The process of developing and implementing a strategy for improving or altering some aspect of the human condition.

Problem solving: The steps followed to resolve some difficulty.

Advocate: One who steps forward on the behalf of the client system in order to promote fair and equitable treatment or gain needed resources.

Mediator: One who resolves arguments or disagreements among micro, mezzo, or macro systems by assuming a neutral role.

Integrator/Coordinator: One who oversees the process of assembling different elements to form a cohesive whole, product, or process (e.g., a new agency policy) and subsequently watches over its functioning to make sure it's effective.

Manager: One who assumes some level of administrative responsibility for a social services agency or other organizational system.

Educator: One who gives information and teaches skills to other systems.

Analyst/Evaluator: One who determines the effectiveness of a program or agency for an organization or community.

Broker: One who links a system of any size (individuals, families, groups, organizations, or communities) with community resources and services.

Facilitator: One who guides a group experience.

Initiator: One who calls attention to an issue or problem.

Negotiator: One who acts to settle disputes and/or resolve disagreements, acting on the behalf of one of the parties involved.

Mobilizer: One who identifies and convenes community people and resources and makes them responsive to unmet community needs.

Critical thinking: The careful scrutiny and analysis of what is stated and what appears to be true, answers, solutions, and opinions concerning an issue.

Social action: Coordinated effort to advocate for change in a social institution to benefit a specific population, solve a social problem, enhance people's well-being, or correct unfairness.

Social planning: A "technical process of problem-solving with regard to substantive social problems, such as delinquency, housing, and mental health" (Rothman, 2001, p. 31).

Locality development: Emphasis on a broad spectrum of people at the local level defining goals and working to achieve them.

Advocacy: Stepping forward on behalf of the client system in order to promote fair and equitable treatment or gain needed resources.

Chapter Summary

The following summarizes this chapter's content as it relates to the learning objectives presented at the beginning of the chapter. Objectives include the following:

LO 1-1 Define and explain the macro social environment.

The macro social environment is the configuration of communities, organizations, and groups within the latter that are products of social, economic, and political forces and institutions. A community is "a number of people who have something in common that connects them in some way and that distinguishes them from others" (Homan, 2011, p. 8). Organizations are "(1) social entities that (2) are goal directed, (3) are designed as deliberately structured and coordinated activity systems, and (4) are linked to the external environment" (Daft, 2016, p. 13). Some organizations provide social services. A group is at least two individuals gathered together because of some common bond, to meet members' social and emotional needs, or to fulfill some mutual purpose. Social, economic, and political forces operate within and affect the macro social environment.

LO 1-2 Describe ecosystems theory as a useful conceptual framework for understanding the macro social environment, and discuss relevant concepts derived from systems theory and the ecological perspective.

Ecosystems theory provides one significant means of conceptualizing and understanding human behavior. Concepts taken from systems theory include **system, boundaries, subsystem, homeostasis, role, relationship, input, output, negative** and **positive feedback, interface, differentiation, entropy, negative entropy,** and **equifinality**. Terms taken from the ecological perspective include the **social environment; energy; input; output; interface; adaptation; person-in-environment fit; stress, stressors,** and **coping; relatedness; habitat;** and **niche**.

LO 1-3 Discuss people's involvement with multiple systems in the macro social environment.

A target of change is the system that social workers need to change or influence in order to accomplish

goals. A micro system is an individual. A mezzo system refers to any small group. A macro system is any system larger than a small group, including organizations and communities. A client system is any individual, family, group, organization, or community that will ultimately benefit from social work intervention. Macro client systems include communities, organizations, and larger groups of clientele who have similar issues and problems and are potential beneficiaries of positive change.

LO 1-4 Describe generalist practice and explain the relationship between some of its major concepts and the macro social environment.

Generalist practice is the application of an extensive and diverse knowledge base, professional values, and a wide range of skills to promote human well-being for individuals, families, groups, communities, and organizations. The following concepts involved in generalist practice are discussed: targeting any size system for change; working within an organizational structure; using a planned change process; adopting a wide range of professional roles; applying critical thinking skills; and incorporating research-informed practice. Other generalist practice concepts concern adherence to professional values, the understanding of human diversity, emphasis on client empowerment, and advocacy for human rights.

LO 1-5 Define critical thinking and discuss its use in generalist practice.

Critical thinking is (1) the careful scrutiny of what is stated as true or what appears to be true and the resulting expression of an opinion or conclusion based on that scrutiny, and (2) the creative formulation of an opinion or conclusion when presented with a question, problem, or issue. Generalist practitioners can use a Triple A approach to assess information and situations: (1) Ask questions; (2) assess the established facts and issues involves; and (3) assert a concluding opinion.

LO 1-6 Discuss critical thinking questions that will be raised throughout the book.

This section on critical thinking questions addresses evaluation of one's geographic community and the frequency of using critical thinking.

LO 1-7 **Identify differences between historical approaches to social work practice in the macro social environment and contemporary macro practice.**

Traditional methods of macro practice include social action, social planning, and locality development. In contemporary macro practice, social advocacy replaces social action, planning and policy practice replace social planning, and community capacity development replaces locality development.

Looking Ahead

This chapter described the macro social environment as the context for generalist social work practice. Some of the major concepts involved in generalist practice were described and discussed.

The next chapter will continue the explanation of generalist practice by examining the values and principles that guide such practice in the macro social environment.

Competency Notes

This section relates chapter content to the Council on Social Work Education's (CSWE) *Educational Policy and Accreditation Standards* (EPAS) (CSWE, 2015). One major goal of social work education is to facilitate students' attainment of the EPAS-designated nine core competencies and their 41 related component behaviors so that students develop into competent practitioners. As indicated in the beginning of this chapter, *competencies* are basic capabilities involving social work knowledge, skills, and values that can be demonstrated and measured by component behaviors. Competencies reflect more general expectations for proficient social workers. *Component behaviors*, on the other hand, are measurable actions that demonstrate the application of social work knowledge, skills, and values for effective social work practice. Component behaviors are more specific and are used to measure competency. The goal in competency education is to ensure that students demonstrate the ability to integrate and apply the competencies in practice with all size systems.

Students require knowledge in order to develop skills and become competent. Our intent here is to specify what chapter content and knowledge coincides with the development of specific competencies and component behaviors. (This ultimately is intended to assist in the accreditation process.) Therefore, the following listing first cites the various Educational Policy (EP) core competencies and

their related component behaviors that are relevant to chapter content. Note that the listing generally follows the numerical order in which competencies and component behaviors are cited in the EPAS. Also note that component behaviors cited under each competency are bulleted in the EPAS. For clarity, the bulleted component behaviors are alphabetized here under each of the nine competencies.

 We have established that "helping hands" icons such as that illustrated in this paragraph are labeled and interspersed throughout the chapter, indicating where relevant accompanying content is located. The page numbers noted in the listing indicate where icons are placed in the chapter. Following the icon's page number is a brief explanation of how the content accompanying the icon relates to the specified competency or practice behavior.

As mentioned earlier, the EPAS competencies and component behaviors are summarized in a chart on the inside cover of this book. The chart also indicates in which chapters icons for specific competencies and component behaviors are located throughout the book.

The content of this chapter prepares students to apply knowledge of human behavior and the social environment. The following identifies where Educational Policy (EP) competencies and component behaviors are discussed in the chapter.

EP 1 (Competency 1)—Demonstrate Ethical and Professional Behavior. *(p. 30)*: Attending to professional roles and behaviors is part of generalist practice. *(p. 36)*: Contemporary macro practice is discussed in contrast to traditional models. Social workers should respond to changing contexts that shape practice so that they may update their approaches. *(p. 30)*: Social workers assume defined professional roles within the organizational structure

EP 1a Make ethical decisions by applying the standards of the NASW Code of Ethics, relevant laws and regulations, models for ethical decision-making, ethical conduct of research, and additional codes of ethics as appropriate to context. *(p. 27)*: Adherence to professional values and ethics is key to generalist practice.

EP 1b Use reflection and self-regulation to manage personal values and maintain professionalism in practice situations. *(p. 7)*: Practicing personal reflection about one's own community can begin the process of understanding communities and their significance for clients.

EP 1c Demonstrate professional demeanor in behavior; appearance; and oral, written, and electronic communication. *(p. 30)*: Practitioners should demonstrate professional behavior while functioning within the organizational structure. *(p. 35)*: Social workers should know the profession's history, including that of macro practice.

EP 1e Use supervision and consultation to guide professional judgment and behavior. *(p. 28)*: Social workers should use supervision as it is configured within the organizational structure and supervisory hierarchy.

EP 3 (Competency 3)—Advance Human Rights and Social, Economic, and Environmental Justice. *(p. 28)*: Social workers should advocate for policies that advance social well-being.

EP 3a Apply their understanding of social, economic, and environmental justice to advocate for human rights at the individual and system levels. *(p. 9)*: Social workers must first understand social, economic, and political forces in order to advocate for and advance social, economic, and

environmental justice. *(p. 3)*: Generalist practitioners should advocate for human rights, and social, economic, and environmental justice.

EP 4 (Competency 4)—Engage in Practice-Informed Research and Research-Informed Practice. *(p. 34)*: Generalist practitioners use research to guide their interventions with client systems.

EP 4a Use practice experience and theory to inform scientific inquiry and research. *(p. 34)*: Research should focus on issues related to practice so that it is directly relevant to practice effectiveness.

EP 4c Use and translate research evidence to inform and improve practice, policy, and service delivery. *(p. 34)*: Social workers should utilize research on practice effectiveness to make informed practice decisions.

EP 5 (Competency 5)—Engage in Policy Practice. *(p. 37)*: "Policy practice that aims to help relatively powerless groups, such as women, children, poor people, African Americans, Asian Americans, Latinos, Native Americans, gay men and lesbians, and people with disabilities improve their resources and opportunities" (Jansson, 2012, p. 1).

EP 5b Assess how social welfare and economic policies impact the delivery of and access to social services. *(p. 28)*: Assessment is a key step in determining whether social, economic, and environmental policies support or detract from social well-being.

EP 6 (Competency 6)—Engage with Individuals, Families, Groups, Organizations, and Communities. *(p. 12)*: Social workers can use theoretical and conceptual frameworks such as ecosystems theory to guide the processes of assessment, intervention, and evaluation. *(p. 27)*: Generalist practitioners use a planned change process in their interventions with client systems. Client systems may be individuals, families, groups, organizations, or communities. *(p. 23)*: Social workers must have knowledge and skills to practice with individuals, families, groups, organizations, and communities. *(p. 28)*: Social workers should follow the planned change process that includes the stages of engagement, assessment, intervention, and evaluation with individuals, families, groups, organizations, and communities.

EP 6a Apply knowledge of human behavior and the social environment, person-in-environment, and other multidisciplinary theoretical frameworks to engage with clients and constituencies. *(p. 6):* Social workers should be knowledgeable about the range of social systems in which people live and how these systems promote or deter people in maintaining or achieving health and well-being. Large (macro) systems include communities, organizations, and groups. People are involved with a wide range of systems in the social environment.

EP 7a Collect and organize data, and apply critical thinking to interpret information from clients and constituencies. *(p. 7):* Generalist practitioners emphasize client strengths. *(p. 34):* Social workers must learn to collect, organize, and interpret appropriate data about communities to conduct relevant assessments concerning clients

EP 7c Develop mutually agreed-on intervention goals and objectives based on the critical assessment of strengths, needs, and challenges within clients and constituencies. *(p. 27):* Generalist practitioners establish goals with their client systems.

EP 7d Select appropriate intervention strategies based on the assessment, research knowledge, and values and preferences of clients and constituencies. *(p. 37):* Three models of intervention in macro practice are discussed.

EP 8 (Competency 8)—Intervene with Individuals, Families, Groups, Organizations, and Communities. *(p. 30):* The planned change process helps clients resolve problems.

EP 8a Critically choose and implement interventions to achieve practice goals and enhance capacities of clients and constituencies. *(p. 27):* Distinguishing and appraising multiple sources of knowledge will help social workers better understand how communities function. *(pp. 7, 34):* Critical thinking questions are posed. *(p. 34):* As generalist practitioners, social workers should use critical thinking as they work with client systems. *(p. 34):* As generalist practitioners, social workers should use critical thinking skills to evaluate and integrate multiple sources of knowledge to make decisions, come to conclusions, and differentiate facts from fiction.

EP 8d Negotiate, mediate, and advocate with and on behalf of diverse clients and constituencies. *(p. 28):* Social workers should advocate on the behalf of their clients.

EP 8e Facilitate effective transitions and endings that advance mutually agreed-on goals *(p. 28):* Two of the steps in planned change involve termination and follow-up.

EP 9 (Competency 9)—Evaluate Practice with Individuals, Families, Groups, Organizations, and Communities. *(p. 28):* One of the steps in planned change involves evaluation of interventions.

EP 9b Apply knowledge of human behavior and the social environment, person-in-environment, and other multidisciplinary theoretical frameworks in the evaluation of outcomes. *(p. 34):* Evaluation of practice throughout the intervention process can help determine whether a worker is really helping a client.

Media Resources

MindTap for Social Work

 Go to MindTap® for digital study tools and resources that complement this text and help you be more successful in your course and career. There's an interactive eBook plus videos of client sessions, skill-building activities, quizzes to help you prepare for tests, apps, and more—all in one place. If your instructor didn't assign MindTap, you can find out more about it at CengageBrain.com.

2 | Values and Principles That Guide Generalist Practice in the Macro Social Environment

Values and principles concerning human rights guide generalist social work practice.

LEARNING OBJECTIVES

After reading this chapter you should be able to...

2-1 Describe the values that characterize generalist practice and explain the relationship between these concepts and the macro social environment.

2-2 Identify the National Association of Social Workers (NASW) *Code of Ethics*, summarize professional ethical responsibilities, and resolve ethical dilemmas.

2-3 Explain the importance of identifying with the social work profession.

2-4 Describe human diversity with its multiple, overlapping factors (Council for Social Work Education [CSWE], 2015, EP 2).

2-5 Explain diversity with respect to gender, sex, and culture.

2-6 Define cultural competence and address four competencies involved.

2-7 Analyze various critical thinking questions.

2-8 Review the significance of client empowerment, strengths, and resiliency.

2-9 Explain the importance of advocacy for human rights and social and economic justice.

2-10 Discuss some of the dynamics involved in oppression.

2-11 Demonstrate awareness of ethical topics.

EP 1, 2

What values are most important to you? Caring for others? Self-preservation? Charity? Fairness? Equality? Material possessions? Financial stability? Honesty? Loyalty? Freedom of speech?

How do you make decisions about what is right and what is wrong? Do you have a personal code of ethics that guides your behavior? Do you consider yourself more of an independent thinker? Or do you tend to go along with the crowd and usually do what you're told?

What are your thoughts about the value of human diversity? Is it some vague concept that is difficult to relate to? Do you think of specific groups of people? Are there any groups about whom you harbor some negative feelings—for example, people with physical or intellectual disabilities (mental retardation), older adults, religious organizations or sects, certain racial groups, migrants and people who immigrate illegally, or people with a sexual orientation different from yours? If so, what are these negative perceptions?

Do you have thoughts about the status of human rights in the world today? Are there oppressed populations? If so, who are they? What do you think are the causes of oppression? Should it and can it be stopped? If so, how should it be stopped? Who should stop it?

We all have values and opinions about what is good and bad, right and wrong. We each have an individualized view of how the world goes round and how it ideally should go round.

Social work as a profession also promotes professional values. Additionally, the profession requires ethical conduct on the part of practitioners. Therefore, to understand the dynamics involved in the macro social environment, it's crucial to understand the values and principles that guide generalist practitioners in their work.

EP 2

LO 2-1 Chapter 1 introduced generalist practice as the application of an extensive and diverse knowledge base, professional values, and a wide range of skills to promote human well-being for individuals, families, groups, organizations, and communities. It also elaborated on a range of other concepts characterizing generalist practice. This chapter will explore the professional principles and beliefs that distinguish generalist practice.

These include professional values and ethics, the understanding of human diversity, an emphasis on client empowerment, and the pursuit of social, economic, and environmental justice.

Describing Generalist Practice: Adherence to Professional Values and the Application of Professional Ethics LO 2-2

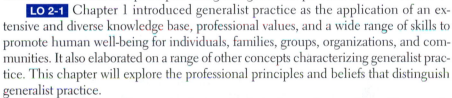

EP 1

Professional values and ethics are at the heart of social work. Thus, these characterize the next significant dimension in the definition of generalist practice. **Values** involve what you do and do not consider important. They concern what is and is not considered to have worth. They also involve judgments and decisions about relative worth—that is, about what is more valuable and what is less valuable.

Ethics concern principles that specify what is good and what is bad. They clarify what should and should not be done. The NASW *Code of Ethics* (2008) is based on professional values and provides guidelines for what practitioners should do when confronting a range of difficult situations.

Highlight 2-1

The Importance of Identification with the Social Work Profession LO 2-3

EP 1

While working within an organization, a generalist practitioner should maintain and demonstrate a professional identity. *Identification with the social work profession* means that as a social worker, you must represent the profession and support its mission and core values. Such identification includes a commitment to the profession's enhancement and to your own professional conduct and growth, in addition to knowledge of the profession's history. Identification, then, involves adherence to professional ethics, demonstration of professional roles (discussed in Chapter 1), and participation in lifelong learning to enhance knowledge and skills (CSWE, 2015).

Ethics and values are clearly related, although they are not synonymous. Dolgoff, Loewenberg, and Harrington (2012) explain, "Ethics are deduced from values and must be in consonance with them. The difference between them is that values are concerned with what is *good* and *desirable*, while ethics deal with what is *right* and *correct*" (p. 25). Values determine what beliefs are appropriate. Ethics address what to *do* with, or how to *apply*, those beliefs.

Cournoyer (2014) summarizes the momentous importance of social work ethics as he directs his comments to generalist practitioners working in the macro social environment:

> We must consider every aspect of practice, every decision, every assessment, every intervention, and virtually every action you undertake as social workers from the perspective of our professional ethics and obligations. This dimension supersedes all others. Ethical responsibilities take precedence over theoretical knowledge, research findings, practice wisdom, agency policies, and, of course, our own personal values, preferences, and beliefs. (p. 144)

Because of the core significance of professional values and ethics for social workers, their identification with the social work profession is a necessity (CSWE, 2015). Highlight 2-1 underscores the importance of this identification as generalist practitioners work in groups, organizations, and communities in the macro social environment.

The NASW *Code of Ethics*

EP 1a

Simply put, ethics guide professional behavior. The mission of the **Code of Ethics** "is to enhance human well-being and help meet the basic human needs of all people, with particular attention to the needs and empowerment of people who are vulnerable, oppressed, and living in poverty" (NASW, 2008). The six core values are as follows:

1. *Service*: Providing help, resources, and benefits so that people may achieve their maximum potential.
2. *Social justice*: The philosophical perspective that all people have the right to enjoy equal opportunities in economic, political, and social realms.

3. *Dignity and worth of the person:* Holding in high esteem and appreciating individual value.
4. *Importance of human relationships:* Valuing the dynamic reciprocal interactions between social workers and clients, including how they communicate, think and feel about each other, and behave toward each other.
5. *Integrity:* Maintaining trustworthiness and sound adherence to moral ideals.
6. *Competence:* Having the necessary skills and abilities to perform work with clients effectively.

The most extensive portion of the *Code* is devoted to specific "Ethical Standards." It encompasses 155 specific principles clustered under six major categories: social workers' ethical responsibilities to clients, to colleagues, in practice settings, as professionals, to the social work profession, and to the broader society. Focus on Ethics 2-1 summarizes the major concepts involved in each of the six broad areas. The entire *Code* is available from NASW online at http://www.socialworkers.org/pubs/code/code.asp.

Social Workers' Ethical Responsibilities to Clients

The first category of ethical standards identifies social workers' 16 ethical responsibilities to clients. How should practitioners behave with respect to clients? What aspects of worker/client interaction are most significant within an ethical context? The standards range from supporting client **self-determination** (everyone's right to make his or her own decisions) to maintaining the highest possible level of **confidentiality** (the principle that workers should not share information provided by or about a client unless they have the client's explicit permission to do so) to avoiding sexual relationships with clients.

Social Workers' Ethical Responsibilities to Colleagues

The *Code* specifies 11 areas in which practitioners have ethical responsibilities to colleagues. These areas focus on having respect for colleagues, even when differences of opinion arise. The areas also address working cooperatively on the behalf of clients. Social workers should make referrals to professionals with other areas of expertise when necessary. Finally, social workers should address situations when colleagues are functioning ineffectively due to personal problems or unethical conduct.

Social Workers' Ethical Responsibilities in Practice Settings

This section of the *Code* focuses on 10 standards for appropriate behavior in practice settings. Social workers who supervise others should be competent and evaluate supervisees fairly. Any information or data that any social worker records should be accurate. Social workers should advocate for increased funding both inside and outside their agencies when resources are needed for clients. Social workers should "act to prevent and eliminate discrimination in the employing organization's work assignments and in its employment policies and practices" (NASW, 2008, 3.09e). Finally, practitioners should make sure their employers are aware of unethical practices.

Focus on Ethics **2-1**

A Summary of Ethical Standards in the NASW *Code of Ethics*

1. Social Workers' Ethical Responsibilities to Clients
   - 1.01 Commitment to Clients
   - 1.02 Self-Determination
   - 1.03 Informed Consent
   - 1.04 Competence
   - 1.05 Cultural Competence and Social Diversity
   - 1.06 Conflicts of Interest
   - 1.07 Privacy and Confidentiality
   - 1.08 Access to Records
   - 1.09 Sexual Relationships
   - 1.10 Physical Contact
   - 1.11 Sexual Harassment
   - 1.12 Derogatory Language
   - 1.13 Payment for Services
   - 1.14 Clients Who Lack Decision-Making Capacity
   - 1.15 Interruption of Services
   - 1.16 Termination of Services
2. Social Workers' Ethical Responsibilities to Colleagues
   - 2.01 Respect
   - 2.02 Confidentiality
   - 2.03 Interdisciplinary Collaboration
   - 2.04 Disputes Involving Colleagues
   - 2.05 Consultation
   - 2.06 Referral for Services
   - 2.07 Sexual Relationships
   - 2.08 Sexual Harassment
   - 2.09 Impairment of Colleagues
   - 2.10 Incompetence of Colleagues
   - 2.11 Unethical Conduct of Colleagues

3. Social Workers' Ethical Responsibilities in Practice Settings
   - 3.01 Supervision and Consultation
   - 3.02 Education and Training
   - 3.03 Performance Evaluation
   - 3.04 Client Records
   - 3.05 Billing
   - 3.06 Client Transfer
   - 3.07 Administration
   - 3.08 Continuing Education and Staff Development
   - 3.09 Commitments to Employers
   - 3.10 Labor–Management Disputes
4. Social Workers' Ethical Responsibilities as Professionals
   - 4.01 Competence
   - 4.02 Discrimination
   - 4.03 Private Conduct
   - 4.04 Dishonesty, Fraud, and Deception
   - 4.05 Impairment
   - 4.06 Misrepresentation
   - 4.07 Solicitations
   - 4.08 Acknowledging Credit
5. Social Workers' Ethical Responsibilities to the Social Work Profession
   - 5.01 Integrity of the Profession
   - 5.02 Evaluation and Research
6. Social Workers' Ethical Responsibilities to the Broader Society
   - 6.01 Social Welfare
   - 6.02 Public Participation
   - 6.03 Public Emergencies
   - 6.04 Social and Political Action

Social Workers' Ethical Responsibilities as Professionals

Social workers' ethical responsibilities as professionals include eight broad dimensions by which they should judge their behavior and responsibility. First and foremost, they should be competent to do their jobs. If they are not, they should either seek out the education and learn the skills needed to become competent or get another job. Social workers should not "practice, condone, facilitate, or collaborate with any form of discrimination on the basis of race, ethnicity, national origin, color, sex, sexual orientation, gender identity or expression, age, marital status, political belief, religion, immigration status, or mental or physical disability" (NASW, 2008, 4.02). They should be honest, avoid fraud, and seek help when personal problems begin to interfere with their professional effectiveness. They should represent themselves and their qualifications accurately, and never take credit for someone else's work.

Social Workers' Ethical Responsibilities to the Social Work Profession

Ethical responsibilities to the social work profession focus on two dimensions: integrity, and evaluation and research. First, **integrity** refers to social workers' adherence to and promotion of high moral and ethical standards. Social workers should consistently strive to practice in accordance with ethical principles. They should also work hard to enhance their effectiveness. Social workers should participate in activities aimed at professional contributions, such as "teaching, research, consultation, service, legislative testimony, presentations in the community, and participation in their professional organizations" (NASW, 2008, 5.01c).

The second dimension concerning responsibility to the social work profession concerns the use of evaluation and research in practice. Social workers should scrutinize and assess the effectiveness of policies that guide their work and of the work itself. When possible, social workers should aid in contributing to the social work knowledge base. For example, they might submit data or participate in research studies. Social workers should keep themselves updated regarding research about practice and practice effectiveness. When conducting research, practitioners should follow "responsible research practices" as specified in the *Code* (NASW, 2008, 5.0.2p).

Social Workers' Ethical Responsibilities to the Broader Society

Ethical responsibilities to the broader society include four areas that reflect the basic core of social work—namely, to advocate and work for people's general welfare. This responsibility surpasses those merely listed in most job descriptions. First, social workers should promote people's general welfare on all levels from the local to the global. Second, they should encourage people's up-to-date involvement in the formulation of public policies and practices. Third, practitioners should eagerly offer their services during community crises (e.g., floods, tornadoes, earthquakes, or terrorist attacks). Fourth, social workers should actively participate in improving social and political policies that are fair, equitable, and beneficial.

It is beyond the scope of this book to elaborate on each specific ethical standard here. However, several designated standards and ethical issues will be discussed through various Focus on Ethics perspectives periodically portrayed throughout the book. Focus on Ethics 2-2 introduces the concept of ethical dilemmas.

Professional ethical standards always stand at the forefront of effective generalist practice. To understand the dynamics and issues characterizing the macro social environment, it is necessary to identify and assess various potential ethical pitfalls. Later chapters will continue to discuss the importance of values and ethics.

Focus on Ethics **2-2**

Ethical Dilemmas

EP 1, 1a

Note that from a superficial perspective, professional judgments may look like a simple matter of common sense. Just do the right thing, right? However, in real-life decisions, values and ethical principles constantly conflict. This can result in **ethical dilemmas**, namely, problematic situations where one must make a difficult choice among two or more alternatives where ethical standards conflict. No one perfect answer can conform to all the ethical standards involved. Sometimes, there is substantial personal or professional risk for the practitioner who raises unpopular questions.

Consider the following two examples occurring in the macro social environment:

- One practitioner, Bruce, reflects on his predicament, "I work in an agency that is not providing the services agreed to in exchange for grant money. Its brochures advertise the services as available and the agency documentation shows the services as provided, so the grantor believes the services are in place. The staff doesn't have the necessary resources, so those directly responsible for the care of the individuals who should be receiving the services are under a lot of stress. The consumers were promised something and are not getting it" (Kenyon, 1999, p. 213).

Answer the following questions:

1. What major issues are involved here?
2. What alternatives are available to Bruce?
3. What are the pros and cons of each alternative?

4. What do you think is the "right thing" to do?
5. What would you do if you were Bruce?

- Adriana works in a community mental health clinic, and most of her time is devoted to dealing with immediate crises. The more she works with people in crisis, the more she is convinced that the focus of her work should be on preventive programs designed to educate the public. Adriana comes to believe strongly that there would be far fewer clients in distress if people were effectively contacted and motivated to participate in growth-oriented educational programs. She develops detailed, logical, and convincing proposals for programs she would like to implement in the community, but they are consistently rejected by the director of her center. Because the clinic is partially funded by the government for the express purpose of crisis intervention, the director feels uneasy about approving any program that does not relate directly to this objective (Corey, Corey, & Callanan, 2011, p. 533).

Answer the following questions:

1. What major issues are involved here?
2. What alternatives are available to Adriana?
3. What are the pros and cons of each alternative?
4. What do you think is the "right thing" to do?
5. What would you do if you were Adriana?

This brief discussion simply introduces the concept of ethical dilemmas.

Describing Generalist Practice: Understanding and Appreciating Human Diversity LO 2-4

EP 2, 6a

Another important value inherent in generalist practice is the appreciation and engagement of human diversity (CSWE, 2015). **Human diversity** refers to the vast array of differences among human beings, including such factors as gender, ethnicity, values, culture, spiritual/religious beliefs, sexual orientation, and both mental and physical health. Lum (2011) reflects:

Human diversity involves the recognition of differences and similarities in the experiences, needs, and beliefs of people. (p. 75)

Social work by nature addresses virtually any type of problem posed by any type of person from any type of background. To help people, practitioners must be open-minded, nonjudgmental, knowledgeable, and skilled to work with any client. Social work education is charged with teaching knowledge, skills, and values concerning "the intersectionality of factors including age, class, color, culture, disability, ethnicity, gender, gender identity and expression, immigration status, political ideology, race, religion, sex, and sexual orientation" (CSWE, 2015, EP 2).

Intersectionality of Diverse Factors

The concept of **intersectionality** involves the idea that people are complex and can belong to multiple, overlapping diverse groups. "The intersectional perspective acknowledges the breadth of human experiences, instead of conceptualizing social relations and identities separately in terms of either race *or* class *or* gender *or* age *or* sexual orientation"; rather, an intersectional approach focuses on the "interactional affects" of belonging to multiple groups (Murphy, Hunt, Zajicek, Norris, & Hamilton, 2009, p. 2). People may experience injustice from a combination of reasons. The concept of intersectionality "underscores the complex nature of cultural and personal identities and human experiences that cannot be defined simply by one dimension of inequality or difference—either race or gender or sexual orientation or ability. The social worker, who is involved in working with individuals, families, groups, and communities belonging to diverse groups, must develop the cultural competence to work with people at the intersections of the multiple dimensions of diversity" (Murphy et al., 2009, p. 42).

Murphy and her colleagues (2009) provide the following case example demonstrating the complexity of intersectionality:

The Vue family emigrated from Laos six months ago. They were happy to find a small apartment that is convenient to a grocery store and meat-packing plant where Mr. Vue works long hours. They have three daughters, aged five years, four years, and six months. Shortly after they moved in, a neighbor called the local Department of Human Services (DHS). The neighbor, Mrs. Smith, had spotted one of the girls sitting alone in front of the apartment door one afternoon. Mrs. Smith was surprised to see the front door open, the younger girl on the couch, and the infant sleeping. The police arrived on the scene about the same time Mrs. Vue returned home, carrying grocery bags. She was taken aback to see the police in her apartment. Mrs. Vue said she had left the children for 30 minutes to buy milk. The children were taken into DHS custody, and Mr. and Mrs. Vue were told that they would have to appear in court three days later.

The Vue family will be assigned a case worker who is responsible for understanding how race, ethnicity, and class affect this family. Moving from a small village in Laos, could this family have understood the new dangers and expectations that come with parenting in the United States? How does their economic position affect their ability to find appropriate child care? What other factors affect their needs as a family? (p. 42)

Types of Human Diversity

We will arbitrarily spend some time here discussing selected aspects of human diversity, namely concepts related to gender and sex, in addition to culture. It is beyond the scope of this chapter to discuss each aspect of human diversity. Highlight 2-2 does offer definitions for each concept. Chapter 12 explores and discusses various diverse facets in greater detail. Additionally, a range of issues concerning human diversity is addressed throughout the book.

Human Diversity: The Complexity of Gender and Sex   `LO 2-5`

Gender is an aspect of diversity that is much more complex than it may initially seem. **Gender**, a broad concept, is the cluster of psychological, behavioral, social, cultural, physical, and emotional traits commonly linked with being a male or female. A related term is **gender role**. Gender roles "are culturally defined behaviors that are seen as appropriate for males and females, including the attitudes, personality traits,

---

Highlight 2-2

Definitions for Aspects of Human Diversity

EP 2

Age: Some time period during a person's lifespan. Age is often considered an important aspect of human diversity for older adults, as they experience *ageism*, discrimination based on preconceived notions about older people, regardless of their individual qualities and capabilities.

Class (or social class): People's status or ranking in society with respect to such standards as family background, income and wealth, education, prestige, or power.

Race: A socially created system of categorization that purports to identify people by shared characteristics such as common genetic or geographical background, physical features, or attributes that distinguishes them from other people.

Ethnicity: The affiliation with a large group of people who share such characteristics as tribal, racial, cultural, linguistic, national, or religious backgrounds.

(People of) color: "A collective term that refers to the major groups of African, Latino and Asian Americans, and First Nations People [Native Americans] who have been distinguished from the dominant society by color" (Lum, 2011, p. 129).

Culture: The customs and ways of doing things such as shaking hands when greeting others.

Disability: A physical or mental impairment [or ongoing health or mental health condition] that substantially limits one or more of the major life activities of an individual.

Gender: The cluster of psychological, behavioral, social, cultural, physical, and emotional traits commonly linked with being a male or female.

Gender identity: A person's internal psychological view of self as being either a male or a female, or, possibly, some combination of both.

Gender expression: The way we express ourselves to others in ways related to gender that include both behavior and personality.

Sex: The biological aspects of being either male or female, including anatomical and genetic traits.

Sexual orientation: Sexual and romantic attraction to persons of one or both genders.

Immigration status: A person's position in terms of legal rights and residency when entering and residing in a country that is not that person's legal country of origin.

Political ideology: The "relatively coherent system of ideas (beliefs, traditions, principles, and myths) about human nature, institutional arrangements, and social processes" that indicate how a government should be run and what principles that government should support (Abramovitz, 2010, p. 131).

Religion: People's spiritual beliefs concerning the origin, character, and reason for being, usually based on the existence of some higher power or powers, that often involves designated rituals and provides direction for what is considered moral or right.

emotions, and even postures and body language that are considered fundamental to being male or female in a culture. Gender roles also extend into social behaviors, such as the occupations we choose, how we dress and wear our hair, how we talk . . ., and the ways in which we interact with others" (Carroll, 2013, pp. 89–90). Rosenthal (2013) continues that "these socially stipulated expectations about gender are usually based on the notion of opposites; anyone who moves away from one extreme must, by definition move toward the other. Thus, a woman who acts in a way that is considered not traditionally feminine is considered to be acting more masculine" (p. 102).

Other important concepts related to gender are gender identity, gender expression, and gender-role socialization. *Gender identity* is the way people view themselves as being male, female, or some combination of both.

Gender expression concerns how we express ourselves to others in ways related to gender that include both behavior and personality. *Gender-role socialization* is the process of conveying what is considered appropriate behavior and perspectives for males and females in a culture.

We will differentiate the concepts of gender and sex. *Sex* refers to the biological aspects of being either male or female, including anatomical and genetic traits. Gender, then, emphasizes social and psychological aspects of femaleness or maleness; sex, on the other hand, focuses on the biological qualities of being male or female. Subsequent sections address sexual orientation, intersex, and transgenderism.

Sexual Orientation A significant aspect of diversity in some ways related to gender, **sexual orientation** is sexual and romantic attraction to persons of one or both genders. Terms concerning sexual orientation are important to understand. Puglia and House (2006) explain:

> Language is important for what it communicates as well as what it implies. Throughout their lives, gays, lesbians, and bisexuals hear biased and offensive street language such as "queer," "faggot," "homo," "dyke," and "queen." This language affects the self-esteem of gays, lesbians, and bisexuals, stigmatizes them, and is just as offensive to these populations as ethnic slurs are to various ethnic populations. (p. 516)

People having a sexual orientation toward the same gender are generally referred to as *gay* if they are male and *lesbian* if they are female. However, many people use the term *gay* to refer both to lesbians and gay men. The older term referring to same-gender sexual orientation is *homosexual*. People having a sexual orientation toward persons of the opposite gender are *heterosexual*, also referred to as *straight*. People sexually oriented toward either gender are referred to as *bisexual*.

It's difficult if not impossible to state exactly how many people are lesbian or gay. Many lesbian and gay organizations maintain that they make up 10 percent of the population. One lesbian and gay organization is called "The Ten Percent Society." Carroll (2013) reflects:

> Although there is much work to be done in determining the prevalence of homosexuality, scholars generally agree that between 3% and 4% of males are predominantly gay, 1.5% to 2% of women are predominantly lesbian, and about 2% to 5% are bisexual. (p. 272)

Variations in the Expression of Gender: Intersex and Transgender People   In an overly simplistic, naïve view of the world, one might think, "You're either a male or you're a female. Period." However, neither gender nor sexual orientation is a simple concept. Money (1987) proposes nine factors of gender that more fully portray some of the complexity of gender. The first seven are physical variables: chromosomal predisposition to gender; the presence of either ovaries or testes; exposure to male or female hormones prior to birth; brain differentiation resulting from hormones prior to birth; the presence of female or male internal reproductive organs; exterior genital appearance; and the production of either male or female hormones during puberty. The two psychological variables are the gender assigned at birth ("It's a boy" or "It's a girl") and the person's *gender identity* (one's perception of oneself as being either "female" or "male").

It is estimated that 1 out of every 1,500 to 2,000 babies born has some combination of physical characteristics demonstrated by both sexes (Crooks & Baur, 2014; Intersex Society of North America [ISNA], 2008). Such a person is referred to as *pseudohermaphrodite* or **intersex**. A true **hermaphrodite** is a person "born with fully formed ovaries and fully formed testes," a condition that is extremely rare (Carroll, 2013, p. 86). Another variation in the expression of gender involves **transgenderism**, or *transgender identity*, including "people whose appearance and/ or behaviors do not conform to traditional gender roles" (Crooks & Baur, 2014, p. 129). These people may feel that the gender assigned at their birth is false or at least incomplete as a description of who they are.

Among these people are *transsexuals*, people who feel they are imprisoned in the physical body of the wrong gender. Because their gender identity and sense of self are at odds with their biological inclination, they often seek to adjust their physical appearance closer to that of their gender identity through surgery and hormonal treatment. Many transsexual people prefer to be referred to as *transgender* people. The word *transsexual* emphasizes "sexual," whereas *transgender* emphasizes "gender" identity, which they say is the real issue.

Because lesbian, gay, bisexual, and transgender people face some of the same problems, when referring to them as a group, we will use the term **LGBTQ** (i.e., lesbian, gay, bisexual, transgender, and questioning). Highlight 2-3 discusses gayphobia or homophobia, which is often experienced by LGBTQ people.

Human Diversity: Culture   LO 2-6

Another crucial aspect of human diversity involves culture, a term often used with respect to the macro social environment. *Culture* includes customs and ways of doing things. Our culture defines what we think is good or bad, true or false, and influences what we do on a daily basis. It involves a constantly changing "integrated pattern of human behavior that includes thoughts, communications, actions, customs, beliefs, values, and institutions of a racial, ethnic, religious, or social group" (Lum, 2011, p. 17).

Culture is evident in both communities and organizations. For example, a geographic community's culture may be based on Hispanic, Jewish, African American, or White Anglo customs and expectations. Or, it may reflect a mixture of cultural traditions and heritages.

| Highlight **2-3** |

Gayphobia (Homophobia)

A major problem LGBTQ people face is *gayphobia* or *homophobia*, the irrational fear and/or hatred toward people who are gay, lesbian, bisexual, and transgender. Although not all LGBTQ people suffer from gayphobia in all its forms every day, all LGBTQ people must endure some forms at some times (Petrocelli, 2012; Tully, 2001). In order to help LGBTQ people cope with the results of gayphobia, social workers must understand their life situations and environmental issues.

Petrocelli (2012) explains that gayphobia is an "updated label" for homophobia. She revised "the term because today, most people identify more positively with the word *gay* than with the word *homosexual*. The reason for the two different connotations is simple. The word *gay* originated during a time when people were more pro-gay. On the other hand, the word *homosexual* evolved out of a more homophobic time and environment" (p. 98). Petrocelli (2012) continues:

Gayphobia reflects irrational fear because it is solely based on stereotypes and myths and a lack of real gay education and contact. Consequently, some heterosexual gayphobic people exhibit increased levels of gayphobia when attracted mentally, socially, or emotionally to members of the same sex. The increase in fear in this particular kind of scenario is triggered by the irrational fear that they are gay, when in fact they are not. They mistakenly confuse social feelings for gay attraction, and they fear thinking of themselves as gay. This type of fear [is labeled] . . . *gaysocialphobia*. (pp. 98–99)

LGBTQ people may suffer from gayphobia in at least three ways, one of which is *overt victimization.* Dworkin (2000) remarks:

Anti-LGB[TQ] violence is more common than most people realize. . . . All the symptoms commonly associated with posttraumatic stress [a condition in which a person continues to reexperience some traumatic event like a bloody battle or a sexual assault] are likely to follow a physical or verbal attack, in varying degrees of intensity, depending on the circumstances of the attack and the vulnerability of the victim. (p. 170)

A second way LGBTQ people encounter gayphobia involves *covert victimization*, where discrimination occurs that is not obvious. For instance, Erik, a 21-year-old gay man and college student, applies for a part-time job at Bubba's Big Burgers, a local fast-food restaurant. Bruce, the manager, somehow found out that Erik is gay. He chooses to hire another applicant for the position who is heterosexual (or so Bruce thinks) because that applicant is more "appropriate."

A third way LGBTQ people suffer from gayphobia involves internalizing it. If most those around them are gayphobic, making fun of and severely criticizing LGBTQ people, it's fairly easy for LGBTQ people to start believing it themselves. As a consequence, these individuals may develop feelings of isolation, clinical depression, a poor sense of self-esteem, thoughts of suicide, and substance abuse. Others may engage in acting out behaviors.

Organizations also have culture. On one level, organizational culture involves the diversity and backgrounds of its staff. On another level, **organizational culture** is defined as "the set of key values, beliefs, understandings, and norms shared by members of an organization" (Daft, 2016, p. 89). Later chapters further discuss organizational culture.

Cultural Competence   *Cultural competence* is "the mastery of a particular set of knowledge, skills, policies, and programs used by the social worker that address the cultural needs of individuals, families, groups, and communities" (Lum, 2005, p. 4). Social workers must develop cultural competence to work effectively with clients from various cultural, ethnic, and racial backgrounds.

Cultural competence, strongly supported by the NASW *Code of Ethics*, involves several dimensions (Lum, 2005; NASW, 2008, 1.05). Workers should strive to develop an awareness of personal values, assumptions, and biases. They should establish a positive approach toward and an appreciation of other cultures. They should work to understand how their own cultural heritage and belief system differ from and may influence interaction with clients who have a different cultural background. Workers should recognize the existence of stereotypes, discrimination, and oppression for various diverse groups. They should develop a nonjudgmental attitude and learn about the cultures of their clients. Finally, practitioners should develop attitudes that respect differences and do their best to learn effective skills for working with people from other cultures. Highlight 2-4 describes four competencies or goals concerning how a generalist practitioner might strive for cultural competence.

Highlight 2-4

Competencies for Cultural Competence

EP 1b, 2a-c, 6a

Sue, Rasheed, and Rasheed (2016) suggest that social workers should have four competencies (i.e., appropriate skills, knowledge, ability, and understanding) around cultural competence.

Competency One: Becoming Aware of One's Own, Values, Biases, and Assumptions about Human Behavior

What biases, stereotypes, and beliefs do you hold about various diverse groups? Everyone has them. Social workers must take care not to make automatic assumptions about diverse groups in the social environment. They must strive to appreciate human differences, yet view each client system as an individual. It's an ongoing, endless process to identify, clarify, and evaluate your own values.

Competency Two: Understanding the Worldviews of Culturally Diverse Clients

Before social workers can work objectively and effectively with clients, they must try hard to become aware of the lens through which they view the world. *Worldview* concerns people's perceptions of the world around them and how they fit into that world. Perceptions include awareness of the surrounding environment, social status, social roles, legal rights, and economic status, among the many other variables characterizing people's lives. Not only do worldviews consist of "our attitudes, values, opinions, and concepts, but they also affect how we think, define events, make decisions, and behave" (Sue & Sue, 2016, p. 166). Slattery (2004) explains:

> Our worldview influences whether we see the glass as half full or half empty or even whether it contains fluid

at all. . . . [It] is a way of organizing and distilling huge amounts of complex material into simple and understandable forms, which allows us to respond to the world more rapidly and efficiently. Imagine the feeling of having to pay attention to every piece of information that was received every minute of the day. The sound of the rain on the window, the temperature of the room, the feel of a book, the sound of pages being turned, and one leg on the opposite knee with one foot on the floor. The amount of information sensed at any moment is overwhelming. So, we perceive only part of it and use a still smaller portion. . . . Our worldview serves as a filter, accepting information that makes sense and discarding information that does not fit. (pp. 88–89)

Social workers must be aware of their own values and biases so that they don't impose their ideas on clients. They must also explore carefully with clients the clients' own worldviews. It is a practitioner's job to try to

---

Critical Thinking Questions 2-1 LO 2-7

EP 8a

Do you automatically make assumptions about any group based on race, culture, gender, sexual orientation, religion, economic status, or ability level? If so, what are these assumptions? To what extent are they fair or accurate?

continued

Highlight 2-4 *continued*

view the social environment from the client's perspective in order to help that client make the most effective decisions.

Competency Three: Developing Appropriate Intervention Strategies and Techniques

Sue, Rasheed, and Rasheed (2016) explain:

Social work and social workers must begin the process of developing appropriate and effective helping, teaching, communication, and intervention strategies in working with culturally diverse groups and individuals. This competency means . . . systems intervention as well as traditional one-to-one relationships. It is important that the social worker have the ability to make use of indigenous helping and healing approaches and structures that may already exist in the minority community. . . . The concept here is to build on the strengths of a community and to empower [its residents] . . . in their ability to help themselves. . . . Effectiveness in helping clients is most likely enhanced when the social worker uses intervention modalities and defines goals that are consistent with the life experiences and cultural values of clients. (pp. 64–65)

Competency Four: Understanding Organizational and Institutional Forces That Enhance or Diminish Cultural Competence

Communities may not be tolerant or supportive of various diverse groups:

In many cases, organizational customs do not value or allow the use of cultural knowledge or skills. Some social service organizations may even actively discourage, negate, or punish multicultural expressions. Or client problems may be the result of institutions that oppress them. Thus, it is imperative to view cultural competence for organizations as well. . . . Developing new rules, regulations, policies, practices, and structures within organizations that enhance multiculturalism is important. (Sue, Rasheed, & Rasheed, 2016, p. 65)

Critical Thinking Questions 2-2

 How would you describe your own worldview? What are the major values and beliefs that support this worldview?

EP 8a

Describing Generalist Practice: Focus on Empowerment, Strengths, and Resiliency   LO 2-8

Another vital concept in the definition of generalist practice and an ongoing theme throughout social work is **empowerment**, which involves ensuring that others have the power, ability, and authority to achieve self-determination.

The empowerment approach is a perspective on practice that includes how we think about social work practice as well as actual steps we pursue in practice. Throughout the assessment process and our quest to understand human behavior in macro systems, it's critical to emphasize, develop, and nurture strengths and positive attributes in systems of all sizes to empower people. Empowerment aims at enhancing individuals', groups', families', and communities' power and control over their destinies. Empowerment involves social workers striving to improve the following traits:

- *Positive sense of self-worth and competence* ("I am important." "I am capable of getting things done.")
- *Ability to influence the course of one's life* ("I have control over what I do." "I can make and follow plans to accomplish my goals.")

- *Capacity to work with others to control aspects of public life* ("I am an important part of my community and other larger systems, and can work with others to improve our quality of life." "In collaboration with others, I can make improvements in my community, in the organization where I work, and in other groups to which I belong.")
- *Ability to access the mechanisms of public decision making* ("I vote and communicate my expectations to decision makers at all levels.")

Walsh (2013) explains:

> Many clients do not, or perceive that they do not, have power, either over themselves, their significant others, or the agencies and communities in which they reside. This sense of powerlessness underlies many problems in living. It can be internalized and lead to learned helplessness and alienation from one's community. An empowerment orientation to practice represents the social worker's efforts to combat the alienation, isolation, and poverty . . . in clients' lives by positively influencing their sense of worth, sense of membership in a community, and ability to create change in their surroundings. (p. 25)

Empowerment in generalist practice involves critical thinking about how macro systems affect people. To what extent are people getting the resources and support they need from their communities and organizations within their communities? Why or why not?

The Strengths Perspective

Focusing on strengths can provide a sound basis for empowerment. Sometimes referred to as the *strengths perspective*, this orientation focuses on client resources, capabilities, knowledge, abilities, motivations, experience, intelligence, and other positive qualities that can be put to use to solve problems and pursue positive changes (Sheafor & Horejsi, 2015).

EP 7c

Assessment of human behavior establishes the basis for understanding people's problems and issues, and subsequently helping them improve their lives. Social workers address people's problems every day, but it's the identification of people's strengths that provides clues for how to solve these problems and improve their life situations. Saleebey (2013) cites the following principles involved in the strengths perspective:

- *Every individual, group, family, and community has strengths.* Even during people's darkest times, it's important to identify and emphasize strengths. Strengths include intelligence, good character, close family, good friends, spiritual faith, a job, a place to live, talent, personality, and any other positive thing you can think of.
- *Trauma and abuse, illness, and struggle may be injurious, but they may also be sources of challenge and opportunity.* Think of one of the worst experiences you've ever had. Regardless of how terrible it was at the time, were you able to turn it around and learn something from it? To some extent, did it make you a stronger or wiser person?
- *Assume that you do not know the upper limits of the capacity to grow and change,* and *take individual, group, and community aspirations seriously.* It's impossible to foresee the future and know all the opportunities you will encounter and the

barriers you will face. A strengths perspective emphasizes that it's important to set goals and to eagerly pursue opportunities when they occur.

■ *We best serve clients by collaborating with them.*

Saleebey (2013), a social worker, reflects about a client he knows:

> Mrs. Johnson knows more about thriving in a public housing project than anyone I can think of. Over the course of 35 years, she successfully raised 11 children. She maintained a demeanor of poise, and she demonstrated intelligence and vigor, even as her community underwent dramatic, often frightening changes. Her contributions to the community are, simply put, amazing. She has much to teach us and other residents of her community. I certainly would not presume to work *on* Ms. Johnson but would be privileged to work *with* her. (p. 19)

Critical Thinking Questions **2-3**

**EP 1b,
8a**

What Are Your Strengths?

Individual Strengths

- What do you see as your most significant personal strengths?
- What challenges have you overcome about which you're especially proud?

Family Strengths

- What strengths do you see in your own family?
- In what ways does your family put these strengths to use?
- In times of trouble, how does your family contribute to your own personal sense of strength?

Group Strengths

- To what social, work, and other types of groups do you belong?
- Do you have special people upon whom you can rely? If so, who are they, and in what ways do they support you?
- What are the strengths inherent in these groups?
- How do these group strengths contribute to your own personal sense of strength?

Organizational Strengths

- To what organizations do you belong (e.g., clubs, work settings, churches, recreational groups, sports groups, volunteer groups)?
- What are the strengths in these organizations?
- How do these organizational strengths contribute to your own personal sense of strength?

Community Strengths

- What are the strengths in the community where you live?
- How do these strengths contribute to your own quality of life?

- *Every environment is full of resources.* Resources can provide great strengths. One of social workers' major roles is to link clients with the resources they need to empower them to improve their lives.
- *Caring, caretaking, and context are key.* Social workers care about others. They are concerned about the environment or context in which people live. They recognize that communities and social service organizations should, respectively, take care of their citizens and the people they serve (Saleebey 2013, pp. 17–20).

Individuals, families, groups, organizations, and communities all have strengths. It's a goal of generalist practice to identify these strengths and use them to solve problems and make effective plans to enhance people's well-being.

Resiliency: Using Strengths to Combat Difficulty

A concept related to the strengths perspective and empowerment is resiliency. **Resiliency** is the ability of an individual, family, group, community, or organization to recover from adversity and resume functioning, even when suffering serious trouble, confusion, or hardship. Whereas the "strengths perspective focuses on capabilities, assets, and positive attributes rather than problems and pathologies," resiliency emphasizes the use of strengths to cope with adversity and survive, despite difficulties (Gutheil & Congress, 2002, p. 41).

Norman (2000) provides an illustration of the concept of resiliency:

When a pitched baseball hits a window, the glass usually shatters. When that same ball meets a baseball bat, the bat is rarely damaged. When a hammer strikes a ceramic vase, it too usually shatters. But when that same hammer hits a rubber automobile tire, the tire quickly returns to its original shape. The baseball bat and the automobile tire both demonstrate resiliency. (p. 3)

Resiliency involves two dimensions—risk and protection (Norman, 2000). In this context, **risk** involves "stressful life events or adverse environmental conditions that increase the **vulnerability** [defenselessness or helplessness] of individuals" or other systems (p. 3). **Protection**, on the other hand, concerns those factors that "buffer, moderate, and protect against those vulnerabilities" (p. 3).

One example of a community organization that builds on the strengths and resiliency of residents is Unitas. Unitas is a social service organization promoting and supporting social and emotional well-being of families by empowering youth to become change agents, and create self-sustaining communities (Unitas, 2016). Its goal is to help at-risk children and their families avoid such negative experiences as juvenile delinquency, drug use, violence, and dropping out of school. The Unitas Extended Family Circle (UEFC) conducts outreach to Hispanic youth in the South Bronx of New York City. UEFC builds on strengths that emanate from the Hispanic culture's core values of *personalismo* (i.e., "valuing and building interpersonal relationships") and respect, familism (i.e., "a preference for maintaining a close connection to family"), and spirituality (Santiago-Rivera et al., 2002, p. 42, 44).

It "recognizes the devastating effects of urban ghettos on people, particularly children and youth, and firmly believes in the healing power of all people, in their strengths, capacities, aspirations, and the availability of internal and external resources" (Perez-Koenig, 2000, pp. 143–144):

> Each individual is respected and valued, regardless of status. Respect emphasizes "being" and "who," rather than competition and "what." There is a substantial reverence for life, and for living in the moment. Familism locates the family, rather than the individual, as the most important social system. The family is a source of identity and support. Familism for most Hispanics includes the entire extended family. This extendedness emphasizes strong feelings of identification, loyalty, and solidarity. Extended family refers not only to the traditional kin, related by blood or marriage, such as aunts, uncles, and cousins, but also includes non-blood, non-marriage related persons who are considered family—compadres and comadres (godfathers and godmothers) and *hijos de crianza* (children who are raised as members of the family). The extended family provides an indispensable source of instrumental and expressive support. . . .
>
> UEFC invites children and adolescents to become members of symbolic small families and of the large, agency-wide, extended family. . . . Through corrective make-believe family relationships (in small groups as well as in the larger group of the community) participants develop better adaptive or coping mechanisms. . . . The large family circle is decentralized into small symbolic families, to permit an individual sense of belonging without anonymity. . . . UEFC meetings reinforce in each participant their identity as a member of this extended family (a make-believe extended kinship network), as well as their membership in their small symbolic families. The use of rituals, stories, group discussions, and clear norms and rules maintain a milieu necessary for healing relationships to be experienced in an emotional climate of mutual trust and peaceful, nonviolent transactions. (Perez-Koenig, 2000, pp. 145–149)

The importance of spirituality, which "lies at the core of the Hispanic culture," is stressed (Perez-Koenig, 2000, p. 146). In addition:

> [T]he make-believe parents, aunts, and uncles (caretakers) participate in an ongoing weekly training program led by a professional social worker. The goal of these sessions is to enable "helpers of children" to learn interpersonal skills which will encourage children to be effective, happy, and cooperative. Through training they learn skills to raise children's self-esteem and feelings of competency; skills to communicate effectively with children; skills to help children resolve conflicts and solve problems. (Perez-Koenig, 2000, p. 149)

The formulated families meet weekly. Children are encouraged to share their feelings and ideas. Caregivers work to meet children's and adolescents' needs by nurturing them, teaching them communication and problem-solving skills, and providing an environment where they feel important and safe. The basic idea is to enhance children's natural resiliency by stressing and developing their strengths.

Describing Generalist Practice: Advocacy for Human Rights and Social and Economic Justice [LO 2-9]

EP 3, 3a, 3b

Advocacy for human rights and social and economic justice represents the final dimension in the definition of generalist practice. The pursuit of these goals should characterize generalist practice in the macro social environment. Several important concepts are involved.

Advocacy

The first concept is that of **advocacy**, which has been defined as the act of stepping forward on behalf of the client system to promote fair and equitable treatment or gain needed resources. NASW policy states:

> Professional social workers value social justice, alleviating social ills and oppression at all levels of society. As such they are uniquely qualified to provide advocacy at micro, mezzo, and macro levels of practice. (NASW, 2012, p. 319)

Human Rights

Generalist practitioners have the responsibility of advocating for human rights. **Human rights** are those rights that all people are entitled to regardless of race, culture, or national origin. Reichert (2006) cites three facets of human rights. The first set of rights includes "political and human freedoms that are like what U.S. citizens view as human rights. Political and civil human rights include the right to a fair trial, freedom of speech and religion, freedom of movement and assembly, and guarantees against discrimination, slavery, and torture" (p. 3).

The second set of rights involves "attempts to ensure each resident of a country an adequate standard of living based on the resources of that country. Under this second set, everyone 'has the right to a standard of living adequate for the health and well-being of himself and of his family, including food, clothing, housing and medical care and necessary social services.' In addition, 'motherhood and childhood are entitled to special care and assistance,' and everyone has the right to a free education at the elementary level (United Nations, 1948, arts. 16–27)" (Reichert, 2006, p. 3).

The third set of human rights involves "rights among nations" on a global basis where "everyone is entitled to a social and international order in which human rights can be fully realized" (Reichert, 2006, pp. 3–4). This includes international cooperation for "environmental protection and economic development," and avoidance of exploitation of some countries by others (Reichert, p. 4). Chapter 13 further explores these concepts in addition to social and economic justice on a global basis.

Social, Economic, and Environmental Justice

Generalist practitioners also have the responsibility to advocate for social, economic, and economic justice (CSWE, 2015; NASW, 2012). **Social justice** exists when every individual has opportunities, rights, and responsibilities equal to those

EP 3a, 5b, 5c, 8d

of all other members of a society. **Economic justice** concerns the distribution of resources in a fair and equitable manner. **Environmental Justice** is a state of being in which all people are treated fairly in the establishment and enforcement of environmental policies and laws.

In life, social, economic, and environmental justice are hard goals to attain. Rarely are rights and resources fairly and equitably distributed. Even the definitions of *fair* and *equitable* are widely debated. What does *fair* mean? Does it mean that all people should receive the same income regardless of what they do, or even whether they have jobs at all? The point is that social workers must be vigilantly aware of the existence of injustice. It is our ethical responsibility to combat injustice whenever it is necessary and possible to do so.

We have already indicated that the NASW *Code of Ethics* stresses that workers' ethical responsibility to the broader society is to advocate and work for people's general welfare. This responsibility reflects the basic core of social work, although most job descriptions do not specifically reflect this. The *Code* reads:

> Social workers should promote the general welfare of society, from local to global levels, and the development of people, their communities, and their environments. Social workers should advocate for living conditions conducive to the fulfillment of basic human needs and should promote social, economic, political, and cultural values and institutions that are compatible with the realization of social justice. (NASW, 2008, 6.01)

Living conditions may encompass everything from low-quality housing and dangerous neighborhoods to environmental issues such as clean water and air, and the location of hazardous industries and conditions that undermine health or safety (e.g., confined animal feed operations (CAFOs), landfills, and others).

The *Code* continues that as part of their professional responsibility, social workers should pursue social and political action seeking fair and equal access to resources and opportunities. They should actively support policies to improve the human condition and promote social justice for all. Practitioners should especially work to enhance opportunities for "vulnerable, disadvantaged, oppressed, and exploited people and groups" (NASW, 2008, 6.04b). Social workers should support conditions and policies that respect cultural diversity. Similarly, they should work to prevent and eliminate conditions and policies discriminating against or exploiting people, especially vulnerable populations.

Oppression LO 2-10

When talking about issues involving fairness, justice, and human rights, many other concepts come into play. Advocacy for people who need to be empowered implies that people belonging to some groups experience a significant lack of power. In other words, people belonging to some groups are oppressed. **Oppression** entails "putting extreme limitations and constraints on some person, group, or larger system" (Kirst-Ashman, 2017, p. 66). Essentially, oppression occurs when one group acts to prevent or limit access to resources for some other group. This is achieved by impeding the other group's freedom or by otherwise diminishing their value. Examples of this were evident in the 2016 presidential election campaign when candidate Trump said of undocumented Mexican immigrants, "They're bringing drugs, they're bringing crime, they're rapists" (Donald Trump/Immigration, 2016). Statements like this are intended to devalue a specific group. Similar events were also evident, including attempts to limit access to the polls for people of color because they were assumed to vote for Democratic Party candidates (Brennan Center for Justice, 2016). Several courts have struck down these efforts noting that they were intentionally discriminating against black voters and Native Americans.

Power, Privilege, and Acclaim   Such dominating groups are often characterized by power, privilege, and acclaim. **Power** is the ability to move people on a chosen course to produce an effect or achieve some goal (Homan, 2016). **Privilege** entails special rights or benefits enjoyed because of elevated social, political, or economic status. **Acclaim** is enthusiastic public praise. People who experience acclaim, such as high-level politicians, well-known professionals, and famous entertainers, maintain broad influence over what other people think. Subsequently, people with much privilege and acclaim have greater power to influence and control their destinies and those of others.

Marginalization, Alienation, and Poverty   People with lesser power, usually falling into some category of distinguishable characteristics (e.g., race, ethnicity, income, religion, political party, age, or disability), may be denied rights, treated unfairly, or put down by a group holding greater power. People in downtrodden groups often suffer marginalization and alienation. **Marginalization** is the condition of having less power and being viewed as less important than others in the society because of belonging to some group or having some characteristic (e.g., being poor). **Alienation**, related to marginalization and occurs when a person or group does not feel a part of the larger group in a society. This sense of not fitting in may also be accompanied by discriminatory treatment. Often, victims of oppression also suffer **poverty**, the lack of money or material goods available to other members of a society. Lack of money, for example, prevents one from purchasing goods or services that most people would consider necessary. Highlight 2.5 introduces the issue of global poverty.

Populations-at-Risk, Stereotypes, and Discrimination   **Populations-at-risk** are populations or groups of people who share some identifiable characteristic that places them at greater risk of social and economic deprivation and oppression than the general mainstream of society. Often, those in power harbor stereotypes about oppressed groups that result in discrimination against them. A **stereotype** is "a fixed mental picture of a member of some specified group based on some attribute or attributes that reflect an overly simplified view of that group, without consideration or appreciation of individual differences" (Kirst-Ashman, 2017, p. 67). Stereotypes may relate to any of the factors indicating types of diversity. We have established that these include "age, class, color, culture, disability and ability, ethnicity, gender, gender identity and expression, immigration status, marital status, political ideology, race, religion/spirituality, sex, sexual orientation, and tribal sovereign status" (CSWE, 2015, EP. 2). **Discrimination**, a concept closely related to that of oppression, is "the act of treating people differently based on

Highlight **2-5**

Global Poverty and Social Injustice

EP 3a, 5c, 8d

Global problems shared by many countries necessitate cooperation by many nations to solve them; the problem of poverty is widespread and insidious (Healy, 2008). Although significant disparities in income and wealth exist in the United States, when looking at the global community, discrepancies are even greater among nations (Kendall, 2013). Kendall (2013) explains:

- Richer nations are those that are highly industrialized, are technologically more sophisticated, and have higher levels of income per person. Examples are New Zealand, Japan, and the United States.

- Nations in the middle of the economic continuum are in the process of converting from an agricultural to an industrial focus. Examples include Mexico, Venezuela, the Russian Federation, and China.

- Poorer nations have mainly agricultural economies, a minor industrial base, low levels of income per person, and fewer national resources. Examples include countries in sub-Saharan Africa, Afghanistan, Bangladesh, and Haiti.

The problem of global poverty is huge, and multinational macro tactics to address it must still be developed. However, various less-all-encompassing strategies have been somewhat successful in helping reduce poverty (Healy, 2008). For example, some nations have provided grants to help individuals and families that are impoverished. In Mexico, one program paid fees to mothers in order to finance their children's school, food, and health care costs. Another project in Brazil provided financial support to families when they maintained their children's school attendance and made certain the children received health care consistently.

Other nations have provided small grants to individuals to finance small business start-ups. Such projects could include a wide range of efforts. They might involve such conventional endeavors as craft production or raising chickens to sell eggs. Or they could entail more contemporary projects such as helping finance a cell phone that the grant recipient could rent out to fellow residents in a small rural village.

Chapter 13 discusses further the problem of global poverty.

---

the fact they belong to some group" rather than on their individual merit (Kirst-Ashman, 2013, p. 66).

For example, harboring the false stereotype that people with physical disabilities also have intellectual disabilities might result in job discrimination against people with physical disabilities. Similarly, maintaining the false stereotype that women are too emotional to be effective leaders might result in discrimination against a woman in her pursuit of a powerful political position.

Common Elements in Oppression   Van Soest and Garcia (2003) introduce at least three elements that are common to all oppression:

First, oppression always bestows power and advantage on certain people who are regarded as the norm and denied to others based on status as the "other" or different. The defined norm (i.e., White, male, heterosexual) is the standard of *rightness* against which all others are judged; the "other" (i.e., not White, not male, not heterosexual) is not only different from the norm, but is also believed and perceived to be inferior and deviant, which then justifies conferring advantage on those who fit the norm and disadvantaging the other. . . .

EP 8a

At a Glance **2-1**

Concepts Related to Social and Economic Justice

Acclaim: Enthusiastic public praise.

Advocacy: The act of stepping forward on the behalf of the client system in order to promote fair and equitable treatment or gain needed resources.

Discrimination: The act of treating people differently based on the fact they belong to some group rather than on their individual merit.

Economic justice: The distribution of resources in a fair and equitable manner.

Human rights: The premise that all people, regardless of race, culture, or national origin, are entitled to basic rights and treatment.

Marginalization: is the condition of having less power and being viewed as less important than others in the society because of belonging to some group or having some characteristic (e.g., being poor).

Oppression: Putting extreme limitations and constraints on some person, group, or larger system.

Power: The ability to move people on a chosen course to produce an effect or achieve some goal (Homan, 2016).

Privilege: Special rights or benefits enjoyed because of elevated social, political, or economic status.

Social justice: The philosophical perspective that all people have the right to enjoy equal opportunities in economic, political, and social realms.

Alienation: Occurs when a person or group does not feel a part of the larger group in a society.

Poverty: The lack of money or material goods available to other members of a society.

Populations-at-risk: Populations or groups of people who share some identifiable characteristic that places them at greater risk of social and economic deprivation and oppression than the general mainstream of society.

Stereotype: A fixed mental picture of a member of some specified group based on some attribute or attributes that reflect an overly simplified view of that group, without consideration or appreciation of individual differences.

A second element common to all oppressions is that they are held in place by ideology [i.e., a systematic manner of thinking, in this case, about people and their behavior] and violence or the threat of violence. The ideology on which racial oppression is based is that of superiority based on race (i.e., White supremacy). Likewise, the ideology on which sexual oppression is based is that of superiority based on gender (i.e., male) and the basis for homosexual oppression is an ideology of superiority based on sexual orientation (i.e., heterosexual). Violence is used to enforce and maintain all oppressions. Violence comes in many forms and may be physical and direct (e.g., lynching, rape, battering, gay bashing), or personal and psychological (e.g., name-calling based on dominant ideology and negative stereotypes). Violence may be indirect and/or institutionalized. For example, it may be associated with high poverty rates, the predominance of men of color in the criminal justice system and on death row, and the reality of police brutality.

A third common element of all oppressions is that they are institutionalized. This means that racism, sexism, and heterosexism are built into the norms, traditions, laws, and policies of a society so that even those who have non-racist, non-sexist, and non-heterosexist beliefs are compelled to act in accordance with institutional interest. (pp. 35–36)

LO 2-11 A major thrust of social work, embedded in the profession's ethical code, is to combat oppression and advocate on the behalf of oppressed groups. It has been stressed that advocacy is the act of speaking up, pushing for change, or pleading clients' causes. It is workers' ethical responsibility to actively thwart any cruelty, unfairness, or discrimination they observe. This standard places the ultimate responsibility on the individual worker to make certain that service is provided fairly and people are treated justly. This doesn't relinquish the responsibility of agency administrators. However, individual professional social workers also have a responsibility to advocate for and pursue positive change.

Chapter Summary

The following summarizes this chapter's content as it relates to the learning objectives presented at the beginning of the chapter. Objectives include the following:

LO 2-1 Describe the values that characterize generalist practice and explain the relationship between these concepts and the macro social environment.

Generalist practice involves the application of an extensive and diverse knowledge base, professional values, and a wide range of skills to promote human well-being for individuals, families, groups, organizations, and communities. Concepts involving values that characterize generalist practice include adherence to professional values and the application of professional ethics; understanding human diversity; emphasizing client empowerment, strengths, and resiliency; and advocating for human rights and social and economic justice. Social workers conduct generalist practice with an emphasis on these dimensions in the context of the macro social environment.

LO 2-2 Identify the National Association of Social Workers (NASW) *Code of Ethics*, summarize professional ethical responsibilities, and examine ethical dilemmas.

The NASW *Code of Ethics* has six core values: service, social justice, dignity and worth of the person, importance of human relationships, integrity, and competence (NASW, 2008). Social workers' ethical responsibilities include those to clients, to colleagues, in practice settings, as professionals, to the social work profession, and to the broader society. Ethical dilemmas are problematic situations where one must make a difficult choice among two or more alternatives where ethical standards conflict.

LO 2-3 Explain the importance of identifying with the social work profession.

Identification with the social work profession means that "social workers [should] serve as representatives of the profession, its mission, and its core values" (CSWE, 2015, EP. 1c).

LO 2-4 Describe human diversity with its multiple, overlapping factors.

Human diversity refers to the vast array of differences among human beings, including such factors as gender, ethnicity, values, culture, spiritual/religious beliefs, sexual orientation, and both mental and physical health. Aspects characterizing human diversity include "age, class, color, culture, disability and ability, ethnicity, gender, gender identity and expression, immigration status, marital status, political ideology, race, religion/spirituality, sex, sexual orientation, and tribal sovereign status" (CSWE, 2015, EP. 2).

LO 2-5 Explain diversity with respect to gender, sex, and culture.

Gender and sexuality are aspects of diversity that are much more complex than they may initially seem. Inherent concepts include gender, gender identity, gender expression, gender roles, gender-role socialization, sex, sexual orientation, intersex, and transgender people. Gayphobia or homophobia is the irrational fear and/or hatred toward people who are gay, lesbian, bisexual, or transgender.

Culture includes customs and ways of doing things. Our culture defines what we think is good or bad, true or false, and influences what we do daily. Culture is evident in both communities and organizations.

LO 2-6 **Define cultural competence and address four competencies involved.**

Cultural competence is "the mastery of a particular set of knowledge, skills, policies, and programs used by the social worker that address the cultural needs of individuals, families, groups, and communities" (Lum, 2005, p. 4). Competencies involved in cultural competence include self-awareness, understanding the worldview of culturally diverse clients, developing appropriate intervention strategies, and understanding organizational and institutional forces that enhance or negate cultural competence.

LO 2-7 **Analyze various critical thinking questions.**

Critical thinking questions addressed personal assumptions about human diversity, personal worldview, personal and related strengths, and oppressed groups.

LO 2-8 **Review the significance of client empowerment, strengths, and resiliency.**

Empowerment aims at enhancing individuals', groups', families', and communities' power and control over their destinies. The strengths perspective focuses on client resources, capabilities, knowledge, abilities, motivations, experience, intelligence, and other positive qualities that can be put to use to solve problems and pursue positive changes (Sheafor & Horejsi, 2015). Resiliency

is the ability of an individual, family, group, community, or organization to recover from adversity and resume functioning, even when suffering serious trouble, confusion, or hardship. Empowerment, strengths, and resiliency can be used to help clients combat difficulty.

LO 2-9 **Explain the importance of advocacy for human rights and social and economic justice.**

Advocacy is the act of stepping forward on the behalf of the client system to promote fair and equitable treatment or gain needed resources. Human rights involves the premise that all people, regardless of race, culture, or national origin, are entitled to basic rights and treatment. Social justice is the philosophical perspective that all people have the right to enjoy equal opportunities in economic, political, and social realms. Economic justice concerns the distribution of resources in a fair and equitable manner. Generalist practitioners should advocate for human rights and social and economic justice (CSWE, 2015; NASW, 2012).

LO 2-10 **Discuss some of the dynamics involved in oppression.**

Oppression entails putting extreme limitations and constraints on some person, group, or larger system. Dominating groups often are characterized by power, privilege, and acclaim. People with lesser power often suffer marginalization and alienation. Stereotypes and resulting discrimination often affect populations-at-risk. Common elements in oppression include assuming standards of "rightness," an established ideology, and institutionalization of beliefs.

LO 2-11 **Demonstrate awareness of ethical topics.**

Ethical topics included the NASW *Code of Ethics* and ethical dilemmas occurring in the macro social environment.

Looking Ahead

This chapter completed discussion of the definition of generalist practice. It focused on values and principles that guide generalist practice in the macro social environment.

The next chapter will discuss the theories and dynamics of how generalist practitioners function in small groups in the macro social environment.

Competency Notes

The following identifies where Educational Policy (EP) competencies and component behaviors are discussed in the chapter.

EP 2.0 Generalist Practice *(p. 43 ff)*: Generalist practice provides the foundation for social work practice and is grounded in the liberal arts and the person-and-environment construct. This chapter discusses concepts concerning values that characterize generalist practice and their relationship to the macro social environment.

EP 1 (Competency 1)—Demonstrate Ethical and Professional Behavior *(p. 43)*: Professional values and ethics are at the heart of social work. Thus, these characterize the next significant dimension in the definition of generalist practice. **Values** involve what you do and do not consider important. They concern what is and is not considered to have worth. *(p. 44)*: Identification with the social work profession involves adherence to professional ethics, demonstration of professional roles, and participation in lifelong learning to enhance knowledge and skills. *(p. 48)*: **Ethical dilemmas** are problematic situations where one must make a difficult choice among two or more alternatives where ethical standards conflict. No one perfect answer can conform to all the ethical standards involved.

EP 1a Make ethical decisions by applying the standards of the NASW *Code of Ethics*, relevant laws and regulations, models for ethical decision-making, ethical conduct of research, and additional codes of ethics as appropriate to context *(pp. 44–47)*: The significance of adhering to professional values and applying professional ethics is discussed. The concepts of identification with the social work profession and professional conduct are introduced and emphasized. The NASW *Code of Ethics* is summarized and discussed. Addressing ethical dilemmas involves tolerating ambiguity. Questions are posed to encourage principled decisions. Critical thinking questions are posed.

EP 1b Use reflection and self-regulation to manage personal values and maintain professionalism in practice situations. *(p. 54)*: Practitioners must practice personal reflection about their own worldview so that they don't impose it upon their clients. *(p. 57)*: Assessment of one's own strengths by practicing personal reflection helps a social worker better understand the strengths of other systems.

EP 2 (Competency 2)—Engage Diversity and Difference in Practice. *(p. 42)*: Oppression and discrimination are defined and discussed. *(p. 43)*: The concepts of advocacy, human rights, and social and economic justice are introduced. *(pp. 48–50)*: Social workers should advocate for human rights, and promote social and economic justice.

EP 2a Apply and communicate understanding of the importance of diversity and difference in shaping life experiences in practice at the micro, mezzo, and macro levels. *(p. 54)*: Social workers should examine the importance of difference in shaping people's lives. Practitioners should recognize the extent to which worldviews of various diverse groups shape these groups' life experiences.

EP 2b Present themselves as learners and engage clients and constituencies as experts of their own experiences. *(p. 54)*: Social workers should view themselves as learners and actively seek out information about their clients' worldviews.

EP 2c Apply self-awareness and self-regulation to manage the influence of personal biases and values in working with diverse clients and constituencies. *(p. 54)*: Practitioners must work hard at self-awareness regarding their own worldviews to avoid imposing these views upon clients.

EP 3 (Competency 3)—Advance Human Rights and Social, Economic, and Environmental Justice. *(p. 60)*: Social workers should engage in practices that advance social and economic justice. The global problem of poverty is introduced.

EP 5b Assess how social welfare and economic policies impact the delivery of and access to social services. *(p. 61):* The *Code* continues that as part of their professional responsibility, social workers should pursue social and political action seeking fair and equal access to resources and opportunities. Social workers should support conditions and policies that respect cultural diversity. Similarly, they should work to prevent and eliminate conditions and policies discriminating against or exploiting people, especially vulnerable populations.

EP 5c Apply critical thinking to analyze, formulate, and advocate for policies that advance human rights and social, economic, and environmental justice. *(p. 61):* Practitioners should advocate for policies and services that are respectful and appreciative of diverse worldviews. *(p. 63):* The importance of advocating for social and economic justice, and the enhancement of social well-being, is stressed.

EP 6a Apply knowledge of human behavior and the social environment, person in environment, and other multidisciplinary theoretical frameworks to engage with clients and constituents. *(pp. 48–50):* Social workers should understand the importance of human diversity and the intersectionality of multiple factors in people's lives. Specific dimensions of diversity cited in this competency are defined. *(p. 54):* Social workers should recognize the extent to which organizations and communities may impose their worldviews upon diverse populations, resulting in oppression. *(p. 61–64):* The concepts of oppression, poverty, marginalization, alienation, privilege, power, and acclaim are introduced and defined.

EP 7c Develop mutually agreed-on intervention goals and objectives based on the critical assessment of strengths, needs, and challenges within clients and constituencies. *(p. 56):* Practitioners should assess both clients' limitations and strengths as they proceed with the helping process.

EP 8a Critically choose and implement interventions to achieve practice goals and enhance capacities of clients and constituencies. *(pp. 54–58):* Social work and social workers must begin the process of developing appropriate and effective helping, teaching, communication, and intervention strategies in working with culturally diverse groups and individuals. This competency means . . . systems intervention as well as traditional one-to-one relationships. Social workers must recognize the client system's resiliency and build on those strengths.

EP 8d Negotiate, mediate, and advocate with and on behalf of diverse clients and constituencies. *(pp. 61–63):* Generalist practitioners also have the responsibility to advocate for social, economic and economic justice (CSWE, 2015; NASW, 2012). **Social justice** Exists when every individual has opportunities, rights, and responsibilities equal to those of all other members of a society. **Economic justice** concerns the distribution of resources in a fair and equitable manner. **Environmental justice** is a state of being in which all people are treated fairly in the establishment and enforcement of environmental policies and laws.

Media Resources

MindTap for Social Work

Go to MindTap® for digital study tools and resources that complement this text and help you be more successful in your course and career. There's an interactive eBook plus videos of client sessions, skill-building activities, quizzes to help you prepare for tests, apps, and more—all in one place. If your instructor didn't assign MindTap, you can find out more about it at CengageBrain.com.

3 | Human Behavior in Groups: Theories and Dynamics

Communication, cooperation, and conflict may be part of the dynamic group process.

LEARNING OBJECTIVES

After reading this chapter you should be able to...

3-1 Explain major theoretical perspectives on groups, including field, social exchange, learning, psychoanalytic, systems, empowerment, and feminist theories.

3-2 Apply critical thinking skills to various critical thinking questions.

3-3 Identify basic concepts inherent in interpersonal group dynamics, including communication, interpersonal interaction, norms, roles, and group cohesion, in addition to power and status.

3-4 Discuss the ethical issue of confidentiality in groups.

3-5 Describe the concept of leadership, including leadership styles and characteristics of successful leaders.

3-6 Identify and describe the phases of task group development.

LaTonya, the university's Social Work Club (SWC) president, called the full membership meeting to order. The SWC had much to accomplish tonight. The goal was to identify a range of volunteer activities in which members could participate. At the last meeting, the club passed the requirement that all members participate in at least 30 hours of volunteer activities. Now it was up to the club to identify volunteer possibilities in the university's small town and help members get involved.

The SWC board consisted of LaTonya, Bert (vice-president), Ernie (secretary), Sallie (treasurer), and Morticia (activities director). Board meetings were held every other Tuesday night, with full membership meetings on alternate Tuesdays.

LaTonya thought the SWC board generally got along well except for periodic minor conflicts between herself and Bert. Bert liked to vie for power and control of both board and membership meetings. LaTonya felt Bert somewhat resented her election as SWC president.

LaTonya, however, had assessed their interpersonal dynamics the first time the newly elected board met. From the second board meeting on, whenever Bert got on a control kick, LaTonya tactfully cut him off, regained control, and got the meeting back on track. After all, interpersonal feuding just consumed unnecessary energy and ate away at the SWC's process and effectiveness. LaTonya took her role as president very seriously. She and the SWC membership had a lot to do tonight to get the volunteer program on its feet and running.

The above scenario highlights how groups consist of people having unique personalities, issues, and concerns. On the one hand, a group must accomplish its purpose as a unified entity. On the other, individual members come to a group with their own desires and needs. As in organizations and communities, human behavior in groups is complex.

A *group* is at least two individuals gathered together because of some common bond, to meet members' social and emotional needs, or to fulfill some mutual purpose. Social work practitioners must understand human behavior in groups for many reasons. Working with others to get something done is a core component of generalist social work practice in organizations and communities.

There are four main reasons why groups are relevant in social work. First, sharing interests and mutual activity provides a group of individuals with support, information, and motivation. It is also likely that a group of people can exert greater influence on the social environment than a single individual.

Second, groups enhance the ability to solve problems and develop creative solutions. Groups allow a venue where members can share their ideas, challenges, and experiences while also learning new ways of doing things. Exposure to perspectives different from one's own can initiate ideas and enhance creativity.

A third reason groups are important involves the dynamics of small groups in which members, working together, exert social pressure and influence on each other. A group member is accountable to other members for assuming responsibility and getting things done. In this way, members can empower each other to make progress and achieve goals.

The fourth reason groups are important to social work is the convenience factor. When numerous individuals are involved in decision making, planning, advocating, or intervening, groups often provide the most efficient way of communicating, solving problems, and making decisions.

EP 1, 7

Chapter 3 will describe the types of groups relevant to generalist social work practice. Several theoretical perspectives can conceptualize any group's functioning, regardless of type. Theory provides a framework for understanding how groups work. Additionally, some concepts characterize interpersonal group dynamics such that you can use them in conjunction with any theoretical perspective. The greater your comprehension of group functioning, the more effectively you will be as leader or member.

Conceptual Frameworks and Theories Concerning Groups **LO 3-1**

A **conceptual framework** is a collection of organized hypotheses, ideas, and concepts intended to describe and explain some observable occurrence, event, trend, or fact. Other terms for conceptual framework are **theoretical perspective** and **theory**. Conceptual frameworks can provide avenues for understanding how any system functions in the macro social environment. For the purposes of this book, we have established that such systems include groups, organizations, and communities. This chapter focuses on groups. We define *group* is at least two individuals gathered together because of some common bond, to meet members' social and emotional needs, or to fulfill some mutual purpose. Conceptual frameworks discussed here include field, social exchange, learning, psychoanalytic, systems, empowerment, and feminist theories.

Field Theory

Field theory, initially developed by Kurt Lewin (1951), views a group as an entity moving through its immediate environment in pursuit of its goals. A major strength of field theory is that it stresses the importance of examining the relationship of the group to its environment (Corey, 2016; Toseland & Rivas, 2017). Picture a bowling ball rolling down an alley or a soccer ball speeding down a field. Each ball rolls or reacts within its own context or field. Movement involves the force and direction with which it was propelled and the ruts, gutters, or impediments encountered along the way. This is overly simplistic, however, as field theory sees groups as dynamic entities whose members constantly adapt to their environments. Observing stationary bowling or soccer balls is about as dynamic as watching rocks.

Field theory emphasizes how groups function to achieve designated goals. It views groups as progressing or failing to progress because of positive and negative forces acting on them both internally and externally in the environment. These forces can either help or hinder the group's advancement. Field theory predicts that groups experiencing numerous positive forces, rewards, and encouragements will continue functioning. Groups encountering primarily negative forces will probably fail if positive forces don't counterbalance the negative. Such forces that push toward or pull one away from group involvement and participation are called **valences** (Martin, 2003).

An important concept in field theory is **cohesion**, the collective sum of forces affecting individuals that encourage them to remain group members (Toseland & Rivas, 2017). Examples of positive forces might be how much group members like each other and enjoy each other's company, or members' commitment to the group's purpose. Negative forces might include inconvenient meeting times or other pressures on members' time external to the group. Consider a recent public example of this involving the team appointed by Donald Trump to handle the transition from candidate to president. Originally, Governor Chris Christie was appointed chairman and the team consisted of 6 vice-chairs along with other members. Christie was later replaced by Senator Mike Pence and the number of vice-chairs increased to 13. Representative Mike Rogers, the vice-chair leader dealing with national security, withdrew unexpectedly. A lobbyist on the team, Matthew Freedman, was fired after in-group disagreements with other members. Several other members, including the transition executive director and general counsel, were fired or removed for various reasons, including loyalty to Christie (DeYoung & Miller, 2016). A task group with multiple potential leaders, many jockeying for position or with conflicting agendas, is often a recipe for problems.

Field theory views leadership within a group as being of three types: democratic, authoritarian, or laissez-faire (Toseland & Rivas, 2017). Leadership, discussed more thoroughly later, significantly affects how the group functions and moves along toward accomplishing goals. **Authoritarian leaders** take control of group functioning and make decisions with little or no input from other group members. Needless to say, group members may seriously resent this approach. They may balk at group goals, behave in ways that obstruct group progress, or quit the group altogether. On the other hand, some groups may require such strong leadership when members lack necessary knowledge, skill, or direction.

In contrast, **democratic leaders** maximize member input and participation. They emphasize open discussion of issues, even uncomfortable ones such as disagreements among group members or hostility toward the group leader. Advantages of a democratic approach are equal input for all and open knowledge of the issues. Disadvantages include the fact that members may not really be equal in terms of motivation, competence, skills, or participation.

Finally, **laissez-faire leaders** assume a laid-back, nondirectional approach where the group is left to function or struggle on its own. This approach usually doesn't work unless group members are highly knowledgeable, competent, and independent, requiring little guidance to accomplish tasks.

Field theory also introduced several concepts regarding the importance of internal group interaction. In the context of a small group, **roles** are expected behavior patterns based on individuals' status or position within the group. **Norms** are collective rules and expectations held by group members concerning what is appropriate behavior within the group. *Power* is the ability to move people on a chosen course to produce an effect or achieve some goal (Homan, 2016). **Consensus** is the extent to which group members concur about group goals and other aspects of group interaction.

At a Glance **3-1**

Field Theory

Conceptual framework: A collection of organized hypotheses, ideas, and concepts intended to describe and explain some observable occurrence, event, trend, or fact.

Field theory: The view that a group is an entity moving through its immediate environment in pursuit of its goals.

Valences: Forces that push one toward or pull one away from involvement and participation.

Cohesion: The collective sum of forces affecting individuals that encourages them to remain group members.

Authoritarian leadership: Taking control of group functioning and making decisions with little or no input from other group members.

Democratic leadership: Maximizing member input and participation.

Laissez-faire leadership: Assuming a laid-back, nondirectional approach where the group is left to function or struggle on its own.

Role: Expected behavior patterns based on individuals' status or position within the group.

Norms: Collective rules and expectations held by group members concerning what is appropriate behavior within the group.

Power: The ability to move people on a chosen course to produce an effect or achieve some goal.

Consensus: The extent to which group members concur about group goals and other aspects of group interaction.

Social Exchange Theory

Field theory views a group as a single entity, stressing its functioning as a unit. Although some attention is given to interpersonal dynamics within the group, the focus remains on how the group functions as a unit. **Social exchange theory**, on the other hand, stresses the importance of the individual within the group context. It views the group as the place where social exchange takes place. **Social exchange** at its most basic level refers to interpersonal interaction, which involves both rewards and costs. **Rewards** are the pleasures, fulfillment, enjoyment, and other positive emotions that a person experiences when involved in a relationship. Social exchange theory suggests that individual group members continue in the group because they receive social rewards for group membership. This membership is based on receiving more rewards than experiencing costs. **Costs** include negative experiences, the expenditure of time and energy required to maintain a relationship, or the loss of rewards because of making ineffective choices (e.g., spending time talking with a group member you don't like much instead of one you do).

Garvin (1987) explains:

People enter into social interactions with the expectation of rewards. Because each person in the interaction has the same motivation, it logically follows that each must offer something of value to the other in the exchange. . . . What an individual offers another in an exchange—whether energy, time, or resources—is referred to as a "cost."

Social exchange theory focuses on interactions between and among individuals. Each interaction can be broken down into a series of behaviors and responses. Each behavior or response is evaluated in terms of how rewarding or punishing it is to the other members in the group. When group members experience more rewards and fewer costs, the social exchange is likely to be positive and to reinforce group participation.

At a Glance 3-2

Social Exchange Theory

Social exchange theory: Theory that stresses the importance of the individual within the group context.

Social exchange: Interpersonal interaction, which involves both rewards and costs.

Rewards: The pleasures, fulfillment, enjoyment, and other positive emotions a person experiences when involved in a relationship.

Costs: Negative experiences, the expenditure of time and energy required to maintain a relationship, or the loss of rewards because of making ineffective choices.

Several assumptions are inherent in exchange theory. First, relationships have an interdependent dimension. That is, the ability of each participant to receive rewards is dependent on that person's ability to bestow rewards. If you can't give rewards to others, they probably won't give any to you. Second, the process of social exchange is governed by values and expectations such as fairness and the importance of a mutual sense of give and take. It follows, then, that giving rewards should result in eventually receiving rewards. Third, "trust and commitment" develop as more social exchanges occur over time, which tends to "stabilize" relationships. As people get to know each other and expectations become established, relationships become more predictable. Highlight 3-1 analyzes a conversation using social exchange theory.

Highlight 3-1

Analysis of a Conversation Using Social Exchange Theory

Francine and Horace, members of a volunteer community group whose goal is to maintain cleanliness on four city-block sidewalks, have the following conversation. Each response is followed by a brief analysis according to social exchange theory.

Francine says to Horace, "Did you finish your assigned block yet?" *(Neutral question, although a minor cost to Francine in terms of effort expended)*

Horace responds, "Heck, yes. I appreciate your suggestions about removing the dog dirt. I just don't know why people keep big dogs in the city." *(Reward for Francine; minor cost for Horace for effort expended)*

Francine states, "Yeah, that Super Dooper Pooper Scooper really works. Will you be cleaning your assigned sidewalks on a weekly basis?" *(Minor cost to Francine for effort expended)*

Horace replies, "Nah, once a month is plenty. Don't want to wear myself out." *(Cost to Francine because it's not what she wants to hear; minor cost to Horace for effort expended)*

Francine vehemently states, "What! This neighborhood will be a pig sty if you don't clean up the sidewalk more than monthly." *(Cost to Horace because Francine criticized his behavior; cost to Francine because of her anger and for effort expended)*

Horace huffily retorts, "You can't tell me what to do. This is a voluntary neighborhood group. Keep bossing me around like that and I quit." *(Cost to Horace because of his anger; cost to Francine because she doesn't want Horace to quit, as she would probably have to do his work)*

"I'm sorry," Francine humbly replies. "I just get so upset when people mess up the neighborhood so." *(Reward for Horace because he appreciates Francine's apology; cost to Francine because of the effort it took to apologize)*

"Oh, don't worry about it," Horace says. "We're all in this together. You're probably right. I'll do my part and clean up at least every two weeks. The Super Dooper Pooper Scooper does make it easier." *(Reward to Francine because she appreciates Horace's effort; cost to Horace for effort expended)*

Learning Theory

Learning theory is a theoretical orientation that explains the social environment in terms of behavior, its preceding events, and its subsequent consequences. It posits that behavior can be learned, and therefore, that maladaptive behavior can be unlearned. Learning theory provides a framework for understanding how behavior develops. Like social exchange theory, learning theory focuses on individual group members rather than the entire group's process and functioning. It is usually applied to treatment groups involving therapy for individual clients rather than task groups in macro settings. However, because of learning theory's significance in understanding human behavior and the increasing body of research documenting its effectiveness in many settings, it merits brief discussion here (Miltenberger, 2015; Sundel & Sundel, 2005).

Learning theory proposes three primary means of affecting people's behavior within groups. First, **respondent conditioning** refers to the elicitation of behavior in response to a specific stimulus. If a group member suddenly screams, "FIRE!" (a stimulus), other group members will probably run for their lives out of the room (response). Another example is a group of social workers receiving in-service training on solving ethical dilemmas. When the group leader gets up and goes to the chalkboard (stimulus), other group members dig out notebooks from their briefcases to take notes (response).

A second type of learning is **modeling**, the learning of behavior by observing another individual engaging in that behavior. For example, a social worker leads an educational group of community residents interested in writing their legislators about some hot political issue. The worker can serve as a model by writing to designated legislators herself. She can model what to write and how to say it.

A third type of learning is **operant conditioning**. In this type of learning, people engage in behaviors largely because of consequences that occur immediately following the behavior. One type of behavioral consequence is **reinforcement**, a procedure or consequence that increases the frequency of the behavior immediately preceding it. **Positive reinforcement** is the positive event or consequences that follow a behavior and act to strengthen or increase the likelihood that the behavior will be repeated in the future. Consider an agency task group working to establish a new recording format for monitoring clients' progress. Karl, one group member, states to Max, another, "Thanks so much for sharing your ideas. They're great." Max likes the compliment, which is positive by nature. If Karl's response increases Max's future sharing of ideas, it is positive reinforcement.

Negative reinforcement is the removal of a negative event or consequence that serves to increase the frequency of a behavior. First, something must be removed from the situation. Second, the frequency of a behavior is increased. In this manner, positive and negative reinforcement resemble each other. Both function as reinforcement that serves to increase or maintain the frequency of a behavior. Highlight 3-2 provides an example of negative reinforcement in a macro setting.

Learning theory describes another type of consequence, **punishment**, which is the presentation of an aversive event or the removal of a positive reinforcer that results in a decrease in frequency or elimination of a behavior. In a way, punishment

---

Highlight **3-2**

An Example of Negative Reinforcement in a Macro Setting

An example of negative reinforcement in a macro setting involves a group of community leaders. An ancient tradition for the group is to read both the meeting's minutes and any new reports at the beginning of the meeting. Because this is so excruciatingly dull, most group members come about 45 minutes late, or don't show up at all. Matt Tress, the group's chairperson, decides that reading all that boring material is a waste of time and is really turning people off. Matt sent an email to all group members stating that minutes and new reports will no longer be read during meetings because it wastes precious time. Rather, members will receive the material as email attachments that should be read in advance of meetings. It was amazing how group members started showing up on time after only a meeting or two when the meetings dealt with business items instead of boring reading. Halting readings (removing a negative event) reinforced group members' punctuality and attendance (increased frequency of behavior).

---

is the opposite of reinforcement in that it weakens or decreases the frequency of behavior instead of increasing it. Highlight 3-3 provides an example of punishment in a macro setting.

Cognitive-Behavioral Theory

Cognitive-behavioral theory combines components of learning theory and cognitive theory. Behavioral theory (also known as behavioral therapy) involves the practical application of learning theory principles to changing behavior. Cognitive theory emphasizes people's ability to make rational decisions and alter their behavior.

Cognitive-behavioral theory has been used extensively in treatment groups. As with learning theory, it has rarely been applied to task groups and other groups operating in macro settings.

Four basic assumptions are involved in cognitive-behavioral theory. First, it's relatively optimistic, as it asserts that people can make positive changes in their lives. Most emotions, thought processes, and behavior have been learned; therefore, they can also be changed through new learning (Corey, 2017). New ways of thinking and more effective behaviors can be learned to replace those that are

At a Glance **3-3**

Learning Theory

Respondent conditioning: The elicitation of behavior in response to a specific stimulus.

Modeling: The learning of behavior by observing another individual engaging in that behavior.

Operant conditioning: In this type of learning, people change their behaviors largely because of consequences that occur after the behavior.

Reinforcement: A procedure or consequence that increases the frequency of the behavior immediately preceding it.

Positive reinforcement: The positive event or consequences that follow a behavior and act to strengthen or increase the likelihood that the behavior will occur again.

Negative reinforcement: The removal of a negative event or consequence that serves to strengthen or increase the frequency of a behavior.

Punishment: The presentation of an aversive event or the removal of a positive reinforcer that results in the decrease in frequency or elimination of a behavior.

Highlight **3-3**

An Example of Punishment in a Macro Setting

Punishment can occur in groups. Consider Yaakov, a social services supervisor, who's holding a group supervisory meeting with his financial assistance workers. Yaakov often tends to drone on when trying to make a point. Akuba, one of the workers, interrupts, tactfully in her perception, and asks a question for clarification before discussion moves on and the question becomes irrelevant. Obviously annoyed,

Yaakov sharply retorts, "Never, never interrupt me again in the middle of a thought!"

Akuba learns. She never, ever interrupts Yaakov again. In fact, she hesitates to speak to him at all unless she must. Yaakov's sharp rebuttal is punishment because Akuba's interrupting behavior never occurs again (decreased frequency or, in this case, elimination of behavior).

---

problematic. Within treatment settings, group members are taught new ways to approach problems, issues, or relationships.

A second assumption inherent in cognitive-behavioral theory is that problematic behavior is the focus of change (Corey, 2017). Many other theoretical approaches consider behavior only as a symptom of deeper, underlying psychological problems. Therapists who practice based on cognitive-behavioral theory "operate on the premise that changes in behavior can occur prior to or simultaneously with understanding oneself and that behavioral changes may well lead to an increased level of self-understanding" (Corey, 2012, p. 349).

The third supposition involved in cognitive-behavioral theory is that thinking (**cognition**), feeling (emotions), and acting (behavior), interact and communicate with each other. By doing so, they all individually and collectively contribute to our overall sense of well-being as well as the outcomes we experience. When we change any part of this (thoughts, feelings, or behavior), it can lead to changes in the others. For instance, if you feel depressed (emotion), you might think very negative thoughts about yourself (e.g., "I'm such a rotten person") (cognition), and may avoid friends to isolate yourself (behavior). Similarly, if you studied very hard (behavior) and received 98 percent after taking a recent exam, you might think very positive thoughts about yourself (e.g., "I'm so smart") (cognition), and feel extremely happy (emotion). Hence, the three subsystems can influence or affect each other.

The fourth premise is that a wide range of approaches under the umbrella of cognitive-behavioral theory can be chosen and used to change behavior (Corey, 2017, pp. 354–358). For example, **modeling** is often employed by a group leader or other group members to demonstrate and teach appropriate behavior. **Coaching** is also used to help group members acquire new behaviors. **Behavioral rehearsal** is the act of practicing a new behavior, interaction, or manner of communication in a group setting. This can help a person become accustomed to a new approach to prepare for a subsequent real-life situation. For example, behavioral rehearsal can be useful in seeking goals of improved assertiveness or conflict management skills. **Social (positive) reinforcement** by a group leader or other group members in the form of "praise, approval, support, and attention" can also be powerful in changing cognition and behavior (Corey, 2017, p. 356).

At a Glance **3-4**

Cognitive-Behavioral Theory

Cognition: The act of thinking.

Modeling: The learning of behavior by observing another individual engaging in that behavior (e.g., coping strategies).

Coaching: Used to help group members acquire new behaviors.

Behavioral rehearsal: The act of practicing a new behavior, interaction, or manner of communication in a group setting to prepare for subsequent real-life situations.

Social (positive) reinforcement: "Praise, approval, support, and attention" (Corey, 2016, p. 356).

Cognitive restructuring: "The process of identifying and evaluating one's cognitions, understanding the negative behavioral impact of certain thoughts, and learning to replace these cognitions with more realistic and adaptive thoughts" (Corey, 2016, p. 356).

Finally, **cognitive restructuring** "is the process of identifying and evaluating one's cognitions, understanding the negative behavioral impact of certain thoughts, and learning to replace these cognitions with more realistic and adaptive thoughts" (Corey, 2017, p. 356). For example, cognitive restructuring has been used effectively with troubled young people, people experiencing depressive disorders, social anxiety, and PTSD (Corey, 2017; Barrera, Szafranski, Ratcliff, Garnaat, & Norton, 2016; Norton & Abbot, 2016). Goals might include improved skills for problem solving, managing one's own life, cognitive coping, and relating to others. Group members are taught how to identify their thoughts about how they value themselves. They also learn to identify what they're thinking in problematic situations (e.g., when they're angry and act out violently). They then help each other learn how to change self-destructive or self-defeating thoughts, and replace such cognitions with more effective ones. This can result in positive behavioral change.

Many other techniques are also applied, but these are beyond this book's focus on groups in macro versus treatment contexts.

Psychoanalytic Theory

Psychoanalytic theory emphasizes the impact of early life experiences on current feelings and behavior. It has been applied to individual and group situations, although it is primarily used in treatment instead of macro contexts. Because of its significance in the conceptualization of group work, however, it merits some attention here.

Psychoanalytic theory focuses on three major aspects of group functioning. The first is how group members act out in the group context unsettled issues encountered early in life, usually within their own families (Corey, 2017; Toseland & Rivas, 2017). Yalom and Leszcz (2005) comment, "The great majority of clients who enter groups. . .have a background of a highly unsatisfactory experience in their first and most important group: the primary family" (p. 15). For example, a group member may have had difficulties communicating with his father, who ruled the family with an iron fist. That group member might then come to see the group's leader as another powerful father-like figure who will rule the group in a like manner.

A second aspect of group functioning emphasized by psychoanalytic theory is the attention given to the emotional reactions group members have to other members

Highlight **3-4**

Case Example—Id, Ego, and Superego

Pearl, a member of a community action group to prevent drug abuse, is one example of how these three mental dimensions might conflict. She attends a planning meeting to designate responsibilities for implementing a drug-prevention program. Unfortunately, she was so busy she skipped both breakfast and lunch, so she is ravenously hungry at the 1:30 P.M. meeting. Her id tells her to leave the meeting and get something to eat immediately.

However, her ego tells her it isn't socially appropriate to leave the meeting abruptly and get something to eat. She should have thought ahead rationally and brought a sandwich. Finally, her superego says she must stay and participate to the best of her ability because of her strong belief in controlling illegal drug use. The right thing to do is to help the community's children and, despite her hunger, remain at the meeting.

and to the group leader. These may include utter dependence on the leader(s) who group members see as being very powerful; actual defiance of the leaders who may be seen as threatening their rights and autonomy; varying degrees of competition among group members vying for attention from the leader(s) and other group members; attempts to form subgroups of allies in order to gain power against the group leader(s) or other members; and extreme selflessness when trying to meet other group members' needs at the expense of their own (Yalom & Leszcz, 2005).

Psychoanalytic theory's third focus on groups involves the distortions in their perceptions of other deriving from past life experiences. Psychoanalytic theory poses several concepts used to explain such personality forces. For instance, it views people as experiencing frequent conflict among three levels of consciousness— the id, the ego, and the superego. The **id** is the primitive force operating in the unconscious arena of the brain that represents basic primitive drives such as hunger, sex, and self-preservation. The **ego** is the rational component of the mind that evaluates consequences and determines courses of action in a logical manner. The **superego** is the conscience, which decides what actions and behaviors are right and wrong. Highlight 3-4 presents a case example illustrating these concepts.

Another concept important in understanding a psychoanalytic perspective on group functioning is the **defense mechanism**, any unconscious attempt to adjust to conditions such as anxiety, frustration, or guilt that are painful to experience. For example, without realizing it, to cope with her anxiety about group involvement, a group member is excessively quiet and withdrawn (a defense mechanism).

Psychoanalytic theory emphasizes scrutiny of individual members' feelings, behaviors, and interactions. These are then closely examined while the group leader and other members give feedback. The intent is for group members to attain **insight**, an understanding of their motivations, emotions, behaviors, and issues, a primary goal of the group process.

Systems Theory

We have established that systems theory provides an exceptionally useful means for understanding and describing human behavior in many contexts, including the

At a Glance **3-5**

Psychoanalytic Theory

Id: The primitive force operating in the unconscious arena of the brain that represents basic primitive drives such as hunger, sex, and self-preservation.

Ego: The rational component of the mind that evaluates consequences and determines courses of action in a logical manner.

Superego: The conscience, which decides what actions and behaviors are right and wrong.

Defense mechanism: Any unconscious attempt to adjust to conditions such as anxiety, frustration, or guilt that are painful to experience.

Insight: An understanding of one's motivations, emotions, behaviors, and issues, a primary goal of the group process.

interactions of individuals, groups, families, organizations, and communities in the macro social environment. For example, groups are an entity with features such as boundaries, a purpose, and ways of seeking and maintaining equilibrium in the face of ongoing change.

A group is a **system**, a set of related elements that are orderly, interrelated, and a functional whole. The group is distinguished by **boundaries**, borders or margins that separate it from other groups or the external environment and helps give it an identity. Think of the group as a living cell having a membrane or boundary around it. This boundary determines who is a group member and who is not.

Subsystems are subordinate or secondary systems within the group system. Each member of the group is a subsystem and two group members who form a special friendship in the group may become a subsystem.

Group systems strive to maintain a state of **homeostasis**, the tendency for a system to maintain a relatively stable, constant state of balance. Groups must maintain some homeostasis—or status quo—to survive and thrive.

Group members assume roles within the group. We have established that *roles* are expected behavior patterns based on an individual's position or status within the group. These roles may include leader, emotional supporter, idea person, task director, and so on.

Group members have relationships with each other. A **relationship** is the dynamic interpersonal connection between two or more persons or systems that involves how they think about, feel about, and behave toward each other. Relationships among various group members may be cooperative, friendly, helpful, hostile, or strained, depending on group members' patterns of interactions.

Objectives of Groups in Systems Theory   Group systems strive to attain four primary objectives, including **integration**, **pattern maintenance**, **goal attainment**, and **adaptation** (Toseland & Rivas, 2017; Corey, 2016). First, they seek **integration**, the means whereby group members fit and work together. Group members must get along and communicate well enough to get things done.

Second, group systems pursue **pattern maintenance**, how the group adheres to its basic processes and procedures. Group members establish procedures and expectations for ongoing interaction, such as how members should relate to each other, how decisions are made, or how and/or when members are given opportunities to voice opinions.

Third, group systems strive for **goal attainment**, achievement of their ultimate tasks and goals. Group systems exist for a purpose. To be worthwhile, the group must achieve its goals.

Fourth, group systems seek **adaptation**, the group's capacity to adjust to surrounding environmental conditions through an ongoing process of change. For example, if the building in which the group meets is condemned to be torn down, the group must adapt by finding another meeting location. If the room temperature is uncomfortable, someone will need to adjust the HVAC accordingly.

Balance between Task and Socio-Emotional Functions in Systems Theory

Generally, group systems strive to maintain a balance between two basic functions: task functions and socio-emotional functions. This is true for all groups, although the relative balance will differ for task and treatment groups. Task functions, which pursue goal attainment and adaptation, include exchanging information, establishing plans, and evaluating progress toward goals. They concern work and responsibility in groups. Socio-emotional functions, on the other hand, represent the feelings and emotional needs of group members. Such functions, geared to maintaining the group system's integration and pattern maintenance, are positive when they help lower tensions and increase mutual agreement and group solidarity. Negative socio-emotional functions, by contrast, increase conflict, tension, and disagreement.

Group Functioning in Systems Theory To understand how group function is viewed within systems theory, we need to recognize four concepts. These include activities, interactions, sentiments, and norms.

1. **Group activities** are the happenings and actions conducted in a group.
2. **Interactions** are the reciprocal behaviors and communications engaged in by group members.
3. **Sentiments** are the emotions and reactions manifested by group members.
4. **Norms** are the expectations held by group members regarding how they should behave in the group.

These four dimensions are critical to a group system's ongoing health and well-being. In the process of existing, groups must contend with both its internal and external environments. Group system activities, interactions, sentiments, and norms are oriented to and affect the internal group environment when they relate to group members' adaptation to each other.

These same variables are oriented to and affect the external environment when group members must adapt to pressures posed by that environment. For example, consider a group that holds its annual soup and sandwich supper, which helps fund the local homeless shelter. Group activities, interactions, sentiments, and norms may focus on the internal group relationships and process when two members are arguing about who has the best chunky chicken soup recipe. The internal group environment is the focus of attention. However, when the group finds out that its treasurer has absconded to Mexico with the proceeds from the fundraiser, it must turn its attention to the external environment. Its activities, interactions, sentiments, and norms must now focus on obtaining new funding to support the homeless shelter.

Critical Thinking Questions 3-1 LO 3-2

EP 8a

Picture some formal group with which you've been involved (e.g., a student organization, religious group, class group project, recreational group, or sports team).

- In what kind of specific *activities* did the group participate?
- How would you explain the *interactions* of group members?
- How would you describe the *sentiments* experienced by yourself and other group members?
- What *norms* did the group assume for how you should behave?

At a Glance 3-6

Systems Theory

System: A set of related elements that are orderly, interrelated, and a functional whole.

Boundaries: Borders or margins that separate one group from another.

Subsystem: Subordinate or secondary systems within the group system.

Homeostasis: The tendency for a system to maintain a relatively stable, constant state of balance.

Role: A culturally expected behavior pattern for a person having a specified status or being involved in a designated social relationship.

Relationship: The dynamic interpersonal connection between and among group members.

Integration: The means whereby group members fit and work together.

Pattern maintenance: How the group adheres to its basic processes and procedures.

Goal attainment: Achievement of a group's ultimate tasks and goals.

Adaptation: The group's capacity to adjust to surrounding environmental conditions through an ongoing process of change.

Group activities: The happenings and actions conducted in a group.

Interactions: The reciprocal behaviors and communications engaged in by group members.

Sentiments: The emotions and reactions manifested by group members.

Norms: The expectations held by group members regarding how they should behave in the group.

Empowerment Theory

EP 2

We have defined *empowerment* as the enhancing of individuals', groups', families', and communities' power, ability, and control to determine their own destinies. Groups are particularly appropriate for empowerment as they can strive "to change oppressive cognitive, behavioral, social, and political structures or conditions that thwart the control people have over their lives, that prevent them from accessing needed resources, and that keep them from participating in the life of their community" (Breton, 2004, p. 59). We will discuss five dimensions regarding how empowerment theory applies to groups: social justice, consciousness raising, mutual aid, power, and multicultural socialization (Breton, 2004; Finn & Jacobson, 2008; Gutierrez & Lewis, 1999; Robbins, Chattejee, & Canda, 2012).

EP 3

Social Justice   **Social justice** is the broad philosophical perspective that all people have the right to enjoy equal opportunities in economic, political, environmental, and social realms. An underlying theme of empowerment theory is that society is structured so that some groups are oppressed and denied their right to resources, free choice, and equal opportunity. Action groups can be formed to address these issues and advocate for positive change. (Of course, treatment groups also can and should assume an empowerment approach, but here we're focusing on macro settings.)

Consciousness Raising   **Consciousness raising** is the process of enhancing people's awareness of themselves, of others, or of issues in the social environment (Robbins et al., 2012). It occurs when they either have not thought of these ideas before or have made superficial assumptions about them, not having used critical thinking to evaluate the ideas' validity. People often tend to blame an oppressed group for that group's oppression (blaming the victim). People may think that it's the group members' fault that they are subject to social injustice. People feel group members should've worked harder. Or that they're too stupid to do better. Or that they're immoral. Because the oppressed group members are part of and influenced by the macro social environment, they may also fall into the trap of blaming themselves (Breton, 2004; van Wormer, 2006).

Consciousness raising helps people ask themselves questions about their personal predicament. Facts and ideas are brought to their attention regarding why they, in addition to numerous others, are experiencing social injustice. This process helps people link issues such as poverty and racism to the social, political, and economic configurations in which they live. Essentially, consciousness raising empowers people to view themselves more positively and realistically. Through consciousness raising they identify their strengths and see their capabilities for action. They become stronger, both personally and politically. Consciousness raising "provides group members opportunities to begin to see themselves as members of a community and eventually to fully participate in the life of that community"; they "begin to identify themselves as citizens—political beings—who, in a democracy, have the right and responsibility to participate on the sociopolitical scene, to be heard, and to influence policies so that they can access the resources they need" (Breton, 2004, pp. 60, 63).

Mutual Aid   Empowerment stresses how group members can help and empower each other through **mutual aid**, the act of providing support, feedback, and information within a group context (Breton, 2004; Parsons, 2008). Group members may see themselves as "a group of peers perceived as equal partners striving and helping each other to gain control over their lives" (Breton, 2004, p. 67). They come to recognize that they have the power and capacity to actively use the group to help themselves and each other. They use the bonds with other members and their own empathy to support differences as they seek to balance the needs of both the individual members and the group as a whole.

EP 2

Power   We have established that **power** is the ability to move people on a chosen course to produce an effect or achieve some goal. Potential power discrepancies exist within virtually any group (Robbins et al., 2012). Some members may be more assertive, knowledgeable, skilled, or have greater status for any variety of reasons. If a leader has been designated in a group or if a leader emerges, there is a natural power discrepancy that may work against mutual aid and empowerment.

Five styles of communication in groups affect the potential for empowerment through mutual aid in a group (Wood & Tully, 2006; Toseland & Rivas, 2017):

1. **Maypole.** The leader (e.g., a social worker) remains at the center of the group, controlling the members and paying attention to everyone separately. Group interaction among members is discouraged.
2. **Round robin.** The leader maintains control but each group member takes turns speaking.
3. **Hot seat.** The leader maintains control by directing all attention to one group member (in the hot seat) while the other members watch.
4. **Agenda-controlled.** The leader maintains strict order by using Robert's Rules of Order or some other structured form of running a meeting.
5. **Free form.** No leader emerges and group members feel free to contribute at will.

The most empowering communication style is the *free form*, where members empower themselves and are free to support each other (Wood & Tully, 2006). A disadvantage of this style might be a lack of structured order. It's possible that group members can get off track, thus interfering with the achievement of group goals. Suggestions for dealing with this challenge include asking two group members to share the leadership role. This may prevent a dominant and controlling leader from emerging. Another option is to simply rotate the leader's role among all group members. Group members can learn from others who can model leadership approaches, and power is distributed more equally among members. Greater empowerment of each member should result.

EP 2, 2a

Multicultural Socialization   Empowerment in any group also involves multicultural understanding and socialization. Group leaders and members should strive to identify, be sensitive to, and appreciate any differences that might exist among members including such factors as ability, race, class, gender, sexual orientation, and age. For heterogeneous groups to prosper, leaders must empower member differences and recognize that there are multiple ways to achieve a group's goals. **Socialization** is the process by which a group or society conveys its knowledge, values, beliefs, and expectations to its members.

Use of false assumptions and stereotypes can hastily serve to "turn off" group members, disrupting group cohesion and empowerment. **Group cohesion** is the extent to which group members feel that they belong in a group and desire to continue being members. Cohesion can be undermined by a group member or leader using obvious stereotyping based on characteristics supposedly associated with a specific group to which the member belongs.

Jiwan and Imani, the two lesbian women in Liz and Anna's group, sat together during the first group meeting. No mention of it was made. As the second group convened, however, these same two women moved to occupy adjacent seats. Jean [another group member], said aloud to Anna, "Why is it that the lesbians always sit together?" Liz overheard the remark and responded, "Probably for the same reasons that all the heterosexual women have sat together." Somewhat perplexed, Jean then looked around the room at how others had chosen to arrange themselves and found that group members had indeed

Critical Thinking Questions **3-2**

EP 2, 8a

To what extent do you feel you have multicultural knowledge and awareness? In what group situations involving people from diverse backgrounds, if any, might you feel uncomfortable and why? What things might you do to enhance your own multicultural knowledge, awareness, and sensitivity?

At a Glance **3-7**

Empowerment Theory

Empowerment: Enhancing individuals', groups', families', and communities' power and control over their destinies.

Social justice: The philosophical perspective that all people have the right to enjoy equal opportunities in economic, political, and social realms.

Consciousness raising: The process of enhancing people's awareness of themselves, or others, or of issues in the social environment.

Mutual aid: The act of providing support, feedback, and information within a group context.

Power: The ability to move people on a chosen course to produce an effect or achieve some goal.

Socialization: The process by which a group or society conveys its knowledge, values, beliefs, and expectations to its members.

Group cohesion: The extent to which group members feel that they belong in a group and desire to continue being members.

organized themselves in this fashion. She responded, "I never thought of it that way before!" Liz and Anna then began the group with a discussion of choices and their multiple interpretations, using the seating experience as an illustration. As all members of the group began to understand their collective lack of comfort in this new situation, they also began to gain additional information about choices others made that they had previously misunderstood. Seating options in later group sessions began to vary from the pattern exhibited during the first two weeks. [In other words, after addressing and thinking about this aspect of diversity, sexual orientation no longer dictated who sat together and who did not.] (Gutierrez & Lewis, 1999, pp. 74–75).

Feminist Theories

EP 2, 2c

Feminist theories involve "the liberation of women and girls from gender-based discrimination. The goal of feminist theories and practice is women's *self-determination* or the right to make one's own decisions" (Kirk & Okazawa-Rey, 2010, p. 4). For some feminists, this means "securing equal rights for women within existing institutions—from marriage and the family to government policy and law. For others, it means fundamentally changing these institutions" (Kirk & Okazawa-Rey, 2010, p. 4). Many feminist theories "were developed in the context of women's organizing for change—for the abolition of slavery, for women's suffrage, for labor rights, the civil rights of people of color, women's rights, and gay/lesbian/ bisexual/transgender rights. Feminist theories have been concerned with fundamental questions: Why are women in a subordinate position in our society and, indeed, worldwide? What are the origins of this subordination, and how is it perpetuated? How can it be changed?" (Kirk & Okazawa-Rey, 2007, pp. 14–15).

Note that feminist theories vary in terms of the concepts they emphasize (Kirk & Okazawa-Rey, 2010, pp. 10–14; Robbins et al., 2012, pp. 111–113). The following are a few examples. **Liberal feminism** "grew out of liberalism, a theory about individual rights, freedom, choice, and privacy" (Kirk & Okazawa-Rey, 2010, p. 10). Women are considered equal to men and, therefore, should have equal rights (Robbins et al., 2012). **Socialist feminism** grew out of Marxist economic theories and is "particularly concerned with the economic aspects of women's lives" (Kirk & Okazawa-Rey, 2010, pp. 12–13). It typically focuses on "women's relationship to the market including unpaid work in the home, childcare, and unequal wages in the paid labor market" (Robbins et al., 2012, p. 111). **Radical feminism** views women as "an oppressed class" (Robbins et al., 2012, p. 111). It emphasizes how male domination "manifests itself in gender roles, and family relationships, heterosexuality, and violence against women, as well as the wider male-dominated world of work, education, government, religion, and law" (Kirk & Okazawa-Rey, 2012, p. 12). **Postmodern feminism** stresses "the particularity of women's experiences in specific cultural and historical contexts. . . . [It] seeks to account for differences among women based on age, race, culture, national origin, ability, and other attributes" (Kirk & Okazawa-Rey, 2012, p. 17). Gender is viewed as a continuum rather than two separate states (Robbins et al., 2012).

Here we will arbitrarily select some of the major themes characterizing most feminist theories and apply them to group functioning in macro contexts. These include using a gender filter, assuming a pro-woman perspective, empowerment, consciousness raising, viewing personal issues as political concerns, stressing the importance of process, seeing "unity in diversity," and "validation" (Gutierrez & Lewis, 1999; Robbins et al., 2012). Often these themes have common characteristics.

Using a Gender Filter   **Using a gender filter** to view the plight of women in the macro social environment establishes a new way of looking at the world, with women and their issues becoming the focus of attention (Robbins et al., 2012). Such a filter emphasizes that women are not only part of the larger community, but themselves make up a community of women within that larger community.

Assuming a Pro-Woman Perspective   A major misunderstanding regarding feminist theory and practice is that it has an anti-male focus. Rather, it is a **pro-woman perspective**, concerned with such things as the experiences, development, resiliency, strengths, and histories of women. It recognizes that oppression is a factor that influences the outcomes that women experience but offers opportunity for achieving justice in all the relationships in which women are involved. Feminist theories maintain that women should have equal rights, responsibility, and opportunity, and call for a social order that offers equality and rejects exploitation.

Empowerment   Feminist *empowerment* involves women coming together around a common cause and promoting human rights and liberation. The emphasis here, of course, is the empowerment of women by focusing on their strengths. Use of collaboration and consensus building is emphasized; democratic processes and procedures are stressed.

Consciousness Raising   **Consciousness raising**, an important principle in empowerment theory, has been a significant aspect of the feminist perspective (Hannam, 2012). In this context, consciousness raising is the development of personal awareness and understanding of the cultural, personal, economic, and political conditions that mold women's reality. Furthermore, it involves undertaking a serious examination of a woman's self and her feelings about a range of issues affecting women. Women must become aware of the issues engulfing them in their environment before they can take steps to address them. A basic approach for consciousness raising entails asking oneself a series of questions and considering potential answers. Questions include:

- Who am I? What are my needs, my desires, my visions of a life that is safe, healthy, and fulfilling?
- Who says? What is the source of my self-definition and that of my reality? Does it conform to my experience of self and the world?
- Who benefits from this definition? Does it conform to my needs, my "truths"? Is it possible for me to live by these definitions? If not . . .
- What must change, and how?

Answers to these questions should focus on defining a woman's self-worth, what she values, and how fairly the world is treating her. If she determines that her treatment is unfair or inadequate because she is a woman, how can she make changes in her macro environment to receive better or more fair treatment? Consciousness raising thus can become a foundation of empowerment. First, a woman explores herself. Next, she examines issues and appraises her status. Finally, she proposes plans to improve her life and her environment.

For example, LaShondra is a single mother of two children, ages 2½ and 4. She can support her children well enough by working as an optometrist's assistant. However, she must work some evenings, in addition to 9:00 a.m. to 5:00 p.m. on most weekdays. One of her problems is finding adequate and flexible daycare. Another problem is receiving court-mandated child support payments from her ex-husband. He just can't seem to hold down a job for very long. Still another problem is her high rent for a tiny apartment due to lack of adequate affordable housing. Other problems are lack of a social life and difficulties in obtaining credit to buy a sorely needed new car. Her "ex" ruined her credit rating while they were married.

Alone, LaShondra feels stuck. She views her problems as personal and individual. She tends to blame herself after the fact for making the "wrong decisions." However, talking to other women, getting information, and discussing issues can help to raise LaShondra's consciousness. She can become aware of how she is not alone, but shares her plight with many other women in similar situations. She can come to realize that many things in her world are not her fault. Rather, they result from basic social conditions working against her.

The final facet of consciousness raising involves proposing and working toward positive changes in the macro environment. With others, LaShondra can confront community leaders and politicians about the lack of adequate child care. Can community funds be directed to help subsidize centers? Can she and other local women establish their own center, together paying for staff and volunteering their free time to help cut costs?

How can LaShondra and other women not receiving child support from itinerant ex-husbands or partners seek their fair share? Is there some community agency available to help them search for missing fathers and require payment? If not, why not? Can such a service be developed?

LaShondra discovers that other community women share similar concerns regarding the lack of adequate reasonable housing. How can the community address this problem? Can community leaders help? Can private developers be encouraged or subsidized to build housing community mothers need?

Together, LaShondra and other women can address their social issues. Can they organize and sponsor community events to fulfill social needs and decrease isolation? Can they form clubs or groups to help them "get out" regularly and feel less alone?

Finally, can LaShondra and other community women work together to find ways to establish credit? Can they as a group approach local banks and businesses to discuss the issues? Can processes be established to determine when credit problems are not their fault, but rather, the fault of ex-spouses?

The Personal as Political   Viewing **the personal as political** is a major aspect of consciousness raising from a feminist perspective; "individual and collective pain and problems of living always have a cultural and/or political dimension" (Bricker-Jenkins & Netting, 2009, p. 279; Fisher & Burghardt, 2008; Robbins et al., 2012). GlennMaye (1998) defines the personal and political facets of consciousness raising:

> The personal dimension of consciousness raising involves (1) identifying one's own feelings, perceptions, and needs from the vantage point of one's own experiences, (2) naming or defining one's experiences in one's own language, and (3) telling one's own life story. . . . The political dimension of consciousness raising involves (1) linking one's personal experiences to one's position as a woman in a male-dominated society, (2) identifying oneself as a woman who shares a common fate with all women, and (3) taking action to change oneself and the social structures that oppress women.
>
> The personal and the political aspects of consciousness raising cannot really be separated. They exist as [an intellectual, logical process of reasoning] . . . in which personal experience and social reality are discovered, tested, and recreated. The full meaning of feminist consciousness resides in apprehending the complex reality of one's situation as a woman with the faith in one's ability and right to a fully human existence. (p. 37)

Thus, a feminist perspective proposes that all women are connected, that there are no personal private solutions, and that growth as a person can only be attained through action in the political realm.

The Importance of Process   Feminist theories emphasize that the **process** of *how* things get done is just as important as *what* gets done. A traditional patriarchal perspective that stresses male dominance focuses on the significance of end results and goal achievement. For example, consider a wealthy male politician who readily gets elected to the position of state senator after spending a huge amount of money on his political campaign. A patriarchal perspective emphasizes the importance of having won the election. It does not focus on how the election was won. Attention centers neither on the amount of money that was spent nor what contributions the senator received from large corporations expecting to receive privileged treatment.

Feminist theories stress that decision making is based on equality and the participation of all. All group members' input is important. No one should have power over another. Feminist theories focus on aspects of process such as making certain all participants have the chance to speak and be heard, adhering to principles of ethical behavior, working toward agreement and consensus, and considering personal issues as important.

Unity in Diversity: "Diversity Is Strength"   Feminist theories stress unity and harmony, on the one hand, and appreciation of diverse characteristics on the other (Bricker-Jenkins & Netting, 2009). Gutierrez and Lewis (1999) explain that "efforts are made to bridge differences between women based on such factors as race, class, physical ability, and sexual orientation with the principle that **diversity is strength**" (p. 105). Women working together can achieve a better quality of life for all. To remain unified, women must appreciate each other's differences. Diverse characteristics are sought out and welcomed. New ideas to improve old ways of doing things are encouraged.

Validation   **Validation** is the process of accepting a person and a person's actions as justifiable and relevant. A feminist perspective does not exclude factors such as critical thinking, analysis, and efficiency. However, it also includes validation of the nonrational, that is, aspects of life and human interaction that go beyond structured scientific reasoning. Feelings, emotions, and intuition are also important concerns. Spirituality is another dimension given precedence. Spirituality "includes one's values, beliefs, mission, awareness, subjectivity, experience, sense of purpose and direction, and a kind of striving toward something greater than oneself" (Frame, 2003, p. 3).

Validation can occur through group experiences as we come to recognize that some of our perceptions about our lives and environment are legitimate, valid, and worthy of discussion. Recognizing through collective experience that others have similar problems or challenges helps reduce self-blaming while also looking at aspects of the environment that contribute to those experiences. This helps raise one's consciousness and energizes the group to pursue collective action designed to change those factors. This may entail seeking change in aspects of the family, societal institutions, the community, or the larger environment.

EP 8a

Critical Thinking Questions 3-3

To what extent do you agree with the concepts inherent in feminist theories? To what extent do you feel you are or are not a feminist, and why?

Of all the theories discussed here (field, social exchange, learning, psychoanalytic, systems, empowerment, and feminist), which concepts do you think are most relevant in understanding how groups work? Explain why.

At a Glance 3-8

Feminist Theories

Self-determination: Everyone's right to make his or her own decisions.

Using a gender filter: Viewing the world with women and their issues becoming the focus of attention.

Pro-woman perspective: The perspective that "women's diverse histories, conditions, developmental patterns, and strengths are shaped and subjugated under conditions of oppression but can be reshaped through collective work" to achieve justice in relationships (Bricker-Jenkins & Netting, 2009, p. 279).

Empowerment: The process where women come together concerning a common cause and promote human liberation

Consciousness raising: The development of personal awareness and understanding of the cultural, personal, economic, and political conditions that mold women's reality.

The personal as political: The view that "individual and collective pain and problems of living always have a cultural and/or political dimension" (Bricker-Jenkins & Netting, 2009, p. 279).

Process: The perspective that *how* things get done is just as important as *what* gets done.

"Diversity is strength": The view that aspects of diversity should be appreciated as strengths and used to establish unity.

Validation: The process of accepting a person and a person's actions as justifiable and relevant.

Understanding Groups in the Macro Social Environment: Task Group Dynamics LO 3-3

EP 6

Because this book focuses primarily on working with other systems in the macro social environment, the following sections will focus on task groups. A **task** or **work group** is a collection of people that applies the principles of group dynamics to solve problems, develop innovative ideas, formulate plans, and achieve goals within the context of an organization or a community.

What goes on in task groups? What do you need to know about task groups to understand how they work so you can be an effective task group member or leader? At least six concepts tend to characterize groups—communication, interpersonal interaction, norms, roles, group cohesiveness, and power and status.

Communication

EP 1c

Communication, the exchange of information, is the heart of a group. Communication may be *verbal*, using spoken or written words, or *nonverbal*. **Nonverbal communication** includes any means by which information is conveyed not using spoken or written words. Group members must communicate effectively to get things done.

Wheelan (1999) explains:

You would be surprised at the number of groups . . . encountered whose members receive feedback about group performance but do not use that feedback to implement constructive changes. In most cases, this is due to a simple flaw in the group's internal processes. Groups that do not utilize feedback constructively usually do not have a mechanism [or procedure] in place to evaluate the validity of the feedback and to make decisions about what changes they should make based on that feedback. An example of such a mechanism might be that internal and external feedback is sought on a regular basis and that the feedback is discussed and evaluated at the beginning of the next meeting. If the feedback is judged to be valid and helpful, members discuss ways to improve team performance, decide what changes to make, and implement those changes.

This may seem like an elaborate process, but in reality, it usually takes 10 minutes or less. The trick is to collect the feedback from internal members at the end of one session and discuss it at the beginning of the next. Feedback from external sources should be collected between meetings. (p. 43)

Positive Verbal Communication in Effective Task Groups   Four aspects tend to characterize verbal communication in effective task groups functioning in macro settings (Wheelan, 1999). First, they should "have an *open communication structure* that . . . [encourages] all members to participate. Individuals are listened to regardless of their age, title, sex, race, ethnicity, profession, or other status characteristics. This enhances productivity since all ideas and suggestions get heard" (p. 42).

Second, effective groups regularly seek out feedback about the efficiency and success of their process and output. In successful groups, members accurately can evaluate themselves, their interaction, and their results. They ask for feedback both from each other and from outside sources with whom the group is involved.

Third, in effective task groups, members provide each other with feedback that is practical and useful. Useful feedback satisfies one of two criteria. First, it can help the group achieve its goals. Second, it can provide information to members about improving their individual performance within the group.

Fourth, effective task groups actually use both the internal and external feedback they receive. Group members not only seek out and obtain information about group functioning, but they implement recommendations to improve the group's performance.

Nonverbal Communication in Task Groups   We've established that nonverbal communication includes any means by which information is conveyed not using spoken or written words. Eye contact, facial expressions, body positioning (e.g., relaxed or extremely tense), and posture all can convey vital information among group members. Nonverbal communication can give important clues about what's really going on in group members' heads. Sometimes a group member will say one thing but mean another and provide nonverbal evidence for the latter. For example, a task group member might say while grimacing and looking desperately at her watch, "That's a great idea, but we should really save our discussion for when we have more time." The nonverbal cues may indicate that the member really means that she's quite annoyed that the other group member introduced the topic so late in the meeting. She really doesn't think it's a "great idea" at all—or certainly not at this time.

Carroll, Bates, and Johnson (2004) discuss the importance of nonverbal communication, particularly from the perspective of group leaders. (This information is just as important for group members who are not leaders to comprehend what's really going on in a group.) They write:

> Nonverbal [communication] . . . is a particularly important source of information for group leaders. Alertness and sensitivity to nonverbal data can provide group leaders with a rich source of interactive material. The thumb tucked tightly inside a fist, a flexing jaw muscle, arms folded tightly across the chest, the drumming of an index finger . . . all represent important messages to group leaders. Although leaders may not always respond immediately to verbal or silent signals such as tight fists, drumming fingers, excessive yawns, inappropriate smiles, or a flushed neck, leaders observe and draw tentative meaning from them. When verbal and nonverbal cues . . . [do not coincide], when the tone of voice insinuates one thing while the words say another, when lips are smiling but hands are clenched, the leader is watchful. The language of nonverbal communication in a group is rich with silent signals that can be received by a leader's [and other group members'] sensitive antennae. The leader "hears" as many of these signals as possible, then responds selectively and in a responsible manner.
>
> Group leaders [and other group members] also may note changes of posture, rates of speech, direction of gaze, length of messages and silences, and changes in facial expression" to provide indications of what members are thinking. (p. 68)

Cross-Cultural Differences in Communication   Note that it's important to be sensitive to cultural differences concerning the meaning of specific nonverbal and verbal communication in task group settings. Corey, Corey, and Callanan (2015) explain:

> Many cultural expressions are subject to misinterpretation, including appropriate personal space, eye contact, handshaking, dress, formality of greeting, perspective on time, and so forth. Western countries often feel uncomfortable with periods of silence and tend to talk to ease their tension. In some cultures silence may be a sign of respect and politeness rather than a lack of a desire to continue to speak. Silence may be a reflection of fear or confusion, or it may be a cautious expression and reluctance [to participate further in discussion.] (p. 123)

Eye contact provides an example of diverse cultural expectations for this type of nonverbal communication. Cormier and Hackney (2008) explain:

> In some cultures . . . eye contact is appropriate when listening. In other cultures, an individual may look away as a sign of respect or may demonstrate more eye contact when talking and less eye contact while listening. Good eye contact [in mainstream American culture]—eye contact that reinforces [attentiveness and makes] . . . communication easier—lies somewhere between the fixed gaze and "shifty eyes," or frequent breaks of eye contact. (p. 45)

For instance, Chinese people speaking together "use much less eye contact, especially when it is with the opposite sex"; thus, a male group participant's direct eye contact with a Chinese woman might be "considered rude or seductive in Chinese culture" (Ivey & Ivey, 2016, p. 54).

Another example of variations in cultural communication involves Hmong people who originated in Southeast Asia. Many have immigrated to the United States. Neuliep (2012) explains:

> Nonverbal gestures used in Hmong culture include twitching the eyes to communicate contempt for another. Twitching the eyes during a long stare is very offensive and may lead to physical confrontation. . . . Kneeling is done only by men when they want to express their thanks or to ask another for mercy and forgiveness. A woman's kneeling has little or no value because of her low rank and position in Hmong clans. (p. 121)

Barriers to Communication   Several barriers can interfere with communication and group progress. Sometimes, the communication sender is unclear, vague, or evasive in terms of what she's saying. For example, a group member says, "That idea is interesting." What does "interesting" mean? What do you mean when you say you got an "interesting" birthday gift? Is it good or bad? Are you happy or unhappy?

Other times, communication barriers are due to the communication's receiver. The receiver may be biased against the sender, more interested in other concerns, or floating off somewhere in Never Never Land. For example, a group member sends the following communication to another group member, "Time is short. We must come to a decision quickly. How do you vote, yes or no?" The receiving group member responds, "Huh?" The receiver had been thinking about how his parking meter was probably overdue and how he hoped he wouldn't get a parking ticket. The last one he got was for $85.

Still other times, communication barriers exist in the group environment, either internally or externally. Examples are noise and distractions in the hallway, phones ringing, interruptions, people looking at their smartphones, and whispering by other group members. A screaming girl outside might distract group members, who wonder what's happening to her. A communication receiver might be unable to clearly hear a sender's message because other group members are rudely talking about their social plans for Friday night. A hearing impairment might affect one or members of the group. A fire alarm might disrupt the group altogether.

Communication is effective in groups when senders' **intent** (what they wish to convey) match their **impact** (what the receivers understand). Groups work most effectively when members pay attention and strive to clarify and understand what each other means.

Self-Disclosure   One other aspect of communication worthy of note is **self-disclosure**, the sharing of personal feelings and information. Self-disclosure can enhance group members' feelings of belonging and acceptance in a group. It forms the basis for members getting to know and trust each other.

Corey, Corey, and Corey (2014) urge that group members use care when self-disclosing. For example, going into intimate detail of some former experience not really related to the group or the group's purpose may detract from the group's effectiveness and annoy other members. These authors make some suggestions for using self-disclosure. Group members should only self-disclose when the information has direct bearing on the group's purpose. Members should use careful discretion regarding what they really want to share with others and what is too private or ir-relevant to reveal. Finally, self-disclosure is often more appropriate after a group has been meeting for a while instead of during its initial sessions. Highlight 3-5 provides a case example of self-disclosure.

Interpersonal Interaction

EP 1c

Interpersonal interaction is the result of verbal and nonverbal communication, ex-pressed emotions and attitudes, and behavior between or among persons. It is much more complicated than communication because emotions, attitudes, and behaviors in addition to reciprocal responses are integrally involved. Interpersonal interaction can reflect mutual respect, liking, dislike, resentment, admiration, encouragement, discouragement, approval, disapproval, or mistrust. Through interaction, group members express ideas, emotions, and attitudes to each other. Highlight 3-6 pro-vides a case example involving interpersonal interaction in a group.

Norms

Norms are unwritten, collective rules and expectations held by group members con-cerning what is appropriate behavior within the group. In essence, norms are informal regulations about what is and what is not supposed to be done within the group's inter-action (Williams, 2016). An example of a group norm is a shared expectation that only one group member speaks at a time. Members should not interrupt each other. Another norm may be that all issues discussed within the group are confidential and therefore should not be shared outside of the group. Cathy's breaking of this norm is described in Highlight 3-6, an illustration of interpersonal interaction in the group context.

Norms are communicated to group members in at least three basic ways (Dumler & Skinner, 2008). First, a group leader may simply and explicitly state the unwritten rules. Second, group members may discuss among themselves and verbally identify norms. Third, incidents occurring in the group's history may shape norms. Dumler and Skinner (2008) propose the following four examples of how events happening in and to a group can mold group norms (p. 328):

1. *Leadership "rotation."* One example involves an early point in a group's his-tory where a group member aggressively tries to establish control and be-come the group's forceful leader. Other group members resent this tack and

---

Highlight 3-5

Case Example—Self-Disclosure

Mindy and Mort are members of a community group in the small town of Big Horn that is trying to raise community residents' awareness about the need for a new elementary school. Big Horn has begun to serve as a bedroom commu-nity for a nearby metropolitan area. Mindy self-discloses to Mort, "Thanks for volunteering to talk to the town board chair-person. It's always so difficult for me to talk to community leaders." Here she takes a personal risk of possible criticism by confessing to Mort a weakness of hers. Mort responds "Oh, no problem. I like talking to that guy and pushing him a little. He always thinks he knows everything." Mort's response to Mindy is pleasant, implies warmth, and avoids criticism. As a result, Mindy's and Mort's relationship is enhanced just a little bit by providing mutual support that increases trust.

Highlight **3-6**

Case Example—Interpersonal Interaction

One group, a foster care unit, provides an example of contrasting interpersonal interaction by various members. The unit is made up of a social work supervisor, Ada, and her five supervisees, Tom, Dick, Harry, Mary, and Herman. Tom, Dick, Harry, and Mary almost worship Ada. They respect her expertise, appreciate her support, and genuinely like her. Herman, on the other hand, harbors bitter resentment toward Ada because she had been chosen unit supervisor over him. Herman typically pouts during group meetings, interspersing occasional negative or critical comments. The other group members simply ignore him.

Another example of how interpersonal interaction affects group process is a group of community residents on a search committee for the neighborhood's youth recreational center. Applicants include both community residents and candidates from other parts of the city. To maintain fairness, avoid hurt feelings, and fulfill legal responsibilities, group members agree that all comments made within the group will go no further.

One group member, Cathy, makes a few comments to Ludwig, one of the applicants from the community who happens to be a good friend of hers. Cathy informs Ludwig of the criticisms made by other group members, implying he shouldn't get his hopes up too high about getting the job. Ludwig irately calls the group members who had criticized him, tells them of Cathy's communication, and angrily complains.

Thereafter, Cathy's credibility within the group is totally blown. When confronted, Cathy refuses to acknowledge that she is the one who blew the whistle to Ludwig. She won't admit to doing it, but she won't admit to not doing it, either. Ludwig told group members she was the one who informed him. Worse yet, group members no longer trust that group discussion will be kept confidential. Productive conversation about the pros and cons of each candidate is severely inhibited. Eventually, the position is filled, for better or worse. However, the other group members swear they will never again serve on another committee with Chatty Cathy.

seek to prevent such an occurrence in the future. Thus, they establish a group norm that leadership will be formally rotated every time the group meets. Such rotation, of course, could also be specified for every month, every other group meeting, or some other designated rotation.

2. *The importance of "timeliness" and punctuality.* Consider a group that misses the important deadline of submitting a report to the agency's executive director (the person highest in the agency's power structure). Consequently, the agency director chews out the group mercilessly about how the agency's funding depends on getting information to funding sources in a timely manner and that this should NEVER happen again. The group then may establish the norm that deadlines absolutely must be met and excuses for lateness will not be tolerated.

   A similar issue involves being late for meetings. If one or two group members typically saunter into meetings 5 or 10 minutes late, the rest of the group is forced to wait, collectively wasting a significant amount of their time. To help prevent this behavior, the group may establish the norm that meetings will start on time. Period. Anyone coming in late will just have to miss anything transpiring during the beginning of the meeting.

3. *Expectations for "loyalty."* In the Highlight 3-6 case example where confidentiality was broken, the group might have openly discussed, changed, and established a new norm requiring loyalty to the group in the form of confidentiality. **Confidentiality** is the ethical principle that workers should not

share information provided by or about a client unless that worker has the client's explicit permission to do so. Within the macro social environment, confidentiality can also be applied to group participation in organizations and communities. Focus on Ethics 3-1 addresses the importance of confidentiality in groups.

4. *The pursuit of "fairness."* Consider a social work unit in a public welfare department. Historically, the first person putting in a request for vacation days automatically gets the days requested. Only a limited number of workers can be on vacation at any one time because enough staff must remain to serve clients adequately. Some of the unit workers who had children in elementary school were unable to put in requests very early because of their children's as yet-unscheduled sports and other activities. The social work unit group determined that the norm governing the vacation request process was unfair and instituted a new one. The new norm established a process where names were rotated on a list. The worker having first choice for vacation this year would be rotated to having last choice next year, thereby giving all workers a chance at getting the vacation days they wanted.

Focus on Ethics **3-1**

Confidentiality in Groups LO 3-4

EP 1a

Confidentiality is very important in groups (Corey et al., 2015). Depending on the group's purpose, information might involve job applicants being discussed and considered (as demonstrated in Highlight 3-6), other administrative decisions and issues that concern people's performance or personal lives, or clients (such as during treatment conferences where staff get together to review clients' progress and goals). Some information shared within a group setting should be kept confidential; that is, it should be entrusted in confidence among group members only. Sharing some types of information outside of a group has the potential of invading people's privacy, harming people's reputation, and causing mistrust among group members and nonmembers. In some cases, an individual who believes he or she was slandered about derogatory comments made by others has the option of suing for damages, yet another reason for observing confidentiality.

An example in an administrative setting might be a group of supervisors reviewing the performance of Amy, a newer staff member near the end of her probationary period who is being considered for permanent status. Even though the supervisors will not engage in gossip about Amy or about other supervisors, they may become careless and share more than they should. Perhaps you've been involved in a study group, religious group, volunteer organization, student organization, or department at work where you found out that another group member had been "talking behind your back." Perhaps it involved criticizing your performance in the group. Or it may have concerned some personal information you shared in the group that you did not want shared outside of the group.

Corey and her colleagues (2014) make the following suggestions regarding confidentiality in groups:

- Confidentiality is critical to a group's success but leaders cannot guarantee that all members will uphold this policy. Members should be told initially and periodically reminded about the importance of confidentiality. This is especially important in the age of social media.

- Leaders must also point out the limitations to confidentiality inherent in laws, professional ethics standards, and the behavior of others in the group.

- Group leaders may establish contracts in which members agree to abide by the expectation of privacy.

- Leaders may need to create sanctions for violations of confidentiality.

Note that norms, once established, are not necessarily static; they often change over time as group purpose, membership, and needs change. Consider an agency work group formed to discuss fundraising mechanisms. Initially, the group maintains a formal dress code norm, the expectation that members wear suits or their equivalent during meetings. As group members get to know each other better and become more comfortable, they start attending group meetings in more comfortable informal attire. The dress code norm could change from formal suits to sweatshirts and jeans.

Roles

EP 1c

Roles are expected behavior patterns based on individuals' position or status within the group. Two types of roles are necessary to achieve group goals effectively on an ongoing basis (Aldag & Kuzuhara, 2005). First, *task-oriented roles* are those with the purpose of conducting tasks to achieve goals. Group members "who initiate tasks, gather information for use by the . . . [group], offer suggestions, and help motivate others" are performing task-oriented roles (p. 446). *Relations-oriented roles* are those with the purpose of keeping group members happy and satisfied with group progress and interaction. Group members "who keep the group harmonious, assist in helping members resolve disputes, and encourage members as they face barriers are engaging in relations-oriented roles" (p. 446). Sometimes, group members also assume *self-oriented roles*, where these members seek their own satisfaction and control, often without concern for other group members' well-being (Aldag & Kuzuhara, 2005, p. 446). For example, a group member might try to bully other group members into accepting him as group leader. People assuming self-oriented roles often disrupt the group's ability to work together and get things done.

Roles may be formal or informal. A formal role is that of a committee chairperson assigned by the agency's executive director. Another formal group role is that of a secretary elected by a group majority vote.

Informal roles vary widely. A group member with established expertise might serve as the group expert on certain matters. A member with a well-developed sense of humor might become the group clown, helping the group dissipate anxiety and interact more comfortably. Group leaders might also develop informally. On a court jury, for example, a task-oriented person with good listening, communication, and organizational skills might emerge as leader by group consent.

Group Cohesiveness

Group cohesiveness is the extent to which group members feel close to each other or connected as group members. It makes sense that in most groups, cohesiveness doesn't occur immediately but rather develops over time (Corey et al., 2014). Indicators of cohesiveness include good attendance and punctuality, efforts by group members to maintain confidentiality and make each other feel safe, use of good listening skills and support among group members, and a willingness to provide feedback and share perceptions about other members' issues (Corey et al., 2014).

Group cohesiveness obviously facilitates a group's ability to function effectively. Effects include members' increased willingness to participate in group activities and functions, encouragement of nonconforming members to get with the program and cooperate, and increased success at achieving goals (Dumler & Skinner, 2008; Williams, 2016).

Power and Status

EP 2

Related concepts to interpersonal interaction and cohesiveness in groups are power and status. **Power** is the potential ability to move people on a chosen course to produce an effect or achieve some goal (Homan, 2016). **Status**, a concept closely related to power, is the relative rank assigned to members within the group. People with higher status usually have more power, and those with lower status have lesser power. People with more power and higher status can exert greater influence on what a group does.

Aldag and Kuzuhara (2005) describe the three ways that power can be used in groups:

- **Power over**. This is power used to make another person act in a certain way; it may be called **dominance**.
- **Power to**. This is power that gives others the means to act more freely themselves; it is sometimes called *empowerment* . . .
- **Power from**. This is power that protects us from the power of others; it may be called **resistance**. (p. 366)

They indicate that "these uses of power suggest that power is more than just a way to change others' behaviors (although that function is certainly important). It may also be used to help others act more freely or to prevent others from forcing us to do things we don't want to do" (p. 366).

Possible Sources of Power in Groups   There are five possible sources of power in groups: legitimate, reward, coercive, referent, and expert (Dubrin, 2016; Dumler & Skinner, 2008; Griffin, 2016). Each can contribute to a group member's potential to influence the group.

Legitimate power is that attained because of one's position and vested authority. Police officers, judges, state governors and agency directors and supervisors have some degree of legitimate power because of their positions.

Reward power is that held because of the ability to provide positive reinforcement or rewards to others. Examples of rewards are raises, "A's" on papers, allowances, promotions, days off, awards, and social praise.

Coercive power is that based on the capability of dispensing punishments or negative reinforcement to influence other members' behavior. Bosses wield coercive power over their employees by reprimanding them or by imposing limitations on what they're allowed to do. In addition to legitimate power, police officers have coercive power over speeders by giving expensive speeding tickets. The head nurse on a mental institution's ward can exert coercive power over uncooperative patients by restricting privileges.

Referent power is that held because of other group members' respect and high esteem. A military hero might have referent power in his platoon because of great

At a Glance 3-9

Group Dynamics

Communication: The exchange of information.

Nonverbal communication: Any means by which information is conveyed other than through spoken or written words.

Self-disclosure: The sharing of personal feelings and information.

Interpersonal interaction: The result of verbal and nonverbal communication, expressed emotions and attitudes, and behavior between or among persons.

Norms: Unwritten, collective rules, and expectations held by group members concerning what is appropriate behavior within the group.

Roles: Expected behavior patterns based on individuals' position or status within the group.

Group cohesiveness: The extent to which group members feel close to each other or connected as group members.

Power: The potential ability to move people on a chosen course to produce an effect or achieve some goal.

Legitimate power: That attained because of one's position and vested authority.

Reward power: That granted because of the ability to provide positive reinforcement or rewards to others.

Coercive power: That based on the capability of dispensing punishments or negative reinforcement to influence other members' behavior.

Referent power: That held because of other group members' respect and high esteem.

Expert power: That based on established authority or expertise in a particular domain.

Status: The relative rank assigned to members within the group.

acts of bravery. Famous actors and actresses, some high-level politicians, famous authors, and well-known playwrights have referent power to the extent that they are admired and command respect.

Finally, **expert power** is that based on established authority or expertise in a domain. A famous family therapist and author of many books on family therapy may have expert power among a group of social work practitioners who work with families. Likewise, a successful investment counselor volunteering to assist a group of urban residents in getting their financial affairs in order has expert power within that group.

As you were reading this, you might have recognized that some people possess multiple sources of power. An agency director or supervisor may have expert power because of their knowledge and expertise and legitimate power because they have been employed to lead this particular group or organization. They likely have both a degree of reward and coercive power as they evaluate their staff members' performance. Finally, to the extent that their staff members look up to them, like them, or value their relationship with the supervisor, they may also have referent power.

Leadership in Task Groups   LO 3-5

Leadership is the act of exerting influence on other group members to direct their behavior, activities, attitudes, or interaction. Leadership may be formally assigned or informally established. How a group runs and whether it's effective depend on its group dynamics and leadership. The previous section discussed group dynamics. The following sections will discuss various aspects involved in leadership. These include leadership and power, "leader-directed" vs. "group-directed" leadership, task-oriented versus relationship-oriented approaches to leadership, personality traits of effective group leaders, and leadership skills.

Leadership and Power

EP 8c, 6

Leadership is related to power and status within a group. For example, the new executive director of a community mental health center has power based on her formal status as a significant administrator—that is, legitimate power. Depending on her qualifications and the parameters of her job description, she may also possess reward, coercive, referent, or expert power.

Informal leaders who gradually develop within a group context might establish their status through referent and expert power. Group members might discover over time that a member is exceptionally responsible, conscientious, considerate of others' feelings, and organized. Such a person might emerge as a group leader by consensus or majority agreement.

"Leader-Directed" versus "Group-Directed" Leadership

One way of looking at leadership within a task group involves "leader-directed" versus "group-directed" approaches (Jacobs, Masson, Harvill, & Schimmel, 2016, p. 22). **Leader-directed** approaches involve greater structure and control imposed by the leader. **Group-directed** methods, on the other hand, allow group members to have greater control over what happens in the group. Jacobs and his colleagues (2016) discuss the differences:

> Effective leaders who follow the leader-directed model never demand that the members follow them as if they were gurus; rather, they lead in a manner that is valuable for the members. The leader-directed style of leadership does not mean that the leader is on an ego trip or that the group must serve the personality of the leader. It simply means that the leader understands the members' needs and structures the group to meet those needs.
>
> Leaders using the group-directed approach often turn the group over to the members and have the members determine the direction and content. This can be quite valuable for some groups. [For example, consider a jury that selects the person to serve as jury foreman, or some other group where all members have equal status and no leader has been appointed.] However, there are times when this approach wastes much time, especially for a group that is meeting only once or for only a few sessions. Often members don't know what they need. . . . A leader-directed style can be of great benefit by providing structure, thought-provoking questions, and [guidance]. . . .
>
> [In summary,] [e]ven though the leader is responsible, the amount of leading will depend on the kind of group and the composition of its members. For certain groups, the leader may primarily want the members to direct the group; for other groups, the leader will want to assume much of the directing. (pp. 22–23)

In conclusion, Jacobs and his colleagues (2016) suggest that *"people don't mind being led when they are led well"* (p. 22).

Task-Related versus Relationship-Related Approaches to Leadership

Another way of looking at leadership style within groups involves task-related versus relationship-related emphases. **Task-related** approaches focus more on adherence to procedures and accomplishment of goals. **Relationship-related** approaches stress the importance of interaction, communication, cooperation, and group members' satisfaction.

Task-Oriented Group Leaders   Northouse (2016) describes a task-oriented leadership style:

> Task-oriented people are goal oriented. They want to achieve. Their work is meaningful, and they like things such as "to do" lists, calendars, and daily planners. Accomplishing things and doing things is the raison d'etre for this type of person. That is, these individuals' *reason for being* comes from *doing*. Their "in-box" is never empty. On vacations, they try to see and do as much as they possibly can. In all avenues of their lives, they find meaning in doing. (p. 106)

Task-oriented leaders tend to assume at least three approaches in working with groups. First, such a leader is very *adaptable* to various group situations (Dubrin, 2016). For example, task-oriented leaders would provide close direction for group members who require such guidance. However, such leaders would provide much less direction to motivated, self-reliant group members, and then only on an as-needed basis. The major goal is to get the job done.

A second practice involved in task-oriented leadership concerns "*initiating structure*, which means the leader organizes work, defines role responsibilities, and schedules work activities" (Northouse, 2016; Dubrin, 2016). Such leaders pay great attention to detail and to the technical aspects of getting goals accomplished.

A third task-oriented leadership practice entails having *high expectations* for group members' performance and accomplishment (Dubrin, 2016). Group members tend to respond positively to leaders who require a lot from them; similarly, when expectations are low, group members' performance tends to be much poorer (Dubrin, 2016).

With respect to task-oriented leaders in general, Northouse (2016) reflects:

> As you would expect, people vary in their ability to show task-oriented leadership. There are those who are very task oriented and those who are less task oriented. This is where a person's personal style comes into play. Those who are task oriented in their personal lives are naturally more task oriented in their leadership. Conversely, those who are seldom task oriented in their personal lives will find it difficult to be task oriented as a leader.
>
> Whether a person is very task oriented or less task oriented, the important point to remember is that, as a leader, he or she will always be required to exhibit some degree of task behavior. For certain individuals, this will be easy and for others it will present a challenge, but some task-oriented behavior is essential to each person's effective leadership performance. (p. 73)

Relationship-Oriented Group Leaders   Relationship-oriented leaders are more interested in relating to others than in completing tasks. Northouse (2016) explains:

> Relationship-oriented people differ from task-oriented people because they are not as goal directed. The relationship-oriented person finds meaning in *being* rather than in *doing*. Instead of seeking out tasks, relationship-oriented people want to connect with people. They like to celebrate relationships and the pleasure relationships bring.
>
> Furthermore, relationship-oriented people often have a strong orientation in the present. They find meaning in the moment rather than in some future objective to be accomplished. In a group situation, sensing and feeling the company of others is appealing to these people. . . . They are the people who are the last to turn off their cell phones as the airplane takes off and the first to turn the phones back on when the airplane lands. Basically, they are into connectedness. (p. 107)

As do task-oriented leaders, relationship-oriented leaders tend to utilize several approaches as they work with groups. First, relationship-oriented leaders *demonstrate concern* for group members and try to be considerate (Northouse, 2016). They try to build "camaraderie, respect, trust, and regard between leaders" and other group members; such leaders also feel that "taking an interest in workers as human beings, valuing their uniqueness, and giving special attention to their personal needs" is vital for the group (Northouse, 2016, p. 111). This may also involve expressing interest in personal matters not directly related to the group's tasks or purpose. For example, a relationship-oriented leader might inquire about a group member's ill child or sibling even though this has nothing directly to do with the group.

A second approach assumed by relationship-oriented leaders is related to demonstrating concern for group members' well-being. Relationship-oriented leaders provide *"emotional support and encouragement"*; this includes encouraging group members "to participate in decision-making" and providing "frequent encouragement and praise" (Dubrin, 2016, p. 118). Dubrin (2016) elaborates:

> Emotional support generally improves morale and sometimes improves productivity. In the long term, emotional support and encouragement may bolster a person's self-esteem. Being emotionally supportive comes naturally to the leader who is empathetic and warm. (p. 118)

A third approach emphasized in relationship-oriented leadership is *"openness to worker opinions"* (Dubrin, 2016, p. 117). Such leaders encourage group members to participate actively in decision making. Encouraging the voicing of opinions makes group members feel valued. They are then more likely to expend greater energy in group participation.

Northouse (2016) summarizes the relationship orientation in terms of four behaviors:

1. Openness to different points of view
2. Treating others with respect and dignity
3. Helping people get along together and improve relationships
4. Striving to make the work environment as enjoyable as possible

"Relationship leadership behavior is a critical component of effective leadership performance" (p. 174).

Task-Oriented versus Relationship-Oriented Leadership: Which Is Best?   Is task-oriented or relationship-oriented leadership more effective? Northouse (2016) notes that research has shown no ideal leadership type but that good leaders often demonstrate both task and relationship orientations. Leaders can benefit from knowing the relative balance of their individual styles of leaderships on the dimensions of task orientation and relationship building.

Personality Traits of Effective Group Leaders

Research associates several personal characteristics with effective leadership in groups. These involve both general personality attributes and traits useful for completing tasks and achieving goals (Dubrin, 2016). Personal characteristics related to good leadership include self-confidence, humility, intelligence, determination, trustworthiness, sociability (and emotional intelligence), and flexibility.

Self-Confidence   First, self-confidence characterizes an effective leader (Dubrin, 2016; Lussier & Achua, 2013; Northouse, 2015). **Self-confidence** is the personal condition of having a positive self-concept and the belief in one's ability to get things accomplished.

One reason for deficient self-confidence might involve lack of experience. For instance, an individual might resist leading a group when that person has little experience interacting in groups. Getting more experience in group participation may build greater self-confidence because such experience might enhance understanding of group dynamics and interaction. In addition, learning skills for leading groups and being given opportunities to practice such skills may help build self-confidence.

Lack of self-confidence might also be related to a poor self-concept. **Self-concept** is a person's overall positive or negative feelings about him- or herself. Self-confidence involves having a positive self-concept. People with self-confidence are more likely to express opinions openly, provide group direction, and help a group navigate through problematic situations. Highlight 3-7 reviews suggestions for enhancing your self-concept and gaining self-confidence.

Appropriate Humility   Although good leaders tend to be self-confident, they should also demonstrate humility when it's appropriate (Dubrin, 2016). **Humility** is a personal condition involving modesty and lack of arrogance. If you're a good leader you will confess "when you do not know everything and cannot do everything, as well as admitting your mistakes . . . A leader, upon receiving a compliment for an accomplishment, may explain that the group [not the leader alone] deserves the credit" (Dubrin, 2013, p. 40). Group members would probably neither like nor respect a group leader who's arrogant, bossy, and dictatorial. Would you?

Intelligence   Intelligence is related to leadership ability (Northouse, 2016). **Intelligence** is the "cognitive ability to think critically, to solve problems, and to make decisions" (Lussier & Achua, 2016, pp. 38–39). Leaders tend to have higher levels of

Highlight 3-7

Enhancing Your Self-Concept and Self-Confidence

Many people, for whatever reason, have a poor self-concept and lack self-confidence. Lussier and Achua (2016) make the following eleven suggestions for improving the ways people view themselves and, thus, enhance their ability to interact, communicate, and lead:

1. *Realize that there are few, if any, benefits to negative, pessimistic attitudes about others and yourself.* Let go of grudges and fear of failure.
2. *Consciously try to have and maintain a positive, optimistic attitude.* It is often our unconscious thoughts and behaviors that undermine us.
3. *Cultivate optimistic thoughts.* Emphasize your strengths. Are you articulate, smart, creative, helpful, or hardworking? Tell yourself, "I can do it," or "I'm worth it." In your mind's eye, "picture yourself achieving your goal."
4. *If you catch yourself complaining or being negative in any way, stop and change to a positive attitude.* "Attitudes *are positive or negative feelings about people, things, and issues*" (p. 48). You will probably get better at identifying your negative thoughts with practice. Gradually, you can change your attitudes and the way you view the world. You can gradually shift to a much more positive perspective.
5. *Avoid negative people, especially any that make you feel negative about yourself.* Associating with positive people who strengthen your self-concept only helps you to focus on the positive.
6. *Set and achieve goals.* Even establishing and accomplishing small goals (e.g., getting to a meeting on time or completing some task you've been avoiding) can make you feel more in control. It can give you a sense of being successful.
7. *Focus on your success; don't dwell on failure.* Emphasize the goal you've achieved, not the one you didn't. "Happiness is nothing more than a poor memory for the bad things that happen to you."
8. *Don't belittle your accomplishments or compare yourself to others.* Each of us has our strengths and weaknesses, so focus on your strengths. Don't dwell on not being "as good" as someone else. Who you are and what you can do is what is important.
9. *Accept compliments.* Recognizing praise can build up your self-concept and self-confidence. Avoid saying clichés such as, "Aw, that wasn't much," or "Anybody can do that." Give yourself credit.
10. *Be a positive role model.* If you think of yourself as someone who demonstrates the right thing to do, you will see yourself in a positive light. Being a positive role model reveals leadership ability.
11. *When things go wrong and you're feeling down, do something to help someone who is worse off than you.* There's almost always someone who has a bigger problem or a worse situation than you have. Focusing your attention on someone else rather than on yourself can get your mind off your negative personal issues. Rather, you can stress the positive things you're doing on someone else's behalf (pp. 48–49).

intelligence than people who are not leaders; however, good leaders should not be too much more intelligent than other group members (Northouse, 2016). If the intelligence gap is too great, then the leader and group members may not be able to communicate well. They may not "be on the same wavelength" as other group members.

Determination Determination is another trait characterizing good leaders (Lussier & Achua, 2016; Northouse, 2016). **Determination** "is the desire to get the job done and includes characteristics such as initiative, persistence, dominance, and drive" (Northouse, 2013, p. 24). Leaders who have determination are willing to persist in the pursuit of their goals despite barriers. They initiate action within the group without having to be told what to do.

Highlight **3-8**

How to Build Trust within a Group

Having a trustworthy leader is so important. This is especially true in these times where mistrust runs rampant concerning powerful business leaders and politicians. Dubrin (2016) suggests that leaders abide by the following suggestions to establish their trustworthiness:

- Make your behavior consistent with your intentions. Practice what you preach and set the example. Let others know of your intentions and invite feedback on how well you are achieving them.

- When your [group] . . . encounters a problem, move into a problem-solving mode instead of looking to blame others for what went wrong.

- Honor confidences. One incident of passing along confidential information results in a permanent loss of trust by the person whose confidence was violated.

- Maintain a high level of *integrity* [solid adherence to moral and ethical principles; emphasis added]. Build a reputation for doing what you think is morally right in spite of the political consequences. . . .

- Listen with compassion and attentiveness when interacting with others. Appear attentive by your body language such as maintaining eye contact, moving toward the person, and put away electronic interrupters such as a smartphone.

- Admit mistakes. Covering up a mistake, particularly when everybody knows that you did it, destroys trust quickly. (p. 41)

Trustworthiness   Research is establishing that trustworthiness is related to good leadership (Dubrin, 2016). **Trustworthiness** is a personal characteristic that inspires confidence and belief by others in one's honesty and dependability. Dubrin (2016) remarks:

> An effective leader . . . is supposed to walk the talk, thereby showing a consistency between deeds (walking) and words (talk). In this context, **trust** is defined as a person's confidence in another individual's intentions and motives and in the sincerity of that individual's word. Leaders must be trustworthy, and they must also trust group members. (p. 40)

Highlight 3-8 provides suggestions for leaders to enhance their trustworthiness as they function in groups.

Sociability and Emotional Intelligence   Sociability tends to characterize leaders (Lussier & Achua, 2016; Northouse, 2016). **Sociability** is the tendency to search out others and form congenial social relationships. Sociable people are "friendly, outgoing, courteous, tactful, and diplomatic" (Northouse, 2013, p. 26). They tend to be good communicators and are perceptive about others' feelings and needs. Their effective interpersonal skills allow them to work collaboratively with others.

Related to sociability is the concept of emotional intelligence. **Emotional intelligence (EI)** is "the ability to do such things as understand one's feelings, have empathy for others, and regulate one's emotions to enhance one's quality of life. This type of intelligence generally [involves] . . . the ability to connect with people and understand their emotions" (Dubrin, 2016, p. 50). EI is related to good leadership and is characterized by the following four features (Dubrin, 2016, pp. 50–52; Lussier & Achua, 2016, p. 37):

1. **Self-awareness** is the ability to perceive one's own emotions and how they affect one's behavior. Leaders who are self-aware can acknowledge their strengths and weaknesses. They can understand how their frame of mind and emotions can affect others.
2. **Self-management** is the ability to control troublesome emotions both in oneself and in others. "Successful leaders . . . don't let negative emotions (worry, anxiety, fear, anger) interfere with getting things done" (Lussier & Achua, 2016, p. 37).
3. **Social awareness** is "the ability to understand others" (Lussier & Achua, 2013, p. 39). It involves **empathy**, which is not only being in tune with how others feel but also conveying to them that you do understand. This enhances a person's ability to form interpersonal relationships.
4. **Relationship management** is "the ability to work well with others, which is dependent on the other EI components. Successful leaders build effective relationships by communicating, responding to emotions, handling conflict, and influencing others" (Lussier & Achua, 2016, p. 37).

Flexibility   Flexibility enhances a leader's competence (Dubrin, 2016; Lussier & Achua, 2016). **Flexibility** is "the ability to adjust to different situations and change" (Lussier & Achua, 2016, p. 52). "Leaders who are flexible are able to adjust to the demands of changing conditions, much as anti-lock brakes enable an automobile to adjust to changes in road conditions" (Dubrin, 2016, p. 52). Groups are dynamic entities where issues and relationships are constantly in flux. Only a flexible leader can make the transition from one scenario to another.

Leadership Skills

In addition to establishing a power base, effective leaders require many skills. These include the following three categories of skills: promoting group functioning, collecting and assessing information, and acting (Toseland & Rivas, 2017).

Promoting Group Functioning   Promotion of group functioning, the first skill category, centers on involving and motivating group members. Earlier discussion stressed many aspects of this. Attending and responding skills are essential. Basic communication skills such as simple encouragement are important. For example, sometimes a simple one-word response or nonverbal head nod while maintaining eye contact is enough to encourage a group member to continue. Another effective communication skill is **rephrasing**, stating what another person says, but using different words than those used by that person. One other useful communication skill is **clarification**, making certain that what a group member says is understood. This is often done by asking a question about a statement. We have established that the group leader must make group members feel they are important group participants. Highlight 3-9 discusses ways that group leaders can empower group members.

Collecting and Assessing Information   The second category of skills in successful group leadership involves collecting and assessing information. This involves soliciting necessary information from group members, synthesizing its meaning, and analyzing its importance. For example, an agency group is established to develop an **in-service training program**. This is a program provided by an employing agency, usually conducted by a supervisor or an outside expert, designed to help agency staff improve their effectiveness (e.g., providing education about specific treatment techniques) or better understand agency functioning (e.g., educating staff about new legal issues or policy changes). An effective group leader asks members "the right questions" to elicit the necessary information. The group leader should help the group address what types of training agency staff require, how the group should solicit this information from staff, who could provide training, and what scheduling would be most convenient. The leader should help the group summarize information and prioritize tasks. Such action may include identifying patterns or gaps in the data as well as suggesting how the additional information may be acquired so that the assessment is complete (Toseland & Rivas, 2017).

Taking Action   The third category of skills necessary for effective leadership involves taking action. These are skills geared to developing plans and assisting group members in plan implementation. An effective leader should encourage members' input, assist them in communication with each other (both of which are discussed in Highlight 3-9), provide direction when necessary, keep the group on task, and resolve conflicts as they arise. Highlight 3-10 urges you to begin assessing your own leadership potential.

Highlight 3-9

Empowerment by Group Leaders

Toseland and Rivas (2017) emphasize that it's critical for group leaders to share power and encourage member participation beginning at the very first meeting. They cite at least six ways that leaders can empower members to become involved, take responsibility for group activities, and feel that they are important contributors to the group:

1. A group leader should promote communication *among group members* instead of structuring communication primarily *between him- or herself and a member*. If members direct attention only to the group leader, it gives that leader great power and control over what happens in the group. When group members communicate with each other, it decreases the leader's power in a positive way. Relationships may then develop among members, they may feel freer to share ideas with each other,

and they may be more willing to work productively together.

2. A group leader should seek input from members regarding developing an agenda and general direction of future meetings. Asking for input implies that the leader respects what group members have to say. A leader who responds to group members' suggestions by incorporating their input can empower group members and make them feel that their participation in the group really matters.

3. A group leader should support group members who have natural leadership potential when they begin to demonstrate an ability to influence the group. A leader should not hoard power and abruptly halt other group members' access to it. Rather, a leader should appreciate group members' strengths and energy, encouraging the use of these qualities to further fulfill group goals.

continued

Highlight **3-9** *continued*

4. A group leader should support group members who engage in mutual support, sharing and aid of other members. We've discussed **mutual aid**—the act of providing support, feedback, and information within a group context—as a process of empowering groups and group members. Spending group time in this way can enhance development of relationships, trust, and competence in working together.

5. A group leader teaches and models for members appropriate leadership skills. A good group leader can use the group context to teach group members effective leadership skills by utilizing such skills early and throughout the group process.

6. Group leaders can help members assume leadership roles by recognizing and building on their strengths, abilities, and problem-solving abilities. For instance, a group leader can encourage a group member to lead a discussion, provide needed information, or assume an active role in addressing and resolving some issue. People need the chance to practice at leading to become effective leaders. First, group members need to identify their potential leadership strengths by trying out attempts at leadership. Then, members need to practice and perfect these approaches to develop leadership skills.

At a Glance **3-10**

Leadership

Leadership: The act of exerting influence on other group members to direct their behavior, activities, attitudes, or interaction.

Leader-directed leadership: Leadership approaches that involve greater structure and control imposed by the leader.

Group-directed leadership: Leadership approaches that allow group members to have greater control over what happens in the group.

Task-related leadership: Leadership approaches that focus more on adherence to procedures and goal accomplishment.

Relationship-related leadership: Leadership approaches that stress the importance of interaction, communication, cooperation, and group members' satisfaction.

Self-confidence: The personal condition of having a positive self-concept and the belief in one's ability to get things accomplished.

Self-concept: A person's overall positive or negative feelings about him- or herself.

Humility: A personal condition involving modesty and lack of arrogance.

Intelligence: "Cognitive ability to think critically, to solve problems, and to make decisions" (Lussier & Achua, 2016, p. 38).

Determination: "The desire to get the job done and includes characteristics such as initiative, persistence, dominance, and drive" (Northouse, 2016, p. 24).

Trustworthiness: A personal characteristic that inspires confidence and belief by others in one's honesty and dependability.

Integrity: Solid adherence to moral and ethical principles.

Sociability: The tendency to search out others and form congenial social relationships.

Emotional intelligence (EI): "The ability to do such things as understand one's feelings, have empathy for others, and regulate one's emotions to enhance one's quality of life" (Dubrin, 2016, p. 50).

Self-awareness: The ability to perceive one's own emotions and how they affect one's behavior.

Self-management: The ability to control troublesome emotions both in oneself and in others.

Social awareness: "The ability to understand others" (Lussier & Achua, 2016, p. 37).

Relationship management: "The ability to work well with others, which is dependent on the other EI components" (Lussier & Achua, 2016, p. 37).

Flexibility: "The ability to adjust to different situations and change" (Lussier & Achua, 2016, p. 38).

Rephrasing: Stating what another person says, but using different words than those used by that person.

Clarification: Making certain that what a group member says is understood, which is often done by asking a question about a statement.

Highlight **3-10**

You and Your Leadership Potential

We have discussed a range of issues and dynamics involved in leadership. Some people naturally have some of the qualities inherent in good leaders. Some people have acquired specific leadership skills. The approach taken here is that leadership capability can be nurtured and developed. Group-leading and communication skills can be learned. At this point in your life, how would you assess your own leadership potential? Answering the following questions may provide you with some insight.

1. In a group leadership position, do you see yourself as being more task oriented or relationship oriented?
2. To what extent do you think you would like to improve your task-oriented and relationship-oriented leadership ability and in what ways?
3. In group situations, to what extent do you assume a leadership role or are accorded that role by others?
4. How would you rate yourself on the following dimensions (1 being very poor and 10 being exceptional)?

a. Self-confidence

1-----2----3----4----5----6----7----8----9----10
Very poor   Average   Exceptional

b. Self-concept

1-----2----3----4----5----6----7----8---9----10
Very poor   Average   Exceptional

c. Humility

1-----2----3----4----5----6----7----8----9----10
Very poor   Average   Exceptional

d. Intelligence

1-----2----3----4----5----6----7----8----9----10
Very poor   Average   Exceptional

e. Determination

1-----2----3----4----5----6----7----8----9----10
Very poor   Average   Exceptional

f. Trustworthiness

1-----2----3----4----5----6----7----8----9----10
Very poor   Average   Exceptional

g. Integrity

1-----2----3----4----5----6----7----8----9----10
Very poor   Average   Exceptional

h. Sociability

1-----2----3----4----5----6----7----8----9----10
Very poor   Average   Exceptional

i. Emotional Intelligence

1-----2----3----4----5----6----7----8----9----10
Very poor   Average   Exceptional

j. Self-awareness

1-----2----3----4----5----6----7----8----9----10
Very poor   Average   Exceptional

k. Self-management

1-----2 --3----4----5----6----7----8----9----10
Very poor   Average   Exceptional

l. Social awareness

1-----2----3----4----5----6----7----8----9----10
Very poor   Average   Exceptional

m. Relationship management

1-----2----3----4----5----6----7----8----9----10
Very poor   Average   Exceptional

n. Flexibility

1-----2----3----4----5----6----7----8----9----10
Very poor   Average   Exceptional

Although the 14 dimensions are not necessarily equal, adding up your total score and dividing by 14 may give you some idea about how you view your own leadership potential. A lower score would indicate having limitations and a higher score would reveal strengths. Reviewing the score of each dimension could help indicate what areas you might work on to improve your leadership ability.

EP 8a

Once again, picture some group with which you've been involved. What kind of group was it? Who was the leader of that group? What kinds of power (legitimate, reward, coercive, referent, and/or expert) did that leader bring to the group? How would you describe the leader's style—more leader-directed or group-directed? To what extent did the leader empower group members? What specific techniques did the leader use to facilitate empowerment?

Stages of Task Group Development LO 3-6

EP 6

Groups usually proceed through several stages as they develop through time. These include composition, beginnings, assessment, stabilization and working, and endings stages (Corey et al., 2014; Toseland & Rivas, 2017).

Stage 1: Task Group Composition

Whether individuals are appropriate for membership in a specific group depends on that group's purpose. There must be a reason for participants to become group members. Therefore, they must share some common purpose or motivation. In treatment groups, it makes sense to select members who are working on common problems or addressing similar issues.

Composing task groups in the macro environment requires different considerations. Task groups may be either formal or informal. **Formal groups** requiring structured representation in membership include **delegate councils** (groups of representatives from a series of agencies or units within a single agency), committees composed of elected representatives, and task forces appointed by administration. Because **informal groups** are groups where participants come together simply because of mutual interests, there may be great diversity in membership.

Definition of the Group's Purpose   A major consideration in task group composition is a definition of the group's purpose to determine who will be the most useful group members (Aldag & Kuzuhara, 2005; Toseland & Rivas, 2017). For example, two social workers bring a group of community members together to address the community issue of sexual assault. Who would logically support or be interested in addressing this issue? Who might have expertise to help define the problems involved and develop plans? Who has potential resources to contribute for plan implementation? The workers identified several potential group members, including the local physician who examines sexual assault survivors; a police officer who has access to legal statistics and is often the first one called to the crime scene; upstanding community leaders, such as the bank president, who lend credibility to the issue and have significant access to resources; and women's studies faculty from the local university, who have natural interest in this women's issue.

The Group's Context   Another factor to consider regarding group composition is the context in which the group meets. Some aspects of this context involve location and sponsorship. Is an agency sponsoring the meeting? If so, what agency representation is required? What resources will the agency provide? If no agency is technically sponsoring the meeting, where in the community will group meetings be held?

Another aspect of group context involves the perceptions held by others in the external environment about the issue and the group's purpose. Consider the community group identified earlier formed to address the issue of sexual assault in the community. Important issues to consider include public attitudes toward assault survivors. Are community residents generally sympathetic toward or blaming of people who have survived assault? Will the community likely support or resent the group and its purpose?

Group Size   Group size is still another element of group composition. There appears to be no magical answer regarding the best size of a group (Corey et al., 2014). The trick is to include enough people to generate ideas and get work done, but not so many that the group process becomes unmanageable. Group membership should reflect a broad enough range of abilities and perspectives to guarantee the generation of diverse ideas and problem-solving suggestions. A group should be "big enough to give ample opportunity for interaction and small enough for everyone to be involved and to feel a sense of 'group'" (Corey et al., 2014 p. 155).

Note that as groups increase in size, they tend to become more formal and develop structures resembling those in larger organizations. For example, a social work student club may have very informal interactions when there are only five members. However, when the group expands to 35, the membership elects officers and follows more formal procedures for running meetings, such as **parliamentary procedure** (a highly structured technique designed to make decisions and conduct business).[1]

Stage 2: Beginnings

During the beginnings stage, group members get to know each other and begin establishing the group's interpersonal dynamics. Initially, introductions are in order. Members begin addressing trust issues so that group cohesion is enhanced. They discuss the group's purpose and goals to establish the group's ongoing direction. A group usually seeks a consensus regarding goals so that it may begin identifying the tasks necessary to achieve those goals. Contracting involves establishing agreements about individual and group responsibilities. Goals, procedures, roles, and basic arrangements such as regularity of meetings and meeting place are established.

The beginnings period allows the group to structure itself in terms of leadership and division of responsibility (Corey et al., 2014). In some groups, one strong authoritarian leader will emerge. Other groups will assume a much more democratic perspective, more evenly distributing responsibility for maintenance and tasks.

---

[1] It should be noted that parliamentary procedure can be and often is used with groups of any size. Major concepts include "motion" (a proposal submitted to the group that requires action), "second" (an indication of approval of a proposed motion), "amend" (to add, delete, or substitute words or portions of a motion), "majority vote" (greater than one-half of the total of persons voting or ballots cast), and "table" (a motion to postpone action indefinitely on a motion already on the floor) (Kirst-Ashman & Hull, 2018, pp. 120–122).

Stage 3: Assessment

We have established that effective group leaders conduct ongoing assessment of group dynamics and functioning. Assessment is cited as stage 3 because it should begin when the group is formed.

Assessment involves all the concepts described earlier in the discussion of group dynamics. Leading a group requires focusing attention on communication, interpersonal interaction, norms, roles, cohesion, power, and status. As group interaction is ongoing, so is assessment. A leader's role involves making certain the group gets along well and remains on task. Assessment of group functioning is important both during initial group involvement and as an ongoing maintenance task.

Conflict, referred to as **storming**, often characterizes both this phase and the beginnings phase of the group (Johnson & Johnson, 2012, p. 2). Members may experience disagreement regarding where they think the group should go or how it should be run. It is important for leadership to address such conflicts for the group to continue and accomplish its goals.

Stage 4: Stabilization and Working

Stabilization and working is the task group's productive period. Order must be established for the group to function and progress. Sometimes, the stabilization process is referred to as **norming**, where group members develop consensus about the members' roles and appropriate group norms. Group members must come to a consensus about how disagreements will be handled so that they may proceed with their assigned tasks.

EP 8e

During the working phase, group leaders must pay special attention to meeting preparation, clear designation regarding how and when tasks will be performed, empowering participants, enhancing motivation, minimizing conflict, keeping members on track, and evaluating the progress of both individuals and the entire group (Toseland & Rivas, 2017). Sometimes, this is referred as the **performing** phase of the group, where the focus is on completing tasks (Johnson & Johnson, 2012).

Stage 5: Endings and Evaluation

Not all groups terminate. Some are ongoing, such as a city council or a civic association like the Jaycees. Even with ongoing groups, membership usually changes. People move away, lose interest, or must attend to other priorities. Endings for individual group members and full groups happen inevitably, just like death.

Some approaches help to facilitate endings in groups. First, leadership can help prepare group members by talking about the group's termination ahead of time. This dulls the surprise factor when a group abruptly ends. It also gives members time to think about the group's end ahead of time, deal with their feelings, and think of alternative ways for spending their time.

Another suggestion for helping groups end is to encourage the sharing of ending feelings. Group members can get negative feelings such as regret and loss out in the open, in addition to receiving emotional support from other group members.

At a Glance **3-11**

Stages of Task Group Development

1. Task group composition

   Delegate council: A group of representatives from a series of agencies or units within a single agency.

   a. Definition of the group's purpose
   b. The group's context
   c. Group size

2. Beginnings

3. Assessment

Storming: A phase in a group where conflict occurs; this characteristic applies to both the beginning phase of a group and the assessment stage.

4. Stabilization and working

   Norming: Group members reach consensus about the members' roles and appropriate group norms; the stabilization and working phase of a group.

   Performing: A phase of the group where the focus is on completing tasks.

5. Endings and evaluation

Finally, evaluating and summarizing the group's accomplishments is helpful. Especially with a successful group that accomplished many or most of its goals, giving the group and its members credit for their achievement can be very rewarding. If goals were not achieved, the group might discuss reasons why and suggest alternative methods to achieve goals in the future.

Chapter Summary

The following summarizes this chapter's content as it relates to the learning objectives presented at the beginning of the chapter. Objectives include the following:

LO 3-1 Explain major theoretical perspectives on groups, including field, social exchange, learning, psychoanalytic, systems, empowerment, and feminist theories.

Important concepts in field theory include valence; cohesion; authoritarian, democratic, and laissez-faire leadership; role; norms; power; and consensus. Significant concepts in social exchange theory include rewards, costs, and social exchange. Learning theory concepts include respondent conditioning, modeling, operant conditioning, positive and negative reinforcement, and punishment. Cognitive-behavioral theory constructs include cognition, modeling, positive reinforcement, social (positive) reinforcement, and cognitive restructuring. Concepts significant in psychoanalytic theory include id, ego, superego, defense mechanism, and insight. Systems theory concepts

include system, boundaries, subsystem, homeostasis, role, relationship, integration, pattern maintenance, goal attainment, adaptation, group activities, interactions, sentiments, and norms. Important concepts in empowerment theory are empowerment, social justice, consciousness raising, mutual aid, power, socialization, and group cohesion. Constructs underlying feminist theories include self-determination, using a gender filter, assuming a pro-woman perspective, empowerment, consciousness raising, the "personal as political" (Bricker-Jenkins & Netting, 2009, p. 279), the importance of process, unity in diversity ("diversity is strength") (Gutierrez & Lewis, 1999, p. 105), and validation.

LO 3-2 Apply critical thinking skills to various critical thinking questions

Critical thinking questions addressed personal formal group involvement, multicultural knowledge and awareness, agreement with feminist theories, the relevance of various group theories, and group leadership.

LO 3-3 Identify basic concepts inherent in interpersonal group dynamics, including communication, interpersonal interaction, norms, roles, and group cohesion, in addition to power and status.

Communication is the exchange of information. Nonverbal communication involves any means by which information is conveyed not using spoken or written words. Self-disclosure is the sharing of personal feelings and information. Interpersonal interaction is the result of verbal and nonverbal communication, expressed emotions and attitudes, and behavior between or among persons. Norms are unwritten, collective rules and expectations held by group members concerning what is appropriate behavior within the group. Roles are the expected behavior patterns based on individuals' position or status within the group. Group cohesiveness is the extent to which group members feel close to each other or connected as group members. Power is the potential ability to move people on a chosen course to produce an effect or achieve some goal. Power can be in the form of legitimate, reward, coercive, referent, or expert. Status is the relative rank assigned to members within the group.

LO 3-4 Discuss the ethical issue of confidentiality in groups.

Confidentiality is the ethical principle that workers should not share information provided by or about a client unless that worker has the client's explicit permission to do so. Within the macro social environment, confidentiality can also be applied to group participation in organizations and communities. Group leaders should stress both the importance and the limitations of confidentiality in groups.

LO 3-5 Describe the concept of leadership, including leadership styles and characteristics of successful leaders.

Leadership is the act of exerting influence on other group members to direct their behavior, activities, attitudes, and interaction. Leadership can be "leader directed" or "group directed" (Jacobs et al., 2016, p. 22). It can also be task oriented, relationship oriented, or both. Personal characteristics related to good leadership include self-confidence, appropriate humility, intelligence, determination, trustworthiness, sociability (and EI), and flexibility. Leadership skills include promoting group functioning, collecting and assessing information, and acting. Leaders can empower group members by sharing power and encouraging member participation.

LO 3-6 Identify and describe the phases of task group development.

Stages of task group development include (1) task group composition, (2) beginnings, (3) assessment, (4) stabilization and working, and (5) endings and evaluation.

Looking Ahead

This chapter discussed the theories and dynamics of how generalist practitioners function in small groups in the macro social environment. The next chapter will discuss the types of groups functioning in the macro social environment.

Competency Notes

The following identifies where Educational Policy (EP) competencies and component behaviors are discussed in the chapter.

EP 1 (Competency 1)—Demonstrate Ethical and Professional Behavior. *(p. 71)*: Engaging in professional behavior in groups requires understanding one's role as group leader or member.

This requires awareness of the function and development of groups.

EP 1a Make ethical decisions by applying the standards of the NASW Code of Ethics, relevant laws and regulations, models for ethical decision-making, ethical conduct of research, and additional codes of ethics as appropriate to context. *(p. 96):* Maintaining confidentiality to the extent that it is possible is an important ethical principle guiding professional practice.

EP 1c Demonstrate professional demeanor in behavior; appearance; and oral, written, and electronic communication. *(p. 90):* Practitioners must understand the dynamics of communication discussed here to demonstrate professional communication when working in and with groups. *(p. 94):* Social workers must understand the dynamics of interpersonal interaction to demonstrate professional demeanor in behavior and communication. *(p. 97):* Roles assumed by social workers in groups are discussed.

EP 2 Generalist Practice. *(p. 83):* Empowerment theory emphasizes building on people's strengths, a basic concept in generalist practice.

EP 2 (Competency 2)—Engage Diversity and Difference in Practice *(p. 83):* The principle of power is discussed. *(p. 85):* It is important to recognize the effects of multicultural socialization, as a culture's structures and values may affect various groups negatively or positively. *(p. 85):* Feminism focuses on oppression, and the enhancement of privilege and power as each of these concepts relate to gender. Various concepts involved in feminism, which addresses the diversity factor of gender, are explored. *(p. 85):* Social workers must understand the concepts of power and status to engage diversity and difference in practice. *(p. 85):* The goal of feminist theories and practice is women's self-determination. *Self-determination* is everyone's right to make his or her own decisions. *(p. 98):* *Status*, a concept closely related to power, is the relative rank assigned to members within the group. People with higher status usually have more power, and those with lower status have lesser power. People with more power and higher status can exert greater influence on what a group does.

EP 2a Apply and communicate understanding of the importance of diversity and difference in shaping life experiences in practice at the micro, mezzo, and macro levels. *(p. 85):* Social workers must recognize how multicultural differences affect life experiences. *(p. 85–90):* Feminism addresses the importance of gender differences in terms of shaping life experiences.

EP 2c Apply self-awareness and self-regulation to manage the influence of personal biases and values in working with diverse clients and constituencies. *(pp. 85–88):* The process of consciousness raising described in feminist theory helps increase self-awareness and is a useful model for social workers seeking to understand their own biases.

EP 3 (Competency 3)—Advance Human Rights and Social, Economic, and Environmental Justice. *(p. 83):* Social justice is defined and emphasized as an important aspect of empowerment theory.

EP 6 (Competency 6)—Engage with Individuals, Families, Groups, Organizations, and Communities. *(p. 90):* Engagement with groups requires understanding how they develop and the stages through which they move. *(p. 100):* Social workers must understand what leadership involves before they can provide it to improve policies and services. *(p. 110):* Groups usually proceed through a number of stages as they develop through time. These include composition, beginnings, assessment, stabilization and working, and endings stages (Corey et al., 2014; Toseland & Rivas, 2017).

EP 6a Apply knowledge of human behavior and the social environment, person-in-environment, and other multidisciplinary theoretical frameworks to engage with clients and constituencies. *(p. 71–113):* Social workers must understand the theories and conceptual models helpful for working with groups. Social workers can use theoretical frameworks to guide the processes of assessment, intervention, and evaluation as they work in and with groups. Understanding the concepts and terminology inherent in systems theory helps social workers prepare for action with systems of all sizes, including groups. *(p. 90)*: Understanding group dynamics prepares social workers for action and intervention with groups. *(p. 110)*: Understanding the stages of task group development helps practitioners prepare for action with task groups.

EP 7 (Competency 7)—Assess Individuals, Families, Groups, Organizations, and Communities. *(p. 71)*: Understanding the concepts and theories used when working with groups is essential for assessment.

EP 7b Apply knowledge of human behavior and the social environment, person-in-environment, and other multidisciplinary theoretical frameworks in the analysis of assessment data from clients and constituencies. *(p. 71)*: Assessing groups and group functioning often requires use of different theories and concepts.

EP 8 (Competency 8)—Intervene with Individuals, Families, Groups, Organizations, and Communities. *(p. 71)*: To intervene effectively with groups requires awareness of their functioning including appropriate theories.

EP 8a Critically choose and implement interventions to achieve practice goals and enhance capacities of clients and constituencies. *(pp. 82, 85, 89, 110)*: Critical thinking questions are posed.

EP 8b Apply knowledge of human behavior and the social environment, person-in-environment, and other multidisciplinary theoretical frameworks in interventions with clients and constituencies. *(p. 71ff)*: All the theories

and concepts described in this chapter are useful for understanding human behavior in the social environment.

EP 8c Use inter-professional collaboration as appropriate to achieve beneficial practice outcomes. *(p. 100)*: Leadership is discussed. Practitioners must understand leadership to collaborate with colleagues and clients for effective policy action. The concept of leadership is explored with respect to task groups. Social workers must understand what is involved in leadership to provide it as they work to improve the quality of social services.

EP 8e Facilitate effective transitions and ending that advance mutually agreed-on goals. *(p. 112)*: Leadership can help prepare group members for endings by talking about the group's termination ahead of time. Another suggestion for helping groups end is to encourage the sharing of ending feelings. Finally, evaluating and summarizing the group's accomplishments is helpful. Especially with a successful group that accomplished many or most of its goals, giving the group and its members credit for their achievement can be very rewarding. If goals were not achieved, the group might discuss reasons why and suggest alternative methods to achieve goals in the future.

EP 9c Critically analyze, monitor, and evaluate intervention and program processes and outcomes *(p. 112)*: Helping the group evaluate the group experience can identify alternative approaches that might be used in other groups.

Media Resources

MindTap for Social Work

Go to MindTap® for digital study tools and resources that complement this text and help you be more successful in your course and career. There's an interactive eBook plus videos of client

sessions, skill-building activities, quizzes to help you prepare for tests, apps, and more—all in one place. If your instructor didn't assign MindTap, you can find out more about it at CengageBrain .com.

4 | Types of Groups in the Macro Social Environment

Many types of organizational and community groups function in the macro social environment.

LEARNING OBJECTIVES

After reading this chapter you should be able to...

4-1 Define task groups and explain their relevance within generalist practice in the macro social environment.

4-2 Describe task groups formed to meet client needs, organizational needs, and community needs.

4-3 Summarize the ethical issue of handling your own negative feelings in task groups.

4-4 Answer critical thinking questions concerning task groups.

4-5 Discuss barriers to successful teamwork and team empowerment.

4-6 Define treatment groups.

4-7 Compare and contrast treatment conferences and treatment groups.

4-8 Identify means to empower a group through good committee leadership.

4-9 Examine how social action groups can empower their members to alter the external social environment.

Sunshine is the social worker on a homeless shelter's assessment team. Other team members are a physician, nurse, psychologist, in-house living supervisor, and vocational counselor. Together, the team works with incoming homeless families, conducting individual and family assessments. Their initial plans involve meeting families' immediate health and survival needs. Long-term planning focuses on permanent housing, access to health care, vocational planning, and counseling needs. Sunshine's been working with the group for almost six years now. She thinks they function together well, as they're used to each other's little personality quirks.

Aaron, a social worker at a group home for adults with chronic mental illness,[1] is leading a treatment conference on behalf of Harry, one of the group home's residents. Aaron is responsible for calling together the home care supervisor, psychiatrist, and daytime care counselors to discuss Harry's case. Aaron will formulate an agenda for the meeting, lead the discussion, solicit feedback from participants, assist the group in establishing intervention plans, and write up the final report, including recommendations.

Giovanna, the supervisor of a hospital social work unit, is a member of an administrative group comprised of the hospital director, the head nursing supervisor, and the physical therapy supervisor. Their purpose is to evaluate the hospital's policies regarding job expectations for members of each professional group and make recommendations for changes.

Javier, a school social worker, was elected by the other workers in his school district to serve as a delegate to the state's School Social Work Advocacy Association. This group meets in the state capitol four times each year to identify common issues, discuss concerns, and make recommendations to state legislators that advocate for school policy improvements.

Ginny, a school worker at a large residential facility for people with intellectual disabilities (formerly mental retardation), is a member of the agency's Facilities Improvement Committee. The group includes representatives from various other agency units such as adult care counselors and educational specialists. The group's task is to evaluate the adequacy of living conditions for residents. Plans include assessment of various institutional facets, including: furniture and paint conditions throughout the institution; food preparation and quality; transportation availability for residents (e.g., to meet health care and recreational needs); regularity of treatment plan updates; and general staff conduct toward residents. Ultimately, the group will make recommendations to the agency's administration for improvements.

Jude, a social worker at a county social services department, organized a group of neighborhood center residents to advocate for a summer sports and recreation program for community youth. The social action group's goal is to persuade elected county officials to divert some funds to the center so that volunteers might develop and run the program.

---

[1] *Mental illness* or *mental disorder* is any of a wide range of psychological, emotional, or cognitive disorders that impair a person's ability to function effectively. Causes may be genetic or biological in origin while others result from chemical, physiological, psychological, or social experiences. *Chronic* mental illness means that it is ongoing or long lasting.

Each of the chapter-opening scenarios illustrates how social workers can be involved in task (or work) groups. Although it is not a focus of this book, social workers, of course, also run treatment groups. For example, a worker might run a group for adult survivors of sexual abuse, adult children dealing with their parents' deteriorating health, or children struggling with their parents' divorce. Or, a worker might lead a group to educate teens about HIV transmission, new parents about the behavioral management of their children, or unemployed adults about job possibilities in their community.

EP 6, 6a, 6b, 7b, 8b

Because groups vary so radically in size, purpose, and process, there are many ways to categorize them. Most of the ensuing discussion will address task groups because of their significance in the macro social environment.

Task Groups LO 4-1

As Chapter 3 indicated, a **task group** is a collection of people that applies the principles of group dynamics to solve problems, develop innovative ideas, formulate plans, and achieve goals within the context of an organization or a community. Task groups in the macro social environment are formed to meet the needs of individuals, families, groups, organizations, or communities. For example, an agency task group might focus on developing strategies to meet the needs of Eastern European immigrants seeking agency resources. This involves helping individuals and families. Another task group might include social services personnel and representatives from community neighborhoods to coordinate a Neighborhood Watch program aimed at preventing crime. This task group works on behalf of various neighborhood groups and the entire community. Still another organizational task group consists of representatives from various departments to review the agency's policy manual and recommend changes. This task group serves the organization.

Eight main types of task groups will be discussed in the following sections. They include groups formed to meet client, organizational, and community needs (Toseland & Rivas, 2017, pp. 28–41).

Groups to Meet Client Needs LO 4-2

Social services organizations structure various types of groups to meet clients' needs. These groups include teams, treatment conferences, and staff development groups (Toseland & Rivas, 2017).

Teams

A **team** is a group of two or more people gathered together to work collaboratively and interdependently in pursuit of a designated purpose. Within the macro environment of social service provision, team members function together to improve client treatment and service provision. Note that not just any old work group is a team. A team consists of committed members working in unison on the behalf of clients (Johnson & Johnson, 2009).

Teams, then, differ from other types of work groups in two major ways (Johnson & Johnson, 2012; Lussier, 2012). First, members depend on each other and clearly acknowledge that fact, whereas other work groups often consist of members working more independently of each other. Second, teams emphasize achievement of team goals, whereas other work groups tend to focus on achievement of individual tasks and goals within the group context. A good way of conceptualizing an effective team is to think of a successful sports team, in which small groups of individuals bring their individual skills to achieve a mutual goal (i.e., winning in their particular sport). Team members have a cohesive, unified identity and see themselves as a unit working together to achieve clearly identified ends.

Teams may be formed internally within an agency environment, or they may include representatives from other systems in the macro environment external to the agency. Six types are described in the literature (Compton, Galaway, & Cournoyer, 2005).

First, a team may consist solely of social work practitioners from the same agency. An example is a team of social workers in a Veterans Health Administration hospital where social workers assigned to the temporary housing unit for homeless vets, a substance abuse counseling unit, and the hospital surgical unit work together on the behalf of a homeless vet who is an alcoholic and has serious kidney disease.

A second type of team is also one composed solely of social workers, but they come from a variety of agencies within the community. An example involves social workers from various agencies including a community recreational center, the school, protective services, and a shelter for victims of domestic abuse. These workers come together as a team to establish a service plan for a family with children ages 7, 9, and 11 and a physically abusive father.

A third type of team involves professionals from a variety of disciplines within the same agency. An example is a social worker, psychiatrist, nursing supervisor, and an occupational therapist working in a nursing home.[2] Together, they function as a team to develop residents' plans involving medication, exercise, activities, and counseling.

A fourth type of team also includes a variety of professionals, but they come from different agencies. Consider a young man with an intellectual disability who lives in a group home and needs to establish a vocational plan for his future. The group home social worker forms a team with an independent psychologist who does ability and achievement testing along with a vocational rehabilitation counselor from a sheltered workshop to establish a plan.

A fifth type of team involves social work practitioners working together with indigenous helpers or paraprofessionals within the parameters of the same agency. An **indigenous worker** is a community member who either volunteers or is employed to assist professionals. Tasks may include conducting basic problem assessments, providing necessary information about available services, or connecting people

---

[2] *Occupational therapy* provides assistance learning or relearning skills of daily living. These may be self-care, communication, social, or employment-related skills to improve an individual's functioning despite physical or mental impairment. It often focuses on enhancing fine motor coordination (such as eye/hand coordination) and sensory integration (the ability to take in, sort out, and connect sensory information gathered from the external environment).

with services. A **paraprofessional** is a person with specialized skills and training who assists a professional in conducting his or her work. Examples include paralegals, social work aides, and physicians' assistants. This type of team might include an agency social worker and a foster parent working together to establish a service plan for a child in foster care (Compton et al., 2005).

The final type of team also involves social work practitioners working with indigenous workers or paraprofessionals, but who come from outside the agency's parameters. An example is a social worker employed by a homeless shelter who forms a team with volunteer community residents to raise funds for area homeless people.

A different type of team format that is becoming increasingly common is the virtual team. Highlight 4-1 defines the virtual team concept, discusses their advantages and disadvantages, and provides suggestions to team leaders for improving team effectiveness.

Focus on Ethics 4-1 addresses how negative feelings might surface in task groups, including teams, and what to do about them.

Creating smooth functioning teams takes careful attention to potential problem areas. For example, even professionals from the same discipline—including social work—might have very different perspectives on how to do things. One social worker might be very behaviorally oriented and feel that all goals and means to achieve them should be clearly defined and started immediately. Another social worker might assume that it's much more important to spend time talking about things and examining goals carefully before proceeding. Have you ever worked on a group project for some class where you and some of the other group members had totally different ideas about how the project should proceed? It is suggested that team members "should recognize the inevitability . . . of diverse perspectives and opinions, and learn to negotiate them, in the best interests" of whomever the team is trying to help or whatever goals it's trying to accomplish (Compton et al., 2005, p. 294).

The next section discusses barriers to successful teamwork and team empowerment.

Highlight 4-1

Virtual Teams and Team Leadership

EP 8b

Virtual teams are becoming more common (Dufrene & Lehman, 2011; Griffin, 2016; Lauffer, 2011; Weinbach & Taylor, 2015). A **virtual team** is "a small group of people who conduct almost all of their collaborative work by electronic communication rather than in face-to-face meetings" (Dubrin, 2012, p. 477). Virtual teams may be dispersed among several locations or organizations. Communication technology utilized by virtual teams includes "e-mail, instant messaging, telephone and text messaging, wikis and blogs, videoconferencing, and other technology tools" (Daft & Marcic, 2017, p. 606).

There are some advantages to virtual teams when organizations and communities have the resources, equipment, and opportunities to use them. Virtual teams generally allow more flexibility and can be more efficient (Williams, 2016a). People from various locations or organizations can communicate or meet virtually without having to travel. They may have more control over when and how they communicate with each other. "Using collaborative software, several people can edit a document at the same time, or in sequence, and also have access to a shared database" (Dubrin, 2012, p. 477). Subsequently, team members can work on their individual tasks in their own locations and may better schedule their time.

continued

Highlight **4-1**   *continued*

There are also potential disadvantages to virtual teams. These include:

- "Lack of cohesion
- Feelings of isolation by members . . .
- Absence of face-to-face contact to facilitate relationship building" (Dufrene & Lehman, 2011, p. 3)

Virtual team members "must learn to express themselves in new contexts. The give-and-take that naturally occurs in face-to-face meetings is more difficult to achieve through videoconferencing or other methods of virtual teaming" (Williams, 2016a, p. 207). The virtual environment is not as conducive to perceiving the nuances of communication, such as the nonverbal behavior of other team members (Weinbach & Taylor, 2015).

Virtual team leaders must pursue multiple tasks to be effective. Although these tasks are also important in nonvirtual task groups, virtual task groups often present a greater challenge. Leaders must:

- "Promote a feeling of inclusion for all members
- Provide the team with necessary information
- Promote trust
- Encourage healthy discussions
- Manage conflict" (Dufrene & Lehman, 2011, pp. 3–4)

There are a few specific strategies leaders can use to complete these and other tasks necessary for effective virtual teams. First, team leaders should "review team communication strategies regularly to determine their effectiveness" (Dufrene & Lehman, 2011, p. 4). For example, if some technological approach is causing confusion or delaying progress, some other method of communication should be selected.

A second strategy for virtual team leaders concerns making certain that goals and expectations for member participation are clearly defined (Dufrene & Lehman, 2011; Williams, 2016a). Team members should know exactly what their responsibilities are to fulfill them.

A third approach to effective virtual team leadership involves leaders holding members responsible for completing assigned tasks on time (Dufrene & Lehman, 2011). Leaders should closely monitor the entire team's progress toward goals to ensure that progress is being made.

Fourth, leaders should regularly give team members feedback about their performance so that they can accurately evaluate their progress toward achieving goals (Williams, 2016b). Leaders should be optimistic and encouraging. They can "reward both individual and team accomplishments through avenues such as virtual award ceremonies and recognition at virtual meetings. They are liberal with praise and congratulations, but criticism or reprimands are handled individually rather than in the virtual presence of the team" (Daft & Marcic, 2017, p. 608).

A fifth strategy for virtual team leaders involves soliciting input from team members on a regular basis (Dufrene & Lehman, 2011). Leaders should ask questions to make certain that members clearly understand team communication and progress. Team leaders should also ask members to share their thoughts about how the virtual team is functioning (Williams, 2016b). Leaders can seek suggestions for how to improve the team. This reinforces members' involvement and communicates to them that they are important, valued components of the team.

A sixth strategy is for leaders to "hold face-to-face meetings, when possible"; they should "use videoconferencing when face-to-face contact is not possible" to maximize the quality of interaction and interpersonal communication (Dufrene & Lehman, 2011, p. 4).

Barriers to Successful Teamwork and How to Address Them

EP 5b

Sometimes a social worker may be hesitant to participate on a team. Compton and her colleagues (2005) propose a scenario that might be used to describe such unwillingness:

A man crossing the street was hit by a truck. When passers-by rushed over to help, they saw the man crawling away as fast as he could, on hands and one knee, dragging one leg helplessly. They said, "Where are you going? Don't you realize you've just been hit by a truck? You need help." The man replied, "Please leave me alone. I don't want to get involved." (p. 293)

The following four dynamics can become obstacles to team participation (Compton et al., 2005, pp. 293–294):

1. *The myth of good intentions.* "Social workers sometimes assume that good intentions and a cooperative attitude are sufficient to ensure effective teamwork. If we are friendly, respectful, and considerate of others, surely good interdisciplinary collaboration must follow? This rests on the assumptions that getting along with others is a relatively simple and natural ability, that teamwork depends primarily on personal characteristics, and that specific knowledge and skills are nonessential" (p. 293). Instead, a team effort should be conducted carefully, as it is a complex process "that involves a great deal more than good intentions and desirable personal qualities. . . . [K]nowledge and skills for effective teamwork must be learned and refined" (p. 293).

2. *Helplessness in the face of authority.* Some social workers practice in settings dominated by other professions. For example, primary and secondary schools are governed by educators, and health care personnel preside over hospital or other health care settings. Being in the minority might discourage a social worker from speaking up and actively contributing on a team. Social workers should be encouraged to develop confidence in their knowledge and skills, and to assertively contribute to the team's process of goal achievement.

3. *Professional boundaries.* "Professionals who serve on helping teams tend to have both distinct and common areas of expertise. Indeed, some tasks can be completed by team members from several professions or disciplines. Because of the overlapping responsibilities associated with these common tasks, specific negotiation is required to avoid misunderstanding, conflict, and duplication of effort. Some professionals, including certain social workers, view their turf as large and expansive. They may consign other team members from other professions and disciplines to peripheral roles. Some other professionals may eschew specialization and insist that all members of the team—regardless of discipline—can deal effectively with any problem. Neither extreme seems especially productive. Teams reflect diverse talents and abilities. Effective service often requires a combination of specialized and general expertise. Teams benefit from recognition and use of members with special competence and clarification about who should do what within those common areas that overlap" (p. 293). Therefore, it's important to discuss and specify who will assume what role in getting things done.

4. *Professional differences.* Professionals from different disciplines may assume different perspectives on the "right" way to accomplish goals. For example, consider a doctor and a social worker who are dealing with an older adult who broke her hip and now must find an alternative supportive living environment. The doctor and other health care personnel might stress her physical needs, her physical limitations, and her medication. A social worker, on the other hand, would probably focus more keenly on the patient's ability to fit into and be comfortable in whatever environment she enters (person-in-environment fit). For instance, who might serve as her support system? How will she get around to conduct her daily living affairs, such as grocery shopping and washing clothes? Who could she call on to help her in the event of an emergency?

Focus on Ethics **4-1**

No One Is Immune from Being Human and Having Human Emotions `LO 4-3`

EP 1, 1c

There is a difference between having normal human feelings and how you choose to behave. Ephross and Vassil (2004) discuss some ethical aspects of working in task groups:

Working effectively with working [task] groups requires a degree of self-awareness, and a sense of one's own dignity and that of others. This allows leaders and members to recognize and understand their own feelings. Like other people, social workers working in groups may get tired, annoyed, and discouraged. Since they are human beings, they are entitled to their hang-ups and feelings. All feelings are acceptable for professionals in groups. All behaviors certainly are not. Understanding and guarding strictly the boundary between feelings and behaviors is called professional skill. It is also called observing professional ethics.

Two examples may make this point clearer. It is quite normal, for example, for a group leader to feel attracted to certain group members. They may see one or more members as attractive, intelligent, witty, or possessing some other desirable characteristic. Recognizing these feelings is ok and demonstrates self-awareness. However, it is not acceptable to act on these feelings, neither to favor some group members over others nor to undertake intimate relationships with a group member while one carries responsibility for maintaining a professional relationship. Conversely, it is normal for a professional to like some group members less than others, even not to like some group members. Again, the principle is that the feeling is acceptable, perhaps to be worked through by introspections, perhaps not. Hostile behavior toward such group members is not acceptable and flies in the face of professional ethics. (p. 408)

The importance of paying attention to these challenges is illustrated by the following example. An agency director wanted a cross-section of agency personnel to serve on a new strategic planning committee. She put out a call for volunteers who would work for the next year or two to develop a strategic plan that would guide the organization for the next five years. She appointed the committee, which was composed of agency social workers, members of the clerical staff, and paraprofessionals. One senior social worker voiced a strong interest in strategic planning and was appointed as chair of the committee. The committee met periodically, and attendance was good at the beginning. Slowly, however, many clerical and paraprofessionals staff began to stop attending. The committee chair gave periodic updates to the director but did not point out that interest in committee participation was waning. After almost two years of work, the committee chair announced at a meeting of the entire agency that his committee had finished its work and identified its sole recommendation: namely, that a strategic planning committee would need to be created to craft a strategic plan for the next five years. The director and other staff were incredulous. How could a committee work for two years and get nothing done? In the autopsy that followed, several things became clear. First, despite the good intentions voiced at the beginning, many members simply lacked the skill to develop a strategic plan. Second, the committee chair had oversold his ability to lead the group. Third, the chair ignored suggestions and ideas offered by clerical staff and most of the paraprofessional members of the committee. He thought that since they lacked his status in the agency, their ideas could not be that useful. These members acted helpless in the face of his authority and did not challenge his leadership. Unwilling to settle for second-class status

EP 8a

Critical Thinking Questions 4-1 LO 4-4

Have you ever been a member of a team or task group? If so, what were the circumstances? What variables acted as barriers to effective teamwork? What factors helped to empower the group to achieve its goals?

in the committee, they just stopped coming. In the end, the chair was unable to maintain committee member interest and commitment and failed to admit that he could not achieve his task.

Team Empowerment LO 4-5

Hellriegel and Slocum (2011) identify several characteristics that are endemic to effective teams. The members:

- Know why it exists and have the shared goals of getting things done (task-orientation behaviors) and building constructive interpersonal ties and processes (relationship-oriented behaviors).
- Support agreed-upon guidelines or procedures for making decisions.
- Communicate openly and have achieved trust among themselves.
- Receive help from one another and give help to one another.
- Deal with conflict openly and constructively.
- Diagnose its own processes and improve their own functioning.
- Experience a sense of freedom to be themselves while feeling a sense of belonging with others (p. 350).

EP 8c

These characteristics reflect the empowerment of individual members and highlight their sense of purpose in belonging to the group. The absence of any of these characteristics is likely to make the group less effective or ineffective.

Treatment Conferences

Clients often have many needs. It's common for professionals from several disciplines, including social work, to work together and provide needed services to a client. Other disciplines may include teaching, occupational therapy, physical therapy,[3] speech therapy,[4] psychology,[5] counseling,[6] medicine, and nursing, among others, depending on the client's needs.

---

[3] *Physical therapy* is the treatment of various problems caused by injury, disease, or deformity using such interventions as exercise, heat and cold treatments, and massage. It may be used in lieu of or in addition to surgery or drugs.

[4] *Speech therapy* is treatment designed to assist clients experiencing language or speech problems to enhance their ability to speak with greater clarity.

[5] *Psychology* emphasizes the study of behavior and cognitive processing; therapeutic work is often associated with treatment of mental disorders or testing people for intelligence or aptitude.

[6] *Counseling* is a field overlapping various other fields, including social work, that focuses on problem solving and providing help to individuals, families, or groups.

Treatment conferences are groups that meet to establish, monitor, and coordinate service plans on the behalf of a client system (Summers, 2009; Toseland & Rivas, 2017). Treatment conferences allow several professionals, operating as a group, to collaborate and offer creative, synchronized services. Such groups "are able to evaluate their own performance and make changes to improve their service delivery. The bottom line is improving the delivery of services to clients" (Woodside & McClam, 2014, p. 19). Treatment conferences may also be called case conferences, case staffings, treatment staffings, or, simply, staffings.

Treatment conferences may involve internal agency professionals and staff, or they may include professionals and staff from different agencies. It depends on which agencies and staff are involved in service provision. Usually, the involvement of all service providers, regardless of their agency affiliation, is encouraged.

Sometimes, clients and their families are invited to attend treatment conferences. Other times, clients are invited to attend only a portion of the conference. Some agencies indicate that having clients and other outsiders present interferes with the frank presentation of information about clients and their families. Other agencies feel that content may be too emotionally stressful for clients and their families to hear.

A treatment conference may be conducted by a team, if the group meets the definition of a team, namely, that members are interdependent and work together toward a unified goal. However, treatment conferences often differ from teams in at least three ways (Toseland & Rivas, 2017). First, group members might not have established a working relationship as a unit. Second, treatment conferences might be held infrequently, such as at six-month or one-year intervals, preventing the bonding necessary to establish a team. Third, treatment conferences might involve a different configuration of participants at each meeting because long periods of time pass, clients' needs change, and staff come and go.

Case Example of a Treatment Conference   The following is an example of a treatment conference in a diagnostic and treatment center for children with multiple physical and psychological disabilities. The client Timmy, age 3, has severe **cerebral palsy**, a disability resulting from damage to the brain before, during, or shortly after birth resulting in problems with muscular coordination and speech. Timmy has very little control of his extremities, torso, face, and mouth. He has some limited control of his eyes.

After Timmy is referred for assessment, extensive testing is performed by speech, occupational, and physical therapists. A physician conducts a thorough physical examination and orders relevant tests. Sometimes, a geneticist is involved to establish the etiology of the disorder. However, Timmy experienced oxygen deprivation at birth due to the umbilical cord being wrapped around his neck. Because the etiology of the disability has been established, the program director, a physician, determines that a genetic assessment is unnecessary. A psychologist conducts perceptual and ability testing. Finally, a social worker carries out a family assessment.

All evaluators subsequently attend the treatment conference. This group cannot be considered a team, because it does not work together on a regular basis. For example, there are five occupational therapists and three social workers. The configuration of participants for any client varies drastically, as only one professional per discipline is involved with each case. During the treatment conference, participants share their

Critical Thinking Questions **4-2**

EP 8a

The agency in the previous case example of a treatment conference has a policy that excludes parents and clients from treatment conferences because of reasons mentioned earlier. Is this appropriate? Is this ethical? How does client exclusion relate to *self-determination* (each individual's right to make his or her own decisions), an important professional value in social work? To what extent do clients have the right to know about and be involved in their own and their families' assessment and intervention planning? What is your recommendation—inclusion or exclusion?

findings and prepare a treatment plan. For children like Timmy, who require ongoing treatment and therapy, an annual treatment conference is automatically scheduled. Only those professionals involved in ongoing treatment attend later treatment conferences. For instance, a speech therapist would no longer be involved with the case if the child did not require speech therapy. Because Timmy has such extensive treatment needs, professionals from all disciplines will be involved in future conferences.

Staff Development Groups

EP 1, 2b

The goal of **staff development groups** is to improve, update, and refine workers' skills to improve client services (Toseland & Rivas, 2017). Staff development groups allow groups within an organization to work on skill enhancement together. Gibelman and Furman (2013) explain staff development:

> Staff development . . . is usually an internal agency program. The goal of staff development is to improve employees' knowledge, skills, and abilities in relation to the agency's programs and services. The scope and breadth of such programs will depend on the agency's size and resources. Smaller agencies may collaborate with other human service organizations to conduct training in areas of mutual interest and in response to similar staff needs. Again, the focus is on the relatedness of the training content to the specifics of the job. . . . [S]taff development may focus on promoting awareness of and sensitivity to the particular characteristics, cultures, and needs of the clients, as well as the practice technologies and methodologies relevant to effective service provision and positive service outcomes. (Gibelman & Furman, p. 106)

Examples of staff development groups include:

- A group of social workers, psychologists, and nurses who attend hospital-sponsored sessions on new drugs introduced in the past year.
- A juvenile-probation unit attending a seminar on changes in the state's children's code.
- Group supervision offered by an experienced social worker for practitioners working with protective service clients designed to help them improve their skills.
- A Planned Parenthood director who meets weekly with volunteers providing services to her agency.

Highlight **4-2**

Treatment Groups LO 4-6

EP 8, 8e

Treatment groups help individuals solve personal problems, change unwanted behaviors, cope with stress, and improve group members' quality of life. Efforts focus on clients solving their personal problems, enhancing personal qualities, or providing each other with support. There are at least six primary types of treatment groups: therapy, support, educational, growth, self-help, and socialization (Toseland & Rivas, 2017, p. 20).

Therapy Groups

Therapy groups help members with serious psychological and emotional problems change their behavior. Led by an expert therapist, emphasis is on helping remedy individual problems and rehabilitating clients (Toseland & Rivas, 2017). Examples of therapy groups are those formed to treat "depression, sexual difficulties, anxiety, and psychosomatic disorders" (Corey, Corey, & Corey, 2014, p. 11). (**Psychosomatic disorders** are physical symptoms [for example, stomachaches, numbness, pain] caused by emotional problems.)

Case Example: Therapy Groups for Women Living with Depression and Anxiety

EP 2

An example of a therapy group is one run in a mental health setting for women living with depression and anxiety (Stauffer, Pehrsson, & Briggs, 2010). Stauffer and his colleagues (2010) describe such a group:

A group of women sat waiting for the first session of an anxiety and depression group to begin.

Angie looked at her fingers guiltily. Despite her best efforts, she had bitten down to the quick of her exposed and raw nailbeds. She did feel good, though, about keeping her appointment for the "class to help me with my nerves." Across the waiting room, Susan leaned against a wall, restless and fidgeting nervously. Thoughts raced through her mind as she wondered, "How has life come to this?"

As Kat hunched in a chair near the exit, her stomach churned with hunger. She had virtually stopped eating a month ago. What little she did eat she vomited.

Kat read books and watched television many hours a day to stop worrying about everything. She often drank wine to forget and to sleep.

Tricia sat in a corner chair, wracked with guilt, believing she was failing her struggling family. "This is a waste of time and money," she thought, while considering her family needs. Yet she lacked the energy to move. She felt exhausted all the time.

Keely sat in a corner opposite Tricia with reddened eyes, trying to hold back tears. She cried easily and too often. Life overwhelmed her. She no longer felt connected to friends and family. Although her involvement in her church had been substantial and important to her, more recently she felt isolated and detached from everyone and everything. (pp. 377–378)

The following are five examples of goals such a group might establish for its members (Stauffer et al., 2010). First, participants might learn to carefully examine their own behavior for symptoms of depression and replace old behavior patterns with new, more functional ones. Second, members might work on decreasing negative thinking about themselves and substituting more positive, objective thinking about their strengths. Third, these women might learn relaxation and stress-reduction techniques. Fourth, participants might provide a supportive environment where they feel free to express their concerns. Fifth, members may use the group as a forum for practicing "positive and assertive communication" that they then could apply to other settings in their lives (p. 380).

Support Groups

Support groups consist of participants with common issues or problems who meet on an ongoing basis to cope with stress, give each other suggestions, provide encouragement, convey information, and furnish emotional support. Such groups vary greatly in process and structure. They may either be run by a trained social worker or by members themselves. Examples include a group of persons living with AIDS, recovering alcoholics, adult survivors of sexual abuse, and veterans experiencing posttraumatic stress disorder.

Support groups differ from therapy groups in two major ways. First, support groups place greater emphasis on members supporting and helping each other. This contrasts

continued

with how a therapy group focuses on the leader assisting members in solving serious personal problems. The second way support groups differ from therapy groups is their emphasis on ongoing coping and support instead of alleviating psychological difficulties.

Case Example: Support Groups for LGBTQ People

EP 2

Examples of support groups include those benefiting LGBTQ (lesbian, gays, bisexual, transsexual, and questioning or queer) people. Gay men and lesbians often are traumatized because of physical, emotional, and verbal abuse they experience in a homophobic culture. These oppressive experiences may contribute to a variety of mental health challenges, including drug or alcohol abuse, depression, or suicide, among others.

Communities and agencies can establish support groups to address any number of issues, depending on needs. Several themes often emerge in gay men's support groups, including the following (Provence, Rochlen, Chester, & Smith, 2014; Puglia & House, 2006):

- Dealing with the stigma and shame associated with being gay that is imposed by the encompassing society
- Managing the coming-out process
- Preventing or managing AIDS/HIV
- Confronting family issues such as acceptance or lack thereof by their family of origin
- Dealing with relationships and intimacy in a society that doesn't foster gay relationships
- Resolving ethnic and cultural identities and the many issues involved

Similarly, Engelhardt (1997) describes common themes addressed in lesbian women's support groups:

- Management of heterophobia
- The "invisibility of the lesbian woman's experience"
- "Safety and vigilance issues . . . ranging from verbal harassment to physical assault"
- "Lesbian relationships and sexual expression"
- "Living with dignity as a declared lesbian woman" (pp. 281–283)

Educational Groups

Educational groups provide information to participants. Information may be of virtually any kind. Examples of educational groups include an informational meeting of parents of children having a rare genetic disorder characterized by extremely frail bones that are easily broken (osteogenesis imperfecta); teens receiving sex education; a presentation by an employment counselor to a group of adults interested in finding jobs; and a group of older adults in a nursing home requesting information about their prescribed drugs.

Toseland and Rivas (2017) explain that all educational groups are designed to enhance the knowledge and/or skills of members. Often, the groups combine presentations of information by specialists with group discussions focused on the new information. The leader is concerned about both the individual member as well as the entire group and see the group as a means of teaching and reinforcing new behaviors, ideas, and skills.

Members share a common interest in the purpose of the group and may also have other similarities such as age, member of a board, or common roles such as foster parent. Selecting members of an educational group requires awareness of the existing knowledge, skills, and experience of all members, with a goal of ensuring that every member has the best chance of learning.

Growth Groups

Growth groups are those aimed at expanding self-awareness, increasing potential, and maximizing optimal health and well-being. Growth groups often emphasize exploring hidden thoughts and emotions in addition to disclosing these to other group members for feedback. Examples include a group of heterosexual singles exploring their attitudes about the opposite gender; a group of adolescents engaging in values clarification, and a group of gay men focusing on gay pride issues (Toseland & Rivas, 2017).

Case Example: Growth Groups for African American Juvenile Offenders

EP 2

Harvey (2011) describes the development and implementation of growth groups for African American juvenile offenders that use an Afrocentric approach. **Afrocentricity** is a worldview focused on the culture, experiences, and history of individuals with black African ancestry. The purpose is to develop understanding of how the world functions and how people are treated. These growth groups provide a good example of how a macro system can develop a program to enhance the well-being of a population-at-risk.

continued

Highlight **4-2**   *continued*

Here, a type of "treatment group" can also address broader needs (i.e., fighting oppression, increasing social awareness, and enhancing self-confidence) in a macro context.

African Americans have endured a turbulent and oppressive history that includes slavery, brutalization, and destruction of family life and yet have made significant strides in improving their own lives as well as those of others. There is a great deal of diversity among this population, as is true for most other cultural groups in our society. This ranges from socioeconomic class, experiences with racism, degree of identity with African American culture, and educational achievement. Despite this diversity, most African Americans have been victims of racism and discrimination at some junction in their life. Persistent disparities continue to exist within African American populations when compared to the White population.

African Americans make up about 13 percent of the US population (or even more when considered in combination with one or more other races); African American people continue to suffer the following injustices when compared with Whites (US Census Bureau, 2016):

- Children are much more likely to live in poor families.
- Infant mortality is more than twice that of Whites.
- African Americans are 31% percent less likely to graduate from college.
- They are 22% less likely to be employed in management, business, sciences, or arts.
- Poverty levels are significantly higher (26.2% compared to 14.8% nationally).
- African Americans are much more likely to be incarcerated in the criminal justice system. The lifetime likelihood of a Black man being imprisoned is 1 in 3 compared to 1 in 17 for white men.

The purposes of forming Afrocentric growth groups of African American juvenile offenders include enhancing members' self-respect; establishing a stronger identity with African heritage and culture; developing ties with a positive peer group; widening vocational aspirations; and strengthening the ability to make socially responsible decisions (Harvey, 2011). In addition to providing a treatment context where they work on developing personal strengths, these groups address and help members cope with broader social issues.

Young African American offenders are viewed within their macro context. Poverty, marital and family dissolution, White oppression and discrimination, the strong social pressure of negative street-corner peer groups and gangs, and

lack of career hopes all contribute to an environment where crime becomes a logical means of survival. These young men typically express several themes (Harvey, 2011):

- Adults around here do it, so why shouldn't I?
- Violence is a way of life. If you don't stand up for yourself, you're history.
- How can I be moral and still survive the horrendous peer pressure to be bad?
- You have to be strong and not express emotion to get any respect and protect yourself (p. 166).
- Shouldn't women be treated as inferior and be handled with violent behavior?
- Police are the bad guys.
- How can I deal with Whites' racist treatment?
- I don't know that much about African culture.

An Afrocentric approach emphasizes both spirituality and connectedness with others in the environment, including individuals, family, and community. Its goal is to engender self-understanding, self-respect, and "a strong sense of responsibility for the well-being and harmonious interconnection between self and others" (Harvey, 2011, p. 268). The Afrocentric approach rests on seven basic principles, called the Nguzo Saba (Harvey, 2011; Karenga, 2000, 2012; Belgrave & Allison, 2014). These include (1) "unity" with "the family, community, nation, and race," (2) "self-determination," (3) "collective work and responsibility," (4) "cooperative economics" (to own and operate a business for profit), (5) "purpose" (to develop a positive and great community), (6) "creativity," and (7) "faith" ("to believe in our parents, our teachers, our leaders, our people, and ourselves, and in the righteousness and victory of our struggle") (Harvey, 2011, p. 268). (Chapter 9 elaborates upon these principles in the context of communities.)

These growth groups, then, are designed to provide members with "a positive perspective on African and African-American culture, assist them in developing their own African-American group identity, . . . and provide them with tools to deal with the oppressiveness of white supremacy" (Harvey, 2011, p. 269). Groups consist of 15 boys ages 14 through 18 who are on probation. Offenses include dope dealing, sexual assault, car theft, armed robbery, burglary, and numerous other criminal acts.

Group co-leaders include social workers or people with other types of expertise such as that in African studies, music, or theater. Group process involves the acquisition of skills such as positive interpersonal interaction, relationship

continued

Highlight **4-2** *continued*

building, communication, and introspection. Groups stress enhancing members' self-concepts, developing "constructive lifestyles and positive solutions to life problems," and appreciating their cultural heritage and personal strengths (Harvey, 2011, p. 272).

During the initial eight-week group phase, coleaders teach members about group process, the Afrocentric perspective, and the important formalized rites of passage involved in group membership. Group members then participate in a weekend retreat where co-leaders and a group of older adult men decide which 15 young men will be included in the group. Chosen members then undergo an initiation ritual where they pledge to uphold the principles of Nguzo Saba, are given an African name, and are presented a "special identifying symbol" they are expected to wear at all group meetings; no new members are admitted after this point (Harvey, 2011, p. 272).

Groups then meet weekly for 90 minutes, as members develop their group identity, learn, and develop skills. Group activities may include videos and music, depending on the topics addressed. Guests are invited to speak on various topics, called "modules," that stress the importance of African and African American culture (Harvey, 2011, p. 273). Modules, which last from four to six group sessions, address any number of topics, ranging from African American culture to relationships between men and women to dealing with racism.

Upon completion of all modules, group members participate in another weekend experience, where they demonstrate their newly learned skills and prepare for the final special recognition ceremony. This ceremony becomes the culmination of the group experience, where members demonstrate before their families and community what they have achieved. They proclaim their sacred name and "receive a symbol and a certificate of sacred transformation" (Harvey, 2011, p. 274).

We have established that this process intends to enhance group members' self-respect, sense of African American identity, and sense of responsibility for and belonging to the African American community. It is hoped that other anticipated effects will include crime reduction, improved school attendance, better grades, and increased employment. Initial results were promising (Harvey, 2011). Family members reported improved behavior at home, and group members expressed enhanced self-respect and appreciation of African heritage. Similar outcomes have been noted in other growth groups of African American males (Wyatt, 2009).

Socialization Groups

Socialization groups help participants improve interpersonal behavior, communication, and social skills so that they might better fit into their social environment. Social activities and role plays are often used for group members to practice new social skills. Members may lack skills in being assertive, handling conflict, or presenting one's self to a supervisor or prospective employer. Examples of such groups include an urban neighborhood's youth activities group, a school-based group of shy teens working to improve interpersonal skills, and a Parents Without Partners group sponsoring various social activities, such as parties and outings (Corey, 2016; Toseland & Rivas, 2017).

The process of leading a socialization group involves several steps:

- Assessment of the members' weakness and strengths in the areas of social skills and communication
- Leader-led instruction on specific topics related to member-identified issues
- Leader-led modeling of appropriate social and communication skills
- Role playing by members applying the skills discussed and modeled by the leader
- Homework assignments that involve members applying the new skills in specific situations
- Follow-up discussions about the homework assignments
- Provision of additional suggestions and feedback to help improve members' skills

Self-Help Groups

Self-help groups are groups most often led by their members who typically have experienced similar life challenges. This includes groups such as Alcoholics Anonymous, whose members have a history of alcohol abuse, and Parents Anonymous, for members who are at risk of engaging in child abuse. Other self-help groups focus on mental health, sexual addictions, or hoarding, and may be focused only on a specific group such as lawyers or nurses with a shared problem. Some self-help groups may involve social workers, while others may be restricted to only members with the specific difficulty for which the group was created.

continued

Highlight **4-2** *continued*

Groups Serving More Than One Purpose

Sometimes, a treatment group will serve more than one function and not fit neatly into a designated category. For example, consider a group of young adults with intellectual disabilities formed to improve group members' assertiveness skills. The group serves as a growth group because it expands members' self-awareness, a socialization group to improve social skills, an educational group to provide members with assertiveness training, and a support group for members to help and encourage each other. Self-help groups often serve multiple purposes such as support, education, and self-awareness.

Leaders of staff development groups generally have an expertise in the topic addressed. Various learning formats are used, including lectures by group leaders or other experts, group discussion, audiovisual presentations, role playing, and modeling of specific behaviors or techniques. Group members can confer about content, practice skills via simulations, and get feedback about their performance from other group members.

Staff development groups may involve an agency unit of staff (e.g., a social work department, or all helping professionals who work with a particular client population). This might become part of the supervisory process for the group where ongoing staff development is provided. One of the authors provided training to foster care staff in a variety of child-focused treatment modalities including play therapy. (Staff development groups may also be composed of new staff who receive orientation and training about job requirements, expectations, and policies (Sheafor & Horejsi, 2012, p. 44)). Another aspect of staff development concerns groups that include most of an agency's staff who attend an in-service training session or series of sessions.

Treatment Groups versus Treatment Conferences **LO 4-7**

Note that agencies, in addition to providing treatment to individuals and families, can also offer counseling and help to a group of people gathered together at the same time. Such groups are called treatment groups. A **treatment group** is a group intended to help individual members solve personal problems, change unwanted behaviors, cope with stress, or improve their quality of life. The major difference between task groups and treatment groups is that the task group's aim is to achieve a desired goal or to implement a change in the group's *external* environment. A treatment group's purpose, on the other hand, is to alter group members' behavior or attitudes in the *internal* group environment for therapeutic, educational, supportive, or social reasons (Toseland & Rivas, 2017). Treatment groups involve clients and establish treatment goals for those clients. Task groups form goals to make changes or implement goals outside of the group (e.g., in the agency or the community). Highlight 4-2 describes five primary types of treatment groups. That content is included here to describe a common aspect of service provision in social service agencies.

Be careful not to confuse treatment groups with treatment conferences. Treatment conferences may be composed of staff and clients with the goal of *externally* monitoring the treatment process. Treatment groups provide treatment *internally* and directly to clients.

Groups to Serve Organizational Purposes

EP 6

A social service organization's administration is expected to maintain effective agency functioning, hire staff competent to do their jobs effectively, plan, provide supervision for employees, manage financial resources, monitor agency functioning, and evaluate the effectiveness of service provision (Lewis, Packard, & Lewis, 2012). At least three types of groups often characterize agency environments: administrative groups, committees, and boards of directors.

Administrative Groups

Administrative groups are various clusters of supervisors and managers organized to maintain and improve organizational functioning (Ephross & Vassil, 2004). Usually, agency lines of authority are described in a hierarchical fashion, as illustrated by an organizational chart described in Chapter 7. Most often, decision makers are clustered into groups so they can communicate about what's happening in the organization, make decisions, and coordinate their leadership. Such groups often include various levels of administrative staff, such as supervisors, directors, managers, and department heads. Such an administrative group usually meets on a regular basis to discuss issues and develop plans for running various aspects of the organization. An example of an administrative group in a residential treatment center for girls with serious behavioral and emotional problems is the assistant director, social work director, home care staff director, and on-grounds school principal. An example in a sheltered workshop serving people with intellectual disabilities is the activities director, vocational director, social work supervisor, and transportation manager. In a public social services agency, the group may include the director, deputy director, and supervisors of the delinquency, foster care, child protective services, adult protective services and TANF services units.

Committees

A **committee** is a group of persons given the authority and responsibility to consider, research, act on, and report on a topic or issue. Committees are common entities in organizations that operate to meet various organizational needs (Toseland & Rivas, 2017). They consist of volunteers, appointees, or elected representatives who meet to address any significant issue concerning the organization's functioning. Sometimes committees are ongoing; other times, they are temporary (also called ad hoc).

Examples of committees include a group of staff representatives appointed to investigate, assess, and make recommendations about the quality of food served to residents in a nursing home. Another example is a large county department of social services that establishes a committee of unit representatives to develop a plan for coordinating and scheduling scarce meeting space within the facility. As the agency is housed in an old Grumbles department store building built many decades earlier, adequate meeting rooms are rare.

Highlight 4-3 discusses how a good leader can empower a committee and enhance its functioning.

Highlight 4-3

Empowerment through Good Committee Leadership   LO 4-8

EP 8c

Brody and Nair (2014) stress how good leadership can help committees and other task groups function more effectively. When a social worker has been designated, appointed, or elected as a committee leader, six tactics facilitate successful meetings:

1. The leader should state the purpose of the meeting immediately at the beginning. All committee members should be on track and know generally what to expect.

2. An agenda for the meeting should be prepared in advance of the meeting and distributed ahead of time to all committee members. An **agenda** is "an ordered list of topics to be covered at the meeting" (Kirst-Ashman & Hull, 2018b, p. 123). Agenda items are usually one to a few words that alert committee members to discussion topics. This allows them to think about the issues ahead of time and possibly bring information that they feel applies to the topic.

3. Ground rules should be clearly explained right at the outset of a committee meeting. The leader (or chairperson) "identifies expectations on how members are to interact with each other and how the business of the meeting would be conducted. This includes clarifying the process for decision making" (Brody & Nair, 2014, p. 198). For example, **Robert's Rules of Order** (Robert, 2016) illustrate one method of running meetings with highly structured techniques such as **formal motions** ("proposed actions that the group is asked to support") and voting procedures (Kirst-Ashman & Hull, 2018b, p. 122).

4. Committee members should get specific assignments so that their understanding of what they need to do by the next meeting is perfectly clear. Sometimes, a leader will ask for volunteers to complete assignments or volunteers will suggest their own assignments. Other times, a leader may make assignments. However, a leader should be very careful that committee members are willing to carry them out, or they probably won't get done.

5. An effective leader should deal with any conflict emerging in the group. Conflicts may arise because of interpersonal or emotional issues occurring among members, differences of opinion regarding how the group should proceed, or competition for control of the group. A good leader will address the conflict and seek a compromise without taking sides.

   Wheelan (1999) remarks, "Some groups navigate their conflicts well, and others disband or become dysfunctional by dealing with their differences ineffectively. What do successful teams do to promote positive conflict resolution? Members of successful teams communicate their views clearly and explicitly. They avoid generalizations and are specific in their communication. They talk about trust and cooperation during the discussion" (p. 65). They also will argue their points straightforwardly so that the group may come to some resolution. A good leader will facilitate this process.

6. Finally, an effective leader will periodically summarize the discussion throughout the committee's meeting. This helps to establish a consensus regarding where the group is going and keep the group on track.

Boards of Directors

A **board of directors** is another type of administrative group (Toseland & Rivas, 2017). It is a group of people authorized to formulate the organization's mission, objectives, and policies, in addition to overseeing the organization's ongoing activities. A board of directors also has ultimate control over the agency's higher administration, including its executive director or chief executive officer. Boards are usually recruited from respected members of the community who hold positions of power and influence or have high status, expertise, or influence. Others may be chosen because they represent a group in the community such as people of color, organization alumni, or others whose ideas are useful to the board. Examples of boards of directors include one overseeing a large private substance abuse treatment center and another governing an organization running seven hospices. (A **hospice** is a nonhospital facility where people having terminal illnesses can die as comfortably as possible with the best quality of life possible.)

Boards of directors can serve many positive functions for agencies. They can:

- Serve as ambassadors to communicate the organization's mission, policies, programs, and services [to clients, community residents, staff, governmental units, and other social services agencies] . . ..
- Interpret and communicate to the organization the needs of the communities served by the organization.
- Define the organization's position on public policies and serve as advocates.
- Protect the organization from inappropriate intrusions by government and special interests.
- Promote the organization to [financial] donors and potential donors (Axelrod, 2005, p. 137; Lewis et al., 2012, p. 40).

Groups to Serve Community Needs

EP 6

At least two types of groups also can be formed to meet community needs—delegate councils and social action groups (Toseland & Rivas, 2017).

Delegate Councils

A *delegate council* is a group of representatives from a series of agencies or units within a single agency. Representatives may be elected by their constituencies or appointed by agency decision makers. Typical goals include enhancing cooperation and communication among professionals in different units or agencies, reviewing issues relevant to service provision, enhancing management approaches, and pursuing social action goals (Toseland & Rivas, 2017).

An example of a delegate council is a group of representatives from four private social service agencies in three states. Each agency provides a range of services, including mental health counseling, substance abuse counseling, group homes for people with various disabilities, residential treatment centers for troubled youth, recreational programs for families, and foreign adoptions. In two agencies, administrators appointed five representatives each. In the other two agencies, representatives were elected by staff in their respective six service divisions. One recent delegate council conference focused on integrating new management principles throughout the agencies' administrative structures.

Another example of a delegate council is a group of professionals working in rape crisis centers throughout the state. Each agency designates a representative to meet in the council to discuss education and treatment issues in addition to interagency cooperation.

Social Action Groups

**EP 3b, 5c,
5b, 8c**

Chapter 1 discussed how generalist social work practice entails using a structured planned change course of action to help clients. **Planned change** is the development and implementation of a strategy for improving or altering one or more aspects of the client's life circumstances or environment. These may include behavioral patterns, problems in functioning, relationship difficulties, or other challenges that impair the client's well-being. **Social action groups** are groups formed to engage in some planned change effort to shift power and resources to modify or improve aspects of the macro social or physical environment (Netting, Kettner, McMurtry, & Thomas, 2017; Toseland & Rivas, 2017). They may consist of professionals, clients, community residents, or some combination of these groups. Social workers can use social action groups to connect people with necessary services and resources, address and solve problematic situations, and alter conditions in the macro social environment to enhance living conditions and quality of life.

Social action groups in communities often involve one of three dimensions—"geographic, issue, or identity" (Staples, 2004, p. 344). First, a group from a *geographical area* (e.g., a neighborhood, a town, a county, a state, or even a whole region) might band together and address issues of concern to them all. Such problems might include "housing, education, recreation, employment, environmental issues, transportation, or health care" (p. 345). One example is a group of agency workers and community residents collaborating to raise funds to establish a neighborhood park. Another example is the Coalition for a Better Acre, a group of primarily Central American and Cambodian residents who live in one of the poorest neighborhoods of Lowell, Massachusetts (Staples, 2004, p. 345). Their goal is social action for neighborhood improvement through cleanup, increasing inexpensive housing availability, and development of programs serving young people.

A second dimension often fueling community social action groups concerns specific social *issues*, regardless of geographic residence. Such issues might include "clean elections, tax reform, women's rights, environmental justice, or [older adult] … issues" (Staples, 2004, p. 345). One example of such a social action group is a coalition of social work practitioners working to improve professional social work licensing standards in their state. Another example is the Massachusetts Senior Action Council (MSAC), which involves members throughout the state. Its goal is social action for improved living conditions for older adults, improved and better-maintained senior housing, improved prescription drug coverage, and "a managed-care patients' bill of rights" (p. 346). (**Managed care** is a health care delivery system designed and organized to control costs, utilization of health services, and the quality of services provided.) The third focus involving community social action groups is "*identity*, for instance, ethnicity, religion, sexual orientation, or physical or mental disability. The Latino Immigrant Committee in Chelsea, Massachusetts, is composed primarily of recent immigrants from El Salvador, Honduras, Guatemala, Colombia, Chile, and Nicaragua. A core group of 30 people is most active and has engaged in social action focused on discriminatory treatment at the local branch of the post office, on worker safety at a local meat processing plant, on gang violence, on immigrant rights, and on increased participation in the political process" (Staples, 2004, p. 346).

At a Glance **4-1**

Types of Groups in the Macro Social Environment

I. **TASK GROUPS:** Collections of people that apply the principles of group dynamics to solve problems, develop innovative ideas, formulate plans, and achieve goals within the context of an organization or a community.

   A. **Groups to meet client needs**

      1. **Team:** A group of two or more people gathered together to work collaboratively and interdependently to pursue a designated purpose.

         a. **Virtual team:** "A small group of people who conduct almost all of their collaborative work by electronic communication rather than in face-to-face meetings" (Dubrin, 2012, p. 477).

      2. **Treatment conference:** A group that meets to establish, monitor, and coordinate service plans on the behalf of a client system.

      3. **Staff development group:** A group formed to improve, update, and refine workers' skills, the goal being improved services to clients.

   B. **Groups to serve organizational purposes**

      1. **Administrative groups:** Various clusters of supervisors and managers organized to maintain and improve agency functioning.

      2. **Committee:** A group of persons given the authority and responsibility to consider, research, act on, and report on a topic or issue.

      3. **Board of directors:** An administrative group authorized to formulate the organization's mission, objectives, and policies, in addition to overseeing the organization's ongoing activities.

   C. **Groups to serve community needs**

      1. **Delegate council:** A group of representatives from a series of agencies or units within a single agency.

      2. **Social action group:** A group formed to engage in some planned change effort to shift power and resources to modify or improve aspects of the macro social, economic or physical environment.

II. **TREATMENT GROUPS:** Groups that help individuals solve personal problems, change unwanted behaviors, cope with stress, and improve group members' quality of life.

   A. **Therapy group:** A group that helps members with serious psychological and emotional problems change their behavior.

   B. **Support group:** Consist of participants with common issues or problems who meet on an ongoing basis to cope with stress, give each other suggestions, provide encouragement, convey information, and furnish emotional support.

   C. **Educational group:** A group that primarily provides information to participants.

   D. **Growth group:** A group aimed at expanding self-awareness, increasing potential, and maximizing optimal health and well-being.

   E. **Socialization group:** A group that helps participants improve interpersonal behavior, communication, and social skills so that they might better fit into their social environment.

Note that sometimes the distinctions among these three dimensions are not that clear. The MSAC example that addresses the concerns of older adults might also be considered an issue of identity. However, the point is that social action groups are formed to improve social, economic and environmental policies, as well as to enhance people's overall well-being.

Social Action Groups and Empowerment   LO 4-9

Social action often means pushing a macro system to change, moving against the mainstream, or making demands on scarce resources. To do this requires substantial effort. Expenditure of output or effort requires adequate energy or strength. Social action groups can be used to empower group members internally, and thus enhance their strength for altering the external environment in at least five ways (Carr, 2004; Staples, 2004; Brueggemann, 2014).

Increasing Understanding

EP 1c

First, communicating with other group members about their perceptions of problems and issues can greatly expand group members' understanding of these issues (Carr, 2004). There may be benefit in challenging perceptions that impede a group from accomplishing their goals. The depth of understanding and insight increases as group members share personal insights about how relatives and friends view these issues.

For example, consider a group of neighborhood residents and agency social workers formed to evaluate the adequacy of neighborhood housing and the extent to which it complies with established building codes. Horace, one group member, lives with his family in a rented home with horribly drafty windows. He understands that problem from personal experience. However, as other group members share their perceptions, Horace's understanding of such problems significantly deepens.

Quanisha, another group member, talks of how her 7-year-old son, paraplegic from an accidental bullet to the spinal cord during a neighborhood gang battle, can't get into their rented home without being carried. Ramps are nonexistent. Quanisha indicates that she can cope with the situation now while the boy is small. However, the bigger he gets, the harder it will be to move him.

Another group member, Robert, discloses information about an additional problem. His aging parents live in a rented home next door to him. He describes how their home has broken windows whose cracks are plastered with masking tape, making it almost impossible for his parents to see outside. Additionally, their two outside doors don't close properly, so that in winter the place is like a wind tunnel. Robert's parents are afraid to tell the landlord, as they fear he will get mad and evict them. In similar cases, neighborhood landlords found reasons to evict tenants or simply shut the properties down, saying that the upkeep wasn't worth the meager rent they received.

Horace's understanding of the neighborhood housing problems and issues is greatly expanded by hearing about other residents' issues and experiences. His individual view is multiplied many times so that he now better understands the nuances and complexities of the housing problem.

Inspiring Others

EP 8c

A second way that social action groups can empower group members is by acknowledging those who have overcome issues of powerlessness. By building on their success, the group may be motivated and encouraged to show similar strength. Those who have successfully achieved their goals can serve as role models, providing emotional support, and sharing relevant skills and knowledge.

For example, Thelma is part of a social action group aimed at increasing voter registration and education about issues in her community. She shares with the group how she was once totally apathetic regarding voting. At the time, she thought no matter how she felt or what she did, it really didn't matter. She felt like a tiny goldfish in Lake Ontario. Thelma then told of how her neighbor Louise got her involved in the social action process. Louise recruited Thelma to get out, pound the pavement, and encourage community residents to vote. Louise also helped Thelma dispense brochures about issues affecting the community. At first, Louise accompanied Thelma to visit community residents. As Thelma gained experience and confidence, she soon went out by herself.

EP 8a

Critical Thinking Questions **4-3**

Consider a social action group working to improve state laws regarding how sexual assault perpetrators and survivors are treated. The group discusses the history, legalities, and oppressive issues involved. In this way, action group members enhance their awareness of issues they never considered before. For example, how fair is it that wives cannot legally prosecute their husbands for sexually assaulting them? When prosecuting an assault case, how rational is it to explore the survivor's detailed sexual history with the perpetrator and with other sexual partners? How significant is the amount of force the perpetrator used against the survivor (e.g., use of a weapon or gang rape)? How relevant is the amount of resistance offered by the survivor to protect herself?

Thelma now helps other action group members become empowered to carry out the group's tasks. She gives them tips about how to handle crabby and irascible residents. She often accompanies new members when they start out. Thelma provides a significant role model of empowerment for other group members.

Consciousness Raising

A third way social action groups can empower members is through consciousness raising, a concept introduced and discussed in Chapter 3 (Carr, 2004). Social workers can encourage group members to relate their personal problems and issues to what's happening around them in the macro social environment (Carr, 2004). For example, Chapter 3 established that group members, like many people in American culture, may feel that poverty is the result of personal failure rather than an institutionalized socioeconomic condition of unfairness and lack of equal opportunity. A social worker might assist group members in looking beyond their own circumstances by asking questions: "Why does poverty, then, affect, so many people?" "Why are so many poor people working, yet still can't make it?" "Why are so many children and older adults poor?" In this way, group members might begin to view poverty as a structural problem that the political and economic system needs to address.

Providing Mutual Support

Provision of mutual aid or support among action group members is a fourth means of group empowerment. Chapter 3 also introduced and discussed this important concept involved in empowerment. The group context is a source of mutual social-emotional support to help clients achieve change in multiple arenas in their own lives (Carr, 2004). Consider an action group working on getting signatures for a petition to improve the quality of health care provided by a managed care organization. When the group experiences extreme resistance to its recommendations, on the part of that organization's administration, group members can turn to each other for support, encouragement, and the generation of new ideas for leveraging the organization.

Another example is an action group of single mothers receiving public assistance whose purpose is to improve benefits, educate recipients regarding their rights, and inform members and others of community resources. Group members become increasingly supportive of each other in addressing related personal problems such as difficulties with men, dealing with substance abuse, assisting with child care, providing financial help, and participating in recreational activities with each other.

Using Cooperation

A fifth means of empowerment within social action groups is ongoing communication and cooperation concerning the macro change process (Carr, 2004; Staples, 2004). It's often easier to work with others toward a designated goal than to pursue it in isolation. The planned change effort is often uneven, having ups and downs in terms of making progress. New impediments can emerge in the political environment. Action group members can work together to adjust to changes in the environment, alter plans accordingly, and continue monitoring progress toward goals.

For example, school social workers from secondary schools in a large metropolitan area form a social action group to seek increased funding for students' extracurricular activities. With shrinking budgets, one special activity after another has been eradicated. These include band, drama club, play productions, debate, golf, and tennis. The workers feel young people require positive activities to experience healthy growth and development. Without such activities, the teachers feel teens are much more likely to turn to gangs, drugs, and crime.

Parents form a similar social action group with the same concerns about their children's school activities. The social workers' group invites the parents' group to merge with it, thereby enhancing both groups' mutual power and influence. Both groups must adjust to the new changes in membership. For example, parents provide a different perspective concerning expectations and needs. The social workers' group will need to learn to encompass this new perspective. Together, social workers and parents develop new cooperative goals.

When the state legislators abruptly decrease property taxes, and, hence, the amount of resources available to schools, the social action group must respond accordingly. With continuously shrinking state funding, the group starts exploring new alternatives. One idea is to form a fundraising Booster Club that sponsors pancake breakfasts and charity concerts, in addition to sending members door-to-door to solicit funds.

The point is that conditions often are in flux for social action groups. A strength of a group context is that members can help each other work out new alternatives and plans of action for accomplishing goals. The group can monitor its progress in a coordinated fashion without full responsibility falling on an individual member.

Chapter Summary

The following summarizes this chapter's content as it relates to the learning objectives presented at the beginning of the chapter. Objectives include the following:

LO 4-1 Define task groups and explain their relevance within generalist practice in the macro social environment.

Task or work groups are those applying the principles of group dynamics to solve problems, develop innovative ideas, formulate plans, and achieve goals. Task groups in the macro social environment are formed to meet the needs of individuals, families, groups, organizations, or communities.

LO 4-2 Describe task groups formed to meet client needs, organizational needs, and community needs.

Task groups formed to meet client needs include teams, treatment conferences, and staff development groups. Task groups formed to meet organizational needs include administrative groups, committees, and boards of directors. Task groups formed to meet community needs include delegate councils and social action groups.

LO 4-3 Summarize the ethical issue of handling your own negative feelings in task groups.

It's normal for negative feelings to surface sometimes while participating in task groups. However, negative feelings should not be manifested in the form of hostile behavior.

LO 4-4 Answer critical thinking questions concerning task groups.

Critical thinking questions concerned involvement in a team or task group, evaluation of an agency policy covering exclusion of clients from treatment conferences, and issues faced by a social action group working to improve state laws regarding how sexual assault perpetrators and survivors are treated.

LO 4-5 Discuss barriers to successful teamwork and team empowerment.

Barriers to successful teamwork include "the myth of good intentions," "helplessness in the face of authority," "professional boundaries," and "professional differences" (Compton et al., 2005, pp. 293–294). In empowered teams, members feel effective, goals are deemed valuable, and members experience adequate autonomy (Hellriegel & Slocum, 2011).

LO 4-6 Define treatment groups.

Treatment groups help individuals solve personal problems, change unwanted behaviors, cope with stress, and improve group members' quality of life. Types of treatment groups include therapy, support, educational, growth, and socialization groups.

LO 4-7 Compare and contrast treatment conferences and treatment groups.

Treatment groups offer counseling to a group of people gathered together at the same time with goals of achieving positive change for members in the internal group environment. Treatment conferences, on the other hand, are task groups with goals of achieving change in the group's external environment such as the client being discussed in the group.

LO 4-8 Identify means to empower a group through good committee leadership.

A good leader clearly and initially states a meeting's purpose, establishes an agenda, explains ground rules, clarifies specific group member assignments, deals with conflict, and periodically summarizes the ongoing discussion.

LO 4-9 Examine how social action groups can empower their members to alter the external social environment.

Social action groups can increase members' understanding of issues, inspire others, raise consciousness, provide mutual support, and use cooperation to achieve macro change.

Looking Ahead

This chapter discussed the various types of groups existing in the macro social environment. The next chapter will introduce knowledge and theories about organizations in the macro social environment.

Competency Notes

The following identifies where Educational Policy (EP) competencies and component behaviors are discussed in the chapter.

EP 1 (Competency 1)—Demonstrate Ethical and Professional Behavior. *(p. 127):* Staff development groups can provide regular opportunities to engage in career-long learning. *(p. 127)*: Working in task groups requires adherence to professional ethics.

EP 1c Demonstrate professional demeanor in behavior; appearance; and oral, written, and electronic communication. *(p. 127)*: In task groups, professional roles and boundaries must be established and maintained. *(p. 138)*: Communication among action group members should be effective and increase members' understanding of issues. Professional demeanor can be demonstrated through communication among action group members.

EP 2 (Competency 2)—Engage diversity and difference in practice. *(p. 130)*: Gender is a dimension of diversity. *(p. 129)*: Sexual orientation is a dimension of diversity. *(p. 130)*: Age, color, culture, and race are dimensions of diversity.

EP 3b Engage in practices that advance social, economic, and environmental justice. *(p. 136)*: Social action groups advocate for human rights, social, economic, and environmental justice.

EP 5b Assess how social welfare and economic policies impact the delivery of and access to social services. *(p. 137)*: Social action groups can analyze and advocate for policies that advance social well-being. *(p. 137)*: Suggestions for successful teamwork are discussed. This prepares social workers for collaboration with colleagues to pursue effective policy action. Social action groups can involve collaborating with colleagues for effective policy action. Participating in social action groups often requires collaboration with colleagues and clients in the pursuit of effective policy action. This can be done by inspiring group members, enhancing consciousness raising, providing mutual support, and using cooperation.

EP 5c Apply critical thinking to analyze, formulate, and advocate for policies that advance human rights and social, economic, and environmental justice. *(p. 139)*: Social action groups often engage in practices that advance social, economic, and environmental justice.

EP 6 (Competency 6)—Engage with Individuals, Families, Groups, Organizations, and Communities. *(p. 129)*: Social workers must be knowledgeable about the various types of groups to prepare for action with groups. *(p. 129)*: Social workers must understand how groups serve organizational purposes to prepare for work with groups and organizations. *(p. 135)*: Generalist practitioners must understand how groups serve community purposes to prepare for work with groups, organizations, and communities.

EP 6a Apply knowledge of human behavior and the social environment, person-in-environment, and other multidisciplinary theoretical frameworks to engage with clients and constituencies. *(p. 119)*: Social workers must understand how task groups develop and function, and how they are used within a macro environment.

EP 6b Use empathy, reflection, and interpersonal skills to effectively engage diverse clients and constituencies. *(p. 119)*: Social workers use a variety of interpersonal skills to work with group members to help them succeed at their task.

EP 7b Apply knowledge of human behavior and the social environment, person-in-environment, and other multidisciplinary theoretical frameworks in the analysis of assessment data from clients and constituencies. *(p. 121)*: Team leaders need to assess carefully the characteristics of members that will contribute to or interfere with a group achieving its purpose.

EP 8 (Competency 8)—Intervene with Individuals, Families, Groups, Organizations, and Communities. *(p. 128)*: Treatment groups can help clients resolve problems.

EP 8a Critically choose and implement interventions to achieve practice goals and enhance capacities of clients and constituencies. *(p. 125, 127, 139)*: Critical thinking questions are raised.

EP 8b Apply knowledge of human behavior and the social environment, person-in-environment, and other multidisciplinary theoretical frameworks in interventions with

clients and constituencies. *(p. 121):* Generalist practitioners should keep abreast of technological developments such as the use of virtual teams. *(p. 127):* Staff development groups can provide opportunities for staff to keep abreast of new ideas, trends, policies, and treatment approaches.

EP 8c Use inter-professional collaboration as appropriate to achieve beneficial practice outcomes. *(p. 134):* Effective committee leadership can result in sustainable changes in service delivery and practice that improve the quality of services. *(p. 125):* Treatment conferences are opportunities to collaborate with other professionals on behalf of services to clients. *(p. 136):* Collaborating with other professional and nonprofessional groups is often a way of increasing the effectiveness of social action groups with similar goals.

EP 8e Facilitate effective transitions and endings that advance mutually agreed-on goals. *(p. 129):* Participation in treatment groups can teach group members prevention interventions that enhance their capacities.

Media Resources

MindTap for Social Work

 Go to MindTap® for digital study tools and resources that complement this text and help you be more successful in your course and career. There's an interactive eBook plus videos of client sessions, skill-building activities, quizzes to help you prepare for tests, apps, and more—all in one place. If your instructor didn't assign MindTap, you can find out more about it at CengageBrain.com.

5 | Knowledge and Theories about Organizations

Kablonk Micro/Fotolia LLC

Organizations and people's statuses within them may be viewed in many ways.

LEARNING OBJECTIVES

After reading this chapter you should be able to...

5-1 Define organizations.

5-2 Describe organizations providing social services.

5-3 Discuss several major organizational theories.

5-4 Answer various critical thinking questions.

5-5 Describe the dynamics of gender-based power in organizations.

5-6 Provide examples of ethical issues that may arise in organizations.

5-7 Demonstrate the application of ecosystems concepts to organizations and social agencies.

Beverly Hill received her social work degree last month and was ecstatic. She just got the job of her dreams as a counselor at Gridlock Meadows (GM), a residential treatment center for adolescent males with serious behavioral and emotional problems. She would be doing individual and group counseling with residents, providing consultation for behavioral planning on two residential units, and running some parent groups. Beverly loved working with young people and their families. She couldn't wait to start. It was too good to be true.

Three weeks after her first day on the job, Beverly knew the job was too good to be true. She was seriously wondering whether accepting the position was such a wise idea. Her experiences at GM were unlike any she had before in work, educational, or volunteer positions. Every morning when she arrived at GM, she felt like she was in jail. GM required all employees to sign in and out. One minute late meant being docked a half hour's pay.

But that was only a minuscule part of the problem. Beverly felt she couldn't breathe without her supervisor Bambi's approval. Bambi insisted on attending all Beverly's adolescent and parent group sessions and proceeded to take over running them. Beverly had little chance to get a word in edgewise.

Every progress note, letter, and report Beverly wrote, Bambi insisted on seeing, approving, and initialing. Beverly felt like Bambi thought her an incompetent idiot. Beverly had little chance to get a cup of coffee without Bambi's explicit approval.

When Beverly gently approached Bambi about these and several other similar issues, Bambi blew up. "How dare you contradict me after being here less than a month," she exclaimed. "You're under a strict three-month probationary period. I can fire you anytime. You'd better start paying attention to company policy and be happy you have a job."

Beverly never thought an organization could be run like that. She felt thwarted and trapped. She didn't know if she could work under such circumstances even for a short time. Maybe she should quit and start her job search over again. Now, she felt she knew much more when considering a job about what to look for in an agency and how it was run. She would give the possibility of quitting very serious thought.

Organizations—including social service agencies—vary dramatically in structure and managerial style. Perhaps Beverly would not have been so shocked had she better understood organizational dynamics and the potential problems she might encounter. No organization is perfect. Some organizations are more productive and better places to work than others.

Human behavior in organizations involves people using their skills and working together to meet goals and provide services. Communication channels and a hierarchy of authority coordinate this process. Understanding how organizations function requires a focus on the behavior, activities, performance, outlooks, and attitudes of the people who work in them.

Social service organizations, as macro systems in the social environment, have major impacts on clients and other community residents. They establish services and develop means to deliver them. Because the organizational environment provides the context and structure for social workers to provide services, it is critical for workers to understand organizations' internal functioning.

When there are difficulties, people within organizations can work to improve organizational effectiveness and efficiency. Social workers have the serious ethical responsibility to enhance agency functioning. The National Association of Social Workers (NASW) *Code of Ethics* states that "social workers should work to improve employing agencies' policies and procedures and the efficiency and effectiveness of their services" (NASW, 2008, 3.09b).

We have established that this book does not try to teach *how* to do social work practice and implement changes in communities, organizations, or groups. However, it does intend to provide a *foundation* upon which to build such system-changing skills. Before you can plan and implement changes in organizations on clients' and communities' behalf, you must understand how these macro systems work. This and the next three chapters will address a range of problems and issues relevant to how organizations function in the macro social environment.

This chapter focuses primarily on organizations related to social services. However, much of the content also is relevant to understanding any type of organization as a macro system.

Defining Organizations LO 5-1

Organizations are "(1) social entities that (2) are goal directed, (3) are designed as deliberately structured and coordinated activity systems, and (4) are linked to the external environment" (Daft, 2016b, p. 13). Four elements stand out in this definition.

First, organizations are **social entities**. That is, organizations are made up of people, with all their strengths and failings. Organizations dictate how people should behave and what responsibilities employees must assume as they do their jobs. Individuals bring to their jobs their own values and personalities. Thus, patterns of behavior develop in organizational environments, which Chapters 7 and 8 discuss further.

Second, organizations are **goal-directed**. They exist for some specified purpose. An organization specializing in stock brokering exists to help clients develop financial investments that make money. Social service organizations exist to provide services and resources to help people with designated needs. An organization must clearly define its goals so that workers can evaluate the extent to which they are achieved.

The third key concept in the definition is that organizations are *deliberately structured and coordinated activity systems*. **Activity systems** are clusters of work activities performed by designated units or departments within an organization. Such systems are guided by a *technology*, the practical application of knowledge to achieve desired ends. Organizations coordinate the functioning of various activity systems to enhance efficiency in attaining desired goals. Organizations have structures that include policies for how the organization should be run, hierarchies of how personnel are supervised and by whom, and different units working in various ways to help the organization function.

An intake unit for a large county Department of Social Services is an example of an activity system. Workers under supervision process new cases by following established procedures, obtaining required information, and making referrals to the appropriate service providers.

Another example is a family services organization that has several activity systems, including one staff unit providing marriage and family counseling, another providing family life education,[1] and still another focusing on community activities aimed at family advocacy, recreation, and support. Each unit pursues different functions to achieve the agency's general goal of providing family services.

Of course, organizations other than those providing social services also have activity systems. For example, consider a yogurt company, also an organization, that specializes in producing frozen yogurt. One activity unit is responsible for developing new flavors of yogurt, one for manufacturing them, and another for marketing them.

The fourth concept inherent in the definition of organizations is *linkage to the external environment*. Thus, an organization is in constant interaction with other systems in the social environment, including individuals, groups, other organizations, and communities. Agencies providing social services interact dynamically with clients, funding sources, legislative and regulatory agencies, politicians, community leaders, and other social service agencies.

Organizations Providing Social Services LO 5-2

This and the next three chapters focus on organizations that provide social services to clients. **Social services** include the tasks that social work practitioners and other helping professionals perform with the goal of improving people's health, enhancing their quality of life, increasing autonomy and independence, supporting families, and helping people and larger systems improve their functioning in the social environment. That is quite a mouthful. In essence, social services include the wide range of activities that social workers perform in their goal of helping people solve problems and improve their personal well-being.

Social services may be **institutional**, that is, those provided by major public service systems that administer such benefits as financial assistance, housing programs, health care, or education. They might also include **personal social services** that address more individualized needs involving interpersonal relationships and people's ability to function within their immediate environments. Such services usually target specific groups (such as children or older adults) or problems (such as family planning or counseling).

Social Agencies

A **social agency**, or **social services agency**, is an organization providing social services that typically employs a range of helping professionals, including social workers in addition to office staff, **paraprofessionals** (persons trained to assist professionals), and sometimes volunteers. Social agencies generally serve some

---

[1] *Family life education* is a group learning program that addresses multiple life issues and crises. It is typically led by a social worker or other helping professional in any of a variety of settings, including health care centers, schools, churches, and community centers. Virtually any important life issue can be addressed, ranging from newborn care to child management to preparation for retirement.

Highlight 5-1

Common Social Services Terms

EP 1c

Note that the terms *social services, human services*, and sometimes *social welfare* are often used interchangeably when referring to organizations, agencies, and agency personnel. **Human services** include organizational programs that are created to assist people in achieving well-being in society. This may do so by providing social support, financial assistance, and other needed programs. Because the terms **social services agency**, **social services organization**, and *social agency* mean essentially the same thing, these three terms will be used interchangeably.

Social welfare in the broadest sense is the entire system of services, benefits, and programs designed to help people sustain themselves and their families. Ultimately, the social welfare system provides a wide variety of assistance that encompasses financial, health, economic, and educational programs required to support and maintain society. Social welfare, then, is a broad concept related to the general well-being of all people in a society. As practitioners, we are most likely to be concerned about two basic dimensions of social welfare: (1) what people get from society (in terms of programs, benefits, and services) and (2) how well their needs (including social, economic, educational, and health) are being met.

designated client population experiencing some defined need. Services are provided in accordance with a prescribed set of policies regarding how the agency staff should accomplish their service provision goals. Highlight 5-1 discusses some related terms.

Several concepts can describe social agencies. For example, social agencies can be either public, private, or proprietary. **Public social agencies** are run by some designated unit of government and are usually regulated by laws impacting policy. For example, a county board committee oversees a public welfare department and is responsible for establishing its major policies. (Of course, such a committee must function in accordance with state or federal governments, which often provide a portion of the money for the agency's programs.)

Private social agencies, on the other hand, are privately owned and run by people not directly employed by some level of government. Some are classified as **nonprofit social agencies**. That is, they are run to accomplish some service provision goal, not to make financial profit for private owners. They usually provide some type of personal social services. Funding for services can include tax moneys, private donations, grants, and service fees. A board of directors presides over a private agency, formulating policy and making certain that agency staff run the agency appropriately. An example of this type of organization would be Lutheran Social Services or Goodwill Industries.

Proprietary, or **for-profit**, **social agencies** provide some designated social services, often quite like those provided by private social agencies. However, a major purpose for the existence of a proprietary social agency is to make a profit for its owners. An example would be an agency owned by a social worker that provides therapy for clients having sexual-related problems or another owned by a group of physicians that provides services to older adults to help them stay in their own homes as long as possible.

Organizational Theories and Conceptual Frameworks LO 5-3

EP 6

Organizational theories are ways to conceptualize and understand how organizations function by identifying specific concepts and explaining how these concepts relate to each other. They provide a lens through which to view the organizational environment and direct you as to which aspects of that environment should be your focus of attention. The remainder of this chapter explores a range of ways in which organizations can be viewed and examined.

Organizational behavior "is the study of human behavior in the workplace, the interaction between people and the organization, and the organization itself. . . . The major goals of organizational behavior are to explain, predict, and control behavior" (Dubrin, 2007, p. 2). What components in the organizational environment are significant to those who work there? What issues do they face, and how do they tend to react? **Management** "is the attainment of organizational goals in an effective and efficient manner through planning, organizing, leading, and controlling organizational resources" (Daft, 2016a, p. 4). Here, attention is focused on the interaction between managers, those in power, and workers, those who directly accomplish the organization's goals by performing various tasks. Later chapters will further explore organizational behavior, dimensions and structure of the organizational environment, and management.

To work within organizations, evaluate them, and sometimes change them, it is helpful to understand the major theories regarding how organizations operate. Such a perspective is also useful to determine what kinds of organizational structures are most effective for specific client situations.

Many organizational theories have been borrowed from the business and management literature. Businesses and social service organizations have much in common. Both need resources, namely money, to function. Likewise, both produce results or products via some process. For example, among other products, Honeywell manufactures burglar alarms. The Family Service Agency of Bay County provides clothing, medical equipment, food, and other items needed to assist individuals and families.

There is a wide range of theories concerning how organizations work. Some of them directly contradict others, probably because there is such a vast array of organizational structures, functions, and goals. There are tremendous differences among social service organizations in terms of structure and function, and more so among all types of businesses and organizations. The important thing for you is to think about how organizations work, because you will be working in one.

Some theories emphasize similar dimensions, such as expectations for staff treatment, the importance placed on profits, or the degree to which new ideas are encouraged. However, each theory stresses various concepts somewhat differently.

One means of considering the wide variety of organizational theories is to place them on one of two continuums (O'Connor & Netting, 2009). One is adherence to traditional rigid structure, on the one hand, versus seeking fundamental change for the better on the other. The second continuum involves a focus on human individuality and well-being on one side, and a focus on objective, efficient completion of tasks on the other.

The following theories are reviewed here. Classical organizational theories developed early in the last century include scientific management, the administrative theory of management, and bureaucracy. They reflect rigid structures in addition to emphasis on productivity and task completion. Human relations theories portray a later shift in perspective to theory that's more oriented toward human relationships and motivation. Feminist theories also stress the importance of the human component in organizational functioning and, of course, focus on the empowerment of women. The cultural perspective emphasizes the importance of expectations in the organizational environment and culture to maintain the organization's status quo. Political-economy theory emphasizes how organizations must adapt to their external environments, stressing the effects of resources and power. The institutional perspective also focuses on external pressures—not resources and power, but social institutions and their demands. Contingency theory stresses careful analysis of all variables to determine those that relate directly to an issue or problem (which could concern either the personal traits of people involved or other elements related to the specific situation). Culture-quality theories, characterizing the end of the last century, emphasize the importance of establishing a positive organizational culture that promotes worker motivation and improves the quality of their work. Finally, ecosystems theory provides a perspective for understanding organizational functioning that fits well with social work. It provides a structured way of viewing organizations, yet focuses on how change might occur. It also can take into account both the importance of human well-being and the accomplishment of organizational tasks and goals.

Classical Organizational Theories

Classical management theories emphasize that specifically designed, formal structure and a consistent, rigid organizational network of employees are most important in having an organization run well and achieve its goals (Griffin & Moorhead, 2014). In general, these early theories saw each employee as holding a clearly defined job and straightforwardly being told exactly how that job should be accomplished. These schools of thought call for minimal independent functioning on the part of employees. Supervisors closely scrutinize the latter's work. Efficiency is of utmost importance. Performance is quantified (i.e., made very explicit regarding what is expected), regulated, and measured. How people feel about their jobs is insignificant. Administration should avoid allowing employees to have any input regarding how organizational goals can best be reached. Rather, employees should do their jobs as instructed and as quietly and efficiently as possible.

Scientific Management   Frederick W. Taylor introduced the concept of **scientific management** (Daft, 2016a; Nelson & Quick, 2013a). Developed in the early twentieth century, it reflected a time when there was often great hostility between management and employees. Management pushed employees to work as hard as possible to maximize company profits. In response, employees, to protect themselves, worked as slowly and did as little as possible. They figured that working faster and becoming more productive would endanger their own and other workers' jobs if management could get more work out of fewer people. Management sought high profits and workers wanted high wages. Both were working against each other.

Four principles characterize Taylor's scientific management style (Daft, 2016a; Williams, 2016a):

1. Jobs and tasks should be studied scientifically to identify and create standardized work procedures and expectations.
2. Workers should be chosen on a scientific basis to maximize their potential for being trained and turned into productive employees.
3. Management and employees should cooperate with each other and work together following standardized procedures.
4. Management should be responsible for planning and assigning tasks that workers were then to carry out as instructed.

The Administrative Theory of Management   Also in the early twentieth century, Henri Fayol proposed an **administrative theory of management** (Williams, 2016a). His ideas focused on the administrative side of management rather than the workers' performance. He proposed five basic functions that management should fulfill. These included planning, organizing, command, coordination, and control (Williams, 2016a). He concluded that all managers should abide by the following six basic principles, although he did indicate that they should use **discretion** (the opportunity to make independent judgments and decisions) concerning the intensity of their actions (Williams, 2016a; p. 34):

1. *Division of work.* Workers should be divided up into units so that they might perform specialized instead of more general tasks. He posed that specialization would lead to greater productivity.
2. *Authority and responsibility.* A chain of authority exists from the top to bottom of any organization and includes each worker. Management should have the authority to give orders to workers, oversee their activity, and make them comply with these orders. In response, workers would assume responsibility for completing their assigned work.
3. *Centralization.* Depending on which would maximize productivity, management should centralize authority (i.e., place decision-making power and responsibility at the top of the organization's power hierarchy) or decentralize such authority (give power and responsibility to lower-level managers and workers in the organization's power hierarchy).
4. *Delegation of authority.* Upper-level management should have the responsibility of delegating responsibility and work assignments to managers and workers lower in the power hierarchy. Management should carefully analyze organizational processes and delegate authority as it saw fit.
5. *Unity of command.* Each worker should have one designated supervisor to whom he or she should report. This should avoid confusion and give consistent messages and orders to workers.
6. *Unity of direction.* Each unit in the organization (which is specialized under the division of labor) should have a single designated goal. This also should avoid confusion and inconsistency.

Ideally, these principles should work together. High-level management should give authority to lower-level management (authority and responsibility) as it saw fit (centralization or decentralization; delegation of authority). Workers should be specialized (division of labor) and work in designated units. There should be a clear hierarchy of authority regarding who is responsible for each worker (unity of command) and each unit (unity of direction) to avoid confusion, enhance consistency, and maximize productivity.

Bureaucracy   Described by Max Weber in the early twentieth century, **bureaucracy** encompasses formal administrative structure with clearly defined boundaries, units or functions, and hierarchical relationships among the functions. Every function or unit has well-defined responsibilities, tasks, and rights. The successful functioning of a unit is not dependent on the individual holding a position. Bureaucratic relationships are impersonal and decisions are based on policies, rules, and procedures that have been articulated to all employees. The bureaucracy achieves its goals efficiently with precision and reliability. In summary, traditional bureaucracies emphasize the following (Griffin & Moorhead, 2014):

- Highly specialized units performing clearly specified job tasks
- Minimal discretion on the part of employees
- Numerous specific rules to maintain control

The Social Security Administration, the Detroit Department of Social Services, and the Federal Bureau of Investigation are examples of large bureaucracies. Chapter 8 will address what it's like to work in an organization with a bureaucratic style of management.

Human Relations Theories

A major change in theoretical perspective concerning organizations and performance occurred in the 1920s and 1930s after a series of studies conducted at an electric plant in Hawthorne, Illinois (Netting, Kettner, McMurty, & Thomas, 2017; O'Connor & Netting, 2009; Phillips & Gully, 2014). There researchers observed workers who were exposed to several different conditions. One of the variables tested was the lighting provided during workers' shifts. Researchers first found that workers performed better when exposed to dimmer lighting. They then were surprised to discover that workers were also more productive when lighting was increased. In other words, any change in lighting resulted in increased production. They concluded that workers' performance improved simply because they were being observed.

Phillips and Gully (2014) explain:

> The reason that workers are motivated by informal things is that individuals have a deep psychological need to believe that their organization cares about them. Essentially, workers are more motivated when they believe their organization is open, concerned, and willing to listen.

The Hawthorne studies prompted further investigation into the effects of social relations, motivation, communication, and employee satisfaction on factory productivity. Rather than viewing workers as interchangeable parts in mechanical organizations as the scientific management movement had done, the **human relations movement** viewed organizations as cooperative systems and treats workers' orientations, values, and feelings as important parts of organizational dynamics and performance. The human relations movement stressed that the human dimensions of work, including group relations, can supersede organizational norms and even an individual's self-interests.

Unsophisticated research methods did render some of the conclusions of human relations researchers incorrect. For example, the relationship between employee satisfaction and performance is more complex than researchers initially thought. Nonetheless, the movement ushered in a new era of more human, employee-centered management by recognizing employees' social needs, and highlighted the importance of people to organizational success. (pp. 12–13)

Chester I. Barnard was one of the early leaders of the human relations movement (Phillips & Gully, 2014). He viewed organizations as "systems of cooperative human activity" with an emphasis on working together (p. 13). He also stressed the importance of "two-way communication" between workers and management (p. 13). Prior to this, classical organizational theories focused only on one-way communication—management would tell workers what to do.

Griffin and Moorhead (2014) explain that human relations theories assume

that employees want to feel useful and important, that employees have strong social needs, and that these needs are more important than money in motivating employees. Advocates of the human relationship approach advised managers to make workers feel important and allow them a modicum of self-direction and self-control in carrying out routine activities. The illusion of involvement and importance were expected to satisfy workers' basic social needs and result in higher motivation to perform. For example, a manager might allow a work group to participate in decision making, even though he or she had already determined what the decision would be. The symbolic gesture of seeming to allow participation was expected to enhance motivation, even though no real participation took place. (p. 85)

Likewise, the immediate work group, a mezzo system, is critical in human relations theories. If workers were satisfied with their interpersonal relationships with their supervisors and in their work groups, they would become more productive; in this context, virtually all workers theoretically could become productive employees (Dubrin, 2007).

Theory X and Theory Y   The management styles of administrators and supervisors in organizations have considerable impact on the productivity and job satisfaction of employees. Douglas McGregor (1960) developed two theories of management style. He hypothesized that management thinking and behavior are based on two different sets of assumptions, which he labeled **Theory X and Theory Y**. Theory X reflects aspects of classical scientific management in its focus on hierarchical structure, providing a contrasting approach to Theory Y, which focuses on human relations. These theories are addressed here because they emphasize the treatment of employees.

Theory X managers view employees as being incapable of much growth. Employees are perceived as having an inherent dislike for work, and it is presumed that they will attempt to evade work whenever possible. Therefore, X-type managers believe that they must control, direct, force, or threaten employees to make them work. Employees are also viewed as having relatively little ambition, wishing to avoid responsibilities, and preferring to be directed. X-type managers therefore spell out job responsibilities carefully, set work goals without employee input, use external rewards (such as money) to induce employees to work, and punish employees who deviate from established rules. Because Theory X managers reduce responsibilities to a level where few mistakes can be made, work can become so structured that it is monotonous and distasteful. The assumptions of Theory X, of course, are inconsistent with what behavioral scientists assert are effective principles for directing, influencing, and motivating people.

In contrast, Theory Y managers view employees as wanting to grow and develop by exerting physical and mental effort to accomplish work objectives to which they are committed. Y-type managers believe that the promise of internal rewards, such as self-respect and personal improvement, are stronger motivators than external rewards (such as money) and punishment. A Y-type manager also believes that under proper conditions, employees will not only accept responsibility but seek it. Most employees are assumed to have considerable ingenuity, creativity, and imagination for solving the organization's problems. Therefore, employees are given considerable responsibility in order to test the limits of their capabilities. Mistakes and errors are viewed as necessary phases of the learning process, and work is structured so that employees can have a sense of accomplishment and growth.

Feminist Theories and Organizations

Chapter 3 discussed feminist theory with respect to groups and established that there are a range of feminist theories that emphasize various concepts (e.g., women's individual rights, economic status, or cultural contexts). Feminist theories emphasize interpersonal relationships and respect for each other's right to be heard and contribute. Highlight 5-2 discusses the dynamics of gender-based power in organizations.

EP 8

Critical Thinking Question 5-1   LO 5-4

Compare and contrast classical organizational theories and human relations theories. What are the strengths and weaknesses of each?

Highlight 5-2

The Dynamics of Gender-Based Power in Organizations   LO 5-5

Burk (2012) proposes and discusses some of the dynamics involved in organizations that sustain men in positions of power. To begin with, "males, much more so than females, are conditioned almost from birth to view the world in terms of hierarchies, power relationships, and being winners" (p. 436). Consider the following five dynamics:

1. *"Power re-creates itself in its own image"* (Burk, p. 436). Burk states that, psychologically, people

continued

Highlight **5-2**   *continued*

tend to be drawn to other people who resemble themselves. Therefore, in organizations where men already assume most of the powerful positions, there is a tendency to promote other men to maintain that status quo. Often, diversity in terms of gender and race characterize the lower echelons of organizational power structures. The higher up in management you go, the less diversity there is. Consider how there are only 21 women chief executive officers (CEOs) in all the Fortune 500 companies (Zarya, 2016).

2. *"Power elites enforce norms and systems that guarantee continued power"* (Burk, p. 437). Boards of directors (as discussed in Chapter 4) often govern organizations, select top administrators, and recruit for their own replacements. Therefore, a board of White males (who make up most boards) will tend to seek other White males to "fit in" with the board culture. Even when diverse people in terms of gender or race are brought into a board, they are 'trained' through mentoring and role "modeling" regarding how to act (p. 437). Thus, they will be taught board expectations and be encouraged to conform. This would likely serve to discourage people characterized by some aspect of diversity from bringing in other people like themselves. They would not want to be seen as someone who will cause trouble and "rock the boat."

3. *"Power creates a sense of entitlement"* (Burk, p. 437). People who are in powerful positions become accustomed to having that power. They begin to assume they are naturally entitled to maintain that power over others. Consider how the average pay of a CEO in 2014 was more than 303 times that of the average employee, up from 20 times more in 1965 (Hodgson, 2015). Such huge salaries become a general expectation.

4. *"Power creates invulnerability, leading to a flaunting of society's standards"* (Burk, p. 437). People with great power have the authority to exercise their own will. They can surround themselves with people who flatter and reinforce them because of their power. Powerful leaders can isolate themselves from authorities that could affect or sanction them. They may feel invulnerable and capable of doing whatever they choose, regardless of the rules. A former Illinois governor, a person with significant power, comes to mind who allegedly participated in a wide range of illegal activities. One of these alleged activities involved trying to sell President Barack Obama's prior Senate seat to the highest bidder. Or consider the mortgage companies' CEOs, also very powerful leaders, who received huge bonuses upon their already huge salaries after allowing their companies to verge on or fall into bankruptcy. I never cease to be amazed at what some people (who already have so much) think they can get away with (and often do).

5. *"Loyalty to power overshadows other loyalties, including gender"* (Burk, p. 438). Women who attain higher levels of authority and power tend to lose their interest in helping other women advance (Burk, 2012, p. 438). Perhaps, the dynamics involve how more powerful women begin to identify with others in the power structure, primarily White men. Such women may seek validation from their powerful peers and assume attitudes more like these peers in order to increase their own personal power.

Critical Thinking Questions **5-2**

EP 8a

What do you think of these five proposed dynamics of gender-based power in organizations? Do they make sense to you, or are they too extreme? Explain why. What are the reasons women comprise such a relatively small percentage of people with the greatest political and corporate power, despite making up more than half the population?

The Application of Feminist Principles to Organizations   In order to counter-act the types of gender-related power dynamics discussed in Highlight 5-2, a num-ber of feminist principles can be applied to organizations.

At least five basic feminist concepts and related recommendations for organiza-tional improvements are relevant:

- *Using a gender filter.* Feminist theories focus on the rampant sexism existing in the macro social environment and the need to stress women's conditions, needs, and opportunities. Therefore, within organizational contexts, man-agement and workers must be vigilant regarding the treatment of women in a fair, nondiscriminatory manner.

  Powell and Graves (2003) recommend that organizational leaders:

  promote nondiscrimination in treatment of people and decisions about people. This means promoting compliance by all employees with federal, state, and local equal employment opportunity (EEO) laws. Such laws ban discrimination based on sex, race, ethnicity, national origin, age, religion, and other personal characteristics that are not relevant to the job at hand. It also means refraining from discrimination based on job-irrelevant personal characteristics even if it is not illegal. For example, there is no U.S. federal law banning discrimination based on sexual orientation,[2] but such discrimi-nation is just as unacceptable as sex or race discrimination. (p. 218)

- *Empowerment.* Power should be distributed and equalized to whatever ex-tent possible within an organization. This would support a decentralized organizational structure that provides great discretion on the part of workers throughout the organization. Organizations should also empower women to be promoted and assume leadership positions.

  Gutierrez and Lewis (1999) suggest that "attention should be paid to staff development," including "access to conferences, training workshops, and other educational opportunities . . . Staff can also be supported through flex time and other policies that encourage flexibility and self-care. Simi-larly, providing opportunities for staff to develop programs and professional skills that match their own personal interests is an important part of the em-powerment of staff within an agency" (pp. 83–84).

- *The personal as political* (Bricker-Jenkins & Netting, 2009, p. 279; Fisher & Burghardt, 2008). Feminist theories emphasize that women become aware of their own opinions, feelings, and situations (consciousness raising). They stress that the condition of women goes beyond one's personal situation and that women should strive to improve conditions for all women. The impli-cation is that workers should try to combat sexism wherever it occurs in an organization, not just on their own personal behalf.

- *The importance of process.* Feminist theories emphasize that the process of *how* things get done is just as important as *what* gets done. The im-plication in an organizational context is that management should involve

---

[2]Twenty states and the District of Columbia banned employment discrimination based on sexual orien-tation, and 11 states and the District of Columbia forbid it based on gender identity (FindLaw, 2016).

workers in decision making and planning to the greatest extent possible. Workers should feel like important participants in the organizational environment.

Organizational administrations should "*promote inclusion* of employees from all groups in the organizational culture. The focus of promoting inclusion is on the nature or *quality* of work relationships between employees who belong to different groups" (Powell & Graves, 2003, p. 219). Teamwork should be emphasized (Gutierrez & Lewis, 1999).

■ "*Diversity is strength*" (Bricker-Jenkins & Netting, 2009). Feminist theories stress unity and harmony, on the one hand, and appreciation of diverse characteristics on the other. Women should appreciate each other's differences and work together for the benefit of all. In organizational contexts, diversity (e.g., gender, race, ethnicity, age, and sexual orientation) should not only be appreciated but actively sought out and encouraged.

Administrations should "*promote diversity* among employees in all jobs and at all levels. The focus of promoting diversity is on the number or *quantity* of employees from various groups in different jobs and at different organizational levels" (Powell & Graves, 2003, p. 218).

In summary, Powell and Graves (2003) recommend that "*all* organizations— large or small, public or private, profit or nonprofit—set the goals of being nondiscriminatory, diverse, and inclusive in their employment practices. . . . [Organizational] communications should convey the message that promoting nondiscrimination, diversity, and inclusion are important organizational goals. These communications may include speeches by top executives, with transcripts or videos available to internal and external groups, newsletters, status reports, recognition events, special awards, and publicity for employees who have done good work toward these goals. The **mission statement** [a declaration of an organization's purpose and goals] of the organization should state that the organization regards achievement of these goals as critical to its success" (emphasis added, pp. 231–232).

The Cultural Perspective

EP 2, 2a

Organizational culture is the constellation of "beliefs, norms, attitudes, values, assumptions and ways of doing things that is shared by members of an organization and taught to new members" (Lussier & Achua, 2016, p. 359). The cultural perspective on organizations assumes that each organization develops a unique mixture of values, standards, presumptions, and practices about how things should be done that eventually becomes habit.

EP 8

Critical Thinking Question 5-3

How do men fit into the application of feminist theories to organizations?

Management and other personnel may not be consciously aware that such patterns and expectations have developed. They become ingrained in established means of accomplishing tasks and goals. If it worked before, it'll work again. "If it ain't broke, don't fix it." The result is the establishment of an ideological structure that frames how organizational members think about the organization and how it should work. This perspective not only guides people's view of current practices but also shapes how they think about new issues. Employees tend to view new ideas by shaping them to conform to old, tried-and-true practices.

An advantage of the cultural perspective may be that performance becomes predictable, thus requiring less effort to develop new approaches. However, a disadvantage is that such an established view may squelch innovative ideas. There's pressure to retain the old way of thought. For example, an energized worker in a social services organization might come to a staff meeting with a brilliant new treatment approach with excellent evaluation results. The cultural perspective suggests that staff will tend not to evaluate the new approach fairly and impartially. Rather, they might nod pleasantly in feigned mild agreement and proceed to recycle the new approach into the same old routine.

It should be noted that the organization's culture might support creative innovation and risk-taking instead of the status quo. If this were the case with the group just discussed, staff would enthusiastically welcome the new treatment idea the worker presented. Personnel would shy away from old techniques and search for new ones. In this case, the advantages and disadvantages would be reversed. An advantage, then, would be development of fresh, more effective intervention modalities. A disadvantage would be lack of stability and predictability.

Political-Economy Theory

Political-economy theory emphasizes how organizations must adapt to their external environments, stressing the effects of resources and power. To prosper and provide services, an agency must have three basic kinds of resources (Schmid, 2009). First, it must have **legitimacy** (having appropriate legal status and justification for existence). Second, it requires **political power** (the ability to influence entities that make decisions concerning the organization's ability to function) (Emphasis added) (p. 418). Third, an agency needs economic resources (e.g., to maintain its location, provide services, and pay staff).

Political-economy theory stresses how an organization is dependent on external resources for survival. Therefore, it is subject to pressure from resource providers in terms of how it functions. "The greater the resource dependency of the organization on an element in the environment (e.g., governmental funding agency, regulatory organization, professional association, providers of clients), the greater the ability of the element to influence organizational policies and procedures" (Hasenfeld, 2009, p. 62).

Therefore, an organization is in a constant struggle to negotiate with resource providers and other controlling systems to gain as much control over its functioning as possible (Hasenfeld, 2009). An organization can do this in various ways. To gain power, an organization will strive to compete effectively with other agencies providing similar services. Or an organization might form **coalitions**, alliances of individuals, groups, and organizations with similar goals that become more influential and powerful when united.

Focus on Ethics **5-1**

Power versus Service Provision `LO 5-6`

EP 1

Political-economy theory has been criticized for the emphasis placed on power and access to resources instead of effective service provision to clients. This theory obviously poses difficulties for social workers who maintain professional values and ethics. How does the use of power and its relationship to resources relate to saving a 3-year-old from neglect and abuse? Or how do you determine the significance and cost of helping an adult with bulimia nervosa control the disorder? (**Bulimia nervosa** is a condition occurring primarily in females that is characterized by uncontrolled overeating followed by purging activities such as self-initiated vomiting and the use of diuretics, as well as excessive guilt and shame over the compulsive behavior.)

Organizational leaders might bargain with external controlling elements to negotiate for more power and control in exchanges of services for resources.

Political-economy theory also characterizes the internal agency environment. Hasenfeld (2009) explains:

> The internal dynamics of the organization will also reflect the power relations of different interest groups and individuals within the organization. Some of these groups (e.g., professional staff, executive[s] . . .) derive their power from relations with important external organizations, others because they possess personal attributes, control internal resources (e.g., information and expertise), or carry out important functions (e.g., manage the budget). (p. 62)

Focus on Ethics 5-1 raises some ethical questions concerning political-economy theory.

The Institutional Perspective

Like political-economy theory, the institutional perspective emphasizes the importance of external pressures on an organization. However, instead of focusing on power and resources, this perspective accentuates the pressures imposed by social institutions. **Social institutions** are established constellations of roles, expectations, values, groups, and organizations that are instituted to meet basic societal needs. Typical institutions include formal ones like government, social welfare institutions, and the military, as well as more informal ones like the family or religion. Social institutions are reinforced by various "social rules"; social rules govern society's expectations for behavior through laws, regulations, values, and assigned statuses (Hasenfeld, 2009, p. 65).

The institutional perspective assumes that "the more organizations adhere to the rules of these institutions—by embedding the rules in their structures—the greater will be their legitimacy and chances of survival" (Hasenfeld, 2009, p. 65). Schmid (2009) explains the application of an institutional perspective to social services agencies:

> For example, to ensure a steady flow of resources, human services organizations often adopt the espoused ideologies and goals of the government, which are not always attainable. These ideologies and goals can be expressed as

"closing social gaps and reducing inequality between haves and have nots," "the need to redistribute power and transfer it to peripheral units," "integration of [diverse] populations," and "changing attitudes toward minorities." Organizations that succeed in achieving those goals increase their legitimacy and, consequently, their prospects for survival, irrespective of the immediate efficacy of the required practices and procedures. (p. 421)

In other words, these ideals and social rules may sound good. However, for an organization to comply with them and achieve actual results through service provision is often a difficult, and perhaps impossible, task (Hasenfeld, 2009; Schmid, 2009). Thus, what often really happens is that organizations establish goals in concordance with social rules and receive the resulting legitimacy and support. However, such stated goals may have little to do with actual results achieved.

Contingency Theory

Contingency theory maintains that each element involved in an organization depends on other elements; therefore, there is no one perfect way to accomplish tasks or goals (Daft, 2016b; Hasenfeld, 2009; Schmid, 2009). Each organization with its units or subsystems is unique. Thus, the best way to accomplish goals is to make individual determinations in view of the goal's context. The behavior of personnel is too varied and complicated to be easily explained by a few simple notions. Daft (2016b) clarifies:

> **Contingency** means that one thing depends on other things, and for organizations to be effective, there must be a "goodness of fit" between their design and various contingency factors [inside and outside of the organization]. What works in one setting may not work in another setting. There is no one best way. Contingency theory means *it depends*. (p. 28)

Therefore, different means are required to solve various problems depending on all of the variables involved. Daft (2016b) continues:

> For example, a government agency may experience a certain environment, use a routine technology, and desire efficiency. In this situation, a management approach that uses bureaucratic control procedures, a hierarchical structure, and formalized communications would be appropriate. Likewise, a free-flowing design and management processes [with few standardized routines and much worker discretion] work best in a high-tech company that faces an uncertain environment with a non-routine technology. The correct [management] approach is contingent on the organization's situation. (p. 28)

A strength of this theory is its flexibility. It can be applied to any situation in any organization. However, a potential weakness is its lack of direction. The core idea suggests that all variables should be evaluated and any may be significant. Where does one start when evaluating a problem or planning a procedure? Staff? Input? Output? Process? It's difficult to determine.

Focus on Ethics **5-2**

Organizational Theories and the NASW *Code of Ethics*

EP 1b

Chapter 2 introduced the following six core values emphasized in the NASW *Code of Ethics* (NASW, 2008):

1. *Service*: Providing help, resources, and benefits so that people may achieve their maximum potential.
2. *Social justice*: The broad philosophical perspective that all people have the right to enjoy equal opportunities in economic, political, and social realms.
3. *Dignity and worth of the person*: Holding in high esteem and appreciating individual value.
4. *Importance of human relationships*: Valuing the dynamic reciprocal interactions between social workers and clients, including how they communicate, think and feel about each other, and behave toward each other.
5. *Integrity*: Maintaining trustworthiness and sound adherence to moral ideals.
6. *Competence*: Having the necessary skills and abilities to perform work with clients effectively.

To what extent do the following theories comply with these professional values? Explain.

- Classical organizational theories
- Human relations theories
- Feminist theories
- The cultural perspective
- The institutional perspective
- Contingency theory

Focus on Ethics 5-2 addresses evaluating a few the theories we've discussed concerning the application of social work values and ethics.

Culture-Quality Theories

Theories stressing organizational culture and quality improvement characterized the final two decades of the twentieth century and paved the way for future approaches (Vecchio, 2006). These views

> focused on how to build a strong set of shared positive values and norms within a corporation (i.e., a strong corporate culture) while emphasizing quality, service, high performance, and flexibility. Simultaneously, Western industry developed an interest in designing an effective response to growing global competition. High quality was seen to be related to high employee commitment and loyalty, which were believed to result, partially, from greater employee involvement in decision making. To establish new mechanisms for employee involvement, changes were seen as being necessary in existing corporate cultures, and the establishment and maintenance of new cultures became the goal. Some organizations now seek to have employees openly discuss aspects of corporate culture and suggest techniques for achieving a culture that emphasizes greater teamwork and cooperation. (Vecchio, 2006, p. 12)

One application of culture-quality theories is total quality management, described in Chapter 8.

Ecosystems Theories

Chapter 1 established that ecosystems theory serves as an umbrella approach for defining and understanding the functioning of macro systems, including organizations. We have established that ecosystems theory assumes a systems theory perspective but integrates several relevant ecological concepts. Other theories can be explained using concepts and terms inherent in ecosystems theory.

Ecosystems theories focus on how organizations take resources (input) and process them into a product or service (output). They emphasize how all parts of the organization (subsystems) are interrelated and function together to produce output (Daft, 2016b).

Ecosystems theories stress the interactions of the various subsystems involved. Additionally, the importance of the environment and the impacts of other systems upon the organization are also stressed. In some ways, ecosystems theories are more flexible than many other theories. Irrational, spontaneous interactions are expected rather than ignored. Ecosystems theories emphasize constant assessment and adjustment.

LO 5-7 **Undertaking Organizational Change from an Ecosystems Perspective** Social workers want to provide clients the best services they can. Because practitioners generally work under the auspices of organizations, they want those organizations to be as effective as they can be. Other organizations with which clients have transactions should also be as effective as possible. The underlying theme is to provide the best resources and services possible to help clients.

For whatever reasons, organizations may not provide the best service possible. An agency director may make decisions in the best interest of a grant funding source instead of clients. Procedures may be out of date and bogged down. Resources might shrink so critical decisions must be made about which programs to support and which to cut. The NASW *Code of Ethics* states that social work practitioners should advocate for "open and fair" resource allocation procedures; "when clients' needs can be met, an allocation procedure should be developed that is non-discriminatory and based on appropriate and consistently applied principles" (NASW, 2008, 3.07b). Thus, practitioners have an ethical responsibility to advocate on the behalf of clients when those clients are not being served adequately. Social workers are expected to work with larger systems to improve service provision. If the agency isn't doing its job well enough, then it's the worker's responsibility to initiate and undertake positive changes. To undertake such change, you must understand how organizations function as systems. Highlight 5-3 applies ecosystems concepts both to organizations and social service agencies.

Which Organizational Theory Is Best?

EP 6

No one really knows which organizational theory is best. As time passes, theoretical perspectives rise and fall in terms of their popularity. The reality is that all organizations must contend with uncertainty in their environments, engage in constant adjustments in their operations, and be flexible in how they approach change and challenges.

Highlight **5-3**

Applying Ecosystems Concepts to Organizations and Social Service Agencies

Ecosystems concepts can be applied to social service and other organizations such as businesses and industry. We've established that they help structure ways to think about how any organization works. Organizations in general take *input*, process it, and produce some *output*. Input is the energy, information, or communication flow received from other systems. Output is what happens to input after it has gone through and been processed by some system.

Consider an industrial organization that manufactures earplugs called Plugitup. Plugitup is a *system*, a set of elements that are orderly, interrelated, and a functional whole. The system's purpose is for its elements, including employees, management, and machinery, to work together to manufacture earplugs. The system is delineated by its **boundaries**, the repeatedly occurring patterns that characterize the relationships within a system and give that system its identity. People working for Plugitup are within the system's boundaries. People not working there are outside those boundaries. Boundaries determine who is and is not part of the system. Within these boundaries are various **subsystems**, secondary or subordinate systems. These include employees working on the plant floor, engineers, and management.

Plugitup's *input* is raw materials necessary for producing earplugs. Processing involves converting raw materials into a liquid formula, pouring it into molds, and refining the final product in preparation for sale. Plugitup's *output* is the final earplug products ready for sale.

As does any company, Plugitup has a *relationship* with its consumers. A relationship is the dynamic interpersonal connection between two or more persons or systems that involves how they think about, feel about, and behave toward each other. To establish **homeostasis**—the tendency for a system to maintain a relatively stable, constant state of balance—the company must preserve lines of communication with its public and respond to the public's wants.

A *role* is an expected behavior pattern based on individuals' positions or status within the group. Part of Plugitup's management's role is to monitor public demand. Management finds that the public desires more variety in earplugs than it did two decades ago. It sponsors market surveys to get **feedback** from consumers. Feedback is a special form of input by which a system receives information about that system's own performance. Sometimes consumers give **positive feedback**,

the informational input a system receives about what it is doing correctly in order to maintain itself and thrive. For example, consumers say they particularly love fluorescent orange earplugs. This tells Plugitup what it is doing well and encourages the company to continue producing orange ones. **Negative feedback**, on the other hand, is informational input received by a system that criticizes some aspect of its functioning. For instance, consumers might indicate that the earplugs are too small for people with exceptionally large ear canals. Plugitup would then have to address the issue of earplug size. It might start offering earplugs that are more flexible in terms of size or provide a range of earplug sizes.

That there are many ways of producing and marketing earplugs reflects *equifinality*, the notion that there are many different means to the same end. Earplugs can be made in various colors and shapes, and with varying pliability. Various production procedures can be employed. In Plugitup's case, the end or goal is to produce marketable earplugs regardless of the final product's specifications and how that product is made. Therefore, instead of manufacturing only one type of earplug as it originally did decades ago, the company sustains six different lines of earplugs using somewhat different production procedures. This reflects **differentiation**, a system's tendency to move from a more simplified to a more complex existence.

The **interface** between the company and earplug consumers is the stores selling earplugs to the public. An interface is the point where two systems (including individuals, families, groups, organizations, or communities) meet each other, interact, or communicate.

If Plugitup's management does not effectively respond to public demand, the company may experience **entropy**, the natural tendency of a system to progress toward disorganization, depletion, and death. Rather, management strives to achieve **negative entropy**, the process of a system moving toward growth and development. Company management wants to continue growing and increasing earplug profits. Failing to fight entropy can result in a company going out of business or losing dominance in its field. Examples include Blockbuster Videos and Kodak.

Now compare Plugitup with a counseling center called Happyhelp. Happyhelp is a *system* whose purpose is to help clients solve problems. People working for Happyhelp

continued

Highlight **5-3** *continued*

are within the system's *boundaries*. People not working for Happyhelp are not part of the system. Various *subsystems*, including social workers, accounting staff, support staff, and management, work within Happyhelp's boundaries to provide service.

Happyhelp's *input* into the helping process includes its staff and all their skills. Plugitup's process is the conversion of raw materials into earplug products. Happyhelp's process is the application of intervention skills to help clients with many different problems, including depression, mental illness, eating disorders, and substance abuse. Happyhelp's *output* is the extent to which clients' goals are achieved and problems alleviated.

Relationships are formed between Happyhelp's social workers and its clients. Relationships are also formed among staff and between practitioners and management. Practitioners' *roles* include helping clients work on and solve problems. Role expectations include having effective skills in addition to conducting oneself professionally and ethically.

Goals include helping clients regain their *homeostasis* so that they might maintain stable and productive lives. Happyhelp also strives to maintain its own homeostasis so that it can continue to function as a helping agency. Happyhelp seeks to avoid *entropy* because it wants to continue functioning as a productive system. Thus, it strives for *negative entropy* by adding new staff, creating innovative programs, and providing for staff development. Such development reflects *differentiation* as service provision becomes more complex.

The *interface* is the contact between client and social worker, the agency's representative. Workers provide clients with *feedback* about their thoughts and behavior. Workers endeavor to give *positive feedback* to clients whenever possible to reinforce clients' strengths and positive efforts.

Various Happyhelp social workers use different treatment approaches and techniques to help people solve problems. This reflects *equifinality*, as there are many ways to conceptualize issues and pursue goals.

Critical Thinking Questions **5-4**

EP 8a

Which organizational theory or theories do you think are most effective and practical? What are your reasons for thinking so? What concepts do you think are most important? What type of organizational environment would you prefer to work in? What experiences in working for businesses or organizations have you had that influence your opinions?

Most organizations probably reflect a mixture of concepts derived from various theories. It is outside the scope of this text to explore organizational theory beyond providing a foundation to help you understand human behavior within the context of organizational macro systems.

Because of its flexibility and the complexities of working with real clients, this book will primarily view organizations from an ecosystems perspective. As we have discussed, various organizational theories emphasize different aspects of organizations in terms of how you should view their functioning and what you should consider most significant. Regardless of the theory chosen, you can use an ecosystems approach to readily describe the processes involved in organizational life. Social work literature stresses the significance of systems theories and the ecological perspective in framing social work practice, including social services management. Each management theory can be examined using concepts inherent in ecosystems theories.

At a Glance **5-1**

Organizational Theories

Theories	Major Concepts
Classical Organizational	Specifically designed formal structure
	Consistent, rigid organizational network of employees
	Clearly defined job descriptions with little discretion
	Efficiency; close supervision
Human Relations	Focus on human relations
	Strong emotional needs of employees
	Symbolic participation by employees in decision making
Feminist	Dynamics of gender-based power
	Using a gender filter
	Empowerment
	The personal as political
	The importance of process
	Diversity is strength
	Promotion of nondiscrimination, inclusion, and diversity
Cultural Perspective	Organizational development of a unique mixture of values, standards, presumptions, and practices about how things should be done
	Predictable performance
Political-Economy	Organizational adaptation to the external environment
	Emphasis on resources and power
	Constant struggle to gain power
Institutional Perspective	Organizational adaptation to the external environment
	Responses to social rules imposed by social institutions
	Search for external legitimacy and support
Contingency	All organizational elements dependent on all other elements
	Complexity of employee behavior
	No one best approach
Culture-Quality	Emphasis on organizational culture and quality improvement
Ecosystems	System
	Boundaries
	Input and output
	Interrelated subsystems
	Relationships
	Homeostasis
	Roles
	Positive and negative feedback
	Equifinality
	Differentiation
	Interface
	Entropy and negative entropy

Chapter Summary

The following summarizes this chapter's content as it relates to the learning objectives presented at the beginning of the chapter. Objectives include the following:

LO 5-1 Define organizations.

Organizations are "(1) social entities that (2) are goal directed, (3) are designed as deliberately structured and coordinated activity systems, and (4) are linked to the external environment" (Daft, 2016a, p. 13).

LO 5-2 Describe organizations providing social services.

Social services include the tasks that social work practitioners and other helping professionals perform with the goal of improving people's health, enhancing their quality of life, increasing autonomy and independence, supporting families, and helping people and larger systems improve their functioning in the social environment.

LO 5-3 Discuss several major organizational theories.

Organizational theories include classical organizational theories that reflect rigid structure in addition to emphasis on productivity and task completion. Examples are scientific management, the administrative theory of management, and bureaucracy. In contrast, human relations theories and feminist theories stress the importance of the human component in organizational functioning. Human relations theories stress people's social needs, motivation, and behavior. Feminist theories, of course, focus on the empowerment of women. The cultural perspective emphasizes the importance of expectations in the organizational environment and culture to maintain the organization's status quo. Political-economy theory focuses on how organizations adapt to external systems in the macro environment that have resources and power.

The institutional perspective also focuses on organizations' adaptation to the external environment, but in response to social rules imposed by social institutions. Contingency theory stresses careful analysis of all variables to determine those that relate directly to an issue or problem involving either personal or other organizational factors. Culture-quality theories, characterizing the end of the last century, emphasize the importance of establishing a positive organizational culture that promotes worker motivation and improves the quality of their work. Finally, ecosystems theory provides a perspective for understanding organizational functioning that fits well with social work. It provides a structured way of viewing organizations, yet focuses on how change might occur.

LO 5-4 Answer various critical thinking questions.

Critical thinking questions addressed comparing and contrasting theories, evaluation of the dynamics of gender-based power in organizations, the application of feminist theories to men, and the usefulness of organizational theories.

LO 5-5 Describe the dynamics of gender-based power in organizations.

Dynamics include: (1) "Power re-creates itself in its own image"; (2) "power elites enforce norms and systems that guarantee continuous power"; (3) "power creates a sense of entitlement" (4) "power creates invulnerability, leading to a flaunting of society's standards"; and (5) "loyalty to power overshadows other loyalties, including gender" (Burk, 2012, pp. 483–484).

LO 5-6 Provide examples of ethical issues that may arise in organizations.

Ethical issues addressed included power versus service provision in political-economy theory, and the relationship between organizational theories and the NASW *Code of Ethics*.

LO 5-7 Demonstrate the application of ecosystems concepts to organizations and social agencies.

The ecosystems concepts—including system, boundaries, input, output, subsystem, relationship, homeostasis, role, positive and negative feedback, equifinality, interface, entropy, and negative entropy—were applied to an industrial organization and to a social service agency.

Looking Ahead

This chapter discussed the various theories concerning how organizations function. The next chapter will address social service organizational settings, goals, and contexts in the macro social environment.

Competency Notes

The following identifies where Educational Policy (EP) competencies and component behaviors are discussed in the chapter.

EP 1 (Competency 1)—Demonstrate Ethical and Professional Behavior. *(p. 146)*: Social workers have the serious ethical responsibility to enhance agency functioning. *(p. 150)*: Political-economy theory has been criticized for the emphasis placed on power and access to resources instead of effective service provision to clients. This theory obviously poses difficulties for social workers who maintain professional values and ethics.

EP 1a Make ethical decisions by applying the standards of the NASW *Code of Ethics*, relevant laws and regulations, models for ethical decision making, ethical conduct of research, and additional codes of ethics as appropriate to context. *(p. 146)*: The NASW *Code of Ethics* requires social workers to strive to improve social policies and services. *(p. 159)*: Questions are raised concerning professional ethics and the issue of power versus service provision. *(p. 161)*: Questions are raised concerning the organizational theories discussed here and their compliance with the NASW *Code of Ethics*.

EP 1b Use reflection and self-regulation to manage personal values and maintain professionalism in practice situations. *(p. 161)*: The Code of Ethics includes six core values that require the social work to use reflection and management of personal values when working with clients. These include service, social justice, dignity and worth of the person, importance of human relationships, integrity, and competence.

EP 1c Demonstrate professional demeanor in behavior; appearance; and oral, written, and electronic communication. *(p. 148)*: Social workers must understand the meaning of terms commonly used in practice to demonstrate effective communication.

EP 2 (Competency 2)—Engage Diversity and Difference in Practice. *(p. 156)*: Feminist theories address issues concerning gender, a dimension of diversity. The application of feminist principles to understanding organizations addresses oppression, privilege, and power as they relate to gender. *(p. 157)*: The cultural perspective addresses culture (within the context of organizations), a dimension of diversity.

EP 2a Apply and communicate understanding of the importance of diversity and difference in shaping life experiences in practice at the micro, mezzo, and macro levels. *(p. 156)*: The application of feminist principles to understanding organizations involves examination of the effects of gender in shaping life experiences within organizations. *(p. 157)*: Organizational culture affects life experiences within the context of organizations.

EP 3 (Competency 3)—Advance Human Rights and Social, Economic, and Environmental Justice. *(p. 156)*: The application of feminist principles to understanding organizations concerns assessing and understanding the forms and mechanisms of oppression and discrimination as they relate to gender.

EP 6 (Competency 6)—Engage with Individuals, Families, Groups, Organizations, and Communities. *(p. 146)*: Engaging with organizations requires understanding that they are social entities, goal directed, deliberately structured, and linked to the external environment. *(p. 149)*: *Organizational theories* are ways to conceptualize and understand how organizations function by identifying specific concepts and explaining how these concepts relate to each other. They provide a lens through which to view the organizational environment and direct you as to which aspects of that environment should be your focus of attention. *(p. 162):* No one theory is always the best or most applicable to understanding any organization. The reality is that all organizations must contend with uncertainty in their environments, engage in constant adjustments in their operations, and be flexible in how they approach change and challenges.

EP 6a Apply knowledge of human behavior and the social environment, person-in-environment, and other multidisciplinary theoretical frameworks to engage with clients and constituencies. *(p. 146):* Social workers must understand the theoretical and conceptual frameworks concerning organizations to guide the processes of assessment, intervention, and evaluation in the context of organizations. A range of such conceptual frameworks are discussed here. Discussion focuses on the critique and application of knowledge to understand person and environment within the organizational context.

EP 7b Apply knowledge of human behavior and the social environment, person-in-environment, and other multidisciplinary theoretical frameworks in the analysis of assessment data from clients and constituencies. *(p. 149):* Generalist social work practice requires a wide knowledge base including a broad range of theoretical frameworks

for assessment. *(pp. 162–165):* Systems theory provides a useful theoretical framework for guiding the assessment process. *(p. 162):* The ecological perspective provides a useful theoretical framework for guiding the assessment process. *(p. 162):* Knowledge about human behavior and the social environment is critical for effective assessment in social work practice. Generalist practitioners must have knowledge to assess the involvement of systems of all sizes, including macro systems, when considering a planned change process.

EP 8 (Competency 8)—Intervene with Individuals, Families, Groups, Organizations, and Communities. *(p. 146):* Social workers must have knowledge about organizations to prepare themselves for interventions with organizations and communities.

EP 8a Critically choose and implement interventions to achieve practice goals and enhance capacities of clients and constituencies. *(pp. 154, 157, 164):* Critical thinking questions are raised.

EP 9b Apply knowledge of human behavior and the social environment, person-in-environment, and other multidisciplinary theoretical frameworks in the evaluation of outcomes. *(p. 146ff):* Familiarity with theories and conceptual models is critical for all steps in the planned change model, including evaluation.

Media Resources

MindTap for Social Work

 Go to MindTap® for digital study tools and resources that complement this text and help you be more successful in your course and career. There's an interactive eBook plus videos of client sessions, skill-building activities, quizzes to help you prepare for tests, apps, and more—all in one place. If your instructor didn't assign MindTap, you can find out more about it at CengageBrain .com.

6 | Social Service Organizational Settings, Goals, and Environmental Contexts

Organizations respond to human needs. Here people demonstrate on the behalf of Social Security to emphasize the importance of saving it.

LEARNING OBJECTIVES

After reading this chapter you should be able to…

6-1 Contrast primary and secondary agency settings.

6-2 Define and discuss organizational mission statements, goals, and objectives for achieving goals.

6-3 Describe faith-based services.

6-4 Discuss goal displacement.

6-5 Explain the external macro environment of social service organizations, including resources, legitimation, client sources, and relationships with other organizations.

6-6 Present an example of a humanitarian organization in the context of the global macro environment.

6-7 Explain the impact of social and economic forces on social service organizations.

6-8 Describe how federal social legislation, Temporary Assistance to Needy Families (TANF), and managed care impact agency service provision.

6-9 Answer various critical thinking questions.

6-10 Provide examples of ethical issues that may arise in managed care.

A pink slip. Perry could not believe it. He went to his office mailbox today just like he did every weekday, and there it was. The pink slip said he was being laid off in two weeks.

Perry had been a social worker for a Protective Services unit at Rutabaga County Department of Social Services for four years. Although very demanding, he loved his job. He worked in a special program stressing family preservation that emphasized keeping families together if possible. It involved intensive work with families over limited time periods. Perry's goal was to help families get back on their emotional feet and function permanently without social service assistance.

With a relatively small caseload of families, Perry could provide the intensive services families at risk of child abuse or neglect desperately needed. Sometimes, he served as an educator, providing help with child management, anger control, or budgeting. He usually served as counselor and support system, focusing on family strengths and assisting with members' problem solving. Other times, he was a broker, linking families with needed resources like health care or grants for paint and home repairs to comply with building codes. He even helped families paint rooms and fix windows to avoid having children removed for neglect because of inadequate housing conditions. The intent was to help families in crisis and under extreme economic and emotional pressure become stronger, healthier, and independent. As a result, the risk for child abuse or neglect was significantly decreased and the need for placement of children in foster care at the county's great expense eliminated. Perry felt he had provided enormous help to many families over the years.

In the past, getting people off expensive assistance and service-provision rolls had delighted county administrators gravely focused on budget crises. The external environmental climate, however, had abruptly changed. Severe budget cuts forced agency administrators to make tough decisions. They decided Perry's family preservation program was much too expensive to continue. He served too few clients to warrant his salary. Perry no longer had a job. His clients would no longer receive the services they needed.

It was not Perry's fault that he lost his job. Nor was it his fault that he could no longer help his clients, as he had in the past. His agency's external environment had shifted, and resources had been reduced. The result was a change in the agency's goals that no longer made his program a priority. Forces in the external environment directly affected his agency's ability to provide services.

Chapter 5 discussed organizational theories and some basic knowledge about organizations. This chapter will continue examining organizations within the social environment, both internally and externally. Two important concepts concerning the internal environment are agency setting and organizational goals. A range of variables in the external environment directly affects structure and human behavior in the internal environment.

The Importance of Organizations for Social Workers

EP 6, 7c

Organizations are particularly important to practitioners for three basic reasons. First, they employ workers. An organization's policies, goals, and restrictions will directly affect what work practitioners can and cannot do with clients. The second reason for an organization's significance is that sometimes the organization and not the client will be the source of problems. Workers therefore need to evaluate how well their organizations are functioning to do their own work effectively. Third, it's necessary to analyze and understand an agency's functioning prior to undertaking any macro-level changes. We have established that the NASW *Code of Ethics* obligates social workers to advocate and work for improvements in their agency settings when necessary.

Social workers may need to participate in organizational change to enhance agency functioning and effectiveness. This section's purpose is not to provide a detailed explanation of organizational behavior. Rather, it is to alert new social workers to internal organizational factors that can affect their ability to do their jobs. Two primary concepts important in understanding the internal environment of organizations are agency settings and organizational goals.

It is necessary to briefly comment about the terms used in this book. Organizational theories are taken primarily from the business and management literature. However, they apply to all organizations, including social services agencies. For our purposes, we will use the terms *organization, social services agency, social service agency, social agency,* and *agency* interchangeably. The chapters on organizations in this book focus on the social services agencies in which social workers practice and clients receive services.

Agency Settings LO 6-1

Social workers usually work within one of two types of organizational settings, primary or secondary. Each type of setting has implications for effective practice and for how workers experience their work environment.

Primary Settings

Primary settings are those agencies where social work is the main or primary profession employed. Most public social service agencies are primary settings. It is common for the administrators, supervisors, and most of the workers to be social workers with social work degrees and titles. Although there may be other occupations or professions present (e.g., homemaker service providers[1] or psychologists), they represent a minority of the staff.

Because most of the staff and administrators are social workers, they tend to share similar professional values and perspectives. Their education and training are typically similar. One benefit of these settings is that workers never must explain what social workers do. Everyone knows and understands the social work role. This cannot be said for secondary settings.

Secondary Settings

Secondary settings are characterized by the presence of a variety of professional staff. The main service provided by the agency is not social services. Typical examples are hospitals and schools. In a hospital, medical care of patients is the primary

---

[1] *Homemaker services* help clients remain in their homes by offering assistance in a variety of activities, including shopping, laundry, housework, preparation of meals, and sometimes transportation to medical or other appointments.

service. Medically trained personnel (e.g., nurses and physicians) comprise the largest segment of the professional staff. Most of the administrative staff and supervisors will have a medical background. Social work is just one of several ancillary professions contributing to the overall goal of medical care provision. Other professions include dietitians, pharmacists, and chaplains, to name a few.

The wealth of disciplines and professional perspectives can produce a challenging environment for social work. Typically, social workers must learn the language (for instance, medical terminology or relevant abbreviations) used by the other professions. Unlike primary settings, a secondary setting such as a hospital is usually operated within a definite pecking order controlled by other professions. Physicians are at the top of that hierarchy. Social workers are not. This sometimes means that social work values and perspectives will clash with those of the physicians and other medical personnel. Highlight 6-1 provides an example illustrating how this can work.

Highlight 6-1

Case Example—Working in a Secondary Setting

Cristina, a hospital social worker, was working with Tyrone, a 61-year-old patient with Parkinson's disease, along with his family. **Parkinson's disease** is a chronic, progressive disorder that may produce tremors in various part of the body, muscular rigidity, slowed movement, and balance and coordination impairments. Signs of the impairments may differ from one person to another and tend to be experienced in the middle to later years of life. Tyrone had been hospitalized for a malfunctioning of his kidneys that had nothing to do with his Parkinson's disease. However, nurses referred Tyrone to Cristina when they observed him falling several times while walking from his bed to the bathroom. These nurses felt that Tyrone would have difficulty returning home without special equipment such as a walker or a wheelchair. They indicated he might even require some special placement instead of returning to his home.

Cristina met with Tyrone. She found it very difficult to understand him, as the Parkinson's disease was seriously affecting his ability to formulate words. However, with some difficulty she could discuss his situation with him. He stated vehemently that he wanted to return home. He emphasized how the disease "wasn't that bad." He stressed that he would be all right now that the kidney problem had subsided, if he could just get home!

Cristina also spoke alone with Tyrone's wife, Ursula, age 59. Ursula felt that Tyrone was denying the seriousness of his condition. She said that his muscular control and balance had deteriorated significantly in the past four months. Ursula told Cristina that Tyrone had been a university engineering professor at a prestigious private college. She explained that it was very difficult for him to admit to his increasingly serious weakness. Ursula also expressed concern about her ability to care for him adequately at home. Tyrone was a large hulk of a man. Ursula indicated that it was impossible for her to lift him if he should fall. She felt that someone needed to be with him always. Yet, she hesitated to take him out of the home and place him in a health care facility. She felt it might break his spirit and his heart.

Cristina met with Tyrone and Ursula individually one more time and, finally, together for their last encounter. She discussed with them a variety of possibilities. These included obtaining supportive equipment, widening the doorways in their home, installing ramps for wheelchair accessibility, and referring them to various other supportive service providers. The latter included a beeper Tyrone could use to call for help in the event he fell. Additionally, Cristina began arranging for a visiting nurse to assist Ursula with Tyrone's care and to provide respite care one afternoon each week to give Ursula a break.

Cristina felt good about her work with Tyrone and Ursula. She felt she had helped them establish a viable plan for the present. It could maintain Tyrone in his own home until his increasing disability required more extensive treatment and, possibly, placement in some special facility. Cristina had already contacted the recommended services to establish their availability and viability in Tyrone's case. The next step

continued

Highlight 6-1 *continued*

was to finalize the plans and put them into place before Tyrone's upcoming discharge.

Cristina came to work the next morning and went around as usual, checking her patients' charts to see what was happening and monitor progress. When she got to Tyrone's room, it was empty. Initially, Cristina assumed that a nurse or volunteer had taken him for a walk to get some daily exercise.

However, Cristina was shocked as she found and read his chart. It stated he was being transported this very day to a health care facility. What about the plans she had made with Tyrone and Ursula? What about Tyrone's adamant feelings about remaining in his own home? In disbelief, she stared at the signature of Tyrone's attending physician, Dr. Strangelove. Dr. Strangelove had totally ignored all that she had written in the chart about Tyrone's discharge planning. A deepening fury began to paint her emotions. How dare Dr. Strangelove do this! How dare he act as if she did not even exist!

Luckily, Cristina became so busy that day that she had little more time to think about Tyrone, Ursula, or Dr. Strangelove. By the next morning, she had simmered down quite a bit. After all, Tyrone and Ursula had the right to choose their own destinies. She was just there to help them if she could.

When she later talked to the head nurse about the matter, Cristina was enlightened about what it meant to work in a secondary setting. She abruptly found out that the physician's word ruled in a medical facility. Apparently, Dr. Strangelove was personal friends with Ursula's son Devin, who was also a physician. Dr. Strangelove and Devin sat down first with Ursula and later with Tyrone to discuss their feelings about Tyrone's condition and his and Ursula's future. Both physicians felt strongly that it was ridiculous for Tyrone to return home. Both felt it was far beyond Ursula's marital responsibility to "sacrifice" herself for Tyrone. They apparently had urged and eventually persuaded Ursula to pursue placing Tyrone in a residential facility. It was the head nurse's opinion that Tyrone felt too weak to fight all three of these people and voice his own desires. So, defeated, he complied with their recommendations.

Cristina was not convinced that the decision was the correct one for either Tyrone or Ursula. However, she understood that they had every right to make their own decisions, regardless of the dynamics involved in the decision-making process. Cristina also learned that she had significantly less status than physicians did in this secondary setting.

Mission Statements, Goals, and Objectives   LO 6-2

EP 6, 7c

Many, if not most, social services agencies have a **mission statement**, a declaration of the organization's purpose that "establishes broad and relatively permanent parameters within which goals are developed and specific programs designed" (Kettner, Moroney, & Martin, 2017, p. 109). It also includes what client populations are to be served, what needs should be met, and how that will occur. For example, the Center for Youth and Family Solutions, a private nonprofit social services agency, has a mission statement saying it will "engage and serve children and families in need with dignity, compassion, and respect by building upon individual and community strengths to resolve life challenges together" (Center for Youth and Family Solutions, 2017, p. 1). This is a broad statement that encompasses a range of programs, including the following:

- Comprehensive behavioral health counseling
- Foster care services
- Adoption services
- Youth intervention programs and services
- Guardian angel residential services for youth
- In-home counseling for seniors and volunteer companions (p. 1)

Kettner and his colleagues (2017) provide two other examples of mission statements. One concerns a family service agency whose mission is "to promote family strength and stability in a manner that allows each individual to achieve his or her potential while, at the same time, supporting strong and productive interrelationships among family members" (p. 110). Still another mission statement involves an agency offering services to alcohol and drug addicts. Its mission is "to promote and support the achievement of a positive and productive lifestyle, including steady employment and stable family and human relationships, for those formerly addicted to chemical substances" (p. 110). The "key" to a mission statement is that it "should focus on what lies ahead for its clients or consumers if the agency is successful in addressing their problems and meeting their needs" (Kettner et al., 2017, p. 110).

Organizational Goals

Mission statements identify the organization's basic goals. In addition, most agencies also have a set of **organizational goals**. These goals typically relate back to the mission statement. Kettner and his colleagues (2017) offer this definition of organizational goals and discuss their purpose:

> Goals are statements of expected outcomes dealing with the problem that the program is attempting to prevent, eradicate, or ameliorate. They are responsive to problems and needs, and represent an ideal or hoped-for outcome. . . . Goals provide a [general] sense of programmatic direction and need not be measureable or achievable. . . .
>
> Goal statements provide a beacon that serves as a constant focal point and lends a sense of direction to the program. They are the reasons for which the program is funded and implemented. They are statements of preferences or values. (p. 112)

How does an organization establish its mission statement and goals? As services must be in line with current social welfare policy and legislation, so must the mission statement and official goals. Mission and goals will also reflect the organization's stance in terms of treatment modality in addition to its values.

Social service organizations and agencies, then, formulate goals to address any of a wide range of needs and problems concerning human well-being. Social service organizations are supposed to use their resources to address these needs and remedy problems. The establishment of goals directs this process.

To understand an organization's functioning, it is helpful to think in terms of "official" and "operational goals"; Lauffer (2011) explains:

> Agencies use their *official* goals to say something about where they are headed. These goals are used to explain agency purposes and to gather support and legitimacy for their operations. They are often found in such formal documents as agency mission statements, incorporation papers, Web sites, annual reports, and promotional materials.
>
> In contrast, *operational* goals are likely to be inferred from actual practices. Operational goals can be explicit or implicit. They are explicit when spelled out in departmental program objectives, project proposals, or program priorities. They are implicit when inferred from staff and departmental behaviors. [In other words, implicit goals, although not spelled out, reflect actual work and performance in the agency on an everyday basis.] (p. 27)

Why must we make the distinction between official and operational goals? The problem is that official goals may have very little to do with an agency's actual operational goals. Reasons for this will be discussed more thoroughly later when we address the concept of goal displacement.

Goals provide social services agencies with general direction concerning *what* should happen, but not with specific guidance regarding *how* it should be done. Highlight 6-2 discusses how agencies structure the process of carrying out goals by identifying objectives.

Highlight **6-2**

Objectives Indicate How to Achieve Goals

EP 7c

Goals are general statements about what an organization wants to accomplish. They usually don't specify exactly how to achieve them. **Objectives** are smaller, behaviorally specific sub-goals that serve as stepping stones on the way to accomplishing the main goal. Brody and Nair (2014) explain:

Typically, goals represent long-term endeavors, sometimes as long as three to five years, and may even be timeless. Examples of these goals statements would be "improving access to health care services for low-income persons" or "reducing racism in our community." . . . Objectives represent relevant, attainable, measurable, and time-limited ends to be achieved. They are relevant because they fit within the general mission and goals of the organization and because they relate to problems identified by the organization. They are attainable because they can be realized. They are measurable because achievement is based upon tangible, concrete, and usually quantifiable results. They are time limited (usually a year); this time frame helps the organization demonstrate concrete results within a specified period. (p. 55)

Kettner and his colleagues (2017) recommend that the following questions be asked to establish "clear, specific measurable, time-limited, and realistic" objectives that the agency is committed to achieve:

- *Use of clear, unambiguous terms.* Is the objective clear? Does it mean the same thing to anyone who reads the statement?
- *Expected results.* Does the objective specify results to be achieved, including numbers and changes in conditions?

- *Measurable results.* Is the objective written in such a way that it can be measured? Are measurement criteria incorporated into the objective?
- *Achievability.* Does the statement indicate a time limit within which or a target date by which the objective will be achieved?
- *Accountability.* Is the objective realistic, given our technology and knowledge as well as available resources? (p. 134)

Brody and Nair (2014) identify four basic types of objectives used in social service agencies—*impact, service, operational,* and *product.*

Impact objectives specify outcomes to be achieved as a result of program activities. They detail the return expected on the organization's investment of time, personnel, and resources. The following are examples:

- To place 20 children in adoptive homes in one year
- To secure jobs for 35 juvenile delinquents in 5 months
- To increase the number of foster children reunited with their natural parents from 40 to 50 by June 30

Service objectives are the organization's tally of activities provided or services rendered. Sometimes these are referred to as **activity or process objectives**. Examples include the following:

- To serve 300 clients in the program year
- To conduct 680 interviews
- To provide 17 neighborhood assemblies
- To interview 20 children needing foster homes

Operational objectives convey the intent to improve the general operation of the organization. Examples include the following:

continued

Highlight **6-2** *continued*

- To sponsor four in-service training workshops for 40 staff
- To obtain a pilot project grant of $10,000 within 6 months
- To increase the number of volunteers by 150
- To reduce staff turnover from 20 percent to 10 percent annually

Operational objectives are essential to enhance the way an organization functions. They are a means to the end for which the organization was established. By providing in-service training, for example, an organization improves the way it serves its target populations.

Product objectives "are designed to provide a tangible outcome to benefit a target population or a community. . . . The following are examples of product objectives:

- To obtain passage of House Bill 41
- To develop a neighborhood family support system
- To review and critique a specific piece of legislation
- To open four schools in the evening for recreation
- To provide a media effort on teen pregnancy prevention
- To coordinate a communitywide campaign on mental health." (Brody, 2014, pp. 56–57)

One aspect of many private organizations that involves organizational goals concerns a spiritual dimension. Some social service organizations are faith-based—that is, sponsored by or affiliated with a religious or spiritual organization. Such organizations often state in their mission, goals, and objectives the assumptions that undergird their services. The following section discusses faith-based social service organizations.

EP 2

LO 6-3 **Mission and Goals Involving Spirituality: Faith-Based Social Services** A common context in which social workers address issues in spirituality and religion involves faith-based organizations. **Spirituality** concerns people's "values, beliefs, mission, awareness, subjectivity, experience, sense of purpose and direction, and a kind of striving toward something greater than oneself"; **religion** is "a set of beliefs and practices of an organized religious institution. . . . It is important to note that *religion* is one form of spirituality. The two concepts are not mutually exclusive" (Frame, 2003, pp. 3–4).

To varying degrees, faith-based social services often incorporate aspects of spirituality and religion into their mission statement and goals. For example, a mission statement might include "spiritual nurture" as one of the agency's goals or describe a "program as 'Christ-centered'" (Hartford Institute, 2017).

Although the United States has slowly become less religious over the past 30 years, faith-based social services remain a significant factor in meeting social welfare needs. Because it is possible that you will either work in faith-based agencies or be working with them in some capacity, we will spend some time discussing them here.

Faith-based organizations may offer a broad assortment of services. These can include assistance in preparing for obtaining employment, literacy training, child care, and English as a Second Language (ESL) classes and those that will help a person complete the requirements for a GED (General Education Development). The GED is a means for obtaining the equivalent of a high school diploma for those who have never achieved this milestone. Some organizations provide transportation, temporary or permanent housing, food, shelter, clothing, and a variety of social services.

Tangenberg (2005) provides some examples of how diverse faith-based programs can be in terms of service programming, conceptualization of faith, and expression of spirituality:

The Daylight Shelter organization provides overnight shelter and meals to homeless individuals and families. Prayer occurs before meals, and evening worship services open to the public are offered five times each week. Engagement in religious activities is optional. Men and women also may choose to participate in 12-step recovery programs that are separated by gender and have a strong religious focus. Religious activities in the recovery programs are required and are discussed before participation so referrals to secular programs can be made if necessary. . . . Describing the program's spiritual base, the Director said:

"Our program is Christ-centered. . . . [Program participants] have to go to church—they pick their own churches—we do devotions every morning, we have Bible studies three times a week, we have Bible classes." . . .

[In contrast,] [t]he Jackson Community Center is an organization with no religious references in its name or program activities, although it is closely affiliated with a large Protestant denomination. Primary services include adult basic education and employment preparation. . . .

Some board members must be members of the founding Christian denomination, and ties to the denomination are strong, although there are no expectations regarding the faith commitments of staff members. Values of dignity, care, and compassion are emphasized rather than a specific religious ideology, and financial and volunteer support is frequently sought from the religious community. . . .

[Yet, another example involves] Peace House [which] is a drop-in center that provides meals and emergency services for homeless men and women and outreach to former center guests who are in jail or prison. . . .

Although it originated under Catholic auspices, Peace House includes staff from various faith traditions sharing spiritual values of compassion and service. No organized religious programs are available for guests, and no religious symbols are displayed, although staff meet daily for meditation and prayer and have a small weekly liturgy. (pp. 203–204)

Many issues can surface when social workers enter the realm of spirituality in a faith-based setting. Questions can arise regarding how the worker's own sense of spirituality coincides or contrasts with the host agency's perspective. There are no easy answers to such questions. A worker may struggle with personal views that are at odds with the agency's. A practitioner must always address such issues in an ethical and professional manner. If views between the agency and the worker are too incongruent, leaving the agency may be an appropriate solution.

EP 6b

Canda and Furman (2010) comment on spirituality and social work:

Spirituality is the heart of helping. It is the heart of empathy and care, the pulse of compassion, the vital flow of practice wisdom, and the driving energy of service. . . . There is mounting empirical evidence and practice wisdom that a person's sense of positive spiritual meaning, purpose, and connectedness along with participation in supportive aspects of religious communities are associated with enhanced well-being" (pp. 3–4). It is important to be clear that the social worker's role is not proselytizing or converting clients in a specific spiritual or religious direction or derogating anyone else's religious or spiritual beliefs. Rather, it is recognizing the important impact that spirituality and religion have on some individuals and building on the strengths and resources that are available to improve the quality of the client's life.

Multiple Goals

Social service organizations usually are complex entities. Therefore, they frequently aim to accomplish multiple goals. There are many reasons for this. First, agencies must hold themselves accountable to legislative requirements and constraints. For instance, an organization providing group homes for children with intellectual disabilities must conform to a range of state licensing rules that mandate the minimum standards for service provision. These include the maximum number of clients in any residence, the amount of space required per child, the staff-to-client ratio, how the kitchen and dining areas should be equipped, and even the requirement that toilet seats be open or split in the front instead of closed.

Multiple goals also occur because many social service agencies may serve a range of client groups. For example, one organization may provide daycare services, vocational training, adoption services, and foster care all at the same time. The Center for Youth and Family Solutions, described earlier, provides another example of an organization sponsoring a wide range of programs pursuing many goals. Each segment of the agency pursues its own goals within the context of the larger organizational environment that has more encompassing organizational goals.

Additionally, organizations may be held accountable to different segments of the public, each making its own demands upon an agency's performance and subsequently its goals. Such public entities may include other social service agencies, groups formed because of common goals or pursuits (**interest groups**), legislative entities, licensing and regulating bodies, and professional organizations. For example, a child advocacy interest group may pressure a social services agency specializing in helping survivors of domestic violence to increase its standards for temporary shelter of mothers and their children. Likewise, professional organizations may require the same agency to provide minimum in-service training sessions for staff in various job positions. We have established that in-service training is instructional programming provided by an employer that brings in experts to help employees develop skills and understanding intended to help them improve their work performance. Hence, the agency must pursue both goals in addition to many other goals established for numerous other reasons.

Goal Displacement   LO 6-4

EP 6

A major problem encountered by workers in organizations involves **goal displacement**. Goal displacement was originally defined as "substitution of a legitimate goal with another goal which the organization was not developed to address, for which resources were not allocated and which it is not known to serve" (Etzioni, 1964, p. 10). Goal displacement can occur whenever an organization pursues goals that are inconsistent with their mission or original reason for existing. This can happen when the original goal has been met and a new one must be identified or when other factors move the organization off course. Many nonprofit agencies have accepted grants that required them to pursue courses of action that are different from their original goals. Sometimes, it occurs when the agency is in financial trouble and the grant appears to offer a means to continue operation. It can also occur when an organization begins pursuing its leaders' personal interests rather than achieving its official goals (Netting, Kettner, McMurty, & Thomas, 2017).

Goal displacement is a common problem for bureaucracies because of their size and scope of responsibilities. An organization with multiple goals can simply end up focusing on the means to an end rather than the end itself. For example, a desire to maintain appropriate records as the organization achieves its goals can become its primary focus. Then, maintaining accuracy and getting information recorded as soon as possible starts consuming time originally spent on achieving the goal of serving agency clients. Many times, this occurs slowly over the years and is not discovered until a new staff member, director, or consultant points it out.

In summary, goal displacement occurs when an organization continues to function but no longer achieves the goals it's supposed to. Sometimes, it happens when the *process* of achieving goals takes precedence over the actual goal *attainment*. A typical scenario in social service organizations is when the rules and following those rules become more important than providing services to clients.

It should be noted that goal displacement can also involve positive changes in goals. A classic example is the March of Dimes, which began as an organization dedicated to raising money to eradicate polio, historically a major childhood disease. With the discovery of a polio vaccine, the disease ceased to be a major health problem in the United States and Canada. Instead of going out of business, however, the organization shifted its goal to raising money to combat birth defects. The new goal had one advantage over the polio-related goal. Instead of focusing on a single disease, the organization now directed its attention to a large category of problems. With such a broad scope, the organization would probably never run out of new childhood health problems to combat. Therefore, it would be unlikely that it would ever again face a similar dilemma of goal displacement.

This commentary is not intended to be critical of the March of Dimes, or any other organization. It is a fact of organizational life that agencies seldom go out of existence. Once a goal is achieved, most organizations do not disappear. Instead, they shift their attention to new goals. This process only becomes a problem when the means to the goals assume a life of their own. When this happens, agencies may place greater emphasis on crossing T's and dotting I's than on providing effective service to clients.

For instance, consider the example concerning the county social services department in Highlight 6-3. As a worker in that agency, there are several things you might target for change. These include working with other workers and administration to significantly shorten the tedious forms. You might also explore ways to get information out to community residents regarding the documentation and needed information they must bring when applying for services. Simple things like putting up clearly visible signs instructing people where to go when they first enter the building might be helpful. Even advocating for waiting room chairs made to make people comfortable might be useful.

Highlight **6-3**

An Example of Goal Displacement—Process Supersedes Progress

EP 5b

A large county Department of Social Services (previously referred to as "the public welfare department") comes to mind. It is located in the shell of an old department store with high ceilings and a myriad of small worker cubicles somewhat resembling a mammoth beehive. All outside windows have been sealed with bricks because of "the heating and ventilation problems." No one really knows what that means. However, everyone inside the building knows that the building's interior is isolated from the outside world.

When entering the main door of the building, it is extremely difficult to figure out where to go for what kind of services. This is true even if you're a professional social worker, let alone if you're a client entering the building for the first time. Consider what it would be like if you were a client applying for services from this agency. You probably must stand in line for 15 or 20 minutes simply to get the information you need to find out where to go.

When you finally wander into a waiting area for the services you need, you must stand in line again for another 20 minutes or so to get the forms you must fill out for the services you need. You then take the 20 pages of complicated forms, which you must fill out meticulously, and take a seat. The chairs are made of hard plastic. There are large "dust bunnies" (sometimes referred to as "dinosaur dust

bunnies") rolling around your feet. It takes approximately an hour to fill out the forms. This is assuming you can read well in English. You probably do not understand some of the questions, so you leave the spaces blank. You then take the forms up to the desk, where they are placed in a pile. You must wait your turn to see an intake worker (i.e., someone who begins the process to provide services). You wait two to three hours.

Finally, your name is called and you are instructed to go to Cubicle 57 to see Ms. Hardmoney. You enter Cubicle 57 and see Ms. Hardmoney sitting at her desk and reading your forms. You then begin a discussion with her concerning the additional information she needs to process your application for services. It seems, she indicates, that several critical elements of information are missing. Look at those blanks. She then says you must get the critical information before you can continue the application process. The critical information is somewhere at home. Well, that's all right. Just go home, get it, and start this whole process over again tomorrow. At least you know where the waiting room is now.

In this example, the organization was supposed to be providing services to people in need. However, the complicated process, commonly called *red tape*, became much more important to the organization's staff than whether clients received needed services.

Ecosystems Theory, Organizations, and Goal Displacement

EP 6

We have established that it is helpful to view social service organizations in terms of ecosystems theories' concepts. Many of the notions involved are like those used in reference to business and industry. For example, in industry, resources or *input* are *processed* by the organizational system, which turns out some product or *output*. Figure 6-1 illustrates this sequence as *ecosystems concepts*. Essentially, the same thing happens in social service organizations. They take resources (*input*) and, in response to social forces and institutionalized values, apply some *process* (procedures for providing services) to produce *output* (actual service provision or some other benefits for clients).

Often when goal displacement occurs, however, the emphasis is placed on the process rather than the product. The organizational system begins to consider the rigid process of providing services as its major function. The *process*, rather than effective provision of services, then becomes the organization's *product*.

Goal attainment comprises what is supposed to happen through the intervention process. Illustrated in Figure 6-1, the input (in the form of resources) is supposed to be used on behalf of clients in the intervention process. Hence, "$" refers

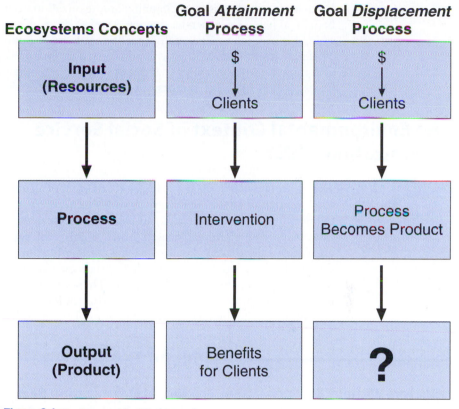

Figure 6-1 The Process of Goal Displacement

to resources with an arrow pointing to "clients" in the top box in the goal attainment process. The result is supposed to be positive benefits for clients. Thus, an arrow points from the "$ to clients" box to the middle box that refers to the "intervention" process. The intervention process involves whatever treatment process or technology the organization uses to help its clients. Finally, an arrow points from the "intervention" box down to the "benefits for clients" box, illustrating what is supposed to happen in an agency's goal attainment process.

Figure 6-1 also illustrates *goal displacement* on the far right. Here, input (in the form of resources) is used to maintain the *process* of what is done with those resources. In essence, the process becomes the *product*. The positive impacts on clients are somehow lost and forgotten as agency personnel strive to maintain and complete the process. Figure 6-1 depicts this with arrows leading down from the "$ to clients" box to the "process becomes product" box. The arrow leading from the latter box down to the "?" box reflects how the actual results for clients become relatively unimportant and possibly unknown.

Goal Displacement and Generalist Practice

This discussion's intent is to enhance your awareness of problems often encountered in organizational service provision. Understanding the dynamics of organizational behavior is a prerequisite to changing an organization's behavior for the clients' benefit. When a social service agency ceases to serve clients as effectively as possible, it is your job as a generalist practitioner to try to improve service provision. This may involve advocating with administrators for a new program, suggesting and promoting agency policy changes, or initiating a fundraising project to provide Christmas toys for needy families.

The Environmental Context of Social Service Organizations LO 6-5

EP 8b

The environmental context in which a social services organization functions is critically important to the organization's ability to pursue and attain its goals. This is not only true for local, statewide, and national organizations, but also for organizations that are internationally based. Much of this book addresses organizations as we perceive them every day in our local community environment. However, we should also attend to organizations that operate internationally. Such international organizations are abundant and thriving. Therefore, it is important to establish a perspective regarding how international organizations may function in the global environment. Highlight 6-4 provides an example of an independently functioning

---

Highlight 6-4

Doctors Without Borders—An International Organization Seeking Improved Health and Social Justice in the Global Macro Environment LO 6-6

EP 3, 3a, 3b, 5b, 5c, 8, 8b, 8c, 8d

It's easy to concentrate on your own country and how organizations function within your own national context. However, as you know, the world now is a heavily interrelated global community. It's important for social workers to "understand the global interconnections of oppression and human rights violations" and be knowledgeable about organizational "strategies to promote social and economic justice and human rights" around the world (CSWE, 2015, EP 3). Therefore, a good example of such an organization—Doctors Without Borders/Médecins Sans Frontières—will be described here.

Doctors Without Borders, or Médecins Sans Frontières (MSF), is a private international organization that was created by doctors and journalists in France in 1971. In 2015, it provided medical and health services to 69 different countries. As an independent organization, it helps people whose very existence is threatened by war, illness, epidemics, natural disasters, famine, and other catastrophes. In addition to

physicians and other health care providers, MSF also is open to other professionals. While MSF does not take sides in disputes, it does describe the conditions and plight of people it serves, with a goal of ending the crisis (MSF, 2016).

Since 1980, MSF has opened offices in 28 countries. Today, MSF employs more than 35,000 people across the world. Since its founding, MSF has treated over a hundred million patients—with 8.6 million outpatient consultations being carried out in 2015 alone.

MSF remains fiercely independent of both governments and institutions. MSF also reserves the right to speak out to bring attention to neglected crises, challenge inadequacies or abuse of the aid system, and advocate for improved medical treatments and protocols.

MSF rejects the idea that poor countries deserve third-rate medical services and strives to provide high-quality care to patients. Simultaneously, and with equal vigor, MSF continuously seeks to improve the organization's own practices. (MSF, 2017, p. 1) humanitarian international organization. Chapter 13 focuses on social justice and the global community.

Regardless of the scope of an organization, at least four environmental dimensions directly affect that organization's ability to survive and prosper: available resources, legitimation, client sources, and relationships with other organizations. The following sections examine the significance of each of these factors.

Resources

Social service agencies must have financial support to survive. They must have access to at least two types of resources—financial and personnel.

There are no less than five potential types of financial resources for agencies (Weinbach & Taylor, 2015). First, the government may allocate money for services or financial payments.

Second, private agencies and foundations may contribute to agency service provision. An example of a private funding agency is the **United Way**, an international alliance of 1,800 local organizations that raises funds for allocation to various social service organizations and other projects; goals include enhancing education, attaining financial stability, and promoting healthy lives. It raises in excess of $5 billion per year (United Way, 2017). **Foundations** are organizations that collect private funds and distribute them for a variety of purposes. These may include artistic, educational, health, social welfare, and other causes that meet the foundation's criteria. A third funding resource for agencies involves fees (collected directly from clients or from third-party payments) (Weinbach & Taylor, 2011, p. 273). **Third-party payments** are reimbursements to service providers from government agencies or insurance companies.

A fourth source of financial support includes grants and contracts. A **grant** is "a sum of money given to individuals or organizations to perform work in their areas of expertise. . . . [In this context, grants] are sums of money awarded competitively to agencies to initiate, expand, or help to support a social program" (Weinbach & Taylor, 2011, p. 247). **Contracts** "are agreements between two organizations or bodies that specify that one will provide certain services in exchange for payments from the other" (Kirst-Ashman & Hull, 2018a, p. 540). In other words, one organization pays another organization to provide services.

A fifth funding source for agencies involves financial gifts and contributions provided by businesses, corporations, or individual donors (Weinbach & Taylor, 2015). Agencies may undertake **fundraising**, the process of soliciting and raising financial resources through any of a variety of means. Such means may include soliciting donations, sponsoring participatory activities, or organizing sales of donated items, among many other approaches.

Other than financial resources, a second type of resource critical for a social services agency involves personnel. What kind of staffing does the agency have? What are their professional credentials? Are staff qualified and plentiful enough to carry out their duties effectively? Highlight 6-5 provides a case example involving personnel resources.

Legitimation

Another environmental dimension impacting social service agencies is **legitimation** (Schmid, 2009, p. 412). We have already briefly mentioned the importance of

---

| Highlight **6-5** |

Case Example—Personnel Resources

A debate raged in one state between professional social workers, on the one hand, and certain county social services agency administrators on the other. (It might be noted that many of the latter administrators were not social workers by profession.) The battle ensued when professional certification for social workers was first initiated in the state. Most professional social workers adamantly maintained that it was critically important for workers calling themselves "social workers" to have graduated from accredited social work programs and have the requisite experience.

Some rural county social service agency administrators, on the other hand, staunchly maintained that there were not enough graduates from professional social work programs to fill all the positions available in their rural agencies. They declared that the only workers they could attract to fill their agencies' job positions were graduates having other degrees, such as those in sociology and psychology. These administrators emphasized that most social work graduates were attracted to the state's larger, more exciting urban areas.

Much to the dismay of professional social work educators, a faction of sociologists teaching in local universities supported the county administrators' view and politically lobbied on the former's behalf. These sociologists were concerned that graduates with sociology degrees would be able to find employment as easily as graduates with social work degrees. To a great extent, this approach coincided with the sociologists' own interests, namely, to maintain a higher number of sociology majors.

Most professional social workers and social work educators were appalled. None of the sociology programs were accredited. Therefore, these programs were held accountable to no standards such as those mandating the teaching of practice skills, the infusion of professional values and ethics throughout the curriculum, a substantial field internship, and a focus on human diversity. All social work programs, on the other hand, were required to adhere faithfully to such standards.

Upon further investigation, the state association of social workers established that the major reason the complaining rural county administrators were unable to recruit social work graduates was that these administrators paid near-to-minimum-wage salaries. Additionally, the state Social Work Education Association determined that virtually hundreds of graduates were being turned out from several state universities within 100 miles of these counties. There were plenty of graduates available to fill positions—that is, if the counties would pay salaries appropriate for professional social workers.

This environmental dimension substantially affected the ability of county social service agencies to provide professional services. If agencies were not required to hire professional social workers, but could employ sociology or psychology graduates, regardless of their training in skills and values, quality of service would be seriously curtailed. The agencies' personnel resources would directly affect the agencies' ability to provide service to clients.

---

legislative requirements and constraints with respect to an agency's organizational goals. Legitimation is the condition where the external environment provides an agency with the appropriate status or authorization to perform agency functions and pursue agency goals. An agency must be legally viable. Once established, the agency must continue to abide by the rules upon which its existence is based.

Consider, however, if an agency does not follow the appropriate rules and regulations. For example, a health care center for older adults failed to follow the rules concerning maintenance of its bedridden patients, especially those with Alzheimer's disease. Clients' relatives visiting the center reported to the state's licensing agency that they had observed several seriously disturbing incidents during their visits. These observations included clients having wallowed in their own feces for over a day, staff slapping clients in the face when these clients refused to cooperate, and employees depriving clients of food to punish them for poor behavior. Once the health care center's practices became known and were investigated by state authorities, the agency was closed. It no longer possessed the legitimation and accountability needed to support its existence.

Client Sources

The third environmental dimension affecting agencies involves the availability of clients. A range of client resources is necessary to provide enough clients to keep the agency financially afloat. Client resources include other public and private agencies that make referrals. They also include individual potential clients who seek services for themselves. In other words, an agency cannot last very long without enough clients to sustain it.

One agency, for example, provided special therapy services (including social work, occupational, speech, and physical) to schoolchildren in a variety of rural counties. The counties initially did not each have enough clients to hire their own full-time therapists. Therefore, each county respectively purchased from the agency whatever therapists' time was needed.

For instance, a social worker or occupational therapist might serve clients in county A only one or two days each week. Because of a limited number of clients, this might be all the service that the county needed. Together, the counties provided enough work for the agency to maintain several full-time therapists in each discipline. However, new state requirements to provide adequate service to children were put into place. More children became eligible for service. The counties also began to develop enhanced assessment techniques and procedures. Over time, a number of counties subsequently identified enough of their own clients to hire their own full-time therapists. Hence, the agency providing special services no longer had access to enough clients in enough counties. It simply had to shut down.

Relationships with Other Organizations

EP 8c

The fourth environmental dimension affecting organizations involves relationships with other agencies in the macro environment. Analysis of this organizational environment is essential to understand any organization's functioning. How does the social service agency interact with other organizations within its macro environment? Such relationships may fall under the category of *detached*, *collaborative*, or *competitive*. Each type will be discussed below.

Detached Relationships among Organizations Some agencies are integrally involved with each other and can't function without each other. Other organizations are highly competitive with each other, while de*tached* agencies have virtually nothing to do with each other except for brief, haphazard encounters. While we will not focus much attention on such uninvolved relationships, it is important to note that few agencies can continue to exist without developing relationships with others in their service area.

Collaborative Relationships among Organizations *Collaborative* organizations are different agencies that work together in some way. They cooperate to address the external task environment—for example, lobbying for legislation that supports social services or working together to serve the same clients with multiple needs. "Organizations must build collaborations and networks with other organizations to manage the external task environment, adapt to fast-changing conditions, and acquire resources essential for the organization's survival" (Alter, 2009, p. 435). Agencies are not islands. Often, they cannot function in isolation. They need referral sources for clients. Alternately, they need appropriate resources to which they can refer clients whose needs they cannot meet.

Consider a sheltered employment facility where adults with intellectual disabilities are trained in basic work skills and function under comprehensive supervision. Such an agency needs other agencies that run group homes and institutional facilities where clients can reside when not at work. If clients have nowhere to live, then they can't take advantage of the sheltered employment facility activities.

Another example is an organization providing in-service treatment for alcoholic clients. This organization receives virtually all its referrals from local family services agencies providing family counseling and local hospitals. Without the cooperation of these referral agencies, the inpatient program would cease to exist. Likewise, the local family services agencies and hospitals would be unable to serve alcoholic clients adequately if the in-service alcohol treatment program did not exist.

Competitive Relationships among Organizations   *Competitive* social service agencies may vie with each other for clients (Alter, 2009). If the number of clients is relatively limited, the competition may be quite fierce. We have established that agencies need clients to survive and thrive. Highlight 6-6 provides a case example of competitive relationships among organizations.

The Impact of Social and Economic Forces on Social Service Organizations: The Shifting Macro Environment LO 6-7

EP 8b

Social service organizations function within the larger macro environment and must respond to shifting social and economic forces. Social forces include societal expectations regarding who is eligible to receive benefits and what types of benefits are appropriate. People vote for politicians who support their ideas and, it is hoped, will implement social policies agreeing with these conceptions. Economic forces involve how many resources are allocated to agencies for service provision. Social service agencies can only provide resources that are available and administer services in legally prescribed ways.

Social and economic forces may affect social service provision in at least three major ways. First, resources and funding may be limited. For example, a funding cut may result in the elimination of one of several programs in a domestic abuse shelter. Second, policies, regulations, and the wishes of political leaders determine what agencies can and cannot do. For instance, a child protection agency may be required by law to address a child maltreatment complaint within 24 hours. Third, social service agencies may be pressured to conform to public expectations. For example, the encompassing community might respond negatively when a mental health agency decides to locate group homes within residential neighborhoods.

Highlight 6-6

Case Example—Competitive Relationships among Organizations

One state supported several privately run residential treatment centers for boys, ages 12 to 17, with serious behavioral and emotional problems. The state purchased services from these agencies because the state did not provide these services itself. **Purchase-of-service** involves a financial agreement or contract where one agency, often a public agency, agrees to purchase services from another agency. It may be cost effective for the public agency to purchase the services from the other agency rather than to develop and provide those services itself. The agency from which services are purchased then assumes responsibility for developing and overseeing service provision.

For many years, the state and counties provided enough clients to maintain all of the centers. No new centers opened because the number of agencies approximately matched the number of clients. The status quo, or homeostasis, was maintained.

However, when the state decided to build and open its own extremely large treatment complex, the number of clients available to privately run treatment centers was significantly decreased. Thus, approximately half of the residential centers were forced to close. They could not solicit enough clients to sustain themselves. The other half of the centers that continued to exist did so because they quickly decided to specialize their services. For instance, one center specialized in serving clients who had dual diagnoses of both behavioral disorder and intellectual disability. Another center specialized in boys needing treatment because they had been sexually abused.

The new state treatment complex was large but not extensive enough to accommodate all the state's clients who needed treatment. These clients had to go somewhere. The state determined that it was in the state's best fiscal interest to continue purchasing services for some clients who fell in certain categories. The fact that various centers decided to specialize in treating certain problems facilitated the state's decision-making process concerning which clients to treat in its own facility and which to refer elsewhere. Children with special needs and problems were referred to those centers that specialized in the treatment of those respective needs and problems.

Another case involved Granite, a private mental health agency providing comprehensive services for an entire county. The agency had a contract with county government to provide these services and had received this funding for many years. As is common, the contract was renewed periodically. One year, when the contract was up for renewal, another provider of mental health services decided to compete for the same funding. Despite having a long-standing relationship with the county, Granite lost the contract to its competitor who offered to provide the same services for less money. Even in social services arenas, being competitive is a strength.

This situation is sometimes referred to as **NIMBY** (Not in my backyard) because though community members may in theory support the idea of group homes or homeless shelters, they prefer these be located elsewhere.

As the population continues to expand worldwide, resources continue to shrink. Decreasing resources means that funding and financial support become more and more difficult to get. Changes in political philosophies and leadership in countries can have an impact as support for human services ebbs in favor of frugality and/or competing visions. These factors often mean that competition becomes more and more intense. It then makes sense that organizations producing higher-quality products (more effectively) at lower costs requiring lesser input (more efficiently) will be more likely to survive than those that are less effective and efficient. Likewise, social service organizations providing more effective and efficient services will probably outlive less effective and less efficient counterparts.

Understanding social and economic forces affecting social service organizations provides insights into organizational behavior and individual behavior within organizations. Whenever possible, social workers have a professional obligation to improve organizational systems' performance and enhance service provision to clients. This is difficult to do within the macro context because social service organizations' external environment is constantly in flux. Social forces impact other macro organizations and influence political policies that, in turn, modify the availability of funding. Social service organizations must continue seeking out and nurturing funding resources, while at the same time responding to or opposing changes in legislation and regulation that undermine their missions.

As discussed earlier, funding mechanisms vary widely. Social and economic forces jar social service organizations with unpredictability, suddenness, and severity. Thus, to survive and effectively meet their goals of helping clients, these organizations must maintain keen awareness of external influences and their effects. Organizations must also readily react to changing requirements and demands, as people's needs, values, and conditions change over time. Two major social and economic thrusts seriously impacting and, in many ways, restricting service provision today are federal social legislation and managed care.

Federal Social Legislation: Temporary Assistance to Needy Families (TANF) LO 6-8

EP 3b, 5b

Federal social legislation has major effects on what programs social service agencies can provide. Therefore, when legislation changes, agency services are identified and changed by that legislation. The underlying theme is that social legislation may significantly enhance or severely cut benefits to people in need. Agencies and their workers must comply with regulations whether they like them or not and whether they think such regulations are fair or not. The alternative is to undertake macro change efforts that prevent or ameliorate the damage that may be done to social service funding and support for services in general.

EP 5

The current major public assistance program for children and families living in poverty is Temporary Assistance to Needy Families (TANF), which replaced the former program Aid to Families with Dependent Children (AFDC) in 1996. TANF was created by the Personal Responsibility and Work Opportunity Reconciliation Act of 1996 (also known as PRWORA).

Dolgoff and Feldstein (2013) describe TANF's four major goals:

1. To provide assistance to needy families so that children may be cared for in their homes or in the homes of relatives;
2. To end the dependency of needy parents on government benefits by promoting job preparation, work, and marriage;
3. To prevent and reduce the incidence of out-of-wedlock pregnancies and establish annual numerical goals for preventing and reducing the incidences of these pregnancies; and
4. To encourage the formation and maintenance of two-parent families. (p. 207)

Dolgoff and Feldstein (2013) further elaborate about TANF:

The TANF program was passed to drastically reform the welfare system to place a greater emphasis on work and personal responsibility and to provide states with flexibility to create what they consider to be the best approaches to these aims for their particular circumstances. . . . Major emphases were to reduce projected spending, require work, limit assistance to certain durations, make work pay, improve child support enforcement, encourage parental responsibility, and give more power and authority to states to encourage innovation and creativity in welfare policy. (p. 208)

It's important to review the history of public assistance to understand the issues involved. Americans have a long-established record of ambivalence about providing poor people with financial assistance. Feelings are even more complex now, of course, with the change in political power in Washington, DC. Karger and Stoesz (2013) explain:

EP 2

On the hostility side, the argument goes like this: If privilege is earned by hard work, then people are poor because they are lazy and lack ambition. Those driven by the powerful American spirit of competitiveness see the inability of the poor to compete as a serious character flaw. On the other hand, only a few paychecks separate the welfare recipient from the average citizen—thus the compassion. Although democratic capitalism is rooted in the belief that hard work guarantees success, real life often tells a different story. (p. 242)

AFDC, originally established as Aid to Dependent Children (ADC) by the Social Security Act of 1935, was a program providing payments funded by federal and state governments to children deprived of parental support because a parent was absent from the home, had died, or was incapable of managing the household for physical or mental reasons. Most families receiving benefits were single mothers whose partners were not in the home.

AFDC established eligibility standards based on income level, family configuration, number and age of children, motivation to participate in work programs, and other factors. Eligible families passed an *income test*—that is, an eligibility guideline that establishes the maximum amount of income a family may earn without losing benefits. Those who made too much money were ineligible for benefits.

Eligible families could potentially receive financial assistance for many years in addition to Medicaid,[2] food stamps,[3] and partial financial support for housing, (with the exception of a few states that subtracted the amount received in food stamps and housing assistance from the AFDC grant). Note that how long families can continue receiving public assistance is a matter of strong debate. Facts indicate that before TANF, half of all AFDC recipients left welfare rolls within one year, the number rising to 70 percent after two years; however, over 75 percent of welfare recipients did eventually return to AFDC rolls (Karger & Stoesz, 2013).

Many issues characterize the public assistance debate concerning the effectiveness, fairness, and humaneness of TANF and its effects on children and families in need. Several have arbitrarily been selected to be addressed here. They include adequacy of funding, time limits, work requirements, child care, education and training for better jobs, job quality and availability, and equitable treatment by states.

---

[2] *Medicaid* is a program funded by federal and state governments that pays for medical and hospital services for eligible people who are unable to pay for these services themselves and are determined to be in need.

[3] *Food stamps* are coupons distributed through a federal program to people in need who use them like cash to purchase primarily food, plants, and seeds.

Adequacy of Funding   The adequacy of funding under TANF is below that previously available in its predecessor, AFDC. While a couple of states provide assistance at 1996 levels, most do not. Only 10 states adjusted their benefits in the period of 2015 to 2016, while most allowed benefits to lose value through inflation (Center on Budget and Policy Priorities, 2016). As Jansson (2014) points out, even with the addition of SNAP (Supplemental Nutrition Assistance Program), all the recipients remain below the poverty level, regardless of where they live in the United States. In fact, "every state's TANF benefits for a family of three with no other cash income were below 50 percent of the poverty line, measured by the Department of Health and Human Services' (HHS) 2016 poverty guidelines" (Center on Budget and Policy Priorities, 2016, p. 1). (The **poverty line or poverty threshold** is the minimal annual cash income level established by the federal government, which is based on family size, that determines whether people are living in poverty.)

In 2016, the maximum benefit for a family of three ranged from a low of $170 per month in Mississippi to a high of $923 in Alaska. In many cases, those amounts have not changed in the 20 years since the creation of TANF. With state budgets continuing to shrink, it's highly unlikely that states will divert proportionately more funding than they have in the past to address additional public assistance needs. Instead, they are likely to supply only the minimal funding required, which means fewer resources for potential recipients. TANF also permits states to impose tighter restrictions regarding who is eligible for benefits. Additionally, many states have established family caps that ban families from receiving additional benefits for any children born after the family's initial involvement in the program. Many social service agencies providing benefits have serious concerns about these restrictions and the negative effects on clients.

Time Limits   TANF also establishes time limits for receipt of benefits. Clients can receive no more than five years of benefits in their lifetime. Beyond five years, states may opt to extend assistance to no more than 20 percent of their caseload. They may also continue funding recipients through state funds alone. This is a huge change from AFDC, which allowed recipients to receive assistance if they remained eligible. TANF allowed states to reduce their time limits and curtail

EP 8a

Critical Thinking Questions 6-1 LO 6-9

Do you feel that children and families living in poverty should be supported by the government? If so, to what extent, and under what circumstances? If not, why not?

EP 8a

Critical Thinking Questions 6-2

Should time limits be imposed on how long a recipient can receive assistance? If so, what should they be?

other provisions that would make exceptions for individual cases. A concern is that agencies might have to turn away people in desperate need because these people have depleted their time allocation. What happens when time limits run out?

Work Requirements   The pressure is on to make states get TANF recipients working and off benefit rolls. TANF establishes the following work requirements:

- With few exceptions, recipients must work as soon as they are job-ready, or no later than two years after coming on assistance.
- To count toward a state's work participation rate, single parents must participate in work activities for an average of 30 hours per week, or an average of 20 hours per week if they have a child under age six. Two-parent families must participate in work activities for an average of 35 hours a week or, if they receive federal child-care assistance, 55 hours a week.
- Failure to participate in work requirements can result in a reduction or termination of a family's benefits.
- States cannot penalize single parents with a child under six for failing to meet work requirements if they cannot find adequate child care.
- States must engage a certain percentage of all families and of two-parent families in work activities or face financial penalty. These required state work participation rates are 50 percent overall and 90 percent for two-parent families; however, states can reduce the targets they must meet with a caseload reduction credit. For every percentage point a state reduces its caseload below its FY 2005 level (without restricting eligibility), the credit reduces the state's target participation rate by one percentage point.

Child Care   Compared to AFDC, TANF maintains strict work requirements to make people eligible for financial assistance. Therefore, TANF recipients must find alternate care for their children. We've established that single parents must work an average of 30 hours per week, or an average of 20 hours per week if they have a child under age six. Two-parent families must participate in work activities for an average of 35 hours a week. Questions concern how parents will cope with child-care needs, work stress, homemaking responsibilities, and parenting.

Although the original funding for child care was increased at the time TANF was created, whether states provide child care services to recipient families is up to them. States may fund child care in a variety of formats, ranging from licensed child-care centers to family caregivers. While funding for child care has increased, that change has not kept up with inflation, resulting in a decrease of over 17 percent (Congressional Research Service, 2016).

Child care remains a problem for working parents in both middle- and lower-income families. Often, quality child care is not available or is too expensive for

EP 8a

Critical Thinking Questions 6-3

Should public assistance recipients be required to work? If so, what do you think the details of this requirement should be?

families to afford. When it is available, it may not meet the needs of parents who work unusual hours. Poor-quality child care can pose a health and safety risk to the child. Because the income and benefits for child-care workers is generally low, high rates of turnover are common.

Education and Training for Better Jobs   Another issue involves the jobs that TANF recipients can get. TANF funds can only be used to provide 12 months of vocational educational preparation, which is often insufficient to develop the skills needed for employment. Many have not earned a high school diploma or GED. Often, those with poor elementary and high school preparation are not prepared for community college or find that work schedules prevent successful completion of their education. Moreover, only about half of students who enter community colleges complete their education (Urban Institute, 2012). TANF rules also limit the amount of post-high school education that will count toward participation rates in the program. In addition, many single parents who are employed find it difficult to reduce their work hours (and their income) or to cut back on time with their families (Urban Institute, 2012). How can former TANF recipients seek better jobs and experience upward mobility with little or no education and training?

Job Quality and Availability   When TANF recipients leave the program, it is often not because they located a job. While a strong labor market helps everyone, a weak one tends to affect low-income families more. As we have discussed, many TANF recipients lack the educational or vocational skills to find jobs paying a living wage. Moreover, many have other barriers to employment, including (Center on Budget and Policy Priorities, 2015):

> mental and physical impairments; substance abuse; domestic violence; . . . learning disabilities; having a child with a disability; and problems with housing, child care, or transportation. TANF has, for the most part, failed this group of families—many of whom have become disconnected from both work and welfare—by providing them with neither a reliable safety net nor employment assistance that adequately addresses their employment barriers. (p. 1)

Critical Thinking Questions 6-4

EP 8a

Who will provide all the additional child care services for newly working mothers?
Will funding be adequate in view of the huge potential influx of children requiring care?
What if no adequate daycare is available?
Will centers or family caregivers accept infants or toddlers who are not yet toilet-trained, children many current child-care facilities reject?
How will these services be monitored for adequacy, safety, and quality?
How will parents adjust to separation from their children?
How will children be affected by limited access to their single parent?
How does this policy affect children's welfare?

Critical Thinking Question **6-5**

To what extent should the public pay for education and training for public assistance recipients?

EP 8a

Critical Thinking Question **6-6**

What could be done to improve the quality of jobs available for public assistance recipients?

Many recipients leave TANF, not because they have found gainful employment but because they have exceeded the mandatory time limit for participation. Others have accepted low-wage employment that does not come near meeting their financial needs. Some accept part-time employment paying minimum wage and remain woefully impoverished.

Realistically, how good is the potential for upward mobility offered by most low-paying jobs? While the economy has recovered from the most recent recession, multiple employment challenges still face recipients of TANF.

Equitability among States   As we have established, the states set their own eligibility standards, and support levels for TANF recipients. This means that a recipient in one state could get a fraction of the income support received in an adjoining state. The fairness of this arrangement is nonexistent and reflects the inherent difficulty of the current system that gives block grants to states along with significant flexibility in how the money is spent. Some states spend the funds on programs with only a tangential relationship to poverty and not focused on welfare recipients. For example, one state may use its funds to reduce the rate of teen pregnancy while another uses its funds to prevent child abuse or neglect.

EP 8a

Critical Thinking Question **6-7**

To what extent should benefits provided to public assistance recipients be equal in all the states?

EP 8a

Critical Thinking Question **6-8**

How would you restructure the public assistance system if you had the power? What are your values concerning what's important?

What Is the Answer?   We have touched on only a few of the many issues involved in TANF. Legislation governs programs and service provision in the macro social environment. The following are suggestions to consider when making future legislative decisions:

1. Provide adequate funding and build in adjustments for inflation in future years.
2. Require states to spend federal TANF funds on promoting and supporting work activities.
3. Reduce current weekly work requirements.
4. Require states to emphasize education and job training that can lead to career advancement and better occupational opportunities.
5. Increase the opportunities that can be involved in work to include enrollment in training or educational programs so that recipients have access to a better, more productive future.
6. Eliminate time limits or make them more flexible so that recipients can have enough time to become educated and develop career skills.
7. Encourage states to develop strategies targeting barriers to employment. (Center on Budget and Policy Priorities, 2015)

Managed Care Reflects Social and Economic Forces

EP 8b

Another major social and economic force that affects many agencies' service provision is managed care. The concept serves as an umbrella for many different types of health agencies and health care services. **Managed care** is "a health care delivery system organized to manage cost, utilization, and quality" (Medicaid.gov, 2017, p. 1). These include decisions about the need for and appropriateness of such things as tests, medical procedures, and treatments provided by health care staff. Mooney, Knox, and Schacht (2015) explain that managed care involves "insurance companies monitoring and controlling the decisions of health care providers . . . [by requiring] doctors to receive approval before they can hospitalize a patient, perform surgery, or order an expensive diagnostic test" (p. 45).

Managed care has become an integral part of social work practice in numerous fields, including health care, mental health, work with older adults, public assistance, and child welfare. All people, including clients, need health care to one extent or another, and most are now enrolled in at least one managed care

At a Glance 6-1

Issues Concerning TANF

- Adequacy of funding
- Time limits
- Work requirements
- Availability of child care

- Lack of education and training for better jobs
- Job quality and availability
- Lack of equitability among states

organization. Health care providers and managed care organization contract with each other to form networks that have consequences for both entities. Providers are given rules and guidelines that they must accept in exchange for funding provided by the health insurance company. While there are benefits to such arrangements, the focus is always on cost. This is a source of criticism from both providers and patients who believe health care decisions should be made by the patient in consultation with the provider, not by faceless insurance bureaucrats.

Today, managed care involves health insurance companies, hospitals, networks of physicians and other treatment providers, health maintenance organizations, preferred provider organizations, and point-of-service plans. **Health maintenance organizations (HMOs)** are group plans requiring monthly premiums in which participants choose a primary care physician who coordinates care; such care is usually only paid for if provided within the service network and emphasizes preventive care (MedlinePlus, 2017).

A **preferred provider organization (PPO)** is groups of hospitals and health care providers who have contracted with a managed care plan to provide services to plan members in exchange for negotiated fees and copayments made by the member (Patient Advocate Foundation, 2017). If plan members wish to receive care from providers that are not part of the PPO, their costs will be higher.

Point-of-service (POS) plans allow participants to choose between an HMO and PPO each time health services are needed (MedlinePlus, 2017).

EP 5

Managed care fundamentally altered traditional relationships between clients and social work practitioners. Historically, social workers in agency settings established treatment plans (that could address health and mental health concerns) in conjunction with clients, in addition to stressing informed consent and confidentiality to comply with ethical standards. Managed care takes these decisions out of workers' and clients' hands and puts them into the hands of removed third-party decision makers. A managed care representative, often a utilization reviewer or case manager, then reviews documentation and regulates what services can be provided to patients and how much will be paid for them. To some, managed care reflects the domination of managed care organizations' financial gain over patients' best interests.

Two primary principles promoted by managed care are *retention of quality and access* while *controlling cost*. That is, health and mental health services should be of high quality and readily accessible to clients, on the one hand. Yet, they should be very cost effective, on the other.

Managed Care's Means of Controlling Costs   Managed care employs several approaches to control costs. One method is the practice of **capitation**, "a system managed care plans use to pay physicians or hospitals, in which the providers receive a fixed, predetermined sum of money, typically on a monthly basis, from the plan to care for plan members. Capitation places providers at-risk for financial losses" but also pays them even if the patient is never seen (Patient Advocate Foundation, 2017, p. 1).

A second approach to controlling costs involves **gatekeeping**, the required authorization by a designated primary care physician to make all decisions about such things as tests, treatments, and the services of specialists. This prevents patients from seeking out alternative care and care providers on their own.

A third cost-preventive mechanism is **utilization management**, where a health provider must receive approval from a utilization manager who assesses "whether the care is medically necessary and appropriate to the patient's needs" (Patient Advocate Foundation, 2017). This reduces the health care provider's autonomy as well as potentially reducing the client's confidentiality. The latter occurs because the person making the review has access to all the patient's health records, not just the ones applying to a particular problem.

The Pros and Cons of Managed Care   The debate about the benefits and consequences of managed care is ongoing. The one obvious problem is that the United States has no better health outcomes than the top 13 industrialized nations, although we spend substantially more on health care services (Squires, 2012). The United States spends 50 percent more than France and about double that spent in the United Kingdom (Commonwealth Fund, 2015). Our rates for life expectancy, chronic conditions, and infant mortality are well below those of other countries, and we charge more for the same tests and procedures used throughout the world. We also spend more per capita, despite not covering millions of citizens. The same is true for costs of prescription drugs, which far outpace the costs of other industrialized countries.

Some argue that we spend more on treatments for various diseases than other countries but ignore the fact that the measure of success should be on outcomes rather than inputs (Business Insider, 2017). Other identified benefits include the following:

- Freedom to sue your doctor or hospital for malpractice
- Access to hospitals and health insurance if you can afford it
- More advanced research
- High pay for doctors
- More MRI and CT scanner machines per million population
- More identification and treatments for mental disorders
- Best treatment of chronic disease
- Highest rates of cancer survival
- More screening for cancer

Focus on Ethics 6-1 discusses some ethical issues in managed care.

The Future of Managed Care: Advocacy for Patients' Rights   Managed care will likely continue to be the nation's primary approach to health care provision; it permeates both inpatient and outpatient contexts for all types of health care. As chronic conditions continue to grow within the US population, managing the costs of treatment will continue to be a challenge. Chronic conditions account for about 75 percent of health care spending (Myers, 2015).

The use of mobile technology will place demands on managed care systems to find more ways to communicate directly with clients, many of whom are already using technology to track their own health data. Adequate security will be required to protect increasingly accessible data systems with critical client health information.

A third trend will be focused on increasing wellness and prevention with a goal of reining in costs. One goal is helping ensure that clients adhere to therapy

Focus on Ethics **6-1**

Ethical Issues in Managed Care

EP 1, 1a

Most generalist practitioners work within social service agencies that employ them. They are supposed to follow agency and other regulatory policy. However, they are also responsible for maintaining ethical practices and making certain clients' needs are met.

Several ethical issues may be raised concerning managed care and how it affects agency service provision:

■ A potential conflict exists with respect to client self-determination. When subject to managed care, clients no longer have the right to choose their service provider. Rather, the managed-care utilization reviewer makes this determination.

■ Clients can be denied the best quality of service when the managed care reviewer refuses to honor the health care provider's recommendations. This may entail the actual treatment recommended as well as the number of times that the client can see the social worker.

■ Confidentiality is at risk when client health information is provided to a third party, the managed care system that might demand client information before agreeing to pay for care.

■ Managed care rules might place limits on what information a practitioner can share with clients.

If a managed care organization demands information before providing services, what should the worker do? What if the worker does not agree with the organization's demand for information and feels the regulations violate clients' rights to privacy?

---

regimens, including medication schedules. A Centers for Medicare and Medicaid Services research study observed that medication nonadherence in 2000 was the cause of 33 to 69 percent of medication-related hospital admissions (Myers, 2015, p. 1). Moreover, only about one-fourth of patients take their medication as prescribed. This suggests the wisdom of communicating with clients the importance of adhering to medication schedules.

At the same time, there is a great deal of unhappiness with the system and some of its activities, some of which have already been mentioned. It remains to be seen what changes to health care services will be generated by a new Congress and president in their efforts to replace or repeal the Affordable Care Act (ACA, or Obamacare).

The opportunity to advocate for clients in the health care arena will continue to exist. This may range from advocacy for individual or groups of clients with unresponsive or unhelpful managed care organizations to advocating with national and state legislators to ensure that the gains achieved by the ACA are not lost because of political unhappiness with some portions of the Act The changes brought about by ACA have significant consequences for clients. Prior to the ACA, health insurance companies could impose annual and lifetime limits on coverage, refuse to cover dependents to age 26, and fail to cover prevention services without cost sharing. They could deny coverage because of preexisting conditions, discriminate based on health history, and establish lengthy waiting periods prior to covering health care costs. They also had no restrictions on how much out-of-pocket spending and cost sharing they required for participants (Scott, Keckley, & Copeland, 2013). These provisions, and in fact, the overall system that may replace or respond to concerns about the ACA, are opportunities for advocacy, particularly on the macro level.

**EP 3a, 5b,
5c, 8c,
8d, 9d**

LO 6-10 NASW policy champions "an equal right to continuous, high-quality care that is effective, efficient, safe, timely, and patient-centered"; it also advocates for "policies and practices that ensure that patients receive necessary and appropriate care and guarantee patient rights protections" (NASW, 2012, p. 170).

In their work with individuals and families, generalist practitioners can help clients understand the rules and regulations involved in managed care so that clients might: (1) better navigate the complex system, (2) get detailed information about treatment options, and (3) have increased ability to fight for the services they need.

In terms of the macro political picture, workers can strive to address the range of issues mentioned earlier. Pursuits may include "lobbying for legislation to regulate managed care, making alliances with other health care providers [to enhance the potential for positive change], and using research and analysis of data generated by their practice" to improve service provision (Dhooper, 2012, p. 283).

Chapter Summary

The following summarizes this chapter's content as it relates to the learning objectives presented at the beginning of the chapter. Objectives include the following:

LO 6-1 Contrast primary and secondary agency settings.

Primary settings are those agencies where social work is the main or primary profession. Secondary settings are characterized by the presence of a variety of professional staff of which social work is one.

LO 6-2 Define and discuss organizational mission statements, goals, and objectives for achieving goals.

An organizational mission statement is a declaration of the organization's purpose that "establishes broad and relatively permanent parameters within which goals are developed and specific programs designed" (Kettner et al., 2017, p. 109). Organizational "goals are statements of expected outcomes dealing with the problem that the program is attempting to prevent, eradicate, or ameliorate" (Kettner et al., 2017, p. 112). Social service organizations are usually complex with multiple goals. Objectives are smaller, behaviorally specific subgoals that serve as stepping stones on the way to accomplishing the main goal.

LO 6-3 Describe faith-based services.

Faith-based social service organizations are agencies sponsored by or affiliated with a religious or spiritual organization. To varying degrees, faith-based social services often incorporate aspects of spirituality or religion into their mission statement and goals.

LO 6-4 Discuss goal displacement.

Goal displacement is the "substitution of a legitimate goal with another goal which the organization was not developed to address, for which resources were not allocated and which it is not known to serve" (Etzioni, 1964, p. 10). A typical scenario in social services is when the rules and following those rules become more important than providing services to clients. Ecosystems concepts can be applied both to social service and business organizations.

LO 6-5 Explain the external macro environment of social service organizations, including resources, legitimation, client sources, and relationships with other organizations.

Social service organizations must have access to adequate resources to function. Legitimation is the condition where the external environment provides an agency with the appropriate status or authorization to perform agency functions and pursue agency goals. A range of client resources is necessary to provide enough clients to keep the agency financially afloat. Social service organizations may experience uninvolved, complementary, or competitive relationships with other organizations in the macro social environment.

LO 6-6 Present an example of a humanitarian organization in the context of the global macro environment.

Doctors Without Borders, or Médecins Sans Frontières (MSF), is an international humanitarian organization with associative offices in 19 countries. Its primary goals include provision of medical aid to people anywhere in the world who are in direst need and speaking out on people's behalf about neglected crises, concealed human rights abuses, and inappropriately restrictive national policies.

LO 6-7 Explain the impact of social and economic forces on social service organizations.

Social service organizations function within the larger macro environment and must respond to shifting social and economic forces. Resources and funding may be limited. Policies and regulations determine what agencies can do. Social service organizations may be pressured to conform to public expectations.

LO 6-8 Describe how federal social legislation, Temporary Assistance to Needy Families (TANF), and managed care impact agency service provision.

TANF replaced Aid to Families with Dependent Children (AFDC) as one primary means of reducing poverty. Major issues include adequacy of funding, time limits, provision of child care, education and training for better jobs, job quality and availability, and equitability of benefits among states.

Managed care is "a health care delivery system organized to manage cost, utilization, and quality" (Medicaid.gov, 2017, p. 1). These include decisions about the need for and appropriateness of such things as tests, medical procedures, and treatments provided by health care staff. Mooney, Knox, and Schacht (2015) explain that managed care involves "insurance companies monitoring and controlling the decisions of health care providers . . . [by requiring] doctors to receive approval before they can hospitalize a patient, perform surgery, or order an expensive diagnostic test" (p. 45). Managed care has become an integral part of social work practice in many fields. Managed care organizations attempt to retain quality by controlling costs. Means of controlling costs include capitation, gatekeeping, and utilization management. Physicians and patients generally feel that health care has declined since the advent of managed care. Managed care will likely continue, although many difficult issues are involved. Social workers can actively advocate for improvements.

LO 6-9 Answer various critical thinking questions.

Critical thinking questions focused on various aspects of TANF (including public support, time limits, work requirements, working mothers, education and training, job quality, equitability among states, and restructuring the public assistance system).

LO 6-10 Provide examples of ethical issues that may arise in managed care.

Ethical issues in managed care include the potential clash between gatekeeping, on the one hand, and client self-determination, informed consent, and client confidentiality on the other.

Looking Ahead

This chapter addressed social service organizational settings, goals, and contexts in the macro social environment. The next chapter will explore organizational structure and dynamics.

Competency Notes

The following identifies where Educational Policy (EP) competencies and component behaviors are discussed in the chapter.

EP 1 (Competency 1)—Demonstrate Ethical and Professional Behavior. *(p. 195):* Ethical issues in managed care are identified.

EP 1a Make ethical decisions by applying the standards of the NASW Code of Ethics, relevant laws and regulations, models for ethical decision-making, ethical conduct of research, and additional codes of ethics as appropriate to context. *(p. 195):* Ethical issues involved in managed care that conflict with the NASW *Code of Ethics* are discussed.

EP 2 (Competency 2)—Engage Diversity and Difference in Practice. *(p. 177):* Religion and spirituality are aspects of human diversity that can affect service provision. *(p. 189):* The concept of privilege is addressed.

EP 3 (Competency 3)—Advance Human Rights and Social, Economic, and Environmental Justice. *(p. 182):* MSF exposes forms and mechanisms of oppression and discrimination on a global basis. *(p. 193):* Several suggestions are provided for improving the TANF system to make it economically and socially just.

EP 3a Apply their understanding of social, economic, and environmental justice to advocate for human rights at the individual and system levels. *(p. 182):* Global interconnections of oppression are discussed; an international humanitarian agency addressing these issues is described. *(p. 194):* Means of advancing human rights in managed care are discussed.

EP 3b Engage in practices that advance social, economic, and environmental justice. *(p. 182):* MSF demonstrates organizational advocacy for human rights and social justice. *(pp. 188–194):* Before generalist practitioners can advocate for policies that advance the human rights of TANF beneficiaries, they must understand the TANF policies involved. *(pp. 193–194):* Social workers can advocate for the policy changes concerning TANF that are discussed here to enhance human rights for TANF recipients. *(p. 196):* Practitioners should advocate for organizational and legislative policy changes that advance human rights in managed care.

EP 5 (Competency 5)—Engage in Policy Practice *(pp. 193–194):* Social workers must understand the history of social policies and services involved in public assistance to engage in policy practice and improve service delivery. *(pp. 196–197):* Social workers must understand the history of social policies and services involved in health care provision to engage in policy practice and improve service delivery.

EP 5b Assess how social welfare and economic policies impact the delivery of and access to social services. *(p. 180):* Goal displacement in social service organizations can undermine the delivery of and access to social services. *(pp. 193–194):* Social workers must understand the issues involved in TANF in order to analyze and formulate policies that improve agency service provision and advance social well-being. *(p. 182ff):* MSF provides an example of how an organization can formulate and advocate for policies that advance social well-being. *(pp. 196–197):* Generalist practitioners should analyze the policies involved in TANF so that they can formulate and advocate for policies that advance the social well-being of TANF recipients. Policy changes are suggested that could advance the social well-being of TANF recipients. *(pp. 196–197):* Suggestions are provided for policy advocacy that advances social well-being for managed care recipients.

EP 5c Apply critical thinking to analyze, formulate, and advocate for policies that advance human rights and social, economic, and environmental justice. *(p. 182):* MSF provides an example of an organization that engages in practices to advance social justice. *(p. 196):*

Suggestions are made for practices that advance social and economic justice for managed care recipients.

EP 6 (Competency 6)—Engage with Individuals, Families, Groups, Organizations, and Communities. *(p. 171)*: Social workers must understand the organizational goals of their agency to evaluate program outcomes. Generalist practitioners should evaluate the extent to which organizational goals are achieved. When goal displacement occurs, specified goals are less likely to be attained. *(p. 180)*: The ecosystems theoretical framework is applied to understand the processes of assessment, intervention, and evaluation in the context of organizations.

EP 6a Apply knowledge of human behavior and the social environment, person-in-environment, and other multidisciplinary theoretical frameworks to engage with clients and constituencies. *(p. 180)*: Social workers must be knowledgeable about systems of all sizes, including organizations.

EP 6b Use empathy, reflection, and interpersonal skills to effectively engage diverse clients and constituencies. *(pp. 177–178)*: Canda and Furman (2010) comment on spirituality and social work: "Spirituality is the heart of helping. It is the heart of empathy and care, the pulse of compassion, the vital flow of practice wisdom, and the driving energy of service. . . . There is mounting empirical evidence and practice wisdom that a person's sense of positive spiritual meaning, purpose, and connectedness along with participation in supportive aspects of religious communities are associated with enhanced well-being".

EP 7c Develop mutually agreed-on intervention goals and objectives based on the critical assessment of strengths, needs, and challenges within clients and constituencies. *(p. 171)*: Social workers must understand their agency's mission statement, goals, and objectives in order to develop appropriate intervention goals and objectives with clients. *(p. 174)*: Generalist practitioners must

understand how to formulate goals and objectives to develop them with clients.

EP 8 (Competency 8)—Intervene with Individuals, Families, Groups, Organizations, and Communities. *(p. 194)*: MSF provides an example of how to initiate actions to achieve organizational goals.

EP 8a Critically choose and implement interventions to achieve practice goals and enhance capacities of clients and constituencies. *(pp. 190–194)*: Critical thinking questions are raised.

EP 8b Apply knowledge of human behavior and the social environment, person-in-environment, and other multidisciplinary theoretical frameworks in interventions with clients and constituencies. *(p. 170)*: Practitioners should continuously appraise and respond to the changing agency environment to provide relevant services. *(p. 182)*: Social workers should continuously keep abreast of how international organizations like MSF attend to emerging societal trends in health and human rights to provide relevant services. *(p. 186)*: Generalist practitioners should maintain continuous awareness of the shifting macro environment that affects service provision. *(p. 198)*: Social workers should keep abreast of changing developments in managed care to provide relevant services.

EP 8c Use inter-professional collaboration as appropriate to achieve beneficial practice outcomes. *(p. 194ff)*: MSF provides an example of how an organization can collaborate internationally with colleagues and clients for effective policy action concerning health and human rights. *(p. 185ff)*: Social workers should understand their agency's relationships with other organizations to collaborate with colleagues in these agencies to pursue effective policy action. Practitioners are encouraged to make alliances with other health care providers to enhance the potential for effective policy action. *(pp. 182)*: MSF provides an organizational example of promoting changes in service delivery to improve service provision. Social workers are encouraged

to provide leadership in improving managed care policies and services.

EP 8d Negotiate, mediate, and advocate with and on behalf of diverse clients and constituencies. *(p. 182)*: MSF provides an example of organizational advocacy for clients.

EP 9d Apply evaluation findings to improve practice effectiveness at the micro, mezzo, and macro levels. *(p. 171)*: Workers need to evaluate how well their organizations are functioning to do their own work effectively.

Media Resources

MindTap for Social Work

 Go to MindTap® for digital study tools and resources that complement this text and help you be more successful in your course and career. There's an interactive eBook plus videos of client sessions, skill-building activities, quizzes to help you prepare for tests, apps, and more—all in one place. If your instructor didn't assign MindTap, you can find out more about it at CengageBrain .com.

7 | Organizational Structure and Dynamics

Interpersonal communication and dynamics characterize organizations.

LEARNING OBJECTIVES

After reading this chapter you should be able to...

7-1 Describe organizational culture and structure, and discuss how lines of authority and channels of communication are involved.

7-2 Discuss centralized versus decentralized organizations.

7-3 Respond to various critical thinking questions.

7-4 Examine interpersonal communication within social services agencies.

7-5 Describe the perceptual process during communication.

7-6 Identify interpersonal barriers to communication.

7-7 Summarize ethical issues concerning the use of distortion, enhancement of ethical communication, political behavior, and problematic unethical behavior.

7-8 Distinguish supervision and consultation in organizational settings.

7-9 Describe the importance of power in organizations and identify its various types.

7-10 Explain organizational politics and their dynamics.

7-11 Suggest tactics for using agency politics for positive change.

7-12 Explore the concept of organizational justice as it relates to social, economic, and environmental justice.

"I just can't tolerate Biff," Brunhilda proclaims to Stanwood, one of her social work colleagues. They both work in a large private social services organization providing numerous services, including counseling, substance abuse programs, vocational training, and community-based facilities for people with intellectual disabilities. Biff, whose real name is Bufford Bifford, is the manager of the agency's accounting department. Biff is very impressed with his own accomplishments, but unfortunately has extremely poor social interaction skills. With a superior demeanor, he typically commands Brunhilda and other social workers to scurry about and do his bidding when he determines that some billing matter needs instant attention. He expects workers to drop everything else they're doing and meet his needs immediately.

Stanwood tries to soothe Brunhilda's ruffled feathers. "After all," he stresses, "Biff is not our immediate supervisor, Bruny." He reminds Brunhilda that social workers must maintain positive working relationships with other agency staff, including Biff, because financial accountability is so important. Biff, like other staff, have little direct power over what social workers in the agency can, cannot, will, or will not do. Social workers are directly responsible to their own supervisor to develop appropriate treatment and referral plans and respond to agency needs. Stanwood urges Brunhilda to "be cool." He adds, "Our supervisor's a pretty good egg. The bottom line is you don't have to obey Biff's every wish. You could just choose to smile, nod, and ignore him. Remember, there are no jerk-free work environments."

This vignette does not imply that all organizational environments have Biffs, although many probably do. However, it focuses on the importance of agency expectations, structure, and interpersonal dynamics when you're trying to get your job done. Depending on your agency environment, you can feel supported and energized or angry and thwarted.

Chapter 5 defined *management* as "the attainment of organizational goals in an effective and efficient manner through planning, organizing, leading, and controlling organizational resources" (Daft, 2016b, p. 4). Management, then, is the art of getting things done in an organization by directing and synchronizing the performance of its workers. Managers accomplish this by setting goals for the entire organization or agency units, acquiring and allocating resources, coordinating employees' work, monitoring progress, and improving efficiency and effectiveness where possible (Daft, 2016b; Daft & Marcic, 2017). This says *what* management does, but it doesn't say *how* managers do it. This is where management style comes in. Equifinality applies here in that there are many ways to manage an organization. (*Equifinality* is the notion that there are many different means to achieve the same end.)

Ginsberg (1995) maintains "that strict adherence to a hierarchy often is dysfunctional, and the bureaucratic element of organizations can be harmful" (p. 15). However, he continues that "the principle of maintaining some unity of command is important, and failure to maintain a division of labor can lead to conflict and to some functions not being performed. The need for an organizational structure that separates tasks and maintains distinct responsibilities is probably as important as it always was" (p. 15).

Thus, elements of organizational structure are necessary to hold an agency together, regardless of variations in management style, that is, how staff and clients are viewed and services provided. This chapter investigates organizational culture, structure, and interpersonal dynamics. Chapter 8 will further explore management approaches and means of empowering staff.

Organizational Culture LO 7-1

EP 6a, 6b

Organizational culture is "the set of key values, beliefs, understandings, and norms shared by members of an organization.... Culture is a pattern of shared values and assumptions about how things are done within the organization. This pattern is learned by members as they cope with external and internal problems, and taught to new members as the correct way to perceive, think, and feel" (Daft & Marcic, 2017, p. 76). Many aspects of culture entail unwritten rules, traditions, and practices that hold the organization together (Hellriegel & Slocum, 2011). Organizational culture can include expectations for level of performance, interpersonal communication and interaction, management style, and appropriate dress.

Organizational culture, then, involves many facets. For example, what kind of attire is expected and considered appropriate within the organization's cultural environment—suits or jeans? A hospital social worker might choose to dress more formally because the environment is full of uniformed professionals. Contrasting informal dress might appear "unprofessional." A residential treatment center for males with behavioral disorders, on the other hand, might manifest a very informal organizational culture, at least concerning dress. The latter culture expects social workers and counselors to participate in a range of activities, including informal group sessions in the living units, recreational activities, and administration of consequences for poor behavior. It makes sense to dress comfortably and informally in such an environment.

Another facet of organizational culture is the agency's "personality." Each agency has its own personality. That is, it is more formal or informal, structured or unstructured, innovative or traditional than other agencies. From the first day of work within an agency, it is important to explore and begin understanding that agency's character. What tasks are considered the most important (e.g., documentation of treatment effectiveness, other record keeping, administrative conferences, or number of hours spent with clients)? How much freedom do workers have in conducting daily professional activities? Daft and Marcic (2017) comment:

> In some organizations, a basic assumption might be that people are essentially lazy and will shirk their duties whenever possible; thus, employees are closely supervised and given little freedom, and colleagues are frequently suspicious of one another. More enlightened organizations operate on the basic assumption that people want to do a good job; in these organizations, employees are given more freedom and responsibility and colleagues trust one another and work cooperatively. (p. 76)

Organizational culture is a common concept addressed in studying organizations, regardless of the theoretical perspective assumed. The cultural theoretical perspective on organizations discussed in Chapter 5, of course, emphasizes culture as the primary dimension for understanding organizational functioning. Other theories give the concept of culture less emphasis in relationship to the numerous other dimensions involved in organizations.

Organizational Structure

EP 6

Organizational structure is "the set of formal tasks assigned to individuals; formal reporting relationships including lines of authority, decision responsibility, number of hierarchical levels, and span of manager's control; and the design of systems to ensure effective coordination of employees across departments" (Daft & Marcic, 2017, p. 272). All large agencies (and many smaller ones, as well) have a *formal* structure specifying how management thinks the organization should be run. Most often, formal structure is explicated in an organizational chart showing who reports to whom. Such charts depict designated lines of authority and communication within the agency. A later section of this chapter will discuss organizational charts more thoroughly. Frequently, the agency operates in accordance with this chart, at least with respect to some functions, such as how information is disseminated, either from the top down or bottom up. For example, a social work supervisor might be expected to give appropriate information directly to supervisees. Likewise, those supervisees might expect the supervisor to convey their concerns up the administrative ladder. Highlight 7-1 discusses an important dimension of agency structure—the degree to which the organization is centralized or decentralized.

Agencies also develop informal structures and lines of communication. For example, it is typical for an agency to structure its units so that all workers in the unit report to one supervisor. Consider the case of the Humdrum County Foster Care Unit. Five workers and a supervisor comprise this unit. When workers have questions or problems, they are supposed to bring these to Henry, the Foster Care Unit supervisor. Often, however, Henry's supervisees discuss their cases with other workers in the unit or with Tiffany, the senior worker in the agency's Adoptions Unit. This means that the Foster Care Unit supervisor is deprived of information

---

Highlight 7-1

Centralized versus Decentralized Organizations   LO 7-2

One other aspect of agency structure merits brief commentary. A continuum can depict organizations and their degree of centralization. On one far side are extremely centralized organizations. These organizations resemble those run based on classical scientific management theories. Lines of authority are clearly established. There is a strict hierarchy designating who has power over whom. The units in centralized organizations are clearly defined and cleanly separated. Workers have little discretion to make their own decisions. Responsibilities are defined and overseen from above.

A probation and parole department provides an example of centralization. Clients assigned to workers in a designated unit reflect very similar characteristics. Procedures and treatment plans are relatively uniform in approach. Clients

and workers must abide by clearly defined rules and regulations. Little worker discretion is possible.

On the opposite side of the centralization continuum are extremely decentralized organizations, contrasting sharply with centralized organizations in flexibility. Decentralized organizations provide and encourage broad worker discretion. They likely serve a wide variety of clients with vastly different problems, issues, and backgrounds. Workers in such organizations need discretion to make plans for viable solutions. For example, extreme decentralization might characterize a community crisis-intervention organization. Clients coming in for help might have problems ranging from depression to illness to job loss to executive-level stress. Workers need a broad range of discretion to address a wide variety of problems.

that might be important to doing his job. At the same time, the unit workers gain consultation from peers and lessen the need for the supervisor's time.

Unfortunately, getting advice from others can lead to problems. For example, Bob, a new supervisor, on the job for two days, was given an extensive form to use for a referral to another agency. Once he looked over the form, he was uncertain whether the form was to be filled out or was a guideline or template for a lengthy narrative style referral. Wary of displaying his ignorance to his supervisor, he asked Jonah, another social worker in the agency with whom he had earlier worked. Jonah told Bob that he was pretty sure the form was to be filled in and no narrative was needed. Bob went ahead, filled out the form, and forwarded it to his supervisor. Within an hour or two, the form was back on his desk with a note that said, "What the hell is this?" Bob made a mental note that if he did not understand something, he would be better off asking his supervisor.

Although superficially confiding in Tiffany or Jonah might seem like a bad arrangement, it has some beneficial aspects. Workers who are sometimes uncomfortable talking with their supervisor can get help from other more experienced workers. Maybe Henry is not competent to provide answers or is too lazy or busy to take the time. Tiffany or Jonah might be an extremely knowledgeable, pleasant people who like to help their colleagues. Sharing ideas and problems helps to produce a camaraderie among the workers. This decreases their stress levels and often leads to better job performance. Human relations theories stress the importance of such interpersonal communication and support in organizations.

The point here is not to praise or criticize the existence of informal structures and communication channels. Instead, it is to acknowledge that they do exist and are a reality that practitioners must deal with in social services agencies. In practice, awareness of both formal and informal agency channels of communication strengthens social workers' ability to do their job. Once practitioners know the options and alternatives, they can make more informed choices. This is, after all, a major goal of the intervention process.

Three concepts are especially significant when appraising an agency's formal and informal structures. These are *lines of authority*, *channels of communication*, and *dimensions of power*.

Lines of Authority

All large agencies (and many smaller ones) have a formal structure. An agency's formal structure involves **lines of authority** (Daft, 2016b; Griffin & Moorhead, 2014). For our purposes, authority concerns the specific administrative and supervisory responsibilities of supervisors involving their supervisees. Authority entails who is designated to supervise whom. Agency policy usually specifies in writing these lines of authority.

We have established that often an agency's formal structure is explained in an organizational chart. Job positions held by individual staff members are portrayed by squares or circles that are labeled per their respective job positions. A formal hierarchy of authority in an organizational chart is depicted by vertical lines leading from supervisors down to supervisees (Griffin & Moorhead, 2014; Jansson, 2014). Generally, job positions higher on the chart have greater authority than those placed lower on the chart. Lines drawn from higher figures to lower figures identify the supervisors of staff holding job positions located lower on the chart and having less responsibility and power. These lines represent who oversees and assumes direct responsibility for the specified employees directly below them. The formal organizational structure as demonstrated by an organizational chart, then, dictates how control and supervision are *supposed* to flow.

A Case Example: The Idle Ness Center

The chart in Figure 7-1 reflects the hierarchy of authority for the Idle Ness Center for Diagnosis and Treatment, an agency providing assessment and therapeutic treatment to children with multiple developmental and physical disabilities. Parents bring children with a wide range of physical and behavioral difficulties to the agency to assess the children's abilities in a variety of areas, plan treatment programs, and provide the appropriate therapies.

The rectangles in Figure 7-1 designate those job positions having some degree of administrative responsibility within the agency system. The bolder the rectangle, the more authority and responsibility the position entails.

The executive director has the most authority and is responsible for the overall performance of the Idle Ness Center. Below him are five agency directors, including the medical director (a physician), and those for accounting, maintenance engineering, food services for clients and staff, and transportation services for clients. Each director (except accounting) is, in turn, responsible for the supervision of other staff further down the hierarchy of authority. The medical director is responsible for overseeing the entire clinical program, including the work of the various departmental supervisors. Departments include occupational therapy, physical therapy, speech therapy, psychology, and social work. The circles at the very bottom of the chart represent line staff who are providing services directly to or concerning clients.

By examining this chart, it is painfully clear how this agency is run, correct? If you look at the Social Work Department, there are two direct service workers who report directly to their social work supervisor. It is obvious how these social workers go about their business of providing services to clients, look to their own supervisor for direction, and live happily ever after, right? The chain of command is so blatant you may think this entire discussion borders on, if not engulfs itself in, monotony.

The "catch" is that formal organizational charts depict lines of *formal* authority within agencies. Such formal lines of authority dictate how communication and power are *supposed* to flow. Sometimes, an agency's actual chain of command follows the formal chart closely. Equally often, however, agencies develop *informal* channels of communication and power that are very different from those stated on paper. As an example, we will explore the Idle Ness Center's informal channels of communication and dimensions of power.

Channels of Communication

EP 1c

All agencies have numerous **channels of communication**, which are, complex systems of communication whereby staff members convey and receive information. *Communication*, of course, is "the process of transmitting information from one person or place to another" (Williams, 2016a, p. 619). This may involve verbal and written means as well as the use of behavior, symbols, or signs. Communication,

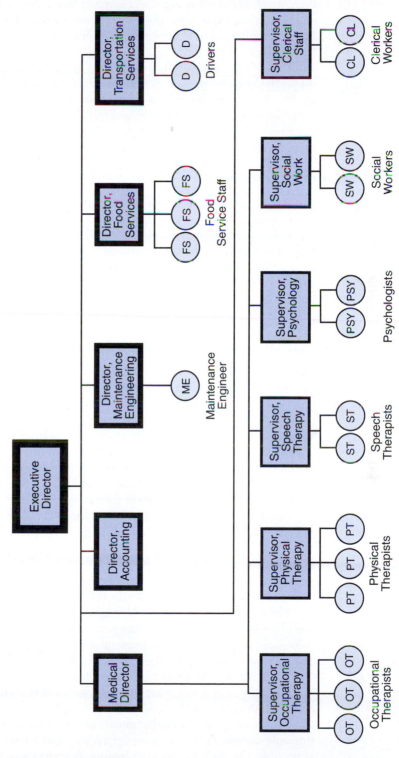

Figure 7-1 Idle Ness Center for Diagnosis and Treatment—Example of a Formal Organizational Chart

then, involves the many nuances regarding how information is conveyed verbally and nonverbally. It entails subtle inflections, comfort level between communicators, and multitudes of minute gestures. Communication is explored in more depth later in the chapter.

Formal lines of authority might imply that such communication channels are supposed to flow harmoniously and synchronously along with these lines of authority. In other words, supervisees are *supposed* to communicate primarily with their identified supervisors for direction and feedback. Likewise, supervisors are *supposed* to communicate directly with their supervisees and the managers who supervise them. As we will see, this is not the case in the Idle Ness Center.

Power in the Formal Structure

EP 1c, 2

Power is the potential ability to move people on a chosen course to produce an effect or achieve some goal (Griffin & Moorhead, 2014; Homan, 2016). Like channels of communication, dimensions of power are supposed to follow the established lines of authority. In the organizational chart, those in supervisory positions above their employees are supposed to have actual power (i.e., clear-cut influence and control) over those employees. In real-life agency environments, this may or may not be the case. Note that many other facets of power and organizational politics will be explored later in the chapter.

Example of Informal Structure: The Idle Ness Center

Direct your attention to the Social Work and Psychology Departments illustrated in Figure 7-2. We will concentrate on this smaller portion of the organizational chart concerning the informal structures of communication and power within the agency. Figure 7-2 contrasts the formal and informal structures for these two agency departments. The *real* channels of communication and dimensions of power among supervisors and direct service staff are very different from those illustrated in the formal organizational chart. The real relationships reflect the personalities and interactions among people who have unique perspectives and identities, strengths, weaknesses, problems, and needs of their own.

The formal structure pictures Ellen, the Psychology Department supervisor, as being responsible for the administration and supervision of both LaVerne and Shirley's job performance. Both the latter have a master's degree in psychology. Likewise, the formal structure portrays Roseanne, the Social Work Department supervisor, as having direct supervisory authority over both Karen and Susan, each of whom has a master's degree in social work.

The lower box portrays the real-life informal structure of these departments. Karen, one of the social workers, has become good friends with Ellen, the Psychology Department supervisor. Both single, they frequently socialize together and even vacation together. Their positive relationship is reflected by the bold line connecting them in Figure 7-2.

Karen, on the other hand, gets along terribly with Roseanne, her own supervisor. It is difficult to define what "having a personality conflict" really means. However, this concept could be used to define Karen's and Roseanne's relationship. For whatever reason, they do not personally like each other. Additionally, Karen views Roseanne as basically being incompetent, lazy, and interested in doing as little work as possible. On the other hand, Roseanne perceives Karen as an overly energetic,

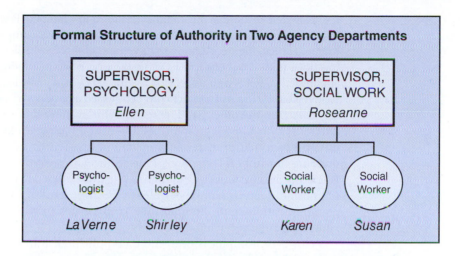

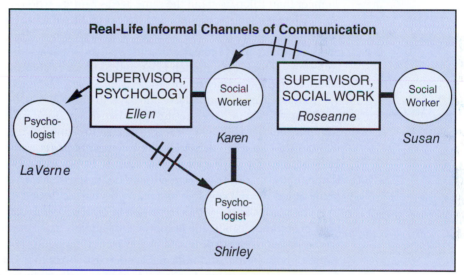

Figure 7-2 Organizational Charts Contrasting Formal and Informal Structures in Agencies

impulsive "go-getter" who acts "like a bull in a china closet." Both interact as little as possible with each other. Most communication between them takes place in email form, with Roseanne issuing Karen direct commands regarding what should and should not be done. Figure 7-2 illustrates Roseanne and Karen's relationship by the arrow that swoops up from Roseanne and down again to Karen. Communication and power consistently flow downward from Roseanne to Karen in a dictatorial, hierarchical fashion. Cross lines on the arrow indicate conflict.

Roseanne, on the other hand, has much in common with Susan, the other social worker. They frequently spend much time together and go out to lunch. Roseanne views Susan as a calmly competent worker who communicates well and is enjoyable company. In effect, Roseanne treats Susan like a friend and equal. Figure 7-2 illustrates this relationship with the thick linear bond linking Roseanne and Susan horizontally.

Now, let's investigate the informal relationship within the Psychology Department. Supervisor Ellen sees LaVerne, one of her supervisees, as a competent professional colleague. Hence, Figure 7-2 portrays LaVerne slightly below Ellen. The connecting arrow flows from Ellen down to LaVerne because Ellen maintains her supervisory and administrative status with respect to LaVerne. They essentially like each other on a professional basis. However, neither considers herself a personal friend of the other.

Ellen, on the other hand, perceives Shirley, her other supervisee, in a much different light. Ellen regrets hiring Shirley and has begun to document Shirley's difficulties in performance in preparation for "letting her go" (dismissing her or firing her from the agency). Thus, Shirley is positioned significantly below Ellen, the arrow connecting them running from Ellen down to Shirley. The chain of communication and power clearly positions Ellen in the more powerful, communication-controlling position, and Shirley in an inferior, less powerful, communication-receiving status.

However, the plot is even more complicated. Karen, who is substantially younger than Ellen, is about the same age as Shirley, who is also single. Karen and Shirley have much in common and have established a firm friendship. They, too, occasionally spend time and socialize with each other. Thus, a bold vertical line connects them. This indicates that they consider each other equals, friends, and colleagues. This is even though Ellen and Shirley's relationship is poor and quickly deteriorating. Cross lines on the arrow again indicate conflict.

Karen is in an uncomfortable and tenuous position. On the one hand, she values her friendship with Ellen. She also sees Ellen as a professional ally within the agency who provides her with some leverage against Roseanne. On the other hand, Karen likes Shirley. Karen understands that Ellen is not perfect (nor is she). Thus, Karen can listen to Shirley's complaints against Ellen and provide some sympathy. Karen, however, must take extreme care not to speak against either Ellen or Shirley to the other. It is not easy to maintain such a balancing act.

The point here is neither to praise nor criticize the existence of informal structures of communication and authority. Instead, it is to acknowledge that they do exist and pose a reality to deal with in any agency, including yours. In practice, being aware of both formal and informal agency structures may strengthen your ability to do your job. Once you know the options and alternatives open to you, you can make better informed, more effective choices.

What eventually happened at the Idle Ness Center described here? Shirley quit and left for another position in a different state. Shirley and Karen soon lost contact. Six months later, Karen also left the agency for another social work position that more closely matched her more energetic, enthusiastic style. She became a counselor for teens with serious behavioral and family problems. Karen and Ellen continued to maintain their personal friendship for many years after Karen left the agency. No one knows what became of Roseanne, Susan, or LaVerne.

Informal assessment of your agency environment can help you determine how you can best do your job. It can help you to decide the extent to which you "fit in" or should look for another job somewhere else.

The next sections of the chapter will explore in greater depth the processes of interpersonal communications, power, and politics as they occur in social services agencies.

EP 8a

> ## Critical Thinking Questions 7-1 LO 7-3
>
> Have you ever worked in an environment where the actual channels of communication differed significantly from those proposed by the formal agency structure? If so, in what ways did they differ?

Interpersonal Communication in Social Service Organizations LO 7-4

EP 1c, 6b

We've established that communication involves "the process of transmitting information from one person or place to another" (Williams, 2016b, p. 415). Such transfer occurs in the context of the perception of both the person sending information and those receiving it. The sender's **intent** is the information that the sender is trying to communicate. The receivers' **impact** is what the receivers actually comprehend. The communication's effectiveness involves the extent to which the sender's intent matches the receiver's impact. The receiver may *perceive* what the sender is saying in a very different way than what the sender is trying to say.

Perception and Communication LO 7-5

Williams (2016b) clarifies:

> **Perception** is the process by which individuals attend to, organize, interpret, and retain information from their environments. And because communication is the process of transmitting information from one person or place to another, perception is obviously a key part of communication. Yet, perception can also be a key obstacle to communication. (p. 416)

People are exposed to multiple stimuli at the same time. They may be talking on the phone while reading their email while someone knocks at their door. They thus must filter all the input they're getting and focus on what they perceive as the most significant or attention-grabbing aspects of that communication. People participating in the same group or watching the same event may have totally different perceptions or be in total disagreement about what's occurring.

Williams (2016b) explains:

> For example, every major stadium in the *National Football League* has a huge TV monitor on which fans can watch replays. As the slow-motion video is replayed on the monitor, you can often hear cheers *and* boos [at the same time], as fans of competing teams perceive the same replay in completely different ways. This happens because the fans' perceptual filters predispose them to attend to stimuli that support their team and not their opponents. (p. 416)

The filtering process involves four phases (Williams, 2016b):

Attention is the process of noticing or becoming aware of particular stimuli. Because of perceptual filters, we attend to some stimuli and not others. . . .

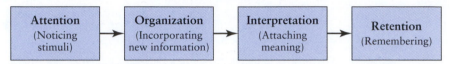

Figure 7-3 The Process of Perception

Organization is the process of incorporating new information (from the stimuli that you notice) into your existing knowledge. Because of perceptual filters, we are more likely to incorporate new knowledge that is consistent with what we already know or believe. **Interpretation** is the process of attaching meaning to new knowledge. Because of perceptual filters, our preferences and beliefs strongly influence the meaning we attach to new information (e.g., "This decision must mean that top management supports our project."). Finally, **retention** is the process of remembering interpreted information. Retention affects what we recall and commit to memory after we have perceived something. Of course, perceptual filters affect retention as much as they do organization and interpretation. Figure 7-3 depicts the process of perception.

In short, because of perception and perceptual filters, people are likely to pay attention to different things, organize and interpret what they pay attention to differently, and, finally, remember things differently. Consequently, even when people are exposed to the same communications (e.g., organizational memos, discussions with [supervisors] … or [clients]) …, they can end up with very different perceptions and understandings. (p. 417)

This difference in perception can also be seen in the criminal justice system when eye witnesses to an event recall vastly different information. When multiple witnesses see the same event, they may identify the alleged culprit as White, Black, or Hispanic, medium build or taller, wearing a blue or green or red jacket, with a full head of hair or balding and driving an SUV or a sedan. These perceptual differences make the job of law enforcement difficult and increase the chances for cases of mistaken identity.

Just as families or couples have misunderstandings (potentially resulting in fights), so do people communicating in organizations have problems "hearing" the meaning of what others are saying. For example, a supervisor may say to her social work supervisees, "The agency director is coming to talk to us tomorrow." One of the workers may perceive that she said, "The director probably wants to break some bad news to us." A second worker might think, "The director's going to pat us on the back for the nice job we did on that fundraising dinner." Still another worker may interpret, "The director's coming, and I never can understand a thing she says because her talks are always so disorganized."

Interpersonal Barriers to Communication in Agencies   LO 7-6

At least four barriers can inhibit effective communication in social service organizations. These include noise, personality factors, individual perceptual errors, and lying and distortion (Hellriegel & Slocum, 2011, pp. 258–259). Figure 7-4 illustrates how each of these barriers can negatively impact effective communication. They distort the congruence between the sender's *intent*, what the sender wants to communicate, and the receiver's *impact*, what the receiver actually interprets.

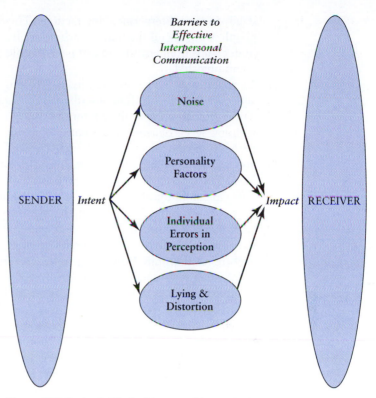

Figure 7-4 Barriers to Effective Interpersonal Communication

Noise The first barrier to effective interpersonal communication in agencies is *noise*, "any interference with the intended message" while a sender is trying to get his or her message across (Hellriegel & Slocum, 2011, p. 258). We've already established that people in work settings must sift through multiple stimuli to focus on, organize, interpret, and retain what has been said. Distractions can involve any number of circumstances. Several people might be talking at once. Someone might drop a large metal box filled with office equipment. Outside an office window, a car might crash into a lamp post. Another example is trying to talk on a cell phone while others in the vehicle are also talking on their cell phones.

Personality Factors Personality factors are the second type of barrier to effective interpersonal communication. We all know people who are popular and others whom everybody tries to avoid. Personality factors are a major dimension in any interpersonal relationship, including those developed in organizations. This is true both for social workers providing direct service and for people holding management positions. Five personality factors can either enhance or interfere with effective communication (Hellriegel & Slocum, 2011):

1. "*Emotional stability* is the degree to which a person is calm, secure, and free from persistent negative feelings" (p. 79). People with high levels of emotional stability can be described as calm, unexcitable, level-headed, and

steady in their interpersonal interactions. They are easier to work with than people who "fly off the handle" when the least bit flustered. Also, people under stress from any source can have trouble understanding what is being communicated.

2. "*Agreeableness* is a person's ability to get along with others" (p. 79). Highly agreeable people are often described as "considerate, friendly, helpful, and willing to compromise their interests" (p. 79). On the other hand, people with low levels of agreeableness are frequently characterized "as short tempered, uncooperative, and irritable" (p. 80). People who are highly agreeable are better at forming relationships with others. Other people are more likely to feel comfortable with them instead of being defensive and are more likely to communicate openly their feelings and ideas.

3. "*Extraversion* is the degree to which a person seeks the company of others" (p. 80). *Extraverts* (people who are socially outgoing) eagerly seek out and socialize with others. They generally develop good interpersonal skills and nurture relationships. *Introverts* (people who are socially withdrawn) tend to isolate themselves and avoid interaction with others.

4. "*Conscientiousness* involves self-discipline, acting responsibly, and directing our behavior" (p. 80). A conscientious person places importance on achieving goals and getting things done. Conscientious people are often described as organized and thorough. They take their responsibilities seriously and can be depended upon to carry out their tasks. A person who lacks conscientiousness tends to assume a laid-back attitude in which promptness and attention to detail are not all that important. It's much more difficult to work with, communicate with, and trust unreliable people than conscientious people.

5. "*Openness* describes imagination and creativity" (p. 80). An open person actively seeks out others' ideas and is open-minded about trying to understand them. Openness implies having the potential to change in response to new concepts and information. An individual who lacks openness can be described as closed-minded and unreceptive to new ways of thinking and doing things. These individuals are unlikely to accept information that disagrees with their already held ideas or positions.

Individual Errors in Perception   Individual errors make up the third category of perceptual mistakes involved in agency interpersonal communication. As people organize and interpret information, inaccuracies and errors in both perception and judgment may occur.

EP 1b

Critical Thinking Questions **7-2**

How would you describe yourself in terms of emotional stability, agreeableness, extraversion, conscientiousness, and openness? How do these personality variables relate to how you see yourself interacting with others in a work setting?

EP 8a

Accuracy of judgment is important because perceptions affect how people are treated in organizations. For example, a supervisor who attends to or emphasizes the wrong factors in a supervisee's performance could cause an inaccurate perception of how well that employee is functioning in the agency. This could result in a poor performance review of that employee instead of a good one. (Note that this book uses the terms *employee* or *worker* to refer to people who directly serve clients and other staff generally at the bottom of an organizational chart. The terms *manager* and *supervisor* refer to people higher in the organizational chart who have supervisory responsibility and authority over other employees. Specific agencies may choose one of the latter two terms over the other in their job titles and descriptions. The term *manager* can also refer to people in management higher in the organizational structure who have direct authority over supervisors or other managers.)

Another example of inaccurate judgment involves an employer interviewing a potential employee for a job. The interviewer may selectively focus on characteristics that are insignificant or simply miss out on the interviewee's best qualities because of perceptual errors and erroneous judgment. Several errors commonly occur in such job interview situations (Hellriegel & Slocum, 2011, pp. 114–115). First, **similarity error** happens when interviewers place too much importance on the similarities and differences between themselves and the interviewees. People are naturally drawn to others whom they perceive as being like themselves. Once, a job candidate was interviewing for a social work position. The candidate had mentioned on his resume that one of his personal areas of interest was flying airplanes recreationally. It just so happened that the interviewer was also a recreational flier. They "hit it off" immediately while talking about flying and the candidate was hired. The candidate, who was qualified for the job along with many others, felt strongly that having flying in common with the interviewer gave him an edge over other candidates and got him the job.

Contrast error, a second type of error of judgment, involves placing too much emphasis on how a job candidate compares with other candidates in the pool of those who applied. Every job search has a pool of candidates who apply. It's unpredictable who will be in the pool. Pools vary dramatically regarding the quality of applicants. An average candidate (in terms of qualifications such as education, experience, and interpersonal skills) may look terrible in a pool composed of applicants with stellar qualifications but look terrific compared to a group of very poorly qualified candidates. Keep this in mind in future searches for employment; much is out of your hands.

Third, **first-impression error** happens when, for whatever reason, an interviewer formulates an initial impression based on the perceptions of some variables and then refuses to change that impression. For example, an interviewee might be wearing orange earrings, a color the interviewer despises. It's neither fair nor logical, but the interviewer forms a negative impression of the interviewee right from the beginning of the interview. This view may be highly resistant to change, regardless of the interviewee's relevant qualifications.

Hellriegel and Slocum (2011) suggest guidelines to help make more accurate judgments in job interviewing situations: "(1) Avoid generalizing from an observation of a single trait (e.g., tactful) to other traits (e.g., stable, confident, energetic, dependable); (2) avoid assuming that a behavior will be repeated in all situations; and (3) avoid placing too much reliance on physical appearance" (p. 115).

Highlight 7-2 reviews several other specific perceptual errors that can occur in interpersonal communication in an agency context.

Critical Thinking Questions **7-3**

EP 8a

We probably have all been interviewed for a job at some time or another. Some of us have had many job interviews. If you've had such experience, picture a specific situation where you were interviewing for a job. To what extent do you think the interviewer's perceptions of you and your abilities were accurate? To what extent do you think that the interviewer made similarity, contrast, or first-impression errors? Did you get the job? Why or why not?

Highlight **7-2**

Specific Types of Individual Perceptual Errors in Agency Settings

EP 1b, 2c

Some other specific types of inaccurate judgments can occur in agency settings and interfere with effective interpersonal communication. These include stereotyping, the halo effect, projection, and assumptions about ethnicity and culture.

Stereotyping

We've established that a **stereotype** is "a fixed mental picture of a member of some specified group based on some attribute or attributes that reflect an overly simplified view of that group, without consideration or appreciation of individual differences" (Kirst-Ashman, 2017, p. 103). For example, if an agency worker maintains the stereotype that women make poor supervisors regardless of their practice and interpersonal skill levels, that worker will probably resent a woman being hired as his or her supervisor. Similarly, consider a young employee who automatically assumes that a person in his or her 70s is probably "getting senile." That young employee is unlikely to place any confidence in colleagues over 70. Additionally, the employee will likely have perceptual distortions about the abilities and strengths of senior clients.

Halo Effect

The **halo effect** is the condition where "one positive or negative characteristic dominates the way that person is viewed by others" (Hellriegel & Slocum, 2011, p. 116). For example, if Jadwiga, an agency worker, perceives her colleague Mohammad as having trouble being

punctual in meeting deadlines, that impression may color her impression of other aspects of Mohammad's personality and behavior. Jadwiga may display impatience whenever Mohammad volunteers to get something done for their *social work department* (a group of social workers clustered together under one supervisor in the organizational power structure and organizational chart). She may not listen to Mohammad's contributions during staff meetings, because she automatically assumes he's a poor worker. She may perceive everything Mohammad does negatively even when his work is done well and punctually.

Projection

"**Projection** is the tendency for people to see their own traits in other people" (Hellriegel & Slocum, 2011, p. 117). This is especially true for negative traits, including hostility, vengefulness, miserliness, disorganization, or the need to control others. In effect, projection reverses the truth. For example, consider a worker who savors manipulating colleagues to do work for him. He may also project this trait onto his colleagues and feel that they are trying to manipulate him into doing their work.

Assumptions about Ethnicity and Culture

EP 2

Hellriegel and Slocum (2011) explain how perceptions are influenced by ethnicity and culture:

Misinterpretation of the situation occurs when an individual gives certain meaning to observations and their relationships.

continued

Highlight **7-2** *continued*

Interpretation organizes our experience and guides our behavior. Read the following sentence and quickly count the number of Fs:

FINISHED FILES ARE THE RESULT OF YEARS OF SCIENTIFIC STUDY COMBINED WITH THE EXPERIENCE OF YEARS.

Most people who do not speak English see all six Fs. By contrast, many English speakers see only three Fs; they do not see the Fs in the word *of*. Why? Because English-speaking people do not think that the word *o* is important for them to understand the meaning of the sentence. We selectively see those words that are important based on our cultural upbringing. (p. 113)

The role of culture is important in organizational settings affecting both staff and staff/client interactions. For example, differences in cultural perceptions exist regarding what is appropriate behavior for people in the United States compared to those in Arab nations (Hellriegel & Slocum, 2011). A common behavior in the United States is to shake hands upon meeting. In Saudi Arabia, a male should not shake hands with a female unless she extends her hand first. Verbal greetings are appropriate. Under no circumstances should a male being introduced to a female greet her by kissing her on the cheek. In the United States, it is generally customary to open a gift in front of the gift giver when it is received. Arabian people do not do so in organizational settings, but open gifts later when the giver is no longer present. Gifts involving alcohol or pork should never be given to Arabian people.

EP 1a

Lying and Distortion   A fourth barrier to effective interpersonal communication in agencies, unfortunately, involves lying and distortion (Hellriegel & Slocum, 2011, p. 259). *Lying* is the use of communication to deceive information receivers into believing something that is not true. In contrast, *honesty* involves stating what one considers to be true in the most straightforward manner possible. **Distortion**, as defined by Hellriegel and Slocum, "represents a wide range of messages that a sender may use between the extremes of lying and complete honesty" (2011, p. 259). The intent is to slant information in a particular direction. An example is a social worker asked by her supervisor whether she has talked to Mrs. Smith today. The worker says, "Yes, I saw her this afternoon." The supervisor is concerned that the worker is maintaining contact with a particular client and the worker knows this. However, the worker's response that she talked to Mrs. Smith today does not tell the whole story. The conversation between the worker and Mrs. Smith came about when they met in the line at the grocery store, an unlikely place to have a typical worker–client interview. This is a distortion on the part of the worker.

The National Association of Social Workers (NASW) *Code of Ethics* instructs social workers to "act honestly and responsibly and promote ethical practices on the part of the organizations with which they are affiliated" (NASW, 2008). Furthermore, it directs social workers not to "participate in, condone, or be associated with dishonesty, fraud, or deception" (NASW, 2008, 4.04).

Critical Thinking Questions **7-4**

EP 8a

Have you had interactions in work settings that involved inaccuracies of judgment such as stereotyping, the halo effect, projection, or ethnic and cultural assumptions? If so, what were they? Did they involve misperceptions on your part or on the part of other staff? If you could go back and improve the communication and interaction both on your part and on the part of the other people who were involved, what would you change?

However, just as organizations are imperfect, so are the people who work in them. The *Code of Ethics* cannot guarantee that all professionals will always function in an ethical manner. We address the issues of lying and distortion because you may be confronted with these in the agency where you work.

Hellriegel and Slocum (2011), commenting from a business management perspective, note that "the use of vague, ambiguous, or indirect language doesn't necessarily indicate a sender's intent to mislead" (p. 259). In fact, they continue:

> This form of language may be viewed as acceptable political behavior. Silence may also be a form of distortion, if not dishonesty. Not wanting to look incompetent or take on a manager [or supervisor] in a departmental meeting, a subordinate may remain quiet instead of expressing an opinion or asking a question. (p. 259)

Sometimes, distortion provides a means of *impression management*, which "is an attempt by an individual to manipulate or control the impressions that others form about them" (Hellriegel & Slocum, 2011, p. 117). In other words, a person tries to manage or influence the *impression* that he or she is making on others. For example, a bartender might put a few big bills in his tip jar. The intent is to give customers the impression that big tipping is the way to go in that bar. The following are five tactics reflecting forms of impression management (Hellriegel & Slocum, 2011, p. 119):

1. **Ingratiation** is the act of seeking acceptance and support through deliberate efforts that aren't totally honest. They include unmeant flattery, support of others' opinions you don't agree with, running errands you really don't want to do, or laughing heartily at jokes you really don't think are all that funny.
2. **Self-promotion** is the act of describing oneself in an unwarranted and overly positive manner. It might be considered a form of bragging. The reason for self-promotion might be to boost self-esteem or to get ahead in some way (e.g., get a promotion or special treatment). An example from the most recent presidential campaign is the statement by one candidate that "I know more about ISIS than the generals do, believe me" (Beutler, 2016, p. 1).
3. **Intimidation** is the use of threatening behavior to make other people feel like something bad might happen to them if they don't do what you want them to. For example, Taylor wants Alfredo's support for an agency policy change. Taylor intimidates Alfredo by threatening that if Alfredo doesn't comply, he will be sorry. Taylor might say that she will never support Alfredo in any of his initiatives again. She might threaten to inform Alfredo's supervisor that he is uncooperative. The key to intimidation is an implied or even overt threat.
4. **Supplication** is behavior that suggests the need for help even though help is not really needed. One reason for supplication involves getting out of doing work a person doesn't want to do. Another reason simply entails getting satisfaction out of indirectly controlling someone else's behavior.
5. **Face-saving** is behavior that attempts to avoid being accountable for the full consequences of one's negative behavior, decisions, and performance (p. 259). People using face-saving strategies will try to make their actions look better than they really are. This might involve making excuses for why things turned out badly, blaming others for negative results, minimizing negative consequences by disguising them as not really being that bad, or denying that the problem really exists at all.

Lying is clearly unethical. Levels of distortion are more complex. For example, you don't necessarily say to someone you really don't like, "I really can't stand you. Shut up." In this instance, it's not that you're lying. Rather, it does not necessarily facilitate an agency's functioning to say every negative thing that comes to mind. However, on the continuum from mild distortion to lying, the more distortion strategies approach lying, the more unethical they are. The more that distortion and lying occurs in an agency environment, the worse the agency's potential for effective interpersonal communication. Focus on Ethics 7-1 addresses the ethics of using distortion. Focus on Ethics 7-2 suggests tactics for enhancing ethical communication in agency settings.

Focus on Ethics **7-1**

Using Distortion to Manipulate Others   `LO 7-7`

EP 1

To what extent do you feel distortion tactics are ethical or unethical? Are any such tactics ever useful or necessary? If so, which ones, and in what situations? Have you ever had experience using distortion tactics? If so, which ones and under what circumstances? Have distortion tactics ever been used on you? If so, what were your reactions?

Focus on Ethics **7-2**

Enhancing Ethical Communication in Agencies: Means to Empowerment

EP 1b,1c, 6b

There are several guidelines to improve ethical interpersonal communication in agencies. These are important both for management and other staff to implement.

1. Be honest. Simply put, honesty enhances open communication and increases trust. Colleagues are more likely to work together when they trust and like each other.

2. Practice empathy in your interpersonal work relationships. As noted, **empathy** is the interpersonal practice not only of *being in tune* with how another person feels, but also *conveying* to that person that you understand how he or she feels (Kirst-Ashman & Hull, 2018b). People are more likely to communicate with you and feel comfortable with you if they think you understand them.

3. Workers should strengthen their skills in listening carefully to each other and trying to understand what each other is really saying. An important aspect of communication is **active listening**. An active listener asks questions, uses paraphrasing to test for accuracy, pays full attention to the speaker, nods to show interest, and maintains appropriate eye contact.

(Daft & Marcic, 2017, p. 561). Both senders and receivers of communication should expend conscientious effort to understand and appreciate each other's point of view.

4. Management should work to establish an environment that encourages a **climate of trust and openness**: Being open with others in your agency or organization helps them feel comfortable communicating honestly with you and with others. This is important because subordinates often fail to transmit negative information for fear of what will happen. An example of this was when President Trump claimed that as many as 5 million illegal votes were cast in the 2016 election despite substantial evidence that this was not true. His press secretary's only response to a question about the obvious invention was, "It's something he believes," suggesting that no one wanted to fact-check the boss (Farley, 2017). In most organizations, a reluctance to be open, honest, and trust one's supervisor or leader contributes to a culture of denial or downplaying of serious problems. (Chapter 8 will discuss management approaches.)

The Social Worker as Employee: Supervision in Organizational Settings   LO 7-8

EP 1e

This book stresses the importance of interpersonal dynamics and relationships in the macro social environment. We have discussed the significance of organizational structure and interpersonal communication in social service organizations. Related to these dimensions is practitioners' use of supervision and their interaction with supervisors. In the organizational context, social workers practice under supervision. **Supervision** is the process by which a designated supervisor watches over and evaluates a worker's performance, directs and coordinates activities, and provides feedback. The goal of supervision is to maximize performance and make certain that activities are conducted and services are delivered effectively and efficiently. A good supervisor can be invaluable in helping practitioners get their work done successfully in agency settings. Generalist practitioners' interpersonal relationships with agency supervisors will always have special significance in the organizational environment (CSWE, 2015, EP 1e). The social work profession has heavily embraced the value and use of supervision.

You've most likely worked in some kind of job or, perhaps, many jobs, although not necessarily in social services. Regardless of what type of job you held, you had a supervisor to oversee your work. The skills used and responsibilities assumed in different jobs obviously vary widely. However, many aspects of the interpersonal relationship between an employee and a supervisor are the same regardless of job setting. You may have had what you considered a good supervisor or a bad supervisor. Such experiences provide you with insight for understanding the importance of supervision in any work environment, including social services settings. Working under and with supervisors is an important facet of the organizational macro social environment.

The following sections will explore administrative, educational, and other functions of supervisors; workers' general expectations of supervisors; how to use supervision effectively; and problems with supervision.

Administrative, Educational, and Other Functions of Supervisors

Supervisors perform a wide range of functions, many of which are not obvious to practitioners working directly with clients. Tasks include administrative and educational responsibilities in addition to a range of other functions.

Administrative Functions   In their administrative function, supervisors do such things as assign cases to workers, review case plans, and discuss progress on individual cases. Accomplishing these functions helps ensure that the agency's work is being completed in a proper and timely manner. Supervisors thus monitor the agency's direct service provision to clients. Supervisors also help workers stay in touch with changes in the agency. In a sense, supervisors occupy a middle ground between the worker and the agency administration. In this role, they serve as a two-way communication link.

We have established that supervisors convey to higher administration how well agency services are being administered. They also convey information from agency administration to workers who provide services directly to clients. Sometimes the information conveyed from the administration is positive. For example, it might be announced that the agency received an award for excellence or that the staff's annual vacation time will be increased. Once, I worked for a private agency whose administration decided to give all staff an extra day off on their respective birthdays. The staff applauded.

Other times, however, the administration will convey information through supervisors that will not be positive. For instance, workers might be told that their caseloads will be increased significantly. They might be instructed that they will have to remain on call and keep their cell phones with them every other Saturday night. Or they may learn that their morning and afternoon breaks will be cancelled despite their union contract providing for such breaks.

In these latter cases, it is helpful to be sensitive to a supervisor and his or her position. Supervisors can be placed in very precarious positions. They may be given directives to convey information to workers that they know workers will not like. Yet they may have had little or no input into the content of such directives. It's easy for you as a worker to become angry or disgusted at hearing bad tidings and direct your negative feelings toward your supervisor. Supervisors won't always be able to quell external demands or help you as much as you need, despite their good intentions. They will have their own job constraints and demands with which to contend.

Supervisors can also assist workers to become more effective in their assigned roles. If a worker is having difficulty, the supervisor should determine the reason. For example, is the problem a lack of knowledge, skill, or attitude? If so, what can the supervisor do to assist the worker in gaining what he or she needs?

Another example of a problem might be that there is no reward system for good job performance. Consider a social worker whose program is repeatedly over budget. Rarely is anything said about this. When the worker finally ends a year within budget, no recognition or acknowledgment is forthcoming. The worker ends up asking herself, "Why should I work so hard at cutting costs and keeping within my budget when no one cares anyway?" The following year, she is once again over budget. A supervisor should know what workers find rewarding and try to build in some type of reward structure.

Consider another issue. Is the worker somehow being punished for doing a good job? This can happen easily with workers who have been staying on top of the workload, getting paperwork completed on time, and otherwise performing in an exemplary fashion. A common reaction is to give this person more to do because "she can obviously handle it." Simultaneously, other workers who are less successful at balancing the job's demands are excused from additional assignments. In effect, such behavior serves to punish the good worker and reward the poor one.

EP 1, 2b

Educational Functions   Supervisors have a multifaceted educational role. They can aid workers by helping them improve their knowledge and skills, establish priorities among work tasks, and develop increased self-awareness. They also orient workers to both agency policy and social work values. This can serve to enhance workers' identification with the profession. Learning from supervisors can help workers engage in ongoing skill development. Supervisors can help new social workers learn about the agency and the clients it serves. This includes such characteristics as cultural heritage, values, and other information helpful for working with the client population.

Other Supervisory Functions Like many middle-management roles, the supervisor's job is not easy. Supervisors are caught between higher-level administration and their own supervisees, who operate at lower levels in the agency's structure of authority. Yet, workers expect a supervisor's assistance in negotiating the very system that pulls supervisors in opposite directions. A case in point involves a field-placement student in a hospital setting who angers a physician by writing something in a patient's chart the physician does not like. The physician misunderstands the student and is going to have the student reprimanded. The student's field instructor (her supervisor) intercedes to clarify the situation. Thus, the matter is resolved to everyone's satisfaction. The student truly needs such supervisory assistance. This illustrates how workers often depend on supervisors to help them deal with real everyday problems.

Workers also expect support from a supervisor. Unfortunately, supervisors must play a combined role as teacher-administrator-supporter. Sometimes the roles of supporter and teacher clash with the supervisor's administrative role. For example, supervisors might be called upon to reprimand or discipline supervisees. Likewise, supervisors might be asked to follow a specific course of action that is inconsistent with workers' needs or wishes.

For example, the upper-level administration of a social service organization abruptly decides to require that workers work an extra day on every other weekend in addition to their regular 40-hour, Monday-through-Friday workweek. Or, administrators might instruct supervisors to inform their supervisees that annual raises will be minimal or even nonexistent due to external funding cuts.

Workers' General Expectations of Supervisors

Supervisors can empower supervisees to become more effective in their practice with clients by providing help, information, and encouragement. The following are some general expectations that workers frequently have of their supervisors (Cassidy & Kreitner, 2010; Dolgoff, 2005; Leonard & Trusty, 2016; Kadushin & Harkness, 2014; Leonard, 2010):

1. *Be readily available to provide suggestions or assistance concerning difficult cases.* Workers expect their supervisors to help them out when they are confronted with a problem or an exceptionally difficult case. Hopefully, supervisors will use their own well-developed interpersonal skills to assist in the communication process. Sometimes, the supervisor's questions alone will help the worker figure out the best approach to take with a case, without the former even providing any specific instructions.

2. *Make certain that workers are knowledgeable about agency policy.* Agency policy tells workers which actions among a multitude of actions they may take and which they may not. Additionally, the policy may specify how an agency is structured, the qualifications of supervisors and workers, and the proper procedures agency staff should follow as they go about their daily work routines. Workers depend on immediate supervisors to keep them abreast of changes in agency policy and to continue monitoring their work to make sure they remain in compliance with policy.

3. *Provide input to higher levels of administration regarding line workers' needs.* Workers rarely have direct formal lines of communication with high-level

agency decision makers. Thus, workers must depend on their supervisors to communicate workers' needs upward so that this information reaches people in power who can make changes and meet needs. We have already discussed formal organizational structure and organizational charts that reflect the formal chain of command and communication.

4. *Facilitate cooperation among staff.* Workers expect their supervisors to coordinate all staff work so that together they can accomplish what they're supposed to do. If workers disagree with each other or enter into some conflict, supervisors will step in and mediate. Workers depend on supervisors to help attain some resolution of any number of problematic issues.

5. *Nurture workers and give them support when needed.* Workers depend on supervisors to encourage them to perform competently. Workers hope that supervisors will praise them when they do their work well. Often, workers look to supervisors when they need to vent feelings or discuss issues.

6. *Evaluate workers' job performance.* Workers expect supervisors to evaluate the strengths and weaknesses they demonstrate while doing their jobs. Workers depend on supervisors to get them back on track when they do something wrong or ineffectively. Workers often need constructive criticism. Frequently, supervisors have direct input in the matter of performance-based raises.

7. *Facilitate workers' development of new skills.* Supervisors assume positions superior to those of workers. Workers depend on their supervisors to be more knowledgeable than they are. Thus, workers look to supervisors to help them develop new skills and improve their expertise.

8. *Demonstrate trustworthiness.* Employees expect to trust their supervisors to be honest, truthful, trustworthy, and ethical.

Using Supervision Effectively

Effective use of supervision hinges partly on your own behavior and characteristics as a worker. Communicating clearly and regularly with your supervisor can get you the help you need to work through exceptionally difficult situations and find resources you would not otherwise know about. The following are some helpful suggestions for maximizing your use of supervision (Kadushin & Harkness, 2014; Sheafor & Horejsi, 2015; Wallace & Masters, 2006).

EP 1c

Use Your Communication Skills with Your Supervisor   Work on using good communication skills with a supervisor. Check to be certain that the messages you hear are clear. Ask questions. Rephrase a question if you don't think your supervisor understands what you mean. Paraphrase your supervisor's answer to ensure you understand what was said. (*Paraphrasing* is restating what the other person has said, but using different words.) Monitor your nonverbal behavior (such as facial expressions and body positioning) to make certain you're giving an accurate impression of how you feel and what you mean.

When your supervisor uses a word you don't understand or one that does not make sense, ask what he or she means. Sometimes people will use letters or acronyms (e.g., NASW, CSWE, OSHA, KUMQUAT, or PIGWART). If you don't know what it means, *ask.*

Plan your messages to your supervisor carefully ahead of time, especially email or written ones. Keep in mind the following questions:

What am I trying to say?

Who is my intended listener?

Is there a best time to communicate?

Is there an ideal place to communicate?

How best should I communicate?

What is the purpose of my communicating?

Written communication is important. Decisions that require a supervisor's agreement should often be put in writing. One way you might do this is by sending an email to your supervisor, summarizing his or her instructions or your mutual decisions regarding some plan of action. This documents the fact that you have your supervisor's support.

 Keep Up-to-Date Records   Agencies run on records. A common source of irritation between coworkers and supervisors concerns recordkeeping. Keeping up-to-date records is frequently difficult. The pressure of ordinary business makes it hard to take time away from serving clients to maintain case records. However, recordkeeping is essential for accountability. You are accountable to your supervisor, and he or she, in turn, is accountable to higher levels of administration. If you fail to keep up with required recordkeeping, it will reflect badly on your supervisor. Additionally, if you eventually leave your position for some reason, your successor will have a tough time figuring out your cases if you haven't kept good records.

Plan Your Supervisory Agenda Ahead of Time   Many workers have a set time to talk with their supervisors. Use this time to the fullest. Think about the topics and ideas you want to discuss. List the questions you have. Make sure you cover the items on your list before you leave the session. If sufficient time is available, you might even email or give your supervisor a copy of your agenda beforehand so that he or she can think about the topics prior to the meeting. However, be sensitive to your supervisor's reactions to this structured approach. Be careful not to be too aggressive or pushy. Coming on too strong threatens some supervisors.

 Put Yourself in Your Supervisor's Shoes   Use empathy with your supervisor. *Empathy* has been defined as the interpersonal practice not only of *being in tune* with how another person feels, but also *conveying* to that person that you understand how he or she feels (Kirst-Ashman & Hull, 2018b). Your supervisor is an individual with his or her own feelings, interests, biases, and opinions. Think about both what he or she needs to know and what he or she needs to communicate to you. It is helpful to get to know your supervisor as well as possible. How might you best respond to your supervisor's needs and issues?

EP 6b

 Display an Openness to Learning and to Improving Yourself   Displaying an openness to learning means that you should be willing to accept criticism and to use it to improve your work. It also means you must be able to admit when you don't know something or even when you have made a mistake. This is often hard to do.

EP 1b

It is difficult to admit to one's lacks or failings. However, the willingness to seek help is basic to learning. Consider your supervisor a resource that you should be willing to use (i.e., of course, if your supervisor is competent).

Demonstrate a Liking for Your Work   Major complainers and whiners are usually very unappealing to both supervisors and others. It is better to emphasize the positive aspects of your work, including those facets you especially like. Generally speaking, if you do not like your work, you should quit and pursue other opportunities. Continuing to hold a position that you find unsatisfying can lead to burnout and a diminished interest in fulfilling your helping role.

An illustration of this point comes to mind. Several years ago, two probation and parole agents came to address an Introduction to Social Work class. Both had been in the corrections field for many years and had talked to other classes several years earlier. During the current talk, they referred to their clients in derogatory terms, criticized their agency and agency colleagues, and displayed a high level of dislike for their work responsibilities in general.

By the end of the class, it was evident that both agents had become burned out from their jobs. They were no longer operating within a social work value system. Following their departure, the instructor had to spend some time undoing the negative impressions the speakers had left regarding what social work was all about. Of course, the instructor never again invited them back to the university, although they might have served as good examples for a class on stress and burnout.

Work Cooperatively with Other Staff   Much of social work requires teamwork, addressed in previous and in future chapters. Your supervisor will expect you to work well with other social workers and with professionals from other disciplines. Be sensitive to how your behavior affects others. Show respect for the competence and talents of your peers and coworkers. Be tolerant of what you see as their shortcomings. Try to see the world from their perspectives and understand why they feel and act the way they do.

Give Your Supervisor Feedback   Supervisors can benefit from feedback as much as workers. Tactfully, let your supervisor know what you like and dislike. If you have specific needs that your supervisor can appropriately fulfill, share them. Use the suggestions for giving feedback found earlier in the chapter in the section "Use Your Communication Skills with Your Supervisor."

Forewarn Your Supervisor about Problematic Situations   Supervisors should be alerted whenever a case becomes especially problematic. When you don't know about the implications of a particular course of action or how it might affect the agency, share this information with your supervisor. Get help. Don't wait until things have developed to crisis proportions before talking to your supervisor.

Learn Your Supervisor's Evaluation System   Ask your supervisor for the basis upon which you will be evaluated. It might be an evaluation form or a description of the evaluation process in the agency's policy manual. Your job description can also help orient you to what you're supposed to be doing and accomplishing. Regardless, you should know far in advance what criteria your supervisor and agency will use to evaluate you. Hopefully, there will be no, or few, surprises during an evaluation meeting.

At a Glance **7-1**

Using Supervision Effectively

— Use your communication skills with your supervisor.
— Keep up-to-date records.
— Plan your supervisory agenda ahead of time.
— Put yourself in your supervisor's shoes.
— Display an openness to learning and to improving yourself.

— Demonstrate a liking for your work.
— Work cooperatively with other staff.
— Give your supervisor feedback.
— Forewarn your supervisor about problematic situations.
— Learn your supervisor's evaluation system.

Evaluation systems may be *formative*, that is, ongoing. Such evaluations provide regular feedback, thereby allowing workers to make corrections as the need arises. *Summative* evaluations are scheduled to occur periodically. These evaluations tend to be more general in that they summarize progress and accomplishments over a longer, designated period, such as a year or six months. Some agencies and supervisors use both formative and summative approaches in conjunction with each other.

Problems in Supervision

Just as there is no perfect world, there is no perfect work environment. Likewise, there are no perfect supervisors. Complaints about supervisors are common. Sometimes they are valid; other times they are not. There will be times when, despite how hard you try, you will be unable to get formal, quality supervision.

There are many reasons why supervisors can be ineffective (Kirst-Ashman & Hull, 2018b). They may have gotten the job for whatever reason, even though they are not competent to do it. Thus, they're incapable of providing you with the help you need. Sometimes, supervisors take credit for their employees' work, which of course causes resentment on the employees' part. Some supervisors don't like to work very hard. You may feel that they're not doing their job the way they should. A supervisor may dislike conflict and shy away from it. Such a supervisor may provide no help in resolving interpersonal disputes among staff. Finally, supervisors may have difficulty delegating work to supervisees. They may not trust in your competence to do a good job. They may monitor your work too closely and "breathe down your neck" at every opportunity. Highlight 7-3 illustrates several unproductive games that can be played in supervisor–supervisee relationships.

Highlight **7-3**

Games Supervisors and Supervisees Sometimes Play

The supervisory relationship can be a complex one. In any supervisory dyad, both people are unique individuals with distinctly different personalities. Communication is rife with the potential for misunderstandings, conflicts, and manipulation. Power, of course, is also involved. As a result, there are a number of games that workers and supervisors play. Because they are games, they prevent real issues from being addressed out in the open. Games can also corrode relationships.

Kadushin and Harkness (2014; Kadushin, 1968) have cited many games worth staying alert to:

1. *I'll be nice to you if you'll be nice to me.* This game involves a supervisory relationship in which both parties are afraid to give any negative or constructive feedback. They avoid real issues by complimenting each other. This is fake interaction. Remarks are rarely genuine. The

continued

Highlight **7-3** *continued*

purposes of supervision are not fulfilled because of the participants' hesitation to assertively confront each other and the issues.

2. *Therapize me.* This game involves the supervisor delving into the worker's personal life and issues. This is inappropriate. If workers need counseling—as many of us do at various times during our lives—they should receive it outside their agency setting from another professional whom they pay. It is also inappropriate for workers to use their supervisors' time in this manner and for supervisors to pry into their workers' personal lives. The purpose of maintaining a working environment is to get the necessary work done, nothing else. If a worker is experiencing personal crises or emotional problems, it is appropriate for a supervisor to provide that worker with feedback. The feedback should focus on the worker's job performance and how personal issues might be affecting that performance. It is also appropriate for a supervisor to suggest that the worker get some counseling to resolve the problems that are affecting his or her work behavior.

3. *Good buddies don't evaluate.* This game usually entails a supervisor who feels uncomfortable holding a superior position over workers. To avoid having to sit down and evaluate workers' performances, the supervisor becomes friends, and, in effect, personal equals with workers. Once again, this game interferes with the purposes of supervision. Workers and supervisors fail to get constructive feedback from each other. Workers are cut off from having access to the supervisor's expertise and assumption of responsibility over them. A worker needs a supervisor, not a friend, to keep him or her on track.

4. *Of course, I know much more than you do.* This is a game of one-upmanship. Either the supervisor or the worker consistently reveals that he knows much more than the other. You might meet people like this in your classes—you know, someone who sits in the front row and, with an exceptionally condescending tone, corrects the instructor at least twice each week.

5. *Poor, helpless, little old me.* In this game, the employee dependently leans on the supervisor for almost everything while the worker "plays dumb."

He asks the supervisor to validate almost everything he does. In this way, he doesn't have to do much thinking. He manipulates the supervisor into doing all of his thinking for him. He can also avoid responsibility for mistakes. If he makes one, he can blame the supervisor because he "said it was OK" or "told me to do it that way."

6. *Information is power.* This game occurs when one or the other in the supervisory relationship withholds information. A worker can withhold information from a supervisor to avoid the supervisor's scrutiny. For example, a worker seriously edits the facts about a particular case. He does so because he feels he should be doing more with the case. Omitting information keeps the supervisor in the dark concerning what the worker is not doing.

Likewise, a supervisor can keep information from an employee to maintain greater control over that employee. Consider a supervisor who keeps one worker from knowing that her colleagues have a considerably smaller caseload than she does. In effect, not telling her that she's doing more than her share keeps her doing it and getting things done for the supervisor.

7. *Avoiding the issue.* This game requires a supervisor or worker who avoids salient issues by using criticism or changing the subject. For example, a worker says, "I am very concerned about my client's alcohol problem. How do you think I should proceed?"

The supervisor responds, "It sounds as if you don't feel very confident in that area." In this way, the supervisor both blames the worker for ignorance and avoids providing any concrete assistance.

8. *Pose questions to answer questions.* As with "avoiding the issue," this game is used to sidetrack real issues. Instead of answering a question, a worker or supervisor responds with another question. This behavior, of course, throws the responsibility for answering a question back to the person who asked it in the first place. For example, a worker might ask a supervisor, "Can I take Friday afternoon off?" The supervisor responds, "What would happen if I let the whole unit off on Fridays? Who would be around to serve clients?" This response avoids giving an answer. Instead, it places the responsibility for finding an answer on the worker.

EP 8a

Critical Thinking Questions **7-5**

Supervision is an important aspect of working in an organizational context, whether it is a social services agency, business, or any other organization. What types of jobs have you held? In what types of organizations (e.g., businesses) have you worked? What were your supervisors like? One by one, picture each supervisor in your mind. Evaluate each according to the following variables and explain your reasons. To what extent was this specific supervisor:

- Competent?
- Capable of providing you with help when you needed it?
- Supportive of your work?
- A good communication link between you and upper levels of management or administration?
- A good facilitator of cooperation among you and other staff?
- Effective at resolving intra-staff conflicts?
- A fair and reasonable evaluator of your job performance?
- Effective at providing you with positive feedback about good performance?
- Helpful in terms of facilitating the development of new skills?

Consultation in Organizational Settings

EP 1e

Consultation is the process of seeking out and receiving expert help from an individual, group, or organization to resolve an identified problem or address a designated issue. Supervision also should provide skilled assistance to improve job functioning. However, the definition of *consultation* used here differs from that of **supervision** in two ways. First, supervision is an ongoing process inherent in an organization's structure that addresses supervisees' overall work performance and many specific practice matters. In other words, the supervisor has some degree of administrative authority over the supervisee. Second, consultation is sought outside of ongoing administrative relationships to address a designated, explicit problem or issue. A consultant has no administrative power over the recipient of consultation. The recipient can choose to use the consultant's input and suggestions or not.

Consultation can be useful when an individual, group, organization, or even a community is addressing a problem that is beyond its ability to solve. Consultation can occur within an agency or expert help can be sought outside of the agency, depending on the assistance needed. Internally, consultation may be provided informally among colleagues. Externally, consultation may also be imparted on a formal contractual basis when one party seeks out the established expertise of another, often at some financial cost.

For example, social work programs seeking accreditation often hire an expert consultant from an outside source to help them through the complex accreditation process. (**Accreditation** is an official body's formal recognition that some organization has met all the standards required by the accrediting body.) Accredited social work programs must provide evidence that their students have mastered various competencies necessary for social work practice (e.g., application of critical thinking skills and ethical principles), and that the learning environment satisfies established standards (e.g., the program has appropriate admissions procedures for students, faculty assignments, and resources) (CSWE, 2015).

Note that social workers have established themselves as consultants in a range of areas; for example, they can assist other professionals in their work or be called upon to provide testimony in court as expert witnesses. The latter requires a formal recognition by the judge that the person is an expert in his or her field.

Power and Politics in Social Service Organizations   LO 7-9

EP 2

We have established that *power* is the potential ability to move people on a chosen course to produce an effect or achieve some goal. Power is an important concept regarding social service organizations. Power in this context extends far beyond the relationships between individual supervisors and supervisees. Who has power and how it's used directly affects how workers can do their jobs. Management has power over workers (including you when you get a job). However, we determined earlier that there are various types of power that don't necessarily coincide with the formal organizational chart. Therefore, a discussion of power in organizations is relevant to you for at least two reasons. First, management has the potential to empower you to do your job well. Second, as a worker you can think in terms of your own power and how you can strive to improve agency functioning. You may also develop tactics to influence people in power when advocating for clients or improved service provisions. For example, you might feel that agency hours should be extended to better accommodate clients' schedules. Or you might feel clients' needs are not being met adequately in some area (e.g., counseling, transportation, financial support) and you decide to advocate on their behalf. Acquisition of a power base may also be useful when requesting benefits such as a raise or prime vacation times.

Types of Power

Chapter 3 discussed the five types of power that group leaders may have. These types of power also apply to people working in organizations (Daft, 2016b; Lussier & Achua, 2016). Sources of power include the following:

- *Legitimate power* (that attained because of one's position and vested authority)
- *Reward power* (that which stems from the ability to provide positive reinforcement and rewards to others)
- *Coercive power* (the capability of dispensing punishments in order to influence others' behavior)
- *Referent power* (that held because of other group members' respect and high esteem)
- *Expert power* (that based on established authority or expertise in a particular domain)

Supervisors and managers usually are given legitimate power. They also often have reward and coercive power. Anyone, including direct service workers and supervisors or managers, can develop referent and expert power.

The concept of power is quite complex. Vecchio (2006) explains:

> Power is an essential feature of a manager's [or supervisor's] role. Without some degree of power, a [supervisor] . . . would find it difficult to direct the efforts of subordinates. Thus, power underlies a [supervisor's] . . . effectiveness. Subordinates also possess forms and degrees of power. For example, subordinates can control the work flow or withhold support from their [supervisor]. . . . Therefore, to some extent, each member of an organization possesses power.
>
> Because power is intangible, it is very difficult to define clearly and precisely. Also, our language has several similar terms that we tend to confuse with power, such as authority and influence. . . .
>
> Power is not always legitimate. Therefore, we speak of *authority* as the right to try to change or direct others. Authority includes the notion of legitimacy. It is the right to influence others in the pursuit of common goals agreed upon by various parties. [For example, supervisors have authority by virtue of their job titles and descriptions.] Power, in contrast, does not always pursue common goals and may, at times, be clearly directed to pursuing only a single individual's goals.
>
> Another term, **influence**, is also frequently used when discussing the notion of power. Influence tends to be subtler, broader, and more general than power. Although both influence and power can be defined as the ability to change the behavior of others, power embodies the ability to do so with regularity and ease. Influence is weaker and less reliable than power. . . . Influence relies on particular tactics and often employs face-to-face interactions. Thus, the exercise of influence tends to be more subtle than the exercise of power. (p. 124)

Determining who has power can be tricky. Sometimes, people with important titles or placement high in the organizational structure have little ability to influence and control subordinates' behavior. Because people in power have the potential ability to influence your work behavior and how clients are served, it's important to know who has this power. Aldag and Kuzuhara (2005) explain:

> How can you tell who has power in an organization? Job titles may help; so may status symbols. Still, we know these things can be deceptive and that some people with a lot of power don't have fancy titles or big offices. Some other signs of managers' power include the abilities to do the following:
>
> - Intercede favorably on behalf of someone in trouble with the organization.
> - Get a good placement for a talented subordinate.
> - Gain approval for expenditures beyond the budget.
> - Obtain above-average salary increases for subordinates.
> - Place items on the agenda at policy meetings.
> - Get fast access to top decision makers.
> - Have regular, frequent access to top decision makers.
> - Obtain early information about decisions and policy shifts. (pp. 370–371)

Politics in Social Service Organizations LO 7-10

Organizational politics are "attempts by individuals to influence the behavior of others as a means to protect their self-interests, meet their own needs, and advance their own goals" (Hellriegel & Slocum, 2011, p. 293). This advantage is achieved "through means other than merit or luck" (Dubrin, 2012, p. 456). Aldag and Kuzuhara (2005) further explain:

> When we hear someone speak of organizational politics, we probably think of such things as "passing the buck," "apple polishing," "backstabbing," and other "dirty tricks" we use to further our selfish interests. We use the term organizational politics more broadly, to refer to activities that people perform to acquire, enhance, and use power and other resources to obtain their preferred outcomes in a situation where there is uncertainty or disagreement. Because the focus is on people's preferred outcomes, rather than organizational outcomes, this may or may not involve activities contrary to the best interests of the organization. (p. 378)

Don't automatically think that organizational politics are always evil and self-serving (Dubrin, 2012; Nelson & Quick, 2015). Sometimes, agency problems or needs should be addressed. A policy might not be working, or a supervisor might not be performing all her responsibilities. It's beyond the scope of this book to teach you *how* to advocate for positive changes, but you should be aware of organizational politics as an important aspect of human behavior in the macro social environment. For one thing, most people prefer to be somewhat "political" by avoiding "criticizing your boss in public, losing control of your emotions during meetings, or challenging sacred beliefs or values of the organization" (Aldag & Kuzuhara, 2005, p. 379). Therefore, being aware of politics might be important, "if only to be alert for the political actions of others and to avoid personal embarrassment" (Aldag & Kuzuhara, 2005, p. 379).

Dynamics Contributing to Political Behavior in Agencies The following are four of the many reasons politics occur in organizations:

1. Organizations are by nature political (Griffin & Moorhead, 2014). They are made up of a range of units or departments, each striving to achieve its own goals and competing for resources. Competition is a fact of life. Power enhances the ability to compete. Power often allows for greater control.
2. Scarce resources intensify the need for power to compete successfully (Nelson & Quick, 2015). Griffin and Moorhead (2014) explain:

> Whenever resources are scarce, some people will not get everything they think they deserve or need. Thus, they are likely to engage in political

---

Critical Thinking Questions **7-6**

EP 8a

Power relationships characterize all organizations, including social services and businesses. Most of us have had work experience. Think of a job you've had. What types of power did your direct supervisor have? Who else in the organization had influence or power, and how did they use it?

behavior as a means of inflating their share of the resources. In this way, a manager seeking a larger budget might present accurate but misleading or incomplete statistics to inflate the perceived importance of her department. Because no organization has unlimited resources, incentives for this kind of political behavior are often present. (p. 388)

3. Uncertainty encourages agency politics (Griffin & Moorhead, 2014; Nelson & Quick, 2015). If organizational goals are vague, people may struggle for greater control over the agency's direction. If lines of authority are unclear, people may contend for control over their own behavior and that of others.

4. Some people are more power-oriented than others (Nelson & Quick, 2015). When power is limited, power-oriented workers, supervisors, or managers will often try to expand their influence. "Power-oriented managers [or supervisors] sometimes cope with the limited amount of power available by expanding their sphere of influence sideways. For example, the director of the SNAP (food stamp) program in a government agency might attempt to gain control over the housing assistance program, which is at the same level" (Dubrin, 2007, p. 270). (*Food stamps* are credits distributed through a federal program to be used like cash to purchase primarily food, plants, and seeds [Barker, 2003]. **Housing assistance** often involves rental subsidies or vouchers by which government programs assist with rent, mortgage payments, and low-rent public housing, or block grants to state and local governments for developing affordable housing [Dolgoff & Feldstein, 2013; Kirst-Ashman, 2013].) Some people who are extremely concerned with gaining power are characterized by "**Machiavellianism**, a tendency to manipulate others for personal gain" (Dubrin, 2007, p. 270). Such people thrive on gaining power for power's sake.

Focus on Ethics 7-3 addresses the issue of political behavior in organizations. Highlight 7-4 explores the concept of organizational justice.

Focus on Ethics **7-3**

Political Behavior in Organizations

EP 1

Champoux (2006) reflects:

Political behavior in organizations raises many questions about what is ethical and what is not. ... Using power and political behavior in an organization to serve self-interest is unethical. ... Similarly, political behavior that uses excessive organizational resources to reach a personal goal is also unethical. These observations suggest that any political strategy and its associated tactics are unethical if they do not serve the organization's goals or at least the goals of a larger group (clients or staff serving clients on the clients' behalf). (p. 372)

Champoux (2006) suggests considering the following characteristics to determine that political behavior in an organizational context is ethical:

■ The behavior should serve people outside the organization [(clients), not just the person using politics for personal gain]. ...

■ Individuals should clearly know the person's intent and give their consent ... to be influenced. ...

■ Administering the organization's resources, procedures, and policies should allow fair treatment of all affected people. (p. 372)

Highlight **7-4**

Organizational Justice LO 7-12

EP 3a, 5c

Social justice has been defined as the broad philosophical perspective that all people have the right to enjoy equal opportunities in economic, political, and social realms. Social justice ensures that all citizens would have the same rights and benefits as well as the same responsibilities and opportunities regardless of their background or membership in diverse groups. Similarly, **economic justice** has been defined as the distribution of resources in a fair and equitable manner. Social and economic justice can also be viewed within the context of organizations. Both can be applied to how workers at various levels in the organization are treated and how they feel about their treatment. This does not mean that each employee should be treated identically. Employees have different responsibilities and receive different salaries for their work. A key concept involved in social and economic justice is fairness, the idea that employees are treated impartially, honestly, and according to the rules (agency policy). The economic aspect concerns receiving compensation related to their role, merit, and significance within the organization.

Organizational justice, then, involves the "perceptions of people in an organization regarding fairness"; organizational justice can be divided into four types—distributive, procedural, interpersonal, and informational justice (Griffin & Moorhead, 2014, pp. 392–394).

Distributive Justice

Griffin and Moorhead (2014) describe distributive justice:

> **Distributive justice** refers to people's perceptions of the fairness with which rewards and other valued outcomes are distributed within the organization. ... Perceptions of distributive justice affect individual satisfaction with various work-related outcomes such as pay, work assignments, recognition, and opportunities for advancement. Specifically, the more *just* people see rewards to be distributed, the more satisfied they will be with those rewards; the more *unjust* they see rewards to be distributed, the less satisfied they will be. Moreover, individuals who feel that rewards are not distributed justly may be inclined to attribute such injustice to misuse of power and/or to political agendas. (p. 392)

Procedural Justice

Procedural justice involves people's perceptions of the fairness of an organization's procedures and processes as well as how the organization carries out tasks and achieves goals (Griffin & Moorhead, 2014). For example, consider the process of evaluating an employee's work. One supervisor is experienced, knowledgeable about the formal evaluation process, and adept at communicating information about that process to supervisees. Supervisees would much more likely consider this supervisor fair and just than a supervisor who was vague, ill-informed about the process, lax about following the prescribed procedure, and poor at communicating information concerning the evaluation.

Griffin and Moorhead (2014) continue:

> When workers perceive a high level of procedural justice, they are somewhat more likely to be motivated to participate in activities, to follow rules, and to accept relevant outcomes as being fair. But if workers perceive more procedural injustice, they tend to withdraw from opportunities to participate, to pay less attention to rules and policies, and to see relevant outcomes as being unfair. (p. 393)

Interpersonal Justice

Interpersonal justice is "the degree of fairness people see in how they are treated by others in their organization" (p. 394). Supervisees will likely perceive a high level of interpersonal justice under the following conditions. First, supervisors and management treat employees with respect. Second, they make employees feel like they have a voice that is heard. Third, supervisors and management communicate information to employees about what is happening in the organization. Fourth, simply put, management is honest.

If the opposite conditions prevail, then supervisees will likely feel the interpersonal atmosphere of the organization is unfair and unjust. That is, if employees don't feel respected by management, think they are treated with contempt or condescension, don't have access to true information, and suspect dishonesty on the part of administration, a low level of interpersonal justice will likely prevail.

continued

Highlight **7-4** *continued*

Informational Justice

Informational justice is "the perceived fairness of information used to arrive at decisions" (Griffin & Moorhead, 2014, p. 394). If an employee thinks that a supervisor or management "made a decision based on relatively complete and accurate information, and that the information was appropriately processed and considered, the person will likely experience informational justice even if they don't completely agree with the decisions. But if [an employee] … feels that the decision was based on incomplete and inaccurate information and/or that important information was ignored, the individual will experience less informational justice" (p. 394).

The Importance of Organizational Justice

Social workers are responsible for advancing human rights and social, economic and economic justice, regardless of the context (CSWE, 2015, EP 3). They are thus responsible for incorporating social justice practices in organizations. Supporting and establishing distributive, procedural, interpersonal, and informational justice within an organization provides a means for accomplishing this.

Environmental Justice

Though not discussed by Griffith and Moorhead, **Environmental justice** has been identified by CSWE as a goal toward which students should be prepared. Environmental justice is a state of being in which all people are treated fairly in the establishment and enforcement of environmental policies and laws. It requires that people do not suffer because of the environment in which they work or live. Examples of environmental injustice include decisions and actions that result in pollutants threatening air, food and water, hazards such as unsafe home insulation and building materials, and the lack of access to healthy and reasonably priced foods. No group in society should experience an unequal share of environmental injustice. Unfortunately, environmentally unjust experiences are most often visited upon people of color and lower income communities. This is because they and their communities are more often targeted for the placement of services and facilities such as landfills, polluting industries, waste treatment plants, toxic waste dumps, and similar hazards (Skelton & Miller, 2016). We will refer to environmental issues and justice in more detail in Chapters 9 and 10.

EP 5, 5b,
8, 8c

Using Agency Politics for Positive Change LO 7-11   We've indicated that as an agency worker, you may be in the position to advocate for positive change on behalf of clients or agency personnel. The following are tactics to establish a power base within an agency setting so that you might have greater influence with decision makers.

First, conduct a **political diagnosis**, an assessment of "the location of power in an organization and the type of political behavior that is likely to happen" identifying "politically active individuals and coalitions in the organization, the amount of power they have, and the likely ways they will use their power" (Champoux, 2006, p. 367).

You can pursue several strategies to identify individuals who have power; start with the "organization chart and a description of titles and duties" (Champoux, 2006, p. 367). Then interview people in various organizational units to determine how decisions are made, who has decision-making responsibility for distributing resources, how identified people generally use their power or are likely to, and what their goals are for their performance and status within the organization.

It is also important to identify any coalitions within the agency. "A *coalition* is an alliance of individuals who share a common goal. Coalitions are also interest groups that try to affect decisions in the organization. Coalitions can have members from widely scattered parts of the organization" (Champoux, 2006, p. 368). An example of a coalition occurred in a social agency upon the arrival of a new executive director. The new executive director decided quickly that every staff member should have his or her own printer instead of everyone using a central printer serving each floor of their building. (She based this need on the time wasted as each worker issued a print command, walked down the hall to see if the document was ready, and oftentimes waited while other print jobs were printing since the printer was being used by as many as 35 people.) When the new executive director made the decision, she was immediately challenged by a coalition that included, the technology supervisor, the office manager, and the deputy director. The three individuals had been in their positions for many years and controlled many aspects of the agency. In fact, the deputy director had been a candidate for the executive director's position. Each felt threatened by the flexibility and freedom that this printer decision offered staff members and decided to use their influence to change the executive director's mind. (Note: The coalition failed in their effort.)

Assessing coalitions should involve the same strategies used in assessing the power of individuals within the organization. This should help establish the agency's "political network," the system of "affiliations and alliances of individuals and coalitions" within the social service organization's environment (Champoux, 2006, p. 368).

A second tactic for enhancing power and influence involves developing contacts and relationships with people in power (Dubrin, 2012). Such people can provide you with support and information to help achieve your goals.

Third, to increase your power base, form coalitions yourself (Lussier & Achua, 2016). This may be as simple a thing as forming a coalition to have enough votes to get a proposal passed in a committee. Or it may involve a coalition approaching an administrator with a new idea to persuade him or her to adopt it. Involving more people tends to enhance your credibility and validity.

Fourth, get information about what's going on (Lussier & Achua, 2016). Keeping current helps you develop believable arguments on your behalf. Being knowledgeable inspires people's confidence in you.

Fifth, provide positive feedback where warranted (Aldag & Kuzuhara, 2005). Positive feedback can be given concerning others' statements, support, and performance. Positive feedback helps to strengthen interpersonal relationships. Persistent complainers tend to turn other people off. People with positive proposals who are known to be supportive are more easily heard.

Sixth, use assertive communication (Dubrin, 2009; Vecchio, 2006). *Assertiveness* is stating your thoughts, feelings, and needs clearly in a straightforward manner. It involves a balance between being too aggressive on the one hand and too timid on the other. Assertive people consider both their own needs and those of others when deciding whether and how to express themselves. Of course, being assertive does not mean that you should avoid tact. Always consider the communication receivers' feelings. Effective assertive communication means thinking about the best way to state your ideas at the most appropriate time.

Focus on Ethics 7-4 describes some tactics *not* to use when engaging in agency politics.

Focus on Ethics **7-4**

Tactics *Not* to Use in Agency Politics: Problematic Unethical Behavior

EP 1

We've noted that behavior can occur in organizations that is inappropriate and unethical. Some political tactics are designed to hurt other people. Others are intended for selfish advancement. Some tactics can ruin your reputation or have very negative consequences in the future. The following six strategies should not be used when involved in agency politics.

1. Don't engage in backstabbing (Dubrin, 2012, p. 459). **Backstabbing** "requires that you pretend to be nice but all the while are planning someone's demise. A frequent form of backstabbing is to initiate a conversation with a rival or someone you dislike about the weaknesses of a common boss. You encourage negative commentary and make careful mental notes of what the person says. When these comments are passed along to the [supervisor]. . . . , the other person appears disloyal and foolish" (p. 459).

   People backstab to make themselves look better or more important, often to get ahead in competitive situations. Backstabbing is devious, self-serving, and unprofessional. It usually results in deterioration of interpersonal relationships and the ability to function as a team.

Dubrin (2012) suggests how to respond to backstabbing:

   A useful counterattack to the backstab is to ask an open-ended question [which requires more explanation than a yes or no answer] such as, "I'm not sure I understand why you sent that e-mail about my not supporting [that treatment goal]. . . . Can you explain why you did that, and what made you think I do not support [that goal]. . . . ?" You might also add, "Do you think this situation is serious enough to discuss with our supervisor?" (p. 460)

2. *Don't set up a person for failure* (Dubrin, 2012, p. 460). "A highly devious and deceptive practice is to give someone an assignment with the hopes that he or she will fail and therefore be discredited" (p. 460). One example is a supervisor who assigns a worker an unusually complicated and demanding case that the supervisor knows the worker will have

great difficulty handling. Another example is when an agency administrator allocates to a supervisor the role of overseeing an exceptionally turbulent and defiant department that the administrator knows the supervisor will be unable to control.

   One other example involves setting someone up to present bad or unwanted news to damage that person's standing or reputation. At one point, I was a newly promoted supervisor of a social work unit in a day treatment center for youth having serious emotional and behavioral problems. The center provided therapy and special education for troubled youth residing in the community. The program's two primary components were social services and therapy under my direction, and the school under its principal's direction. I was young and didn't know much about supervision or agency politics. For whatever reason, the school principal was not supportive of my promotion. The director informed the principal and me (who were equals on the organizational chart) that new recording requirements of clients' progress would require twice as much time and work as before. None of the staff—teachers, teaching assistants, or social workers—would be at all happy about that news. The principal asked me to make the announcement at an all-staff meeting. I foolishly did what he told me to and made the announcement both to my social work supervisees and to his teaching staff. Everyone immediately viewed me as the bringer of bad tidings and "the bad guy," an image that persisted for months. The principal benefited in at least two ways by setting me up for failure. First, he avoided being "the bad guy" himself; second, he enhanced his power base by making me look worse than him.

3. *Don't "divide and conquer"* (Vecchio, 2006, p. 131). This strategy "usually involves creating a feud among two or more people so that they will be continually off balance and thus unable to mount an attack against you" (p. 131). They are essentially kept busy fighting with each other, allowing you to go about your business. Unfortunately, this tactic hurts interpersonal relationships. It also takes time and energy away from doing a good job.

continued

Focus on Ethics 7-4 *continued*

I once worked in a social work department supervised by Fred. Fred's approach to supervision was control by dividing and conquering. Two of the workers, Jethrow and Davida, had been good friends for a long time. Fred told Jethrow that Davida had been criticizing his work. Fred then told Davida that Jethrow had been critical of her work. None of this was true. By disrupting Jethrow's and Davida's friendship, Fred broke up the coalition of support that they formed. In this way, Fred felt he had greater control of what went on in the department. It eventually backfired for Fred, however. A third worker, Cathy, talked both to Jethrow and Davida, who told her what Fred had been saying to each of them. Cathy subsequently told Jethrow and Davida what each other had shared. The result was that they confronted each other and discovered that Fred had been lying. They then confronted Fred, who consistently denied that he had said anything like that. Eventually, the entire department formed a coalition and sought help from the administration concerning Fred for this and many other behavioral problems. Fred was fired.

4. *Don't "exclude the opposition"* (Vecchio, 2006, p. 131). Another underhanded technique is to exclude a rival or adversary from participation in meetings, agency functions, or social events. One approach is to schedule an important decision making meeting "when the opposition is out of town (on vacation . . .) or attending another meeting. With the opposition absent, it is possible to influence decision making or to take credit for a rival's efforts" (p. 131).

5. *Don't go over your supervisor's head without first exhausting all other options* (Vecchio, 2006). There are times when it might be necessary to go over your supervisor's head and complain to his or her supervisor. Some employees do this to complain about the supervisor's performance or how the supervisor is treating them. Consider the earlier example with Fred, Jethrow, and Davida when staff formed a coalition and sought help from administration. However, the staff first confronted Fred, who did not respond. The entire staff formed a coalition to address the issue the only way they knew how. Only then did they "air dirty laundry" about the department to higher levels of administration. Supervisors hate it when supervisees go over their heads and "narc" about their performance. It's much wiser to try to work out whatever the problem is internally before going outside of the department. Making an enemy of a supervisor by making him or her look bad can make your life miserable in the future. Additionally, often administration will side with the supervisor, as people in management tend to stick together. The result might be a decrease rather than an increase in your power and potential to influence.

6. *Don't throw temper tantrums* (Vecchio, 2006, p. 132). Emotional volatility may earn you the reputation of being overly emotional and overreactive. People tend to see the emotions and miss out on the content of what you're trying to communicate. You don't want to establish a reputation of being hard to work with. That will only encourage others to avoid you and not support you when you need it.

Critical Thinking Questions **7-7**

EP 8a

Most of us have likely had work experiences. Have you ever been in a position to observe the use of either the negative or positive tactics described here? If so, explain the circumstances. To what extent were the tactics effective? To what extent were they ethical?

Chapter Summary

The following summarizes this chapter's content as it relates to the learning objectives presented at the beginning of the chapter. Objectives include the following:

LO 7-1 Describe organizational culture and structure, and discuss how lines of authority and channels of communication are involved.

Organizational culture is "the set of key values, beliefs, understandings, and norms shared by members of an organization" (Daft & Marcic, 2017, p. 76). Organizational structure is "the set of formal tasks assigned to individuals; formal reporting relationships including lines of authority, decision responsibility, number of hierarchical levels, and span of manager's control; and the design of systems to ensure effective coordination of employees across departments" (Daft & Marcic, 2017, p. 272). Lines of authority reflect the formal agency structure of administrative and supervisory responsibilities. Channels of communication involve numerous, complex systems of communication in an organization whereby staff members convey and receive information.

LO 7-2 Discuss centralized versus decentralized organizations.

Centralized organizations are clearly defined with a strict hierarchy that allows little discretion. Decentralized organizations have flexibility and allow for greater worker discretion.

LO 7-3 Respond to various critical thinking questions.

Critical thinking questions focus on experiences with supervisors, organizational communication channels, one's own personality factors, job interview experience, experiences with inaccuracies of judgment, power relationships, and observations of positive and negative tactics used in an organizational context.

LO 7-4 Examine interpersonal communication within social services agencies.

The communication sender's intent is the information that the sender is trying to communicate.

The receiver's impact is what the receiver actually comprehends. The sender's intent should closely match the receiver's impact in effective communication. A case example (the Idle Ness Center) provides an examination of formal and informal channels of communication among staff.

LO 7-5 Describe the perceptual process during communication.

Perception is "the process by which individuals attend to, organize, interpret, and retain information from their environments" (Williams, 2016b, p. 435). The process of perception involves attention, organization, interpretation, and retention.

LO 7-6 Identify interpersonal barriers to communication.

Barriers to communication in agencies include noise, personality factors, individual errors in perception, and lying and distortion.

LO 7-7 Summarize ethical issues concerning the use of distortion, enhancement of ethical communication, political behavior, and problematic unethical behavior.

Questions were raised concerning the ethics of distorting communication with the intent of manipulating others. Means of enhancing ethical communication in agencies include being honest, using empathy, employing active listening, and establishing a "climate of trust and openness" (Daft, 2016b, p. 382). Political behavior should not be used in organizations to pursue self-interests at the expense of others. Unethical political tactics include backstabbing, setting others up for failure, creating divisions between other staff, excluding the opposition from decision making, going over your supervisor's head, and throwing temper tantrums.

LO 7-8 Distinguish supervision and consultation in organizational settings.

Supervision is the process by which a designated supervisor watches over and evaluates a worker's performance, directs and coordinates activities, and provides feedback. Supervisors serve administrative and educational functions, in addition to others. Supervisees expect supervisors to help them in their work, communicate with them concerning agency policy, convey concerns to administration, facilitate staff cooperation, provide support, evaluate job performance, and facilitate new skill development.

Using supervision to your benefit as a worker involves using effective communication skills with your supervisor, keeping up-to-date records, planning supervisory agendas ahead of time, empathizing with your supervisor, displaying an openness to learning, demonstrating a liking for your work, working cooperatively with colleagues, providing feedback to your supervisor, warning your supervisor about potential problems, and learning your supervisor's evaluation system.

Problematic situations in supervision may involve a supervisor taking credit for your achievements, supervisory incompetence, laziness, problems with delegation, and inability to deal with conflict, among others.

Consultation is the provision of help by a knowledgeable person to another seeking assistance on a work-related goal or issue. Consultation differs from supervision in that supervision is ongoing and consultation usually is not. Whereas a supervisor has administrative power over a supervisee, a consultant ordinarily does not.

LO 7-9 Describe the importance of power in organizations and identify its various types.

Power is the potential ability to move people on a chosen course to produce an effect or achieve some goal. The concept of power, which can be used in many ways, is complex. Types of power include legitimate, reward, coercive, referent, and expert.

LO 7-10 Explain organizational politics and their dynamics.

Organizational politics are "attempts by individuals to influence the behavior of others as a means to protect their self-interests, meet their own needs, and advance their own goals" (Hellriegel & Slocum, 2011, p. 293). This is achieved "through means other than merit or luck" (Dubrin, 2012, p. 456). The political nature of organizations, scarce resources, uncertainty, and people's varying needs for power all are dynamics contributing to political behavior in agencies.

LO 7-11 Suggest tactics for using agency politics for positive change.

Tactics include conducting a political diagnosis, developing contacts with those in power, forming coalitions, being informed, providing appropriate positive feedback, and using assertive communication.

LO 7-12 Explore the concept of organizational justice as it relates to social and economic justice.

Organizational justice involves the "perceptions of people in an organization regarding fairness" (Griffin & Moorhead, 2014, pp. 392). Types of organizational justice include distributive, procedural, interpersonal, and informational (pp. 393–395).

Looking Ahead

This chapter discussed social service organizational settings, goals, and contexts in the macro social environment. The next chapter will explore human behavior, management, and empowerment in organizations.

Competency Notes

The following identifies where Educational Policy (EP) competencies and component behaviors are discussed in the chapter.

EP 1 (Competency 1)—Demonstrate Ethical and Professional Behavior. *(p. 222)*: A competent supervisor who teaches skills and assists in problem solving can support practitioners' career-long learning. *(p. 223)*: Social workers should be informed and proactive regarding evolving organizational contexts in order to practice effectively. *(p. 234)*: Any political strategy and its associated tactics are unethical if they do not serve the organization's goals or at least the goals of a larger group (clients or staff serving clients on the clients' behalf) Champoux (2006). *(p. 238)*: Some political behaviors should not be used in organizational setting because of their unethical implications.

EP 1a Make ethical decisions by applying the standards of the NASW *Code of Ethics*, relevant laws and regulations, models for ethical decision-making, ethical conduct of research, and additional codes of ethics as appropriate to context. *(p. 221)*: Ethical questions are raised regarding the use of distortion to manipulate others. Ethics and political behavior in organizations are discussed. Social workers should not lie or distort information, as both such practices violate the *Code of Ethics*. *(p. 238)*: Unethical tactics that should *not* be used in agency politics are discussed.

EP 1b Use reflection and self-regulation to manage personal values and maintain professionalism in practice situations. *(p. 216)*: Practitioners must practice personal reflection to correct errors in perception. *(pp. 216ff)*: Social workers should reflect upon their perceptual errors in agency settings to correct them. Generalist practitioners should be aware of the potential for lying and distortion so that professional values involving honesty guide their practice. Social workers should manage personal values so that they communicate ethically in agency settings. *(p. 225)*: Social workers are encouraged to practice personal reflection to improve their practice when working with and learning from supervisors.

EP 1c Demonstrate professional demeanor in behavior; appearance; and oral, written, and electronic communication. *(pp. 206–221)*: Social workers should understand the formal organizational hierarchy of power as well as the informal structure of interpersonal interaction to attend to professional roles and boundaries. Social workers must understand how channels of communication function within organizations to demonstrate professional demeanor in communication. *(p. 213)*: Social workers should understand interpersonal communication in social service agencies and interpersonal barriers to communication to demonstrate professional demeanor in communication. *(pp. 222–228)*: Effectively communicating with supervisors demonstrates professional demeanor in communication. Learning from supervisors can help social workers identify with the profession and learn to conduct themselves in a professional manner. *(p. 219)*: Social workers should demonstrate ethical communication in agency settings as a facet of professional demeanor. Keeping up-to-date records reflects professional demeanor in communication.

EP 1e Use supervision and consultation to guide professional judgment and behavior. *(p. 208ff)*: Various aspects of supervision in organizational settings are discussed. *(p. 230)*: Consultation in organizational settings is discussed.

EP 2 (Competency 2)—Engage Diversity and Difference in Practice *(p. 206)*: The concept of power within organizations is discussed. *(p. 218)*: Ethnicity and culture in organizational settings are dimensions of diversity. Social workers should recognize the extent that factors involving ethnicity and culture can cause oppression, marginalization, or the enhancement of power. *(p. 231)*: The role of power and politics within organizational contexts is discussed, including differential levels of power, types of power, and organizational politics.

EP 2b Present themselves as learners and engage clients and constituencies as experts of their own experiences. *(p. 222)*: Social workers should use the opportunities available from working with supervisors to learn about their social agency and the needs of clients.

EP 2c Apply self-awareness and self-regulation to manage the influence of personal biases and values in working with diverse clients and constituencies. *(pp. 215ff)*: Practitioners should increase self-awareness regarding any stereotypes they may harbor to eliminate personal biases. Social workers should gain self-awareness about their assumptions concerning ethnicity and culture to eliminate the influence of personal biases when working with diverse groups in organizations.

EP 3a Apply their understanding of social, economic, and environmental justice to advocate for human rights at the individual and system levels. *(p. 235ff):* The chapters discuss a variety of justice issues, including organizational, economic, social, distributive, procedural, interpersonal, informational, and environmental justice.

EP 5 (Competency 5)—Engage in Policy Practice. *(p. 231):* Social workers should engage in policy practice to improve agency functioning.

EP 5b Assess how social welfare and economic policies impact the delivery of and access to social services. *(p. 236):* Social workers should analyze, formulate, and advocate for policies that advance social well-being within agencies.

EP 5c Apply critical thinking to analyze, formulate, and advocate for policies that advance human rights and social, economic, and environmental justice. *(p. 235):* Social service agencies should seek organizational justice as described.

EP 6 (Competency 6)—Engage with Individuals, Families, Groups, Organizations, and Communities. *(pp. 205ff):* To work in and with organizations, social workers must understand organizational culture and structure.

EP 6a Apply knowledge of human behavior and the social environment, person-in-environment, and other multidisciplinary theoretical frameworks to engage with clients and constituencies. *(pp. 205ff):* Different organizations have different cultures and approaches to achieving goals. The social worker must understand these characteristics to work effectively in their organization. Generalist practitioners must have knowledge to engage and work with systems of all sizes, including macro systems.

EP 6b Use empathy, reflection, and interpersonal skills to effectively engage diverse clients and constituencies. *(pp. 213ff):* The use of interpersonal skills includes employing effective interpersonal communication. *(p. 226):* Using empathy with a supervisor can improve the supervisory relationship and communication. Gaining the supervisor's help can indirectly enhance practice effectiveness. *(p. 221):* Suggestions for ethical communication are provided. These include the use of empathy.

EP 7b Apply knowledge of human behavior and the social environment, person-in-environment, and other multidisciplinary theoretical frameworks in the analysis of assessment data from clients and constituencies. *(p. 233ff):* A political diagnosis is an assessment of the politics in an organization.

EP 8 (Competency 8)—Intervene with Individuals, Families, Groups, Organizations, and Communities. *(p. 235):* Generalist practitioners should initiate actions to achieve organizational goals that pursue organizational justice.

EP 8a Critically choose and implement interventions to achieve practice goals and enhance capacities of clients and constituencies. *(pp. 213, 216, 218, 219, 230, 233, 239):* Critical thinking questions are posed.

EP 8b Apply knowledge of human behavior and the social environment, person-in-environment, and other multidisciplinary theoretical frameworks in interventions with clients and constituencies. *(p. 225ff):* Understanding agency policies, practice, and politics can be helpful in intervening to bring about change.

EP 8c Use inter-professional collaboration as appropriate to achieve beneficial practice outcomes. *(p. 231ff):* Social workers should provide leadership in promoting improvements in agency service delivery. They can also collaborate with colleagues to establish a power base and pursue effective policy action.

EP 9b Apply knowledge of human behavior and the social environment, person-in-environment, and other multidisciplinary theoretical frameworks in the evaluation of outcomes. (*pp.* 227): An important evaluation system for most workers is the one employed by their supervisors to evaluate a social worker's performance. Ideally, it is one that can fairly evaluate the outcomes of your efforts to serve client systems.

Media Resources

MindTap for Social Work

 Go to MindTap® for digital study tools and resources that complement this text and help you be more successful in your course and career. There's an interactive eBook plus videos of client sessions, skill-building activities, quizzes to help you prepare for tests, apps, and more—all in one place. If your instructor didn't assign MindTap, you can find out more about it at CengageBrain .com.

8 | Human Behavior, Management, and Empowerment in Organizations

Organizations can empower their members. Awards for achievement can enhance internal environments in all types of organizations.

LEARNING OBJECTIVES

After reading this chapter you should be able to ...

8-1 Provide responses to various critical thinking questions.

8-2 Explain the significance of management in social service organizations.

8-3 Describe traditional bureaucracies, orientation discrepancies between social work and bureaucracies, and common behavior patterns found in bureaucracies.

8-4 Critique the US health care system's clash with Asian and Pacific Islander (API) cultural values.

8-5 Discuss problems frequently encountered by and in social service organizations.

8-6 Describe newer concepts involved in management and employee empowerment.

8-7 Discuss the situation encountered by women in social services management.

8-8 Describe two examples of common management and leadership approaches—total quality management (TQM) and servant leadership.

8-9 Examine the perspectives of social workers as employees in terms of using assertiveness and managing conflict.

8-10 Focus on an ethical issue.

Have you ever worked in an organization or business where you heard the following complaints, or perhaps made them yourself?

"My boss is so . . ."

- *Bossy*
- *Inconsiderate*
- *Disorganized*
- *Unfair*
- *Incompetent*
- *Unethical*
- *Screwed up*

All organizations, including social service organizations, are governed by the orientation or style of their management. Supervisors, as part of management, function within the organizational culture and expectations. For any variety of reasons, you may have experienced having a poor supervisor. Management in social service settings can empower practitioners to work more effectively and efficiently, ultimately benefiting their clients. The internal functioning of organizational systems can promote or deter workers' ability to perform effective interventions and link clients with needed resources. Because management is so important for how workers function in organizations, it is critical to understand the dynamics of management and how they relate to worker behavior in the macro social environment.

The Importance of Management LO 8-2

EP 1c, 6, 8

Management is the "attainment of organizational goals in an efficient and effective manner through planning, organizing, leading, and controlling organizational resources" (Daft, 2016a, p. 4). Management involves how employees are thought of and treated. Management style provides important clues for understanding people's behavior in the organizational environment. Often, an organization's management approach reflects one or more the organizational theories described in Chapter 5. Finding that managers operate using a combination of these theories is not uncommon. Numerous bureaucracies continue to exist, with all their strengths and weaknesses, but alternative organizational perspectives and management styles are continuously being developed.

For example, management by objectives (MBO) was a popular approach used in the last quarter of the twentieth century. It focused on goals as the primary

Critical Thinking Questions 8-1 LO 8-1

EP 8a

Have you ever worked in an organization or business where you or other employees had difficulties with a supervisor? If so, what did the problems involve? How might they have been solved and the situation improved?

driving force of agency life, measuring organizational success in terms of how effectively the organization achieved these goals (Kettner, Moroney, & Martin, 2017). MBO encouraged organizational employees to arrive at an agreement about what objectives or results they want to accomplish, specify what organizational resources each goal requires, and establish how long the goal-attainment process should take.

The following sections will address various aspects of management. First, traditional bureaucracy will be discussed. Subsequently, we will address some of the problems organizations face in the macro social environment. The remainder of the chapter will focus on new methods of management aimed at empowering workers to provide better services to clients.

Working in a Traditional Bureaucracy LO 8-3

The concept of bureaucracy was introduced in Chapter 5 under classical management organizational theories. It reflects a traditional approach to management. Because it is such a commonly used concept, we will spend some time here addressing practice within bureaucracies.

What words come to mind when you hear the term *bureaucracy*? Dullness? Tediousness? Boredom? Repetitiveness? Red tape? Sludge?

For whatever reason, most of us have a terrible opinion of bureaucracies. Even one dictionary definition labels bureaucracy "a system of administration marked by officialism (lack of flexibility and initiative combined with excessive adherence to regulations in the behavior of usually government officials), red tape (official routine or procedure marked by excessive complexity which results in delay or inaction), and proliferations ([growth] by rapid production of new parts, cells, buds, or offspring)." Even reading this definition is rather dull.

As classical organizational theories propose, bureaucratic management style emphasizes the importance of a specifically designed, formal structure and a consistent, rigid organizational network of employees to make an organization run well and achieve its goals (Dubrin, 2016; Hellriegel & Slocum, 2011). Each employee has a clearly defined job and is told exactly how that job should be accomplished. This school of thought calls for minimal independent functioning on the part of employees. Supervisors closely scrutinize the latter's work. Efficiency is of utmost importance. How people feel about their jobs is mostly insignificant. Administration avoids allowing employees to have any input regarding how organizational goals can best be reached. Rather, employees are expected to do their jobs as instructed as quietly and efficiently as possible.

Traditional bureaucracies are made up of numerous highly specialized units that are supposed to perform specific job tasks. In the formal structure, there is supposed to be little communication among horizontal units, that is, units of approximately equal status that perform different functions (for example, design and production). Employees are supposed to "stick to their own business" and get their own specifically defined jobs done within their own units. That's it. Discussion is unnecessary.

Traditional bureaucracies allow very little discretion on the part of workers. Policies and procedures for how to accomplish tasks are clearly specified. In other words, what any worker is supposed to do in any particular situation is designated ahead of time. Employees are allowed little, if any, ability and opportunity to be able to think for themselves and make their own decisions concerning their work. They are simply supposed to follow instructions.

The policies and procedures are infinitely complex and detailed. Regardless of what new situation might come up, workers should be able to consult the "rule book" regarding how they should deal with it.

Value Orientation Discrepancies between Workers and "The System"

Helping professionals (including social workers) have a value orientation that can clash with the traditional bureaucracy's reality (Knopf, 1979; Lewis, Packard, & Lewis, 2012). Expecting the values of a large bureaucracy to coincide with your own simply sets you up for disappointment.

Examples of discrepancies are many. For instance, helping professionals believe that the primary goal of bureaucracies should be to serve clients, whereas the actual goal of bureaucracies is to survive. Helping professionals believe bureaucracies should change to meet the emerging needs of clients, whereas bureaucracies resist change and are most efficient when no one is "rocking the boat." Helping professionals believe bureaucracies should personalize services to each client and convey that "you count as a person," whereas bureaucracies are in fact highly depersonalized systems in which clients (and employees) do not count as persons but are only tiny components of a much larger system. Highlight 8-1 lists additional conflicting orientations between helping professionals and bureaucratic systems (Gibelman & Furman, 2013).

Highlight 8-1

Value Orientation Conflicts between Helping Professionals and Bureaucracies

Orientation of Helping Professionals	Orientation of Bureaucratic Systems
Desire a democratic system for decision making.	Most decisions are made autocratically.
Desire that power be distributed equally among employees (horizontal structure).	Power is distributed vertically.
Desire that clients have considerable power in the system.	Power is held primarily by top executives.
Desire a flexible, changing system.	System is rigid and stable.
Desire that creativity and growth be emphasized.	Emphasis is on structure and the status quo.
Desire that communication be on a personalized level from person to person.	Communication is from level to level.
Desire shared decision making and a shared responsibility structure.	A hierarchical decision-making structure and a hierarchical responsibility structure are characteristic.
Desire that decisions be made by those having the most knowledge.	Decisions are made in terms of the decision-making authority assigned to each position in the hierarchy.
Belief that clients' and employees' feelings should be highly valued by the system.	Procedures and processes are highly valued.

Any of these differences in orientation can become an arena of conflict between helping professionals and the bureaucracies in which they work. Some helping professionals respond to these orientation conflicts by erroneously projecting a "personality" onto the bureaucracy. The bureaucracy is viewed as being "mixed in officialism," "uncaring," "cruel," and "the enemy." A negative personality is sometimes also projected onto officials of a bureaucracy, who may be viewed as being "paper shufflers," "rigid," "deadwood," "inefficient," and "unproductive."

One risk associated with impersonal bureaucracies is that people may tend to think of the system as a personality with values. Doing this mistakenly suggests that one can deal with the creature as if it were a person. This leads to becoming angry or upset because the bureaucracy does not respond as another person might. Bureaucratic structures lack a sense of morality or immorality and we waste our time when we treat them like a person. Unfortunately, projection is almost always negative, reflecting the dark or negative aspects of ourselves.

A bureaucratic system is neither good nor bad. It is simply a structure with certain expectations for how to carry out various tasks. However, practitioners may have strong emotional reactions to these orientation conflicts between the helping professions and bureaucracies. Common reactions are anger at the system, self-blame ("It's all my fault"), sadness and depression ("Poor me," "Nobody appreciates all I've done"), and fright and paranoia ("They're out to get me," "If I mess up, I'm gone").

Behavior Patterns in Bureaucratic Systems

Helping professionals often adopt one of several types of behavior patterns while coping with bureaucracies that don't enhance organizational effectiveness; they include "the warrior," "the gossip," "the complainer," "the dancer," "the machine," and "the executioner" (Knopf, 1979, pp. 33–36). Keep in mind that none of these adaptations are usually helpful to the organization nor the clients they serve.

The Warrior   The *warrior* leads open campaigns to destroy and malign the system. A warrior discounts the value of the system and often enters into a win-lose conflict. Warriors loudly and outspokenly complain about almost everything. Because of their overt "bad attitude," warriors rarely, if ever, get promoted. In fact, the warrior generally loses and is dismissed.

The Gossip   The *gossip* is a covert warrior who complains to others both inside and outside of the agency (including clients, politicians, and the news media) about how terrible the system is. A gossip frequently singles out a few officials to focus criticism upon. Bureaucratic administrators generally hate gossips because gossips try to air internal "dirty laundry" outside of the agency. Therefore, supervisors and administrators in bureaucracies often make life very difficult for gossips by assigning them distasteful tasks, refusing to promote them, giving them very low salary increases, and perhaps even dismissing them.

The Complainer   The *complainer* resembles a gossip, but confines complaints internally to other helping persons, to in-house staff, and to family members. A complainer wants people to agree to find comfort in shared misery. Complainers want to stay with the system, and generally do. Because they primarily keep their complaining secretive and internal, they usually avoid antagonizing the administration, and therefore maintain their anonymity (and their jobs).

The Dancer   The *dancer* is skillful at ignoring rules and procedures. Dancers are frequently lonely, often reprimanded for incorrectly filling out forms, and have low investment in the system or in helping clients. However, once inside of a bureaucratic system, dancers often manage to "just get by." They are usually lazy, but dancers generally don't really cause any trouble. They just don't do their jobs very well. It generally goes against the bureaucratic principle of maintaining the status quo to exert the energy necessary to fire a dancer.

The Machine   The *machine* is a "typical bureaucrat" who takes on the orientation of the bureaucracy. A machine's intent is to abide by the official bureaucratic rules no matter what. Machines dislike conflict. To them, obeying the rules to the letter of the law is much safer. Often, a machine has not been involved in providing direct services for years. Machines are frequently named to head study committees and policy groups, and to chair boards. Machines often rise in the organizational power structure to the level of their incompetence ("The Peter Principle"[1]), where they often remain until retirement.

The Executioner   The *executioner* is a tremendously enthusiastic and self-motivated individual who has managed to gain some power, status, and advancement within the bureaucratic organization. Executioners have no real commitment to the value orientations of the helping professionals or to the bureaucracy. However, they have learned how to "play the game." They have managed to hide their anger toward bureaucratic control and red tape. They have succeeded in disguising their manipulative ploys and have fooled many of those around them about their true self-centered, hostile motives. Especially when threatened, executioners attack other targeted persons within an organization with energized, impulsive vigor. An executioner abuses power by not only indiscriminately assailing and dismissing employees but also slashing services and programs.

A Final Commentary on Bureaucracies

The description of bureaucratic systems presented here stresses a number of the negatives about such systems, particularly their impersonalization. In fairness, Lewis and colleagues (2012) stress that there are some positive aspects of bureaucracy, particularly as it "provides a foundation for personnel practices that many workers appreciate" (p. 81). These include "clear job roles and performance expectations, fair treatment, and due process" (p. 81). They continue, however, that it surely doesn't focus enough on the importance of interpersonal processes and the unique differences of individuals. In a later section, this chapter will address newer, more relationship-focused management approaches.

Also note that another advantage of being part of a large bureaucracy is the existing potential for changing a powerful system to clients' advantage. In small or nonbureaucratic systems, a social worker may have lots of freedom but little

---

[1]The Peter Principle was developed by Laurence J. Peter in 1968 (Mish, 2008, 1995, p. 865).

Critical Thinking Questions 8-2

If you were to work in a traditional bureaucracy, what aspects of that bureaucracy would be most difficult for you, and why? How might you cope with the problem?

opportunity or power to influence large macro systems or mobilize extensive resources on behalf of clients. Keep in mind that not everyone working in a bureaucracy adopts the organization's mantra. An example of the potential is the case of Geraldo. He had worked in a large federal government organization and was now being interviewed for a position in a multiunit county social service agency. During the interview, the deputy director asked him about his experiences working in bureaucracies. Geraldo replied, "I have worked in several bureaucracies with multiple rules and know how to do my job within those rules." The deputy director followed up with another query: "What happens when the bureaucracy requirements keep you from serving your clients?" Geraldo responded: "Then I find a way to work around the bureaucracy." Unsure about how the deputy director would respond to this commitment to independence, he was relieved at the end of the interview when he was offered the position.

Highlight 8-2 discusses problems inherent in the US health care system with respect to Asian and Pacific Islander (API) cultural values. In many ways, the health care system functions as a large bureaucracy. Highlight 8-2 also proposes ways to improve its functioning to empower this macro client system.

Highlight 8-2

The US Health Care System, and Asian and Pacific Islander Cultural Values LO 8-4

The system providing health care in the United States is a huge bureaucracy reflecting many of the characteristics of traditional bureaucracies. Although management approaches do vary within its many organizational structures, strict regulations and decision-making hierarchies for health care provision tend to dominate. A problem commonly faced by such bureaucracies is the lack of cultural sensitivity. Rigid rules do not provide flexibility for adapting to culturally diverse values and needs. A major goal in social work is to enhance service provision for clients. Lack of responsiveness to clients' cultural values and belief systems can erect major barriers to receiving effective services.

The US health care provision system has been criticized regarding its responsiveness to Americans of Asian and

Pacific Islander (API) cultural heritage (McLaughlin & Braun, 1999). "There is growing recognition in the United States that culturally sensitive health care and health promotion are critical to reducing health disparities among the multicultural population that constitutes the United States" (Tucker, Daly, & Herman, 2010, p. 505). More specifically, concerns focus on how "the system" emphasizes individual autonomy, which may conflict with "collectivist decision making norms" inherent in API cultures (McLaughlin & Braun, 1999, p. 321).

Choudhouri, Santiago-Rivera, and Garrett (2012) reflect:

Individualism refers to societies where individuals are only loosely connected, and people are expected to be independent and look after themselves and perhaps their immediate families. **Collectivism** characterizes societies where people are a part of cohesive groups

continued

Highlight **8-2** *continued*

from birth onward, and are protected by the group in exchange for loyalty and effort on behalf of the group. Societies tend to fall along a continuum from radical individualism, of which mainstream US society is an example, to extreme collectivism, of which China is an example. (p. 65)

The following discussion first describes five dimensions important in understanding API cultures with respect to involvement in the health care system. Then we identify three conflicts with US health care policy—medical informed consent, advance directives, and decisions about nursing home placement. Finally, we will propose implications for improved health care provision.

Value Dimensions in API Cultures Relating to Health Care Provision

At least five major values inherent in API cultures relate directly to US health care provision: shared decision making in families, "filial piety," "silent communication," "preservation of harmony," and "delayed access but great respect" for health care (Brammer, 2012; Diller, 2015; McLaughlin & Braun, 1999, pp. 323–325; Paniagua, 2014; Weaver, 2005).

Shared Decision Making in Families

In contrast to the individualist perspective emphasized in US health care, Asian Americans and Pacific Islanders rely on the family or larger group to make ultimate decisions about any individual member's care. In the US health care system, individual patients are subject to **informed consent**. That is, physicians and health care staff must inform an individual patient about his or her "diagnosis, prognosis, and alternatives for treatment" (McLaughlin & Braun, 1999, p. 322). A patient then has the right to provide consent for continuation of the treatment process. In many API cultures, this assumption does not comply with values and norms. For instance, "unlike the custom among white people, for whom the individual patient is the decision maker, many Japanese and Chinese families assign decision making duties to the eldest son. In Pacific Islander families, it may be less obvious who the decision maker is" (McLaughlin & Braun, 1999, pp. 323–324). The entire family may share duties and assume designated responsibilities like getting food. Because of the collective nature of decision making, in API cultures it is customary for family members to share information on a family's member's physical or mental health (Paniagua, 2014).

A Cautionary Note

Note that when speaking about any racial, ethnic, or cultural group, it is important not to overly generalize. Here we talk about general value dimensions evident in API cultures. However, individuals or families from any ethnic or racial group may embrace traditional cultural norms to various degrees. They may also experience **acculturation**, "the adjustment and adaptation of the individual from the culture of origin to the dominant culture" (Lum, 2011, p. 55). In other words, members of a diverse group may gradually blend into and adopt the values and customs of the larger society. When thinking about a racial, ethnic, or cultural group, it is therefore important not to assume that all members comply with all cultural values or conform to the same extent. Being of German ethnic heritage does not automatically mean a person loves sauerkraut, liver and onions, blood sausage, and raw ground beef with onions on rye bread just because these are traditional ethnic foods. The trick is to open-mindedly view each person as a unique personality, yet be sensitive to the possible cultural values and beliefs that person may hold.

The other word of caution concerns differences among the many cultures included under the API umbrella. For example, Balgopal (2008) cites several variations evident in specific groups. Japanese Americans are more likely than other Asian-American groups to marry outside of their ethnic group and are more likely to divorce at some point in their lives. Filipino-American couples maintain a more egalitarian relationship than most other Asian-American groups. Indian Americans are more likely to wear clothing based on cultural expectations in India, consume a vegetarian diet, and participate in arranged marriages.

Filial Piety

A second value dimension in API cultures is **filial piety**, "a devotion to and compliance with parental and familial authority, to the point of sacrificing individual desires and ambitions" (Kirst-Ashman & Hull, 2018b, p. 487; Lum, 2011; Brammer, 2012). Paniagua (2014) explains:

> Traditional Asians believe that children's primary duty is to be good and to respect their parents. Parents are expected to determine the course of their children's lives, without consulting the children about their own desires and ambitions, and any failure on a child's part to comply with parent's expectations is seen as a threat to the parents' authority. (p. 120)

continued

Highlight 8-2 *continued*

Silent Communication

A third value inherent in API cultures is silent or nonverbal communication (Leong, Lee, & Chang, 2008). Paniagua (2014) explains:

EP 1c

Asians often respond to the verbal communications of others by being quiet and passive. They may go to a great deal of effort to avoid offending others, sometimes answering all questions affirmatively to be polite even when they do not understand the questions, and they tend to avoid eye contact.

Among Asians silence is a sign of respect and politeness; it also signals an individual's desire to continue speaking after making a point during a conversation (Sue & Sue, 2003). In Western cultures, eye contact during direct verbal communication is understood to imply attention and respect toward others. Among Asians, however, eye contact is considered a sign of lack of respect and attention. Eye contact is particularly a sign of disrespect when it is associated with authority figures (e.g., parents, therapists) and older people. (p. 122)

Leong and colleagues (2008) elaborate:

Asian Americans tend to communicate in a high-context style with context as the primary channel for communication. Direct and specific references to the meaning of the message are not given. Receivers are expected to rely on their knowledge and appreciation for nonverbal cues and other subtle affects for interpreting message meaning. [In contrast,] [t]he Euro-American culture tends to focus on communication through a low-context style, where words are the primary channel of communication. Direct, precise, and clear information is delivered verbally. Receivers can expect to simply take that which is said at face value. The high-context communication style can be seen as an elaborate, subtle, and complex form of interpersonal communication. (p. 117)

Therefore, much can often be learned by carefully observing silent responses and subtle nonverbal gestures. For example, it is "improper" for children "to discuss issues of death and dying with parents, yet concern by either party may be expressed by nonverbal cues such as bowing of the head or eye contact" (McLaughlin & Braun, 1999, p. 324).

Preservation of Harmony

API cultures emphasize **harmony**, the importance of getting along peacefully and not causing trouble for the family (Brammer, 2012; Lum, 2011; Weaver, 2005). This concept characterizes collectivist societies. The implication, then, is "to endure hardship and pain," especially if addressing issues that might cause discomfort or disturbance for other family or group members (McLaughlin & Braun, 1999, p. 325). For example, in Vietnamese culture the "desire to achieve harmony between the self and the non-self remains an essential preoccupation of the Vietnamese in interpersonal relations outside the family group" (Vietnam-culture.com, 2017). Such interpersonal harmony involves being courteous, truthful, and diplomatic. In Hawaiian culture, maintaining harmony in the family is valued above issues of individual success or achievement. These values are expressed in the desire to help others and overall generosity.

There also tends to be respect for clearly defined family structure and hierarchy of authority, arrangements that tend to clarify expectations and encourage predictability of behavior (Sue & Sue, 2016). For instance, Samoan culture stresses "hierarchical systems with clearly defined roles. The highly structured organization of the family defines an individual's roles and responsibilities and guides the individual in interactions with others" (Ewalt & Mokuau, 1996, p. 261).

Delayed Access to But Great Respect for Health Care

API values include emphasis on family, cooperation, harmony, and aversion to causing trouble. All these contribute to avoidance of the US health care system if possible. Asian Americans and Pacific Islanders generally experience shame at the inability to handle their own problems and the need to seek help from formal outside sources (Brammer, 2012; Sue & Sue, 2016). Thus, family and group members strongly prefer to deal with issues and illnesses internally within the family and avoid exposing problems to outsiders. For example, Asian families suffer disgrace when forced to communicate personal information about family problems, including intellectual disability, mental illness, and school or work failures (Lum, 2005).

When it becomes obvious to family members that the family is incapable of resolving health problems, they hesitantly turn to health care providers. Asian Americans may only seek mental health help when the problem becomes

continued

Highlight **8-2**   *continued*

extraordinarily unmanageable and they have exhausted all other sources of assistance (Lum, 2005). Asian and Pacific Islanders who experience mental or emotional stress often transform this into physical symptoms (Lum, 2005).

For physical illness, API families pursue external health services "only if emergency care is needed"; once that step is taken, however, group members view the physician "as a wise and benevolent authority figure" (McLaughlin & Braun, 1999, p. 325). Health care professionals are expected to make collectivist decisions, that is, those "in the best interest of the greatest number of people involved with the patient" (McLaughlin & Braun, 1999, p. 325).

Conflicts between Cultural Values and the US Health Care System

EP 8

Conflicts between API cultures and US health care system policy and practice focus on at least three problematic issues—informed consent, advance directives, and decisions about nursing home placement (McLaughlin & Braun, 1999). The following discussion relates how the five value dimensions discussed earlier can clash with that system. The point is not to condemn the US health care system, but rather, to examine how it can either detract from the health and well-being of Asian Americans and Pacific Islanders or empower them. The subsequent section will suggest recommendations for improvement.

Informed Consent

Several challenging concerns relate to informed consent (McLaughlin & Braun, 1999). First, consider Asian Americans' and Pacific Islanders' emphasis on harmony and conforming to group wishes. Patients may feel obligated to sign consent papers presented to them when they really don't want to. The API cultural orientation is to cooperate and not cause trouble. Second, cultural norms emphasizing silence and inconspicuousness may prevent patients from voicing contrary opinions, asking questions about illnesses, and refusing to sign papers. Third, health care personnel are often unaware of how API cultural values can affect the consent process and interfere with its integrity.

Fourth, although physicians generally tell family members about a terminal illness, informing the patient about ensuing death is taboo for many Asian Americans and Pacific Islanders. Reasons can be "that the family does not want the patient to become disheartened and give up on living, that the family feels it is disrespectful to speak of such things to an elder, or

that talking about death is 'polluting' or will cause bad luck" (McLaughlin & Braun, 1999, p. 330). Health care personnel thus face an ethical dilemma. Policy and professional ethics may assert that a patient be informed of a terminal diagnosis to discuss and weigh treatment options. However, culturally, the patient may not want to know and may well choose ignorance if given that option.

Advance Directives

A second problematic issue concerning API cultures and the health care system involves advance directives. An **advance directive** is a person's formally recognized statement signed before witnesses that gives instructions for what medical alternatives should be pursued if the person becomes incapable of making such choices. Two issues tend to surface here (McLaughlin & Braun, 1999). First, health care facilities are legally required "to approach patients for copies of advance directives" (McLaughlin & Braun, 1999, p. 331). However, in Chinese, Japanese, and Hawaiian cultures, people seriously avoid discussing death for fear of inviting it or suffering negative consequences.

A second issue is that it is pointless for Asian Americans and Pacific Islanders to discuss such issues because of their collectivist approach. They assume that family members will take care of those issues appropriately when the time comes. In addition, even if the client has created an advance directive in one state, it might not be readily accepted in another, a fact of which clients new to the United States may be unaware.

Decisions about Nursing Home Placement

Many Asian Americans and Pacific Islanders embrace filial piety and firmly believe that children should care for aging parents (Brammer, 2012; Chang, Schneider, & Sessanna, 2011). To them, nursing home placements should be avoided at all costs. Thus, there is some tendency for API families to wait until situations reach crisis proportions before initiating possible nursing home placement (Chang et al., 2011). Stress may escalate from economic pressure to work outside the home, caring for both children and aging parents, and increasing physical and cognitive health problems experienced during the aging process.

Interestingly, in contrast to Western culture, many traditional cultures believe that death should occur at home, and relatives may keep the body there until burial (Dew, Scott, & Kirkman, 2016). Thus, ensuing death may not spur API families to remove the dying member to a nursing or hospital facility.

Critical Thinking Questions 8-3

Implications for an Improved Health Care System

EP 8a,
3b, 5b,
8d, 8e

Large service provision systems are never perfect. There are always quirks and problems because such diverse people are involved. Bureaucracies have established rules to assist in their ongoing functioning. A large health care system cannot adapt itself perfectly to all its beneficiaries' needs. However, a continuous concern for social workers is the need to assess large systems' functioning, recommend improvements, and work to achieve positive changes. This is especially true in view of the US population's wide range of cultural diversity.

How can the US health care system become more sensitive to API and other cultures? How would you address this issue? What recommendations would you make to improve service access and provision to people of API cultural heritage?

The challenges described above are complex. However, others have identified four recommendations that may help address these challenges. They are proposed here.

First, training should be provided for health care personnel that sensitizes them to API cultural values and issues (Hogan, 2013; McLaughlin & Braun, 1999; Tucker et al., 2010). Staff should be taught to carefully observe periods of silence, nonverbal behavior, and family or group interaction for clues to understand such behavior.

Second, "Patients, relatives and clinicians [should] engage in discussions about the patient's future well in advance. These conversations ... can be sensitively discussed at appropriate way points" (Price, 2016, p. 380). Agency policy should encourage staff to tune in to cultural values regarding collectivist versus individual perspectives on decision making, and work with families accordingly (Lum, 2011).

Third, the health care system should begin investigating the adoption of family-centered rather than individual-centered decision-making models for virtually any health-related decisions (McLaughlin & Braun, 1999; Sue & Sue, 2016). Health care personnel should seek to understand individual's and family values, and work within that value system to the greatest extent possible. The health care system should respect both the individual's and the family's right to self-determination.

Fourth, social workers should pursue ongoing advocacy for positive policy and practice changes in the health care system. Health care should respect and appreciate cultural diversity and self-determination, not pretend they don't exist.

Problems Frequently Encountered by and in Social Service Organizations   LO 8-5

Regardless of an agency's structural type and managerial approach, several obstacles can hinder social workers' ability to do their best possible job. As social service agencies struggle to provide efficient and effective services within the larger macro environment, they are often plagued by internal problems and issues. These include vagueness of goals, vagueness of process, impersonal behavior, lack of rewards and recognition, agency policy and worker discretion, and traditions and unwritten rules.

Vagueness of Goals

From a social work perspective, **accountability** is the worker's and the profession's responsibility to clients and the community to work effectively and achieve the goals that have been established. Individual practitioners and whole agencies are called upon to prove that their performance is productive and valuable. A major way of doing this is to define specific, measurable goals and monitor the extent to which these goals are achieved. Chapter 1 introduced the concept of **research-informed practice**. This means social workers should use the approaches and interventions in their practice that research has determined are effective. Social workers should "use evaluation findings to improve practice effectiveness at the micro, mezzo, and macro levels" (Council on Social Work Education [CSWE], 2015, EP 9).

Superficially, this sounds good. However, think about it. How can a practitioner prove that a client has been helped? One way is to define specific behavioral goals. This takes substantial time, effort, and expertise.

For instance, if you're teaching physically abusive parents child-management techniques, how do you know when you've been successful? When they can pass a written test quizzing them on specific techniques? When the parents strike their children only on the hands and rump instead of on the head? When they only strike their children once each day instead of at least a dozen times, as they did in the past? Human behavior simply is difficult to define and measure.

Evaluating the outcomes of an entire organization (or even a single program), including goals, effectiveness, and efficiency, is infinitely more difficult than evaluating the outcomes of micro or mezzo interventions. This is because of the strikingly increased number of variables involved. To evaluate program outcomes, first, the program's goals must be clearly specified and understood.

A common problem is that the goals of a program are so unclear and general that they are not helpful in directing the organization's activities. Goals such as improve community health, address homelessness, and enhance treatment services are simply useless because they lack specificity. Brueggeman (2014) notes that an important step in goal setting is to gather stakeholders (those who have a stake or vested interest in the outcome) who will help identify appropriate, achievable, and measurable goals. "Other stakeholders may be people in positions of power, such as representatives from government agencies and corporations that operate in the community but who do not reside there" (p. 182).

Specifying measurable goals is not an easy task, although social service agencies continue to make progress in the area despite all the difficulties involved. Effective definition, measurement, and attainment of goals enhance workers' ability to do their jobs.

Vagueness of Process

Interventions performed by a variety of individual practitioners and other staff are very difficult to measure and monitor. They are not like manufacturing machinery that punches out slabs of metal. Such slabs can be measured. Raw materials can be made uniform. Effectiveness can be evaluated in terms of the machine's accuracy and efficiency (that is, how fast and perfectly the machine can punch out slabs). In this context, unlike that of the social services, work routines are predictable, repetitive, and relatively easy to monitor and control.

Additionally, professional staff in social service organizations vary widely in terms of intervention approaches, techniques used, priorities, and personality styles. Clients probably vary even more widely in terms of characteristics and needs. Therefore, social service organizations bring multiple, immeasurable, human factors to the intervention process. Because people vary drastically, more than inanimate materials like metal slabs, practitioners who work with people must have much more flexibility than metal slab punchers. That is, workers in organizations need to have some degree of discretion in working with their clients. This, in turn, makes the monitoring of the intervention process more difficult. Social service organizations must constantly strive to define the process by which they deliver services to enhance social workers' ability to function effectively.

Impersonal Behavior

The goals of accountability and efficiency can create difficulties for workers and clients. Sometimes agencies engage in behavior intended to be businesslike but perceived by the workers as impersonal. It's easy, for example, for administrators to make arbitrary decisions where the workers feel left out. One agency director wanted to reduce costs such as postage and cut the time workers spent performing clerical tasks. He decided to eliminate the appointment letters that workers would type on their computers and send to clients who lacked phones. The letters told the client when the worker was planning to visit and asked the client to notify the worker if this was not satisfactory.

No one quarreled with the wish to save money, but many workers were upset because the new mandate would force them to make home visits without giving clients prior notice. To many workers, this seemed inappropriate and unprofessional behavior, even a violation of clients' rights. It could also be more time consuming. The director did not share these opinions, and he overruled the workers' objections. Finally, tired of arguing social work values against business values, one worker calculated the cost of driving across the county to see a client who wasn't home. The wasted mileage cost exceeded the cost of sending out the appointment letters. After some discussion and debate, the director canceled the policy and allowed workers to send out appointment cards once again.

Management can minimize impersonal behavior by enhancing workers' involvement in planning and decision making. It can also strive to address and improve internal channels of communication. Newer trends in management discussed later in the chapter address this issue.

Another example of impersonal behavior involves a foreign adoptions unit in a private child welfare agency. Unit staff felt like their supervisor, Keung, was disinterested in their work and their needs. Keung spent most of his time in meetings with administration. Other times, he seemed preoccupied, gave little eye contact to supervisees, and enclosed himself in his office whenever possible. By demonstrating such impersonal behavior, his staff felt he just didn't care. In reality, Keung was faced with some major issues in terms of keeping his unit intact and healthy. International political problems were causing difficulties in foreign adoptions, making many fewer children available for US adoption. Keung was struggling with administration, trying not to lay off workers and instead providing transfer alternatives for them to other agency units. Keung appeared impersonal, but he was really very concerned. He was preoccupied with helping his workers keep their jobs.

Thus, workers should be sensitive to the position and needs of supervisors and administrators. The latter may indeed appear preoccupied or aloof. However, they must attune themselves to external social and economic forces that affect the entire agency and its operation. If they don't keep the agency running, no one has a job.

Lack of Rewards and Recognition

Another impediment in many organizational environments is management's failure to distribute rewards and recognition as frequently and consistently as most workers would like. In school, it is common for you to get periodic feedback on your performance. Papers are returned with comments and/or a grade. Exams are returned soon after they are given with the grade very evidently displayed. After each grading period, instructors give grades in each course. Many people prefer this regular system of positive reinforcement and expect something like it to exist in the agencies where they work.

Unfortunately, much of the good work that social workers do will never be recognized. It is simply not acknowledged in the busy life of the agency. Other good work will be noticed, but for many reasons no one will comment on it. Supervisors may come to take the good work for granted, not believing it needs regular reinforcement. Clients may appreciate our efforts but are too involved in their own situations to show their gratitude. Sometimes, supervisors like practitioners' performance but clients do not. For example, probation and parole workers taking clients back to court because of clients' violations are unlikely to have such clients praise their efforts. Consequently, a good guiding principle is to learn to reinforce yourself. This means you must take pride in work you do well, accepting that your work will not always be acknowledged to the extent you would like.

A guiding principle is for supervisors, managers, and even colleagues to emphasize strengths whenever possible, just as workers should do with clients. In a busy, demanding work environment, they are easily overlooked. However, the extent to which management can emphasize strengths generally enhances workers' morale and ability to function well.

Agency Policy and Worker Discretion

Agency policies and worker discretion can pose another obstruction to effective work. Practitioners may either feel squelched by policy restrictions about what they can and can't do or be floundering because policies don't provide enough guidance.

Agencies establish and operate within a system of policies that guide workers' behavior and provide direction in situations commonly encountered. For example, an agency may have a policy that requires workers to sign out when they leave the building. This policy makes it easier for supervisors, administrators, and clients needing help to know a worker's location at any given moment. In effect, it is a form of accountability and makes sense to most workers.

Many new workers feel overwhelmed with all the policies, rules, regulations, and procedures they must learn and abide by. They may think that policies control or constrain their every action. In reality, workers have enormous discretion about how they do their jobs, because policies, by their very nature, must be general enough to apply in many different situations. This means that no policy can foresee all the possible events, nuances, and complexities that arise in any given case. Policies establish general guidelines, but workers are responsible for using their discretion or judgment with specific cases. Thus, these policies do not present a real barrier to effective social work. Workers must be prepared to apply their professional knowledge and skills and cannot rely on agency policy to dictate each decision in the field.

For example, consider being a practitioner working for a family services agency that specializes in helping parents learn how to control their children's behavior. Agency policy might prescribe eight weeks to work with parents and demonstrate improvements in their children's behavior. However, you and the parents have relatively wide discretion in determining what specific behaviors to work on. Should you focus on the children's tantrums, their refusal to eat anything but pizza and Krispy Kreme double-chocolate cream-filled donuts for supper, or their almost constant nagging for attention? The decision is a matter of discretion.

It is important for management to monitor the effectiveness of policy on all aspects of agency functioning. Outdated policies should be identified and changed. Cumbersome policies should be simplified if possible. Vague policies should be clarified to provide workers with adequate direction, even in view of their need to use discretion.

Traditions and Unwritten Rules

Unobtrusive, hidden traditions and unwritten rules are other potential problems in agency environments. The written rules frequently appear in some sort of regulation manual or personnel handbook. The unwritten rules are related to the organization's informal structure reflecting who has power and who communicates with whom. As in families, the traditions and unwritten rules are often learned only through verbal exchanges with more experienced group members. Sometimes they are learned only when the novice worker inadvertently violates the rule or tradition.

A case in point was a situation that arose when a new master of social work (MSW) graduate, Butch Cassidy, took his first job at a huge state mental hospital. Each Wednesday afternoon at 2:00 p.m., all the social workers at the hospital gathered around a large conference table. The meeting's purpose was to improve communication among the social work staff. The hospital's social services director, Frank Enstein, and formal policy encouraged social workers to feel free at these meetings to raise issues that were causing them problems or making their jobs more difficult. Frank, the supervisor of four social work units, had offered Butch a job right out of graduate school. Butch had done his first field placement at the hospital and Frank had liked the quality of his work.

Butch's direct social work supervisor, Danielle Pricklesteel, seemed distant and acted as though she resented Butch's presence. Although she was always polite and professional, Butch felt Danielle did not really want him around. Finally, Butch

Critical Thinking Questions 8-4

EP 8a

Have you ever worked in an organization or business where you experienced any of these problems—vagueness of goals, vagueness of process, impersonal behavior, lack of rewards and recognition, vague or restrictive work policies, or hidden traditions and unwritten rules? If so, what were the circumstances? How did you deal with the problem?

decided to use the next Wednesday afternoon meeting to discuss his feelings. All social work staff, supervisors, and Frank attended these meetings.

At the meeting, Butch shared his feelings with the assembled group. Danielle tactfully acknowledged she felt as though Frank had "dumped" Butch in her unit without talking to her about Butch's status beforehand. Danielle apologized for taking out her anger at Frank on Butch. Frank apologized to Danielle for not consulting her before assigning Butch to her unit. The air appeared to clear, and Butch felt much better.

After the meeting, Danielle took Butch aside and told him that she was very upset because he had brought the topic up at the meeting. She stressed, "We never discuss anything important at these meetings. We just meet because Frank likes us to get together. If you have a concern, please talk it over with me first and we'll work it out." Later, Butch learned from talking to other workers that Danielle was right. The group had an informal rule that they never discussed anything important at these meetings. To do so was to violate the workers' informal policy and expectations.

The point of this example is that informal rules and traditions can affect social workers' ability to function effectively. We learn best by observing others and asking privately about things that appear to be rules. Learning about informal rules by breaking them can be painful. The extent to which management can identify expectations and clearly communicate them to new staff enhances workers' ability to function effectively.

Newer Approaches to Management and Worker Empowerment LO 8-6

EP 5, 7b

We've discussed bureaucracy and some of the problems inherent in bureaucracies and any organization providing social services, regardless of its management approach. We'll now turn to addressing some of the new management trends in social service and other organizations. In contrast to bureaucracy, numerous new approaches have been developing that serve to empower workers. Here we will explain five of them: constructing a culture of caring, the learning organization, teamwork and team empowerment, managing diversity, and client system empowerment within the organizational context. There are also dozens of specific methods of management. Two will subsequently be explained here—total quality management (TQM) and servant leadership. Note that because these management trends and specific approaches focus on worker motivation, needs, and interpersonal dynamics, there's overlap in some of the concepts involved.

Constructing a Culture of Caring

Chapter 7 defined *organizational culture* as "the set of key values, beliefs, understandings, and norms shared by members of an organization." Organizational culture provides guidelines and establishes expectations for how people should behave while at work. Brody and Nair (2014) recommend developing a "culture of caring" in the social services agency setting. When staff feel connected with and supportive of each other, they can become a strong, cohesive force in achieving agency goals together.

Five core values characterize a caring organization (Brody & Nair, 2014). First, *job ownership* is the situation where workers feel that their job and their work performance is an important part of their identity (Brody & Nair, 2014, p. 89). They will strive hard to achieve goals and excellence in their work.

Organizations can promote job ownership by encouraging a second key value, a *sense of a higher purpose* (Brody & Nair, 2014, p. 380). A caring culture encourages employees to genuinely feel that they're making a difference through their participation. It makes them feel like an integral, important part of a larger system. This can motivate them to work hard and learn new skills, not because management orders them to, but because they have a genuine desire to do so.

A third core value promoting a caring organizational culture is *emotional bonding* (Brody & Nair, 2014, p. 380). This means the organizational culture supports an environment in which people truly care about and experience a vital feeling of connection with each other. This can be especially helpful in agencies where workers experience exceptional pressures to work with demanding clients. An example is the case of a candidate for a position in a social service agency who was waiting for his initial interview to begin. As he waited, he noted several staff checking with each other about whether they were going to play touch football after work that day. The obvious camaraderie among workers was a positive sign about the working environment of the agency and helped the candidate decide he would accept the position if it was offered.

The fourth core value is *trust*, the condition where people feel they can depend on each other to follow through on tasks and be supportive of one another (Brody & Nair, 2014, p. 380). They then don't have to waste energy on negative interpersonal interactions, conflicts, complaints, and criticisms.

Pride in one's work, the fifth core value, is the condition where workers feel high self-esteem regarding and have great respect for their accomplishments at work (Brody & Nair, 2014, p. 380). Feeling good about yourself and being proud of the job you're doing motivates you to continue doing a good job. This is one virtue of organizations who develop a culture of caring.

The Learning Organization

A second management trend related to empowering workers is the concept of the learning organization. The **learning organization** "is one that works to facilitate the lifelong learning and personal development of all of its employees while continually transforming itself to respond to changing demands and needs" (Griffin, 2016, p. 182). Dubrin (2012) continues:

> In the process, the organization profits from its experiences. Instead of repeating the same old mistakes, the organization learns. A *learning organization* is skilled at creating, acquiring, and transferring knowledge. It also modifies its behavior to reflect new knowledge and new insights. These activities are facilitated by effective communication. (p. 443)

At least five primary concepts characterize the learning organization. First, power is redistributed from higher levels to lower levels in the organizational structure through increased worker participation (Lussier & Achua, 2016). Workers providing services directly to clients are given greater discretion to make their own decisions and plans. Power to provide input into and pursue organizational goals is distributed among all staff instead of being concentrated in management. In other words, workers are empowered. Daft and Marcic (2017) explain:

> *Empowerment* is power sharing, the delegation of power or authority to subordinates in an organization. Increasing employee power heightens motivation for task accomplishment because people improve their own effectiveness, choosing how to do a task and using their creativity. (p. 540)

EP 1, 2b

A second concept characterizing the learning organization is the provision of continuous education to employees (Dubrin, 2016). Griffin (2016) explains:

> Although managers might approach the concept of a learning organization from a variety of perspectives, improved quality, continuous improvement, and performance measurement are frequent goals. The idea is that the most consistent and logical strategy for achieving continuous improvement is by constantly upgrading employee talent, skill, and knowledge. For example, if each employee in an organization learns one new thing each day and can translate that knowledge into work-related practice, continuous improvement will logically follow. Indeed, organizations that wholeheartedly embrace this approach believe that only through constant learning by employees can continuous improvement really occur. (p. 183)

Continuous education is very important for social workers. "Social workers recognize the importance of life-long learning and continually updating their skills to ensure they are relevant effective" (Council on Social Work Education [CSWE], 2015, EP 1).

A third feature attributed to learning organizations involves open communication and information sharing (Dubrin, 2016; Lussier & Achua, 2016). Workers are encouraged to be creative and share new ideas with each other.

A fourth trait characterizing a learning organization is the use of teams (Phillips & Gully, 2012). Teams are encouraged to make recommendations and decisions that management takes seriously and implements. Teams are charged with regularly assessing processes and procedures to make improvements. In social service organizations, using teams can help improve insight into service provision. Thus, change occurs continuously. This contrasts strongly with traditional bureaucracies, which usually work to maintain the status quo.

A fifth concept reflected by a learning organization is the emphasis on continually improving quality and achievement of goals (Dubrin, 2016). Social service agencies that are learning organizations emphasize the *effectiveness* of service provision to clients instead of the *process* of service provision. Clients' perceptions about services are sought out so that improvements in quality and effectiveness can be made.

"Learning Disabilities" Working against Learning Organizations   Senge (2006) identifies several "learning disabilities" that may occur in organizations and work against learning organization culture (pp. 18–25):

- *I am my position.* This means that each worker has tunnel vision, focusing only on the tasks required in his or her position. Workers neither feel part of the greater whole nor feel that they have input into the organization's vision for the future.
- *The enemy is out there.* It's not my fault. It's his. Or it's hers. Blaming others for the consequences of your own behavior works against the learning organization. People don't learn from their mistakes and improve their behavior. Blaming others only weakens interpersonal relationships.
- *The illusion of taking charge.* Sometimes it appears that organizational leaders are taking charge of situations when they lash out at others while trying to solve problems. Superficially, they look like they're in control because they're calling attention to themselves. However, people who are really in charge don't react with emotional outbursts. Rather, they carefully think issues through, assess their own conduct, and make rational decisions.
- *The Fixation on Events.* This occurs when people focus on individual events occurring and try to identify the cause. The pattern of becoming concerned with every new event fails to look at the bigger picture. It prevents them from "seeing the longer-term patterns of change that lie behind events and from understanding the causes of those patterns" (p. 21).
- *The parable of the boiled frog.* As unappealing as this analogy is, it paints a poignant picture. If you throw a frog into a pot of boiling water, it immediately reacts by jumping out. However, if you put a frog in cold water and gradually heat it to boiling, the frog will just stay put and come to an unfortunate end. That's because frogs have adapted to react to abrupt changes in temperature, not gradual ones. The analogy between this parable and organizational behavior is that management (like the frog in boiling water) often reacts precipitately to a crisis or some other event but fails to recognize the slow, gradual, changes that pose a more severe threat. Senge (2006) would say that the major issues affecting organizations are ongoing, gradual developments. Of course, management must react to events, but managers should never lose sight of the long haul, ongoing processes, and longer-term, distant goals.
- *The delusion of learning from experience.* Hopefully, each of us learns from our experiences so that we make better, wiser choices in the future. However, after a change (such as making a policy decision or implementing a new program) is made in an organization, it often takes years to determine whether that change was effective. Thus, organizations don't necessarily learn from experience very quickly.

■ *The myth of the management team.* Some teams (defined in Chapter 4 and discussed further in the next section) are made up of members with hidden agendas who engage in power struggles and attempted manipulation. Management should look beyond the external appearance of a team's functioning and carefully evaluate its accomplishments.

Highlight 8-3

Leadership Styles

EP 8c

Leadership is "a process whereby an individual influences a group of individuals to achieve a common goal" (Northouse, 2015, p. 6). Four leadership styles will be described here—directive, supportive, participative, and achievement-oriented (Lussier & Achua, 2016; Northouse, 2015; Williams, 2016a, 2016b). They are based on a theoretical approach to leadership called **path-goal theory**. Williams (2016b) explains:

> Just as its name suggests, *path-goal theory* states that leaders can increase subordinate satisfaction and performance by clarifying and clearing the paths to goals and by increasing the number and kinds of rewards available for goal attainment. Said another way, leaders need to clarify how followers can achieve organizational goals, take care of problems that prevent followers from achieving goals, and then find more and varied rewards to motivate followers who achieve those goals. (p. 300)

As Northouse (2015) explains, the path-goal theory of leadership "is about how leaders motivate subordinates to accomplish designated goals." He continues:

> Path-goal theory emphasizes the relationship between the leader's style and the characteristics of the subordinates and the work setting. The underlying assumption of path-goal theory . . . is that followers will be motivated if they think they are capable of performing their work, if they believe their efforts will result in a certain outcome, and if they believe that the payoffs for doing their work are worthwhile. (p. 116)

The following four leadership styles are based on path-goal theory:

1. "Directive leadership involves letting employees know precisely what is expected of them, giving them specific guidelines for performing tasks, scheduling work, setting standards of performance, and making sure that people follow standard rules and regulations" (Williams, 2016a, p. 301).

2. "Supportive leadership involves being approachable and friendly to employees, showing concern for them and their welfare, treating them as equals, and creating a friendly climate" (Williams, 2016a, p. 301). "Leaders using supportive behaviors go out of their way to make work pleasant for followers" (Northouse, 2015, p. 118). "Supportive leadership often results in employee satisfaction with the job and with leaders. This leadership style may also result in improved performance when it increases employee confidence, lowers employee job stress, or improves relations and trust between employees and leaders" (Williams, 2016a, p. 301).

3. "Participative leadership involves consulting employees for their suggestions and input before making decisions. Participation in decision making should help followers understand which goals are most important and clarify the paths to accomplishing them. Furthermore, when people participate in decisions, they become more committed to making them work" (Williams, 2016a, p. 301).

4. "Achievement-oriented leadership means setting challenging goals, having high expectations of employees, and displaying confidence that employees will assume responsibility and put forth extraordinary effort" (Williams, 2016a, p. 301).

Note that these categories are not mutually exclusive. People's personalities, values, and behaviors vary dramatically. Each person is unique. It is certainly possible, indeed probable, that a leader may reflect aspects of more than one leadership style.

EP 8a

Critical Thinking Question **8-5**

What type or types of leadership do you think characterizes leaders in a learning organization? Explain.

Teamwork and Team Empowerment

Chapter 4 established that a team is a group of two or more people gathered together to work collaboratively and interdependently with each other to pursue a designated purpose. Teams can provide a useful means of empowerment in organizations by giving the responsibility for service provision to designated groups that work together (Daft, 2016a; Daft & Marcic, 2017; Lussier & Achua, 2016; Williams, 2016a). In effect, it means giving power to teams of agency workers rather than individual managers or workers. Teams can identify problems and issues, discuss potential alternatives, make decisions about how to proceed, set goals, and evaluate progress.

Specific teams might consist of groups of staff members who either provide similar services or serve the same category of clients. Teams generally meet regularly and are expected to work cooperatively together on the clients' behalf. Ongoing resolution of any conflicts occurring among team members is emphasized. Negative internal staff conflict does not benefit clients. Therefore, it is not tolerated.

Teams are most effective and empowered when used under four circumstances (Williams, 2016a). First, teams should be used when there is an obvious, appealing reason for them. A team is much more likely to do well if team members have a clear picture of why the team has been formed and what the team's goals are. If team members don't have a clue as to what they should be doing, then the team doesn't have much chance of being successful.

"Second, teams should be used when the job can't be done unless people work together. This typically means that teams are needed when tasks are complex, require multiple perspectives, or require repeated interaction with others to complete" (p. 203). Tasks requiring specific skills that can be undertaken by a single worker don't necessarily require the multiple sources of energy and ideas generated by a team.

"Third, teams should be used when rewards can be provided for teamwork and team performance. Rewards that depend on team performance rather than individual performance are the key to rewarding team behaviors and efforts" (p. 204). An agency might reward teamwork by giving the team's efforts and accomplishments public recognition in the form of praise, progress reports in an agency newsletter, or plaques that can be displayed in an office. Bonuses and raises also provide means of rewarding effective teamwork.

The fourth circumstance under which teams can function well is when they have clear authority to make recommendations or implement their decisions because of their efforts. Teams function most effectively when left to their own devices to determine their own processes and procedures (Williams, 2016a).

Working as a team has several advantages to working as separate individuals. First, a team allows for the presentation and sharing of many ideas, perspectives, and experiences. Second, team members have a wider repertoire of skills than any one individual. Third, the entire team should "own" its conclusions, recommendations, and results. Fourth, members can teach each other skills in addition to sharing knowledge and information.

The *team* concept should be distinguished from that of a *group*. A team is always a group, but a group might not be a team. Groups do not necessarily work cooperatively, individual roles may be unclear, participation of individual members may be hampered or discouraged, and frequently individual group members are seen as "stars" instead of cooperative co-participants. The team perspective, on the other hand, should encourage performance of the team allowing the entire team to gain recognition and respect within the agency environment.

Diversity as a Strength

EP 2

"Diversity exists in an organization when there is a variety of demographic, cultural, and personal differences among the people who work there" and the clients who receive services there (Williams, 2016a, p. 249). Lussier and Achua (2016) reflect:

> The value of diversity is evident in studies that have found, among other things, that a diversified workforce offers an advantage in understanding and meeting the needs of diverse customers; some of the best job candidates are found among women and other culturally diverse groups; embracing and valuing diversity can lower an organization's cost attributed to high turnover and/or absenteeism among minority groups; and diverse work groups are more creative and innovative than homogeneous work groups. (p. 384)

In contrast to traditional approaches to management, which stressed conformity, current thought focuses on the appreciation of diversity. People coming from diverse backgrounds and having various experiences bring with them a wider range of perspectives and views (Daft & Marcic, 2017). There can be greater potential for creativity and responsiveness to different and diverse client groups.

Highlight 8-4 addresses the status of women in social services management.

Highlight **8-4**

Women in Social Services Management LO 8-7

EP 2, 2a, 3, 3b, 5c

In the general US population, the median wage of women who work full-time is 74 to 83 percent of men's median wages; unfortunately, this percentage drops at every educational level, including those women who have less than a high school diploma (76.8 percent of men's median wage), a high school diploma with no college (77.9 percent), some college or an associate's degree (76.8 percent), and a bachelor's degree or higher (75.2 percent) (US Bureau of Labor Statistics, 2017). A recent study by Chamberlain found that the US average was 75.9 percent when comparing average earnings for men and women. Even when comparing "workers with the same job title, employer

and location, the gender pay gap is still 5.4 percent" (Chamberlain, 2016, p. 1). The wage discrepancies are evident in several industrialized countries, ranging from a greater gap of 75.9 percent in the United States to a smaller gap of 85.7 percent in France. The United Kingdom, Australia, and Germany fell between these extremes. This means that women need to work an additional 70 days each year to reach parity with men (US Dept. of Labor, 2016). Interestingly, the wage gap is highest for White, non-Hispanic women and lowest for Hispanic women (US Department of Labor, 2016).

Regrettably, a similar situation exists for social workers and social service managers. According to the National Association of Social Workers (NASW), available data

continued

indicate that 80 percent of all social workers are women; additionally, of all social work students, women account for 87.8 percent of those receiving baccalaureate degrees, 84.6 percent of those earning master's degrees, and 73 percent obtaining doctorate degrees (2012).

Data from the NASW Center for Workforce Studies (2011) indicate that female social workers earn 14 percent less than male social workers. This is true even when other variables are controlled (e.g., age, highest degree, practice area, rural or urban setting, and years of experience). Documentation dating back to 1961 indicates that female social workers have earned significantly less income than male social workers since that time (NASW, 2012). Additionally, women tend to be clustered in the lowest-paying positions, whereas men tend to be clustered in the highest-paying positions (NASW Workforce Studies, 2011). In this study, of the lower-earning social workers, 89 percent were women and only 11 percent were men. On the other hand, 43 percent of the higher earners were men and 57 percent were women. Consider this in the context of there being five times as many women in the profession as men.

Male social workers take on administrative positions much more quickly and much more frequently than female social workers (NASW, 2012). One study found that men in professions dominated by women (including social work) "often received preference in hiring, were closely mentored by other men in the profession, and were actively encouraged to move into leadership positions" (NASW, 2012; Williams, 1995).

Gardella and Haynes (2004) explore some of the reasons why women social workers are less likely to move into management positions:

- Few books encourage women in human services to become leaders.
- Management literature provides more information than inspiration for women with social work values and goals.
- Most research on women leaders has taken place in large corporations, where, in contrast to women in human services, nearly all the managers are affluent and white.

Although corporate managers and human services managers perform many similar tasks, books by and for women corporate leaders do not address the unique challenges of leading human services organizations. Many women who advance into leadership positions have resisted prejudice and discrimination in their careers. That experience may be of assistance as they support the mission of social work by helping to end injustice and oppression within their own organizations.

Management Approaches Used by Women Leaders

To explore further the dynamics of women in social services management, Gardella and Haynes (2004) invited 23 women leaders in the human services to become members in one of three focus groups, two that met face to face and one online. **Focus groups** are groups of 8 to 10 people who come together to discuss a topic in depth. Members are often those with a significant interest or experience in the topic, and their perspectives are considered particularly valuable. Group members in Gardella's and Haynes's groups came from racially diverse backgrounds, and all participants had substantial leadership experience in organizations. These groups were formed to discuss the career paths followed and the issues faced by these women as they progressed up the career ladder.

Findings revealed that group members' leadership experience reflected the theme of "inclusion," a pattern of behavior emphasizing "connection" and "collaboration" with others, "commitment" to professional values, and "optimism" (Gardella & Haynes, 2004, p. 102). "Inclusive leaders cultivate relationships with and among various communities and groups, using relationships to gather information, to enhance resources, and to form political alliances for their organizations" (p. 139). They took their "social responsibility" very seriously and strove to empower their clients, students, staff, organizations, and communities (p. 102). These leaders believed in "participatory decision making" and "an appreciation for diversity," which, of course, coincides with a culture of caring, employee empowerment, and advocating for diversity (p. 102). "Responding to obstacles with perseverance and hope, they were optimists who learned to fit into human services organizations while also trying to change them. ... They advanced their causes along with their careers, pursuing changes to" create a fairer and more inclusive workplace. Austin (2002) comments on how these findings clash with perspectives adopted by many workers and managers in human service organizations:

Executive positions in human service organizations, as well as in much of the rest of society, are still perceived as being embedded in a White, male, heterosexual culture. ... One of the factors in the resistance of many White heterosexual men, who are otherwise reasonable individuals, to the demographic changes that are now taking place within many organizations is anxiety ... [particularly] the possibility of having to adapt to different expectations in organizational

continued

Highlight **8-4** *continued*

settings in which *it is not taken for granted* that the White, male, heterosexual culture is dominant at the executive level. Anxiety may be particularly acute in male-dominated organizations that have traditionally been organized as a hierarchical, command-and-control structure in which a gender change in leadership positions is accompanied by a change to a low-profile interactive management style. Such culture changes have already occurred in some human service organizations in which women predominate in executive and in policy-making roles as well as in direct service roles. (p. 349)

What Organizations Can Do to Empower Women as Leaders

What should be done to empower women as leaders in organizational settings? First, an organization's management should conduct an audit or analysis of the status of women within itself (Powell, 2011). This should go beyond counting the number of women in specific job categories:

> Organization analysis also includes a cultural audit, a snapshot of the current organizational culture. It assesses the nature of the organizational culture as experienced by employees, which is not necessarily what top management thinks the culture is or should be. It also assesses how the organizational culture influences the treatment of members of different groups. Surveys, interviews, focus groups, and meetings may be used to gather information for the audit. A successful audit uncovers obstacles to the full attainment of organizational goals. Obstacles may include stereotypes and prejudices that affect employees' interactions with one another and managers' decisions regarding recruitment, performance appraisals, promotions, compensation, and other employment practices. (Powell, 2011, p. 229)

A second suggestion is for an organization to establish clear-cut objectives for each management unit (Powell & Graves, 2003). "Managers will put more effort into promoting nondiscrimination, diversity, and inclusion if they are expected to meet concrete objectives in pursuit of each of these goals" (Powell, 2011, p. 230).

A third suggestion involves encouraging employee involvement in the diversity-enhancement process by establishing "employee network groups" composed of women or people with the same cultural background (Powell, 2011, p. 230). "These groups provide career development and networking opportunities" (Powell, 2011, p. 232). However, Gardella and Haynes (2004) warn that this process can isolate women or ethnic groups of color. They indicate that "ethnic niche experience is considered marginal experience with little relevance to the rest of the organization. Knowledge related to women or ethnic minority communities is seen as specialized knowledge, applicable only to those groups. Knowledge related to majority or mainstream groups is seen as general knowledge, applicable to all" (p. 111).

Encouraging Women in Social Work to Pursue Careers in Management

Gardella and Haynes (2004) make several suggestions for female social workers to consider in pursuing a career in organizational management or to support other women who want to do so:

- "Identify a woman leader who may be a role model for you in the future or, alternatively, who has been a role model for you in the past. Invite your role model to lunch. Ask about her career path, accomplishments, and future goals, and thank her for her example" (p. 13).
- Develop a list of your personal strengths. What qualities do you have that enhance your ability to set and achieve goals? Go over the list with a person you respect to assess its accuracy and expand it if possible.
- If you ever have the opportunity, "reach out" to another woman "as a mentor" (p. 53). "Offer her support and the chance to solicit information and help from you. Help her integrate herself into a professional network where she can make additional contacts and establish her professional identity." Mentors are very beneficial for helping both women and men in developing their careers. Think about and articulate what "personal and professional goals" you would like to achieve within "the next five years" (p. 76). Identify the "barriers and opportunities" that may confront you. Develop a strategy for how to deal with them (p. 76).
- Select a community club or professional organization and join it. This can expand both your personal and professional networks. Networking often opens exciting opportunities.
- Meet with other women who are in professional circumstances like your own. You can talk about issues, provide support, and make suggestions for how to cope with problems and develop your personal and professional life.

Client System Empowerment by Management

EP 7c, 8

We have defined *power* as the potential to move other people on a chosen course to produce an effect or achieve some goal, and *empowerment* as the "process of increasing personal, interpersonal, or political power so that individuals can take action to improve their life situations" (Gutierrez, 2001, p. 210). Chapter 1 established that a *client system* is any individual, family, group, organization, or community that will ultimately benefit from social work intervention. *Macro client systems* include communities, organizations, and larger groups of clientele with similar issues and problems. Despite typical organizational problems and wide variations in management style, social workers are responsible for client-system empowerment.

By orienting their management approaches, organizations can serve as empowerment mechanisms for large groups of clients. A major goal of social work is to enhance clients' right of choice, participation in decision making concerning their own well-being, and the availability of resources for them. Social work practice does not focus on simply helping a client adapt or cope to their situation; rather, it seeks to empower clients and communities to prevent or change the problems that they are experiencing. How then can organizational management as a mightier force than individual practitioners encourage the empowerment of large groups of clients and citizens?

Empowerment-oriented intervention involves educating clients so that they understand their social environment, helping them acquire the strengths, skills, and power needed to create change. Of course, this is not always an easy task because of a variety of obstacles that impede progress.

Factors Working against Client Empowerment   Common barriers encountered include lack of financial and other resources available to assist clients. Many agencies make no effort to empower their clients or to even encourage them to participate. Reasons for this include concern that clients might demand more than the agency can provide, fear of conflict when clients are unhappy about services provided, and inability to predict the time and staffing needed to involve clients. The more people involved in the process, the greater the cost.

A second obstacle is barriers that exist in the macro environment where other agencies may resist sending clients to, or receiving clients from agencies that are designed to encourage client empowerment.

A third barrier to encouraging an organization toward an empowerment focus involves *intrapersonal challenges.* Not all staff nor all clients will be capable of fully engaging in empowerment activities. Staff may resist the extra time and patience needed for an empowerment process. This is especially true if past efforts to empower clients have been less than successful. Clients, on the other hand, may lack the mental or physical capabilities to participate fully.

Another challenge to creating an empowerment organization is the *interpersonal issues* involving the people themselves. Of necessity, the level of interaction between practitioners and clients is greater and sometimes reveals inherent barriers. Workers may resist giving up some of the power to clients because in their traditional practitioner–client relationships they may have much more control and responsibility for directing the relationship. Empowered clients may make decisions that the practitioner thinks are unwise. While the practitioner may be correct, clients' making their own decisions is what we mean by client **self-determination**. Some clients will choose alternatives that ultimately hurt them or fail to solve long-standing problems. That, however, is a risk in most areas of social work and not unique to empowering organizations.

EP 1, 2b, 8, 8c

Organizational Conditions Enhancing Client Empowerment   To meet the challenges inherent in creating an empowering organization, several steps are self-evident. First, an organization must have leaders who support the goal and take actions that further its achievement. When administrators do this, it sets up the organization with an empowerment environment that is reflected in all its activities.

Another step is the creation of a staff fully dedicated to empowerment. This means hiring, training, and promoting practitioners who identify with the organization's mission. Staff training is a requirement, as practitioners must learn how to solicit and gather client ideas to promote maximum client input.

Finally, a client-empowering agency will benefit from staff collaboration with each other and with their clients. The advantages of teamwork have already been addressed, and it is particularly appropriate in empowering organizations. Such organizations allow workers greater freedom and flexibility to make decisions with strong support from administration

These suggestions sound positive and logical. However, despite good ideas, ethical and other problematic issues may surface during service provision. Focus on Ethics 8-1 considers a scenario where a client is dissatisfied with a social services agency and its worker's approach in dealing with her.

Focus on Ethics **8-1**

Client Dissatisfaction

EP 1

Consider the following scenario.

Yoko is furious. She is the single mother of three young children and a client at Penniless County Department of Social Services. She is currently receiving public assistance and is enrolled in a work preparation program teaching her skills in food preparation.

She has tried to see her assigned social worker, Gunter, eight times without success. The man is simply never there. Twice she's tried to complain to a supervisor but was cut off at the pass by secretarial sentries who adamantly declared that all supervisors were busy at the moment. They added she could make an appointment in three weeks or so.

Yoko's problem is that she discovered she hates food preparation and the training program in which she was arbitrarily placed. She wants to work and needs

training, but couldn't it involve office work or sales or anything but food preparation? She has little time to make a change. She will only qualify for a few more months of assistance before she is required to work and her assistance is terminated.

Yoko doesn't know to whom she can turn. The agency has no client advisory group or formal appeal process for clients to use. Clients must work through their designated worker. Yoko feels frustrated, angry, and powerless.

What is the ethical thing for the Department of Social Services and the social worker to do? How might management improve "the system" to include procedures and opportunities for Yoko's empowerment? How might she be allowed better opportunities to voice her opinions, make her own decisions, and have direct access to people in power making decisions about her?

Specific Management Approaches LO 8-8

EP 6, 5b, 8c

We've discussed some major themes in current management thought. Now we'll turn to two of the dozens of specific management approaches being used today that apply some of these themes—TQM and servant leadership. Note that these two theoretical approaches simply provide examples of how management can be used to empower staff in organizations.

Total Quality Management

The first of two specific approaches to management and leadership discussed here is **total quality management (TQM)**. Developed by W. Edward Deming and others (Daft & Marcic, 2017), TQM is one of several approaches to management used today. It is characterized by three core principles: a focus on customer needs and satisfaction, continuous improvement in service or product, and teamwork. It builds on the philosophy of involving and empowering team members. Unlike some management approaches, TQM is concerned about the line worker who actually produces the product or service that is delivered by the organization: "TQM focuses on the line worker level rather than the larger administrative system. TQM uses structured problem-solving methods to analyze work processes, eliminate unnecessary steps, and improve quality" (Lewis, Packard, & Lewis, 2012, p. 252). In a social services organization, the goal would be finding out what clients need and providing it. In fact, TQM is a management approach especially significant in social service agencies, because many administrators view TQM as an appropriate leadership model. TQM is also often used as a means of organizational development in social services because of its value as a long-term approach to improving service delivery.

Another application of TQM and its principles involves the organizational assessment approach of quality assurance, frequently employed in social services agencies. **Quality assurance** is a technique used to assess "organizational processes and systems" (as opposed to organizational outcomes or goals) to make certain these processes and systems meet expected standards. It also identifies problems, makes changes in organizational practices, and subsequently reassesses those practices to determine whether effective improvements have been made (Lewis et al., 2012, p. 227).

Secret, Bentley, and Kadolph (2016) reported the use of quality assurance to continually improve an online social work education program. Quality assurance typically uses benchmarks or standards to determine whether improvement is occurring.

It is beyond the scope of this book to describe in detail the implementation process of a TQM philosophy and program. However, to begin understanding how TQM is implemented and how it affects human behavior in a real agency, we will discuss several concepts. These include a focus on clients as customers, quality as the primary goal, employee empowerment and teamwork, TQM leadership, and continuous improvement.

A Focus on Clients as Customers   The central theme of TQM is the importance of the customer or client (Daft & Marcic, 2017; Williams, 2016b). The quest for quality should be focused on what clients need and how effective and efficient they perceive service provision to be. Because staff who provide service directly to clients are central to client satisfaction, such staff are considered critical. TQM stresses that they should have high status and receive good, supportive treatment.

TQM maintains that **customer satisfaction**, the condition where an organization's "services meet or exceed customer expectations," is paramount (Williams, 2016b, p. 505). Therefore, agencies must solicit information from customers to strive for greater effectiveness. This can be done in a variety of ways. For one thing, the agency can administer customer satisfaction surveys or community surveys that solicit information from customers or clients about agency services. Staff can also conduct extensive interviews with individual customers to identify and examine their feelings. Likewise, the agency can focus on customer complaints and undertake extensive investigations. Suggestion boxes for anonymous feedback can be placed in accessible places. Finally, the agency can assemble groups of customers (focus groups) to discuss services and to make suggestions for quality improvement.

It should be emphasized that not only is customer feedback regularly solicited, but that the agency *uses* this feedback to improve its service provision. There are many ways an agency might incorporate feedback: by prioritizing client and agency needs, planning new goals, and undertaking new projects and procedures. Because this book's purpose is not to teach you how to be a manager but, rather, how to understand and work within an organizational environment, we will not discuss these processes here.

Highlight 8-5 identifies seven interactions between workers and customers that should never occur in an organization espousing TQM.

Highlight 8-5

"The Seven Sins of Service"

Albrecht (1988) maintains the need to focus consistently on the quality of service provided to customers (or clients). He identifies "seven sins of service" that organizations commonly commit that work against maintenance and enhancement of service quality: "apathy," "brush-off," "coldness," "condescension," "robotism," "rule book," and "runaround" (pp. 14–16).

Of course, professional social work ethics demand that our clients or customers should always be our top priority. In an ideal world, this would be so. In the real world, however, staff members are individuals with individual weaknesses and failings. These seven sins of service can and do occur. From an organizational perspective, of course, "staff" includes everyone from the agency director to various levels of administrative staff to professional social workers and other helping professionals to clerical staff to maintenance staff. Regardless of job title and responsibilities, each is an agency representative. Albrecht maintains that it is essential for all staff to avoid committing any of the seven sins described here.

As professional social workers, we are supposed to be warm, empathic, and genuine. We are to always treat the customer with respect. However, these values are more difficult to maintain when we have 23 customers waiting in line impatiently for service, or we have an excruciatingly painful migraine headache, or we absolutely must finish an eight-page report by 4:30 p.m. and we haven't even started yet. During these times, Albrecht would say that it's especially important to be vigilant about not committing any of these seven sins:

1. **Apathy.** Albrecht describes this as the "DILLIGAD" syndrome, or "Do I Look Like I Give a Damn?"—à la comic George Carlin (p. 15). In other words, it's easy for staff members to focus on getting their jobs over with so that they can go home and live their

continued

Highlight **8-5** *continued*

own lives. Apathy involves boredom with customer interactions and almost total lack of concern regarding the *quality*, usefulness, or effectiveness of the service provided.

2. **Brush-off.** This consists of getting rid of the customer by passing the buck and doing the smallest amount of work feasible. For example, a staff member might tell a customer that he can't answer her questions accurately and send her off to another department, probably on a wild goose chase.

3. **Coldness.** This "kind of chilly hostility, curtness, unfriendliness, inconsiderateness, or impatience" is intended to convey to the customer, "You're a nuisance; please go away" (p. 15). It is difficult to maintain a warm, interested interpersonal stance every minute of the day. Some customers may be hostile, feisty, or demanding, on the one hand. On the other, you as a worker may be tired, fed up, or disgusted.

4. **Condescension.** Treating customers with a disdainful, patronizing attitude implies that you as the worker are more knowledgeable and, essentially, better than the customers are. When you condescend, you treat people as if they're not very bright. It might be characterized by the phrase, "Now don't you worry your stupid little head about it. I know best and I'll take care of everything. Trust me."

5. **Robotism.** When you treat each customer identically, without changes in facial or verbal expression, or ask the same questions over and over to different customers, you are not responding to individual differences. Such differences don't concern you. Your main intent is to get the job done as fast and efficiently as possible while using as little brain power as possible.

6. **Rule Book.** If you want to think as little as possible, use the rule book to give the organization's rules and regulations absolute precedence. "Go by the book" totally and completely without any hint of compromise. I once called a weight-control clinic for information on exercising and maintaining my weight. A young woman answered the phone, obviously reading a boilerplate blurb about losing weight at the clinic. I asked her if the clinic also helped people *maintain* their current weight, not lose anymore. She answered by rereading the identical blurb she just had read to me. I asked her the same question two more times, after which she repeated the same blurb. Finally, exasperated, I said, "Can't you think for yourself or what?" and abruptly hung up. Although this situation does not reflect a social work context, it does exemplify the sin of rule book. The young woman answering the phone apparently was instructed to read her blurb and not say anything else. Consequently, trying to get any help from her (in this case, information) was totally useless and frustrating.

7. **Runaround.** Stalling customers is a common sin. Workers tell a customer to call someone else for the information first, or to go to Window 217 and fill out the appropriate 22-page form. Runaround entails using as little of your own time as possible, on the one hand, and wasting the customer's time, on the other.

Quality as the Primary Goal   In TQM, quality is the primary goal (Williams, 2016b; Weinbach & Taylor, 2015). However, *quality* is a difficult term to define. TQM can be applied to any organization, regardless of its purpose. There is no TQM definition that will apply to all organizations. Consider an organization that manufactures parasailing parachutes. Its definition of quality would be quite different than a social service organization with the goal of providing substance abuse treatment. Each organization must determine for itself what quality means in terms of its own service provision.

For example, a state could use a set of outcome indicators or standards for assessing the quality of child welfare services offered by county child welfare agencies These might include:

- *Six-month recurrence of maltreatment.* During the past six months, no more than 6.1 percent of children previously abused/neglected have another substantiated report of child abuse or neglect (CA/N).

- *Incidence of reports of CA/N while in substitute care*. During the past six months, of all children in foster care, no more than 0.57 percent have had a substantiated report of CA/N involving foster parents.
- *Stability of foster care placements*. During the past six months, no more than 13.3 percent of foster children experienced more than two placements.
- *Foster care re-entries*. No more than 8.6 percent of children who entered foster care in the past year re-entered foster care in a 12-month period.
- *Length of time to achieve reunification*. At least 76 percent of children in foster care were reunified with their parents or caretakers within 12 months of entering care.
- *Length of time to achieve adoption*. At least 32 percent of foster children eligible for adoption will be adopted within 24 months of entering foster care.

Standards like those shown above are appropriate for an agency providing child welfare services but would be of no value for an agency providing substance abuse or marital counseling. It is up to the individual agency to determine the quality indicators that best fit the type of services offered.

Employee Empowerment and Teamwork   We stress repeatedly that empowerment involves providing people with authority or power so that they might have greater control over what they do. A TQM approach means that workers must be empowered to make decisions about how to do their jobs. Lehman and DuFrene (2017) explain:

> In a Total Quality Management environment, decision-making power is distributed to the people closest to the problem, who usually have the best information sources and solutions. Each employee, from the president to the custodian, is expected to solve problems, participate in team-building efforts, and expand the scope of his or her role in the organizations. The goal of employee empowerment is to build a work environment in which all employees take pride in their work accomplishments and begin motivating themselves from within rather than through traditional extrinsic incentives [such as pay raises]. (p. 23)

TQM management in social service agencies places the major responsibility for effective service provision on direct service workers. TQM not only emphasizes the importance of clients or customers but also employees in the agency units providing services directly to these clients. Likewise, other agency units providing input to direct service units are considered important because of their support to the service providers. For example, supervisory input is considered important primarily because it should aid in the service-provision process.

In some ways, you might envision TQM as an upside-down pyramid. In a typical bureaucratic organization, the power structure as reflected in a formal organizational chart is in the form of a triangle or pyramid. The agency director sits at the pinnacle. Below her might be assistant directors, beneath them managers, below them supervisors, and, finally, at the very bottom, the many workers. The pyramid's shape, of course, reflects the relative number of persons involved at each level. There is only one agency director. There are fewer supervisors than direct service workers. Finally, there are fewer direct service workers than there are clients. In TQM, because the client customers or consumers are given precedence, those providing service directly to them are considered, in a way, the most important. The agency's clients thus form the top level of the inverted pyramid because they are considered the most significant. Right below them would be the direct service workers, beneath them the supervisors, and so on in the reverse order of the bureaucratic pyramid. The agency director and, perhaps, the board of directors would be placed at the very bottom of the inverted pyramid.

TQM espouses not only empowerment of individual employees but also team empowerment (Lewis et al., 2012; Lehman & DuFrene, 2017; Williams, 2016b). This involves giving the responsibility for service provision to designated groups that work together. TQM emphasizes cooperation instead of competition. Such teamwork also means that all organizational employees, from top management to direct service workers, must work together and have the authority and responsibility to improve the quality of products or services and to resolve any problems they encounter.

A concept related to team empowerment is the quality circle. Daft and Marcic (2015) explain:

> A **quality circle** is a group of 6 to 12 volunteer employees who meet regularly to discuss and solve problems affecting the quality of their work. At a set time during the workweek, the members of the quality circle meet, identify problems, and try to find solutions. Circle members are free to collect data and take surveys. ... The reason for using quality circles is to push decision making to an organization level at which recommendations can be made by the people who do the job and know it better than anyone else. (p. 647)

Many organizations train employees to work in teams and problem solve so that they can use these skills in quality circles. Quality circles help encourage employee involvement in decision making as well as improving service delivery, and have proved helpful in human service organizations.

A Total Quality Approach to Leadership   Strong support and leadership from top management is critical in implementing TQM (Griffin, 2016; Lewis et al., 2012). Dumler and Skinner (2008) explain:

> Supervision has been widely practiced as a traditional method of keeping an eye on workers—that is, looking for mistakes [a method often practiced in traditional bureaucracies]. Some managers have even resorted to using information technologies to eavesdrop on employees. This type of practice has debilitating effects on performance and is ethically questionable. ...
>
> The responsibility for quality control ultimately rests with management; however, managers must also promote worker self-management. To further employee self-management, managers must develop worker participation programs and policies. With knowledge of the [organization's] ... costs and goals, workers can practice control with minimal supervision. Management's job is to ensure that workers have the knowledge, the tools, and the power to prevent problems from arising. Managers must also encourage employee's suggestions ... by recognizing and implementing worker quality improvement

decisions. And, if there are problems, management should give workers the first opportunity to solve them. (p. 358)

One task that leaders must accomplish is the establishment of a culture of quality. We've established that *organizational culture* is "the set of key values, beliefs, understandings, and norms shared by members of an organization" (Daft & Marcic, 2017, p. 76).

For example, one agency director whose private, nonprofit family services organization had adopted a TQM perspective illustrated her commitment in a very concrete way. Historically, staff would park in the best spots in the parking lot each workday morning because they always got there first. Clients (or customers in TQM terminology), who regularly got there later, would get the parking spots furthest from the building—if there were any spots left at all. Traditionally, the agency director assumed "ownership" of the best parking spot right by the agency's main door. The assistant director (no. 2 in the agency's hierarchy) then took the second-best spot, and so it went on down the line. The daytime janitor was assigned the very worst spot.

Reflecting the TQM philosophy, the director decided to demonstrate the importance of serving customers and giving them priority by ordering that customers should be left the very best parking spots. Staff were relegated to the worst. The director herself chose the spot in the farthest corner of the lot, next to an appallingly foul-smelling dumpster. She also rallied some of the agency's precious funds to purchase extra parking spaces for customers in a lot adjacent to the agency. She felt that clients should no longer suffer from parking scarcity problems.

Another example of how agency leaders can demonstrate their commitment to TQM principles involves a family services agency that had held its board of directors' meetings at noon each Friday since 1966. The boardroom where their meetings were held was the only large meeting facility in the agency. Therefore, it was used for a variety of agency activities and business, including staff meetings, treatment conferences concerning individual cases, and educational activities for clients. When the agency adopted the TQM management philosophy, the board solicited and received feedback from clients. One recommendation was a stress management class that, ideally, would be held at (yes, you guessed it) noon on Fridays. Because TQM emphasizes clients' importance, the board changed its meeting time to another day and another time. This was done despite some inconveniences for board members.

Note that the board of directors in a traditionally bureaucratic agency would likely assume the topmost status in an agency. In effect, the board functions as the agency director's boss. In traditional bureaucracies, top leaders usually receive top priority for access to agency resources such as prime meeting space.

Continuous Improvement   "**Continuous improvement** is an ongoing commitment to increase product and service quality by constantly assessing and improving the processes and procedures used to create those products and services" (Williams, 2016a, p. 383). TQM does not result in instant improvement in an organization. Rather, it involves small changes reflecting improvements in performance throughout an organization on a constant basis. The organization must maintain an ongoing commitment to the TQM principles involved.

EP 8a

Critical Thinking Questions **8-6**

What are the pros and cons of total quality management (TQM)? To what extent would you feel comfortable either being an employee or a manager in an organization employing total quality management principles?

In the context of social service agencies, one indicator of needed improvement is uneven quality in services provided. If service provision is uneven and unpredictable, then attention should be focused on improving the processes concerned to make them more consistently effective. Quality of effective service provision is the ongoing goal.

All organizations require structure, orderliness, and direction. In other words, they need to be managed. The trick is to balance "structure and control," on the one hand, and TQM's culture of quality on the other (Hill & Jones, 2013, p. 436). In the best of situations, this would require continuous improvement as organizations respond to the ever-changing and sometimes turbulent environments in which they struggle to survive and thrive.

While not fully convinced that the TQM model is ideal for many social service organizations, the importance of quality improvement was underscored by Megivern and her colleagues (2007), who noted: "We strongly encourage social workers to become fully engaged in discussions about quality in their practice settings and use their voices for quality social services transformation. To ignore this opportunity is to allow others to define quality social work practice and perhaps to blame social workers for the failures of larger systems" (p. 122).

Servant Leadership

EP 8c

Another approach to the leadership aspect of management that has gained increased attention over the years is servant leadership (Northouse, 2015). Lussier (2012) describes this approach:

> **Servant leadership** is a leadership style based on simultaneously meeting the needs and goals of employees while meeting the goals of the organization. Servant leaders lead from positions of moral influence, not power, and are very follower-centered. They see leadership as an opportunity to serve at the ground level, not to lead from the top. Servant leaders support employees. ...

At a Glance **8-1**

TQM Concepts

— A focus on *clients as customers*, with customer satisfaction being the principal objective

— *Quality of service* as the primary goal

— The importance of *employee empowerment and teamwork,* thereby giving responsibility for decision making to employees

— *Leadership that sustains TQM culture,* which supports employees and their decisions, instead of directing their every move

— Pursuit of *continuous improvement* of the processes and procedures involved in service delivery

They focus on motivating employees by meeting their higher-level needs: valuing employees' input, encouraging participation, sharing power, developing self-confidence, and fostering creativity. By doing so, servant leaders motivate employees to go beyond role requirements and do what it takes to attain the goals of the organization. Servant leaders can be found at all management levels, focusing on helping others, as they put the needs of others and the organization ahead of their self-interest. (pp. 338–339)

Northouse (2016) further explains how the concept of servant leadership:

Servant leadership is an approach focusing on leadership from the point of view of the leader and his or her behaviors. Servant leadership emphasizes that leaders be attentive to the concerns of their followers, empathize with them, and nurture them. Servant leaders put followers first, empower them, and help them develop their full capacities. Further, servant leaders are ethical. (p. 226)

Servant leaders are concerned about those who are less privileged in life, and they oppose social injustice and other forms of oppression. They focus on the needs of followers and help them to become more knowledgeable, more free, more autonomous, and more like servants themselves. They enrich others by their presence.

"A servant leader is therefore a moral leader" who is interested in helping "employees, customers [clients], and community" members "become wiser, healthier, and more autonomous" (Dubrin, 2016, p. 120). In becoming a servant leader, a leader uses less institutional power and less control, while shifting authority to those who are being led. Servant leadership values everyone's involvement in community life because it is within a community that one fully experiences respect, trust, and individual strength.

Qualities of a Servant Leader   Barbuto and Wheeler (2005) and Northouse (2016) cite characteristics that make one a good servant leader. Some are inherent qualities that really can't be taught. Others are behaviors that can be learned and enhanced.

1. *Calling.* Becoming a servant leader is more than just choosing that course. You must have an innate desire to forgo your own needs. Instead, you must put the well-being of others in the organization and the organization itself before yourself. You must have a genuine desire to improve the lives and functioning of workers. Therefore, it's like a calling instead of a choice.
2. *Listening.* We've established that listening is a vital communication skill. Servant leaders are exceptional listeners (Dubrin, 2016). They seek out information from others in the organization and strive to understand what others are trying to say.
3. *Empathy.* Empathy involves not only *being in tune* with how others feel but also *conveying to them* that you understand how they feel (Kirst-Ashman & Hull, 2018b).
4. *Healing.* Servant leaders encourage emotional healing. They are supportive people who are easy to talk to and trust. People are naturally drawn to them.

5. *Awareness.* Servant leaders have a keen awareness of what's going on around them. They look beyond superficial appearances and explore issues and situations in depth.

6. *Persuasion.* Servant leaders are experts at using persuasion. They avoid making commands, but, rather, explain their views carefully and help others see their point of view.

7. *Conceptualization.* Servant leaders look at the organization's total picture and have vision about what the organization might become (Daft & Marcic, 2017). They encourage others to be creative and dream of how things could or should be. Their conceptualization of the organization's operation and environment is clearly articulated to others.

8. *Foresight.* Servant leaders look ahead and prepare for what might happen in the future. Others look to them for guidance and depend on them to anticipate upcoming issues.

9. *Stewardship.* Stewardship is the condition and act of caring for the basic daily needs of others. It involves planning activities, managing processes, and helping to make other people's lives run smoothly. Stewardship involves a strong desire to serve and assist.

10. *Growth.* Servant leaders view others as being capable of growth and improvement. They maintain a positive perspective and encourage skill development and confidence building in others.

11. *Building community.* A "*community* consists of a number of people with something in common that connects them in some way and that distinguishes them from others" (Homan, 2016, p. 10). Servant leaders encourage a sense of community among all the people who work in an organization. They urge others to work together as a part of something bigger and more important than any single individual could be.

Social Workers as Employees: Interpersonal Skills in the Macro Social Environment LO 8-9

EP 1c, 6b

Thus far, this chapter has focused on management's perspective of human behavior in the organizational environment. We talked about management's trends and approaches, many of which focus on empowering employees. We'll now turn our attention to workers' perspectives in organizational life. Employees are not dull automatons wandering aimlessly through the organizational maze, subject to absolute control by management. Rather, employees in organizations have problems, needs,

Critical Thinking Questions **8-7**

EP 8a

What are the pros and cons of servant leadership? To what extent would you feel comfortable either being an employee or a manager in an organization employing servant leadership principles?

and concerns that are like the issues in our own work settings. This is also the case for social workers and their work environments.

Two aspects of interaction are especially relevant to interpersonal relationships and communication—assertiveness and conflict management. This is true both for personal, informal relationships, and for relationships in work contexts. In macro settings, including organizations, appropriate assertiveness and conflict management can be useful skills for working with colleagues, supervisors, and administrators. These approaches can enhance relationships, improve problem solving, and basically make the job easier.

Assertiveness in the Macro Environment: The Assertiveness Continuum

Alberti and Emmons (2017) describe assertiveness:

> Assertive self-expression is direct, firm, positive—and when necessary persistent—action intended to promote equality in person-to-person relationships. Assertiveness enables us to act in our own best interests, to stand up for ourselves without undue anxiety, to exercise personal rights without denying the rights of others, and to express our feelings . . . honestly and comfortably. (p. 8)

Assertiveness can be thought of as a continuum where communication and behavior can range from nonassertive to assertive to aggressive. **Assertive communication** includes verbal and nonverbal behavior that permits a speaker to get her points across clearly and straightforwardly. Speakers who are assertive take into consideration both their own values and the values of whoever is receiving their message. They consider their own points important, but also consider the points and reactions of receivers as significant.

Nonassertive communication comes from speakers who devalue themselves completely. They feel the other person and what that person thinks are much more important than their own thoughts. People who have difficulty being assertive can experience a range of problems. They can be very shy and withdrawn or afraid to express their real feelings. Although they may become increasingly uncomfortable about their failure to be assertive and protect their rights, they rarely can respond assertively.

For example, Pete has a problem. Part of his administrative job involves collecting information about the amount of client contact from practitioners in his social work department and summarizing the data in a monthly report.

Pete's problem is that Gerri, one of the workers, typically fails to respond to his emails and handwritten requests for data until she is at least two weeks late. Gerri's behavior reflects negatively upon Pete's job performance. He is unable to submit the data until he gets all of it. To higher agency administration, Gerri's tardiness makes Pete look like he's the one who's not punctual in doing this part of his job. This infuriates Pete. However, Pete considers himself a relatively shy person. He hates to confront other people, especially people like Gerri, who has an exceptionally outgoing and vibrant personality. Thus, Pete leaves the situation as it is. He maintains his nonassertive position and allows his underlying anger to seethe.

We have indicated that aggressiveness lies on the opposite end of the assertiveness continuum from nonassertiveness. It engenders bold and dominating verbal

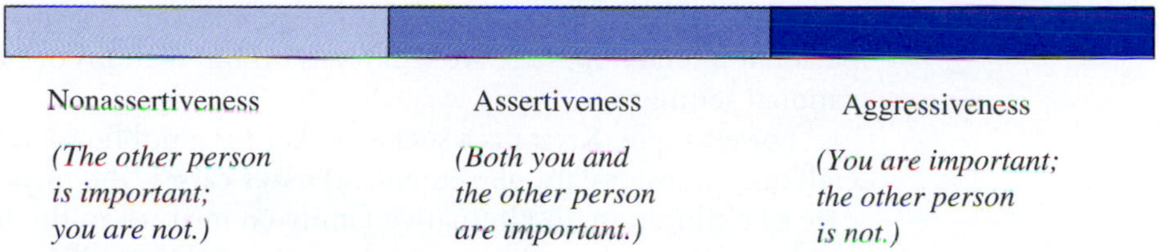

Nonassertiveness	Assertiveness	Aggressiveness
(The other person is important; you are not.)	*(Both you and the other person are important.)*	*(You are important; the other person is not.)*

Figure 8-1 The Assertiveness Continuum

and nonverbal behavior whereby a speaker presses his or her point of view as taking precedence above all other perspectives. An aggressive speaker considers only his or her views important and devalues what the receiver says. Aggressive behaviors are demanding and often annoying.

One example of aggressive behavior would be a fellow worker who consistently talks and occasionally raises his voice during staff meetings so that other staff members have little or no opportunity to "get their two cents in." This worker pays attention only to his own needs, with no consideration for the needs and wants of others. Another instance of aggressive behavior is the employee who consistently makes it a point to get the agency's best vehicle to make home visits. She not only feels it is supremely important for her to get the best available, she also blocks any comments about how consistently getting the best means that other workers are left with the worst on a regular basis.

Figure 8-1 depicts the assertiveness continuum.

Scenarios of Nonassertiveness—Assertiveness—Aggressiveness

An infinite number of scenarios could conceptualize the dynamics involved in assertiveness and various aspects of the assertiveness continuum. Three will arbitrarily be described here. They include passive-aggressiveness, nonassertiveness when being caught off guard, and nonassertiveness leading to an explosion of aggression.

Passive-Aggressiveness   Another form of aggressiveness is **passive-aggressiveness**. Here, an individual is aggressive, but only secretly or covertly so. Often, such a person dislikes confrontation and tries to avoid it at all costs. However, to get their own way, passive-aggressive individuals will go behind others' backs to get what they really want. For example, Donald, a substance abuse counselor, thinks Herschel, a colleague with the same job status, is lazy. Donald would like their supervisor, Maria, to reprimanded Herschel and force him to assume more of the workload. Donald does not want to confront Herschel himself. Therefore, Donald passive-aggressively meets with Maria behind closed doors (literally) to complain about Herschel's laziness and work performance. He encourages Maria to reprimand Herschel. Donald is being passive in that he doesn't confront Herschel. However, Donald is also being aggressive in that he tries to manipulate the situation so that Herschel receives his reprimand. Donald, however, appears (on the outside) to remain uninvolved and blameless.

Nonassertiveness and Being Caught Off Guard   At one time or another, most people wish they had been more assertive instead of acting *nonassertively*. They might have had an experience where they didn't think fast enough to make a suitable reply to a statement or request. Perhaps, they simply had been caught off guard. Although such situations may characterize virtually any type of interpersonal interaction, here we will focus on interactions occurring within organizational settings.

For example, Krysta is a social worker for a public social service agency specializing in foster care placements. (**Foster care** is the physical supervision and care of children in an alternative family context when the biological parents or legal guardians are unable to care for these children.) Krysta is also a member of a *delegate council* (a group of representatives from a series of agencies) called the Interagency Council on Adolescent Pregnancy (ICAP). The council's task is to undertake a major assessment of the area's adolescent pregnancy problem, recommend solutions, and develop a coordinated strategy for the implementation of recommendations.

Krysta is very interested in preventing unwanted teen pregnancy. She is aware of the potentially problematic issues involved in foster care when subsequent out-of-home placements occur for children born to teen mothers.

Krysta is getting out of her car, about to attend one of the council's biweekly meetings. Suddenly, Harold, one of her colleagues and her agency's other council ICAP representative (each agency, including Krysta's, is allowed two delegates), drives up and parks next to her. He says, "Oh, hi. Would you mind writing out that announcement we talked about and circulating it to the other council members?" (The announcement involves a fundraising dinner that an ICAP committee has planned. Harold had promised to write the announcement.) He continues, "I have a court appearance scheduled downtown today, so I can't make the council meeting. I'm glad I ran into you because I have to get going."

Harold catches Krysta by surprise. Then he jumps in his car and drives away. Harold typically "leeches" time, energy, and money from people he works with, including other council members. It may entail just asking for a cigarette from the few remaining colleagues who smoke. Or it might be a request that someone else write up the results of one of the meetings because he doesn't have time (even though it was his turn to function as the meeting's secretary). Sometimes, he asks Krysta to pick him up the next morning because his son needs the car (even though he lives 25 miles out of her way). Another of his favorite ploys is to sheepishly request that Krysta or some other colleague "catch the check" for lunch because he forgot his wallet and doesn't have any cash (he typically says he will pay the lender back later, but never does—at least not without being badgered a half-dozen times). In other words, Harold is downright self-centered and inconsiderate about others' rights.

When he asks Krysta to do this favor, she doesn't have much time to think and almost automatically says, "Oh, yeah, sure." Then, 30 seconds after he's disappeared and it's too late, she thinks, "What did I do that for? I know better than to get sucked in by his requests. Rats!"

The problem is that he surprised Krysta when she least expected it. She had other things on her mind. For one thing, she had been thinking about ideas she wanted to present at the day's ICAP meeting. Krysta had also been preoccupied wondering whether the meeting would be short so she could make her oil change appointment.

Krysta would never impose upon people as Harold does. In his view, not only should she automatically agree to circulate the dinner announcement, but she should also *write* it! She thinks, "Oh, come on. That is his responsibility." She's not certain about all the details for the dinner. She wonders why he didn't call her earlier about the announcement or drop off a note. Not expecting his sudden request, she had been unprepared to respond. She never really thought about such a situation before.

Over the next half-hour, Krysta remains preoccupied about what she *should* have said. For example, she could have straightforwardly exclaimed, "No." Or, maybe she should have compromised and replied, "Sure. You write the announcement, and I'll be happy to circulate it to the council." She continues to stew about her mistake and Harold's inconsiderate behavior for quite a while.

However, it's too late to do anything about it after the fact. Now Krysta has already agreed to do it. She's stuck. She had plainly been too nonassertive in response to Harold's request.

Nonassertiveness Can Build to an Explosion of Aggression   In other situations, people allow their frustration at their own lack of assertiveness to build until they can't stand it anymore and subsequently "lose it." All their emotions explode in a burst of anger. This can readily happen to nonassertive people who allow their discomfort to escalate until they erupt in rage. This display of temper and anger reflects one aspect of the other end of the continuum—*aggressiveness*.

For example, three months ago, Brenna got her first social work position in a sheltered employment facility for adults with intellectual disabilities. One of her male colleagues, a speech therapist also employed by the agency, regularly makes what Brenna considers extremely rude, sexist comments about his female colleagues and even some of the female clients. She feels his behavior has made others so uncomfortable that they find it difficult to work effectively with him in the organizational environment.

Brenna considers herself a confident, straightforward person. Yet she just started this job and does not want to "make waves" or be labeled a troublemaker or whiner. Brenna knows that this man's behavior is inappropriate, derogatory, and clearly wrong. Every time she runs into him at work, he makes one off-color comment or another. Meanwhile, her feelings continue to simmer . . . and SIMMER . . . AND SIMMER. Finally, something snaps and she screams, "I can't stand it anymore! I think you're a disgusting sexist! Just shut up!" Unfortunately, this outburst does little to improve their relationship or his behavior.

Appropriate Assertiveness   LO 8-10

EP 1b

Appropriate assertiveness is a necessity in generalist practice in and with groups, organizations, and communities. Assertiveness involves expressing yourself without hurting others or stepping on their rights. Being assertive means considering both *your own rights* and *the rights of others*. Highlight 8-6 reviews your assertive rights. When interacting with colleagues, supervisors, administrators, staff from other agencies, politicians, or community residents, it is critical to use assertiveness skills.

Highlight 8-6

Each of Us Has Certain Assertive Rights[2]

EP 3a, 5c, 8d

Part of becoming assertive requires figuring out and believing that we are valuable and worthwhile people. It's easy to criticize ourselves for our mistakes and imperfections. It's also easy to hold our feelings in because we're afraid that we will hurt someone else's feelings or that someone will reject us. It's been established that sometimes feelings that are held in too long will burst in an aggressive tirade, which may occur in personal or professional contexts.

A basic principle in social work is that every individual is a valuable human being. Everyone, therefore, has certain basic rights. The following are eight of your assertive rights:

1. *You have the right to express your ideas and opinions openly and honestly.* For example, Manuela, a nursing-home social worker, attends a meeting at another agency which is also attended by workers from a range of community social service agencies. The meeting's purpose is to discuss the possibility of conducting a fundraiser to acquire Christmas presents for low-income children in the community. Each participant has already stated a preference for collecting money from community residents, businesses, schools, and social service agencies. Manuela, however, believes that they would get more if the group asked for donations of *toys* and *clothing* instead of *money*. Even though Manuela is going against the flow, so to speak, she still has the right to voice her opinion straightforwardly and honestly. The final consensus regarding strategy may or may not agree with her proposal. However, she has the right to be heard.

2. *You have the right to be wrong. Everyone makes mistakes.* For example, Mohammed is a school social worker who applies for a state grant to start a summer neighborhood activity program for adolescents in an urban neighborhood. (A *grant* is a funding allocation from one public or private organization or individual to another to undertake some project or achieve some goal.) Mohammed works on the grant every night for two weeks, thinking that such an activity program will keep scores of

children off the streets and out of trouble for at least part of the following summer. His writing task is like trying to compose three 20-page research papers that you've put off until the final two weeks of the semester. This work is *tedious*. Mohammed finally gets the document off and postmarked on the day he thinks it is due. The key word in the previous sentence, of course, is "thinks." Unfortunately, he has read the due date as December 8 instead of December 5. He has probably read that grant application form 30 times. Each time, his mind saw 8 instead of 5.

Unfortunately, the state grant evaluators are strict regarding the timeliness of grant applications. Any grants submitted even one day late are instantaneously dismissed as unacceptable. (This is similar to the practice of many graduate schools concerning application dates: One day late and you're out of luck.) Mohammed is, of course, disappointed and disgusted with himself. He has bragged about his plan to his supervisor and fellow workers. Now he must face the music. What a bummer.

However, Mohammed has the right to make a mistake, even an apparently careless one like this. The cliché that we all make mistakes is exactly right. We all have the right to make mistakes, because even when we try our best we *do* make mistakes.

It is in Mohammed's best assertive interest to chalk his endeavor up as an "experience" and learn from it. On the brighter side, first he has his proposal written up and ready for the next grant opportunity, so all his work has probably not really been wasted. Second, there may be other opportunities for adolescents' summer activities. He can consider other programs and other possibilities. Third, he can learn a specific axiom from the experience: *Always* make certain you know what the deadline is for *any* application.

3. *You have the right to direct and govern your own life. In other words, you have the right to be responsible for*

---

[2] Most of these rights have been adapted from those identified in *The New Assertive Woman* by Lynn Z. Bloom, Karen Coburn, and Joan Perlman (New York: Dell, 1976) and in *Four One-Day Workshops* by Kathryn Apgar and Betsy Nicholson Callaghan (Boston: Resource Communications Inc. and Family Service Association of Greater Boston, 1980).

continued

yourself. For example, Audrey directs a group home for adults with physical disabilities, run by a conservative religious organization. This organization has publicly declared its antiabortion stance. Her direct supervisor, the organization's director, personally maintains a strong antiabortion position. Audrey, however, maintains a solid pro-choice stance on the issue.

A pro-choice rally is being held on an upcoming weekend. Audrey plans to attend and participate. She even expects to hold a pro-choice banner and march in a procession through the main area of town. Audrey believes that such behavior will annoy her supervisor and the agency. However, she believes she has the right to participate in the activity on her own time. This option *is* her right. She is prepared to take responsibility for her behavior and deal assertively with any potential consequences. *Note:* Audrey's assessment of her supervisor's and agency's likely reaction may be wrong. In some organizations, participation in rallies or protests can lead and has led to termination.

4. *You have the right to stand up for yourself without unwarranted anxiety and make choices that are good for you.* For example, Helena works for a child abuse and protection unit with three other workers in a rural social services agency serving several counties. The agency, like many others, is tormented by serious financial problems. Staffing is short. Funding is severely limited. Therefore, work activities outside essential job duties are extremely restricted.

A friend and fellow social worker at an agency in another county calls Helena and excitedly describes an upcoming workshop on new identification techniques for child neglect. Helena thinks it sounds wonderful. She knows that the agency's money is tight, but thinks what a beneficial investment it would be if she and her three unit colleagues could attend the workshop. The workshop would cost the agency $800 at $200 per attendant.

Helena talks to the other workers, who agree that the conference is a great idea. They tell Helena if she can muster agency support, they would love to go. Helena decides to request support from the agency, despite the fact she knows her own supervisor will bristle at the thought of spending

a penny more on anything than the agency absolutely must. Helena determines that she has the right to stand up for herself—and in effect for her unit colleagues—and ask to attend this workshop. She develops a detailed rationale concerning why and how the workshop will benefit workers and enhance agency effectiveness.

Additionally, Helena prioritizes what the agency can potentially do for her and her colleagues. She starts with her first priority and then works down to her last. First, the agency can pick up the entire workshop cost and give her and her colleagues the two days off with pay. Second, the agency can pick up part of the cost for each worker and allow them all to take the two days off without pay. (In this case, Helena and the others will pay the remaining costs themselves.) Third, the agency can allow Helena and her colleagues to attend with pay, but require them to cover the entire workshop cost themselves. Finally, Helena decides that if she has to, she will take the two days off without pay and also pay the entire workshop fee herself. She is uncertain what her colleagues will choose to do in this instance of last resort. Helena assertively proceeds with her request. What do you think will happen?

5. *You have the right not to be liked by everyone. (Do you like everyone you know?)* For example, Hiroko is a public assistance worker for a large county bureaucracy. She is very dedicated to her job and often works overtime with clients to make certain that they receive all the benefits possible. Her colleague, Michael, holding the same job title, thinks this is utterly stupid. He resents that she seems to stand out as a star worker. Michael is not all that much into work himself. As a senior staff member permanently planted in his position, he is not interested in doing any more work than he has to. He often refers to Hiroko as a "drudge."

Hiroko really doesn't care. She knows that effective performance of her job on the behalf of clients is important to her. Frankly (she asserts), it really doesn't matter to Hiroko whether Michael likes her or not. She has the right not to be liked by everybody.

6. *You have the right, on the one hand, to make requests and, on the other, to refuse them without*

continued

Highlight **8-6** *continued*

feeling guilty. For example, Merle is a case manager for veterans who suffer from posttraumatic stress disorder. (A *case manager* is a practitioner who, on the behalf of a specific client, coordinates needed services provided by any number of agencies, organizations, or facilities.) **Posttraumatic stress disorder (PTSD)** is a disorder that develops in some people who have experienced a shocking, scary, or dangerous event (National Institute of Mental Health, 2017, p. 1). Its symptoms include: "flashbacks, bad dreams, [and] frightening thoughts." Those who have experienced a traumatic event—which might include warfare, assault, rape, or natural disaster—might re-experience the event. Part of Merle's job requires that one week each month he take turns with four other staff members to have his cell phone with him and be on call in case of an emergency.

Merle's family is staging a reunion at a ranch resort in Colorado. It happens to be set for a week when Merle is on call and he would not ordinarily take his vacation time. Merle has the right to assertively ask one of the other three staff members on call to switch weeks. His colleagues, on the other hand, also have the right to refuse. From another perspective, consider what would happen if the situation were reversed. Merle then would have the right either to accept or to refuse a request to switch on-call weeks in a similar manner.

7. *You have the right to ask for information if you need it.* For example, Louise is a financial counselor at a private mental health agency that provides therapy for a wide range of emotional problems. She is aware that the agency has access to special funding for persons "with exceptional needs." She knows this only informally via the agency grapevine. Therefore, she is not certain that the term *exceptional needs* means the same to her as it does to agency administrators. Because the agency is privately run, it is not subject to the same requirements to reveal funding sources as are similar public agencies. (The public, which pays for public agencies, has the right to scrutinize budgets and spending.)

Louise is working with several families whom she feels are in dire need of special help. Problems in the families include unemployment, depression, mental illness, poverty, unwanted pregnancy, and truancy. Louise knows that her agency administrator discourages workers from seeking this relatively secret special funding. Available amounts are probably very limited, so the administration must disperse these funds with discretion. Although Louise knows that the administration will not look kindly on her request, she decides to approach the agency's executive director to seek funding for the families in need and find out what requirements make clients eligible for this special funding. She feels that she has the right to ask for this information, even though the agency administration would rather she did not.

8. *You have the right to decide not to exercise your assertive rights.* In other words, you have the right to choose not to be assertive if you don't want to. For example, Horace, a state parole officer, is a member of a task force to curb substance abuse in his state. (**Parole officers** supervise criminal offenders who have been released on the likelihood of good behavior; the officers' goal is to avert future criminal activity.) A **task force** is a team or committee, often made up of representatives from different units within an organizational or community context, who come together on a temporary basis to serve some designated purpose or achieve a particular goal (Daft, 2016b).

Horace attends the last of a series of meetings aimed at facilitating a range of educational prevention and treatment thrusts to diminish substance abuse among youth, especially delinquents. Horace feels that the task force has made great strides. It established goals, developed plans, carried out initiatives, and evaluated its results. Throughout the process, however, he felt that the task force chairperson, Tobin, who happens to be an administrator in Horace's own state Division of Probation and Parole, was being much too pushy. Horace thinks Tobin frequently tried to coerce the group into following Tobin's own agenda. Although the group frequently ignored Tobin's ploys, Horace thinks Tobin's actions were inappropriate and perhaps even unethical.

After careful deliberation, Horace decides that it is not worth it to confront Tobin assertively about Tobin's behavior. Horace decides not to be assertive. After all, Tobin, as task force chairperson, has led the group to achieve great things. The moral here is that you don't have to be assertive every single time the opportunity presents itself.

There's no perfect recipe for what to say when you are trying to be assertive. The important thing is to take into consideration both your own rights and the rights of the person with whom you are interacting. Following are a few examples.

Situation 1: The Grant Proposal   Amorette is a social worker at a residential treatment center for adolescents with severe emotional and behavioral problems. She completes the draft of a grant application for funds to start a sex education program in the center. The proposal includes the sponsorship of experts to provide both educational programming and contraceptives. Agency policy requires that all grant proposal drafts be reviewed by an agency grants committee before being submitted outside the agency. Prunella, one of the center's teachers, is a member of the grants committee.

When Prunella sees the proposal, she flies through the roof. She feels that for this population, talking about sex in such explicit terms will only encourage them to engage in it. She cannot believe that the proposal also includes providing contraceptives directly to the girls. "Why not show them pornographic movies, too?" she thinks to herself.

Prunella approaches Amorette and declares, "That grant proposal you wrote is totally inappropriate. Under no circumstances will I condone it!" How should Amorette reply?

> *Nonassertive response*: "You're probably right. I'll just forget about it."
>
> *Aggressive response*: "What's wrong with you? Are you still living in the dark ages or something? Maybe what you need is a little action yourself."
>
> *Assertive response*: "I understand your concerns. However, I still think this is an important issue to address. Let's talk more about it."

Situation 2: Increasing Services   Gigette is a social worker for a public agency providing supportive home-based services for older adults. The agency's intent is to help people maintain their independence and reside in their own homes as lo whenever possible. A county policy states that clients may receive a maximum of eight service hours from Gigette's agency or others like it each month. Gigette works with numerous clients who require more help than this. She understands that the rationale for the policy is to manage costs. However, she feels that changing the policy to increase potential service to a maximum of 16 instead of 8 hours would allow many clients to remain in their own homes much longer. Providing or subsidizing the nursing-home care clients subsequently need is very expensive.

Gigette works through her agency's administration and gains its support. With the agency's sanction, she approaches Biff Bunslinger, the county board chairperson, and shares with him her proposal and its rationale. She has determined that his support would be the most beneficial in changing the county's restrictive policy. Biff responds, "It's a good idea, but where will you get the money for it? What else do you want to cut? Do you have any idea what repercussions such a major policy change would have?" How can Gigette respond?

Nonassertive response: "I don't know. I'm sorry. Let's forget it."

Aggressive response: "You haven't heard a word I've said. Get off your butt, Biff, and start thinking about those people out there who really need help!"

Assertive response: "I know funding is tight and that you have many financial needs you're trying to balance right now. Let me show you why I think this plan will both save the county money and help your older adult constituents in the long run."

Situation 3: Communication Issues   Bo, an outreach worker for urban homeless people, is on the board of directors of another agency called the AIDS Support Network. (A **board of directors** is an administrative group authorized to formulate the organization's mission, objectives, and policies, in addition to overseeing the organization's ongoing activities.) Another board member, Eleni, a local lawyer, bluntly states to Bo, "I wish you would be more specific when you make your comments during meetings. I can never understand what you're talking about." What can Bo reply?

Nonassertive response: "Yes, you're right. I'll try to speak more clearly in the future."

Aggressive response: "I'm not nearly as unclear as you are, nor, by the way, as arrogant!"

Assertive response: "I'm sorry you feel that way. I would welcome your questions when you don't understand something during a board meeting. Your feedback will help us communicate better." (Highlight 8-7 provides a few practice examples.)

Highlight 8-7

What Would You Do?

How would you respond assertively to each of the following scenarios?

Scenario A

You are a social worker for Heterogeneous County Department of Social Services. Paperwork recording your activities with clients is due promptly the Monday following the last day of each month. For whatever reason, you just forget to get it in by 5:00 p.m. Monday, the day it's due. Your supervisor, Enrique, calls you at noon the next day. He raises his voice and reprimands, "You know that reports are due promptly so that funding is not jeopardized! How many times do I have to tell you that?" You assertively respond …

Scenario B

You work with a colleague who consistently comes late to your social work unit's biweekly meetings. He typically saunters leisurely into the meeting room with a cup of decaf in hand, noisily situates himself in a chair at the rectangular meeting table, and casually interrupts whoever is speaking, asking for a brief review of what he missed. You are sick and tired of such rude, time-wasting behavior. Finally, after the last meeting, you pull this colleague aside and assertively state …

Scenario C

You represent your social service agency at a community meeting where 12 community residents and five workers from other agencies are discussing what additional social services the community needs. Some possible grant funding has become available to develop services. The person chairing the meeting asks for input from each person present except you. Apparently, she simply overlooked that you had not gotten an opportunity to speak. You assertively state …

The Advantages of Assertiveness

There are many benefits to developing assertiveness skills (Egan, 2014; Ivey & Ivey, 2016). For one thing, you can gain more control over your work and other interpersonal environments. Assertiveness may help you avoid uncomfortable or hostile interactions with colleagues, administrators, other agency personnel, politicians, and community residents. You will probably feel that other people understand you better than they did before. You can enhance your self-concept and interpersonal effectiveness as the result of this increased control. In the past, bottled-up feelings may have resulted in psychosomatic problems like piercing headaches or painful stomach upsets. Appropriate assertiveness helps to alleviate the buildup of undue tension and stress and such psychosomatic reactions will probably subside and eventually cease.

Finally, other people may gain respect for you, your strength, and your own demonstration of respect for others. People may even begin to use you as a role model for their own development of assertive behavior.

Assertiveness Training

Assertiveness training leads people to realize and act on the assumption that they have the right to be themselves and express their feelings freely. They also learn the critical difference between assertive and aggressive behaviors—an important distinction.

As we know, social work is practical. Therefore, you can use the suggestions provided to enhance your own assertiveness in a wide range of macro settings. Alberti and Emmons (2008) suggest following several steps to help establish assertive behavior:

1. Scrutinize your own actions and evaluate how effective you are using the assertiveness continuum.
2. Make a record of situations in which you feel you could have been more effective (either more assertive or less aggressive).
3. Select and focus on some specific instance when you felt you could have been more appropriately assertive.
4. Analyze how you reacted in this situation. Critically examine your verbal and nonverbal behavior.
5. Select a role model and examine how she handled a similar situation requiring assertiveness.
6. Identify a range of other new assertive verbal and nonverbal responses that could address the original problem situation you targeted.
7. Picture yourself in the identified problematic situation.
8. Practice the way you've envisioned yourself being more assertive.
9. Once again, review your new assertive responses. Emphasize your strong points and try to remedy your flaws.
10. Continue practicing Steps 7, 8, and 9 until your newly developed assertive approach feels comfortable and natural to you.
11. Try out your assertiveness in a real-life situation.
12. Continue to expand your assertive behavior repertoire until assertiveness becomes a part of your personal interactive style.
13. Give yourself a pat on the back when you succeed in becoming more assertive. It's not easy changing long-standing patterns of behavior.

EP 8a

You and Assertiveness

How assertive do you consider yourself? In what situations, if any, do you find that you tend to be either unassertive or aggressive?

Select a situation in which you feel you could have been more assertive (versus unassertive or aggressive). If you were to experience a similar situation again, how would you prefer to respond?

A Final Note on Assertiveness Training   Remember that you choose whether to be assertive in any given situation. You always have a choice. Making an assertive response to a boss who fires people for speaking up may not be the best plan. You must decide about how to respond. No one else can make that decision for you. Also, recognize that, like any other solution to human problems, being assertive may not always work: Some people don't respond to assertiveness. They may get angry or continue to make inappropriate requests. When assertiveness does not work for you, accept this fact, praise yourself for your progress, and identify areas where you can still improve.

Conflict and Its Resolution

EP 7d

An **interpersonal conflict** is a controversy that occurs whenever two or more people involved in some relationship have incompatible or contradictory needs, expectations, desires, or goals. Words commonly associated with conflict include fighting, struggle, competition, incompatibility, clash, argument, and discord, among others. Conflict can occur in an infinite number of ways and an unending array of situations within an organizational context. No organizational environment is continuously conflict-free. Some people inevitably will clash. It may involve a "personality conflict," a glaring disagreement about some agency matter, or resentment of one against another for whatever reason. Conflict can occur among colleagues or between management and employees. The following sections will discuss the pros and cons of conflict, personal styles of addressing conflict, and the steps in conflict resolution.

The Pros of Conflict

Conflicts in organizational work settings are difficult for many people. It is easy to view conflict and confrontation as being negative, something to avoid at all costs. This is not necessarily the case. Conflict has some positive aspects, including the following (Daft, 2016b; Lussier & Achua, 2016; Johnson & Johnson, 2012):

1. *Conflict can help us explore a situation more thoroughly.* It can force us to more extensively evaluate issues and problems involved in interpersonal communication, such as identification of what problems are, who participants in the conflict, and what can be done to achieve resolution.

2. *Conflict can cause us to make improvements in our behavior and communication.* Change is frequently avoided because it requires some energy to accomplish. When a conflict arises, you may be forced to address an issue and make changes—whether you like them or not.

3. *Conflict can generate new energy to solve a problem.* Conflict increases our awareness of issues and thus may motivate us to make changes in our behavior.

4. *Conflict can make daily routines more exciting.* Disagreements can stimulate creative thinking to develop new solutions. Argument and debate can spawn new, sometimes exciting ideas that we might never have thought of had the conflict not occurred.

5. *Conflict can improve the quality of problem resolution and decision making.* Conflict encourages exploration of ideas and options as well as more critical evaluation of these options.

6. *Conflict can release emotional "steam."* Pent-up feelings simmer and build. Release and resolution through conflict can be constructive in maintaining interpersonal relationships.

7. *Conflict can enhance our own self-awareness.* What issues bother us the most? How do we respond to conflict? Can we identify what "buttons" people can press in us to get us going?

8. *Conflict can be fun when it is not taken too seriously.* Many people enjoy hearty discussion and debate. Games are often based on conflict that is supposed to be fun. The game of "Risk" comes to mind. It is a board game in which the world is divided up into 42 countries or regions. To win, one player must conquer and destroy all the others. Explaining the details would take too much space here. However, even though no actual blood is spilled, emotions are heightened as one player "slaughters" another. One author has been known to violently hurl the board in the air when feeling betrayed by another player who has methodically and unemotionally triumphed. Yet such conflict is *fun* (although it tends to be more fun when you win).

9. *Conflict can facilitate the development and depth of relationships.* Working through conflicts provides opportunities to get to know another person in a deeper, sometimes very meaningful way. What things are the most important to the other person? How does that person feel about and react to these important issues? What is that person really like in situations that are not entirely positive? Additionally, conflict can dispel negative feelings when conflict resolution is achieved.

The Cons of Conflict

Conflict also can have downsides. When considering confrontation as a response to some conflict, it is important to weigh at least three potential losses in an organizational context (Daft, 2016a). First, conflict takes energy. Energy and resources are always limited. You have just so much time, enthusiasm, effort, and initiative. What you expend in one endeavor, you will not have available to use for some other task. Therefore, you must make certain that the targeted conflict is significant enough to merit your efforts.

Second, conflict may result in winners and losers. Adequate compromise might not be possible or realistic. One opponent in the conflict may feel demoralized and unfairly treated by the resolution.

Third, conflict may result in decreased collaboration and teamwork. Losers of conflicts often become uncooperative and cease to concern themselves with colleagues' rights and wants. Extreme conflict may end in almost total lack of communication. Concern for the opponent's welfare may vanish. When workers are totally immersed in intense conflict, their anger might prevent them from working toward compromise. Preoccupation with conflict can even obstruct their ability to do their jobs.

In summary, it is very important to consider both the potential positive and negative consequences of conflict. Results of conflict can range from being extraordinarily positive to absolutely destructive.

Personal Styles for Addressing Conflict

Just as each of us has a unique personality, each has an individualized style for addressing conflict. There are at least four personal styles for managing conflict—withdrawal, aggression, "smoothing," and compromise (Johnson & Johnson, 2012, pp. 252–253).

People who use withdrawal generally dislike conflict and simply avoid it. They will give in, give up, and walk away. They are nonassertive.

Those who use aggression in dealing with conflict want to get their own way at all costs. They display pushiness and aggressiveness on the assertiveness continuum. They value their goals and consider the relationship between themselves and the other party as unimportant.

People who are smoothers value relationships above all else. They would sacrifice their own opinions and goals to preserve their relationship with the other party. Smoothing is usually a poor choice when you have opinions and goals that are very important to you.

Finally, compromisers are assertive. They consider their own feelings and values and those of their opponents important. Compromisers assume the attitude that both parties should voice their opinions, use problem-solving techniques, and relinquish some of their demands to come to a reasonable compromise.

Generally, it is more effective to take both your needs and those of your opponents into consideration. In addition, both your goals and your relationships with your opponents merit your attention.

Steps in Conflict Resolution

Seven steps are involved in conflict resolution (Ivey & Ivey, 2016; Ivey, Ivey, & Zalaquett, 2014; Johnson & Johnson, 2012). Although it is not always possible to go through each one, it is important to keep them in mind. Emphases are on both communication and coordination with the opponent. The steps presented here are among the many approaches to dealing with conflict.

For the purposes of illustration, an extensive case example involving the process of conflict resolution will be presented and discussed. An intent is to give you some insight into the interpersonal dynamics occurring in the social services setting described. Note that such a scenario certainly does not take place in every setting. This just provides one example of conflict in an organization.

Critical Thinking Questions **8-9**

How Do You Handle Conflict?

EP 8a

We've stressed that it's crucially important for you to get to know yourself and your reactions. Personal reflection and self-correction are ongoing aspects of your professional development.

How do you generally respond in conflictual situations? How do you view your personal style for addressing conflict? Might it be some blend of the styles mentioned here?

Have you ever encountered conflict in a work situation with a fellow employee or someone in management? What happened? How did you respond? Now that you think back, what response might have been more effective?

Step 1: The Confrontation   The first step in resolving any kind of conflict is to confront the opponent. A **confrontation** is a face-to-face encounter where people come together with opposing opinions, perspectives, or ideas to scrutinize or compare them. Confrontation, intended to resolve or combat some conflictual situation, means that one or more people disagree with others and make a point of asserting that disagreement. This, of course, may inspire a negative or hostile reaction by the person you're confronting.

People handle conflict and confrontation very differently. As already noted, they have widely varied interpersonal styles and skills. Usually, when engaging in a confrontation, it is wise to keep two major issues in mind. First, clearly identify and examine your personal goals. Conflicts can arise because of differences, often concerning goals or perceptions of goals. How important to you are these goals? Are they very important or only minimally so?

The second major issue to keep in mind when beginning a confrontation is the nurturance of your interpersonal relationship with the other person. Clearly showing respect for the other person's feelings, beliefs, and needs helps to sustain the ongoing relationship. Yes, you have a disagreement and you feel some degree of intensity about your position. However, to what extent are you willing to jeopardize your relationship with this person to win the conflict? To what extent will you be able to compromise? How can you balance conflict resolution with maintaining a positive relationship with your opponent? You do not need any more enemies than you absolutely must have.

A major tenet in organizational contexts is the need to muster support from others to achieve your specified goals. Therefore, the more strongly you can sustain your various relationships with others in the organizational environment, the better you will perform your job and achieve your intervention goals.

CASE EXAMPLE: The Confrontation.   Brainard supervises a 10-person unit that serves clients receiving public assistance in an urban county's social services department. Brainard's problem is Cheryl, one of his 10 supervisees. Essentially, Cheryl is incompetent. She consistently makes decisions that negatively affect clients, fails to complete her paperwork, and effectively disrupts any unit meetings and projects in which she participates. Scores of clients have complained pointedly about her work and her treatment of them.

Brainard, who is newly hired as unit supervisor, inherited Cheryl from the unit's former supervisor, Charlie, who had originally hired her. Cheryl is not only incompetent, she is also a bitter fighter. Two years earlier, when Charlie noticed Cheryl's difficulties in completing her work adequately, he tried to help her solve her problems and improve her performance. However, she bristled defensively and fought him every step of the way. The agency has a strong union, of which Cheryl, of course, is a member. Once employees pass their probationary period of one year, they essentially gain permanent status, after which it is extremely difficult, if not impossible, to terminate their employment. During Cheryl's probationary period, she accused Charlie of harassment and hired legal counsel to represent her. At the time, the agency was suffering some severe public criticism and resultant budget cuts. Therefore, higher administration commanded Charlie to leave Cheryl alone and not cause any trouble. Charlie, who was not renowned for his strength of character or ability to pursue open conflict anyway, backed down in withdrawal mode and soon thereafter transferred to another agency unit.

Now Brainard, stuck with Cheryl, continues to see the problem more clearly as the months pass. Brainard prides himself on his commitment to advocate on the behalf of clients and consistently work in their best interest. He feels it is his responsibility to do something about Cheryl and her incompetence. He, too, initially tried to help her through her difficulties, making numerous specific recommendations for how she might improve her job performance.

Every one of the other nine unit members has similar concerns about Cheryl. They all feel that Cheryl is a blight on their unit. However, she is a permanent employee and hostile. Colleagues are at a loss about what to do.

Brainard, a competent supervisor, begins to clearly document his efforts at helping Cheryl and her failures to perform her job adequately. After several dozen incidents are noted, Brainard brings the situation to the attention of higher administration. The agency administration has a history of disagreement and conflict with the agency's union. Therefore, the administration feels the wisest alternative is to bring in a neutral trained mediator from outside the agency to help both parties settle their differences. Obviously, there is quite a dispute between Cheryl and Brainard.

Step 2: Establish Common Ground   Establish an acceptable common definition of the problem (Johnson & Johnson, 2012). Such a definition should make neither you nor your opponent defensive or resistant to working out a mutually agreeable compromise. Emphasize how important the conflictual issue is to both of you. Be as clear and specific about your concerns as possible. Express and clarify your own feelings, while drawing out those of your opponent. Most important, keep trying to empathize with your opponent's position.

CASE EXAMPLE: *Establish Common Ground.*   The mediator, Jimmy Hoffa, interviews each of the 10 unit personnel, including Cheryl. He also talks extensively to Brainard. He scrutinizes and begins to bring together the evidence. Jimmy establishes a common ground between Cheryl and the rest of the unit. All involved staff, including Cheryl, are unhappy with the conflictual situation. They all feel both their individual performance and that of the unit in general suffers significantly because of it.

EP 1c

Step 3: Emphasize the Importance of Communication   When pursuing conflict resolution, it is crucial for you to establish and nurture communication channels between you and the person(s) with whom you are in conflict. The following seven general communication guidelines are good to keep in mind (Sheafor & Horejsi, 2015):

1. *Do not begin a confrontation when you are angry.* Anger makes you lose your objectivity. You may lose sight of both your goals and the welfare of your opponent and focus instead on punishing or beating your opponent.

2. *Do not provoke a conflict unless you have a clearly established reason for doing so.* Unless you are willing to try to resolve the conflict, do not bother confronting your opponent. Such confrontation will only waste both your and your opponent's time and energy.

3. *If you absolutely despise your opponent or have immense difficulty reaching for any positive, empathic feelings about him or her, do not confront the opponent.* If you do not respect your opponent, a confrontation will only waste your time and energy and that of your opponent. Rather, explore other ways of addressing the conflict (such as calling upon the support of others) or drop the matter completely.

4. *Include positive statements and feedback along with the negative aspects of confrontation.* For example, you might emphasize your opponent's strengths before beginning the confrontation, thereby minimizing his or her perception of being attacked. You might say, "I know you are very knowledgeable and have strong ideas on this subject. I would like to discuss with you some alternative thoughts I've had about it. I know you're busy, but might you have some time to talk?"

   This example first gives the opponent a compliment. ("I know you are very knowledgeable and have strong ideas on this subject.") Compliments, by the way, should be honest, believable ones so that you do not sound insincere. Next, the preceding example introduces the issue in a general way. ("I would like to discuss with you some alternative thoughts I've had about it.") Finally, it implies respect for the opponent's time and work efforts. ("I know you're busy, but might you have some time to talk?")

   In some ways, giving your opponent positive feedback or complimenting him or her is like confrontation. Both complimenting and confrontation provide people with feedback or information about their behavior. Confrontation, of course, incorporates negative feedback, whereas compliments involve positive feedback. It makes sense to provide some of both during the conflict resolution process.

5. *Avoid judgmental or pejorative terms when discussing the conflict.* Prepare details in your head beforehand to explain and clarify the issues and behaviors involved. In the same way, try to present your stance objectively and factually. Avoid overly emotional appeals. If your opponent hears your emotions talking instead of you, he or she may react to your emotions instead of to what you are intending to say.

6. *Supply relevant data in support of your stance.* Articulate your position clearly. Describe the issue straightforwardly. In other words, make sure you

know what you're talking about. Have your facts straight. Have both your ideal solution and some potential compromises clearly established in your mind.

7. *An additional suggestion is to use "I-messages" frequently.* Merely rephrasing your thoughts to include the word "I" enhances the quality of personal caring and empathy. This technique can emphasize the fact that you are trying to address a conflictual issue and are seeking a mutually agreeable solution, instead of criticizing or blaming. For example, you might say, "*I* would like to share with you some inconsistencies in my perception of what you've been saying and what you've actually been doing." This is far more personal and far less blaming than a statement such as, "*You* have been saying one thing and doing another."

CASE EXAMPLE: *Emphasize the Importance of Communication.* Jimmy helps people on both sides of the conflict begin to talk about their feelings and think about suggestions for improvement. By the time Jimmy arrives, the situation is so tense and threatening that communication between Cheryl and Brainard has stopped. Cheryl has also ceased to communicate with her other unit colleagues. A typical comment by other workers at unit meetings reveals that they hesitate to say anything because of Cheryl's threats to sue them. It has been very difficult to get anything accomplished in the unit for a long time.

Jimmy's approach is to use positive feedback as much as possible. He talks of how committed Cheryl is to maintaining her job at the agency. Likewise, he emphasizes that Brainard and the other workers want to function as well as they can in providing services to clients.

Step 4: Emphasize Your Willingness to Cooperate Emphasize your willingness to work with your opponent to find some mutually satisfactory solution. By definition, conflict is staged in the context of disagreement. To minimize the disagreement or, at least, to develop a viable, agreeable plan of action, stress the commonalities you have with your opponent.

CASE EXAMPLE: *Emphasize Your Willingness to Cooperate.* Jimmy encourages Cheryl and the rest of the staff to work toward some solution. He has already established the common ground of a miserable working environment. This motivates participants to cooperate and work toward a mutually satisfying decision about what to do.

Step 5: Empathize with Your Opponent's Perspective Work to understand why your opponent feels the way she does. What is her motivation for taking the stand she does? How does the conflict affect her feelings and her work? How can you express to her that you are sincerely trying to understand her side of the conflictual issue?

CASE EXAMPLE: *Empathize with Your Opponent's Perspective.* As participants become motivated to cooperate and begin to discuss their feelings, Jimmy helps each side see the other's point of view. He holds several meetings with all unit staff present and gives everyone the opportunity to air their views. On the one hand, Brainard and the unit staff are terribly frustrated with Cheryl's inability to work up to the unit's standards. On the other hand, Cheryl has become so ostracized that Jimmy has some concern that she might jump off the eight-story building in which the agency is housed. Cheryl is isolated, lonely, and unhappy.

Step 6: Evaluate Both Your Own and Your Opponent's Motivation to Address the Conflict   You and your opponent may view a conflict very differently. For instance, you may feel the conflict is of extraordinary importance. Your opponent, on the other hand, may think that it's silly to even bring up the issue because it's so minor. Essentially, you need to evaluate whether it is worthwhile to expend the energy to resolve the conflict. Maybe it would just be easier to maintain the status quo and leave the whole thing alone.

For example, the chairperson of a social work department in an undergraduate program felt it was very important to emphasize that each of the six faculty members should be able to teach any course in the program. This chairperson typically spent 15 minutes to an hour at each faculty meeting chit-chatting about how important such flexibility was. One faculty member thought the whole issue was blatantly absurd. Different faculty had specified areas of interest in which they both studied and published. Why should faculty be forced to teach in areas they knew very little about instead of in areas in which they had established some degree of expertise? Would it be good for students to be taught by people who knew little of what they were talking about? Of course, not. However, the faculty member chose to let the entire issue rest since all the faculty taught the same classes they requested each semester anyway, making the issue moot. The faculty member acknowledged the chairperson's strong feelings and decided that confronting the chairperson on this issue would simply not be worth the effort. The faculty member didn't think he could win anyway. Besides, the worst thing that occurred was wasted time at faculty meetings.

Note that in many situations it is possible to change the degree of motivation on your or your opponent's part. In this situation, the department chairperson might have begun to implement what the faculty member termed the "absurd idea" of forcing faculty to teach outside their respective areas. Subsequently, the concerned faculty members might be extremely motivated to address the conflict and pursue some resolution.

CASE EXAMPLE: Evaluate Both Your Own and Your Opponent's Motivation to Address the Conflict.   As both sides air their feelings and frustrations, Jimmy helps them verbalize their motivation for change. Both express sincere interest in halting the conflict. All unit members are getting tired. Therefore, Jimmy determines that both parties are eager to pursue a viable alternative if the group can come up with one.

Step 7: Come to Some Mutually Satisfactory Agreement   The final step in conflict resolution is to come to some mutually satisfactory agreement. To do this, follow these five suggestions (Johnson & Johnson, 2012). First, articulate exactly what your agreement entails. Second, indicate how you will behave toward the other person in the future as compared with the past. Third, specify how the other person will behave toward you. Fourth, agree on ways to address any future mistakes (that is, if you or the other behaves differently than you have agreed to). Fifth, establish how and when you and the other person will meet in the future to continue your cooperative behavior and minimization of conflict.

CASE EXAMPLE: *Come to Some Mutually Satisfactory Agreement.*　It looks to Jimmy as if no agreement can be reached to resolve the situation if Cheryl remains in the unit. Feelings are so strongly directed against her that it is unlikely they would change. Major supervisory efforts to help Cheryl improve her work performance have hopelessly failed. Therefore, it does not look as if a change in Cheryl's behavior is a viable alternative.

Cheryl is a permanent employee and refuses to leave the agency without a major battle. Thus, the only remaining alternative is to transfer her to another position. Cheryl, Brainard, and the other unit workers first breathe a sigh of relief and then are ready to cheer when they examine this alternative. Jimmy works with Brainard and the agency's administration to implement this plan. The administration arranges for the necessary retraining Cheryl needs to assume her new position.

Cheryl happily transfers to another unit. She retains a job in the agency and no longer must deal with colleagues whom she considers irascible, irritable, faultfinding, and backbiting. Likewise, relative peace descends upon the public assistance unit, and workers can once again focus their energies on their jobs.

Cheryl is not heard from by anyone in the unit again except when her name occasionally appears in an agency newsletter, as all agency staff names do at one time or another. Brainard, despite his immense relief at Cheryl's departure, soon becomes bored at the lack of challenge and leaves the agency for a higher paying, more demanding job.

Highlight 8-8 explores suggestions for communication when someone confronts *you.*

Highlight **8-8**

What Do You Say and Do When Someone Confronts You?

EP 1c

What about when someone confronts you? Much of this discussion involves initiating a confrontation with a colleague, supervisor, agency, administrator, some other agency representative, community leader, or the like. What about your own feelings, communication, and behavior when someone confronts you? Your opponent may or may not have well-developed conflict resolution skills. There are at least five useful approaches to use in responding to a confrontation:

1. *Listen closely to what the other person is saying.* Make certain you listen to the specifics of the message. Focusing on the specific words being said can improve your understanding. Don't

react to the emotions expressed if possible. Getting caught up in the emotion and your own reactions of anger or resentment often prevents clear reception of the message and may elicit emotions in yourself that will make resolution of the confrontation difficult or impossible. Becoming overly emotional and losing track of your objectivity does not help you evaluate the situation or help resolve the conflict.

For example, suppose a colleague approaches you and flatly states, "You really are pretty intimidating." The confronter's accusation is imprecise. By listening, you can clarify the negative feedback while the confrontation is occurring. Exactly whom

continued

Highlight **8-8** *continued*

do you intimidate? This person who is confronting you? Other agency staff? Agency administration? Everybody? Similarly, do you make some unidentified other(s) fearful, or are you making threats? In either case, in what way? What verbal and/or nonverbal behaviors does your confronter feel elicit an intimidating reaction? In what contexts does intimidation occur?

2. *Explain to the confronter exactly how you will respond to his or her feedback.* For instance, in the intimidation example just provided, you might tell the confronter that you will approach the people who feel intimidated and help them resolve their negative feelings. You can elaborate upon what you will do to correct the problem. Think about what else you will say and do. In what contexts will you make the changes? Staff meetings? Interviews with community leaders? Casual lunchtime interactions with colleagues?

Sometimes, you can be caught by surprise when someone confronts you. Under these circumstances, you might not be able to think quickly enough to respond immediately. Then it's no problem simply to say something like, "Oh, that surprises me. Give me some time to think about it, and I'll get back to you later."

3. *Thank your confronter for the feedback and his or her willingness to share concerns.* This is not always an easy suggestion to follow. Being criticized can be hard to take. It's really easy to get defensive: "What do you mean I'm intimidating? You have some nerve! You have a pretty noxious personality yourself!"

Feedback can almost always be helpful. Even if you don't agree with what the confronter says, at least you know how he or she feels. In the worst case, the interaction gives you some information concerning how to operate with the confronter in the future. In the best case, you can receive some constructive feedback that may help in your future communications and interactions.

4. *Approach your confronter later, and tell him or her how you have responded to the feedback.* Explain how you have changed your behavior or attitude. You might thank the confronter once again for his or her effort.

Most people are hesitant about this suggestion. It is important to consider and evaluate the confronter's feedback as carefully and objectively as possible. However, if you decide in good conscience that he or she is inaccurate, you obviously will not alter your behavior in future situations. In effect, you will not believe your behavior requires change (at least not the behavior that was criticized). In that case, you can choose either to confront him or her about the inappropriateness of the remarks or just let the matter drop. It might not be worth your effort to extend the confrontation.

Also, be careful of the multi-confronter, the person who regularly tells you all the things that are wrong with you. Such individuals might do this only in their interactions with you, or they might interact in this manner with almost everyone. In any case, depending on your own motivation, you may decide to address such individuals concerning their own overly confrontational behavior. As our discussion illustrates, the possibilities for confrontation are endless.

5. *At the time of the confrontation, do not criticize the confronter by pointing out his or her shortcomings.* That type of response is usually petty and inappropriate. Address the issue at hand first. Settle that. Then, as we discussed in suggestion number four, you might decide to confront the person about his or her own behavior at another time.

A Final Note on Conflict Resolution

As we stated at the beginning of this section, conflict is natural and predictable. Anticipating it, learning about the various types of conflict, and considering ahead of time the possible approaches to conflict management can only increase your effectiveness as a generalist social worker.

Chapter Summary

The following summarizes this chapter's content as it relates to the learning objectives presented at the beginning of the chapter. Objectives include the following:

LO 8-1 Provide responses to various critical thinking questions.

Critical thinking questions in this chapter address difficulties working in an organization, working in a traditional bureaucracy, implications for an improved health care system, working in organizations experiencing problems, leadership in a learning organization, the pros and cons of TQM servant leadership, personal assertiveness, and handling conflict.

LO 8-2 Explain the significance of management in social service organizations.

Management is the "attainment of organizational goals in an efficient and effective manner through planning, organizing, leading, and controlling organizational resources" (Daft, 2016a, p. 4). Management style provides important clues for understanding people's behavior in the organizational environment, including social service agencies.

LO 8-3 Describe traditional bureaucracies, orientation discrepancies between social work and bureaucracies, and common behavior patterns found in bureaucracies.

Bureaucratic management style emphasizes the importance of a specifically designed, formal structure and a consistent, rigid organizational network of employees to make an organization run well and achieve its goals. This allows for very little discretion on the part of workers. Value orientation discrepancies between social work and bureaucracies focus on decision making, distribution of power, flexibility, communication, and consideration of people's opinions and feelings. Common behavior patterns manifested by bureaucrats include the "warrior," the "gossip," the "complainer," the "dancer," the "machine," and the "executioner" (Knopf, 1979, pp. 33–36).

LO 8-4 Critique the US health care system's clash with Asian and Pacific Islander (API) cultural values.

Important values in API culture include shared decision making in families, filial piety, silent communication, preservation of harmony, and delayed access to but great respect for health care. Conflicts between API cultural values and the US health care system include those focusing on informed consent, advanced directives, and decisions about nursing home placement. Suggestions for improvement include providing training for health care personnel, addressing end-of-life issues with whole families, adopting family centered versus individual-centered decision-making models, and pursuing ongoing advocacy for positive changes.

LO 8-5 Discuss problems frequently encountered by and in social service organizations.

Problems frequently encountered by social service organizations include vagueness of goals, vagueness of process, impersonal behavior, lack of rewards and recognition, agency policy and worker discretion, and traditions and unwritten rules.

LO 8-6 Describe newer concepts involved in management and employee empowerment.

Newer management concepts include constructing a culture of caring, the learning organization, teamwork and team empowerment, diversity as a strength, and client system empowerment by management. According to path-goal theory, leadership styles include "directive," "supportive," "participative," and "achievement-oriented leadership" (Williams, 2016a, pp. 299–301).

LO 8-7 Discuss the situation encountered by women in social services management.

Women managers tend to assume management styles that focus on "inclusion," "connection," "collaboration," "commitment" to professional values, and "optimism" (Gardella & Haynes, 2004, p. 102). Organizations can empower women by analyzing women's status within the organization, establishing clear objectives for improvement, and encouraging employee participation in the diversity-enhancement process.

LO 8-8 Describe two examples of common management and leadership approaches—total quality management (TQM) and servant leadership.

"TQM is a philosophy or overall approach to management that is characterized by three principles: customer focus and satisfaction, continuous improvement, and teamwork" that entails employee involvement and empowerment (Williams, 2016a, p. 382). Important principles inherent in TQM include a focus on clients as customers, quality as the primary goal, employee empowerment and teamwork, a total quality approach to leadership, and continuous improvement.

Servant leadership emphasizes providing service by empathizing with, supporting, and nurturing employees. Such leaders place others' needs before their own. Important concepts include calling, listening, empathy, healing, awareness, persuasion, conceptualization, foresight, stewardship, growth, and building community (Northouse, 2016).

LO 8-9 Examine the perspectives of social workers as employees in terms of using assertiveness and managing conflict.

Assertive communication includes verbal and nonverbal behavior that permits a speaker to get points across clearly and straightforwardly, maintaining high regard for both self and the communication receiver. Nonassertive communication occurs when a speaker devalues him- or herself completely, holding the communication receiver in much higher regard. Aggressive communication engenders bold and dominating verbal and nonverbal behavior whereby a speaker presses his or her point of view as taking precedence above all other perspectives.

Every individual has assertive rights. There are advantages to being assertive within the macro environment. People can enhance their assertiveness skills by following a few steps.

Conflict has various pros and cons. Pros of conflict include the potential for gaining new information and resolving problems. Cons may entail wasting energy and harming relationships. People may adopt various styles of addressing conflict. Conflict resolution involves seven steps: the confrontation; establishing common ground; emphasizing the importance of communication; emphasizing willingness to cooperate; empathizing with the opponent's perspective; evaluating the motivations of both sides involved; and coming to a mutually satisfactory agreement.

LO 8-10 Focus on an ethical issue.

An ethical issue involves a scenario where a client is dissatisfied with the social service agency and its worker's approach in dealing with the client.

Looking Ahead

This chapter discussed human behavior, management, and empowerment in organizations. The next chapter shifts the focus from organizations to communities. It examines theoretical perspectives on communities, and explores variations in geographic, rural, urban, and nongeographic communities.

Competency Notes

The following identifies where Educational Policy (EP) competencies and component behaviors are discussed in the chapter.

EP 1 (Competency 1)—Demonstrate Ethical and Professional Behavior. (*p. 255*): Social workers should be informed and proactive regarding the evolving processes of health care provision to make such care provision are culturally competent. *(p. 262):* Continuing education is very important to social workers. *(p. 254):* Ethical questions are raised regarding how an agency should respond to client dissatisfaction.

EP 1a Make ethical decisions by applying the standards of the NASW *Code of Ethics,* relevant laws and regulations, models for ethical decision-making, ethical conduct of research, and additional codes of ethics as appropriate to context. *(p. 280–290):* Development of appropriate assertiveness allows practitioners to practice personal reflection and improve their interactions with others in macro contexts. Subsequent sections provide opportunities to appraise scenarios and demonstrate appropriate responses, in addition to suggesting an approach to assertiveness training.

EP 1b Use reflection and self-regulation to manage personal values and maintain professionalism in practice situations. *(p. 283):* When interacting with colleagues, supervisors, administrators, staff from other agencies, politicians, or community residents, consider both their values and your own when deciding to use assertiveness skills.

EP 1c Demonstrate professional demeanor in behavior; appearance; and oral, written, and electronic communication. *(p. 246):* Social workers should understand the dynamics involved in management to attend to professional roles and boundaries. Management is an integral part of work in professional settings. Social workers should understand the dynamics involved in management to demonstrate professional demeanor in behavior, appearance, and communication. *(p. 255):* Social workers should understand and demonstrate appropriate communication when working with API people. *(p. 290):* Appropriate assertiveness and conflict resolution reflect professional conduct. The appropriate, effective use of both assertiveness skills and conflict resolution demonstrate professional demeanor in behavior and communication. *(p. 291):* Effective communication in conflict resolution demonstrates

professional demeanor. Effective communication is crucial for successful conflict resolution when working with colleagues, supervisors, managers, groups, and organizations. (p. 292): Suggestions for effective communication when involved in a confrontation are given.

EP 2 (Competency 2)—Engage Diversity and Difference in Practice. *(p. 255ff):* Mainstream values concerning health care provision can conflict with the values of a diverse group such as API Americans. This can result in oppression and marginalization of the diverse group concerning medical informed consent, advance directives, and decisions about nursing-home placement. *(p. 251):* Race, culture, and age are dimensions of diversity. *(p. 266):* Gender is a dimension of diversity. *(p. 266):* Social workers should recognize the strength of diversity in organizations. Gender affects privilege and power for women in social services management.

EP 2a Apply and communicate understanding of the importance of diversity and difference in shaping life experiences in practice at the micro, mezzo, and macro levels. *(p. 251):* Cultural differences in expectations regarding health care provision can shape life experiences. *(p. 266):* Gender shapes life experiences in social services management.

EP 2b Present themselves as learners and engage clients and constituencies as experts of their own experiences. *(p. 261):* The learning organization concept of encouraging continuous learning coincides with social workers' responsibility to engage in career-long learning. *(p. 262):* Staff development supports career-long learning for social workers. *(p. 262):* Learning is encouraged in environments dedicated to empowering their workers and clients.

EP 3 (Competency 3)—Advance Human Rights and Social, Economic, and Environmental Justice. *(p. 251):* The oppression of API Americans in terms of culturally insensitive health care provision is discussed. *(p. 266):* This highlight discusses some mechanisms of oppression of women in social services management.

EP 3a Apply their understanding of social, economic, and environmental justice to advocate for human rights at the individual and system levels. *(p. 284):* Rights involved in assertiveness are human rights.

EP 3b Engage in practices that advance social, economic, and environmental justice. *(p. 251):* Practitioners should advocate on the behalf of culturally sensitive health care provision. *(p. 266):* Social workers should advocate for the rights and advancement of women in social services management.

EP 5 (Competency 5)—Engage in Policy Practice. *(p. 251):* Social workers must understand how policy affects health care delivery to pursue policy practice and advocate for improvements in service delivery. Social workers should strive to establish policies, including health care policies, that are culturally sensitive and appropriate to advance social well-being. *(p. 255):* Practitioners should advocate for health care provision that is culturally sensitive. *(p. 260):* Management can formulate agency policies that advance the well-being and effectiveness of employees. Two specific management approaches are discussed.

EP 5b Assess how social welfare and economic policies impact the delivery of and access to social services. *(p. 251):* Social workers recognize that culturally sensitive health care and health promotion are critical to reducing health disparities among the multicultural populations. *(p. 255):* A continuous concern for social workers is the need to assess large systems' functioning, recommend improvements, and work to achieve positive changes. *(p. 246):* Social workers benefit in their assessments of organizations if they understand specific management approaches being utilized.

EP 5c Apply critical thinking to analyze, formulate, and advocate for policies that advance human rights and social, economic, and environmental justice. *(p. 266):* Social workers should engage in practices that advance social and economic justice for women in social services management.

EP 6 (Competency 6)—Engage with Individuals, Families, Groups, Organizations, and Communities. *(p. 269):* Various aspects of management are discussed. Generalist practitioners should critique and apply such knowledge to understand people's functioning in organizational environments. *(p. 271):* Understanding management, a vital part of the agency environment, should help generalist practitioners prepare for action and service provision.

EP 6a Apply knowledge of human behavior and the social environment, person-in-environment, and other multidisciplinary theoretical frameworks to engage with clients and constituencies. *(p. 271):* Social workers should be knowledgeable about human behavior in organizations, of which management is a fundamental aspect.

EP 6b Use empathy, reflection, and interpersonal skills to effectively engage diverse clients and constituencies. *(p. 279):* Assertiveness and conflict management in organizational environments reflect the use of empathy and other interpersonal skills.

EP 7b Apply knowledge of human behavior and the social environment, person-in-environment, and other multidisciplinary theoretical frameworks in the analysis of assessment data from clients and constituencies. *(p. 246):* Social workers can use theoretical and conceptual frameworks describing management to understand management and how it guides the processes of assessment, intervention, and evaluation. Examples of conceptual frameworks for management are discussed. Management provides guidance for the processes of assessment, intervention, and evaluation in social service organizations.

EP 7c Develop mutually agreed-on intervention goals and objectives based on the critical assessment of strengths, needs, and challenges within clients and constituencies. *(p. 260ff):* Social workers should assess client system strengths to emphasize empowerment.

EP 7d Select appropriate intervention strategies based on the assessment, research knowledge, and values and preferences of clients and constituencies. *(p. 290):* Conflict resolution can be an effective strategy to address arguments and controversies encountered when working in and with organizations and communities.

EP 8 (Competency 8)—Intervene with Individuals, Families, Groups, Organizations, and Communities. *(p. 255):* Social workers can help clients resolve problems concerning conflicts between API cultural values and the US health care system. *(p. 270):* Various factors regarding client system empowerment are reviewed. The end intent is to help clients resolve problems. *(p. 269):* Various suggestions are made concerning the initiation of actions to achieve organizational goals.

EP 8a Critically choose and implement interventions to achieve practice goals and enhance capacities of clients and constituencies. *(pp. 246, 251, 255, 260, 265, 277, 279, 290, 293):* Critical thinking questions are posed.

EP 8c Use inter-professional collaboration as appropriate to achieve beneficial practice outcomes. *(p. 264):* Leadership styles are described. Practitioners must understand leadership to become effective leaders. *(p. 260):* Suggestions for client system empowerment include collaborating with colleagues and providing leadership. *(p. 261):* Management can provide leadership in promoting changes regarding how staff members are treated and services are delivered effectively. *(p. 277):* Servant leadership emphasizes the provision of support and service to employees. Servant leaders help their supervisees improve their work. In social services, this would serve to improve the quality of service provision.

EP 8d Negotiate, mediate, and advocate with and on behalf of diverse clients and constituencies. *(p. 266):* Social workers should advocate for positive changes in health care provision concerning cultural competence. *(p. 290):* Part of being assertive is using judgment about when to express your opinion and when to not to exercise your assertive rights.

EP 8e Facilitate effective transitions and endings that advance mutually agreed-on goals *(p. 252):* One suggestion discussed here is to facilitate end-of-life decisions for families.

Media Resources

MindTap for Social Work

Go to MindTap® for digital study tools and resources that complement this text and help you be more successful in your course and career. There's an interactive eBook plus videos of client sessions, skill-building activities, quizzes to help you prepare for tests, apps, and more—all in one place. If your instructor didn't assign MindTap, you can find out more about it at CengageBrain.com.

9 | Communities in the Macro Social Environment: Theories and Concepts

Student members of a Hispanic community demonstrate at a rally on the behalf of immigrants.

LEARNING OBJECTIVES

After reading this chapter you should be able to...

9-1 Explain the concept of community.

9-2 Describe the following theories as applied to communities: social systems, human ecology, social-psychological, structural, functionalist, conflict, symbolic interaction, and empowerment.

9-3 Summarize ethical issues involving homelessness, corporate responsibility, and dual and multiple relationships in rural communities.

9-4 Provide responses to various critical thinking questions.

9-5 Differentiate geographical and nongeographical communities.

9-6 Discuss nongeographical communities, including professional, spiritual, ethnic and racial, and those based on sexual orientation.

9-7 Differentiate rural and urban communities with respect to population trends, employment issues, and some inherent problems.

9-8 Contrast generalist social work practice in rural versus urban setting.

9-9 Explain people's membership in multiple communities.

Thinking about creating change in a community may sound daunting or overwhelming, but it need not be. Many change projects are the culmination of the work of multiple individuals. Look at the following list of community change activities and check those in which you, as a new social worker, believe you could participate:

- *Interview employees of fast-food restaurants about their efforts to unionize.*
- *Gather data on the existence of income inequality in your community and prepare a report.*
- *March with a group opposing a city law that discriminates against transgender individuals.*
- *Distribute campaign literature door to door for a senatorial candidate.*
- *Participate in a voter registration drive.*
- *Research two propositions that would change the state constitution to determine how they would affect low-income community residents.*
- *Join a protest against a pipeline that threatens to pollute the water source for your community.*
- *Participate in a sit-in at a business that discriminates against gay and lesbian employees.*
- *Speak at a city council meeting against a business that is discharging chemical waste into a stream running through your community.*
- *Help prepare a neighborhood garden plot where residents can plant and reap fresh vegetables.*
- *Raise money to refurbish a prominent community landmark.*
- *Sing, play an instrument, or otherwise entertain residents in a local nursing home.*
- *Organize a meeting of students unhappy with the high cost of student housing in their community.*
- *Prepare flyers about fraud targeting older adults and distribute them to their homes.*
- *Help build a Habitat for Humanity home for a low-income family.*

Each of the above activities are designed to have a positive impact on one or more segments of a community. They also are well within the ability of most social workers and many citizens. Beginning to participate at this level often leads to other opportunities to become involved in large projects. Communities are primary settings for human behavior in the macro social environment. Understanding communities is essential for understanding why people behave as they do. This book does not try to teach how to do social work practice and implement changes in communities, organizations, or groups. However, it does intend to provide a foundation upon which to build such system-changing skills. Generalist practitioners are then better prepared to plan for and implement changes in communities to enhance people's well-being and improve their quality of life.

Defining Communities LO 9-1

EP 6, 6a, 7

We have established that a *community* is "a number of people who have something in common with one another that connects them in some way and that distinguishes them from others" (Homan, 2016, p. 10). A key feature of a community is the fact that participants share some mutual characteristic. Those factors might include shared culture, activities, interests, or location.

Thus, communities can be of two primary types—those based on geographic vicinity and those based on common ideas, interests, loyalty, and a feeling that one belongs. Locality-based communities include smaller towns such as Crouch, Idaho; Eggemoggin, Maine; and Necessity, Louisiana. Larger communities include huge cities such as the greater Los Angeles Metropolitan Area or New York City. Still other locality-based communities include smaller portions of larger cities, such as a struggling inner-city ghetto or a posh suburban neighborhood.

Nongeographical communities are based on some commonality other than location. For example, African Americans might form a community based on racial identification, mutual history, and culture. Similarly, a community of professional social workers shares common values, beliefs, and generalist practice skills. Additionally, there are gay communities and military communities where members share many common goals, values, and functions. Even scuba divers make up a community based on common interests, activities, and experiences.

A major social work perspective views communities as entities where citizens can organize or be organized in order to address mutual concerns and improve their overall quality of life. As a social worker, you have the responsibility to examine the community macro environment in which your clients reside. Certainly, you are concerned about how specific clients will function as individuals. However, the effects of the environment in which they live, such as access to resources, cannot be ignored. Assessment of human behavior within the community context is necessary to propose solutions in your practice that address larger issues affecting a broad range of clients. Social workers can use generalist practice skills to mobilize citizens within communities to accomplish the goals these citizens define for themselves.

Theoretical and Conceptual Frameworks of Communities LO 9-2

EP 6, 8b

Theoretical frameworks provide means to view, analyze, and understand communities. You might think of them as theories offering a wide range of lenses, each focusing on alternate aspects or characteristics, and thus affording different perspectives. Viewing the same picture through a red wide-angle lens poses a distinctly different picture than looking at the same scene through a dark blue telephoto lens. Because theories may be applied either to geographical or nongeographical communities, the term *member* rather than *resident* will be used regarding people involved. The eight theoretical frameworks introduced here are social systems, human ecology, social-psychological, structural, functionalist, conflict, symbolic interactionist, and empowerment.

Social Systems Theories

EP 7b

The first theoretical framework identified here concerning communities involves thinking of them as social systems. This perspective is based on systems theory, the major concepts of which were introduced in Chapter 1. We defined a **system** as a set of elements that are orderly, interrelated, and a functional whole. Each community has **boundaries**, borders or margins that separate one entity from another, that define it. For example, a specific location lies within city limits or a specific county. Or you are either a member of the National Association of Bungee Jumpers or you are not. Anderson, Carter, and Lowe (1999) comment on the internal boundaries of geographical communities:

Boundaries within the community include those between [social] institutions that differentiate tasks. (Remember from Chapter 1 that a *social institution* is an established and valued practice or means of operation in a society resulting in the development of a formalized system to carry out its purpose.) These horizontal boundaries include, for example, the uniform worn and the choice of specific colors and tasks. Firefighters' gear is adapted to their task, but it also distinguishes them from police. Their distinctive gear says, "We fight fires. We don't baptize children with our hoses, pick up garbage with our trucks, or fight off mobs with our axes and poles!"

Of course, boundaries between institutions are not always clear. One example is the participation of police in teaching drug abuse prevention (DARE Program) in schools. Does this blur the boundaries between law enforcement and education institutions? What about requirements that agencies must not spend funds to help undocumented immigrants? Does that make social agencies an agent of federal immigration agencies? Sometimes, logical boundaries that naturally would delineate an institution are redrawn. For example, one might surmise that local police are responsible for enforcing all laws whether federal, state, or local. You might expect that local police departments would arrest undocumented immigrants because the federal government defines them as criminals. However, in what is known as sanctuary cities, local law enforcement agencies refuse to enforce federal immigration laws. With respect to immigration, those law enforcement agencies have taken the position that they are not part of the larger law enforcement institution. For the most part, this stance is related to local priorities because police departments must rely on citizens (documented and undocumented) to report crime. Arresting undocumented individuals reduces the willingness of these community members to report being victimized. In sanctuary cities, police want to ensure that the boundary between local law enforcement and federal immigration enforcement agencies is clear.

The social systems perspective emphasizes analyzing how the various social *subsystems* within the community interact with each other. A subsystem is a secondary or subordinate system within a larger system. How well a community functions has much to do with the ability of its systems and subsystems to achieve their mission and goals. Units within the subsystem include such things as churches, educational institutions, health care facilities, businesses, government agencies, and social welfare institutions.

In addition, families, friendship groups, and other informal groups play a role in helping systems and subsystems perform their functions. A breakdown or problem in any of the systems or subsystems can impair the success of a community in achieving its mission.

Viewing communities from a social systems perspective can aid you in assessing your clients' community and their involvement in that community. A social systems perspective can help you formulate a range of questions to help you assess your clients' situations and figure out what you can do to assist them among your various options (*equifinality*). You might ask yourself what *inputs* the community has in terms of resources available to clients and other citizens. How effectively does the community process these *inputs* into *outputs* to meet its citizens' needs? Are enough resources entering the community to keep it healthy and thriving (thereby experiencing *negative entropy* and growth)? Is the community or possibly some of its subsystems progressing toward disorganization and *entropy*? For instance, are farmers moving out of a rural community because they can no longer make ends meet on family farms owned for generations? Are high crime rates driving residents out of a large segment of an urban community, leaving behind deserted, dilapidated shells of buildings? How do the answers to these questions affect your clients' *homeostasis*? What clues do they provide concerning what you can do on your clients' behalf? What actions might you consider taking (a form of output on your behalf that results in input into the community) to improve the community and how it affects your clients' quality of life?

Human Ecology Theories

Recall the ecological concepts reviewed in Chapter 1. A human ecology perspective of community looks at how populations relate to their immediate environments. Of concern is how well services are provided and to whom. This view emphasizes the complexity of communities. Their members are integrally involved in transactions with each other in the surrounding social environment. How clusters of people and organizations are arranged in the community's space becomes important.

Demographics, facts about population characteristics and distribution, are very important from the human ecology perspective. Environmental issues such as pollution, depletion of scarce resources, and overpopulation are especially relevant. Problems in these areas contribute to environmental injustice.

For example, a human ecology approach might focus attention on the exodus of community residents from inner-city neighborhoods to outlying suburbs. Emphasis is placed on the relationship between people and their environment, including the resources available in that environment. Inner-city buildings might be deteriorating rapidly. Businesses and industries might be moving to new, more spacious facilities allowing for more parking, greater growth potential, better consolidation of shopping areas, and improved access for workers and consumers. Often when jobs—and hence, resources—leave an area, so do residents. People move where they can find work. The human ecology perspective might help frame subsequent questions. For example, how can the inner-city environmental deterioration be reversed and necessary resources be provided to allow people to thrive there once again?

Competition, Segregation, and Integration In addition to some basic ecological concepts identified in Chapter 1, three more terms based in human ecology that apply to community macro systems include *competition*, *segregation*, and *integration*. **Competition** concerns the condition where community members struggle for control over various aspects of their environment. For example, while many communities establish laws governing such things as land use, building safety, locations for industry, and other purposes, other communities see these restrictions as unnecessary. The tug of war between those who want few, if any, restrictions and those who see land use rules, building codes, and other laws as helping improve the safety, attractiveness, and livability of their community is ongoing. Space and resources within communities are inevitably limited. Therefore, individuals and groups within a community must typically vie for them. Community members with greater resources and power can gain greater space and additional resources. It follows, then, that poorer residents have access only to less desirable space and significantly fewer resources. For example, richer community members can afford to acquire grander houses in the suburbs while poorer residents might be clustered in crowded urban ghettos.

Competition is often related to **social class**, the ranking of people in society based on their wealth, power, and family background. Indicators of social class usually include job type, educational level, amount of income, and typical lifestyle. People of higher social class generally have a higher standard of living than those of lower social class.

Segregation is the detachment or isolation of some group having certain common characteristics, such as race, ethnicity, or religion, through social pressure, restrictive laws, or personal choice. **Integration**, on the other hand, refers to the process of bringing together and blending a range of groups (including people of different races and ethnic backgrounds) into a unified, functional whole.

Such ecological concepts as competition, segregation, and integration can help social workers analyze a community in terms of its fairness and support to all of its members. Community members are involved in multiple groups and that membership can be both beneficial or negative. Members whose characteristics are different from others in the community may experience discrimination, prejudice, reduced success in life, lack of opportunities, and restricted access to important resources.

Viewing communities from a human ecology perspective helps you to focus on the inequities and problems faced by people who have fewer resources than others in the community. It provides a useful assessment mechanism for understanding why people act as they do within the context of the larger community macro system.

Social-Psychological Theories

A social-psychological perspective emphasizes how community members feel about themselves and how they interact with others. Beyond mere structural, territorial, or functional concerns, this perspective views community members as bound together for psychological and social reasons (Longres, 2008). People feel they are part of a community to experience a sense of belonging, importance, and being part of "we."

One aspect, then, of a social-psychological approach involves the extent to which community members feel they have similar concerns. Do people perceive that the

At a Glance **9-1**

New Human Ecology Concepts

Demographics: Facts about population characteristics and distribution.

Competition: Community members for control over various aspects of their environment.

Social class: The ranking of people in society based on their wealth, power, and family background.

Segregation: The detachment or isolation of some group having certain common characteristics, such as race, ethnicity, or religion, through social pressure, restrictive laws, or personal choice.

Integration: The process of bringing together and blending a range of groups into a unified, functional whole.

community has a sense of identity? Do individuals feel that they are truly a part of the community along with the other members? To what extent do community members agree about how well the community is running or how it should be run?

Another aspect of the social-psychological perspective involves individuals' sense of well-being within the community. Do people feel protected and secure? Or, do they feel they imperil themselves by just walking the streets? Are fellow community members perceived as "friends" or as "foes"?

Still another social-psychological approach to communities involves the standards, expectations, routines, and practices that community members expect of each other (DeFilippis & Saegert, 2008). How do community members expect each other to behave? Which behaviors and attitudes are considered appropriate, and which are not? To what extent do community members feel that they fit into the community social environment?

Typically, membership in a community has an influence on one's identity and expectations for themselves and others. The connection that members have with each other help support community norms and shared rituals that link the present with the past. Communities without such connections provide little guidance to members regarding norms, traditions, or other expectations. Within many cultural groups, these rituals and norms help members connect to the past, feel a part of the present, and hope for the future. *Cinco de Mayo* celebrations, PRIDE marches, and pow-wows often offer members this link between the past and future.

Structural Theories

Generally, the term *structure* refers to how the parts of any community are organized to become one whole. Additionally, structure involves how the components of the whole relate to each other. Although a bit vague, the point is that there are many ways of viewing a community's structure, three of which we identify here.

The first structural approach is the *political perspective* that focuses on various units defined by law, such as village, town, municipality, and county. Each legal entity has its own governing political structure that oversees individuals and links them with state and national government. Communities, then, are smaller political subsystems within larger systems, namely, state and national governments. When thinking about such entities, concepts such as the public, taxes, and voting come to mind.

A second means of viewing communities from a structural perspective focuses on *geographical organization*. How are properties and tracts of land arranged within the community's geographical area? How are roads arranged? Is the community geographically organized like Tokyo, which developed over centuries and is composed of an endless maze of winding, confusing streets and alleys? Or, is the community structured in terms of equally square blocks of land where an address such as "South 2230 East 14791" pinpoints an exact location?

A third way of viewing the community from a structural perspective stresses *power structure*. A community can be assessed according to which of its units have the most power and influence over what happens within it. For instance, wealthier residents typically have greater power. It's likely, then, that they will exert greater influence over decisions made in the community than will the community's poorer citizens. "Power groups" within a community involve members who hold social status and important positions that give them the ability to control access to resources,

Highlight 9-1

Structural Theories and Social Action

**EP 3, 3a,
3b, 5b,
5c, 8d**

Healy (2005) maintains that social workers adopting a structural perspective "are primarily concerned with analyzing and confronting structural injustices, particularly 'how the rich and powerful within society constrain and define the less powerful'" (p. 178; Martin, 2003, p. 24). She continues that "structural social workers draw on the insights of a range of critical social work theories including ... anti-racist and feminist social work, noting that structural social workers 'promote consciousness' because the social structure may hide inequities from people" (p. 178). Social workers serve as catalysts to mobilize people to change the power structure to make it more equitable.

Critical Thinking Questions 9-1   LO 9-3

EP 8a

In what ways are social systems, human ecology, social-psychological, and structural theories similar? In what ways do they differ?

influence critical decisions, and move other people to achieve a goal. These individuals may hold elected positions, own important businesses or industries, or otherwise are regarded as influential. Highlight 9-1 addresses the relationship between structural theories and social action.

Functionalist Theories

Functionalist theories emphasize a community's purpose or *function* and how that community can continue working to attain that purpose. A community must operate well enough to maintain its population, such as having enough food and other resources available. The functionalist perspective views society as "a stable, orderly system composed of a number of interrelated parts, each of which performs a function that contributes to the overall stability of society" (Kendall, 2013, p. 9; Parsons, 1951).

A functional community is one that has groups with a shared purpose or function. The purpose or function may include providing religion, education, or welfare services available to either the entire community or some segment. The primary functions of the community over time directly impact the actions a community chooses to take. For instance, historically, farming community members would assist a new neighbor in building a barn. The community's *function* focused on farming. Community *actions* were used to support that function.

Another example concerns looking at various dimensions of an individual's life in a geographical community, including family, schools, the economy, the political system, and religion. It involves "how the family is a system to ensure the care and raising of children, how schools provide young people with the skills they need for adult life, how the economy produces and distributes material goods, how the political system sets national goals and priorities, and how religion gives our lives purpose and meaning" (Macionis, 2010, p. 9). Each dimension of life serves some function to sustain an individual as a member of a community.

A functionalist approach also focuses on how the community has grown, acted, and matured over time. Because decisions and maneuvers change as time passes, taken collectively the actions become a process. These processes are intimately linked to a wide range of the community's structures, all serving to carry out designated functions. For example, churches of various denominations in a community may informally work together to raise funds and provide food, shelter, and clothing to the community's homeless population. More formal community structures include school boards to supervise the provision of education and social service agencies to provide services and resources.

Manifest and Latent Functions   Not all social functions work out as they're planned. Kendall (2013) explains:

> **Manifest functions** are intended and recognized consequences of an activity or social process. A manifest function of education, for example, is to provide students with knowledge, skills, and cultural values. In contrast, **latent functions** are the unintended consequences of an activity or social process that are hidden and remain unacknowledged by participants (Merton, 1968). The latent functions of education include the babysitter function of keeping young people off the street and out of the full-time job market and the matchmaking function whereby schools provide opportunities for students to meet and socialize with potential marriage partners. These functions are latent because schools were not created for babysitting or matchmaking, and most organizational participants do not acknowledge that these activities take place. (p. 9)

Positive and Negative Social Functions   A society's functions can be either positive or negative. **Positive functions** are purposeful dynamics that serve to sustain people in the community context (Macionis, 2010). **Negative functions**, or **dysfunctions**, according to Kendall (2013), "are the undesirable consequences of an activity or social process that inhibit a society's ability to adapt or adjust (Merton, 1968). For example, a [positive] function of education is to prepare students for jobs, but if schools fail to do so, then students have problems finding jobs, employers must spend millions of dollars on employee training programs, and consumers have to pay higher prices for goods and services to offset worker training costs. In other words, dysfunctions in education threaten other social institutions, especially families and the economy" (p. 9).

Sometimes, trying to address and fix a social dysfunction results in unpredictable other problems. As Coleman and Kerbo note (2009):

> Things get out of whack. Even when things are going well, changes introduced to correct one imbalance may produce other problems. … [Education for all citizens is a valued social function. The educational system develops programs to train people for jobs. However,] educators may train too many people for certain jobs. Those who cannot find positions in their area of expertise may become resentful, rebelling against the system that they feel has treated them unfairly. Thus, "over-education" may be said to be a dysfunction of our educational institutions. Functionalists also realize there are sometimes unintended consequences from

our efforts to change society. For example, the effort to reduce the amount of drugs available on the street may work to push up the crime rate. As the supply of illegal drugs is reduced, the street price of drugs goes up, and addicts may have to commit more crimes to pay for their drug habit. (p. 9)

The functionalist perspective stresses that before making major changes in society, it is vital to analyze carefully the potential repercussions. Bad consequences or dysfunctions may result from well-intended attempts at making positive changes. Highlight 9-2 discusses the relationships among social dysfunctions, social problems, and social disorganization.

Focus on Ethics 9-1 addresses the ethics of assuming a functionalist perspective about homelessness.

Highlight 9-2

Social Dysfunctions, Social Problems, and Social Disorganization

Coleman and Kerbo (2009) describe the relationship between social dysfunctions, social problems, and social disorganization from a functionalist perspective:

Functionalists see a common set of norms and values as the glue that holds groups, [social] institutions, and whole societies together. Small tribal societies in which everyone is in constant close contact usually have little difficulty in maintaining these common ideals, but as the great French sociologist Emile Durkheim pointed out, as societies have become ever larger and more complex, it has become increasingly difficult to maintain a social consensus [agreement by all of society's members about what's valued and what's not] about basic norms and values [Durkheim, 1947]. Thus, one of the major sources of contemporary social problems is the weakening of the social consensus. [**Social problems** are conditions in a society that many people believe should be changed.] Functionalists can cite considerable evidence to show that when the social rules lose their power to control our behavior, people become lost and confused and are more susceptible to suicide, mental disorders, and drug problems. Functionalists also feel that social problems arise when society, or some part of it, becomes disorganized. This **social disorganization** involves a breakdown of social structure, so that its various parts no longer work together as smoothly as they should.

Functionalists see many causes of social disorganization: Young people may be inadequately socialized because of problems in the institution of the family, or society may fail to provide enough social and economic opportunities to some of its members, thus encouraging them to become involved in crime or other antisocial activities. Sometimes a society's relationship to its environment may be disrupted so that it no longer has sufficient food, energy, building materials, or other resources. However, in modern industrial societies, one cause of social disorganization—rapid social change—promotes all [the other social problems]. (pp. 10–11)

Leon-Guerrero (2011) adds:

The *functionalist perspective*, as its name suggests, examines the functions or consequences of the structure of society. Functionalists use a macro perspective, focusing on how society creates and maintains social order. Social problems are not analyzed in terms of how "bad" it is for parts of society. Rather, a functionalist asks: How does the social problem emerge from the society? Does the social problem have a function?

… [For example,] [a] social problem such as homelessness has a clear set of dysfunctions but can also have positive consequences or functions. One could argue that homelessness is clearly dysfunctional and unpleasant for the women, men and children who experience it, and for a city or community, homelessness can serve as a public embarrassment. Yet, a functionalist would say that homelessness is beneficial for at least one part of society, or else it would cease to exist. The population of the homeless supports an industry of social service agencies, religious organizations, and community groups and service workers. In addition, the homeless also highlight problems in other parts of our social structure, namely the problems of the lack of a livable wage or affordable housing. (pp. 13–14)

Focus on Ethics **9-1**

A Functionalist Perspective on Homelessness LO 9-4

EP 1

To what extent do you think it is ethical to view the social problem of homelessness from a functionalist perspective that focuses on its positives? Explain. To what extent are "social service agencies, religious organizations, and community groups and service workers" dependent on the homeless for their existence (Leon-Guerrero, 2011, p. 14)?

At a Glance **9-2**

Functionalist Theory Concepts

Manifest functions: "Intended and recognized consequences of an activity or social process" (Kendall, 2013, p. 9).

Latent functions: Unintended consequences of an activity or social process that are hidden and remain unacknowledged by participants.

Positive functions: Purposeful dynamics that serve to sustain people in the community context.

Dysfunctions (negative functions): "The undesirable consequences of an activity or social process that inhibit a society's ability to adapt or adjust" (Kendall, 2013, p. 10).

Social problem: Conditions in a society that many people believe should be changed.

Social disorganization: "A breakdown of social structure, so that its various parts no longer work together as smoothly as they should" (Coleman & Kerbo, 2009, p. 10).

Conflict Theories

Conflict theories pose direct opposition to functionalist theories. Kendall (2013) explains:

> The conflict perspective is based on the assumption that groups in society are engaged in a continuous power struggle for control of scarce resources. Unlike functionalist theorists, who emphasize the degree to which society is held together by a consensus on values, conflict theorists emphasize the degree to which society is characterized by conflict and discrimination. According to some conflict theorists, certain groups of people are privileged while others are disadvantaged through the unjust use of political, economic, or social power. (Emphasis omitted.) (p. 11)

Functionalists assume that society maintains itself on the basis of a configuration of stable rules and consensus. In contrast, Robbins, Chatterjee, and Canda (2012) reflect:

> Conflict theorists see stability as a temporary and unusual state. ... [C]onflict rather than consensus is assumed to be the norm, and coercion rather than cooperation is considered the primary force in social life. Conflict theorists are primarily interested in two phenomena—power and change. More specifically, they are interested in the ways that people use power to resist or create change. (p. 60)

An example of how functionalism and conflict theories starkly contrast involves how people view the law (Coleman & Kerbo, 2009). Functionalists maintain that people obey laws because they value them and know they're supposed to do the right thing. There is a social consensus that law is important to maintain the social structure. Conflict theorists, on the other hand, affirm that people avoid committing crimes because they're afraid of the negative consequences such as jail. It's not so much that they want to be "good," but rather that they want to avoid potential conflict.

Four concepts are vital dimensions of all conflict theories—conflict, power, minority, and change; Robbins and her colleagues (2012) define them from the conflict perspective:

> **Conflict** is a clash or struggle between opposing forces or interests. **Power** is the ability to control and influence collective decisions and actions. **Minority** refers to groups that have limited access to power, even when they represent a numerical majority. **Change** is a transition or transformation from one condition or state to another. Change can be either rapid or slow, radical or conservative, evolutionary or revolutionary. Some conflict theories perceive change as rapid and radical while others see slow, incremental change as the norm. Change, however, is seen as normative and healthy, and the central propositions listed above are at the core of most conflict [theories]. (p. 62)

Society is viewed as being composed of various competing groups. These groups are in constant conflict, grappling with each other for power and resources. Some groups such as minority groups have less access to power, which means they must struggle to get it. Such struggling results in ongoing conflict. Ongoing conflict, in turn, means constant pressures for change in the distribution of power and resources.

Class Conflict   Conflict theories can be divided into two broad categories—those focusing on "class conflict and the other on interest group conflict" (Robbins et al., 2012, p. 62). Karl Marx (1818–1883), a German philosopher, economist, and activist, began to conceptualize conflict theory based on class differences and conflict. Marx identified basic differences in **social class**, which we have established as the ranking of people in society based on their wealth, power, and family background. He proposed that society was basically divided into the "haves," those with access to wealth and power, and the "have-nots," those with little or no access to such resources. Marx theorized that the wealthy, whom he called the capitalist **bourgeoisie**, owned the factories and businesses, and ran the government. (**Capitalism** is "an economic system in which businesses are privately owned by people called **capitalists** who operate them for profit" [Macionis, 2010, p. 11].) The bourgeoisie then wielded power over the workers, whom he called the **proletariat**, and exploited them at low wages for profit. Marx maintained that the capitalist system only resulted in the exploitation and poverty experienced by the proletariat.

Robbins and her colleagues (2012) explain the resulting conflict:

> Because a small privileged group owns the means of production and exploits others for their profit, a class struggle becomes inevitable as people struggle against exploitation. During this struggle, the owners and the

laborers become increasingly polarized and antagonistic toward each other. A class consciousness—an awareness of class position—develops among the bourgeoisie, who consolidate their common interests based on their need to exploit others for profit. Their economic monopoly, however, manifests itself not only in the work arena but also in the political arena. Through their consolidation of interests they transform their economic power into political power and dominate the political institutions that then become subservient to them. (p. 63)

The result is ongoing conflict between various groups in society based on their social class and the resulting access to power. Marx proposed that the only solution would be revolution and the demise of capitalism so that resources and power could be more equally distributed (Robbins et al., 2006). This, of course, has not happened.

Out of the perspective of conflict theory comes the troubling idea that capitalism encourages **corporate violence** (Mooney, Knox, & Schacht, 2015, p. 10). Mooney and her colleagues (2015) reflect:

Corporate violence can be defined as actual harm and/or risk of harm inflicted on consumers, workers, and the general public as a result of decisions by corporate executives or managers. Corporate violence can also result from corporate negligence; the quest for profits at any cost; and willful violations of health, safety, and environmental laws (Reiman, & Leighton, 2010). Our profit-motivated economy encourages individuals who are otherwise good, kind, and law-abiding to knowingly participate in the manufacturing and marketing of defective products, such as brakes on American jets, fuel tanks on automobiles, and salmonella-contaminated peanut butter. In 2010, a British Petroleum (BP) oil well off the coast of Louisiana ruptured, killing 11 people and spewing millions of gallons of oil into the Gulf of Mexico . . . Evidence suggests that BP officials knew of the unstable cement seals on the rigs long before what is now being called the worst offshore disaster in US history (Pope, 2011, p. 10).

Focus on Ethics 9-2 addresses the ethical responsibilities of corporations concerning production of goods.

Interest Group Conflict   The second broad category of conflict theories involves those focused on conflict resulting from *contradictory values and interests among social groups* rather than among *social classes*. Such groups and coalitions may

Focus on Ethics **9-2**

Corporate Accountability for Production

To what extent should corporations be held accountable for the production and distribution of harmful goods nationally and internationally? If they should be held accountable, in what ways? Who should hold them accountable?

EP 1

be based on race, ethnicity, gender, sexual orientation, religion, politics, or values (e.g., the National Rifle Association or the National Abortion and Reproductive Rights Action League).

For instance, consider the abortion controversy. Along a spectrum of beliefs, people who maintain the strongest antiabortion stance believe that a fetus is a human being from the moment of conception when sperm meets egg. Those who maintain the strongest pro-choice positions, on the other hand, emphasize that a woman has the basic right to choose what she wants done with her own body, regardless of the stage of fetal development. In between these positions are many who think there should be various levels of restrictions on abortion, depending on fetal development.

Another example involves **affirmative action**, the extensive array of policies and other "efforts to correct historical imbalances in opportunities based on race and sex" in work and educational settings (Segal, 2013, p. 149). "Affirmative action is based on the notion that women and minorities should be admitted, hired, and promoted in proportion to their representation in the population" (DiNitto & Johnson, 2012, p. 283). People who support affirmative action often feel that it's a necessary approach to fight discrimination against people of color, promote equality, and to help level the playing field for oppressed populations. People against affirmative action often maintain that it's unfair to provide privileges unavailable to White people because that in itself is a form of discrimination.

EP 8a

Critical Thinking Question **9-2**

What are the similarities and differences between functionalist and conflict theories with respect to communities?

At a Glance **9-3**

Conflict Theory

Conflict: "A clash or struggle between opposing forces or interests" (Robbins et al., 2012, p. 60).

Power: "The ability to control and influence collective decisions and actions" (Robbins et al., 2012, p. 62).

Minority: "Groups that have limited access to power even when they represent a numerical majority" (Robbins et al., 2012, p. 62).

Change: "A transition or transformation from one condition or state to another" (Robbins et al., 2012, p. 62).

Social class: The ranking of people in society based on their wealth, power, and family background.

Corporate violence: The "actual harm and/or risk of harm inflicted on consumers, workers, and the general public as a result of decisions by corporate executives or managers" (Mooney et al., 2013, p. 10).

Bourgeoisie: Wealthy, powerful people who own factories and businesses, and run the government.

Capitalism: "An economic system in which businesses are privately owned by people called *capitalists* who operate them for profit" (Macionis, 2010, p. 11).

Proletariat: Workers who live in poverty and earn low wages, and whom the bourgeoisie exploit for profit.

Interest groups: Groups and coalitions based on race, ethnicity, gender, sexual orientation, religion, politics, or values.

Affirmative action: The extensive array of policies and other "efforts to correct historical imbalances in opportunities based on race and sex" in work and educational settings (Segal, 2013, p. 149).

Still another conflict-laden issue concerns same-gender marriage. People supporting it feel that marriage is a basic right regardless of sexual orientation and that it is discriminatory to deny that right to people of the same gender. On the other hand, people against gay marriage may claim that marriage, often portrayed in a biblical context, can only occur between a man and a woman.

Symbolic Interactionist Theories

Both functionalists and conflict theorists maintain a macro focus on communities and the total society. In contrast, symbolic interactionist theories emphasize using "a microlevel analysis of how people act toward one another and how they make sense of their lives. The symbolic interactionist perspective views society as the sum of the interactions of individuals and groups" (emphasis omitted; Kendall, 2013, pp. 13–14).

Leon-Guerrero (2011) explains:

An **interactionist** focuses on how we use language, words, and symbols to create and maintain our social reality. This microlevel perspective highlights what we take for granted: the expectations, rules, and norms that we learn and practice without even noticing. In our interaction with others, we become the products and creators of our social reality. (p. 16)

Our communities and our society, therefore, are based on how we construct and perceive what exists, what is important, and what is expected behavior. "The concept of role is central to symbolic interactionism"; "a *role* is a social category or position with a set of expected behavior patterns. Roles, however, do not exist in isolation and are, to a great extent, defined by their relationship to one another" (Robbins et al., 2012, p. 309). Therefore, according to symbolic interactionist theories, social interaction molds our identity. "Interactions with others" show us "how to define a particular social situation" and "the world in general"; social interactions are "the basis for the ideas we develop about who and what we are" (Coleman & Kerbo, 2009, pp. 13–14). We then label ourselves and our behavior. This guides our expectations for how we and others should act in various social situations. It's almost like we are actors playing a part, trying to "present a self that will be accepted by others" (Robbins et al., 2012, p. 306).

Leon-Guerrero (2011) continues:

How does the self emerge from interaction? Consider the roles that you and I play. As a university professor, I am aware of what is expected of me; as university students, you are aware of what it means to be a student. There are no posted guides in the classroom that instruct us where to stand, how to dress, or what to bring into class. Even before we enter the classroom, we know how we are supposed to behave and even our places in the classroom. We act based on our past experiences and based on what we have come to accept as definitions of each role. But we need each other to create this reality; our interaction in the classroom reaffirms each of our roles and the larger educational institution. Imagine what it takes to maintain this reality: consensus not just between a single professor and her students but between every professor and every student on campus, on every university campus, ultimately reaffirming the structure of a university classroom and higher education. (p. 16)

Deviant Behavior   Appropriate behavior can be interpreted and learned, but so can deviant behavior. Consider drug addiction or delinquency (Leon-Guerrero, 2011). Symbolic interaction theory maintains that no one begins life as a drug addict or a delinquent. Rather, such behavior is perceived and learned. Drug addicts and delinquents learn and establish their destructive behaviors through interaction with others. They construct and view their realities to support their patterns of behavior.

Labeling Theory   **Labeling theory**, which has developed from symbolic interactionism, indicates that no behavior is inherently bad (Leon-Guerrero, 2011; Robbins et al., 2012). Rather, society determines which behaviors it considers deviant and labels them as such. Thus, when an individual is labeled as "being mentally ill" or a "criminal," these labels reposition that person from being thought of as normal to being considered deviant. Robbins and her colleagues (2012) note that a deviant role then carries with it a special status and role expectations and the deviant person is expected to fulfill the role requirements of, for example, a "patient" or "prisoner." Often, these role expectations become a self-fulfilling prophecy for both the individual and the social audience. Further, labeling theorists point out that these roles are stigmatized and are usually not reversible. Thus, once labeled, the stigmatized person is rarely, if ever, allowed to resume a normal role or position in society (p. 309).

Empowerment Theories

Chapter 2 introduced the concepts of empowerment, strengths, and resiliency, the latter two being important aspects of empowerment theories. Chapter 3 related empowerment theory to groups. The concept of empowerment was integrated through much of Chapter 8, focusing on its importance for both workers and clients in the organizational context. Empowerment is just as important in the context and understanding of communities.

We have established that empowerment involves supporting the development of self-confidence, establishing control over one's life, working together to improve the quality of life, and gaining political power to enhance input and equality. Empowerment theories support the attainment of these goals in communities. Chapter 10 explores community empowerment in greater depth.

Critical Thinking Question 9-3

EP 8a

To what extent do you agree with the comment, "Once a person is labeled as having a deviant role, that label is impossible or nearly impossible to escape"? Explain.

EP 7c

The Strengths Perspective and Communities   The strengths perspective, which provides a basis for empowerment, focuses on a community's assets rather than its problems. Here, six principles championed by the strengths perspective are applied to communities (Saleebey, 2013, pp. 17–20):

1. Each community has assets and strengths. The important thing is to identify them, then use them.
2. Community problems (e.g., crime, delinquency, drug addiction, unemployment, poverty, lack of resources and services in a geographical community, and conflict among factions in a nongeographical community) may be detrimental to the community's well-being, but they can also be viewed as jumping-off points for improvement and growth. For instance, if crime and delinquency are problems in a geographical community, then one option for citizens is to band together to form neighborhood watch organizations to look out for each other. (As noted in an earlier chapter, Neighborhood watch organizations are voluntary groups of neighborhood residents who help each other by keeping a careful eye on each other's property for potential damaging criminal activity, and report any suspicious incidents to each other and police.) Residents can work together to advocate for youths' recreational opportunities and job training to provide positive alternatives to delinquency and employment potential. Citizens can work with school personnel to educate children about drugs, abuse, and prevention. Residents can work together with various facets of the community for improved services and resources.

   Similarly, the strengths perspective views conflict in a nongeographical community such as a professional or special interest organization as providing the opportunity to address differences, make compromises, and collaborate to improve the community's functioning. For example, two factions in a professional organization that differ regarding preferred meeting times—mornings or evenings—may need to meet and discuss a potential compromise. This provides the opportunity for both factions to explain their needs, get information on the other's perspective, review the purpose for meetings, and make compromises with which both factions can live.
3. You never can fully realize how far a community can grow and improve itself. Instead of focusing on limitations and what a community cannot do, the strengths perspective seeks out and enhances ideas about what it can do.
4. Social workers are most effective when working together collaboratively with clients. Social workers can work with community members to identify issues, develop plans, and achieve results.
5. Each community has multiple resources. The trick is to identify them and establish ways to use them.
6. It's critical to care about the community's overall well-being and provide community members with support and help.

Resiliency, a concept introduced earlier in the book, is related to the strengths perspective. Highlight 9-3 discusses how community resiliency can be enhanced through the celebration of Kwanzaa.

Highlight 9-3

Using Resiliency to Enhance Communities: Kwanzaa as an Example

EP 2

Chapter 2 defined *resiliency* as the ability of any size system, including a community, to recover from adversity and resume functioning even when suffering serious trouble, confusion, or hardship. Ayner (2013) discusses how one means of strengthening and developing a community is to combine the seven resiliencies of Kwanzaa. Kwanzaa, meaning "first fruits of the harvest" in Swahili, is a week-long celebration of life, culture, and history for many African Americans. Ayner (2013) indicates that geographical communities and their members can become more resilient when they abide by the tenets inherent in Kwanzaa (Canda & Furman, 2010; Karenga, 2012):

1. *Umoja* (Unity)—to strive for and maintain unity in the family, community, nation, and race (i.e., the world African community)
2. *Kujichagulia* (Self-determination)—to define ourselves, name ourselves, create for ourselves, and speak for ourselves instead of being defined, named for, and spoken for by others . . .

3. *Ujima* (Collective work and responsibility)—to build and maintain our community together and make our sisters' and brothers' problems our problems and to solve them together
4. *Ujamma* (Collective economics)—to build and maintain our own stores, shops, and other businesses and to profit from them together—to share work and wealth, and build and control the economy of our community
5. *Nia* (Purpose)—to make our collective vocation the building and developing of our community to restore our people to their historical greatness
6. *Kuumba* (Creativity)—to do always as much as we can in the way we can to leave our community more beautiful and beneficial than we inherited it
7. *Imani* (Faith)—to believe with all our heart in our people, our parents, our teachers, our leaders, and the righteousness and victory of our struggle—faith in ourselves, in our Creator, in our mothers and fathers, our sisters and brothers, our grandfathers and grandmothers, our elders, our youth, our future and faith in all that makes us beautiful and strong (emphasis added; Karenga, 2000, pp. 58–59)

Which Theoretical Framework Is Best?

EP 8b

There is no answer to this question. Theoretical frameworks simply give you ways of examining things. They give you ideas about how to think and what to look for. Thinking about communities or assessing them in different ways can give social work practitioners ideas about what could be done to improve life for large groups of people in communities. Highlight 9-4 provides a summary of the theories identified here, their foundation principles, and some of their major concepts.

Highlight 9-4

Comparison of Community Theories

Community Theories	Foundation Principle	Some Major Concepts
Social Systems	A system as a set of elements that are orderly, interrelated, and a functional whole.	Boundaries Subsystems Inputs/outputs Entropy Negative entropy Homeostasis Equifinality

continued

Highlight 9-4 *continued*

Human Ecology	Emphasis on the relationship between populations and their environment, especially regarding how resources are distributed.	Competition Segregation Integration
Social-Psychological	Emphasis on how community members feel about themselves and their interactions with others.	Sense of "we" Having similar concerns Sense of well-being
Structural	Emphasis on the structure of the community and how various parts are organized to make a unified whole.	Political structure Geographical structure Power structure
Functionalist	Emphasis on a community's purpose or function and how the community works to continue functioning.	Functions ■ Manifest and latent ■ "Positive and negative" (dysfunctions) Social problems Social disorganization
Conflict	Emphasis on how groups in communities and society are in constant conflict and in a power struggle for scarce resources.	Conflict Power Minority Change Class conflict Interest group conflict
Symbolic Interaction	Emphasis on interpersonal interaction and how communities and society in general are based on people's interpretations of these interactions.	Roles Defining deviant behavior Labeling theory
Empowerment	Emphasis on supporting the development of self-confidence, increased control over personal destiny, working together, and increased political power.	Strengths Resiliency

Critical Thinking Questions 9-4   LO 9-5

EP 8a

Of the theories portrayed in Highlight 9-4, which theories and concepts do you think have the most relevance to social work practice in communities? Explain your reasons. Which theories and concepts do you think have the least relevance? Explain.

Community Context: Nongeographical Communities   LO 9-6

We have established that in addition to geographical communities such as a small town or large city, a community may also be based on some commonality other than location, such as a belief system, cultural background, area of interest, or common experience. These communities of interest include professional communities, racial-ethnic communities, religious groups, friendship networks, groups of patients experiencing common problems, and groups of workplace colleagues (Longres, 2008).

Nongeographical communities can serve a number of purposes to enhance members' sense of well-being, all relating to each other. First, they provide an arena for forming relationships where a person can receive support, encouragement, praise, and information. Relationships can provide feelings of belonging and connectedness that most people seek in one way or another. Second, nongeographical communities can also offer a sense of identity, of who members are. People can view themselves as Roman Catholics, gay men, lesbians, Chicanos/Chicanas, massage therapists, or rocket scientists, depending on the communities to which they belong. Third, nongeographical communities make people feel that they belong and are an integral part of the community even when apart from other members. You don't have to be standing next to another member to experience being part of the community. Regardless of where nongeographical community members are, their community membership and its contribution to their identity as community members remains intact.

Four examples of nongeographical communities will be presented here. These include professional communities (specifically, the National Association of Social Workers), spiritual communities, ethnic communities and communities of people of color, and communities based on sexual orientation.

Professional Communities: The National Association of Social Workers

**EP 1, 1a,
1c, 2b,
5b, 5c, 8c**

One type of nongeographical community is a professional or special interest organization. The National Association of Social Workers (NASW) has already been mentioned several times, especially with respect to its *Code of Ethics*. Established in 1955, NASW is the major social work organization with the largest and broadest membership in the profession. Persons holding bachelor's or master's degrees in social work and students in accredited social work programs can join. It is called an "organization" and does have an internal management structure. However, like many other professional and special interest organizations, it also provides a community for members to share information concerning common issues and to provide each other with support. Like other professional organizations, NASW fulfills at least five purposes in establishing a professional community. First, membership in such a professional organization lends credibility as a social work professional. Most, if not all, established professions have an organization to which members can belong. Such membership bolsters members' professional identity, helps them identify with other members, and enhances the visibility of a profession.

NASW's second purpose is to provide opportunities for networking. State, regional, and national conferences and meetings enable members to talk with each other and share news and ideas. Such meetings provide a means for collaborating with colleagues in pursuit of effective policy action. They present opportunities for planning to advocate for client access to social work services. They also offer occasions for finding out about new career and job opportunities.

NASW's third purpose is to provide membership services. These include *Social Work*, a quarterly journal that addresses various aspects of practice; the *NASW News*, a national newspaper published almost monthly that focuses on relevant research, social welfare policy and service issues, and social workers' accomplishments around the country and the world; and newsletters published by some state chapters.

NASW's fourth purpose is to sponsor organized efforts for lobbying on behalf of socially responsible social welfare policies and services. NASW exerts influence in support of causes and political agendas concurrent with professional social work values. It has also helped states establish licensing or certification regulations for social workers.

NASW's fifth purpose is to publish policy statements on various issues (e.g., youth suicide, health care, people with disabilities, affirmative action, and environmental policy) to help guide members in their practice (NASW, 2012) and a professional *Code of Ethics* (NASW, 2008).

A number of other organizations reflect more specific facets or subsets of social work. Examples include the Association of Community Organization and Social Administration (ACOSA) and the National Association of Black Social Workers (NABSW).

Spiritual Communities

EP 2, 2a

Religion and spirituality reflect yet another aspect of human diversity (Dudley, 2016). *Religion* involves people's spiritual beliefs concerning the origin of, character of, and reason for being, usually based on the existence of some higher power or powers, that often involves designated rituals and provides direction for what is considered moral or right. *Spirituality*, a related concept, is "a search for purpose and meaning in life, a sense of being connected with self, others, and the universe, and an ability to transcend our immediate experience to something larger known by many to be a Higher Power beyond human power" (Dudley, 2016, p. 4). Religion implies membership in a spiritual organization with customs, traditions, and structure. Spirituality may involve religion, or it may reflect a personal, internalized view of existence.

Gotterer (2001) explains: "For some people, religion fosters a spirituality that serves as a bastion of strength. It can provide emotional consolation, inspiration, guidance, structure and security. It can foster personal responsibility, identity, respect for ethical codes, meaningful ritual, and community building" (p. 188).

People involved in formally organized religious denominations or sects become part of that religious community. Hugen (2001, p. 11) cites five ways religion can maintain a sense of community:

1. Religion serves an integrative function by establishing norms and values, making for moral character and for ethical relations with others.
2. Religion serves a social control function by fostering order, discipline, and authority.
3. Religion provides the individual believer with emotional support when needed.
4. Religion confers on believers a sense of identity.
5. Religion can serve as a source of positive physical and mental health. It can contribute to happier, more stable families, marriages, and communities (p. 11).

Religion may also provide an important source of community for ethnic and racial groups. Solomon (2002) describes the church's importance for many African Americans:

No African religious cults were established in the United States during slavery. However, with the coming of Baptist and Methodist missionaries, the slaves found an avenue for the expression of emotion as well as bonds of kinship with their fellow slaves. After emancipation, the enlarged church organizations played an even more important role in the organization of the African American communities. They promoted economic cooperation for the purpose of erecting and buying churches, establishing mutual assistance and insurance companies, and building educational institutions. As the main form or focus of organized social life, the church has been both a secular and a religious institution, a fact that may well account for its playing a broader role in African American communities than in white communities. …

   The spiritual side of the African American church is far more personal than that of the traditional white church: God is never an abstraction apart from the here and now. He is personalized and included in daily life situations. … Prayer is a frequent response to everyday crisis, even by those who do not profess to any deep religious convictions. Comments like "I prayed that my husband would find a job," or "I prayed that my child would get well," may be heard. The church provides significant services in African American communities that can be utilized by creative social work practitioners seeking to enhance social functioning in those communities. For example, Leigh and Green [1982] point out that churches have served to develop leadership skills and mutual aid activities, as well as emotional catharsis for those in need of some release of emotional tensions. If social workers routinely assess the significance of the church in the lives of African American clients, they may find avenues for enhancing their service effectiveness through collaborative activity. (pp. 302–303)

As indicated, spirituality can also be expressed in ways other than those determined by formal religions. Another example is **Kwanzaa**, described earlier in its role of providing a source of strength and resilience. We described how Kwanzaa "emphasizes spiritual grounding" for many African Americans in their communities (Karenga, 2000, p. 62). Karenga (2000) explains its conceptualization and how it is key to a sense of community:

Kwanzaa [first celebrated in 1966] was created first as a fundamental way to rescue and reconstruct African culture in the midst of a movement for re-Africanization. It was to recover a valuable and ancient way of building family and community, shaped so it spoke to current needs and aspirations as a paradigm of possibility. Second, I created it to introduce the Nguzo Saba (The Seven Principles [noted earlier]) and to reaffirm the centrality of communitarian values in building and reaffirming family, community and culture. Kwanzaa was also created to serve as a regular communal celebration which reaffirmed and reinforced the bonds between us as African people both nationally and internationally. And finally, Kwanzaa was created as an act of self-determination as a distinct way of being African in the world. It was conceived as a cultural project, as a way to speak a special African truth to the world by recovering lost models and memory, reviving suppressed principles and practices of African culture, and putting them in the service of the struggle for liberation and ever higher levels of human life. (p. 57)

Sometimes, people's spiritual community involves a combination of religion and spirituality. Consider the First Nations people, the Lakota (Teton Sioux). (Other terms that refer to the indigenous people of North America include American Indians and Native Americans.) Brave Heart (2001) describes the spiritual orientation of the Lakota people:

> For the Lakota and many other Native peoples, spirituality is an integral part of culture and of one's sense of self and worldview. Lakota spirituality is based upon the Seven Sacred Rites brought by the White Buffalo Calf Woman. ... Inherent in this spiritual tradition are the sacredness of women, the sacred relationship with the Buffalo Nation, the values manifested in the ceremonies of self-sacrifice for the good of others, and the importance and sacredness of relationship with all of creation. The Seven Laws (*Woope Sakowin*) of the Lakota include generosity; compassion; humility; respect for all of creation; the development of a great mind through observance, silence, and patience; bravery in the face of adversity in order to protect the nation; and wisdom. The Lakota embrace principles of **noninterference** [the concept that people should be able to make their own decisions without meddling from others (emphasis added)] and tolerance. ... Traditionally, all decisions are made with the next seven generations in mind. (p. 19)

Ethnic Communities and Communities of People of Color

EP 2, 2a

People may also be part of nongeographical communities based on ethnicity or race. For example, many large cities sponsor a range of ethnic festivals such as Italian Fest, Polish Fest, or African American Fest. People who identify with their ethnic heritage may belong to an organized community group that celebrates its heritage and provides opportunities for socializing.

People may also feel part of that community based on their race. However, it may depend on the degree that an individual continues to identify with that racial group's traditional heritage and customs. **Acculturation**, as defined by Lum (2011), is an ethnic person's adoption of the dominant culture in which he or she is immersed. There are several degrees of acculturation; a person can maintain his or her own traditional cultural beliefs, values, and customs from the country of origin to a greater or a lesser extent (p. 55).

For example, people initially immigrating to the United States from Mexico might maintain a strong identity with their Mexican heritage and culture when they first arrive. However, the subsequent generations may lose some of their adherence to traditional culture as they become acculturated.

Weaver (2005) describes how First Nations people often strive to maintain their sense of traditional community:

> Native communities continue to exist as distinct cultural entities with many strengths. Even when federal policies interrupted values transmission, wisdom, beliefs, and practices are strengths that have survived (Long & Curry, 1998). Communities are striving to revitalize traditions through programs that teach language and culture. Many youth now participate in kindergarten or grade school immersion programs that teach language. The importance of the group reinforces socially acceptable behaviors and

emphasizes the value of learning traditions (Swinomish Tribal Mental Health Project, 2002).

First Nations people of all ages are seeking and reclaiming cultural knowledge and traditions. A study of Native women (predominantly Oneida) revealed they handle multiple roles through integration and balance of traditional and contemporary feminine strengths in a positive, culturally consistent manner. Healing the spirit is done through returning to traditions to reclaim the self (Napholz, 2000, p. 94).

Communities Based on Sexual Orientation

EP 2, 2a

Communities based on sexual orientation reflect another type of nongeographical community (Longres, 2008). Chapter 2 introduced terminology used in referring to gay, lesbian, bisexual, transgender, and questioning (GLBTQ) people and explained the concept of homophobia. Because GLBTQ people live in a world that's primarily heterosexual, they frequently seek out others of the same sexual orientation.

They then often can feel more comfortable, feel free to be themselves, and avoid the scrutiny of critical heterosexuals. Hunter and Hickerson (2003) discuss the significance of community for many GLBTQ people:

> The lesbian and gay community is essentially based on a shared sense of identity instead of on residential areas or territories (Bernard, 1973). The solidarity of an identificational community flourishes in large part through its culture or the values, common experiences, and sentiments that it produces (Gruskin, 1999). This includes art, music, literature, and jewelry; groups and organizations, including political associations, baseball teams, and choruses; and special events including music festivals and marches. The lesbian and gay community is also a subculture of the larger American culture and thus shares many broader social values (Murray, 1992).
>
> Just as no unified American culture or community exists, no monolithic gay and lesbian culture or community exists. "Community" can mean different things to different persons, for example, being a member of the worldwide population of lesbian and gay persons versus the population of lesbian and gay persons in the San Francisco Bay area. It can mean participation in a social network, the social "scene," or the lesbian and gay institutions operating in a certain area (Saulnier, 1997). Cultural norms and behaviors also vary because of factors including social class, ethnicity, and residential area (Appleby & Anastas, 1998). Diversity is evident in large events such as Lesbian and Gay Pride Day that is celebrated every year across the United States with parades. Although "solidarity" is present in rhetoric, considerable diversity and pluralism are evident among the parade participants (Herrell, 1992). (p. 22)

Hunter and Hickerson (2003) note that GLBTQ people can reach out in a number of ways to become part of a community:

> In this time of expanding technology and media, LGBTQ persons have been able to interact with others in their groups via print publications,

email, and the Web. Yet, the most enduring connection of these groups remains proximity as they gather in urban areas and neighborhoods to build an infrastructure that offers not only individual support, but also public identity and a sense of pride. Intersex persons also experience these kinds of connections. (p. 29)

Community Context: Geographical Communities

EP 2a

Geographical communities, the second major type of community, are based on location. Most are described based on such variables as the population size, density, and heterogeneity of residence. **Population size**, of course, is the total number of persons living in a designated community. The communities may be large, widely spread out farming areas or counties within an urban area.

Density is the ratio of people living within a particular space. The density of a heavily populated inner-city area is much higher than a suburb where all residences contain single families and are built on half-acre lots. Population size and density are often closely related. Extremely dense areas usually have high populations.

Heterogeneity refers to the extent to which community members have diverse characteristics. A community may vary in its level of heterogeneity, depending on its residents' socioeconomic status, racial and ethnic background, or age range.

The largest communities are **metropolitan**, traditionally those with at least 50,000 people (Ginsberg, 2005). The US Census Bureau now uses a more complex definition that divides urban areas into metropolitan and micropolitan areas (US Census Bureau, 2017). **Metropolitan statistical areas** are locales that have at least one urbanized area of 50,000 or more inhabitants. **Micropolitan statistical areas** have an urban core of at least 10,000 but less than 50,000 population. At last count, there were 381 metropolitan statistical areas and 536 micropolitan statistical areas in the United States. In addition, there were seven metropolitan statistical areas and five micropolitan statistical areas in Puerto Rico (US Census Bureau, 2013).

This book will consider both metropolitan and micropolitan areas as **urban** communities. Rural communities, discussed later, are generally considered as having 2,500 residents or less (Ginsberg, 2005). Because communities differ so widely, Highlight 9-5 identifies a number of terms that reflect some of the differences in communities that don't necessarily fit clearly the categories we've identified thus far.

Urban communities, then, are usually composed of many smaller neighborhoods, communities, and even smaller cities enveloping a central nucleus of social, business, and political activity. Cities making up a large metropolis may include suburban and satellite communities. Suburban communities directly adjoin large urban centers, whereas satellite communities are located near but not directly next to the metropolitan area.

Highlight 9-5

Variations in Communities

Communities vary widely. The following are terms used to identify some of these distinctions (Johnson & Yanca, 2010, p. 118):

1. *Small cities* are units of 15,000 to 20,000 people. They generally have internal operations, with their own police department, post office, and other systems (Kirst-Ashman & Hull, 2018a). They may be satellite communities to metropolitan areas such as Middleton, Wisconsin, adjacent to the state capital, Madison.

2. *Small towns* have between 8,000 and 20,000 people. Unlike small cities, they do not operate independently. Services are few, with residents depending on the encompassing county or larger cities close by. One such small town is Elk Ridge, Utah.

3. *Bedroom* (or *satellite*) *communities* usually evolve near larger urban areas. They are what the name implies, primarily residential communities where people reside, sleep, and enjoy recreational activities. Residents work in nearby urban centers that harbor businesses and industry. Parkville, Missouri, is an example of a bedroom committee to the Kansas City.

4. *Institutional communities* typically are characterized by an institution of substantial size that employs most of the communities' residents. The institution can be a prison, mental hospital, college or university, or a large government entity, as in a state capital. Smaller communities with large universities or prisons are other examples. Residents in such communities are dependent on the institution for their economic well-being. Most often, these are in rural environments. An example is Ossining, a village in New York state, and the home of Sing Sing Correctional Facility.

5. *Reservation communities* are areas that are recognized by the federal government where First Nations people reside. The largest concentrations of their population are in California, Oklahoma, and Arizona, respectively (US Census Bureau, 2012). Note the significance of the concept of *sovereignty* with respect to First Nations peoples. Sovereignty means that they are considered part of separate nations, and so maintain a distinctly different legal standing from other ethnic groups. Thus, tribal governments control some aspects of tribal life, such as law enforcement. The federal government has a role in assisting their communities "by providing financial and medical services" (Kirst-Ashman & Hull, 2018a, p. 300). An example of a reservation community is the Pine Ridge Reservation in South Dakota.

For example, Milwaukee, a large metropolitan area of 2 million people, comprises numerous smaller communities, including downtown Milwaukee, Wauwatosa, Cudahy, and Wayside. Directly adjacent to the central Milwaukee area are less densely populated suburbs with generally higher socioeconomic levels, including Mequon, Pinegrove, and Menomonee Falls. Satellite communities located 30 to 40 miles from central Milwaukee are Sheboygan, Oconomowoc, and Ixonia. Many people working in central Milwaukee actually live in these outlying communities and commute. Suburbs and satellite communities often offer less population density, more services, and a generally higher quality of life. They also usually cost much more to live in.

Heterogeneity or the opposite, *homogeneity* (having like or similar characteristics), also comes into play. Returning to the Milwaukee example, South Milwaukee, the southern portion of the central city, comprises mostly Hispanic residents; Babblebrook Grove, a northern suburb, people of Jewish descent; Pinegrove, a western suburb, White Anglo-Saxon Protestants; and the old fifth ward in the central city, people of Italian descent. Wayside on the east side of central Milwaukee is the home of a large university, and hence is a congregating place for intellectuals, artists, and more trendy people. It is known for great diversity in its racial, ethnic, and vocational composition.

Rural Communities LO 9-7

EP 8

We've established that rural communities have traditionally been characterized as having 2,500 residents or less. They usually include a small town, which might consist of a grocery store, gas station, and tavern. However, such communities often do not offer a wide variety of specialized services. Residents depend on the county and neighboring towns for resources.

People in a rural social environment live under very different circumstances than those in urban areas. These conditions directly affect resource availability, and hence the way social workers practice. Three variables tend to characterize communities in rural areas. First, population density is low, as people either live relatively far apart or relatively few people populate the entire community area. Second, rural communities tend to be geographically distant from larger urban areas. Third, rural communities tend to be more specialized in function than urban centers, which have both population and room to achieve diversity. For example, a farming community's resources would focus on those supporting farming needs, such as feed, seed, and farm implements like tractors and harvesting equipment. Such a community would probably not be able to support a gourmet jellybean and cappuccino shop. There would be too few people to support such a specialized interest. A generic Super Duper Value grocery store offering a wide range of basic daily foods would probably achieve greater success. In some cases, traditional country stores have been replaced by discount "dollar" stores, which are a common sight in rural communities.

Population Characteristics and Trends in Rural Areas   Cromartie (2013) and the US Census Bureau (2016b) report the following population trends in rural areas:

1. Population in rural counties declined between 2010 and 2012, the first time this has happened since census-taking began. Up to 2010, the population had been increasing slowly, making rural areas more popular.
2. About 60 million people reside in rural areas.
3. Rural counties are very diverse, with some focused heavily on recreation, while others see farming and manufacturing as their primary source of jobs.
4. Rural areas focused heavily on recreation experienced the biggest change from previous growth patterns.
5. People living in rural areas are more likely to own their homes.
6. Rural dwellers are more likely to live in their state of birth.
7. Those living in rural areas are more likely to have served in the military compared to urban dwellers.
8. Rural areas comprise 97 percent of the US land area but have only about 19 percent of the population.
9. The average age in rural areas is 51 compared to 45 in urban areas.
10. Rural residents have lower rates of poverty (11.7 percent) compared to 14 percent in urban areas.

11. Rural residents are less likely to hold a bachelor's degree or higher (19.5 to 29 percent).
12. Seventy-six percent of children residing in rural areas live with married couples as opposed to 67 percent in urban settings.
13. Income levels in rural counties ranged from a high of $93,382 in Connecticut to a low of $40,200 in Mississippi.
14. Poverty rates in rural counties ranged from 4.6 percent in Connecticut to about 22 percent in New Mexico.

When we talk about the rural social environment, we're referring to a significant number of people. We've defined the rural community in terms of numbers, but looking at the microcosm of life there is much more complex. The next sections will discuss employment issues, problems faced, and generalist social work practice in rural communities.

Employment Issues in Rural Communities   As might be expected, employment trends and experiences differ between rural and urban areas. For example, military veterans are less likely to be working if they live in rural counties compared to those living in cities (US Census Bureau, 2017b). Laughlin (2016) notes that, contrary to popular thinking, the largest employment area in rural areas is not farming. Rather, it is in the category of educational services, health care, and social assistance at more than 22 percent of the workforce. Manufacturing is next with 12 percent and retail trade is third at about 11 percent. Farming is in fourth place with less than 10 percent of rural residents employed in this area, which also includes forestry, fishing, hunting, and mining.

The location of rural areas also shows differences in employment. For examples, manufacturing is more common in the Midwest, South, and Northeast and less so in the West. In the West and Midwest, more workers are employed in agriculture, forestry, fishing, hunting, and mining than is the case in the Northeast and South.

Nationally, the demand for educators and health care practitioners is high in both rural and urban regions. This is being driven by increased school enrollment and an aging population.

The percentage of foreign-born residents also differs from rural to urban areas (Gryn, 2016). The clear majority of foreign-born population lives in counties that are mostly urban, with less than 3 percent each living in mostly or completely rural counties. Those rural counties with higher percentages of foreign-born residents are in states with strong computer-related employment opportunities, such as Texas and North Carolina, and in the case of Texas, an adjacent foreign country.

Social welfare programs remain a significant economic factor for rural communities (RHIhub, 2017). Income support programs like TANF, the Earned Income Credit, and SNAP are still helping rural families ameliorate the influence of poverty. Participation rates for means-tested state and federal government assistance programs has remained higher for rural than urban residents. Child care services tend to be less common in rural areas, and parents are more likely to rely on family and friends to provide this service. Rural areas have a much lower rate of licensed day care facilities and caregivers. Travel to receive a variety of health care and other social welfare services is more of a problem in rural areas that lack public transportation systems found in urban areas. Attempts to co-locate these services to assist families in need have been implemented in multiple rural locations with mixed success.

Ginsberg (2005) reflects on the rural employment scene:

> Many small communities are one- or two-industry towns ("company towns").... However, there are many other kinds of rural community industries, such as tourism, services to retirees, and, to some extent, warehousing and manufacturing. Many smaller communities do not provide a diversity of employment, though, and young people often find that they must either find a job within the limited number of local industries or move elsewhere for work. Rural employment for well-educated people is often available only in public schools, churches, colleges and universities, or social service agencies. Much employment in rural areas may also require extensive commuting. Trains and buses are not generally available in smaller towns, particularly in the South and West. Therefore, commuting is often by private automobile, which is expensive and often unreliable. Therefore, transportation resources are often considered a major deficiency in rural areas. (p. 8)

Other Problems and Issues Faced by Rural Communities   People have similar problems whether they live in rural or urban environments. However, there are generally fewer services available in rural areas, and those that do exist are often not readily accessible. Therefore, it's often more difficult for rural residents to get what they need. Mackie, Zammitt, and Alvarez (2016) describe some of the problems that rural and small-town residents must cope with, including low-paying jobs, social isolation, less access to services, absence of health and mental health facilities leading to fewer choices regarding treatments, and lack of coordination among service providers. In addition, many rural areas have an aversion to and resist using outside services. The sheer physical distance encountered in rural areas makes even the task of delivering meals to residents and picking them up for church and similar events difficult.

The influx of immigrant families who are now living in rural areas often is a challenge because non-Christians do not have access to institutions such as churches. This is a problem because in the past, churches have frequently been a resource for immigrants providing both tangible and intangible assistance, help with acculturation, and social connections.

Carlton-LeNey, Murty, and Morris (2005) cite three additional issues characterizing rural communities. First, it's difficult to maintain privacy and anonymity in rural environments. People tend to communicate with each other in an open communication system where any word of residents' "comings and goings" travels fast (p. 407). This can result in problems regarding confidentiality.

Another characteristic of rural communities is a strong "good ol' boy" network where the local power structure often permits a few individuals to exercise a lot of power over everybody else (Carlton-LeNay et al., 2005, p. 407). Often, leaders are people who come from what are considered "the best families" (p. 407). This controlling group, whose members essentially are from the most respected families,

EP 2

usually are wealthy White males. Consequently, persons of color can be left out of the power network. At times, people who don't conform to the controlling group's expectations and values may be subjected to suspicion, hostility, and potential rejection.

One other feature characterizing rural communities is a mistrust of government and external interference. Rural residents may try to keep their problems and issues in-house without turning to outsiders (such as social workers and social services agencies) for help.

EP 1b, 1c, 2a, 2b

Generalist Social Work Practice in Rural Communities Social workers practicing in rural communities must address at least five special issues: the importance of generalist practice, interagency cooperation, understanding community values and developing relationships with community residents, emphasizing community strengths, and community building.

First, rural social workers must be true generalists who are prepared to work with individuals, families, groups, local organizations, and the community; they should be primed to use a wide range of skills to meet clients' diverse needs (Mackie, Zammitt, & Alvarez, 2016; Ginsberg, 2005; Lohmann & Lohman, 2005). We've established that because of lower population densities, rural environments usually have fewer resources.

EP 5b, 6, 7c, 7d, 8, 8c, 8e

Unlike rural areas, a large metropolitan area with dense population generates lots of tax money and resources. Such a county can afford to support a large urban department of social services that may have many workers. Large numbers enable such a department to diversify. For example, public and private social service agencies might provide specific, separate services such as substance abuse counseling, protective services for older adults, services for people with intellectual disabilities, foster care, crisis counseling for victims of sexual assault, shelter for victims of domestic violence, and so on. Urban workers may become more specialized in the problems they address, depending on their assigned unit.

In contrast, rural environments usually can't sustain large social services departments with numerous workers. Rather, practitioners must be "multitalented and multiskilled" to help clients address a broad arena of issues (Ginsberg, 2005, p. 5). In a single day, a rural worker may deal with child maltreatment, older adult abuse, substance abuse, and foster care issues.

A second special issue for social workers in rural communities involves *interagency cooperation*. Because fewer, more general services are usually provided by rural public agencies, it's critical for agencies and their staffs to work more closely together than in many urban communities. It's common for practitioners and agency administrations serving rural areas to know their professional colleagues and to collaborate when needed to address client needs. In urban areas with hundreds of available services, this may not be the case.

A third issue involving social work in rural communities is the importance placed on understanding the community, knowing its values, and developing relationships with rural residents (Daley & Avant, 2004). People living in rural communities have different life experiences than those living in bustling cities. Because there are fewer people, social interaction and relationships tend to be much more informal. Rural social workers and their family members might attend the same church or school, participate in the same civic clubs and organizations, and shop at the same grocery store as clients. Therefore, a rural practitioner must be careful to portray an image that reflects positively on his or her agency (Daley & Avant, 2004).

Practitioners' private lives might be more public. For example, it would not be impressive for a social worker counseling a client with an alcohol problem to be cited in the local newspaper for driving under the influence (DUI). Ginsberg (2005) comments regarding the visibility of social workers:

> Social workers are part of the community gossip system. Personal behavior is often a terribly important issue to those one is committed to serve. Personal conduct in matters such as alcohol, dating, religious affiliation and attendance, and purchasing (small town people want their professionals to make purchases from local merchants, for example) are important elements in effectively working in a rural community. (p. 6)

Focus on Ethics 9-3 addresses the ethical issue of dual and multiple relationships in rural communities.

Focus on Ethics **9-3**

Ethical Issues Involved in Dual and Multiple Relationships in Rural Communities

EP 1, 1a, 1b

Because of the close interpersonal nature of rural communities, there is a strong likelihood that dual relationships exist. **Dual** or **multiple relationships** "occur when professionals assume two or more roles at the same time or sequentially with a client" (Corey, Corey, Corey, & Callanan, 2015, p. 254). *Dual* refers to assuming two roles, and *multiple,* of course, to more than two roles. Such relationships may include intermingling professional and nonprofessional roles with clients, such as social worker and business associate, neighbor, parent–teacher association member, or member of the same church, temple, mosque, or synagogue. Multiple relationships may also involve socializing with clients. Furthermore, multiple relationships may extend to having personal or professional relationships with relatives or friends of clients.

The NASW *Code of Ethics* clearly states that "social workers should not engage in dual or multiple relationships with clients or former clients in which there is a risk of exploitation or potential harm to the client" (NASW, 2008, 1.06c). It continues that when dual or multiple relationships are inevitable, practitioners should be extremely careful in maintaining professional roles and boundaries.

Some ethical dilemmas are unique to rural communities. "For example, if a [social worker] ... shops for a new tractor,

he risks violating the letter of the ethics code if the only person in town who sells tractors happens to be a client. However, if the [social worker] ... were to buy a tractor elsewhere, this could strain relationships with the community because of the value rural communities place on loyalty to local merchants" (Corey et al., 2015, p. 267).

Especially in rural communities, dual and multiple relationships may be unavoidable. Watkins (2004) suggests that social workers in such situations "above all, do no harm; practice only with competence; do not exploit; treat people with respect for their dignity as human beings; protect confidentiality; act, except in the more extreme instances, only after obtaining informal consent; [and] practice, insofar as possible, within the framework of social equity and justice" (p. 70).

It's very important for workers to separate their personal from their professional relationships to the greatest extent possible. For example, consider a worker and a client who attend the same church and serve on the same committee there. This does not mean that the worker should become "friends" with the client. That would bias the worker's objectivity and threaten the effectiveness and fairness of the worker–client relationship.

continued

Focus on Ethics **9-3** *continued*

A Case Example of a Dual Relationship in a Rural Community

Corey and colleagues (2015) present and discuss the following case example. It concerns a dual relationship occurring in a rural community and how the situation was handled:

> Millie, a therapist in a small community, experienced heart pain one day. The fire department was called, and the medic on the team turned out to be her client, Andres. To administer proper medical care, Andres had to remove Millie's upper clothing. During subsequent sessions, neither Andres nor Millie discussed the incident, but both exhibited a degree of discomfort with each other. After a few more sessions, Andres discontinued his therapy with Millie.

- Can this case be considered an unavoidable dual relationship? Why or why not?
- What might Millie have done to prevent this outcome?
- Should Millie have discussed her discomfort in the therapy session following the incident? Why or why not?
- If you were in Millie's situation, what would you have done? (p. 268)

Commentary: This case scenario reflects how an unanticipated dual relationship occurred between worker and client in an emergency situation. Sometimes, dual or multiple relationships just cannot be avoided, especially in small communities or rural settings where people are more likely to be in contact with each other. Despite the awkwardness of Andres and Millie's situation, there are some suggestions for how it could have been addressed (Corey et al., 2015). First, Millie should probably have discussed with Andres early on in their professional relationship how they should handle chance encounters in their small community. Should they acknowledge knowing each other? If so, in what way? However, they could hardly have anticipated such a physically oriented example. A second suggestion involves how Millie could have dealt with her own embarrassment and anxiety by processing it with another colleague in a counseling context. Finally, Millie could have openly discussed the event with Andres to get feelings out in the open and, hopefully, to disperse reactions of discomfort. They then may have been able to get on with the professional relationship and pursue counseling goals. In summary, Millie should have addressed the issue in some way for Andres's benefit as her client instead of avoiding it and pretending that the elephant was not in the living room.

Highlight 9-6 discusses potential advantages for social workers in rural environments.

Highlight **9-6**

Advantages for Social Workers in Rural Environments

Despite the challenges inherent in working in rural environments, there are often several positive aspects as well (Ginsberg, 2005). First, workers usually have greater independence because of broader job descriptions and less complex bureaucratic structures in social service organizations. This may be a great advantage for people who appreciate having discretion in what they do and how they accomplish goals. A second advantage is that it may be easier to advance in the social services organizational power structure and get a management position. Competition may not be nearly as strong or plentiful. Third, social workers may be more likely to see the fruits of their efforts with clients more quickly and clearly. "The dearth of services and the smaller scale, which often permits rapid implementation of plans, can allow social workers to see what they have done early in their assignments" (p. 10).

The fourth issue important for social work in rural communities involves emphasizing the strengths inherent in rural communities. Because of the informal nature of relationships, rural clients are often integrally involved with informal support systems or social networks of other people willing to help them out—sometimes referred to as **natural helping networks** (Carlton-LeNay et al., 2005; Tracy, 2002; Watkins, 2004). Such networks can include family members, neighbors, coworkers, fellow church members, community benefactors, and others not providing formal agency services who are willing to volunteer assistance. For example, churches often provide needed help in rural communities (Carlton-LeNay, 2005). They may sponsor community events such as vacation Bible school for children in summer and regular Bible study sessions for nursing home residents. Churches may also provide child care, food and shelter during emergencies, and volunteers who drive people to necessary medical appointments.

A fifth issue concerning rural areas concerns "community building," which is "the process of developing and sustaining partnerships between groups of citizens and practitioners to bring about planned change for the public good" (Poole, 2005, p. 125). There are several key concepts in this definition. First, practitioners work together with community residents as *partners* to improve service delivery and reach out to citizens in remote areas. Practitioners assume their professional roles while citizens volunteer to work with them in all stages of the community-building process.

Another concept inherent in the definition of community building involves **planned change**. Chapter 1 defined **planned change** as a seven-step process of developing and implementing a strategy; the goal is to improve or alter a behavior pattern, condition, or situation so that it improves the well-being of the client. The behavior to be altered may be that of the client or someone else and the condition or situation may exist somewhere in the client's environment. Steps include engagement, assessment, planning, implementation, evaluation, termination, and follow-up.

Yet another important concept in community building is change on behalf of the *public good*. It is social workers' responsibility to improve the communities in which they work whenever possible. As we know, a major social work value is to improve human well-being.

Several projects reflect examples of community building in rural areas (Poole, 2005):

- One group of citizens and social workers improved the coordination of regular food pantry supplies to rural people in need. The original process had been irregular and unpredictable, and the nutritional quality of the food was often poor.
- A group involving practitioners and citizens worked together to improve access to and synchronization of mental health and other health care to rural residents. Prior to the group's efforts, many residents found it difficult to locate available services and service providers found it difficult to coordinate care with each other.
- One rural community decided to examine why community children were experiencing school failure early in the educational process. A planning group made up of citizens—including parents, teachers, other school personnel, professionals from various disciplines in the community, and social workers—assessed the problem, made recommendations for improvements, and monitored the plan's progress.
- A group of social workers and rural women came together to investigate the effectiveness of prenatal assessment processes and systems in the community. They surveyed residents to determine what obstacles women were experiencing. They then worked together to improve publicity about available services, recruitment of patients, and coordination of service provision.

Urban Communities[1]   LO 9-8

EP 2a

Urban communities provide very different settings for generalist social work practice than rural communities. **Urban social work** is practice within the context of heavily populated communities, with their vast array of social problems, exceptional diversity, and potential range of resources. Phillips and Straussner (2002) stress how urban social workers "need to be sensitive to the situations commonly found in the cities and to be knowledgeable about the nature of urban life and the range of impact that the urban environment can have on people" (p. 20). Work in urban communities is important in view of how both the national and global population has been shifting from rural to urban settings. People often flock to cities in search of new opportunities, higher-paying jobs, and greater access to activities and services. Many times, although hopes are high, actual opportunities are scarce or nonexistent, which results in a "disproportionate number of the poor" in the "country's largest cities" (p. 107).

Urban communities are characterized by a number of conditions including higher population density and more diverse population subgroups (e.g., ethnic, racial, cultural, age, sexual orientation). In addition, urban economic conditions involve a range of industries, businesses, rent levels, and transportation availability and costs. Urban communities often involve a bustling tangle of concrete, traffic, noise, and questions about air quality—in sharp contrast to the more natural rural environment. Of course, an urban lifestyle entails more condensed interaction and contact with many people. Finally, the political situation may be intense, with many layers of bureaucracy and numerous people in "the system" who have various amounts of power. Sometimes crime, corruption, and social injustice are evident.

Watkins (2004) explains:

> Urbanization brought dramatic changes in the way people interacted with each other. Individuals moved away from extended family and other primary relationships to cities where primary relationships were replaced by more role-based interactions [for example, employee, renter, customer, student]. Population density and crowding were accompanied by emotional distancing to preserve a sense of privacy and individuality. In low-income neighborhoods, needs overwhelmed the resources of neighbors. Many persons in need were new to the cities and had no support networks. Formalized or institutionalized social services were a rational response to the peculiar social patterns and needs of these urban residents. . .. However, when federal, state, and local governments increased their role in providing services, the programs were no longer tailored to a specific community. In efforts to increase efficiency and fairness, services became more bureaucratic and standardized. The new model of service delivery that developed preferred secondary, "professional" relationships and interactions that were rule- and role-based rather than more personal [and individualized]. Needy individuals were depersonalized into "clients." (p. 67)

---

[1] Note that many of the ideas in this section are taken from *Urban Social Work: An Introduction to Policy and Practice in the Cities*, by N. K. Phillips and S. L. A. Straussner (Boston: Allyn & Bacon, 2002), unless otherwise indicated.

EP 2, 2a

Problems Inherent in Urban Communities   At least five problems tend to characterize urban areas more than rural areas (Phillips & Straussner, 2002). First, even though "problems such as poverty, discrimination, overcrowded housing, crime and violence, homelessness, high rates of school dropouts, substance abuse, and HIV/AIDS exist in communities of all sizes," it is important to note that "they occur with greater frequency and therefore are more visible in the cities" (Phillips & Straussner, 2002, p. 25).

A second problem is the widespread occurrence of discriminatory behavior because of the wide variety of ethnic, racial, religious, and cultural groups living in cities. Groups may be in conflict and fighting for power and resources. Often, public schools are disadvantaged because of inadequate funding, resulting in poorer buildings, libraries, laboratory equipment, and technology, as well as underpaid staff.

"Migration of people unprepared" for the pressures and demands of urban living is a third problem characterizing cities; Phillips and Straussner (2002) explain:

> With their promise of freedom and opportunity, the cities have always been magnets for both the adventurous and the desperate. Most people move to urban areas in search of better opportunities for work or for education, either for themselves or their families, and for many, the cities have served and continue to serve as gateways to success.
>
> However, some who migrate to urban areas, whether from other parts of the United States or from other countries, are faced with unemployment, underemployment, discrimination, poor housing, and language barriers. Those without families or social supports to help them make the transition to the new culture and to city life are at greater risk for poverty, social isolation, and personal and family problems. (p. 27)

As Phillips and Straussner (2002) point out, financial shortfalls or unavailability of resources make up a fourth problem characterizing urban areas:

> Some cities do not have the financial resources to provide services that would assist people in maximizing their potential, while other cities may have the resources, but do not choose to provide services, particularly for the poor. Consequently, there may be a lack of affordable, good-quality housing, or a lack of adequate police protection, schools, or recreational facilities. For example, preschool children and their parents are underserved in many urban communities. (p. 28)

Because of cities' dense population, service gaps can affect huge numbers of people.

The fifth problem characterizing cities involves greater amounts of psychological stress. Stressors including noise, dirty streets, abandoned buildings, overcrowded housing, lack of geographic mobility, and substance abuse can impose psychological pressure and increase general anxieties (Phillips & Straussner, 2002, p. 29).

Highlight 9-7 describes some of the skills involved in urban social work practice.

Highlight 9-7

Generalist Social Work Practice in Urban Communities

**EP 1c, 2,
3b, 8, 8c,
8d**

As in other types of social work, urban social workers use micro practice skills in their work with clients in the community, including establishing and working toward goals, using effective communication and interviewing techniques, respecting client values and perspectives, emphasizing strengths, expressing empathy, and "developing self-awareness" to combat biases and effectively understand clients' perspectives (Phillips & Straussner, 2002, p. 201). Thus, "social workers need to constantly reflect on their work, talk with supervisors or consultants, discuss their concerns with colleagues, and, as students, engage in classroom discussion and exercises that promote the development of self-awareness" (Phillips & Straussner, 2002, p. 201).

Additionally, urban social workers must focus on using skills in at least four major arenas (Phillips & Straussner, 2002):

1. *Paying close attention to human diversity.* Because urban environments more likely have a wider variety of ethnic, racial, and religious backgrounds, urban social workers must be sensitive to the wide range of cultural differences, become knowledgeable about their various clients' cultures, and focus on the identification and use of clients' respective cultural and personal strengths. Urban practitioners must also be attuned to the potential discrimination experienced by people "based on race, ethnicity, culture, age, gender, religion, sexual orientation, disability, poverty, or language spoken. While historically various immigrant groups such as the Irish, the Jews, the Italians, the Chinese, and the Japanese have experienced discrimination in the United States, the most persistent discrimination today is experienced by Native Americans; blacks, including African Americans, people from the Caribbean, and people from Africa; Latinos; Asians; and people of Middle Eastern backgrounds" (p. 26).

2. *Understanding their agency environment.* Urban agencies may be large and complex, or may serve large client populations. Urban workers must understand the intricacy of their agency's power structure, who has decision-making power about what they can and can't do, and where resources are located. Large bureaucracies are often highly impersonal. They tend to emphasize following rules and regulations to coordinate their complex maze of service provision. Often workers are called on to work with other personnel they don't know. Workers must then be sensitive to other staff's roles and use good communication skills to work effectively in collaboration with other service providers. Even smaller agencies in urban settings must work within a complex interplay of numerous organizations also addressing client needs. Urban social workers must understand the functioning of other agencies serving the same clients and work carefully with other staff to coordinate service provision.

3. *Seeking resources in the external urban environment.* Urban social workers often function in a complex labyrinth of many public and private agencies, each providing specialized services in one of a broad range of areas (e.g., mental health counseling, administration of public assistance, domestic violence shelter, sexual assault hotline, or adolescent pregnancy prevention). This differs from rural agencies, which frequently provide a broader range of services to a smaller population; in other words, they are less likely to specialize to the degree that urban agencies can. In their broker role, urban social workers must often seek resources in a confusing tangle of red tape and available services.

4. *Using advocacy.* Note that just because urban areas tend to have larger and more numerous services, this does not mean that there are no significant gaps in service due to limited or lacking resources. Such gaps may involve massive numbers of people. At the agency level, an urban practitioner may need to develop a coalition with colleagues and approach decision-making administrators with suggestions for positive changes. On another level, public policy may not serve clients' best interests. Therefore, strategies to change legislation may include the use of letter-writing or e-mail campaigns to lawmakers, *lobbying* (seeking direct contact with legislators to influence their opinions), or using the mass media to publicize clients' needs and issues to gain public support for positive change.

EP 8a

Critical Thinking Question 9-5

To which geographical and nongeographical communities do you belong? Describe each.

Membership in Multiple Communities   LO 9-9

Remember that each individual is probably a member of multiple communities. You are probably a member of the university or college community, your residential community, the social work professional community, possibly a work group community, and any number of others. Involvement in multiple communities reinforces an individual's sense of belonging and expands potential access to resources and support provided by various communities. For example, the college community provides you with access to library resources and knowledge about values and skills. The residential community gives you neighborly support and potential friendship. The professional community furnishes you with information about jobs, ethical decision making, relevant legal issues, and new work skills.

Chapter Summary

The following summarizes this chapter's content as it relates to the learning objectives presented at the beginning of the chapter. Objectives include the following:

LO 9-1 **Explain the concept of community.**

A community is "a number of people who have something in common with one another that connects them in some way and that distinguishes them from others" (Homan, 2016, p. 10). Communities include those that are geographic and nongeographic.

LO 9-2 **Describe the following theories as applied to communities: social systems, human ecology, social-psychological, structural, functionalist, conflict, symbolic interaction, and empowerment.**

Theoretical frameworks offer theoretical ways to view, analyze, and understand communities. Social systems theories emphasize the concepts of system, boundaries, subsystem, input and output, entropy, negative entropy, homeostasis, and equifinality.

Human ecology focuses on the relationship between populations and the environment. Major concepts include competition, segregation, and integration.

Social-psychological theories stress how community members feel about their interactions with others in the community and their overall sense of well-being.

Structural theories underscore various structural aspects of communities, including political, geographical, and power structures.

Functionalist theories focus on the community's purpose and dynamics. Major concepts involve manifest and latent functions, positive functions, dysfunctions, social problems, and social disorganization.

Conflict theories emphasize how various community groups are in constant conflict in a power struggle over scarce resources. Primary notions include conflict, power, minority, change, class conflict, and interest group conflict.

Symbolic interaction theories stress interpersonal interaction and the interpretation of this interaction for defining roles and deviant behavior. They also emphasize the labeling of behavior.

Empowerment theories emphasize strengths, resiliency, and the development of self-confidence, increased control over personal destiny, working together, and increased political power.

LO 9-3 Summarize ethical issues involving homelessness, corporate responsibility, and dual and multiple relationships in rural communities.

Ethical issues discussed involved a functional perspective on homelessness, corporate accountability for the safe production of goods, and dual and multiple relationships in rural communities.

LO 9-4 Provide responses to various critical thinking questions.

Critical thinking questions addressed comparing and contrasting various theories, the labeling of an individual as "deviant," and the relevance of various theories to social work.

LO 9-5 Differentiate geographical and nongeographical communities.

Geographical communities are described based on such variables as the population size, density, and heterogeneity of residence. Nongeographical communities are based on some commonality other than location, such as a belief system, cultural background, area of interest, or common experience.

LO 9-6 Discuss nongeographical communities, including professional, spiritual, ethnic and racial, and those based on sexual orientation.

Professional communities such as the National Association of Social Workers are based on membership and professional status. Spiritual communities are based on having common "values, beliefs, mission, awareness, subjectivity, experience, sense of purpose and direction, and a kind of striving toward something greater than oneself" (Frame, 2003, p. 3). For example, Kwanzaa "emphasizes spiritual grounding" for many African Americans in their communities (Karenga, 2000, p. 62). People involved in formally organized religious denominations or sects become part of that religious community.

Nongeographical communities may also be based on common racial identity or ethnicity. Communities based on sexual orientation include people with common orientations, values, and a sense of identity.

LO 9-7 Differentiate rural and urban communities with respect to population trends, employment issues, some inherent problems.

Rural communities have traditionally been characterized as having 2,500 residents or less. Although the actual number of rural residents has increased, the proportion of people living in rural areas has decreased. Rural areas often suffer unemployment problems and decreased access to resources. Other issues include concerns about privacy, "good ol' boy" power structures, and mistrust of government.

Urban locales include metropolitan and micropolitan communities (US Census Bureau, 2011). Metropolitan communities are those with at least 50,000 residents. Micropolitan communities are characterized as having one or more urban clusters of at least 10,000 but less than 50,000 people (US Census Bureau, 2013). Multiple problems often characterize densely populated urban communities. Urban social workers should closely attend to aspects of human diversity, understand their agency environment, actively seek out resources available from other agencies, and advocate for improved policy, services, and resources.

Other types of community variations include "small cities," "small towns," "bedroom communities," "institutional communities," and "reservation communities" (Johnson & Yanca, 2010, p. 142).

LO 9-8 Contrast generalist social work practice in rural versus urban setting.

Generalist social workers in rural communities should be prepared to work with a wide range of clients and issues, readily work together with other social service organizations, understand the community and its values, emphasize the strengths inherent in rural communities, and work in partnership with community citizens and groups to undertake community building. Dual and multiple relationships can be a concern more so than in urban setting.

LO 9-9 **Explain people's membership in multiple communities.**

Any individual is likely to be a member of many kinds of communities at once, including geographical and nongeographical communities.

Looking Ahead

This chapter shifted the focus from organizations to communities. It examined theoretical perspectives on communities, and explored variations in geographic, rural, urban, and nongeographic communities. The next chapter discusses power and empowerment in communities, including mapping community assets.

Competency Notes

The following identifies where Educational Policy (EP) competencies and component behaviors are discussed in the chapter.

EP 1 (Competency 1)—Demonstrate Ethical and Professional Behavior. *(pp. 315, 317, 324, 335)*: Ethical questions are raised regarding the functionalist perspective on homelessness, corporate accountability for production, and ethical issues involved in dual and multiple relationships in rural communities.

EP 1a Make ethical decisions by applying the standards of the NASW *Code of Ethics,* relevant laws and regulations, models for ethical decision-making, ethical conduct of research, and additional codes of ethics as appropriate to context. *(p. 324)*: Attending local, state, and national conferences sponsored by NASW helps practitioners engage in career-long learning. NASW has an established *Code of Ethics* to guide professional practice. *(p. 335ff)*: The NASW *Code of Ethics* indicates that practitioners should avoid dual or multiple relationships that place clients at any risk. A case example illustrating an ethical dilemma is described and suggestions for its resolution provided.

EP 1b Use reflection and self-regulation to manage personal values and maintain professionalism in practice situations. *(p. 334)*: When

working in rural communities, generalist practitioners must practice personal reflection and self-correction to ensure compliance with professional values. *(p. 340)*: In addressing potential dual and multiple relationships in rural communities, generalist practitioners must recognize and manage personal values in ways that allow professional values to guide practice.

EP 1c Demonstrate professional demeanor in behavior; appearance; and oral, written, and electronic communication. *(p. 324)*: Membership in the National Association of Social Workers and the connection it offers with the professional community enhance professional identity. *(p. 334)*: In the often-transparent context of rural communities, it is important to demonstrate professional demeanor in behavior, appearance, and communication. *(p. 340)*: When addressing potential dual or multiple relationships in rural communities, generalist practitioners should take great care in attending to professional roles and boundaries. The importance of the broker's role in urban settings is emphasized.

EP 2 (Competency 2)—Engage Diversity and Difference in Practice. *(p. 322)*: Color, culture, and race are dimensions of diversity. *(p. 325, 327)*: Religion and spirituality are aspects of diversity. *(p. 328)*: Sexual orientation is a dimension of diversity. *(p. 338)*: Social workers practicing in urban communities must be aware of the many aspects of diversity characterizing such environments. *(p. 333)*: A rural community's culture can make some groups powerful and oppressive to other groups. *(p. 334)*: Social workers should recognize the extent to which the conditions that may be evident in urban culture can oppress residents.

EP 2a Apply and communicate understanding of the importance of diversity and difference in shaping life experiences in practice at the micro, mezzo, and macro levels. *(p. 340)*: Religion and spirituality reflect yet another aspect of human diversity. *(pp. 327–328)*: Acculturation, as defined by Lum (2011), is an ethnic person's adoption of the dominant culture in which he or she is immersed. There are several degrees of acculturation; a person can maintain his or her own traditional cultural beliefs, values, and customs from the country of origin to a greater or a lesser extent. *(p. 328)*: Communities based on sexual orientation reflect another type of nongeographical community. *(p. 329)*: Heterogeneity refers to the extent to which community members have diverse characteristics. A community may vary in its level of heterogeneity depending on its residents' socioeconomic status, racial and ethnic background, or age range. *(p. 334)*: Rural communities represent another form of diversity and difference in life experience. *(p. 338)*: Social workers are likely to find more diversity in urban versus rural communities. *(p. 339)*: A problem often encountered in urban communities is the widespread occurrence of discriminatory behavior because of the wide variety of ethnic, racial, religious, and cultural groups living in cities.

EP 2b Present themselves as learners and engage clients and constituencies as experts of their own experiences. *(pp. 324–328)*: Differences in spirituality and religion shape life experiences. *(pp. 334ff)*: Color, culture, ethnicity, and race shape life experiences. Sexual orientation shapes life experiences. Variations in geographical location can shape life experiences. It is essential for practitioners in rural communities to recognize how such rural environments shape life experiences. Generalist practitioners working in rural environments should view themselves as learners

and engage community residents as informants. Practitioners working in urban communities should recognize that urban environments shape life experiences. Social workers in urban environments should recognize differences inherent in urban communities that shape life experiences.

EP 3 (Competency 3)—Advance Human Rights and Social, Economic, and Environmental Justice. *(p. 312)*: A structural theoretical framework focuses on social and economic justice.

EP 3a Apply their understanding of social, economic, and environmental justice to advocate for human rights at the individual and system levels. *(p. 324)*: Social workers serve as catalysts to mobilize people to change the power structure to make it more equitable.

EP 3b Engage in practices that advance social, economic, and environmental justice. *(p. 324)*: A structural theoretical framework supports social workers' use of advocacy to advance human rights, and social and economic justice. *(p. 340)*: Social workers in urban communities often must advocate for human rights and needed services.

EP 5b Assess how social welfare and economic policies impact the delivery of and access to social services. *(p. 312)*: A structural theoretical framework helps social workers analyze, formulate, and prepare to advocate for policies that advance social well-being. *(p. 324)*: Involvement in NASW provides opportunities to analyze, formulate, and advocate for policies that advance social well-being. *(p. 337)*: As they practice community building, social workers in rural communities should analyze, formulate, and advocate for policies that advance residents' social well-being.

EP 5c Apply critical thinking to analyze, formulate, and advocate for policies that advance human rights and social, economic, and environmental justice. *(p. 312)*: Social workers serve as catalysts to mobilize people to change the power structure to make it more equitable. *(p. 324)*: Membership in NASW provides one means for social workers to develop plans together to advocate for client access to social work services.

EP 6 (Competency 6)—Engage with Individuals, Families, Groups, Organizations, and Communities. *(pp. 306–307)*: Various theoretical frameworks for viewing and understanding communities are discussed. Social workers practice by working with systems of all sizes, including communities. *(p. 334)*: In community building, rural social workers should follow the planned change process, including engagement, assessment, intervention, and evaluation.

EP 6a Apply knowledge of human behavior and the social environment, person-in-environment, and other multidisciplinary theoretical frameworks to engage with clients and constituencies. *(p. 306)*: Generalist practitioners must have knowledge and theories to engage and work with systems of all sizes, including macro systems.

EP 6b Use empathy, reflection, and interpersonal skills to effectively engage diverse clients and constituencies. *(p. 331)*: As in other types of social work, urban social workers use micro practice skills in their work with clients in the community, including establishing and working toward goals, using effective communication and interviewing techniques, respecting client values and perspectives, emphasizing strengths, expressing empathy, and "developing self-awareness" to combat biases and effectively understand clients' perspectives (Phillips & Straussner, 2002, p. 201).

EP 7 (Competency 7)—Assess Individuals, Families, Groups, Organizations, and Communities *(p. 306)*: Assessment of human behavior within the community context is necessary to propose solutions in your practice that address larger issues affecting a broad range of clients.

EP 7b Apply knowledge of human behavior and the social environment, person-in-environment, and other multidisciplinary theoretical frameworks in the analysis of assessment data from clients and constituencies. *(p. 307)*: Data acquired during the assessment process can be analyzed using any of several theoretical perspectives.

EP 7c Develop mutually agreed-on intervention goals and objectives based on the critical assessment of strengths, needs, and challenges within clients and constituencies. *(p. 321)*: It's important to assess community client systems' strengths when working in and with communities. *(p. 334)*: In community building, social workers should develop a mutually agreed-on focus of work and desired outcomes with rural community residents. Rural social workers should assess community strengths in order to emphasize and enhance community capacities. In community building, rural practitioners should work with community residents to develop mutually agreed-on interventions.

EP 7d Select appropriate intervention strategies based on the assessment, research knowledge, and values and preferences of clients and constituencies. *(p. 334)*: In community building, rural social workers should work with community residents to choose appropriate intervention strategies.

EP 8 (Competency 8)—Intervene with Individuals, Families, Groups, Organizations, and Communities. *(p. 331)*: Generalist practitioners should substantively and affectively prepare for action in rural communities by understanding community values and developing relationships with community residents. *(p. 334)*: In community building, rural social workers help clients and community residents make plans to resolve problems. *(p. 340)*: Social workers in urban communities should initiate actions to achieve organizational goals in complex organizational contexts.

EP 8a Critically choose and implement interventions to achieve practice goals and enhance capacities of clients and constituencies. *(pp. 312, 318, 320, 323, 341)*: Critical thinking questions are posed.

EP 8b Apply knowledge of human behavior and the social environment, person-in-environment, and other multidisciplinary theoretical frameworks in interventions with clients and constituencies. *(p. 307)*: Working with macro-level clients requires understanding the theories and concepts that characterize large systems and how those are used in interventions. *(p. 322)*: Thinking about communities or assessing them in different ways can give social work practitioners ideas about appropriate interventions that will improve life for large groups of people in communities.

EP 8c Use inter-professional collaboration as appropriate to achieve beneficial practice outcomes. *(p. 324)*: Involvement with NASW provides opportunities to communicate and collaborate with colleagues for effective policy action. *(p. 334)*: In community building, it's critical for rural social workers to use interagency cooperation and collaborate with both colleagues and community residents. *(p. 340)*: Social workers in urban communities must often collaborate with colleagues while advocating for clients.

EP 8d Negotiate, mediate, and advocate with and on behalf of diverse clients and constituencies. *(p. 312)*: Social workers in urban

communities must often collaborate with colleagues while advocating for clients. *(p. 340)*: At the agency level, an urban practitioner may need to develop a coalition with colleagues and approach decision-making administrators with suggestions for positive changes. On another level, public policy may not serve clients' best interests. Therefore, strategies to change legislation may include the use of letter-writing or email campaigns to lawmakers, lobbying (seeking direct contact with legislators to influence their opinions), or using the mass media to publicize clients' needs and issues to gain public support for positive change.

EP 8e Facilitate effective transitions and endings that advance mutually agreed-on goals. *(p. 334)*: In community building, rural social workers should work with community groups to implement prevention interventions that enhance client capacities.

Media Resources

MindTap for Social Work

 Go to MindTap® for digital study tools and resources that complement this text and help you be more successful in your course and career. There's an interactive eBook plus videos of client sessions, skill-building activities, quizzes to help you prepare for tests, apps, and more—all in one place. If your instructor didn't assign MindTap, you can find out more about it at CengageBrain .com.

10 | Assessment of Geographic Communities and Empowerment

Jim West/Alamy Stock Photo

Communities can help and empower their residents. Here volunteer college students help build a Habitat for Humanity home on the Martin Luther King holiday.

LEARNING OBJECTIVES

After reading this chapter you should be able to...

10-1 Describe the significance of power in communities, who has it, and why.

10-2 Respond to critical thinking questions dealing with communities.

10-3 Discuss the importance of citizen participation and social support networks.

10-4 Describe ethical issues when engaged in assessment of geographical communities.

10-5 Explain natural helping networks.

10-6 Describe personal empowerment, social empowerment, and the relationship between the two.

10-7 Utilize a format for assessing communities and describe data-gathering procedures.

10-8 Explain community building and highlight the primary principles involved.

10-9 Provide examples of community building in rural communities.

10-10 Explain mapping community assets and suggest methods for collecting information.

10-11 Provide examples of how individuals, groups, associations, organizations, and social institutions can work together for community empowerment.

10-12 Explain social work roles in macro practice.

Brutus, age 77, lives in a rundown, two-story home in an ancient residential section of Bumrap, a large metropolitan city. Chenequa, his neighbor, is very concerned about Brutus and his situation. Twice she found Brutus had fallen helplessly on the ground while walking out to get his mail. She practically had to drag Brutus into the house. Brutus has rheumatoid arthritis, which makes it very difficult to walk even with his two canes. Additionally, his eyesight is poor. Chenequa has questions about Brutus's ability to shop and cook for himself.

Brutus's wife, Olive, died two years ago after a long bout with colon cancer. Since her death, Brutus has remained isolated and alone. His two children live in other states and are busy with their own families and careers.

Brutus considers himself an intelligent, independent man who worked hard most of his life as a house painter. However, since his arthritis took a turn for the worse 10 years ago, he has had to stop actively working. He is now facing financial difficulties. He's experienced many years of little income and high health costs for both he and his wife. He is becoming increasingly depressed about his failing health. However, he clings doggedly to the notion he must remain in his home. To do otherwise, he thinks to himself, would mean giving up and accepting certain death. Brutus is aware of the Heavenly Happy Haven Health Care Center, the only nursing home in the area. He has sadly watched some of his friends enter it and dreads the thought of having to go himself. He misses the old days when he was an active breadwinner who loved to play stud poker and drink Miller GD.

Luckily for Brutus, Chenequa is a natural helper[1] who is concerned about her neighbors' well-being and is familiar with a series of neighborhood services available for older adults. Chenequa made a "neighborly visit" and forced Brutus to address his needs and situation. Although reticent at first, Brutus succumbed to her persuasive encouragement that his life could be better than it is. She emphasized he would not have to enter a nursing home if he didn't want to.

Chenequa made several suggestions regarding how Brutus might tap community resources. First, a local neighborhood center sponsored hot meals each weekday noon for senior residents at nominal cost. Volunteers were available to transport people like Brutus who had difficulty walking even a couple blocks. Brutus had to admit he was tiring of his repetitive diet of baked beans and sauerkraut. Hot cooked meals with meat sounded pretty good to him. Some company with others his age didn't sound that bad, either. The center also sponsored a cooking group that taught citizens basic cooking techniques and provided some free canned goods and other staples.

Chenequa was also aware of a special outreach program sponsored by a local hospital that provided affordable basic medical care for seniors. Seeing a physician there might help Brutus deal more effectively with his arthritis, or, at least, get him some pain medication for those days when it was bad. The local library sponsored a day periodically when practitioners from a local eyecare center volunteered their time to screen seniors for glaucoma and cataracts" and provide updated eyeglass prescriptions. The center subsequently discounted seniors' fees for new glasses.

---

[1] Natural helpers are "'ordinary' individuals identified by others in the community as being good listeners and helpers"; natural helpers typically "provide social support consisting of alleviation of social isolation, emotional support (encouragement, reassurance), communication activities (confidante, listening), and problem-centered services (light housekeeping, errands, transportation, cooking)" (Biegel, Shore, & Gordon, 1984, p. 97).

Chenequa indicated that a local church sponsored biweekly lectures and discussion groups on wellness for senior citizens. Brutus expressed some interest in this but indicated he would rather play poker and drink beer. Chenequa noted that another church sponsored bingo parties for seniors, which held more appeal for Brutus.

Chenequa kept popping in on Brutus to see how he was doing. Because of her efforts and his involvement with a range of neighborhood services and activities, he attained a consequentially better quality of life for a number of years. He significantly benefited from community empowerment.

Chapter 9 provided descriptive and theoretical information about communities and how they function. This chapter focuses on community empowerment. It emphasizes the importance of assessing a geographic community, not only in terms of its problems and needs, but also concerning its strengths and assets.

People and Power in Communities   LO 10-1

EP 2, 2a, 6, 6a

As a generalist practitioner, to engage and assess at the macro level requires a variety of skills. Not only must you employ the interpersonal skills that you use with other-size systems, but you must understand how communities work. Accurate assessment of community functioning can provide you with a foundation to initiate community change. One aspect of communities that you must understand is power. *Power* is the potential ability to move people on a chosen course to produce an effect or achieve some goal (Homan, 2016). Three concepts are important in this definition. First, power involves *potential ability,* or other people's perception that power exists. Even if power is not used, the potential for use is there.

For example, a major religious leader may have the power to heavily influence a decision regarding whether to allow women in the clergy. He might have the power to make this decision independently or to exert pressure on others to comply with his wishes. However, that same leader might choose to remain neutral on the issue and, hence, not use his potential power. Potential ability means the opportunity to use power is there, but there is no guarantee regarding whether this power will be used or to what extent it will work.

The second concept involved in the definition of power is that of *moving people on a chosen course.* People having power can influence, that is, direct or sway, people's actions, thoughts, or decisions in some desired direction. Consider a practitioner working for a private social service agency who wants that agency to earmark more resources for poor people in the community. She must somehow engender some power to obtain that end. She must write a grant for funding, persuade the agency's board of directors[2] and administrative leaders of the idea's value, or lobby with local politicians to divert funding for her proposal.

The third important concept in the definition of power involves the idea that power is used to *produce an effect or achieve some end.* The worker just described might have specific programmatic ideas about helping poor people in her

---

[2] Chapter 4 established that a *board of directors* is a group of people authorized to formulate an organization's mission, objectives, and policies, and to oversee the organization's ongoing activities.

community. For example, she might think a community food pantry or a homeless shelter is the best way to meet a community's needs.

A community's power structure includes who makes decisions about what can and can't be done in a community. It is important for social workers to understand the power structure—including who may potentially be helpful and valuable allies, and who may be potential causes of problems experienced by the community. Such information is vital for establishing effective strategies for positive change.

Who Has Power in Communities, and Why?

At least seven rationales explain why some people in communities have greater power than others. Remember these reasons only reflect potential power. Even a person who has power may or may not get what he or she wants in the end. The rationales are information, wealth, reputation, high status, decision-making positions, laws and policies, and interpersonal connections.

1. *Information* (Homan, 2016, p. 207; Hardcastle, 2011). You might think of the old cliché, "Knowledge is power." Information provides insight into an issue. It might provide greater access to ideas or help one choose allies to enhance power. For example, perhaps you happen to be a great grant writer and can expertly use the Internet to locate information such as grant sources. This gives you an advantage over someone without this knowledge. It gives you greater power to achieve your goals for acquiring funds. Other examples of people whose access to information gives them power includes "newspaper editors, talk show hosts, educators, gossips, gatekeepers (those who control the flow of information to decision makers), preachers, computer wizards, and political confidants" (Homan, 2016, p. 208).

2. *Wealth* (Homan, 2016). Think of another old cliché, "Money is power." People with lots of money have many more choices regarding how they will live their lives than poor people. Rich people can choose to live in Boca Raton, Florida; Beverly Hills, California; or Aspen, Colorado, if they want. Money provides them with that power.

   Likewise, having money affects interaction with those who don't have it. People without enough money must go to other people who have money to get what they need to achieve goals. For example, people who can't afford to pay cash for a home must go to a bank or mortgage broker and apply for a loan. The lending institution has power over those requesting money. It can determine whether a potential borrower is a good credit risk or not. The lender also has the power to determine conditions for the loan—namely, how much down payment and interest the borrower must pay in order to use the borrowed money for some designated time period.

3. *Reputation* (Hardcastle, 2011). People who are highly thought of have greater power to influence others than people with shoddy reputations. Consider the many media advertisements where famous athletes, celebrities, and others endorse a product. The advertisers obviously are trying to communicate nonverbally that the product is good for you. You're supposed to believe this based on the celebrities' great reputations.

Liking and respecting a person probably makes you more likely to go along with that person's ideas. This reflects one type of interpersonal power. On the other hand, a politician who you feel has lied to you or participated in some sleazy, unethical behavior probably would not command much of your support.

4. *High status* (Hardcastle, 2011; Homan, 2016). People who have high social status can command power over those with less social status. Sometimes, such people are in professional or work positions commanding respect because of their high earnings, their degrees, the difficulty it takes to get these degrees, or their sterling accomplishments. They might be CEOs of huge corporations, Supreme Court justices, physicians specializing in breakthrough health care arenas, nuclear physicists, astronauts, or university presidents. Other times, people have high status because of popular political support and acclaim. At varying levels, presidents of nations, state governors, and town board chairpersons have positions assuming status because of the popular support necessary to achieve such positions.

   Sometimes, conditions for enhancing power overlap. For example, an extremely wealthy automobile manufacturer with a high public profile might command power based on wealth, reputation, and resulting high status. Similarly, the director of the CIA might command power based on ready access to lots of information, popular reputation, and high status related to that position.

5. *Decision-making positions* (Hardcastle, 2011; Homan, 2016). People holding important positions in organizational hierarchies have automatic decision-making power as part of their job descriptions. Agency executive directors, company or professional organization presidents, elected politicians, and labor leaders have power and decision-making authority over those below them in their respective hierarchies. People in lower positions depend on those above to make effective decisions regarding how organizations and communities are run.

6. *Laws and policies* (Hardcastle, 2011; Homan, 2016). Public laws and organizational policies dictate how such macro systems are organized and run. "The ability to make, interpret, and enforce the policies governing a community confers a great measure of authority" (Homan, 2016, p. 208). A law or policy can swiftly determine whether you win or lose a child custody suit or an agency grievance concerning sexual harassment. Being associated with formal legal processes gives politicians power. Greater knowledge about legal issues gives lawyers power. Ability to enforce laws gives police officers power. If the blue and red flashing lights have ever overtaken you as you were passing on a curvy rural road on the yellow line, you would be well aware of how it feels to be at the mercy of legal power. It is even worse when the middle-aged officer says, "You're getting a ticket, young lady," when the "young lady" is 47.

7. *Connections* (Hardcastle, 2011; Homan, 2016). Interpersonal connections and affiliations with others in the community can enhance your power base. This is true concerning both large numbers of contacts and supporters, on the one hand, and fewer but more powerful contacts, on the other. "Good ol' boy" networks are alive and well, while good ol' girl connections are developing (Homan, 2016). When trying to change a community policy or

EP 8a

Critical Thinking Question **10-1**   LO 10-2

Think of a person in your own geographical or university community who has power. What are the sources of that power in terms of the seven sources just described?

develop a community service, soliciting others' collaboration and support can significantly strengthen a macro change effort. Other people can provide support, money, votes, information, and extended networking contacts (that is, people they know but you don't).

Citizen Participation   LO 10-3

Individuals and people banding together in community groups can develop and wield significant power. **Citizen participation** is the dynamic, voluntary involvement of community members to address issues and concerns affecting their community and improve social policies, laws, and programs. Several aspects of this definition are significant. First, participants are voluntary—that is, they are committed to expend their efforts. Second, the focus is on the community members themselves, not on outside help. Community members work to make their own changes and improvements. Third, members are aware of issues and problems confronting the community. Often, this requires the education of community members by providing factual information and discussing specific change tactics. Fourth, citizen participation targets laws, rules, and regulations affecting the community to make them better serve the community and its members.

Social workers who strive to improve community macro systems often employ the concept of citizen participation. Social workers can encourage and enable community members to improve community conditions for themselves. Highlight 10-1 provides examples of how young people can contribute to their communities. Focus on Ethics 10-1 explores the issue of informed consent when pursuing community action.

Highlight **10-1**

The Power of Youth

Community involvement is not limited to adult residents. Creative, energetic, concerned young people can also provide great citizen participation and service. Young people can potentially undertake many projects and should not be ignored because of their age.

Janet, age 8, noticed some of her classmates were going without the clothes, toys, and attention she so much enjoyed. The inequities continued to bother her until age 15, when she took the initiative to visit a shelter for homeless people. There she met many children and gave them gifts of colorful crayons, markers, and paper with which they could draw. Some of the drawings, reflecting their life experiences, were intense, moving, and distressing. For the next half of a year, she continued to visit the shelter on a weekly basis, playing with and reading to the children. Then she got an idea. She organized a group at school to help her carry it out. First,

continued

Highlight **10-1** *continued*

she took the pictures the children had drawn and used them as illustrations on calendars. Her start-up money was about $300, most of which she had earned working part-time. She then organized her schoolmates to sell them. The two purposes were to raise money for the shelter and to educate the public about homelessness. When Janet left for college, she made certain that the club would continue. She trained officers, transferred records, and recruited a faculty advisor.

Jacques, age 15, knew that the Special Olympics existed for people with intellectual disabilities, but he never really attended functions or helped out. Jacques was very active in high school basketball, football, and tennis. Accidentally, he found out about Unified Sports, a Special Olympics program that paired people who had a disability with those who performed actively in competitive sports. The intent was to provide opportunities for sports participation and simply to have fun. As Jacques's mother was a special education teacher, he put up a sign-up sheet in her classroom. Seven students with various learning and intellectual disabilities were interested. Jacques then recruited two friends and established the community's first Unified Sports team. Now, 200 community citizens are actively involved in Unified Sports basketball, track, soccer, bowling, baseball, and tennis. Jacques still allocates 15 hours each week in a variety of sporting activities.

Yael, age 17, attended a multiracial high school in which the student population was 45 percent Hispanic, 24 percent Asian, 25 percent African American, and 6 percent White. She became increasingly distressed by the serious racial tensions engulfing all aspects of school life. Racial groups put pressure on individuals, including Yael, not to associate across racial lines. More and more fights were breaking out. Finally, Yael had enough. She started with 6 interested people, a number that grew to over 40. Every day they have lunch together, discussing issues and ideas. She also started publishing an online newsletter where students could share their ideas and suggest improvements.

Margo, a 15-year-old, heard another student talking about a peer mediation program that was being started in her school. The program was designed to help manage conflicts between students. Interested, Margo participated in training to be a peer mediator and learned the importance of "critical thinking, problem solving, and self-discipline" (McWhirter et al., 2013, p. 356). As part of her training, she learned communication skills, role playing, and the steps in getting peers to agree to use mediation to settle their disputes. Over the next two years, Margo worked with

11 dyads, helping all but one through to an agreeable outcome. She also participated in training additional students as mediators during her senior year.

Abdu, age 16, was saddened at the condition of a triangular plot of city land compressed where two city streets came together. It was scattered with junk—old refrigerators, tires, twisted pieces of metal that came from who knows what, and basic garbage. One day while surfing the Internet, Abdu ran across an article describing a national organization aimed at helping poor neighborhoods improve their conditions. It sparked an idea. Why couldn't he get some volunteers and money together to help fix up that miserable piece of property? Abdu worked with school officials, city administrators, other students, teachers, and community residents to completely refurbish the lot into an attractive, well-kept little park. He managed to solicit over $10,500 in donations, grants, and material contributions and helped organize volunteers to develop and use skills. Together, they seeded grass, planted shrubs, erected basketball hoops, and installed playground equipment. Thanks to Abdu's efforts, the community could be proud of its new park.

Miles, a 12-year-old, loved playing baseball, but neither he nor any other kids in his neighborhood could do this on a regular basis because there was no nearby park or ballfield. After griping with other neighbor kids about the problem, he came up with an idea. There was a large abandoned field full of six-foot-tall weeds on the Northside of the neighborhood. It had once been part of a farm but now was simply vacant and awaiting commercial development sometime in the future. It could be a good baseball field if somehow the weeds could be managed. The kids discussed options and decided to present the problem to their parents. Within a week, one of the parents borrowed a tractor with a mower attachment and cut the weeds down to a level where the neighborhood kids could play baseball. Once in use, other parents and kids took turns mowing the field with their own lawn mowers.

Many **social support networks** are informal or more casual associations comprised of individuals or groups who share a connection with others and who provide support to one another in times of need. The connection may be based on membership in a family or other social institution (such as church or school), friendship, shared culture, or geography. Usually, there is no formal membership list or hierarchy of authority. An example is an Internet talk group or "chat room" addressing some common interest such as Christmas ornament collecting or the hottest Hawaiian fishing spots.

Focus on Ethics **10-1**

Informed Consent and Community Action LO 10-4

EP 1

Citizen participation is an essential aspect of community improvement. Yet, what does this really mean? Does it mean community members with the most *power*, the *majority* of community members, or *all* community members? What about community members who simply don't care about the issue one way or another? Dolgoff, Loewenberg, and Harrington (2012) address the ethical issue of informed consent when pursuing community action:

> The ethical dimensions of obtaining informed consent are especially problematic when the client is a community or a neighborhood, as may be the case for social workers engaged in community organizing. A social worker involved in a neighborhood renewal program must consider whether the elected representatives really represent all residents. Does their informed consent suffice or must every resident consent? What is the situation when the initiative for intervention comes from the outside? What does it mean to obtain informed consent when the social worker's initial objective is to raise the residents' consciousness to the fact that there is a problem in their community and that they can do something about it? Requiring every person's consent in this latter situation may be tantamount to ruling out any intervention activity, yet intervening without

informed consent is a violation of professional ethics. What should a social worker do in these circumstances? Hardina (2004) suggests that the best method for ensuring that most participants agree with an approach is to hold a "meeting in which all members debate risks and benefits of the proposed action and attempt to reach a consensus" (p. 599). This approach can be time consuming, and there is no guarantee that consensus can be reached, however "constituents should be fully informed about the consequences of their actions, especially when personal sacrifices (such as job loss, arrest, or social stigma) are great" (Hardina, 2004, p. 599). (p. 166)

It's no newsflash that people in general are complex. Social workers' charge is to work with client system (be it a community, organization, group, family, or individual) to determine the most effective course of action that will protect people's lives, equality, autonomy, and rights; improve their quality of life; yet cause the least harm (Dolgoff et al., 2012). Even elected representatives at the state and national levels rarely have 100 percent consensus among their constituents. Is there any issue that would receive this level of support? The best decision needs the consensus of the beneficiaries of the change effort but unanimity may be impossible.

Social Support Networks LO 10-5

We have established that interpersonal connections provide people with one source of power. The extent of support, both formal and informal, evident in any community usually contributes strength to its citizenry. When residents work together, it's usually easier to get more accomplished than when isolated individuals work alone.

A term related to interpersonal connections is that of a social support network. For any individual, a *social support network* is individuals or groups who share a connection with others and who provide support to one another in times of need. These networks may be informal, as in families, or formal, as might be the case with organizations. In either case, the network members share information, skills, contacts, and other resources that are intended to benefit others in their network. A core concept is the establishment of communication channels with others based on common characteristics, interests, or needs.

Social support networks vary according to the number of people involved, the frequency of their contact or communication with each other, how strongly members feel

EP 8a

| Critical Thinking Questions **10-2** |

With what social support networks are you involved? In what ways do they serve to support you?

about being part of the network, strength of common bonds or characteristics (such as religious commitment, age, or cultural heritage), and geographic distance among members. An example of a formal social support network is a professional association such as the American Public Human Services Organization. Formal social support networks may have established membership dues, prerequisites for membership, or lists of members' names. Note that professional organizations also serve as professional communities. Social support networks, however, imply more intercommunication and interaction than the concept of community. One can be a member of a professional community, for example, and have very little involvement with other members.

The Relationships among Power, Citizen Participation, and Social Support Networks   LO 10-6

The concepts of power, citizen participation, and social support networks often intersect. Community members come together in citizen participation. They form a social support network for each other and establish their power base. They then can confront a formal power structure (e.g., the mayor's office) and pressure this structure to make policies fairer and to distribute community resources more equitably.

Social Networks and Use of the Internet

Like most of the world, social workers are using the Internet frequently and for many reasons. "This includes doing research, accessing national and state databases, communicating through e-mail, accessing groups and organizations with interests that may be of benefit to clients, and carrying out discussions with colleagues around the world" (Kirst-Ashman & Hull, 2018a, p. 529). In addition, social workers are using Internet capability to provide social work services to clients located at a distance, educating others, and expanding the reach of the profession.

The Internet and Social Change   Use of the Internet can greatly facilitate the use of social networks to connect people with similar beliefs and issues. Members of social networks can share information and make plans to advocate and fight for positive change. They can readily communicate with each other in efforts to lobby for change, initiate protests, or meet with decision makers to press for change. One example, Asian Americans for Civil Rights and Equality (founded in 2012), is an organization whose mission is to "connect communities, ideas, and action to inspire a collective movement for positive change" (AACRE, 2017). AACRE (see aacre.org) is networked with other organizations or activities that support its mission, including:

- APEX Express: A weekly radio show providing stories and information about Asians and Pacific Islanders.

- Asian Prisoner Support Committee: Focuses on the increasing numbers of Asians and Pacific Islanders in the United States being detained, imprisoned, and deported.
- Alliance of South Asians Taking Action: Educates, organizes, and empowers communities to stop violence, oppression, racism, and exploitation within and against diverse communities.
- Asian Pacific Islander Equality—Northern California: Advocates and organizes for fairness and equality for Asian and Pacific Islander and Lesbian, Gay, Bisexual, Transgender, and Queer communities.
- Chinese for Affirmative Action: Protects the civil and political rights of Chinese Americans to advance multiracial democracy in the United States.
- Hmong Innovating Politics: A grassroots organization focused on strengthening the political strength of Hmong and other disenfranchised communities through civic engagement and grassroots mobilization.
- Hyphen: A magazine covering news and culture about Asian Americans.
- Network on Religion and Justice for Asian and Pacific Islander Lesbian, Gay, Bisexual, Transgender, and Queer People.
- Visibility Project: A video project dedicated to Queer Asian American Women, Trans, and Gender nonconforming communities.

(More information can be found at http://aacre.org/about/)

Communication and connection via the Internet can be used for any number of purposes. For example, Austin Lee, age 17, of St. Cloud, Minnesota, was able to rally enough support via Facebook and email to convince the city council to approve a skate plaza for $500,000 (Unze, 2011). Lee managed to gather together 60 of his 1,085 followers to attend a city council meeting to advocate for their request. This, in addition to the flood of emails the council received, proved to council members that this was a serious, popular idea that was worth funding.

Globally, the Internet and use of cell phones has allowed individuals and groups to convey information in oppressive dictatorial nations, organize demonstrations, and initiate protests. Kirst-Ashman and Hull (2018a) reflect:

> Technology such as Facebook has been employed to launch protests in Croatia, and computer-savvy individuals have created blogs in counties such as Fiji, Malaysia, Egypt, and Iran to protest government laws, policies, and practices. Messages and photos have been posted on YouTube and Twitter that call attention to events that have not been covered by mainstream media. The use of technology has allowed groups with limited or no power to organize and demand changes in organizations, communities, and countries and has provided yet another tool for social workers pursuing societal change. (p. 533)

EP 1

Information Sources on the Internet   The information to be found on the Internet is endless. Topics can range from community building to mental health to GLBTQ (gay, lesbian, bisexual, transgender, questioning) issues. Highlight 10-2 identifies a number of sites that may be useful for social workers. Be wary, however, about the validity of websites. A friend had a teenage daughter who started looking at websites because she was interested in becoming a model. She ended up being linked to several pornography sites that were really hard to get rid of.

| Highlight **10-2** |

Websites Potentially Useful for Social Workers

Topic or Group	Website
Advocacy for children (Children's Defense Fund)	www.childrensdefense.org
Center for American Women and Politics	www.cawp.rutgers.edu
Community Organizations International	www.acorninternational.org
International Association of Schools of Social Work (IASSW)	www.iassw-aiets.org
International Federation of Social Workers (IFSW)	www.ifsw.org
National Association of Social Workers (NASW)	www.naswdc.org
Networks for social workers sharing specific interests	www.socialworkcafe.net
Social welfare blog	www.socialwelfarespot.blogspot.com
US Census Bureau	www.census.gov
Information for Practice	lfp.nyu.edu

Learning about and using technology is a lifelong process. New programs and applications are rapidly being developed. Sources of information are mushrooming in number. It's critical for social workers to use technology to keep abreast of new knowledge that applies to their clients and their clients' communities.

Natural Helping Networks

One form of informal social support network is the **natural helping network**, a group of nonprofessional people volunteering their time and resources to help either an individual or group of people in need; this might involve providing child care, loaning small amounts of money, offering support in overcoming alcoholism, or providing short-term lodging. The emphasis here is on a network *helping* designated individuals who require resources or support instead of a group networking on the basis of some other common interest. The kind of help available is designed to provide support, either emotional or in the form of resources. For example, Zebb, a young man leaving prison on parole, has a natural helping network back in his home community consisting of concerned family members and clergy. Zebb depends on his family to provide a place to live, food, clothing, and emotional support to help him get back on his feet and live independently. A second function of natural helping networks is to provide information and help connect people with other needed resources. Zebb can rely on his rabbi to help link him with potential jobs made available by other members of the synagogue.

One example of establishing a natural helping network in a community neighborhood involves a protective services worker, Olga, who "was aware that a particular neighborhood needed more day care services and had a high incidence of child abuse" (Halley, Kopp, & Austin, 1998, pp. 407–408).[3] Olga received a number of referrals to investigate alleged child maltreatment. She made numerous visits to the neighborhood and talked to many residents. Olga found out that many residents had an excellent grasp of what was happening there, including incidents of family violence and neglect. Olga thought that if she could find out about potentially explosive situations before they "blew," she could help prevent placement of many neighborhood children in foster care.

Several residents often referred to two strong, independent community women, Lolita and Pat, as "people in the know." They were **natural helpers**, that is, they were ordinary citizens who other community residents considered as people with good listening and problem-solving skills. Natural helpers typically offer support that may include friendship, social and emotional supports such as encouragement, and an ear, with a goal of reducing isolation. Some will also provide concrete services such as help with shopping, cooking, housekeeping, and transportation.

Lolita and Pat, who were good friends, each managed an eight-family rental property located near a large public housing project. Apparently, community residents, including those in the project, knew that they could turn to Lolita and Pat for help and support when they were down and out. For example, one resident, Jewel, mentioned to Olga that when her 13-year-old daughter became pregnant last year, Lolita lent Jewel money for an abortion. Another neighborhood resident, Lakeesha, told Olga how Pat helped her out last year. When Lakeesha couldn't make the rent one month and was evicted from her tiny apartment, Pat let Lakeesha stay with her for a couple weeks until Lakeesha found another place to live.

Olga contacted Lolita and Pat, set up informal meetings, and talked to them about neighborhood issues. Olga slowly approached them about the possibility of becoming identified neighborhood helpers. She explained that residents would informally come to know such helpers as people to whom they could turn for help, advice, information, and support. Lolita and Pat could act as brokers to link community residents with needed daycare services and other resources aimed at combating child maltreatment. Olga emphasized that she would continue to be available to Lolita and Pat to provide information about resources or intervene in crisis situations they felt were too difficult to handle.

Both Lolita and Pat were wary at first. However, upon understanding Olga's idea more fully, Lolita was flattered. It surprised her that a person representing "the system" would recognize her in this manner. Pat was more hesitant. She didn't feel she was qualified to pull off such a role. After all, Pat told Olga, she only had a high school education.

Olga, Pat, and Lolita continued to talk. They discussed how Pat and Lolita were essentially neighborhood helpers already. The new ideas Olga was suggesting were to reinforce this fact, help spread the word farther, and have Olga provide them with help from a formal institution when they needed it. Pat's and Lolita's relationship with Olga evolved and was strengthened. They effectively put the plan into action for the general betterment of community residents' health and well-being.

---

[3] This vignette is loosely adapted from one described in *Delivering Human Services: A Learning Approach to Practice* (4th ed.), by A. A. Halley, J. Kopp, and M. J. Austin (New York: Longman, 1998).

EP 8a

Critical Thinking Question **10-3**

Are you aware of any natural helping network in your community? If so, describe it and how it works.

The extent of support, both formal and informal, evident in any community usually contributes strength to that community. When residents work together, it's easier to get more accomplished than when isolated individuals work alone.

Empowerment and Communities

We have established that *power* is the potential ability to move people on a chosen course to produce an effect or achieve some goal (Homan, 2016). We have also defined *empowerment* as the "process of increasing personal, interpersonal, or political power so that individuals can take action to improve their life situations" (Gutierrez, 2001, p. 210). It involves purposeful, continuous process in communities where people possessing less or unequal resources gain greater access to the community's total resources. Mutual respect and cooperation should characterize the process. Social workers seek to empower client systems, including individuals, families, groups, organizations, and communities, depending on who benefits from the change effort.

Keep in mind that social workers do not hand power over to people. Rather, they help people identify potential courses of action and make decisions about which options result in greater benefits, giving them more power over their own lives and futures. In community settings, social workers can help people become empowered in two basic ways, through personal empowerment and social empowerment (Anderson, 2016).

Personal Empowerment

People have **personal empowerment** when they can directly control what's happening in their own lives. For example, on a simple level, a person can choose whether to order a cherry-chocolate double-nut ice cream cone topped with butterscotch-flavored jimmies or a peanut butter and pumpkin cone covered in chopped walnuts. Likewise, people are empowered when they can choose in which neighborhood they want to live or which job offer to accept.

Social Empowerment

Social empowerment is the condition in the social environment where people have access to opportunities and resources to make personal choices and maintain some control over their environment. Personal empowerment is limited if people don't first possess social empowerment. Laws and policies often regulate people's ability to make choices. For example, people under age 18 do not have the right to vote. Thus, they do not have the social empowerment necessary to provide input for selecting government officials.

Similarly, several decades ago many southern states restricted the use of water fountains either to people of color or White people. People were not empowered in the social environment to make their own decision regarding which water fountain to use. People choosing to use the one not designated for persons with their skin color potentially subjected themselves to severe criticism, ridicule, and even physical endangerment.

Still another example involves professional women working in an agency setting. Agency decision makers follow an unspoken rule that women make ineffective supervisors and administrators because of stereotyped gender-related characteristics. For example, administrators think women get crabby when they have their periods or they aren't strong enough to back up their decisions. Thus, women in that agency are not empowered to move up the career ladder. They do not have social empowerment.

The prior examples of social empowerment or the lack thereof primarily involve opportunities. People can also gain social empowerment by having adequate access to resources. Resources and opportunity are often integrally entwined. For example, people who earn minimum wages do not have the option of buying Rolex watches and Porsches or of living across from Central Park in Manhattan (unless they're servants or enjoy rent freezes established many years ago).

Likewise, consider people who live in poverty-stricken areas that provide relatively poor educational backgrounds. Often, these areas are digital deserts—families and sometimes entire communities lack access to the Internet, and thus the tools that are available to more affluent areas. School systems might have extremely large class sizes, giving teachers little chance of providing students with individual attention. Scarce resources result in fewer educational supplies and limited access to current technology, both in the classroom and in the home. Because of poorer educational preparation, students attending such schools are less likely to do as well on college entrance examinations, and therefore are less likely to be accepted into college. Additionally, the poorer people are, the more difficulty they have paying for higher education and vocational training. Statistics clearly establish that the more education you have, the higher your income is likely to be. Lack of current resources subsequently blocks the acquisition of future resources.

The Interrelationship of Personal and Social Empowerment

Individual and social empowerment are interrelated. It is often hard to determine where one leaves off and the other begins. When a person has social empowerment, it is much more possible to enjoy personal empowerment by exercising personal choice. More personal choices are available.

Community empowerment is a primary social work task. We have established that people are not isolated individuals doing whatever they want like mosquitoes buzzing around potential targets. Rather, each aspect of life depends on people's involvement in the communities, organizations, and groups encompassing them. The macro social environment sets the stage for what resources and opportunities are available. A focus on community empowerment enhances professional social workers' ability to help people gain better access to resources, opportunities, and, subsequently, choices.

Assessment of Communities LO 10-7

EP 6, 7a, 7b, 8

Essentially, there are two ways of looking at a community to understand it (McKnight & Block, 2010; Saleebey, 2016). First, there is the traditional focus on *community problems and needs*. This problem- or deficit-based perspective directs social workers' focus to stressing what's wrong or missing in a situation. "**Need identification** describes health and social service requirements in a geographic or social area, whereas *need* [or *needs*] *assessment* is aimed at estimating the relative importance of these needs" (Siegel, Attkisson, & Carson, 2001, p. 105).

Think about terms such as public housing, Harlem, or Watts that for many, prompt immediate thoughts of areas with a host of problems—gangs, poverty, substance abuse, crime, unemployment, welfare, homelessness, truancy, slums, child maltreatment, broken families, and poor health care. This predilection to focus on the challenges facing these areas ignores the very positive characteristics evident in every community in America. An analogy is looking at a glass as being half empty instead of half full. Not only is this problem-focused perspective overwhelming, but it encourages a spectrum of segmented services each aimed at addressing some designated, isolated problem or need. Service is provided to eligible individuals who may see themselves as service consumers or victims with little or no power to control their own destiny.

For example, a protective services agency may see Nicole, age 20, as a client who appears to be using illegal drugs and is neglecting her two small daughters. The agency's primary goal is to stop the neglect. Its purpose is to ensure survival rather than to improve Nicole's overall quality of life. Agency workers may refer Nicole to counseling, a parent effectiveness training group, or a substance abuse program, and help her receive a public assistance grant. They might consider placing her children in foster care. However, with large caseloads, there may be little they can do to help Nicole get her GED (general education diploma or high school equivalency), seek employment with good health care benefits, find adequate daycare, locate better housing, improve her cooking and child care skills, or connect with an improved social support system. With Nicole, service provision to meet specific individual needs or address designated problems is the focus.

An alternative to viewing a community and its residents from a problem-focused perspective is appraisal of and emphasis on *assets and strengths*. **Mapping assets** is an assessment of a community that emphasizes that community's strengths, capabilities, and assets instead of the community's problems and weaknesses (Community Tool Box, 2016). This approach stresses the importance of looking at the strengths of individuals, community organizations, and social institutions when analyzing any community.[4] It helps practitioners focus on what's going right for people in a community, what resources exist, and what opportunities might be developed. Capacity

---

[4] We've established that a social institution is an established and valued practice or means of operation in a society resulting in the development of a formalized system to carry out its purpose. Examples of social institutions are families, the military, religion, education, social welfare systems, and government.

building then can result. **Capacity building** "is the ability to increase the leadership and organizational skills of local people for the purpose of strengthening their own organizations and networking capacities" (Gamble & Hoff, 2005, p. 178). By identifying and focusing on a community's and its residents' assets, you can build people's capacity to empower themselves and improve their lives and living conditions.

Nicole, introduced earlier, for example, has strengths including love for her children, a foundation of parenting and homemaking skills upon which to build, friends and two sisters in the community who might help and support her, completion of her sophomore year in high school, and a strong desire to keep her two little girls. Potential community organizations to which she might turn for support include an outpatient substance abuse clinic, a vocational education and job placement program, daycare centers, support groups for single mothers held at the local YWCA,[5] and a church to which she belongs. Local institutions potentially available for her and her children's use include public social services, the school system (including an adult education program), hospitals, libraries, and parks.

The following sections will discuss community assessment. First, the many dimensions of a community will be identified to help you understand its essence and how it functions. This kind of information forms the basis for a needs assessment. The final two sections will focus on approaches concerned with community empowerment, community building, and mapping assets.

Understanding the Dimensions of a Community

There are many dimensions of a community to explore that are important to fully understand that community. Questions posed here should provide a foundation for how to identify and subsequently assess community needs. Consider the following aspects of a community (Sheafor & Horejsi, 2012, pp. 169–170):

1. *Demographics.* What are the community's boundaries and basic demographic characteristics (Kettner, Moroney, & Martin, 2017; Burghardt, 2017)? Think about the type of community it is. This includes determining the community's **population size** (the total number of persons living in a designated community), **density** (the ratio of people living within a particular space), and **heterogeneity** (the extent to which community members have diverse characteristics). What ethnic groups live in the community? Do they speak languages other than English?

   Identify the names given to various parts of the community. Are different areas known for having their own characteristics? For example, if it's a larger community, is there an industrial area with several factories? Are there some neighborhoods characterized by blue-collar families and others by wealthy professionals and businesspeople? Does one section have a university with its accompanying academic and student populations and

---

[5] YWCA (Young Women's Christian Association), established more than 150 years ago, refers to organizations around the world that serve to "eliminate racism and empower women" by providing education, social activities, recreation, and other types of support (YWCA, 2006b) in the pursuit of "justice, peace, health, human dignity, freedom, and care for the environment" (YWCA, 2006b).

activities? Where is the community located with respect to other communities, towns, and cities? Is it relatively isolated or close to other communities that could provide resources and services?

What is the area's history? How old is the community? How has it developed over time? What changes have occurred regarding who has populated the area? Have certain groups moved away and others moved in? If so, why?

2. *Geography and environmental influences on community.* What kind of environment characterizes the community (Rubin & Rubin, 2008)? Is it in the middle of the central prairies, connected by interstate highways with other communities at great distances? Is it located on an ocean, major river, or one of the Great Lakes, where shipping and boating are primary economic and recreational activities, respectfully? Is it located in the mountains where winter might cause transportation difficulties? Are there recreational areas such as parks available? To what extent is the community experiencing environmental hazards such as pollution, smog, or tainted water, or deprivations such as power shortages? We must realize that the decisions and actions that result in these and other challenges are often made in the contexts of organizations. The organizations may be businesses looking to make a larger profit by avoiding environmental laws in the United States by moving their industries to countries that lack such restrictions. They may be local companies that try to reduce cost by dumping toxic chemicals into the public sewer system or by burying it in low-income neighborhoods. Other sources may include community planning commissions, city councils, and governing bodies who avoid locating hazards in middle and upper income sections of the community but have few, if any, qualms about siting them in low-income areas. If organizations or organizational figures, public or private, makes a decision that exposes a portion of the population to environmental hazards or risks, they are engaging in environmental injustice. Knowing the source of a problem may help in solving it.

3. *Beliefs and attitudes.* What are the traditions, beliefs, and values that characterize the population or segments of the population (Netting et al., 2017)? What are the spiritual and political values of the various factions of community residents? What social service agencies are available in the community, and how do residents receive and value them? To what extent do residents feel an integral and supported part of the community? Or do they feel isolated and alone?

4. *Local politics.* How is the government structured? For example, cities, towns, and counties can be structured quite differently in terms of who has decision-making power and control. Are there any major issues currently under debate? For example, residents might have conflicting views regarding paying for a new middle school or rezoning a residential area to a business one.

5. *Local economy and businesses.* What businesses, factories, and other sources of employment characterize the community? Is the local economy thriving or in a major slump? Are businesses owned by local residents or huge conglomerates based in other states? What kinds of jobs exist in the community? Do people work inside the community or simply live here and work

somewhere else? Is there adequate public transportation for people to get to and from work? What is the unemployment rate?

6. *Income distribution.* To what extent do community residents receive cash and in-kind (goods and services) public assistance benefits? What are the median income levels for men, women, and various ethnic groups? Does it vary by area within the community? What percentage of people live in poverty?

7. *Housing.* What are housing conditions like in the community? Is it a relatively new community with low population density? Or it is an aging, poor community with high population density and deteriorating, dilapidated housing? What are the "types of housing" characterizing the area (e.g., "single-family dwellings, apartments, public housing") (Sheafor & Horejsi, 2012, p. 169)? What are average rents and costs for real estate? Is there a shortage of low-income housing?

8. *Educational facilities and programs.* An educational system can be assessed in at least four ways. The first involves its context. What is the educational system like? Are schools well supported by the community, or are they experiencing repetitive funding cuts? Where and in what types of neighborhoods are schools located? Are they public, private, or charter schools? A *charter school* is a public school supported by tax dollars but allowed to be managed (chartered) outside of the jurisdiction of the local school board but in accordance with state regulations; its curriculum, targeted population, or educational philosophy usually diverges from other schools in the system (Massat, Constable, McDonald, & Flynn, 2009).

The second way an educational system can be assessed involves its treatment of special populations of children and its attention to cultural differences. How are children with special needs treated? To what extent are programs available for preschool children to prepare them for school entry? For instance, are Head Start programs available? Are there diagnostic and treatment services available for children who have developmental disabilities? Are schools perceptive regarding the ethnic and cultural makeup of their students? Do they celebrate or discourage diversity? If needed, are bilingual programs available?

A third way to assess the functioning of a community's educational system is the extent to which the school system enables students to reach their potential. How do children typically score on standardized achievement tests compared to other communities in the United States and Canada? How well do community students compete with students from other communities in events such as science fairs, spelling competitions, and other contests? How well prepared are students for high school and college? How many students graduate and go on to college? Does elementary school provide them with a solid foundation for future levels of higher education, vocational education, and job training? What is the dropout rate?

A fourth assessment aspect concerns an educational system's concern and focus on adults in the community. On the one hand, to what extent do parents understand their children's development? On the other, how well do community educational programs adequately prepare adults to enter the labor force?

9. *Health and welfare systems.* A community's strengths concerning residents' health primarily involve access to and quality of care. Are there adequate

numbers of health professionals and specialists? Are hospitals and clinics readily accessible to area residents? Are there services available to address problems specific to low-income and students-of-color who experience disproportionate rates of certain illnesses or conditions?

What social service programs are available and where are they located? What specific types of services exist (e.g., crisis intervention, substance abuse treatment, and public assistance)? How accessible and well publicized are these programs? To what extent are they adequate, or are there substantial gaps in service? To what extent do service providers respect the needs and values of minority populations? If the community has non-English-speaking residents, are translators available? Are "self-help groups and informal helping networks" available in the community (Sheafor & Horejsi, 2012, p. 170)?

To what extent are fire and police protection adequate? To what extent is the environment safe? Are housing standards and codes being followed? How do community residents view the justice system and feel they are treated by it and by police officers? Are the public safety and justice systems sensitive to the needs and issues faced by minorities in the community?

10. *Sources of information and public opinion.* Are there "influential TV and radio stations and newspapers to which the people look for information and perspectives on current events" (Sheafor & Horejsi, 2012, p. 170)? We have established that knowledge is power. It is therefore important to ask how members of the community learn what is going on in the community as well as in the world at large (Rubin & Rubin, 2008). Are there neighborhood organizations or other active community groups whose purposes are to keep on top of what's going on within the community? For example, are residents aware that commercial developers are planning to build a toxic waste plant in the near vicinity? Do residents know the student-to-teacher ratio in classrooms? Do community members know about a job-training program subsidized by the county and targeting people in need?

To what extent does the community have human resources? **Human resources** are the knowledge and abilities characterizing some people that can be used to enhance other people's quality of life. Human resources are people who can act as advocates, initiators, planners, educators, leaders, and workers for positive social changes. Are there significant community political, religious, or other informal community leaders who speak for various subgroups and minorities in the population and to whom people look to for help and support?

11. *Summary assessment of community issues.* What is your overall assessment of the community's functioning? To what extent is it good or inadequate? What serious social problems (e.g., "inadequate housing, inadequate public transportation, insufficient law enforcement, lack of jobs, youth gangs, poverty, teen pregnancy, domestic abuse") do community residents face (Sheafor & Horejsi, 2012, p. 170)? What primary "gaps" are evident in "social, health care, and educational services" (Sheafor & Horejsi, 2012, p. 170)?

Highlight 10-3 discusses ways to gather data about a community.

EP 8a

Critical Thinking Questions **10-4**

How would you analyze your own community in terms of these 11 criteria? How would you summarize the information? What are your community's primary problems, needs, and strengths?

| Highlight **10-3** |

How to Gather Data about a Community

EP 7a

There are many ways of collecting data to assess a community. Four will be introduced here that are often used in conducting a needs assessment.

First, you can hold a **public forum** (Burghardt, 2014; Lewis, Lewis, Daniels, & D'Andrea, 2011). This is an open event where all community residents are invited and encouraged to attend. Any community member may serve as a significant source of information. Community members know firsthand what the community's strengths, needs, and issues are. They can also indicate how easy it is to get the services and resources they need within the community. Although probably no individual can give you the "total picture" of what a community needs, he or she might provide some valuable insights. Getting information from a variety of residents can result in a general picture of community needs.

Reviewing **social indicators** is a second means of assessing a community's needs. "Social indicators include demographic characteristics, health and education statistics, socioeconomic variables, employment patterns, and family patterns" (Lewis et al., 2011, p. 272). The focus of attention would depend on what community issues were being addressed. For instance, if you wanted to investigate the needs of community teenagers, you "might begin by reviewing local statistics, such as the juvenile delinquency rate, suicide rate, school dropout rate, or divorce figures" (Lewis et al., 2011, p. 272).

A third needs assessment approach is the **nominal group technique** (Toseland & Rivas, 2008, 2012). Here, group members are gathered and asked to silently write down the needs that exist in their community. This elicits a large list of individually identified needs without any group discussion that might interfere with generating an individual's true feelings. After members have completed their lists, the group leader asks them to go around one at a time and share one of their ideas with the rest of the group. Ideas are then recorded on a whiteboard, on large sheets of paper, or electronically so that they are visible to the group. After all ideas have been recorded, group members participate in a discussion regarding their feelings about the needs that have been shared. After the leader determines that discussion has been adequate, he or she asks group members to prioritize and write down what they feel are the community's most pressing needs. The leader then collects the lists and can combine them to determine the group's overall impression of community needs. This is often followed by a prioritization of the list to identify those the group feels are most important.

A fourth needs assessment approach is the **key informant** technique (Kirst-Ashman & Hull, 2018a; Netting et al., 2012). Key informants are select individuals in the community who have extensive knowledge and understanding of the community's needs and issues. Participants might include service providers such as police officers or teachers, residents who have resided in the community a long time and have been active in community events, and workers in community service agencies. Participants who serve as key informants are then interviewed in depth concerning their perceptions of community needs. A summary regarding their impression of community needs can subsequently be established.

Community Building   `LO 10-8`

EP 5b, 8b, 8c

Community building is a vital concept in an empowerment approach. Chapter 9 discussed it in the context of generalist practice in rural communities. Community building involves the process of enhancing a community's strengths by linking community residents, organizations in the community, and external resources to tackle community problems and work together toward positive change (Briggs, 2008; Milligan, 2008; Rubin & Rubin, 2008). All communities obviously have problems and needs. The trick is to scrutinize potential strengths, often easily overlooked, and to get relevant entities to work together on behalf of community growth and improvement. Saleebey (2006) explains:

EP 7c, 7d, 8, 8d

> Community building refers to the reality and possibility of restoring or refurbishing the sense and reality of community in neighborhoods. It involves among other things helping neighbors—individuals, families, and associations—in a community to strengthen relationships with one another usually around mutually crafted projects. The idea is to replace the notion that they must be completely dependent on outside or professional organizations and institutions for help with the assumptions that they have internal assets and capacities that can be developed and used in increasing the human and social capital of the community. The upshot of this is an increase in the sense of self-efficacy and power in the individuals, families, and associations of the community—they believe that they can make things happen! (p. 255)

Chapter 1 introduced the concept of community organization. Essentially, community building is a dimension of community organizing and macro practice. Highlight 10-4 discusses President Barack Obama's experience in community building in his role as a community organizer.

| Highlight **10-4** |

President Barack Obama's Experience in Community Organization and Community Building

Some might say that an effective community organizer is "a combination of educator, confessor-priest, social activist, motivational expert, mediator, and campaign leader"; thus, one of his colleagues described President Barack Obama during Obama's experience in community organizing and community building (Walsh, 2007).

Walsh (2007) depicts Obama's history. Obama graduated from Columbia University in 1983, having majored in political science. Initially, he worked in New York City as a financial consultant, a job of which he soon tired. He then moved to Chicago in 1985 to work for the newly established Developing Communities Project (DCP) as a community organizer. DCP was "a community group based in the churches of the region, an expanse of white, black and Latino blue-collar neighborhoods that were reeling from the steel-mill closings" (Moberg, 2007). His salary was $10,000 a year with an additional $2,000 thrown in to purchase "a beat-up blue Honda Civic" (Moberg, 2007) so he could get around and do his job. There Obama worked among the "seemingly endless clumps of drab brick apartment buildings and patchy lawns on Chicago's South Side" (Walsh, 2007). He served among the 5,300 African Americans who lived "amid shuttered steel mills, a nearby landfill, a putrid sewage treatment plant, and a pervasive feeling that the white establishment of Chicago would never give them a fair shake" (Walsh, 2007).

continued

Highlight **10-4** *continued*

Obama (1990) comments on the meaning of community organizing:

> In theory, community organizing provides a way to merge various strategies for neighborhood empowerment. . . . This means bringing together churches, block clubs, parent groups and any other institutions in a given community to pay dues, hire organizers, conduct research, develop leadership, hold rallies and education campaigns, and begin drawing up plans on a whole range of issues—jobs, education, crime, etc. Once such a vehicle is formed, it holds the power to make politicians, agencies and corporations more responsive to community needs. Equally important, it enables people to break their crippling isolation from each other, to reshape their mutual values and expectations and rediscover the possibilities of acting collaboratively—the prerequisites of any successful self-help drive.

Obama (1990) speaks of DCP's accomplishments that include establishing job training programs in schools, repairing and restoring housing, improving city services, developing parks, and curbing crime and drug trafficking. He worked on such issues as getting potholes filled, developing summer jobs for youth, and urging housing managers "to repair toilets, pipes, and ceilings" (Walsh, 2007). Possibly, Obama's most contentious experience involved organizing residents to confront public housing administrators about removing dangerous asbestos from area housing (Walsh, 2007). He led residents—although "far fewer than Obama had anticipated—to challenge authorities downtown. Ultimately, the city was forced to test all the apartments and eventually begin cleaning them up" (Moberg, 2007).

Ultimately, Obama left DCP for other pursuits (Walsh, 2007). In 1988 he began law school at Harvard, in 1990 he "became the first African-American president of *Harvard Law Review*," and in 1991 he graduated with his law degree (Walsh, 2007). He then became a civil rights lawyer in Chicago and taught law at the University of Chicago. In due course, he became an Illinois state senator and eventually a US senator in 2004.

Some claim Obama's community-organizing work taught him how to listen well, minimize conflict, and involve a wide range of people in establishing a consensus (Lawrence, 2008; Moberg, 2007). This experience may be what made him decide to devote his life to public service (Moberg, 2007).

Developing a healthy, productive and integrated community involves four major principles. These include working together, creating new connections and coalitions, targeting specific neighborhoods, and building on their strengths (Saleebey, 2016; Kirst-Ashman & Hull, 2018a).

Working Together

First, community building involves many components of a community and other systems with which it's involved working synchronously together. If community resource systems don't work together, nothing much gets done. For example, a community high school may have a strong vocational component aimed at training for and placing students in jobs upon graduation. Related components are adequate employment opportunities and affordable housing. The high school's efforts are virtually useless if no adequately paying jobs for high school graduates exist in the area and no public transportation is available for workers to get to jobs located elsewhere. What good is a job if no affordable housing is available? Where would workers live?

New Alliances and Cooperation

A second principle basic to community building is that it requires new alliances and cooperation. These relationships involve both those among agencies within the community and those between community agencies and external, larger systems.

The first dimension of this principle, *internal cooperation* among community organizations and groups, might involve new creative ways in which they can work together to serve residents. For example, a church, YMCA,[6] and outpatient substance abuse counseling center might combine their efforts in outreach for youth. They might work together contributing staff time, resources, and space to establish a program offering a series of services. These may include drug education provided by counseling center staff at the church and the YMCA, supervised social activities cosponsored by all three agencies, space provided by the YMCA for recreational activities for youth involved in both church groups and abuse counseling, and publicity developed and distributed by the church and the YMCA. These three agencies have no formal connections with each other. Yet, they could potentially work together to establish a unified program available to a wide spectrum of community youth.

Another dimension of establishing new alliances in community building is *external cooperation*. This concerns how organizations and groups in the community must work well together with external macro systems in order to meet community needs. Community residents know what they need and are experts on how public resource systems work or do not work on their behalf. A high-level White male policy maker in Washington, D.C., likely has little insight into the life of a single African-American mother of three who has an 11th-grade education and lives in a tiny two-room apartment in a huge urban hub. How could that administrator know the myriad of details and problems she must address every day to stay alive? There's a crack house next door. She's afraid of what would happen to her kids if they wander too near the dealers and the addicts. Prostitutes walk the streets every night. She's not certain how well her baby-sitter attends to her kids while she's at work. She can just barely make the rent and the grocery bill each week. She's afraid to tell the landlord someone broke her back window because she fears he might evict her. Sometimes, she's late with the rent and doesn't want to make any waves.

The point is that community residents usually have the best understanding about what affects their lives. They really need to provide input into decisions made far above in the bureaucratic structure that have major and sometimes ominous effects on their lives. Hence, we heavily emphasize community resident involvement and leadership.

However, major resources flow into communities from larger city, state, and national macro systems. Communities depend on these resources. Bureaucratic structures are complicated, and regulations for funding distribution are complex. Communities don't have the power and influence to formulate policies and make decisions about how public funds at national and state levels are spent. Community residents and leaders generally have a more limited perspective on what's going on outside of their community. Thus, their focus is more likely to be on community- or neighborhood-specific issues rather than addressing large-scale policy issues and more complex situations. Therefore, community residents and leaders must work together with decision makers in external systems to understand processes and obtain resources the community deserves.

---

[6] YMCA (Young Men's Christian Association), initiated over 150 years ago, refers to organizations in over 120 countries that provide a wide range of educational, recreational, social, and supportive services to community residents, including "all people of all faiths, races, ages, abilities and incomes" (YMCA, 2006a).

The Importance of Targeting Neighborhoods

The third principle involved in community building is the importance of targeting neighborhoods to undertake positive change on behalf of the community. Successful macro changes tend to be geographical-specific, focused on neighborhoods where clients live and the local institutions with which they are already connected. This means involving community services, centers, churches, schools, and other resources already present. Chapter 11 examines more thoroughly how neighborhoods function and can empower residents.

Building on Neighborhood Strengths

Neighborhoods are central to the fourth salient principle in community building. The foundation for positive macro change rests on neighborhood strengths and assets. Neighborhood residents know the most about their needs. They have much in common in that they experience similar living conditions. The basic social work values of self-determination and empowerment dictate that neighborhood residents should have maximum choices about what happens in their own lives.

Mapping assets is a tool to prepare for community building. A subsequent section elaborates upon this approach.

Focus on Ethics 10-2 helps explore the extent to which community building in all its facets complies with professional ethics.

Community Building in Rural Communities   LO 10-9

Much of the literature on community building is oriented toward urban development (Merritt & Collins, 2008; Messinger, 2004). Therefore, we will spend some time here elaborating on the potential for community building in rural communities. First, we will review briefly the context of the rural community. Then we will provide some examples of community-building approaches that have been used effectively in rural communities.

Focus on Ethics **10-2**

Community Building and Professional Ethics

EP 1, 1a

We have established that the six core values in the NASW *Code of Ethics* are (NASW, 2008):

1. *Service*: Providing help, resources, and benefits so that people may achieve their maximum potential.
2. *Social justice*: The philosophical perspective that all people have the right to enjoy equal opportunities in economic, political, and social realms.
3. *Dignity and worth of the person*: Holding in high esteem and appreciating individual value.

4. *Importance of human relationships*: Valuing the dynamic reciprocal interactions between social workers and clients, including how they communicate, think and feel about each other, and behave toward each other.
5. *Integrity*: Maintaining trustworthiness and sound adherence to moral ideals.
6. *Competence*: Having the necessary skills and abilities to perform work with clients effectively.

To what extent does the concept of community building comply with these principles? Explain.

Chapter 9 examined rural communities and identified some of the differences between them and urban environments. Population density is low in rural communities compared with urban. They tend to be located far from urban centers and lack much diversity in functioning. For example, a farming community and any services it has would be oriented toward the support of farming. Similarly, a mining community would focus on sustaining mining. Additionally, lack of employment and poverty often characterize rural areas (Merritt & Collins, 2008). Resources are scarcer than in urban hubs, and therefore services are fewer and less specialized.

Rural residents often have a different perspective on life and the environment than their urban counterparts. Merritt and Collins (2008) remark that it is:

> possible that rural residents define their relationship with the natural environment differently than urban residents. For a trivial, but maybe meaningful example, consider the nicknames of rural high school sports teams such as the Farmington Farmers and the Hoopeston Cornjerkers in Illinois, the Hematites [a type of local mineral often used in making jewelry] of Ishpeming, Michigan and the Biglerville Canners in the apple orchards of Pennsylvania. These nicknames denote rural communities closely connected to their surrounding natural environment and economic base. (p. 151)

Subsequent sections provide case examples of and suggestions for rural community building.

Case Example: The Warren Family Institute

EP 7a, 7c, 7d, 8, 8e

Messinger (2004) describes a grant-funded demonstration project that established the Warren Family Institute (WFI) in Warren County, a rural county in eastern North Carolina. As a **comprehensive community initiative** (CCI), WFI "strategy uses coalitions of public and private agencies, religious organizations, neighborhood groups, community leaders, and individuals in the community to work together on neighborhood councils, task forces, planning committees, and advisory boards to identify needs in the community and to develop and implement a comprehensive plan for multisystem change. . . . Rather than using a single strategy targeting one 'cause' of a social problem, CCIs offer a comprehensive systems approach that attacks complex problems on a variety of fronts" (p. 535).

Messinger (2004) describes the context of Warren County:

> Like many rural areas in the southern United States, Warren County suffers from the replacement of small family farms by corporate agribusiness, sparse economic development, and substandard and inadequate housing. The county's poverty is evidenced by the dubious honor of having the highest percentage of privies [outdoor toilets or, in more colloquial language, outhouses] in the state. (p. 537)

Many of the impoverished residents were isolated and located far apart. Whereas much "community building" is oriented toward empowering urban neighborhoods (as Chapter 11 will explain), the neighborhood concept doesn't readily apply to many rural communities because of the demographics. Rural residents generally don't live that close together.

Social services agencies serving Warren County also often were responsible for several other counties on a regional basis. This resulted in sparse service provision in Warren County. There were only a few small manufacturers in the county that served as employers and provided some tax revenues, although there was a prison, some nursing homes, and some small businesses.

Community strengths included "the presence of good neighbors," the quiet rural setting, and, for some, the support of an extended family network (Messinger, 2004, p. 540).

The WFI planning group initially included representatives from nonprofit social services agencies, "churches, and service organizations, along with county officials" (Messinger, 2004, p. 538). Low-income county residents at first participated by conducting a door-to-door needs assessment. Because citizen participation is so essential, eventually residents became involved at all levels of the organization. Some became members of the board of directors. Others served as representatives at public meetings. Still others became employed as WFI staff.

> The institute attacked the roots of the social and economic problems of low-income families through a three-pronged approach. They partnered low-income families with the institute's family services coordinators, caseworkers who provided support to family members, advocated on the families' behalf with local agencies' staffs, and mentored family leaders to help them be more self-sufficient. The institute also facilitated interorganizational collaboration and coordinated joint projects among local agencies to make better use of their combined resources. Finally, the institute worked to change policies at local and regional agencies that were damaging to low-income families, collaborative planning efforts, and overall development of the county. (Messinger, 2004, p. 538)

Issues that WFI addressed included "unemployment and underemployment, lack of education, poor health care, lack of community involvement, disorganized service provision, and inadequate and substandard housing, with the ultimate purpose of helping low-income families become self-sufficient" (Messinger, 2004, p. 536).

WFI was able to implement a range of programs and projects, including:

- housing repair days
- a first-time homebuyer education and counseling program
- a locally administered, tenant-based rental assistance program
- tenant–landlord mediation services
- transitional housing services
- re-establishment of a county housing authority
- creation of evening family health assessment
- information and referral services
- leadership development training with low-income residents
- the establishment of a summer program for youths
- the creation and coordination of VISTA[7] . . . volunteer opportunities

---

[7] *VISTA* is a national service program to fight poverty in the United States, established in 1965, in which volunteers "commit to serve full-time for a year at a nonprofit organization or local government agency, working to fight illiteracy, improve health services, create businesses, strengthen community groups, and much more" (Corporation for National & Community Service, 2009b).

- the creation of instructional programs and community-building events
- the purchase of a van to transport low-income residents to and from job training and community college classes (Messinger, 2004, p. 541)

Enhancing Rural Youths' Interest in Higher Education

Poole and More (2004) address the problem of encouraging rural youths' interest in higher education. "Rural youth are half as likely to obtain a college degree as their peers in urban and suburban communities. The situation is worse for rural African Americans and Hispanics, only 4% of whom graduate from college" (p. 147).

Reasons Why Rural Youth May Not Seek Higher Education A wide range of factors operates against rural young people aspiring for college degrees (Poole & More, 2004). *Institutional factors* include:

- "As a group, rural youth tend to be less academically prepared for college than their peers in urban school systems. Rural students generally have lower achievement scores on standardized tests and less access to advanced preparatory courses, which deter them from attending college" (p. 148).
- Rural students may experience less encouragement from teachers to attend college and may not receive adequate information about college and potential careers initiated in college.
- College costs may be prohibitive to rural youth, who are more likely than many urban and suburban youth to come from families with lower incomes.

Community factors working against college enrollment include:

- Because many jobs in rural areas do not require a college education, rural youth may not have adequate exposure to role models—people with a college education. Youth may not clearly see the benefits of attaining a college degree.
- "Community members without a college degree sometimes do not recognize the benefits of higher education" (p. 149). Therefore, they would be less likely to encourage college attendance. Community residents may also be hesitant to encourage youth to leave the rural community because it further depletes the population and potential community resources.
- Often, rural communities are located far from colleges and universities, posing geographical obstacles to college attendance.

Family factors against higher education include:

- If parents don't have college degrees, they may be less likely to encourage their children to pursue them.
- "Rural parents often lack information about available resources for college" (p. 150).
- Rural families may have less access to financial resources.

Individual factors inhibiting college enrollment include:

- "Many rural youths are not confident that they can compete successfully in a college environment" (p. 150).

- "Rural students often have low educational and occupational aspirations" due partially "to socioeconomic status" (p. 150).
- "Educational achievement levels are low among rural females," many of whom decide to marry early (p. 151).
- We've already established that rural African American and Hispanic youth are even less likely to get college degrees than their White counterparts.
- It is often very difficult for rural youth to leave their home communities for a radically different college environment, often in an urban setting. They just don't feel they can handle the "culture shock" of it all (p. 151).

EP 7d, 8e

So What Is the Answer?   Poole and More (2004) propose several community-building suggestions to encourage college attendance by rural youth. Educational institutions and the community can address the issue in many ways. Schools can raise expectations for academic performance. They can offer college preparatory courses to begin socializing students for college involvement. One means of doing this is to provide Web-based courses. Schools can also accelerate efforts to provide information about colleges and careers to students early on. Rural students may then be more likely to see college as a viable option. Schools can also provide workshops for school staff, providing them with current information about college and teaching them ways they can portray college attendance in a positive light. Scholarships can be established to assist rural students in financial need. Additionally, schools can identify and link rural students with college-educated mentors where available.

Family strategies include providing workshops for and meetings with rural parents. These can be used to educate parents about opportunities available with a college education, the college application process, and financial planning for college. Individual strategies to encourage rural youths' college potential include inviting college faculty to meet with students and talk to them about the college experience. Students require self-confidence that they can indeed be successful in college. "Tutoring, academic advising, ACT preparation, and [teaching] problem-solving" skills may also enhance motivation to attend college (p. 154). Campus visits also can acquaint students and their families with the college environment and college life. The unknown is often scary. The more familiar students are with the idea of college attendance and what it might be like, the more comfortable they will likely feel.

The idea here is that generalist social workers can help rural communities to develop innovative strategies for addressing problems. This example, of course, focuses on the educational dimensions of a rural community. Highlight 10-5 provides one school social worker's perspective on working in a rural community.

Additional Development Strategies for Rural Communities

EP 7d

Industrialization and capitalist competition have not been very helpful to rural communities. Such "progress" made it difficult for small family farmers to compete with "corporate agribusiness" (Messinger, 2004, p. 537). Merritt and Collins (2008) propose at least three potential ways that rural communities can develop their resources. Generalist social work practitioners can help community members organize themselves and pursue these ideas.

Highlight **10-5**

Working as a Rural School Social Worker

EP 1b, 1c

Line (2005) talks about her experience as a school social worker in the rural Upper Peninsula of Michigan.[8] She describes the area as "about as rural an area as one can get. Some would even call it a wilderness area"; she was one of three school social workers in a three-county school district covering 4,000 square miles that "had more deer than people" (p. 105).

Line (2005) describes the community's residents:

People who lived in this area were very independent and proud. They had been used to working their land, bartering for their needs with their neighbors, and surviving as a result of their own efforts. They all lived like one big, extended family and helped each other without being asked. (p. 106)

It was very difficult for residents to ask for help from "outsiders" whom they neither knew nor trusted; this included school staff although "the school was the focal point for community life" (Line, 2005, p. 106). Having moved from the urban bustle of Detroit, a rural community was quite a change for Line. Because of the huge area and low population density, the job required a lot of driving, both traveling between schools and doing home visits. She remarks:

Some of the home visits were memorable, to say the least. Directions to homes were given by landmarks, not by miles or road names. One went to a home based on: "It is the first white house on the right, after the dairy farm. If you go up the hill, you have gone too far. There is a blue pickup in the driveway." (p. 106)

Line describes some of her various home visit experiences of being welcomed by a flock of lookout geese in addition to "a variety of dogs, goats, and sheep" (2005, p. 107). She indicates that these creatures weren't posted to "get the social worker," but rather they just meandered about the yard at will as a normal part of the scheme of things. She indicated she learned to wear only washable clothing and to not take along anything she "could not do without, in the event it was eaten" (p. 107).

Line stressed that doing her job necessitated true generalist skills in working with various size systems; she was frequently required "to work with individuals, groups of parents, staff or administrators, agencies, and communities" (2005, pp. 107–108). She emphasized how fast information traveled by word of mouth. If something happened one night, the whole community seemed to know about it by the next morning. Because of this communication system, it was very important to establish a good reputation. Only then would community members begin to trust and work with you. Reputation was also important in work with other agencies because networking and working together in rural communities are critical.

Line also underscored the importance of confidentiality. Everyone seemed to know everyone else. So, if one person asked how another was doing, it was important not to violate anyone's privacy. She prepared herself with pat responses like, "I am sorry but I cannot talk about my clients," or, "Isn't the weather awful today?" (the latter is actually answering one question with another question, which is quite a tricky maneuver) (2005, p. 107).

Line indicates that one dynamic in her rural community experience is that "EVERYONE KNOWS your personal beliefs" (2005, p. 109). Therefore, it is important to distinguish personal from professional values, and remain nonjudgmental in interventions with clients. She concludes that she is quite satisfied with her practice in a rural community. To her, "people everywhere are just people and need to be respected for the individuals that they are" (p. 109).

First, "community-supported agriculture" involves:

a consumer cooperative where a farmer sells subscriptions or shares to several dozen households. The farmer takes this money and buys seeds and other inputs to start the growing season. As crops ripen, subscribers can expect a weekly basket of vegetables, fruits, herbs, cut flowers and other items. The farm and subscribers both share the agricultural bounty and the risks. (p. 153)

---

[8] The contents of this highlight are taken from the book *Days in the Lives of Social Workers* (3rd ed.), written by Linda May Grobman (ed.) and published by White Hat Communications in Harrisburg, PA. It provides an excellent source of a wide range of interesting "real-life" stories about social work practice.

A second development strategy concerns "agritourism," where:

> farmers can offer educational experiences to urban tourists who are willing to pay to learn about agriculture and country life. Activities include barn tours, hayrides, u-pick gardens, orchards, hiking, horseback riding, and mountain biking. To teach students where their meals come from, some farmers have planted "pizza farms," a circular plot divided into wedges. Each wedge is planted with an ingredient used to make pizza. One wedge might have herbs; another might have wheat. Yet others might have tomatoes or a grazing dairy cow as the source of cheese. Each wedge is divided by a pathway so tourists can get close to each ingredient. In Massachusetts, the Hyland Orchard and Brewery combines a brewpub with a petting zoo so parents and children can have fun. (pp. 153–154)

A third approach to rural development concerns "producer cooperatives." Merritt and Collins (2008) explain:

> Instead of shipping raw commodities such as soybeans elsewhere for processing, farmers are forming so-called new generation cooperatives (NGCs) to process locally-grown commodities in the community. This increases on-farm profits, generates local jobs, and increases the local tax base, while taking advantage of the rural competitive advantages in crop production. NGCs also lessen the risk of capital flight [where rural residents migrate to cities in search of better jobs and financial prospects] because farmers and other community investors own the processing facilities. (p. 154)

Mapping Community Assets and Empowerment LO 10-10

EP 7a, 7c, 7d

Earlier we discussed the capacity-building approach to community assessment called **mapping assets**. It emphasizes the community's potential based on already present knowledge, skills, and assets rather than focus on the challenges and problems faced by the community. **Assets** are potential persons, groups, and resources in a community that can help it grow and prosper. It contrasts with the community-assessment approach we reviewed earlier that focused primarily on figuring out a community's problems and gaps in services. Three primary principles characterize assets-based community development.

- Identify and describe the current capabilities and capacities of residents, change agents, and local institutions.
- Identify local problems and develop solutions.
- Enhance relationships among residents, change agents, and local institutions.

Mapping assets, then, is devoted to identifying and building the capacities of individuals, as well as empowering community resources to address challenges facing the community.

Identify and Describe Individual Capacities

Each community resident has positive qualities and capacities that can contribute to the community's well-being. If those capacities are identified and appreciated by fellow citizens, the individual will feel like an important community member with a sense of connection to other citizens. These capacities reflect many dimensions of abilities and skills, including the following:

Health/Mental Health   Individuals, family members, neighbors, or volunteers can provide help to community residents who need it. This may take the form of assisting people who are seniors, those who have mental disorders, physical or intellectual disabilities, or other health problems.

Management and Office Work Skills   Individuals may also have organization and office skills they could volunteer to help develop a neighborhood organization or support a social service or health care agency. Such skills might include computer proficiency, budgeting, planning, telephone communication, marketing and sales, writing reports, and organizing data and records.

Building and Repair Skills   Being handy at building and fixing things can be helpful. Repairing buildings, improving homes, and fixing electrical and plumbing fixtures are skills that can contribute to community well-being. Consider Habitat for Humanity, an international organization whose overarching goal is "to accelerate and broaden access to affordable housing as a foundation for breaking the cycle of poverty . . . by helping to build, renovate or preserve homes" (Habitat for Humanity, 2012). To do this, the organization solicits donations from sponsors and help from volunteers. People skilled in construction and repair have valuable assets to contribute. Even if a person lacks the ability to pound a nail, Habitat for Humanity can likely use individuals for picking up discarded material from the building site.

Even without working within a formal structure, community residents can help their neighbors by using specific skills. Staff in one community social services organization wrote and received a grant for starting a tool library. Community residents could "take out" tools and use them for household construction and repair. They later would return them to the tool library, just as they would a book from a traditional library. Another example is an individual who served as a resource for his neighbors doing such as things as installing a mailbox, vacuuming water in the basement from a burst water heater, or resetting circuit breakers for a nearby sorority house when the lights went out.

Cleaning and Maintenance Skills   Community residents may contribute time and effort to help maintain and clean up buildings, parks, and public facilities. For example, various groups, businesses, or families volunteer to clean up garbage along highways in Adopt-a-Highway programs. Or a group of community residents could volunteer to renovate a park area, as did members of a local Kiwanis club. Older adults remaining in their own home may need help mowing grass or shoveling walks or getting to a medical appointment.

Meal Preparation and Food   Some people are skilled at food preparation. People can volunteer to set up, cook, barbeque, and clean up for a neighborhood picnic or other community event. Others may be skilled at gardening and raising vegetables and fruits.

Recreation and Entertainment   Community volunteers could organize sports teams and events for youth or adults. One neighborhood organization in an impoverished community of a large city established sports teams for high-school-age youth. This provided an excellent alternative to participating in illegal and idle activities. All participants were required to maintain at least a B average in school. Volunteer coaches were supportive and worked hard at reinforcing positive behavior, not only on the court, but also in terms of conflict resolution and interpersonal skills. The tallest team member was only 6-foot, 2 inches, which, as we know, is not very tall in the basketball world. However, the team managed to make it to and compete in the national championship against players who loomed above them. Although they didn't win, they became the much-applauded and well-respected underdogs. They beamed with self-confidence and pride at their accomplishments.

Some community residents may be musically talented. They can organize into an orchestra or a band and give concerts or play during parades. One neighborhood resident was highly skilled at playing the piano. She gave monthly concerts to all neighbors who were interested in attending. Even high school students with musical talent can play or perform at nursing homes, assisted living centers, and other congregate sites.

Assistance in Daily Activities   There are many other arenas of life where community residents can help each other. Working parents might provide child care for each other. Or senior residents might volunteer to provide daycare for children. A resident with a car could volunteer to take another resident without transportation to buy groceries. One neighbor could mow another neighbor's lawn or help change the oil in his car. One community member might help another with sewing or mending clothing.

Anything Else   Potential sources of individual assets and contributions are infinite. Asking individuals what they feel their strengths are and how they could help might result in answers that never would've occurred to you. For example, a low-income mother wanted to make clothing for her child but had no sewing machine. Another community member, hearing about the need, volunteered that she had a sewing machine in her basement that she was no longer using and gave it away to the new mother. Another couple learned that a woman was moving into an apartment after leaving a halfway house but had no furniture. They donated a couch that was otherwise sitting unused in their basement. You will never know what assets are available unless you ask.

Highlight 10-6 suggests ways to undertake mapping assets in a community.

Critical Thinking Questions 10-5

EP 8a

How would you assess your own individual capacities with respect to the dimensions of abilities and skills just cited? What do you consider as your most important three assets?

Highlight 10-6

Mapping Assets of Local Associations, Organizations, and Institutions: Gathering Information

EP 7a

In addition to assessing individual capacities, it is important to find out what associations, organizations, and institutions exist in the community and how they function; there are at least four ways to do this. First, look to media such as online resources (most agencies have Web pages), and newspapers and newsletters for printed information. Service directories might be available.

A second way to find out about community services is to use the library. "Your public library has a treasure trove of information about your community, and so does your college or university library"; Homan (2016) reflects:

> Prepare some questions in advance. This will give the librarian a better idea of how to help you. It will also help you focus your inquiry. Most librarians are very helpful. Not only do they know books and where to find them, but they enjoy helping people uncover information and discover the other wonders of their library, such as audiovisual resources, access to databases, maps, and much more. (p. 159)

A third way to gather information about services and organizations is to talk to people in the community. This might include representatives from churches, or social agencies, or people you encounter in the park. To what groups do people belong in the community? These may be political, recreational, volunteer, or social. You can also contact individual leaders of various organizations for their insights. Finally, you can simply start conversations with people you run into as you go about your daily business (Homan, 2016). You might be sitting at the bus stop or standing in line at Walmart. Informal conversation can provide you with valuable insights and ideas.

A fourth means of gathering information about services is to conduct a telephone survey (Homan, 2016). Although even the most scientific surveys can produce incorrect or unreliable results (witness polls taken before the 2016 presidential election), it is important to follow appropriate sampling guidelines so that you can generalize your findings to the population you seek to understand. Of course, you will want to ensure that questions are clearly written and understandable to your audience. Gather only relevant information and avoid asking for data that will be unused. Make sure that the categories of answers are simple and distinct. For example, use, "strongly agree," "mildly agree," "mildly disagree," and "strongly disagree" when this is appropriate. Use open-ended questions carefully because you might get much too much information or information that's irrelevant.

Mapping Assets of Associations, Organizations, and Institutions: Forming Community Linkages

EP 7d, 8c

After it's determined what associations, organizations, and institutions exist in the community by using processes such as those suggested in Highlight 10.6, a list of strengths can be established for each organization. Creative ideas about how to get these systems to work together to provide services and meet needs are endless. For example, each organization may have assets that include people, built assets such as a building or space, equipment or materials, financial resources, and knowledge or skill.

People, of course, are members of an organization or who work for an organization. They reflect a potential for volunteer service. *Built assets* refer to buildings or rooms that are not being used all the time. An organization might give other organizations and groups access to space at unused times. An organization might also have a special space such as a gym that it could share when not in use. *Materials and equipment* include copying machines, writing utensils, computers, kitchens, tables, chairs, DVD equipment, sports equipment, and vehicles. Any of these could be shared with other groups. For example, a community group wanting to plant trees in their town located a business that owned a pickup truck with a Tommy Gate Lift, an attachment that allowed items to be loaded or unloaded by lowering the tailgate. This allowed the group to recruit helpers who otherwise would not have had the physical strength to participate in the tree-planting exercise. *Expertise* means specialized knowledge or skills that also can be shared with other groups and organizations. Finally, *financial resources* mean access to money in some form. Organizations may have membership dues or contributions, grant money, or the ability to conduct fundraising activities.

Community associations, organizations, and institutions can use these assets to work together with other groups and organizations to benefit community residents, both as groups and as individuals. For instance, a religious organization can provide space for Alcoholics Anonymous support group meetings or recreational activities for community youth. (*Alcoholics Anonymous* is a nationwide self-help organization, also sponsoring chapters in many other countries, that provides support, information, and guidance necessary for many recovering alcoholics to maintain their recovery process.) Similarly, a church can sponsor a fundraising drive for a homeless shelter.

Public parks can be used in conjunction with other community groups and organizations to sponsor activities and provide space. For example, a park offered its meeting room facility to a group of seniors for their weekly support meeting; another group held its annual meeting in a local library. A university used a local park for a fair designed to attract underserved students by linking them up with university faculty and students.

Schools provide communities with another source of strengths and assets; consider the following examples. For example, a school can work with a local hospital to provide an opportunity for health professionals to offer pregnancy prevention information. A retired business executive offers to provide tutoring to students at a school. A school's chorus gives concerts to nursing home residents.

Police departments provide yet another source of community assets, as illustrated by the following examples. Police officers distribute Thanksgiving turkeys provided by a local grocery to older community members and to others with a disability. Other police departments sponsor athletic teams for inner city youth. In reaction to an urban community crime wave, police work with neighborhood residents to establish an information network. Residents telephone others they've been assigned to contact and announce when safety meetings are being held in local churches.

Organizations such as the Red Cross have programs and resources to aid community residents during and after disasters. For example, the Ready Neighborhoods program is intended to assist areas strengthen their ability to manage disasters when they strike. The goal is to help residents develop the skills and tools so that they can respond to disasters of any kind (American Red Cross, 2017). It also provides business and organizations with "skills, plans, networks and supplies to mitigate the effects of and safely respond to all hazards."

Hospitals also provide a source of community assets. For example, a hospital works with local churches to sponsor and publicize blood pressure screenings at the religious facilities or supports a Hispanic culture festival with Hispanic neighborhood associations at a local park. Another hospital hires a person with mild intellectual disabilities to do filing in one of its administrative offices.

As Homan (2016) has pointed out, community colleges and universities are yet another source of community assets. For example, faculty can provide educational presentations on any number of topics to community groups. One college established a lecture series presented each fall at a nearby nursing home. One instructor who was certified in sex education volunteered to help a residential treatment center for male adolescents with severe behavioral and emotional problems develop a sex education program. Highlight 10-7 provides a more detailed example of macro systems—including a university—working together.

Highlight 10-7

A Case Example: Macro Systems Working Together   LO 10-11

Improving communities often requires creative thinking about how to use existing political and other public structures, residents' energy, and other resources. One example is the unlikely association between a housing authority in a large, well-established, southern city and a major university in that city—"a highly selective, overwhelmingly white, old-line Southern school situated in a picturesque neighborhood" (Gwynne, 1998, p. 74). The city's "government-subsidized apartments were consistently rated among the country's worst" (Gwynne, 1998, p. 74). One of the largest projects having 1,800 apartment units, ironically named Desire, was infamous as one of the worst in the country.

Gwynne (1998) explains the scenario. The Housing Authority, a 58-year-old agency, was "a political hornet's nest of patronage and chronic mismanagement" that "was so inept at making repairs that tenants routinely waited years for simple services. Hundreds of tenements were literally falling down" (Gwynne, 1998, p. 74). At its wits' end, the Housing Authority had two choices. It could either put the projects under the authority of a federal judge or find some outside agent to take control. A major university in the city turned out to be that outside agent. Many might ask, "What does a university know about running public housing projects?" Apparently, a lot.

University representatives approached the US Bureau of Housing and Urban Development (HUD) with a proposal to assist with one project. HUD and the mayor of the city took it much further and gave the university authority over 10 projects and 55,000 residents. The new association allowed for the newly appointed Housing Authority vice-president to reorganize the agency's total structure and approach.

First tasks included expelling drug dealers and criminals, drastically reducing the backlog of residents' requests for service, and dramatically improving how long it took to get repairs such as plumbing leaks and broken windows accomplished. Instead of months and years, such repairs now might take days or even hours. Future plans included building new, better single-family apartment units after tearing down old, dilapidated ones.

Importantly, the university and the Housing Authority worked closely with the projects' resident association. Community residents became actively involved in running the projects where they lived. Additionally, they helped with maintenance, security, and finding residents employment.

Hundreds of university faculty and students volunteered to provide residents with tutoring and information on "health, parenting, job training, teen pregnancy and high school equivalency" (Gwynne, 1998, p. 74). The volunteers have helped hundreds of adult residents find jobs and placed hundreds of young people in basketball and other sports programs.

Update: In 2001, four years after this article was written, the city of New Orleans demolished the remaining public housing units known as Desire. Subsequently, the city had built 107 rental units on the same site and was building another 318 units when, in 2005, Hurricane Katrina destroyed all of them (African American History, 2017).

> ## Critical Thinking Question **10-6**
>
> In what ways does your college or university work with individuals, groups, and organizations in the community to empower the community?

Social Work Roles in Macro Practice   LO 10-12

EP 1c

We have been talking about community building and mapping community assets based on community strengths. Earlier chapters focused on working in organizations and in groups within the organizational context. You know that generalist practitioners work in the organizations and communities that characterize the macro social environment. As they do so, they may assume several roles to achieve goals, make service provision more effective, and advance social well-being. We have established that a *role* is a culturally expected behavior pattern for a person having a specified status or being involved in a designated social relationship. For social workers, roles involve expectations about how they should act as professionals in their practice.

In order to best understand the various roles generalist practitioners play, it is useful to recall the four types of systems involved in generalist practice. As we discussed in earlier chapters, the **client system** includes those people who will ultimately benefit from the change process. **Macro client systems** can encompass, on the one hand, some number of individuals, families, or small groups, or, on the other hand, communities or organizations. The **change agent system** is the individual who initiates the macro change process. Where the diagrams in Figures 10-1 through 10-12 refer to the "worker," they mean the change agent system who is the social work practitioner. The **action system** includes those people who agree to and will work together to attain the proposed macro change. Finally, the **target system** is the system that social workers must "change or influence in order to accomplish (their) goals" (Pincus & Minahan, 1973, p. 58). In macro practice, the worker's own agency, some subsystem within his or her agency, or the community may become the system at which practitioners direct their intervention efforts.

EP 8d

Chapter 1 briefly mentioned a range of roles social workers may assume. The following sections and Figures 10-1 through 10-12 will elaborate upon social work roles in macro practice. They include enabler, mediator, coordinator, manager, educator, evaluator, broker, facilitator, initiator, negotiator, mobilizer, and advocate. Roles often aren't mutually exclusive and may overlap.

These figures will use circles to represent the worker, macro client systems, and organizational or community macro systems. Lines and arrows depict how systems relate to each other. Note that, unless specified otherwise, a macro system can illustrate interaction with either a community or an organization.

Enabler

An **enabler** provides "support, encouragement, and suggestions" to members of a macro client system so that the system may complete tasks or solve problems more easily and successfully (Kirst-Ashman & Hull, 2018a, p. 97). "Enablers employ such skills

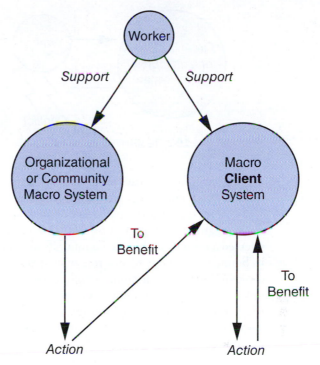

Figure 10-1 The ENABLER Role in Macro Practice

as giving encouragement, identifying and managing feelings, providing hope, identifying strengths, partializing or breaking down problems to make them more manageable, and helping identify options for meeting goals (Kirst-Ashman & Hull, 2018b, p. 20). Enablers, then, are helpers. They assist in the planned change process to achieve community or organizational goals on behalf of the macro client system.

Note that this definition of *enabler* is very different from that used in the topic area of substance abuse. There, the term refers to someone else such as a family member or friend who facilitates the substance abuser in continuing to use and abuse the drug of his or her choice.

Figure 10-1 illustrates the enabler role in macro practice. Arrows point from the worker system to both the organizational or community macro system circle and to the macro client system. These portray the support provided by the worker that assists either macro system in undertaking some action. The latter is depicted by arrows leading from both macro systems to the word "Action." This action, in turn, is intended to result in some benefit for the macro client system. Thus, arrows also lead from the word "Action" back to the macro client system.

Mediator

A **mediator** resolves arguments or disagreements among individuals (micro systems), groups (mezzo systems), organizations, or communities (both macro systems) in disagreement (Cournoyer, 2017; Toseland & Rivas, 2017). At the macro level, mediation involves helping various factions (subsystems) within a community—or

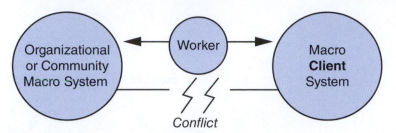

Figure 10-2 The MEDIATOR Role in Macro Practice

helping a community system and some other system (such as another community)—work out their differences. For example, a community (or neighborhood) and a social services organization may require mediation over the location of a substance abuse treatment center. In this case, the social services organization might have selected a prime spot, but the community might balk at having such a center within its boundaries. The mediator role may involve improving communication among dissident individuals or groups or otherwise helping those involved come to a compromise. A mediator remains neutral, not siding with either party in the dispute. Mediators strive to understand the positions of both parties. They may help to clarify positions, recognize miscommunication about differences, and help those involved present their cases clearly.

Figure 10-2 illustrates the mediator role. The worker circle is placed between the organizational or community macro system circle and the macro client system circle. This reflects the worker's neutral stance, requiring that she or he take neither of the involved parties' sides. The broken line beneath the worker circle depicts the two parties' conflicting communication and their inability to settle differences. This diagram depicts a worker mediating between an organizational or community macro system (on the left) and a macro client system (on the right). However, mediation can occur between or among systems of virtually any size.

Coordinator

Coordination involves bringing components together in an organized manner. A **coordinator**, therefore, brings people involved in various systems together and organizes their performance (Cournoyer, 2017). A generalist social worker can function as a coordinator in many contexts, including advocacy pursuits, the synchronization of social service projects, the lobbying of legislators for some policy change, the provision of specialized consultation, or the enhancement of linkages between clients and services.

Figure 10-3 depicts an organizational or community macro system and a macro client system located next to each other. They are both located within a box to illustrate that they are working together. The arrow pointing from the worker to the box portrays the worker's active leadership in bringing together and coordinating the two systems' performances. The arrows circulating around the box reflect the coordination process.

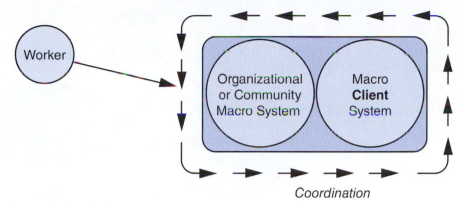

Coordination

Figure 10-3 The COORDINATOR Role in Macro Practice

Manager

A **manager** in social work is one who assumes some level of administrative responsibility for a social services agency or other organizational system (Burghardt, 2014; Kettner, Moroney, & Martin, 2017). Earlier chapters defined *management* as "the attainment of organizational goals in an effective and efficient manner through planning, organizing, leading, and controlling organizational resources" (Daft, 2016, p. 4). Previous chapters also discussed management and leadership in some depth.

Figure 10-4 portrays the manager role. We assume that the organization employs both social workers and various other staff members. The worker circle is located above two staff circles with arrows directed down from the worker circle to both staff circles. This diagram indicates that the worker, having administrative status, has authority over the staff. All three circles are located within the larger organizational environment circle to indicate that the manager role usually occurs within an organizational context.

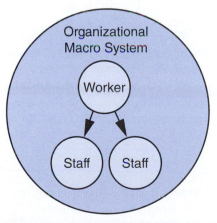

Figure 10-4 The MANAGER Role in Macro Practice

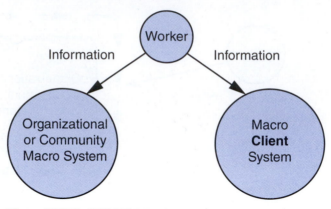

Figure 10-5 The EDUCATOR Role in Macro Practice

Educator

EP 9b

An **educator** gives information and teaches skills to other systems. To be an effective educator, the worker must first be knowledgeable about the topics being taught. Additionally, the worker must be a good communicator so that information is conveyed clearly and is readily understood by the receivers.

In Figure 10-5, arrows run from the worker circle both to the organizational or community macro system circle and to the macro system circle. This depicts that a worker conveys information to these other systems.

Evaluator

An **evaluator** determines the extent to which a program or agency is effective (Brody & Nair, 2014; Kettner et al., 2017). This can occur in an organizational or community context. Generalist social workers with a broad knowledge of how various size systems function can analyze or evaluate their effectiveness. Likewise, they can evaluate the effectiveness of their own interventions with individuals, groups, organizations, and communities.

Figure 10-6 reflects how an evaluator functions. One arrow points from the worker to an organizational or community macro system to illustrate how a worker in an analyst/evaluator role can evaluate a program's or an agency's effectiveness. A second arrow points from the worker to a line that joins another worker to a macro client system. This connecting line illustrates the worker's professional planned change relationship with his or her clients. The arrow illustrates how workers can and indeed should evaluate their own practices with macro client systems.

Broker

A **broker** links the macro client system with community resources and services. Such resources might be financial, legal, educational, psychological, recreational, or health oriented.

In Figure 10-7, the line from the worker circle to the arrow leading from the macro system to the macro client system illustrates the worker's active involvement

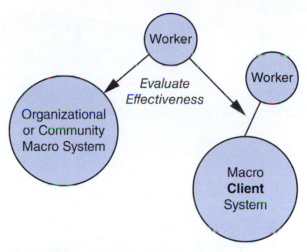

Figure 10-6 The EVALUATOR Role in Macro Practice

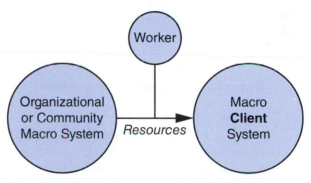

Figure 10-7 The BROKER Role in Macro Practice

in obtaining resources for the macro client system. The arrow points from the organizational or community macro system circle that provides resources to the client system circle that receives them.

Facilitator

A **facilitator** is one who guides a group experience. Although the facilitator role is very common in direct practice with groups, workers also frequently lead groups in macro practice. In the macro context, a facilitator brings participants together to promote the change process by improving communication, helping direct their efforts and resources, and linking them with needed information and expert help.

Figure 10-8 depicts three circles labeled "Colleague" that are connected with each other by lines representing group interaction and communication. Additionally, the linking lines illustrate how colleagues working together form a group or mezzo system. These three colleague circles are enclosed by a larger circle, which refers to a mezzo system that could be a task or planning group within an

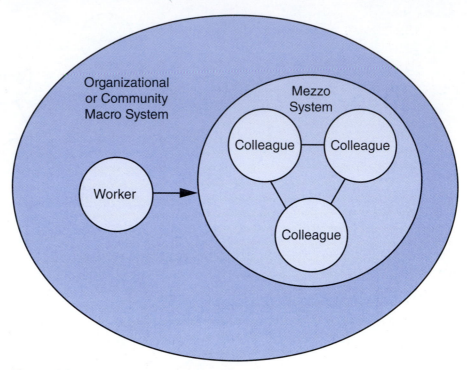

Figure 10-8 The FACILITATOR Role in Macro Practice

organization or a community. The arrow pointing from the worker to the mezzo system depicts the worker's leadership of the group. Hence, the large oval entitled "Organizational or Community Macro System" encompasses all the interaction. The worker facilitates whatever interaction occurs within the mezzo system, which, in turn, occurs within the macro context. Note that although Figure 10-8 arbitrarily depicts three colleagues, in reality, any number of colleagues, clients, community residents, administrators, or politicians could be involved.

Initiator

An **initiator** is the person or persons who call attention to an issue. The issue in the community may be a problem, a need, or simply a situation that can be improved. It is important to recognize that a problem does not have to exist before a situation can be dealt with. Often, preventing future problems or enhancing existing services is a satisfactory reason for creating a change effort. Thus, a social worker may recognize that a policy has the potential to create problems for particular clients and bring this to the attention of her supervisor. Likewise, a client may identify to the worker ways that service could be improved, and the worker then takes it from there. In each case, the worker is playing the role of initiator in terms of beginning the actual change process. Usually, this role must be followed up by other kinds of work, because merely pointing out problems does not guarantee they will be solved.

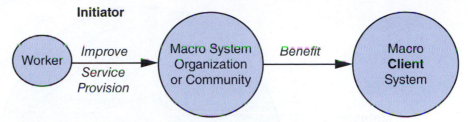

Figure 10-9 The INITIATOR Role in Generalist Macro Practice

In Figure 10-9, an arrow leading from the worker on the far left to the macro system circle in the middle represents the worker's activities directed at improving service provision. Another arrow, which leads from the macro system to the macro client system on the far right, reflects the benefits that the macro system provides for the macro client system as the ultimate result of the initiator's efforts.

Negotiator

A **negotiator** is an intermediary who acts to settle disputes and/or resolve disagreements. However, unlike mediators, negotiators clearly take the side of one of the parties involved.

In Figure 10-10, the macro client system and the worker are located together on the left side of the figure. This indicates that the worker is negotiating on behalf of the macro client system. Two jagged lines with arrows pointing away from them in opposing directions characterize the conflict that has arisen. The macro system on the right side of the figure represents an organization or community engulfed in conflict with the macro client system and the worker/negotiator on the left. The worker/negotiator seeks to resolve the conflict, but does so on behalf of one side of the conflict, namely, the macro client system.

Mobilizer

A **mobilizer** identifies and convenes community people and resources and makes them responsive to unmet community needs (Toseland & Rivas, 2017). The mobilizer's purpose is to match resources to needs within the community context. Sometimes a mobilizer's goal involves making services more accessible to citizens

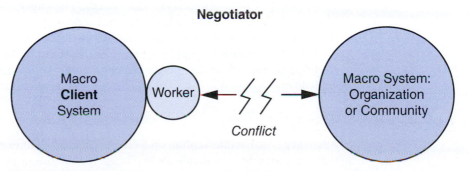

Figure 10-10 The NEGOTIATOR Role in Generalist Macro Practice

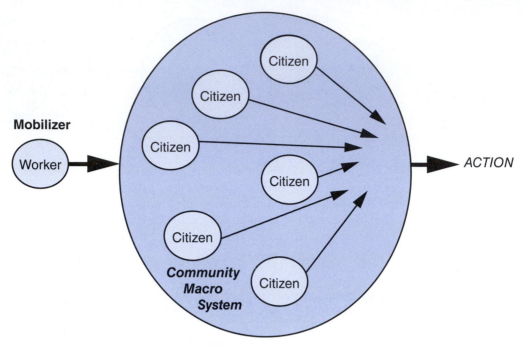

Figure 10-11 The MOBILIZER Role in Generalist Macro Practice

who need them. Other times a goal is initiating and developing services to meet needs that heretofore were unmet.

In Figure 10-11, the worker on the left is assuming a mobilizer role in a macro practice context. The large central circle is labeled *community macro system.* The citizens within the community macro system circle represent an arbitrary number of community residents. (Fewer citizens may be involved, or perhaps thousands of community residents are part of the mobilization process. Ideally, an entire community with virtually all its residents would participate in the macro intervention process.) The arrow leading from the worker (mobilizer) to the community macro system represents the worker's efforts directed toward the mobilization process. The arrows inside the community macro system leading from the citizens toward the word *action* represent the resultant efforts of citizens as they participate in the process of meeting the community's unmet needs. The larger arrow leading from the community macro system circle to the word *action* represents the process of pooling all the citizens' efforts into some coordinated action.

Note that, unlike most of the other roles illustrated in these figures, the mobilizer role occurs *only* in the context of a community. By definition here, it does not apply to organizations.

Advocate

Advocacy is active intervention on a client system's behalf to get needed resources that are currently unavailable, or to change regulations or policies that negatively affect that client system. An **advocate** is one who steps forward and speaks out on

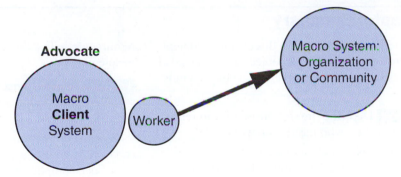

Figure 10-12 The ADVOCATE Role in Generalist Macro Practice

behalf of the client system to promote fair and equitable treatment or gain needed resources. In macro practice, of course, it would be on behalf of some macro client system. This may be especially appropriate when a macro client system has little power to get what it needs. Advocacy often involves expending more effort than is necessary to simply accomplish your job. It also often involves taking risks, especially when advocating on a client's behalf in the face of a larger, more powerful system.

The advocate role is one of the most important roles a generalist social worker can assume, despite its potential difficulties. To emphasize its importance, it is the last macro practice role to be discussed here. It is one of the practice dimensions that makes generalist social work practice unique (Kirst-Ashman & Hull, 2018b). It is part of a generalist social worker's ethical responsibility to go beyond the minimum requirements of his or her job on behalf of a client system when that client system is in desperate need of help or resources.

Figure 10-12 depicts a macro client system and a worker standing together to reflect the worker's alliance with the macro client system during the advocacy process. The bold arrow leading from the worker to the macro system at the right is exceptionally thick, to represent the significant amount of energy it often takes to have an impact on a larger, more powerful system. The elevated location of the macro system above the worker and macro client system illustrates the former's greater power.

Highlight 10-8 discusses the relationship between professional roles and professional identity.

Highlight **10-8**

Professional Identity and Professional Roles

Regardless of what roles social workers assume while working within an organization, generalist practitioners should maintain and demonstrate a professional identity. This means understanding "the profession's history, its mission, and the roles and responsibilities of the profession." It also means knowing and accepting "the value base of the profession and its ethical standards as well as relevant laws and regulations" (Council on Social Work Education [CSWE], 2015, EP 1). Professional identification also requires that social workers "recognize the importance of life-long learning and are committed to continually updating their skills" to ensure relevancy and efficacy (CSWE, 2015, EP 1).

Chapter Summary

The following summarizes this chapter's content as it relates to the learning objectives presented at the beginning of the chapter. Objectives include the following:

LO 10-1 Describe the significance of power in communities, who has it, and why.

Concepts important in the determination of power include potential ability, the movement of people on a chosen course, and the result of producing an effect or achieving some end. Sources of power include information, wealth, reputation, high status, decision-making positions, laws and policies, and connections. These reflect only potential power, not absolute determination of power.

LO 10-2 Respond to critical thinking questions dealing with communities.

Critical thinking questions addressed community power, social support networks, natural helping networks, community analysis, releasing one's own individual capacities, and ways your college can work to empower the community.

LO 10-3 Discuss the importance of citizen participation and social support networks.

Citizen participation is the dynamic, voluntary involvement of community members to address issues and concerns affecting their community and improve social policies, laws, and programs. A social support network is individuals or groups who share a connection with others and who provide support to one another in times of need. The concepts of power, citizen participation, and social support networks often relate to each other. Social networks, use of the Internet, and social change are discussed.

LO 10-4 Describe ethical issues when engaged in assessment of geographical communities.

Ethical issues addressed informed consent and citizen participation, and the extent to which the concept of community building complies with professional ethics.

LO 10-5 Explain natural helping networks.

A natural helping network is a group of nonprofessional people volunteering their time and resources to help either an individual or group of people in need.

LO 10-6 Describe personal empowerment, social empowerment, and the relationship between the two.

Personal empowerment occurs when people can directly control what's happening in their own lives. Social empowerment is the condition in the social environment where people have access to opportunities and resources to make personal choices and maintain some control over their environment. Personal and social empowerment are integrally related and often difficult to distinguish from each other.

LO 10-7 Utilize a format for assessing communities and describe data-gathering procedures.

Mapping assets is an assessment of a community that emphasizes that community's strengths, capabilities, and assets instead of the community's problems and weaknesses. Capacity building "is the ability to increase the leadership and organizational skills of local people for the purpose of strengthening their own organizations and networking capacities" (Gamble & Hoff, 2005, p. 178).

Communities can be assessed in terms of demographics, geographic and environmental influences on community, beliefs and attitudes, local politics, local economy and businesses, income distribution, housing, educational facilities and programs, health and welfare systems, sources of information, and a summary evaluation (Sheafor & Horejsi, 2012, pp. 169–170). Data-gathering techniques include holding a community forum, examining social indicators, using the nominal group technique, and employing the key informant technique.

LO 10-8 Explain community building and highlight the primary principles involved.

Community building involves the process of enhancing a community's strengths by linking community residents, organizations in the community, and external resources to tackle community problems and work together toward positive change. Primary principles include working together, the formation of new alliances, the use of cooperation, the importance of targeting neighborhoods, and building on neighborhood strengths.

LO 10-9 Provide examples of community building in rural communities.

Examples of community building in rural communities include a grant-funded comprehensive community initiative, approaches to enhance rural youths' interest in higher education, "community-supported agriculture," "agritourism," and "producer cooperatives" (Messinger, 2004, pp. 153–154).

LO 10-10 Explain mapping community assets and suggest methods for collecting information.

Mapping community assets is a technique that emphasizes the community's strengths, capabilities, and assets instead of the community's problems and weaknesses. Mapping assets involve both recognizing and drawing out the capabilities and capacities of people and empowering local associations, organizations, and institutions. Drawing out individual capabilities and capacities can include the areas of health, administrative and interpersonal work skills, construction and repair, maintenance, food, recreation and entertainment, and assistance in daily activities, among others. Information for mapping aspects of local associations, organizations, and institutions can be obtained from the media or the local library, by simply talking with people, and by conducting a telephone survey.

LO 10-11 Provide examples of how individuals, groups, associations, organizations, and social institutions can work together for community empowerment.

Examples of how youth can empower the community included raising money for the homeless, providing opportunities for participation in Special Olympics, addressing racial issues in schools, and transforming abandoned community property into a park. An example of a natural helping network involved two natural indigenous leaders in a community neighborhood. Organizations can share assets involving people, built assets, materials and equipment, expertise, and financial resources. One case example reflected how a university worked together with a housing authority to improve living conditions.

LO 10-12 Explain social work roles in macro practice.

Social work roles in macro practice include enabler, mediator, coordinator, manager, educator, evaluator, broker, facilitator, initiator, negotiator, mobilizer, and advocate.

Looking Ahead

This chapter discussed power and empowerment in communities, including mapping community assets and community building. The next chapter will explore various facets of neighborhood empowerment within communities.

Competency Notes

The following identifies where Educational Policy (EP) competencies and component behaviors are discussed in the chapter.

EP 1 (Competency 1)—Demonstrate Ethical and Professional Behavior. (*p. 354*): Ethical issues involved in informed consent and community action are discussed. (*p. 356*): Social workers should continue learning about how to use technology effectively throughout their careers. (*p. 370*): An ethical question is posed regarding the extent to which community building complies with professional ethical principles.

EP 1a Make ethical decisions by applying the standards of the NASW Code of Ethics, relevant laws and regulations, models for ethical decision-making, ethical conduct of research,

and additional codes of ethics as appropriate to context. *(p. 370):* The six core values of the NASW *Code of Ethics* are cited.

EP 1b Use reflection and self-regulation to manage personal values and maintain professionalism in practice situations. *(p. 375):* Social workers practicing in rural communities must be very careful to manage personal values in a way that allows professional values to guide their practice.

EP 1c Demonstrate professional demeanor in behavior; appearance; and oral, written, and electronic communication. *(p. 375):* Attending to professional roles is important for rural social workers. Professional demeanor is important for social workers in rural communities, where word about almost anything, including mistakes or negative remarks, travels fast. *(p. 382):* Professional roles for social workers in macro practice are examined.

EP 2 (Competency 2)—Engage Diversity and Difference in Practice. *(p. 349):* The concept of power in communities is discussed regarding how it relates to privilege.

EP 2a Apply and communicate understanding of the importance of diversity and difference in shaping life experiences in practice at the micro, mezzo, and macro levels. *(p. 349):* People in power experience life differently and have greater control than those not in power.

EP 5b Assess how social welfare and economic policies impact the delivery of and access to social services. *(p. 367):* In community building, social workers should strive to establish community policies and programs that advance social well-being.

EP 6 (Competency 6)—Engage with Individuals, Families, Groups, Organizations, and Communities. *(p. 349):* Social workers should have knowledge about systems of all sizes, including communities. *(p. 361):* Working with communities means recognizing strengths and assets as well as challenges and problems.

EP 6a Apply knowledge of human behavior and the social environment, person-in-environment, and other multidisciplinary theoretical frameworks to engage with clients and constituencies. *(p. 349):* Macro practice in communities requires understanding of theories and approaches to both rural and urban areas.

EP 6b Use empathy, reflection, and interpersonal skills to effectively engage diverse clients and constituencies. *(p. 349):* Engaging macro systems requires the same use of interpersonal skills as when working with other size systems.

EP 7a Collect and organize data, and apply critical thinking to interpret information from clients and constituencies. *(p. 361):* Social workers must collect, organize, and interpret appropriate data about communities in order to work in and with them. *(p. 366):* Data-collection methods are discussed. *(p. 371):* The case example described includes an assessment of community needs. *(p. 376):* Mapping community assets involves collecting and interpreting data about the community. *(p. 379):* Suggestions for collecting and organizing data from local groups and organizations are provided.

EP 7b Apply knowledge of human behavior and the social environment, person-in-environment, and other multidisciplinary theoretical frameworks in the analysis of assessment data from clients and constituencies. *(p. 361):* Understanding rural and urban differences requires knowledge of the characteristics of each locale and appropriate methods of assessment.

EP 7c Develop mutually agreed-on intervention goals and objectives based on the critical assessment of strengths, needs, and challenges within clients and constituencies. *(p. 367):* Generalist practitioners should assess community strengths and limitations for effective community building. Strengths should be emphasized. *(p. 371):* The community's strengths and limitations were assessed in this case example that demonstrates community building. In this case example, professionals worked with community residents and leaders to develop mutually agreed-on intervention goals. *(p. 376):* Mapping community assets emphasizes a community's strengths.

EP 7d Select appropriate intervention strategies based on the assessment, research knowledge, and values and preferences of clients and constituencies. *(p. 367):* Social workers should select the appropriate intervention strategies when working in and with communities. *(p. 371):* This case example identifies appropriate intervention strategies. *(p. 374):* Appropriate intervention strategies for helping rural youths go on to college are discussed. *(p. 374):* Three intervention strategies for rural communities are provided. *(p. 376):* Appropriate intervention strategies are discussed involving the release of individual capacities and how community groups and organizations can work together. *(p. 379):* Appropriate intervention strategies for using a community's assets are provided.

EP 8 (Competency 8)—Intervene with Individuals, Families, Groups, Organizations, and Communities. *(p. 361):* Practitioners must have knowledge about communities in order to prepare for action with them. *(p. 367):* Generalist practitioners help communities and community residents to make plans and resolve problems. *(p. 371):* In this case example, intervention strategies helped organizations in the community improve service provision and achieve their goals. This case example reflects how a community began to resolve its problems.

EP 8a Critically choose and implement interventions to achieve practice goals and enhance capacities of clients and constituencies. *(pp. 352, 355, 359, 366, 378):* Critical thinking questions are posed.

EP 8b Apply knowledge of human behavior and the social environment, person-in-environment, and other multidisciplinary theoretical frameworks in interventions with clients and constituencies. *(p. 367):* Asset mapping is a useful tool to use when identifying the strengths of a neighborhood or community.

EP 8c Use inter-professional collaboration as appropriate to achieve beneficial practice outcomes. *(p. 367):* In community building, social workers collaborate with colleagues and clients for effective community policy action. *(p. 379):* Suggestions are provided for collaboration among various community professionals, groups, and organizations to improve policies and service provision.

EP 8d Negotiate, mediate, and advocate with and on behalf of diverse clients and constituencies. *(p. 367):* One aspect of community building involves advocating for clients. *(p. 382):* The roles of negotiator, mediator, advocate, and others are described.

EP 8e Facilitate effective transitions and endings that advance mutually agreed-on goals. *(p. 371):* Social workers should provide leadership in community building. *(p. 374):* Suggestions presented in this example emphasize prevention of missed opportunity, in this case not going on to college.

EP 9b Apply knowledge of human behavior and the social environment, person-in-environment, and other multidisciplinary theoretical frameworks in the evaluation of outcomes. *(p. 386):* Generalist social workers with a broad knowledge of how various size systems function can analyze or evaluate their effectiveness. Likewise, they can evaluate the effectiveness of their own interventions with individuals, groups, organizations, and communities.

Media Resources

MindTap for Social Work

Go to MindTap® for digital study tools and resources that complement this text and help you be more successful in your course and career. There's an interactive eBook plus videos of client sessions, skill-building activities, quizzes to help you prepare for tests, apps, and more—all in one place. If your instructor didn't assign MindTap, you can find out more about it at CengageBrain .com.

11 | Neighborhood Empowerment

Jim West/Alamy Stock Photo

Neighborhoods and neighborhood residents can improve the quality of life in communities. Here, high school volunteers in Detroit, Michigan, paint a mural on an empty building through the Summer in the City program.

LEARNING OBJECTIVES

After reading this chapter...

11-1 Define neighborhoods and their role in providing a context for human behavior.

11-2 Explain neighborhood functions and how they can enhance residents' quality of life.

11-3 Identify the qualities of strong neighborhoods.

11-4 Respond to critical thinking questions.

11-5 Describe two theoretical frameworks for examining neighborhood structure.

11-6 Discuss neighborhoods, ethnicity, and social class, including the strengths of ethnic and cultural solidarity, and segregation.

11-7 Describe projects that can enhance neighborhood strengths.

11-8 Describe ethical issues involving neighborhoods.

11-9 Describe the invasion-succession, life cycle, and political capacity models of change in neighborhoods.

11-10 Describe neighborhood centers and their origin in the settlement house movement.

11-11 Identify the assumptions upon which neighborhood centers are based today.

11-12 Specify types of activities neighborhood centers can sponsor to improve residents' living conditions.

11-13 Provide examples of neighborhood and community projects reflecting empowerment.

Neighborhood residents can do the following, for example:

- *Register voters in advance of the next election.*
- *Organize to oppose locating a business that will dramatically increase traffic.*
- *Help older adults stay in their homes by doing yard work and other chores.*
- *Teach new immigrants and refugees to speak and read English.*
- *Assist refugees and immigrants with specialized training or education to find employment in their chosen profession.*
- *Initiate a campaign to clean up and preserve a local park.*
- *Help entrepreneurs start up new businesses.*
- *Organize community celebrations and events.*
- *Conduct fundraisers to support community goals and projects.*
- *Identify employers and link them with community citizens needing jobs.*
- *Develop a network of community experts whom residents can contact for help in their areas of expertise (e.g., electrical repair, writing, wellness, or investment).*
- *Create a website and/or computer listserv that will help residents share information, discuss community issues, and stay in touch with each other.*

Because of a neighborhood's critical significance in community building and empowerment, we will discuss neighborhoods in some detail here. The subsequent section emphasizes the importance of neighborhood centers as facilitators of empowerment.

Defining Neighborhoods   LO 11-1

EP 6

A **neighborhood** is a "geographical/residential area in which people share similar values, lifestyles, and housing types, and exhibit a sense of cohesion" (Kirst-Ashman & Hull, 2018, p. 323). There are three important points to this definition. First, a neighborhood is based on a physical area. Second, neighborhoods provide places for people to reside and go about their daily living tasks. Third, neighborhood residents share something in common, such as religious affiliation, racial identity, socioeconomic status, or concerns about encroaching crime. Neighborhood is an especially important concept when talking about geographical communities because of its immediate significance to clients' lives. It is the immediate social environment in which they live, eat, sleep, and interact daily.

A geographical community may consist of several neighborhoods. There are several types of neighborhoods based on size (Fellin, 2001b, p. 127). An **immediate neighborhood** is one consisting of a limited number of family units and lodgings located in a relatively small area. A three-block-long city street might exemplify an immediate neighborhood. An **extended neighborhood** is larger than an immediate neighborhood and might include several square blocks. Finally, a **community neighborhood** includes 30 square blocks or even more.

Neighborhood boundaries are determined in various ways. Neighborhoods are based on residents' common characteristics, values, interests, or lifestyles. Therefore, the concept of neighborhood is more complex than *x* number of square feet, homes, or blocks. For example, Iraqi immigrants might relocate in the same neighborhood based on common heritage, culture, and language. The immediate Iraqi neighborhood might end abruptly in the middle of an urban block where people who are not Iraqi reside.

Likewise, consider a single-home neighborhood populated primarily by older adults. A government housing project for families with young children is built on the next block. The immediate neighborhood for the older residents might end where the housing project begins if the divergent groups have little in common and virtually nothing to do with each other. You might view a neighborhood and its boundaries as how residents define it (Homan, 2016). How would you define the boundaries of your own neighborhood?

Functions of Neighborhoods: Promoting Optimal Health and Well-Being LO 11-2

Neighborhoods can perform a variety of functions (Homan, 2016; Rubin & Rubin, 2008; Warren, 1977; Warren & Warren, 1977). First, a neighborhood can be an arena for social interaction. It can be a place where people feel comfortable and that they belong. Residents might use each other as their primary context for socializing. A neighborhood block party in Madison, Wisconsin, comes to mind. Each year, residents on three blocks of Mifflin Street band together, obtain permission from the city, and host a block party where residents contribute resources and "party hearty" to celebrate the coming of spring.

A second neighborhood function is the provision of mutual aid. Residents can help each other in any number of ways. Homan (2016) reflects:

> Neighbors can provide one another with a range of practical and emotional support. Borrowing a cup of sugar, helping in times of emergency, establishing social contact over a cup of coffee, or helping to fix a leaky toilet are some of the common forms of assistance neighbors provide to each other. The benefits of these commonplace activities, of course, extend beyond eggs and coffee and functional flushing. These connections provide psychological benefits by strengthening our attachments to a wider human community and by helping us recognize the reality and importance of our interdependence. More effectively functioning neighborhoods are more likely to offer their members the benefits of "neighboring." (p. 472)

The following are other examples of mutual aid. A neighborhood in a metropolitan suburb filled with young families who have small children can provide each other child care when they need it. An urban neighborhood can form a "Neighborhood Watch" organization where residents keep a careful eye out on each other's homes to report suspicious strangers and prevent crime. In a northern suburban neighborhood, one neighbor snowplows another's driveway when the latter takes a winter vacation. This helps conceal the fact that residents aren't home and decreases their vulnerability to thieves and vandals.

A third function of neighborhoods is provision of an arena for people to communicate and share information. We have noted that information can provide power. Therefore, neighborhood residents with access to information can share that information and thereby increase their neighbors' and ultimately the neighborhood's power. For example, Harry, a neighborhood resident in a small town, has a good friend, Ernest, a town board member (the decision-making body responsible for planning town projects). Harry finds out from Ernest that the town board is planning to rezone a lot in the neighborhood from residential to commercial, requiring that a business and not a personal residence be built on the lot. The implication for the neighborhood is that property values may plummet. The neighborhood's property is valuable because it boasts a pleasant, laid-back residential area for families. A business in its midst implies more traffic, more congestion, and less daily living appeal. Thus, with this information, Harry and his neighbors can band together, confront the town board, and initiate whatever action is necessary to halt the rezoning plan.

A fourth function of neighborhoods is to allow people to congregate with others having similar status, cultural backgrounds, or interests as themselves (Rubin & Rubin, 2008). For better or for worse, a neighborhood can establish certain standards and strive to admit residents who comply with the prerequisites. A common example is a suburban neighborhood that promotes residents who are White and who have achieved a prescribed level of socioeconomic status. Current residents can work to keep out potential residents who don't comply. High property prices and taxes can exclude people from lower socioeconomic levels. Derogatory comments and even threats can act to deter people of color from moving into such neighborhoods. Obviously, this function does little to comply with the social work values of self-determination and the right to equal opportunity. Preserving social status can be an oppressive function that can counteract optimal health and well-being for people who are excluded from neighborhoods.

Consider one such suburban neighborhood. Neighborhood residents all have one-acre lots on a lake and huge, expensive homes with intricately manicured landscaping. All the neighborhood residents are White. Typically, residents make racial slurs and steadfastly discourage people of color from becoming interested in purchasing homes or empty lots. When one resident family moved because of a job relocation, a rich single White female owner of a large trucking firm, Lullabelle, purchased the family's home.

The neighbors had seen Lullabelle, who was obviously White, and thus had few, if any, initial negative comments to make about her. They were, however, interested in determining what Lullabelle was like and how she would "fit into" the neighborhood. Unfortunately for them, they discovered that Lullabelle was a one-sided, perpetual talker who limited herself to various complaints and excessive detail about how much money she made. Lullabelle also had numerous men friends, ranging in age from about 17 to 71, frequently stay with her and roam about the property. Neighbors were mortified as these men regularly spewed forth vulgarities and felt perfectly comfortable urinating on the garage or on the faultlessly trimmed bushes.

Lullabelle built a small, ugly warehouse-like structure in the front yard to house her old junker cars and used appliances. She kept the remaining three "junkers" out in the driveway. Then she placed several dozen plaster-of-Paris and wooden lawn ornaments about the property. These included the ones where the backsides of "Ma" and "Pa" bending over are viewed so that you can see their polka-dotted underwear. No, the neighborhood residents didn't want any persons of color living in their neighborhood.

A fifth function of neighborhoods is provision of an organizational and political base. Neighborhood residents may choose to join a neighborhood organization or center. Such organizations are groups formed to address common needs of or establish goals for the neighborhood. Examples of goals are cleaning up rubbish, improving the conditions of older buildings, enhancing voter registration and voting, or targeting and abolishing crack houses. This chapter later discusses neighborhood centers much more thoroughly as a means of neighborhood empowerment.

As a group, neighborhood residents may also push politicians and community decision makers to make changes on their behalf. They may seek increased police patrolling or enforcement of building codes requiring such things as repairs to ensure resident safety and health. Social workers can use their listening and questioning skills to engage residents, build trust, identify problems, and suggest solutions.

Qualities of Strong Neighborhoods LO 11-3

Strong, healthy neighborhoods that support residents and enhance their quality of life have the following eight basic characteristics (Grogan-Kaylor et al., 2006; Homan, 2016):

1. A good school system with high standards, good resources, and well-trained teachers who respond to the neighborhood's cultural composition and needs.
2. Good, safe areas for children to participate in play, sports, and other positive recreational and cultural activities.
3. Effective management of children's behavior by presiding adults.
4. Ready availability of and access to good health care facilities and services, especially in times of emergency.
5. Easily accessible public or other community transportation so residents can go to work or school, access health care, and undertake other necessary activities for daily life.
6. Good availability and facilities to meet daycare and other child care needs.
7. Strong support network of families and adults to watch over children, provide support, and serve as positive role models.
8. A reasonably safe environment with low or nonexistent levels of criminal activity, hazardous environmental dangers (such as potholes in streets or bridges lacking railings), and racial conflict.

Describing Neighborhood Structure

Several theoretical frameworks have been developed to describe neighborhoods' structure and composition (Fellin, 2001a, pp. 137–140; 2001b, pp. 123–125). Such approaches focus our attention on various dimensions of neighborhoods so we can evaluate how well they provide for residents' health and well-being. Two will be described here. The first emphasizes interpersonal interaction, identification, and connections. The second approach focuses on neighborhood groups and value implementation.

EP 8a

Critical Thinking Question **11-1** LO 11-4

To what extent does the neighborhood you live in reflect the eight strengths listed above?

EP 8a

> ## Critical Thinking Questions 11-2
>
> To what extent do you socialize with and get support from your neighbors? To what extent do you identify with and feel an integral part of the neighborhood where you live? To what extent is your neighborhood connected with other systems in the larger community environment? Explain your answers.

Theoretical Framework One: Interpersonal Interaction, Identification, and Connections   LO 11-5

One approach to assessing neighborhoods focuses on three conditions (Fellin, 2001a, 2001b; Warren & Warren, 1977). The first is the degree of interpersonal interaction among residents. To what extent do they socialize with each other and provide each other with support? The second condition is the residents' identification with the neighborhood and each other. To what extent do they identify with and feel a part of their neighborhood? The third condition involves the neighborhood's connections with the larger encompassing community. This last variable involving *social connectedness* concerns how neighborhoods have varying degrees of access to politicians who wield power, resources, needed services, and other community systems. Each of these variables can be appraised along a continuum from low to "neutral" to high (Fellin, 2001a, p. 138).

Neighborhoods can then be categorized into six basic types—integral, parochial, diffuse, stepping-stone, transitory, and anomic—based on residents' social interaction, sense of belonging, and connections with others (Fellin, 2001a, pp. 138–139). Highlight 11-1 summarizes how each type of neighborhood reflects the degree of interpersonal interaction, residents' identification with the neighborhood, and social connectedness with other systems outside of the neighborhood.

Highlight 11-1

Communities Based on Interpersonal Interaction, Identification, and Social Connections

	Interpersonal Interaction	Identification with Neighborhood	Social Connectedness
Integral	High	High	High
Parochial	High	High	Low
Diffuse	Low	High	Low
Stepping-Stone	Low	High	High
Transitory	Low	Low	High
Anomic	Low	Low	Low

Integral Neighborhoods   **Integral neighborhoods** are those manifesting high levels of all three conditions. Neighborhood residents are highly involved with each other and readily identify themselves as part of the neighborhood. Helping to produce a sense of cohesion are such factors as pro-education values, involvement in the larger community, shared belief in maintaining and improving their environment and a focus on maintaining law and order. Additionally, an integral neighborhood is clearly linked with the encompassing larger community. For example, neighborhood residents may sit on governing groups or agency boards in their town, city, or state. Or, residents may regularly write letters or editorials for the media.

Parochial Neighborhoods   A **parochial neighborhood** is one high on interaction and identification but low on community connections. In such a neighborhood, residents may interact frequently, identify with each other, and advocate for positive neighborhood goals and changes. Yet, they may neither have any involvement with the larger community nor have access to many resources. For instance, residents in an urban Hispanic neighborhood where most residents speak only Spanish may have little opportunity or ability to communicate with English-speaking decision makers in the larger community. Yet, these residents may feel very bonded with each other and be extremely supportive among themselves.

Diffuse Neighborhoods   A **diffuse neighborhood** offers residents a strong sense of neighborhood identification. However, residents experience little social interaction. They feel they do not need the neighborhood for support or help, and require low levels of connections to resources and services outside of the community. These are usually exclusive suburban neighborhoods or opulent luxury apartment buildings in urban settings. Residents may have money, power, and perceived identification with the neighborhood, yet not feel interaction is essential. They already have what they need and more; therefore, they find it unnecessary to expend energy for advocacy or change.

Stepping-Stone Neighborhoods   A **stepping-stone neighborhood** is characterized by the temporary nature of residents. They may positively identify themselves with the neighborhood but have low levels of commitment to interact with other residents or to work on the neighborhood's behalf because they simply won't be there that long. Residents of stepping-stone neighborhoods often are moving up in their careers and possibly starting and raising families. Because they're "on the way up," they usually have high levels of connection with other resources and systems in the larger community environment. Their efforts are directed elsewhere than neighborhood involvement and improvement. These are poor social environments for people seeking permanent residence or social belonging.

Transitory Neighborhoods   A **transitory neighborhood** resembles a stepping-stone in terms of the transitory nature of residents. However, residents in such neighborhoods have much less access to resources and are probably not moving up in the world. They're just moving. In such a neighborhood, residents have low

EP 8a

Critical Thinking Question **11-3**

Of these seven neighborhood categories—integral, parochial, diffuse, stepping stone, transitory, diffuse, and anomic—how would you describe your neighborhood, and why?

levels of social interaction and identification with the neighborhood. However, because of their serious needs, they frequently have high linkages with the wider community with its resources and services.

EP 6; 6a

Anomic Neighborhoods   Finally, an **anomic neighborhood** is dysfunctional and provides little social support. **Anomie** is a sociological term that means a state of normlessness. It occurs when norms are weak or in conflict leading to alienation and social instability. Despite residents' geographical proximity, the feeling of being in a neighborhood does not exist. It differs from a transitory neighborhood in that people may live here for long periods of time. An example of such a neighborhood is a huge urban low-income public housing project. Gangs, guns, and drugs may infest its corridors. Many residents may feel little identification with other residents yet have nowhere else to go. They may live in constant fear, often for good reason. The larger community may provide little support.

Highlight 11-2 addresses the issue of how neighborhoods don't always fall clearly into one category or another.

Theoretical Framework Two: Neighborhood Groups and Value Implementation

The second approach to describing and understanding neighborhoods focuses on two dimensions—the structure and connections of formal and informal groups in neighborhoods, and how these groups implement the neighborhood's primary values.

Highlight **11-2**

Brief Commentary on the Nature of Neighborhoods

EP 7a

It should be noted that these neighborhood types are not necessarily distinct from each other. The degree to which a neighborhood has social interaction, resident identity, and community linkages varies from one to another. Thus, neighborhood types may overlap or change over time (Fellin, 2001a, 2001b). For example, a stable but not affluent neighborhood that houses families and young couples may decay over time as residents depart and the landlords or owners cannot or choose not to maintain the properties. In less than a decade, the houses may be used by individuals for making or dispensing drugs, taken over by gangs,

or otherwise become unsuitable for the types of families it previously served.

Understanding a neighborhood can help social workers determine an intervention strategy to improve the neighborhood's functioning and enhance residents' quality of life. For example, in an anomic neighborhood, a generalist practitioner might seek to improve residents' involvement and identification with the neighborhood. One way is to identify potential community leaders who are interested and have a stake in community improvement. The worker could then help to train the natural leaders, organize residents, and encourage residents to engage in improving their community.

The basic idea is that formal and informal groups in neighborhoods can assist in achieving both general social goals and those of the individual resident. Such goals may concern "education, participation in community life, community improvement, and maintenance of social order" (Fellin, 2001a, p. 141). Fellin (2001b) explains:

> The organizational base of neighborhoods involves informal contacts and local formal organizations, such as voluntary associations. Neighborhoods can be classified in terms of both their level of organization and their capacity to implement their values, such as orientations toward education, good citizenship, and crime and violence. Recognition of the values of residents in a neighborhood is helpful for both interpersonal and community practice. For example, in areas with high rates of crime and delinquency, the social worker can assess the values of residents toward law and order and toward the tolerance of deviant behavior, and their willingness to organize to implement values to combat violence and crime. (p. 128)

Examples of informal neighborhood groups include groups based on friendship or shared caregiving for children or ailing older adults. Other organized groups might involve support groups, Neighborhood Watch organizations, or social groups such as the Red Hat Society (a nationally based organization with local groups of women who are middle-aged and older that congregate for social activities whose hallmark is the wearing of red and purple clothing—hence the name "Red Hat").

Neighborhood groups can be extraordinarily important in solving community problem. For example, they are often more effective than formal organizations for dealing with short-term relatively simple tasks. For example, if someone needs help moving, child care, or immediate assistance, the neighborhood group often can act faster and more directly than a formal organization. The same is true if the problem requires no specialized knowledge or skill.

On the other hand, complex, large-scale challenges often require the assistance of formal organizations with the knowledge and expertise to deal with such situations. Think of the different needs and possible solutions to the following situations:

- Mrs. Smith, 70-years-old Minneapolis resident has a tree limb fall and break her window in January.
- A tornado destroys the only elementary school in a small town.
- Jose Mendoza is left to care for two school-age children when his wife is deported by US Customs Service because she was here illegally.
- The Mulroney family, while on vacation, had a burglary at their home and lost their television, DVD play, computer, and their daughter's French horn.
- Debraden Smith, age 6, just fell and broke his arm. His grandmother who is caring for him needs transportation to the hospital for her and her grandson.

Which of these challenges would best be met by a neighborhood group, a formal organization, or a combination of both?

EP 8a

Critical Thinking Question 11-4

What are the strengths and weaknesses of the two conceptual frameworks describing neighborhood structure—the first emphasizing interpersonal interaction, identification, and connections, and the second focusing on neighborhood groups and value implementation?

Problems often facing neighborhoods, especially urban ones, include mobility and impersonality. Mobility involves a continuous flux in a neighborhood's population. The idea that a neighborhood is a static entity that exerts a socializing influence on its residents is challenged by the fact that people and families are often on the move. Residents move in and out of neighborhoods, limiting both their socializing influence as well as their ability to help each other. A second problem, impersonality, involves lack of connection and caring among neighborhood residents. It implies deficient social interaction and even isolation from each other. Without cohesion, it's difficult for neighborhood residents to bond together and provide each other with help and support.

By strengthening neighborhood groups and their links with formal organizations, neighborhoods can address and help resolve these problems to empower residents. Social workers can enhance this process. Residents can address the problem of mobility by discussing issues openly, developing welcoming attitudes and behaviors, and using informal groups and local voluntary organizations to reach out to new residents. Neighborhoods can address the issue of impersonality by strengthening their informal group structures, associating and bonding with each other, and offering support.

Neighborhoods, Ethnicity, and Social Class   LO 11-6

Neighborhoods are often characterized by ethnicity and social class (Fellin, 2001a, 2001b; Rubin & Rubin, 2008). Fellin (2001a) explains:

> The most common criteria used for classifying neighborhoods are social class, ethnicity, and culture. Neighborhoods may be distinguished by social class through the use of census data regarding occupational status, household income, education, and lifestyle. Residents usually refer to one or more of these factors in assigning social class names to their neighborhoods. Class names include terms such as wealthy, middle-class, working class, poor, underclass, and skid row neighborhoods. Names for ethnic neighborhoods include those of White ethnic groups, religious ethnic groups, and ethnic minority groups. Use of ethnic/cultural labels for neighborhoods usually indicates that members of a specific group are over-represented in relation to the general population, such as an African American neighborhood or a Hispanic/Latino

neighborhood. Religious or white ethnic labels are usually used when a substantial portion of the population, even if not a majority, are members of a specified group, such as Jewish, Catholic, Italian, Polish, or Irish neighborhoods. (p. 149)

Strengths of Ethnic and Cultural Solidarity

Rubin and Rubin (2008) elaborate on the strengths of community neighborhoods characterized by ethnicity, culture, and religion:

> *Solidarity communities* are constructed as people see themselves, or are labeled by others, as being part of the same racial or ethnic group, or who accept that they share a similar history, cultural traditions, language, or religion [emphasis added] . . . Solidarity ties are usually based on birth, and for some are seen as given. . . . You are born from Irish, or Ethiopian, or Thai ancestry, or your religion of birth is Hindu, Catholic, Dutch Reform[ed], or whatever. . . .
>
> With solidarity communities, cultural pride and ethnic identity provide the social glue that enables people to come together. People are likely to give to charities sponsored by their solidarity group, even if the contributors don't foresee that they themselves are likely to need support. Or people of a given ethnic neighborhood may rally when a hurricane devastates their ancestral homeland, collecting food and clothes in local churches.
>
> Members of solidarity communities reinforce their connectedness through shared rituals, holidays, festivals, and evocations of a common history. To build a sense of community within a solidarity group, organizers encourage social events during which members relate shared historic sufferings to one another. Such narratives replace past traumas and humiliations: forced migrations for Native Americans, incarceration in concentration camps for Japanese Americans during World War II, slavery for African Americans. . . . These historic, mutual experiences can be simultaneously a cause for pride—we went through this and survived—as well as a cause for rebellion. Native American organizers build solidarity within the group by narrating how the mainstream society stole Native American lands and deceived members of the group. Then by orchestrating actions on these same lands, demand that government must now restore traditional hunting, fishing, and land rights that it had taken away.
>
> By reframing how the past is understood, solidarity groups turn prior humiliation into a source of pride. (pp. 82–83)

Understanding the history and interconnections within a solidarity community is vital for social workers. Community organizers such as social workers can identify, convene, and mobilize neighborhood residents and resources both to help celebrate their origins and make them responsive to unmet community and neighborhood needs.

Highlight 11-3 describes three types of projects neighborhoods can undertake to build assets, the first of which emphasizes embracing one's cultural heritage and pride.

Highlight 11-3

Projects to Enhance Neighborhood Strengths LO 11-7

EP 7d

Delgado (2000) suggests at least three types of projects that community neighborhoods can undertake to enhance their strengths and assets. These include murals, gardens, and playgrounds. The idea behind such projects is for neighborhood residents to express themselves and their culture, thereby enhancing their sense of presence, cultural pride, and self-esteem.

The concept of *community built* means that a project is undertaken with the support and under the direction of a community neighborhood (Delgado, 2000, p. 75). This can mean that the entire project is completed by neighborhood residents or that the residents choose to bring in experts to complete a project. To be labeled community built, the project must meet the following 11 criteria . . . (Delgado, 2000):

(1) A concrete product is the end result, (2) the project is built primarily by volunteers, (3) successful completion is dependent on the participation of a wide sector of the community (the wider the better), (4) the project's scale corresponds to the size of the community to increase accessibility, (5) the project has distinct phases (a beginning, middle, and end), (6) the project develops in the community a sense of ownership, (7) the project is spatially defined, (8) the project has significance (social, political, and psychological) for the community, (9) the final form of the project reflects the needs of the community, (10) the final project can last long enough to be enjoyed by future generations, and (11) the project is permanent and creates a sense of permanence and long-term community commitment. (p. 76)

Murals

Large pictures painted or drawn on walls or ceilings, known as murals, can provide an important means of self-expression and cultural pride (Rivera, 2010; Hinton, 2017). Murals are a form of art displayed in grand scale on buildings rather than on canvas. Delgado (2000) explains:

Murals represent a [neighborhood] community effort to utilize cultural symbols as a way of creating an impact internally and externally. Murals should not be confused with graffiti. A mural represents an artistic impression that is not only sanctioned by a [neighborhood] community, but often commissioned by it . . . and invariably involve[s] a team of artists. Graffiti, on the other hand, represent an ar-

tistic impression (sometimes referred to as "tagging") that is individual centered and manifested on subway trains, doors, mailboxes, buses, public settings, and other less significant locations. Their content generally focuses on the trials and tribulations associated with urban living, issues of oppression, or simply a "signature" of the artist. (p. 78)

The content of murals can differ significantly from one another. The first mural type is designed to show ethnic or racial pride, such as Black or Latino history. A second theme often evident in murals involves religious symbols. These are often used in Latino culture because of the importance of religious involvement and influence in this culture. The murals may show spiritual or metaphysical or mystical beliefs associated with the group that painted the mural.

The third type of mural is related to issues of social and economic justice and reflects the experience of the group with institutions within the community. For example, a mural may show conflict and mistreatment by law enforcement, substance abuse, and other themes of concern to the residents. Others may perceive such content as radical or antisocial, but they are realistic perceptions of how it feels to be a member of the community.

A fourth theme displayed in murals involves beautification and decoration for its own sake. Murals don't have to be a statement of great social, political, or religious impact. Rather, they can serve to make a neighborhood a more pleasing and nice-looking place to live. This type of mural has been used in schools to involve students in an art project that beautifies an area of the building.

A fifth type of mural content includes recognition and honoring of others. These could represent a police officer killed in the line of duty, a hometown athlete or soldier, or similar hero. For example, in Sterling, Illinois, there is a mural of all the US presidents who visited there. Murals honoring others is a way for a community or neighborhood to recognize their own experience and heroes.

The sixth theme for a neighborhood mural involves efforts to commemorate community members who have died. This might be a rap star who was killed, local children who lost their lives in a gang shooting, or other local victims. Often, these murals are commissioned by members of the community and are not simply graffiti. In some cases, the depictions on such murals can tell you much about the concerns or issues in a neighborhood.

continued

Highlight **11-3** *continued*

Producing a mural requires a great deal of planning and coordination. Schools and neighborhood centers, for example, have used mural creation as a means of developing skills in those who will contribute to the mural. These include:

- Research on the subject or content of the mural

- Negotiation and discussion with residents about what the mural should show and where it will be located

- Awareness of safety issues involving mural painting

- Collaboration and skills in working with others

- Punctuality and follow-through in beginning and ending the mural

- Training in functional work habits and expectations

- Expansion of skills in verbal and nonverbal communication

- Technical skills involving science and math when designing content and preparing paints

- Money and time management abilities including finding resources to finance the project and scheduling a plan for completion

- Assumption of responsibility as effective contributors to the community and active participants in the project's completion

Gardens

Gardens in urban areas are very important (Hartwig & Mason, 2016; Draper & Freedman, 2010; Ohmer, Meadowcroft, Freed, & Lewis, 2009). Ohmer and colleagues (2009) explain:

While community gardening originally began as a way to improve local food supplies in the early 20th century, it has evolved into a strategy for improving overall community and sustainable development in neighborhoods, including promoting social, environmental, and economic concerns. Prior research shows that community gardening can facilitate social interaction, community involvement and volunteerism, and education of community members regarding horticulture and garden methods. Community gardening has also become an important community development strategy, turning devastated and vacant lots into beautiful spaces with flowers, trees, shrubs, and other vegetation that can be enjoyed by the entire community. (p. 384)

Gardens are grown for four basic purposes (Hartwig & Mason, 2016; Delgado, 2000). First, they can be visually appealing. Second, people can grow gardens as a type of recreation. Third, gardens can be grown for food. Gardens can also be used as a healing space for community members who have experienced past trauma. Sometimes, gardens serve two or more of these purposes.

Neighborhood residents usually get together to develop a garden under four different circumstances (Delgado, 2000). A local empty or cleared plot of land might become available for their use. An institution such as a hospital, church, or school might seek a beautification project. Neighborhood residents might decide to grow a garden for residents in need. Or funding might become available from grants or other public or private sources to support a neighborhood gardening project.

There are many benefits from community gardens (Hartwig & Mason, 2016; Draper & Freedman, 2010; Ohmer et al., 2009). Gardens can provide opportunities for residents to work together toward a common goal. We've already noted that gardens can both provide food and improve a neighborhood's appearance. They can improve residents' sense of self-worth and self-esteem. Gardens can help people living in urban settings experience and appreciate nature.

Neighborhood House of Milwaukee, Inc., a neighborhood center located in an impoverished inner-city community, provides a good example of encouraging urban gardening and the appreciation of nature. (Neighborhood centers established in the settlement house tradition are described later in the chapter.) Neighborhood House's mission is to inspire and connect to strengthen families and the community (Neighborhood House, 2017a).

One of its programs involves Outdoor/Environmental Education (Neighborhood House, 2017a). The agency's property includes a 93-acre Nature Center where "activities include experiential science-based learning with an emphasis on developing critical thinking and a sense of stewardship for the environment" (Neighborhood House, 2017b). A primary purpose is to encourage young people's appreciation and enjoyment of nature. Children ages 6 weeks to 6 years are introduced to this habitat and encouraged to explore. The Gardening Programs offer opportunities for children and teens up to age 18 to participate in all aspects of gardening, from planting to harvesting and eating their produce.

EP 4a;
4c; 9d

One major review of the literature on community gardening found that "youth gardening programs and projects" produce "positive dietary, academic, and developmental results" (Draper & Freedman, 2010). Such programs focusing on nutrition increase "participants' nutrition

continued

Highlight **11-3** *continued*

knowledge; fruit and vegetable consumption, preference, and asking behaviors at home; physical activity; and gardening knowledge and ability" (Draper & Freedman, 2010, p. 478). Draper and Freedman (2010) recommend that further research on community gardening be done; they urge that this "would greatly increase the understanding of the effectiveness of community gardens as a tool for health promotion, fostering positive interracial and intergenerational relationships, creating jobs, increasing food security, and much more. Increased knowledge and evidence in these areas would provide more support for why community gardens should be established, valued, and sustained" (p. 488).

Community Playgrounds

Developing and improving "community playgrounds" can provide excellent opportunities for enhancing a neighborhood's assets. Delgado (2000) explains:

> Although community playgrounds primarily target the recreational needs of children, they also fulfill other functions that rarely get noticed in the everyday life of a community. The structures can play a central role in connecting residents with each other and provide an

outlet for families to do some activity together that does not require the expenditure of funds. (pp. 95–96)

It is vital that neighborhood residents make their own decisions regarding what the playground should be like—what types of equipment should be included and how it should be arranged. It's crucial that the area meet the individual neighborhood's and its residents' needs. Delgado (2000) likens a neighborhood's development of a playground to an old-fashioned barn raising. He continues:

> Simply described, a barn raising brings all members of a rural community, regardless of age, gender, and skills, together for a concentrated period (usually one or two days) to help a fellow neighbor who has suffered some tragedy, like a fire, to build a barn. It serves to help a neighbor in need, reaffirms a community's definition of itself, and ensures the members that they do, in fact, belong to a community that cares. (p. 97)

He concludes, "Community-built playgrounds . . . reflect a community's desire to claim their own space and control the activities within this area. Thus, the presence of such playgrounds can serve as excellent indicators of a community's capacity to rally for a common good" (Delgado, 2000, p. 102).

EP 8a

Critical Thinking Questions **11-5**

Have you noticed any murals, neighborhood gardens, or playground development in your community neighborhood? If so, what were your thoughts about them?

Social Class

"Attention to the social class level of neighborhoods is important for social workers, since neighborhood location and social class have a powerful effect on the resources and liabilities that affect the quality of life of neighborhood residents" (Fellin, 2001b, p. 129). The proportion of homes owned by the residents and the quality of those homes usually reflect the social class-level of a neighborhood. Both social class and home ownership are related "to some combination of occupational status, household income, and educational level of members of a household" (Fellin, 2001a, p. 150).

Houses and social class reflect social status. Higher social status implies greater access to resources. Poorer communities often have both the greatest need and least access to community-based resources to address those needs. **Integration**, the process of assembling diverse groups of people, including different races, into a cohesive whole, sometimes helps to close that resource gap.

Fellin (2001a) reflects:

> Studies of inner-city poverty areas show a decline in status in these neighbor-
> hoods, due to the decline in employment and increase in welfare dependency
> among residents, as well as the departure of upwardly mobile individuals and
> families. . . . At the same time, many working- and middle-class ethnic minority
> neighborhoods have been able to maintain their status because of residential
> stability and strong institutional supports from schools, churches, medical and
> social service institutions, and neighborhood voluntary organizations. Many
> urban neighborhoods that have become more integrated racially have man-
> aged to maintain their class status through institutional and voluntary group
> efforts that support integration. (pp. 153–154)

Segregation

Segregation, the opposite of integration, is separating a group of people based
on race, class, ethnic group, or other characteristic from the general population in society. Segregation, therefore, may be imposed upon a group or it may
be voluntary. Segregation continues to be a major problem in terms of housing
and geographical community location (Mooney, Knox, & Schacht, 2017). Fellin
(2001b) explains:

> The concepts of segregation and integration serve to describe these neighbor-
> hood communities, with segregated neighborhoods having a high proportion
> of ethnic minority and/or cultural group membership . . . Empirical studies of
> housing patterns in North American communities continue to leave no doubt
> that housing segregation is due in large part to discrimination and prejudice
> based on race and/or ethnicity. (p. 129)

There are other rationales for the existence of neighborhoods where residents
have the same racial heritage. Fellin (2001a) explains:

> Some members of ethnic minority groups prefer to reside in neighborhoods
> populated mainly by members of their own group. These individuals . . .
> reside in and are positively identified with the minority community. These
> neighborhoods also receive people who are unable to move into other
> neighborhoods due to economic factors and/or discrimination in housing.
> There is strong evidence that societal and community barriers to residential
> mobility prohibit some persons from "leaving the 'hood'" and [entering more
> mainstream society]. . . . These barriers include . . . financial constraints and
> housing discrimination. (p. 158)

EP 8a

Critical Thinking Questions 11-6

Think of a large city with which you're familiar. To what extent do neighborhoods
reflect ethnic, cultural, and class distinctions? To what extent is segregation apparent?

Focus on Ethics 11-1

Is Segregation Ethical? LO 11-8

What do you think are the dynamics involved in segregation? To what extent is it ethical for communities to allow segregation to continue in neighborhoods? Explain. What, if anything, should be done about segregation?

EP 1b

Processes of Change in Neighborhoods LO 11-9

EP 7b

By nature, systems are subject to change. Levels of input and output change. External factors affecting the system are altered; so it is with neighborhoods. Neighborhoods' social, economic, and political environments are in constant flux. People move in and out. Jobs are developed or businesses leave the area. Buildings get older and require repair. Sometimes, old buildings are torn down and new ones built. Other times, old buildings are refurbished. Still other times, old buildings rot and stagnate in deteriorating states.

Homan (2016) cites three theories that explain neighborhood change: the "invasion-succession," "life cycle," and "political capacity" models (pp. 473–476).

The Invasion-Succession Model

The invasion-succession model is based on the idea that conflict occurs when new groups of people reflecting certain racial, cultural, or religious characteristics move into areas already inhabited by people with different characteristics. A new group will invade and the other will withdraw. **Invasion** *is* "the tendency of each new group" of people coming into an area "to force existing groups out" (Kirst-Ashman & Hull, 2018a, p. 306). **Succession**, then, is "the replacement of the original occupants of a community or neighborhood by new groups" (Kirst-Ashman & Hull, 2018a, p. 306). For example, a neighborhood might first be populated by people of German descent, followed by African Americans, and later by Eastern Europeans. A concern is that "if the withdrawing group takes valuable resources from the community (e.g., family income, shop ownership, political clout) before these can be effectively replaced, the neighborhood is likely to decline" (Homan, 2016, p. 473).

The Life Cycle Model

The life cycle model views neighborhood change as a decline, with a neighborhood undergoing predictable phases from birth until death. These phases include the following five (Downs, 1981; Homan, 2016):

1. A stable and viable neighborhood
2. A minor decline
3. A clear decline

4. A heavily deteriorated neighborhood
5. An unhealthy and nonviable neighborhood (Homan, 2016, p. 475)

Homan (2016) explains:

A stable and viable neighborhood exists when no symptoms of decline have appeared and property values are rising. A period of minor decline may follow in which some minor deficiencies in housing units are visible and density is higher than when the neighborhood was first developed, but property values are stable or increasing slightly. A neighborhood in clear decline is marked by a larger proportion of residents living in poverty. Renters are dominant in the housing market, and landlord-tenant relations are poor because of high absentee ownership. Other factors, such as higher density, low confidence in the area's future, and abandoned buildings, are also associated with this stage. In heavily deteriorated neighborhoods, housing is very run down and even dilapidated. Most structures require major repair. Subsistence-level households are numerous, and profitability of rental units is poor. Pessimism about the area's future is widespread. An unhealthy and nonviable neighborhood is at the final stage of change. Massive abandonment occurs, and those residents who remain are at the lowest social status and incomes in the region. Expectations about the area's future are nil. (pp. 475)

The Political Capacity Model

The political capacity model perceives a neighborhood as having the ability to pass through various stages as it develops its political viability and power (Homan, 2016). Unlike the life cycle model, the focus is on growth rather than deterioration.

Initially, the neighborhood may be disorganized and lacking in leadership. At this stage, someone must function as a community organizer to encourage development of leadership potential in residents. The next stage involves the organizer identifying and working with various social institutions such as schools, churches, and clubs to develop social networking, cooperative interaction, and emerging leadership. The following phase concerns identifying and targeting some neighborhood issues for change. The organizer eventually develops a strong network of neighborhood groups and individuals who begin working together seriously in addressing neighborhood concerns and needs. The final stage involves a neighborhood with a strong leadership and a widespread, inclusive social network that can independently identify neighborhood goals and work cohesively to achieve them.

EP 8a

Critical Thinking Question **11-7**

What do you see as the strengths and weaknesses of each of the three models explaining neighborhood change—invasion-succession, life cycle, and political capacity?

Neighborhood Centers, Empowerment, and the Promotion of Health and Well-Being   LO 11-10

EP 8c

A **neighborhood center** is a community-based agency that advocates for community residents and works with them to provide a wide array of services meeting their needs; it is funded primarily through government agencies, but also through some grants and the United Way. For example, Milwaukee has eight such centers. Services provided by neighborhood centers can potentially address numerous issues, needs, and developmental tasks, from pre-birth to post-death. For example, a neighborhood center might offer family planning information to one family, after-school programming for teens, adult programs aimed at identifying community leaders, and help for another family to plan a funeral.

One such center in Madison, Wisconsin, celebrating its hundredth anniversary, teaches drumming, holds judo classes, helps students learn to sew, provides space for a bluegrass band to practice, and teaches a foreign language course. Other groups that utilize this center include the Hindu Dharma Circle, a Bolivian dance troupe, and African, Ghana, and Nigerian clubs (Worland, 2016, p. A1).

To understand the potential significance of neighborhood centers in the macro social environment, we will discuss three dimensions: a brief history of their development originating with settlement houses, a description of current services and structures and types of activities they sponsor, and a range of case examples.

Settlement Houses: A Response to Changing Social and Economic Forces

EP 1c

Settlement houses of the late nineteenth and early twentieth centuries provided the ideological foundation for today's neighborhood centers. They developed in response to three changing social and economic forces (Garvin & Cox, 1995). The first was industrialization. Mammoth growth in manufacturing and technology brought with it numerous social problems, including unemployment (as the production of goods moved from personal homes to manufacturing plants), and problems with working environments involving poor conditions, long hours, safety issues, and child labor (Day, 2009; Garvin & Cox, 1995).

The second primary change was urbanization. Concurrent with the centralization of industry within urban settings was tremendous growth of urban populations. Masses of people moved from rural to urban areas on quests for work and prosperity. Unfortunately, most were forced to move into the oldest, most crowded, and least sanitary portions of cities.

The third major change during this period was explosive immigration, primarily from northwestern Europe. Immigrants brought with them their own problems. Many came from poor rural environments and had little with which to start their lives in this country. Many became ill during the immigration process. When they arrived, poverty forced many immigrants to live under poor conditions and accept whatever work they could find.

Day (2009) explains that **settlement houses**:

were run in part by client groups, and they emphasized social reform rather than relief or assistance. Three-fourths of settlement workers were women, and most were well-educated and dedicated to working on problems of urban poverty. Early sources of funding were wealthy individuals or clubs such as the Junior League, and at first their founders tried to provide "culture" to members, such as art, music, and lectures. When they found a need, they added new features such as playgrounds, day care, kindergartens, baths, and classes in English literacy. Other services included art exhibits, lectures, and classes in homemaking, cooking, sewing, and shopping, especially for immigrant women who were not used to the facilities available in the United States such as grocery stores and the products they offered (fresh bread, milk, and canned goods). Settlement workers tried to improve housing conditions, organized protests, offered job training and labor searches, supported organized labor, worked against child labor, and fought against corrupt politicians. Over time settlement houses became centers of social reform, and clubs, societies, and political groups . . . used them as bases of operation. (p. 229)

Settlement Houses and Generalist Social Work Practice

Settlement houses formed a strong partial foundation for generalist social work practice within communities in at least three ways. First, the settlement house approach addressed the problems of people in an environmental context instead of focusing on individual pathology. Problems existed in the environment that created difficulties for individuals. Individuals were not viewed as the targets of blame, punishment, and change. Settlements focused on social issues and improving living conditions, especially for those who were poor or less fortunate than most.

Second, an environmental focus led naturally to an emphasis on advocacy and social reform. The macro social environment required change to meet people's needs.

Third, settlement houses emphasized the empowerment of people. At its most basic level, empowerment involves providing people with authority or power. The settlement house perspective viewed people as having strengths and capabilities to effect their own change. Families and neighborhoods were seen as potential vehicles for positive change. The concepts of community organization and group work developed within the settlement house context. Jane Addams and Ellen Gates Starr began, perhaps, the most famous settlement house, Hull House, in Chicago in 1889.

Yan (2004) maintains that settlement houses can continue to provide an important source of strength to neighborhoods and communities. He explains:

The settlement house can provide a physical platform for dialogue. The "neutral turf" of a settlement house allows it to function as a "living room" of the neighborhood, in which all members of the community, of different generations, racial, cultural, gender and political orientation, are welcome. The settlement house's physical presence in the community also represents a symbolic figure of the community. The architectural image of many settlement houses and their history of working with members of the community have been interwoven into the memories of several generations of members of the community. To newcomers in the community, the physical presence of, and the services provided by, a settlement house also provide a physical entry point for integration into the new environment. (p. 62)

Neighborhood Centers Today LO 11-11

EP 7c; 7d;
8; 8c; 8e

Many of the social ills that settlement houses originally addressed no longer exist today. For example, child labor is illegal, and minimum requirements for workplace safety are in place. However, successful neighborhood centers, sometimes called community centers, organize community residents to meet new needs and demands. These include provision of daycare for working parents, preschool programs, home support for older adults, family counseling, substance abuse education and counseling, health services, recreational activities for children and teens, food pantries, temporary shelter, vocational assessment and employment counseling, and meeting locations for various local organizations from the Boy Scouts to Alcoholics Anonymous (Lewis, Lewis, Daniels, & D'Andrea, 2011).

Whereas the initial settlement houses were run by concerned volunteers and community residents, today's neighborhood center is typically run by professionals, although volunteers are often used. The executive director or chief executive officer is often a social worker with a master's degree.

Neighborhood centers are built on four assumptions: the importance of neighborhood residents, an emphasis on neighborhood assets, the potential for various neighborhood centers to work together, and the provision of linkage among various facets of the neighborhood.

Community Neighborhood Residents Are Key Factors The first assumption upon which neighborhood centers are built is that the core of a neighborhood center's existence and success rests on members of the community. It exists only to furnish service and provide a mechanism for community residents to organize themselves to get things done.

Emphasis on Community Neighborhood Assets The second assumption upon which neighborhood centers are built is a focus on community assets. These include strengths and values that contribute to a community's progress, improvement, and development. The focus is on providing residents with what they need to survive and thrive.

For example, working single parents may require daycare and after-school care for their children in order to keep their jobs. Providing such services supports parents' strength in their capacity to work.

Older adults may be able to remain in their own homes if they receive minimal daily support, such as a daily hot meal delivered or someone to transport them to get groceries. A neighborhood center can build on strengths and help maximize people's potential to live independently.

Finally, a neighborhood center may sponsor a gang prevention and youth recreation program. Such a program could focus on the strengths of the community's young people. Services might include counseling children and teens concerning the legal repercussions of gang involvement and redirecting their energies to other, more productive social and recreational activities.

Neighborhood Centers Can Help Neighborhoods Work Together A third assumption regarding neighborhood centers is that they are a means of unifying a neighborhood so it may work together with other neighborhood centers for the betterment of the entire community (Kubisch et al., 2008). The center can serve as the congregating place for residents to organize and hold meetings to address social, economic, and political issues. For example, several neighborhood centers could collaborate to develop a list of the various support services and other opportunities available at each site to broaden the options open to residents of all their neighborhoods. With consolidated resources, the neighborhoods could provide a wider range of services to address more specific identified needs.

One collective also established a landlord assistance project where residents volunteered time and effort to help local landlords. Volunteers identified and made minor repairs on and in neighborhood homes to keep neighborhood residences operational and in compliance with local building codes. Landlords were responsible only for providing required materials at minimal costs. Prior to the landlord assistance project, landlords frequently avoided making or "forgot" to make repairs and improvements, saying that it was too costly to repair old properties in low-rent neighborhoods. They threatened to allow foreclosure for unpaid taxes if upkeep became too expensive. Neighbors volunteering time significantly cut upkeep costs as landlords paid only for supplies, not for the expensive reimbursement required by skilled tradespeople.

Linkage among Neighborhood Units   A fourth foundation principle for neighborhood centers is linkage among various facets of the neighborhood. This includes individual families, local businesses, social service departments, schools, medical facilities, religious organizations, and other public resources. Another neighborhood center established a neighborhood-based group that helped people with mental or emotional help problems. The group identified businesses supportive of providing jobs to people with mental health problems; county social workers to assess, counsel, and refer; school social workers to identify clients and provide group counseling; psychiatrists and other physicians to assess, provide, and monitor appropriate psychotherapeutic drugs; and church groups providing facilities for support group meetings and recreational space and activities. After establishing relationships with relevant service and resource providers, the referral group publicized its existence with fliers to residents and ads in local papers. Neighborhood families with members suffering from mental health problems could then contact the referral group, which, in turn, would link people with necessary resources.

Highlight 11-4 identifies several goals that an effective community center and organization can accomplish.

| Highlight **11-4** |

What Effective Neighborhood Centers and Community Organizations Can Do LO 11-12

EP 8c

Neighborhood centers and community organizations can provide support to residents and improve living conditions in a number of ways (Homan, 2016):

■ *Establishment of a positive and effective sense of self as a neighborhood and as a resident of that neighborhood.* This can be done through publicity in local papers and newsletters, announcements

continued

Highlight **11-4** *continued*

posted in businesses, and decals and emblems placed throughout the neighborhood.

■ *Social activities and celebrations.* Neighborhood centers can sponsor picnics, cultural events, dinners, recreational activities, and entertainment to provide opportunities for positive social interaction, networking, and bonding as a community neighborhood.

■ *Maintenance and clean-up.* Neighborhood centers can form groups to pick up garbage, repair housing, plant trees and gardens, and rejuvenate parks, playgrounds, and other public spaces.

■ *Opportunities for interpersonal interaction.* Neighborhood centers can sponsor and promote any number of chances for social interaction. These include establishing a program where older adults become foster grandparents to lonely children, sponsoring dances, providing information via newsletters about community events, and offering opportunities for residents to participate in the organization's decision-making processes.

■ *Sharing of resources and organizing volunteer help.* Neighborhood centers can sponsor book, toy, or tool libraries. They can identify residents' skills and link these residents with others who need help.

■ *Training and education.* Neighborhood centers can provide educational and training opportunities on any number of topics ranging from how to change the oil in your car to a discussion about a work of classic literature. Many local organizations are helping at-risk youth return to complete high school or other educational opportunities with a goal of ending youth unemployment (Steinberg & Almeida, 2015).

■ *Support for various organized groups.* Neighborhood centers can provide facilities and promote publicity for neighborhood groups, including Boy Scouts, Gamblers Anonymous, or the local theater guild.

■ *Evaluation of services provided by the local government.* The quality of police and fire protection can be monitored, as can the neighborhood's general maintenance.

■ *Protection and safety.* Neighborhood centers can initiate resident participation in crime prevention and monitoring. They can serve as advocates for environmental improvements where dangerous physical conditions exist. This is an area where university and community partnerships have proven helpful in confronting ecological crises (McSpirit, Faltraco, & Bailey, 2012). These alliances offer increased resources not available to a single center or organization.

■ *Provision of various services.* Neighborhood centers can provide a range of services, including counseling, daycare, transportation, and emergency help. They can also partner with universities and colleges to develop more extensive services and linkages, including both health and education assistance. Such alliances offer opportunities for evaluating the effectiveness of services provided (Burbank, Hunter, & Gutiérrez, 2012).

■ *Collaboration with managers of public programs.* Neighborhood centers can work with local government, service providers, and other professionals to develop needed programs and make certain laws and local codes are enforced.

■ *Housing improvement and business development.* Neighborhood centers can advocate for upholding building codes, write grants to develop small businesses to help stimulate the local economy, and encourage resident involvement in public programs providing loans and other assistance.

■ *Enhancement of political clout.* Neighborhood centers can encourage residents to participate in the political process through voting and forming coalitions to advocate for positive change. In addition, joining with other organizations increases opportunity for community-wide changes. For example, a recent study of over 300 community coalitions found that high-functioning community coalitions can effectively produce changes in substance abuse behaviors, particularly underage drinking (Flewelling & Hanley, 2016).

■ *School improvement.* Neighborhood centers can provide feedback to local schools and work with school personnel to develop programs and improve educational processes.

EP 8a

> ### Critical Thinking Questions **11-8**
>
> Are you aware of or familiar with a neighborhood center in your neighborhood or campus community? If so, what types of programs does it provide? If you don't know of one, you might investigate where one exists in a town or city close to you.

Examples of Neighborhood Centers and Community-Building LO 11-13

The following are some examples of the value of neighborhood centers and similar local organizations:

- A Chicago-based program provided young neighborhood boys who were having conduct problems with a group-based training program designed to develop skills and self-control. The group employed modeling, coaching, role playing, and rewards for the boys and caregiver training for parents. Evaluation of the project showed positive changes in criminal behavior and alcohol consumption (Zimmerman, Welsh, & Posick, 2015). This underscores the importance of developing appropriate evaluation measures based on the program's goals.
- A Midwestern neighborhood association with dwindling membership used social media including Facebook, Twitter, and email to inform residents, showcase neighborhood boundaries, and show pictures of past events. It also delivered doorhangers with information about the association and established an annual garage sale day. The neighborhood association varied the means of communication with neighborhood residents by interspersing social media with postal messages and found that multiple communication methods produced a greater response rate (Johnson & Halegoua, 2015).
- Researchers in South Carolina studied residents in 42 neighborhoods to determine the impact of neighborhood organizations on residents' assistance to police in controlling crime. Participants in neighborhood organizations were 54 percent more likely to participate in anti-crime efforts compared to residents who were not involved in these organizations. This can have a positive effect on public safety in the neighborhood (Hawdon & Ryan, 2011).
- Researchers studying the impact of neighborhood youth organizations in Chicago found that the mere existence of these organization may protect residents from being exposed to violence (Gardner & Brooks-Gunn, 2009).
- The Becoming a Man (BAM) program in Chicago provides male students with training and practice in "impulse control, emotional self-regulation, reading social cues and interpreting intentions of others, raising aspirations for the future and developing a sense of personal responsibility and integrity." It represents a recognition that young men of color often lack appropriate role models. Its success has resulted in expansion to 50 schools in the city (Helgeson & Schneider, 2015, p. 17).

Chapter Summary

The following summarizes this chapter's content as it relates to the learning objectives presented at the beginning of the chapter.

LO 11-1 **Define neighborhoods and their role in providing a context for human behavior.**

A neighborhood is a geographic area within a bigger community where residents have some commonalities. It is the significant immediate social environment in which people live, eat, sleep, and interact on a daily basis. Neighborhoods include "immediate," "extended," and "community neighborhoods" (Fellin, 2001b, p. 127).

LO 11-2 **Explain neighborhood functions and how they can enhance residents' quality of life.**

Neighborhood functions include provision of a place for interaction, mutual aid, an arena for people to communicate and share information, an opportunity for people to congregate with others who share similarities, and an organizational and political base.

LO 11-3 **Identify the qualities of strong neighborhoods.**

Strong neighborhoods benefit residents through provision of good resources, strong support networks, and a safe environment.

LO 11-4 **Respond to critical thinking questions.**

Critical thinking questions addressed: neighborhood strengths; neighborhood support systems; description of your neighborhood; comparison of theories describing neighborhood structure; neighborhood projects; ethnic, cultural, and class distinctions with respect to segregation; strengths and weaknesses of models of neighborhood change; and awareness of the existence of neighborhood centers.

LO 11-5 **Describe two theoretical frameworks for examining neighborhood structure.**

One approach to examining neighborhood structure focuses on interpersonal interaction, identification, and connections. Integral neighborhoods are those manifesting high levels of all three conditions. A parochial neighborhood is one high on interaction and identification but low on community connections. A diffuse neighborhood offers residents a strong sense of neighborhood identification, but allows for little social interaction and few connections. A stepping-stone neighborhood is characterized by the temporary nature of residents. A transitory neighborhood also has mainly temporary residents, but they have much less access to resources and upward mobility. Anomic neighborhoods are dysfunctional and provide little support.

A second approach to examining neighborhood structure emphasizes the structure and connections of formal and informal neighborhood groups, and how these groups implement the neighborhood's primary values. Values may focus on goals involving "education, participation in community life, community improvement, and maintenance of social order" (Fellin, 2001a, p. 141).

LO 11-6 **Discuss neighborhoods, ethnicity, and social class, including the strengths of ethnic and cultural solidarity, and segregation.**

Neighborhoods are often characterized by ethnicity, culture, and religion. "Solidarity communities are constructed as people see themselves, or are labeled by others, as being part of the same racial or ethnic group, or who accept that they share a similar history, cultural traditions, language, or religion" (Rubin & Rubin, 2008, p. 82). A focus on social class is important for social workers to understand residents' access to resources and experience with liabilities. It's not news that poor neighborhoods generally have the greatest needs. Segregation is the separation of a group of people based on race, class, ethnic group, or other characteristic from the general population in society.

LO 11-7 **Describe projects that can enhance neighborhood strengths.**

Projects to enhance neighborhood strengths include the use of murals and the development of community gardens and playgrounds.

LO 11-8 Describe ethical issues involving neighborhoods.

Ethical questions concern the extent to which it is ethical for communities to allow or maintain segregation in neighborhoods.

LO 11-9 Describe the invasion-succession, life cycle, and political capacity models of change in neighborhoods.

The invasion-succession model is based on the idea that conflict occurs when new groups of people reflecting certain racial, cultural, or religious characteristics move into areas already inhabited by people with different characteristics. The life cycle model views neighborhood change as a decline, with a neighborhood undergoing predictable phases from birth until death. The political capacity model perceives a neighborhood as having the ability to pass through various stages as it develops its political viability and power.

LO 11-10 Describe neighborhood centers and their origin in the settlement house movement.

A neighborhood center is a community-based agency that advocates for community residents and works with them to provide a wide array of services meeting their needs. Settlement houses were developed in response to industrialization, urbanization, and explosive immigration. Although they provided a range of services, they "emphasized social reform rather than relief or assistance" (Day, 2009, p. 229). They formed a strong partial foundation for generalist social work practice within communities today and provided the underpinning for today's neighborhood centers.

LO 11-11 Identify the assumptions upon which neighborhood centers are based today.

Neighborhood centers are based on four assumptions. First, the core of a neighborhood center's existence and success rests on community people. Second, neighborhood centers focus on community assets. Third, they provide a means for unifying a neighborhood so it may work together with other neighborhood centers for the betterment of the entire community. Fourth, neighborhood centers provide linkage among various facets of the neighborhood.

LO 11-12 Specify types of activities neighborhood centers can sponsor to improve residents' living conditions.

Neighborhood centers can establish a positive sense of neighborhood identity, provide social activities and opportunities for social interaction, assist in neighborhood clean-up, share resources and volunteers, provide training and education, support various established groups, evaluate the local government's services, encourage neighborhood safety, provide various services including counseling, collaborate with managers of public programs, address housing improvement issues, enhance political clout, and work toward school improvement.

LO 11-13 Provide examples of neighborhood and community projects reflecting empowerment.

Examples of empowerment include help with job searches, use of formal professional groups to assist local businesses, identification and provision of space for community events, the offering of opportunities for youth involvement, assistance to homebound older adults, development of neighborhood newsletters and communication channels, and launching of programs to address teen pregnancy and school dropout.

Looking Ahead

This chapter explored various facets of neighborhood empowerment within communities. The next chapter will shift gears and investigate human diversity, populations-at-risk, and empowerment for these populations in the macro social environment.

Competency Notes

The following identifies where Educational Policy (EP) competencies and component behaviors are discussed in the chapter.

EP 1b Use reflection and self-regulation to manage personal values and maintain professionalism in practice situations. *(p. 411)*: Questions are raised concerning the ethics involved in segregation.

EP 1c Demonstrate professional demeanor in behavior; appearance; and oral, written, and electronic communication. *(p. 413)*: Social workers should know the profession's history. This includes information about settlement houses, which were established in the late nineteenth and early twentieth centuries.

EP 4a Use practice experience and theory to inform scientific inquiry and research. *(p. 408)*: According to experience in practice, more social work research needs to be conducted concerning community gardening in order to enhance the effectiveness of such projects.

EP 4c Use and translate research evidence to inform and improve practice, policy, and service delivery. *(p. 409)*: Social workers should utilize research on the effectiveness of community gardening to determine its usefulness in their own practice.

EP 6 (Competency 6)—Engage with Individuals, Families, Groups, Organizations, and Communities. *(p.400)*: Engaging with members and leaders in a community requires the same skills as engaging with individuals and families. This includes good listening skills, ability to ask the right questions, and engendering trust.

EP 6a Apply knowledge of human behavior and the social environment, person-in-environment, and other multidisciplinary theoretical frameworks to engage with clients and constituencies. *(p. 400)*: Social workers can teach neighborhood leaders skills of engagement with other potential advocates.

EP 6b Use empathy, reflection, and interpersonal skills to effectively engage diverse clients and constituencies. *(p. 397)*: Recognition of the values of residents in a neighborhood is helpful for both interpersonal and community practice.

EP 7b Apply knowledge of human behavior and the social environment, person-in-environment, and other multidisciplinary theoretical frameworks in the analysis of assessment data from clients and constituencies. *(p.411)*: Social workers need to evaluate which approach or approaches to use when assessing a community, invasion-succession, life cycle, and political capacity.

EP 7c Develop mutually agreed-on intervention goals and objectives based on the critical assessment of strengths, needs, and challenges within clients and constituencies. *(p. 415)*: Generalist practitioners should work together with neighborhood residents to determine what services neighborhood centers will provide and to develop mutually agreed-on goals for neighborhood centers.

EP 7d Select appropriate intervention strategies based on the assessment, research knowledge, and values and preferences of clients and constituencies. *(p. 407)*: Social workers must have knowledge to practice with systems of all sizes. Neighborhoods reflect an important subsystem of communities. *(p. 407)*: Three approaches to enhance neighborhood strengths are explained. *(p. 415)*: Generalist practitioners working in and with neighborhood centers should select appropriate intervention strategies based on mutually agreed-on goals.

EP 8 (Competency 8)—Intervene with Individuals, Families, Groups, Organizations, and Communities. *(p. 409)*: Social workers who practice in and work with neighborhood centers can initiate actions to achieve these centers' goals. Generalist practitioners working in and with neighborhood centers can help neighborhood residents resolve a range of problems.

EP 8a Critically choose and implement interventions to achieve practice goals and enhance capacities of clients and constituencies. *(pp. 400, 401, 403, 405, 409, 410, 412, 418):* Critical thinking questions are posed.

EP 8b Apply knowledge of human behavior and the social environment, person-in-environment, and other multidisciplinary theoretical frameworks in interventions with clients and constituencies. *(p. 397):* Using appropriate theories and concepts when assessing a neighborhood can help social workers determine an intervention strategy to improve the neighborhood's functioning and enhance residents' quality of life.

EP 8c Use inter-professional collaboration as appropriate to achieve beneficial practice outcomes. *(p. 413):* Social workers can provide leadership as they work in and with neighborhood centers. Neighborhood centers can work with local government, service providers, and other professionals to develop needed programs and make certain laws and local codes are enforced.

EP 8e Facilitate effective transitions and endings that advance mutually agreed-on goals. *(p. 415):* Neighborhood centers can implement prevention interventions such as providing support to older adults in their own homes to prevent their removal from these homes, or providing temporary shelter to prevent homelessness.

EP 9b Apply knowledge of human behavior and the social environment, person-in-environment, and other multidisciplinary theoretical frameworks in the evaluation of outcomes. *(p. 400):* The vast variety of interventions that can be employed in a neighborhood requires careful selection of appropriate evaluation measures based on the program's goals.

EP 9d Apply evaluation findings to improve practice effectiveness at the micro, mezzo, and macro levels. *(p. 417):* Developing alliances and coalitions with universities offers opportunities for evaluating the effectiveness of services provided. These findings can be used to improve organizational programs.

Media Resources

MindTap for Social Work

Go to MindTap® for digital study tools and resources that complement this text and help you be more successful in your course and career. There's an interactive eBook plus videos of client sessions, skill-building activities, quizzes to help you prepare for tests, apps, and more—all in one place. If your instructor didn't assign MindTap, you can find out more about it at CengageBrain .com.

12 | Diversity, Populations-at-Risk, and Empowerment in the Macro Social Environment

The macro social environment is characterized by many kinds of diversity, including diversity that involves race, culture, age, and ability or disability. Here a hospital patient receives hydrotherapy to aid recovery from physical and neurological injuries.

LEARNING OBJECTIVES

After reading this chapter...

12-1   Describe how groups, including African Americans, Hispanics, LGBTQ people, women, and older adults, are populations-at-risk.

12-2   Discuss how empowerment can occur in the macro environment for each group.

12-3   Respond to critical thinking questions.

12-4   Provide examples of how spiritual communities can empower their members.

12-5   Discuss intellectual and other developmental disabilities.

12-6   Identify differences and similarities between the history of how people with developmental disabilities have been treated and current trends.

12-7   Describe ethical issues in diversity and empowerment.

12-8   Describe generalist social work practice with people who have developmental disabilities.

12-9   Summarize avenues of legislative, community, and worker empowerment.

12-10   Examine the macro environment's potential for empowering people with visual impairment and intellectual disabilities.

The following examples reflect empowerment approaches undertaken by various racial and ethnic groups:

- *An urban African American community actively countered drug lords by undertaking an aggressive anti-drug campaign spearheaded by major community leaders.*
- *An African American teacher promised her first-grade class that she would pay for their first year of college education if they maintained "C" averages and made it to college. She saves $10,000 each year from her modest salary to fortify the fund.*
- *Families for Freedom in New York is organizing deportees and families to fight the deportation of undocumented workers.*
- *Isolated, poor urban neighborhoods in major cities throughout the United States have used cooperatives and other development activities to strengthen their ability to control their lives.*
- *Native-American tribes are empowering their members by registering voters, encourage engagement in the political process, and teaching youth about the importance of having a voice in government.*
- *The LEON (Latino Empowerment Outreach Network) in Columbus, Ohio, is working to empower Latinos to become active participants in their own health care by providing educational materials and other resources and educating the community about the health needs of Latinos.*
- *Public housing tenants organized to put pressure on management of local housing authorities to get them to improve and repair the developments and enhance security in the housing units.*
- *The Chicago Anti-Eviction campaign is fighting to end all economically motivated evictions in Chicago. One of its efforts is to have homeless families (especially people of color) move into abandoned homes, fix them up, and live there. The goal is two-pronged: to provide housing for families without any and to move housing into the area of a recognized human rights. Similar empowerment efforts are underway in Los Angeles and Washington, DC.*

Each example above reflects a creative version of empowerment for various diverse populations within the macro social environment. The responses of macro systems to people in need often cannot be categorized neatly as a community, organizational, or group effort. Rather, responses and resulting activities reflect a combination of all three types of systems. Problems ranging from mental health, disabilities, poverty, and homelessness all involve micro, mezzo, and macro variables. A need might be identified within a community context. Organizations and their staff might participate with citizens to develop programs in response to community needs. Task groups are established to initiate, develop, and implement ideas. Sometimes groups focusing on treatment, support, education, personal growth, or socialization are formed to meet identified needs.

Note that it's also important to maintain a multidimensional perspective concerning diversity when talking about any practice approach. These include programs and services developed in organizational and community contexts. Chapter 2 introduced the concept of **intersectionality**, which involves the idea that people are complex and can belong to multiple, overlapping diverse groups. "The intersectional perspective acknowledges the breadth of human experiences, instead of conceptualizing social relations and identities separately in terms of either race *or* class *or* gender *or* age *or* sexual orientation"; rather, an intersectional approach focuses on the "interactional affects" of belonging to multiple groups (Murphy, Hunt, Zajicek, Norris, & Hamilton, 2009, p. 2).

A current example is the challenge of immigration. The only concerns raised about undocumented immigrants appear to be focused on their race or religion. The intersection of race and religion with immigration would likely not be as virulent a concern if the immigrants were coming from Europe or from similar countries. Comments from Representative Steve King, an Iowa member of the House of Representatives, illustrates the blatant use of race to protest immigration. He first said that White Christians have contributed more to Western civilization than any other subgroup, and followed it up later by saying, "We can't restore our civilization with somebody else's babies" (Haag, 2017). Fortunately, many politicians and ordinary citizens repudiated the remarks, and some vacationers threatened to boycott Iowa. Boycotts as a means of forcing change is another form of empowerment.

The comments above are an illustration of some of the challenges facing generalist practitioners. Social work education is charged with teaching knowledge, skills, and values concerning "the intersectionality of multiple factors including, but not limited to age, class, color, culture, disability and ability, ethnicity, gender, gender identity and expression, immigration status, marital status, political ideology, race, religion/spirituality, sex, and sexual orientation and tribal sovereign status" (CSWE, 2015, EP 2).

For example, a person might be Hispanic or Asian American. That individual may also be Muslim or Roman Catholic. Similarly, that person may be a Republican or Democrat, LGBTQ or straight, male or female, age 27 or age 87. Each dimension of diversity intermingles with others to make everyone who he or she is. This chapter provides a range of examples regarding how communities and organizations can respond to the needs of people characterized by any combination of diverse factors.

Populations at Risk in the Macro Environment: African Americans   LO 12-1

EP 2

Consider the status of African American citizens in the United States. Mooney, Knox, and Schacht (2013) remark:

> Despite significant improvements over the last two centuries, race and ethnic group relations continue to be problematic. The racial divide in the United States sharpened in 2005 in the wake of Hurricane Katrina, which left victims—who were predominantly black and poor—waiting for days to be rescued from their flooded attics or rooftops or to be evacuated from overcrowded "shelters" where there was no food, water, medical supplies, or working toilets. (p. 272)

A national survey administered after the disaster indicated that 71 percent of African Americans felt that the Katrina experience demonstrated that racial inequality is still a major problem in the United States; in contrast, 56 percent of Whites indicated that the Katrina disaster provided no real evidence of racism (Mooney et al., 2009). Interestingly, the same survey found that 77 percent of African Americans felt that the hurricane victims would've received better treatment had they been White; this stood in stark contrast with the meager 17 percent of Whites who felt the same way (Mooney et al., 2013).

Despite major triumphs concerning legal and social racial equality, African Americans still fall markedly behind their White counterparts in most measures of social and economic well-being; such indicators include health, educational attainment, employment, and income (Davis, Wallace, & Shanks, 2008).

African American people (making up over 13.3 percent of the US population) continue to suffer a range of injustices (US Census Bureau, 2016c). About one-quarter of African Americans live below the poverty level, compared to 11.6 percent of Whites. Almost 31 percent of African American children live below the poverty level, compared to 16.7 percent of White children. The median[1] family income for African Americans is slightly more than 58 percent of that of their White counterparts. African Americans are more than six times as likely than their White peers to be incarcerated or on death row (Lynch, 2012).

Frequent news reports about Blacks being killed by police officers led to the formation of Black Lives Matter, an organization focused on recognizing that the people being killed or injured in these and other situations matter. While follow-up investigations of these shootings rarely led to charges against the officer involved, they have often uncovered patterns of racism and inadequate police training in the communities where the shootings occurred.

We have established that macro systems can develop policies and programs to enhance the well-being of various groups and populations-at-risk. Groups can be formed and services offered to address larger social issues facing African Americans that benefit individual group participants. An example presented here concerns a program assisting African American and other grandparents who are primary caregivers for grandchildren due to their own children's inability to care for the grandchildren.

Empowerment for African American Grandparents Caring for Grandchildren LO 12-2

EP 2; 7c; 7d; 8

There is a long and strong history of extended family members in African American families supporting each other and helping care for children (Diller, 2015;). According to the US Census Bureau, 6.6 million children under age 18 live with one or both grandparents; grandparent caregivers number 6.2 million (US Census Bureau, 2009). Many of these children live in homes where the biological parent is not present. As has been historically demonstrated, African American children are much more likely to live with grandparents than White children (US Census Bureau, 2016d). These families are often the poorest, with relatively few supports to meet their needs.

One example of a community response to the needs of African American grandparents who have become primary caregivers of their grandchildren is

---

[1] A *median* is the middle number in any ordered list of numbers, with one half of the other numbers below it and one half above it.

Grandparents Raising Grandchildren of Massachusetts. High rates of drug abuse have caused many parents to relinquishing their responsibilities as parents and productive citizens to pursue drug use. Many grandparents have gained custody of their grandchildren because of drug abuse, incarceration because of drug convictions, and the unwillingness to place their grandchildren in the public foster care system.

These grandparents have found themselves in the strange and unusual circumstance of having sudden responsibility for small children at a stage in life when they felt they were done with all that. They face many challenges as they assume this marginalized position in society. (Chapter 2 defines *marginalization* as the condition of having less power and being considered as less important than others in the society, often because of group membership or shared characteristics) (e.g., being poor). In this case, intersectionality involving race, age, class, and status results in multiple challenges.

Grandparents often have a variety of health problems that complicate caring for a child. These include arthritis, coronary disease, and diabetes, and almost 45 percent report that their health is fair or poor (Whitley & Fuller-Thomson, 2017).

As might be expected, the children themselves often come in to the grandparents' care with their own health problems, many arising from their parents use of drugs. In addition, they experience the same normal health problems as other children. Often, the grandparents need day care or special education for the children, and services such as transportation. As caregivers, grandparents may need respite care for themselves and financial support to meet the child's needs.

Grandparents Raising Grandchildren of Massachusetts (2017) pursues multiple efforts to support, assist, and empower grandparents in their new caregiver role. They provide an online list of support groups in the state listed by city, a portion of whom are led by social workers. They also maintain a website highlighting Family Resource Centers that will provide services to grandparents. The website discusses many of the challenges that are faced by parents and grandparents, including substance abuse, gay, and nontraditional parents. It also provides regional workshops and community workshops dealing with the grandparent-grandchild challenge. Moreover, the organization operates a Grandparents Advocacy Program with monthly meetings, monitors legal issues and laws around grandparent-grandchild relationships, and provides links to national and state resources supporting grandparents in their new role.

The value of social support for helping grandparents is high. Jang and Tang (2016) found that such support helps grandparent caregivers cope with the stress and the negative effects of stress arising from their role. Hayslip and Garner (2015) found that social support also positively influenced the health and reduced the likelihood of depression among grandparents.

Similar programs designed to bolster the capacity of and empower grandparents include community-building workshops helping grandparents learn about preparing their grandchild for college and connecting grandparents with other community resources (Bertram et al., 2016). For example, Rhynes, Hayslip, Caballero and Ingman (2013) found that attending and participating in senior center activities had a major positive influence on the "quality of life, caregiver burden, well-being, and role satisfaction" (p. 162) of the grandparents. Although most grandparents were Black, neither ethnicity, age, gender, income, or other factors proved to affect the positive outcome of attendance.

These kinds of projects reflect an empowerment approach, as described by Cox (2002): "The immediate goals of empowerment practice are to help clients achieve a sense of personal power, become more aware of connections between individual and community problems, develop helping skills, and work collaboratively towards social change." Empowerment arises from the combined strength of multiple individuals working to create change in the community.

Policy, Research, and Practice Recommendations to Advance Human Well-Being and Pursue Social and Economic Justice Wilkerson and Davis (2011) make the following recommendations for *policy* change at the state and national levels:

EP 3; 3b; 4a; 5c

Policies should consider greater compensation for kin caregivers over non-kin caregivers because of the benefits of kin care as well as the needs of caregivers. [**Kin caregiving or kinship care** is the provision of caregiving out of the home by relatives, including grandparents.] Public policies are intent on ensuring the welfare of all children and providing assistance that brings kinship families reasonably above the poverty line and gives caregivers adequate support [and] resources to carry out the caregiving tasks. (p. 13)

They continue with the following recommendations regarding research:

EP 5b; 8b; 8c

Currently, data are not sufficient to document current financing of kinship care or the cost of funding kin care providers at the foster care rate. . . . It is also not possible to determine the breakdown of kinship families receiving foster care payments, TANF grants, or even government assistance. There is lack of information regarding the length of kin and non-kin caregivers receiving financial support. Research is needed to assess the current cost of kinship care and make projections regarding the cost of policy suggestions. (p. 13)

Finally, there are several recommendations concerning *practice* regarding how social workers can advance human well-being and pursue social and economic justice (Wilkerson & Davis, 2011). First, practitioners should consider the strengths of the kinship relationship with grandparents who become caregivers. There is often a natural family support network in addition to a mutual understanding of cultural practices and values. Second, social workers should remain abreast of new policies regarding service provision to grandparents and other kin caregivers to make the best use of such services and make appropriate referrals. Third, social workers should learn to view grandparent caregiving not only as alternative family support, but also as part of the formal child welfare support network. Caregiving by grandparents should be considered an aspect of service provision that requires formal resources. Fourth, practitioners should advocate for change in current policies to provide the support necessary for grandparents who care for their grandchildren. Practitioners should also advocate for client access to social work services when appropriate.

An example of such services is a collaborative program between West Virginia State University social work department and the university's extension program offering support and education to grandparents raising their grandkids. It covers such topics as "technology and social media: dangers, pitfalls and plusses, legal issues and documents, negotiating the public school system, and how to help grandchildren with homework" (Quinn, 2016).

Populations at Risk in the Macro Environment: Hispanics/Latinos

EP 2; 2a; 3

Over 56.6 million Hispanic people live in the United States (US Census Bureau, 2016c). The population varies immensely in terms of culture, race, and ethnic origin. Also, note that Hispanic people may also be of more than one race.

Highlight 12-1 addresses identifying terms used to describe Hispanics, and a subsequent section examines the oppression of Hispanic people in the macro environment. The economic and educational picture for the Hispanic population is much poorer than for Whites (US Census Bureau, 2016c):

- There is a significantly higher percentage of families earning lower incomes and a significantly lower percentage earning high incomes as compared to Whites: 39.3 percent of Hispanic families have annual incomes of less than $35,000 compared to 28.3 percent of Whites, and about 27.4 percent of Hispanic families have annual incomes of $75,000 or more compared to 42.9 percent of Whites. The greatest disparities between Hispanics and Whites exist at the highest income levels.
- Of Hispanic families, 21.4 percent have incomes below the poverty level, compared to 11.6 percent of Whites. Of Hispanic groups, the percentage below the poverty level is:

Dominican	26.3 percent
Mexican	24.9 percent
Puerto Rican	25.6 percent
Guatemalan	24.9 percent
Salvadoran	18.9 percent
Cuban	16.2 percent

- The median income for Hispanic families is $45,148 compared to $62,950 for Whites.
- In terms of educational attainment, 66.7 percent of Hispanics graduated from high school or attained more education, compared to 88.8 percent for Whites. Only 15.5 percent of Hispanics graduated from college or attained higher levels of education, compared to 32.8 percent for Whites.

Although there is tremendous variation among Hispanics, several factors may operate to block socioeconomic success. First, lower educational rates fail to prepare Hispanics for higher-paying jobs (Leon-Guerrero, 2011). Second, poverty is related to the undocumented status of many Hispanic immigrants (Delgado, 2007). Without proper documentation, access to higher levels of employment is dubious. Third, some problems may be associated with acculturation issues (Casey et al., 2010; Furman et al., 2009; Shobe & Coffman, 2010). We have noted that

---

| Highlight **12-1** |

Identifying Terms

EP 1c;
2b; 2c

The US government's Office of Management and Budget originally coined the term *Hispanic* in 1978 for use in the census (Green, 1999). The original definition defined Hispanic as "a person of Mexican, Puerto Rican, Cuban, Central or South American or other Spanish culture or origin, regardless of race" (Green, 1999, p. 256). However, the concept is much more complex than this. For example, does this umbrella term include Brazilian people who speak Portuguese, South American Indians whose original language is not Spanish, people from the Philippines who speak Spanish, or immigrants from Spain (Green, 1999)?

An alternate term is *Latino*, which refers both to the Latin languages, including Spanish, and to Latin America. (Note that the term *Latina* is the feminine form of *Latino*.) However, this term omits South Americans who speak English, such as those from Belize or the Guyanas, and "people whose family roots extend to Italy, Germany, and some areas of the Mediterranean" (Green, 1999, p. 256).

Still another term often used is *Chicano*, which refers to US citizens whose heritage is based in Mexico. The obvious disadvantage of this is that it focuses only on Mexico and excludes people with origins in other countries, including those that are primarily Spanish speaking.

Essentially, no one term is acceptable to all groups of people. The four primary Hispanic groups in the United States in terms of size are Mexican Americans (over 64 percent of all Hispanics), Central and South Americans (about 15 percent), Puerto Ricans (almost 9.5 percent), and Cuban Americans (almost 3.5 percent) (US Census Bureau, 2015b). Other groups include those from the Dominican Republic and from other countries in South America (Santiago-Rivera, Arredondo, & Gallardo-Cooper, 2002). However, for any particular family, Goldenberg and Goldenberg (2002) caution, "Socioeconomic, regional, and demographic characteristics vary among Hispanic American groups, making cultural generalizations risky" (p. 326). Santiago-Rivera and her colleagues (2002) reflect:

> Perhaps no other ethnic group in the United States is as heterogeneous in its ethnicity, physical appearance, cultural practices and traditions, and Spanish language dialects as the Latino population. Latinos in the United States are a diverse group of multi-generational.... [people] from different Spanish speaking countries as well as long-term residents in the southwest United States. They all have unique social, economic, and political histories. Latino groups vary in their ancestry, blending indigenous [people originating in an area] (e.g., Aztec and Mayan) and Spanish cultural traditions and, for some Latino groups, African traditions. (p. 56)

It's important not to make stereotyped assumptions about such a diverse group. Santiago-Rivera and her colleagues (2002) continue:

> Although it is not often reported, Latinos may also be of Asian heritage. The Philippine islands, conquered by Spain, were populated by people of Asian heritage. Whereas the native language of the island is Tagalog, Spanish surnames are commonplace, and in the United States, Filipinos may claim either Asian or Latino heritage. In South America and Mexico, there are settlements of Chinese families as well. Peru is one such example. (p. 23)

It's probably best for social workers to listen to their clients concerning language and use the terms those clients prefer when referring to their ethnic heritage (Pew Hispanic Center, 2012). Despite the complexity and the need to appreciate differences within this population, the terms *Hispanic* and *Latino(a)* have generally been used to refer to people originating in countries in which Spanish is spoken. Here the terms *Hispanic* and *Latino* will be used interchangeably unless a specific group (e.g., Puerto Rican Americans) is discussed.

---

acculturation is the degree to which people take on the values and customs of the dominant culture. Recent immigrants or those who have not been acculturated may experience difficulties in feeling as though they fit in; they may receive inadequate support and may isolate themselves from integration into the economic and social structure (Diller, 2015).

Values Often Characterizing Hispanic Families

EP 1;
2a; 2b;
2c

Keeping in mind that more specific variations exist within the many subgroups, we will discuss some cultural themes important to Hispanic families in general. Hispanic heritage is rich and diverse, but the groups tend to share similarities in terms of values, beliefs, attitudes, culture, and self-perception. These include the significance of a common language; the importance of family relationships, including extended family and other support systems; spirituality; and the traditional strictness of gender roles. Carefully listening to clients and learning about their cultural values is a career-long process for social workers.

Significance of a Common Language   The first theme important in understanding the environment for children growing up in Hispanic families is the significance of a common language (Delgado, 2007; Pew Hispanic Center, 2012). One recent major survey reveals several findings (Pew Hispanic Center, 2012). For one thing, most Hispanics "express a strong shared connection to the Spanish language." Eighty-two percent of Hispanics speak Spanish. The survey indicates that 38 percent of respondents speak Spanish as their primary language, 38 percent are bilingual, and 24 percent speak English as their dominant language. Ninety-five percent of respondents, however, say that it's important for future generations to speak English to succeed in the United States. Proficiency in English varies somewhat depending on the generation, as younger generations tend to be more proficient than older ones. Among Hispanics born in the United States, 51 percent speak English as their primary language. This may be due to school attendance and more exposure to the language that occurs earlier in life.

Social workers should "know that there is a growing population of bilingual Latinos who have varying degrees of language proficiencies in English and Spanish" (Santiago-Rivera et al., 2002, p. 121). For instance, recent immigrants may use little if any English, whereas people whose families have been here for centuries may be bilingual or lack any knowledge of Spanish. One strong implication of such diversity is the need for social workers to assess Latino clients' language history and use on an individual basis.

Arredondo and Perez (2003) point out that "language has always been made a political issue in the United States," so that many Latinos may "prefer to speak English versus Spanish" (pp. 120–121). They suggest that practitioners consider the following issues when working with Hispanic clients and communities:

1. Language use can be associated with generation in the United States. Recent immigrants may be monolingual Spanish speakers or speak English as a second language with a wide range of ability.
2. Many Latinos, particularly Mexican Americans, do not speak Spanish at all. These individuals were taught by their parents that to fit in and not be punished in school, as they had been, they could not learn to speak Spanish.
3. Being bilingual or speaking Spanish whenever possible can be viewed as an indication of comfort. However, speaking Spanish in the workplace has often been discouraged so as not to make "others" feel uncomfortable.

4. **Code-switching** refers to the use of Spanish and English in the same sentence [emphasis added]. Individuals engage in code-switching to emphasize a point with a particular English or Spanish word.
5. Bilingualism is an academic, psychological, social and economic asset, not a deficit. The need for Spanish-speaking professionals and workers continues to increase in all work environments in both urban and rural settings. (p. 121)

An important note is the fact that so many cultural activities and aspects of cultural pride are associated with Spanish. Consider the events and holidays (e.g., Cinco de Mayo for Mexican Americans, which refers to the celebrated day a small Mexican army defeated a French army battalion), common history, customs, beliefs, and cooking traditions related to Spanish-speaking origins that are so meaningful in daily cultural life.

The Importance of Family   A second theme reflecting a major strength in many Hispanic families is the significance placed on relationships within the nuclear and extended family, including "aunts, uncles, cousins, and grandparents, as well as close friends," referred to as **familismo** (Diller, 2015; Magaña & Ybarra, 2010; Santiago-Rivera et al., 2002, pp. 42–43; Weaver, 2005):

> Latino families are typically large, intergenerational, and interdependent, and offer an important source of support to their members.... Extended family ties are highly valued and serve as a source of pride and security.... This emphasis on respect and responsibility to family members often leads to . . . [older] adults both being cared for and taking on caregiving responsibilities within the family.... [Older adults] are often cared for within the family rather than through formal social services. When nursing homes are used, family members often continue to fulfill supportive caregiving responsibilities. (Weaver, 2005, p. 148)

Another important related concept reflecting a cultural strength is **compadrazco** (godparentage). **Compadres** (godparents) often serve as substitute parents. According to Santiago-Rivera et al. (2002), godparents "may be prominent leaders or older people who hold some position of authority and respect within the Latino community" and "play an important role in the Latino family's life and are included in all traditional celebrations. The practice of godparentage formalizes relationships between the child's parents and the *compadres* and promotes a sense of community" (p. 44).

Other vital sources of strength involve the community support systems often available to Hispanic families. These include the following:

- **Botanicas:** "small stores located in Latino communities" selling such products as Spanish-language books, records, and herbs.
- **Bodegas:** shall grocery stores that "serve as resource centers for the Hispanic community. They provide information such as the location of folk healers (Mexican, Puerto Rican, and Cuban Hispanic cultures espouse folk healers who help people deal with physical, emotional, and spiritual difficulties.)
- **Club sociales:** Serve as recreational settings as well as helping to link patrons to other community resources.

Personalismo   **Personalismo** is a Latino attitude that recognizes the worth and dignity of others based simply on their humanity (Diller, 2015; Delgado, 2007; Diaz, 2010; Shorkey, Garcia, & Windsor, 2010). Ho, Rasheed, and Rasheed (2004) explain:

> Along with the concept of **familismo**, Latinos define their self-worth in terms of those inner qualities that give them self-respect and earn them the respect of others [emphasis added]. They feel an inner dignity (**dignidad**) and expect others to show respect (**respeto**) for that dignidad. Personalismo is also a cultural trait that reflects a collectivisitic worldview (Levine & Padilla, 1980) in which there is a great deal of emotional investment in the family. Positive interpersonal interaction will help to maintain mutual dependency and closeness for a lifetime. Hence, great importance is given to those positive interpersonal and social skills to facilitate warm, close relationships. (p. 152)

This value can provide a natural predisposition for practice in neighborhoods and communities where people work together and are concerned about each other.

Machismo and Marianismo   **Machismo** is a man's obligation to demonstrate strength, masculinity, dominance, and provide for and protect his family (Diller, 2015). It originates from the Latin word for "male" (Sanchez & Jones, 2010). Although the term emphasizes the value of male bravery and integrity, it also involves "emphasis on traits such as physical aggressiveness, sexual prowess, and alcohol abuse" (Casey et al., 2010, p. 150).

Marianismo is "the counterpart role" to machismo for Latinas, which places "a high value on virginity, purity, and sacrifice for family and children" (Casey et al., 2010, p. 150). Latinas are expected to dedicate themselves to their husbands and family and engage in self-sacrifice for the benefit of their family. The term draws its origin from the traditional idea of the Virgin Mary as a pure, moral, woman.

Santiago-Rivera and her colleagues (2002) reflect: "There is considerable debate over the extent to which Latinos adhere to traditional gender roles in contemporary U.S. society. Although evidence suggests that gender roles are undergoing transformation, the complexities surrounding this phenomenon are far from clearcut" (p. 51).

Weaver (2005) indicates that "although distinct gender roles exist, it is important to recognize that not all Latinas fit these roles to the same extent," and gives the following example:

> Latinas are often stereotyped as passive and submissive, but many changes have taken place in marriages and families in the last decade. Many Latinas now work outside the home and may wield decision-making power about family finances. It is important to understand evolving gender roles within Latino families. (p. 146)

Today over 55.7 percent of Latinas are in the workforce, which is about double the number of 20 ago. This compares to 59.7 percent of African American women and 56.4 percent of White women (US Department of Labor, 2015a, 2015b). From a strengths perspective, Latinas function as socializers, educators, and promoters of values and beliefs within family systems.

Hispanic couples vary widely in terms of who assumes decision-making power and responsibility for family support, as do couples in any other ethnic or racial group. Other factors to consider that influence gender roles include educational level, income, location, history in this country, verbal communication, and family structure (Santiago-Rivera et al., 2002).

EP 2

Spirituality   A third theme characterizing many Hispanic families is the importance of spirituality and religion (Diller, 2015; Delgado, 2007; Shorkey et al., 2010). Weaver (2005) explains:

> Spirituality has a fundamental shaping influence on the lives of many Latinos. Catholicism is a defining force of family and gender roles for Latino people.... Latino Catholicism revolves around the concepts of life and death. This fatalistic belief system emphasizes that God will provide. There is a pervading sense that much of what happens is beyond an individual's personal control. Most Latinos are Roman Catholic, but many espouse beliefs and practices influenced by indigenous and African belief systems. (Santiago-Rivera et al., 2002, p. 147)

Negroni-Rodriguez and Morales (2001) give the following examples of such folk beliefs:

> **Espiritismo** (among Puerto Ricans): "The belief in spirits. Everyone is believed to have spirits of protection, and these can be increased by performing good deeds and decreasing evil. Latinos who ascribe to **espiritismo** believe that loved ones can be around in spirit after death and can lead one's life in times of difficulties. **Espiritistas** (spiritist healers) communicate with spirits and can be incarnated by them. Healing can take place with prescribed folk healing treatment" (p. 135).
>
>   **Curanderismo** (among Mexican Americans and other Central and South Americans): The practice of curing "physical, emotional, and folk illnesses. **Curanderos/as** are healers who use a range of treatments, such as herbal remedies, inhalation, sweating, massage, incantations, and **limpieza** (a ritual cleansing)" (p. 135).
>
>   **Santeria** (among Cuban Americans): Practices that combine "African deities with Catholic saints. The **santeroslas** are priests who function as healers, diviners, and directors of rituals" (p. 135).

Critical Thinking Questions 12-1   LO 12-3

People of color have a long history of discrimination in the United States (Miller & Garran, 2008). How has discrimination and lack of appreciation for diversity negatively affected Hispanic people? How might obstacles to progress be demolished and improvements be made?

EP 8a

At a Glance **12-1**

Values Often Characterizing Hispanic Families

Significance of a **common language:** Eighty-two percent of Hispanics speak Spanish.

The importance of family (familismo): The significance placed on relationships within the nuclear and extended family in addition to others who are close to the family.

Personalismo: A Latino attitude that recognizes the worth and dignity of others based simply on their humanity.

Machismo: A man's obligation to demonstrate strength, masculinity, dominance, and to provide for and protect his family.

Marianismo: "The counterpart role" to machismo for Latinas, which places "a high value on virginity, purity, and sacrifice for family and children" (Casey et al., 2010, p. 150).

Spirituality: Catholicism is a defining force of family and gender roles for Latino people. . . . Latino Catholicism revolves around the concepts of life and death.

Espiritismo: "The belief in spirits" (Negroni-Rodriguez & Morales, 2001, p. 135).

Curanderismo: The practice of curing "physical, emotional, and folk illnesses" (Negroni-Rodriguez & Morales, 2001, p. 135).

Santeria: Practices that combine "African deities with Catholic saints" (Negroni-Rodriguez & Morales, 2001, p. 135).

Empowerment in the Macro Environment for Latinos and Latinas   There are many ways that communities can empower Latinos and Latinas. The next section reviews some research regarding Latinas' perceptions of their means of successfully helping to empower their communities. The subsequent three sections provide case examples of empowerment—one involving Latina immigrants surviving domestic violence, one concerning Latina mothers seeking social justice in housing, and one relating to Latino(a) owned businesses.

Self-Empowerment of Latinas Surviving Domestic Violence   Serrata, Hernandez-Martinez, and Micias (2016) describe the results of an Atlanta-based self-empowerment leadership intervention program for Latina immigrants who have survived domestic violence. Almost 30 percent of Latina women have experienced domestic violence in their lives (Reina, Lohman, & Maldonado, 2014). Many lack knowledge of US legal protections and the availability of other community resources.

One antidote to these problems is the *promotora* approach, which uses peer health promotors to "influence and highlight the strengths of Latina immigrant survivors" (Serrata et al., 2016, p. 38). The model has been used successfully in other area to improve "health care management, . . . improve adherence to diet requirements or medication, . . . promote health lifestyles, as well as access to services for breast and cervical cancer screening, and to prevent chronic disease" (p. 38). The use of peer or lay people works well because they are viewed as community "leaders, trusted advisors, advocates, and role models" (Andrews, Felton, Wewers, & Heath, 2004). The model uses peer workshops that not only transmit information but provide support and connections for those involved. Using a focus that includes emphasizing "intrapersonal (self-perception), interactional (understanding and knowledge about systems and people outside of themselves), and behavioral (specific actions or behaviors), the approach took place over a five-week period" (Serrata et al., p. 38). Training was provided by two facilitators who spoke Spanish, and food and child care was offered.

Critical Thinking Question 12-2

In what ways does the *promotora* model differ from traditional male approaches?

**EP 3; 5b;
5c; 8b;
8c; 8d**

Most participants experienced an increase in self-empowerment in both interactional and intrapersonal areas and all demonstrated increased leadership qualities and engaged "in goal-oriented behavior toward community outreach" (Serrata et al., p. 40). Moreover, subsequent activities by participants included "conducting community workshops and information sharing in the greater Atlanta area" (Serrata et al., p. 44).

Case Example: Latina Mothers Seek Social Justice   Belkin-Martinez (2010) describes a case example of how a group of eight Latina mothers banded together and organized others to pursue social justice. It began when two social workers practicing at a community mental health center started a support group for Latina mothers coping with depression. While conducting an assessment, the workers discovered that the women's most pressing problem was worry about upcoming steep rent increases that they wouldn't be able to afford. The workers also found out that half of the group members lived in the same housing project. Additionally, they discovered that rent there was subsidized by the federal government. Belkin-Martinez (2010) explains:

> For the past thirty years, their landlord had received a voucher from the federal government to charge "market rate" rents in a neighborhood that was not "desirable" for market rate tenants. In other words, the landlord received thousands of dollars every month from the government in order to receive market rate rent for his building. Although the women had been paying below market rate rent, for over thirty years the landlord had been paid extra money by the government to compensate for this. At this point in time, however, the neighborhood had changed significantly, with many newcomers being more affluent and willing to pay higher rents. As a result, the landlord had decided not to renew his government voucher and announced to the tenants that he was planning to double their rents by the end of the year. Being unable to pay the new amount, these women feared that they would be evicted. (pp. 287–288)

This issue involves **gentrification**, "the process in which more affluent people move into an area and rehabilitate its buildings [to enjoy the advantages, activities, and services that can be available in an urban setting.] ... Although the neighborhood grows more attractive, the poor resent the invasion of people with more money. As property values increase, so do taxes and rents, forcing many of the poorer residents to move out to try [to] find lower rent" (Henslin, 2011, p. 397). Although gentrification may breathe new life into an area, it diminishes the availability of affordable housing for people who are poor. Subsequently, gentrification drives many people with low incomes out of the area in search of other inexpensive rentals, which are often very limited.

When exploring the issues involved, group members shared their feelings of helplessness at solving the problem of escalating rents. The sense of community in the area was sorely lacking. Instead, each group member felt it was solely her responsibility to care for her family in reaction to whatever circumstances she was forced to face. As group members continued to discuss and analyze the problem, they "were able to see that their depression was directly related to larger institutional injustices and societal cultural norms and values such as individualism and competition" (Belkin-Martinez, 2010, p. 288). Belkin-Martinez (2010) continues:

> When talking about an action plan, the social workers brought up the idea of trying to resist the upcoming rent increase and to explore ways for the mothers to stay in their homes. Initially, the clients did not believe they had the right to fight for this. Wasn't it the landlord's right to do as he pleased? If it was his building, couldn't he charge whatever he wanted to? What right did they, mere tenants, have to ask him to renew his housing voucher with the federal government? (p. 288)

The social workers contacted an organization in the area whose purpose was to advocate for renters' rights. From the organization's representatives, group members learned more about regulations governing subsidized housing. They examined their prior assumptions that they were individuals powerless to confront "the system." They determined that they did indeed have rights. They were infuriated at how the landlord had been milking the federal government for hundreds of thousands of dollars over the years. As one of the group members noted, "'All of these years, I thought he was doing me a favor by keeping the rent affordable, but now I have learned that I have been paying him double [through both rent and taxes] to stay there!' The women also discussed the racist/classist implications of the landlord's decision to not renew the voucher with the federal government. One said, 'Before any of these rich people wanted to live in our neighborhood, he had no problem taking our money, getting money from the Feds, and renting to us, but now that these rich White people want to move to our neighborhood, all of a sudden we aren't good enough?'" (pp. 288–289).

The group members' worldview had been significantly altered. They were no longer helpless victims of the landlord's whims. Now they were people with rights who could work together to demand change. First, they wrote a letter to the landlord asking him to reconsider and renew the voucher for the subsidy. When the landlord failed to respond to their request, group members solicited signatures from thousands of community residents in a petition calling for voucher renewal. They then sent copies to the landlord, the mayor, and city council members. Still, nothing happened.

Group members subsequently decided to take more extreme action. At the social workers' suggestion, group members and their supporters decided to visit the landlord's headquarters and demand that he discuss the housing issue with them. They wouldn't leave until he did so. However, group members feared that this would result in arrest, which they couldn't afford. Their job responsibilities and scheduling were rigidly in place and they needed the money for their families. They then decided that their supporters who were willing would remain in the office as the police arrived and group members would stage a protest outside to further publicize the issue.

The result was victory! Belkin-Martinez (2010) concludes:

> The police did arrive and indeed arrested about twenty supporters of the women (including many social workers!), and the mothers held a powerful rally outside the building attended by several city council members. The rally and subsequent arrests led to a great deal of press coverage. The following day, the mayor issued a call for the landlord to renew his housing voucher, and the daily newspaper ran an editorial supporting the demand for continuation of the voucher. (p. 289)

This group of Latina mothers empowered themselves and their families. They went from isolated powerlessness to an established strong sense of community. They not only addressed a primary cause of their personal depression, but actually transformed their "world" (Belkin-Martinez, 2010, p. 290).

Case Example: Latina/Latino-Owned Business and Empowerment   We have established that there are many ways to empower people in communities. Some might not be that obvious. For example, one study of Puerto Rican–owned grocery stores and restaurants found that such small businesses can serve their communities in ways far beyond selling food. They can:

- Furnish credit and cash checks when necessary.
- Provide information about community issues and events.
- Supply information about what's going on in their homeland.
- Provide informal counseling to people in crisis.
- Furnish information about relevant, available social services.
- Help community residents interpret and fill out government forms.
- Connect immigrants to their country of origin by selling items such as books, DVDs, and food related to their homeland

Starting a business or service might not seem like an empowering approach for a community; however, immigrants are starting businesses at a faster rate than Americans who were born in the United States. Moreover, the businesses are having an impact on some of the most neglected portions of communities (Renuka, 2007). Main-street businesses owned by immigrants grew to about 90,000 by 2015 and accounted for "all the growth … for most of the nations' metro areas, including New York, Chicago, and Dallas." Small stores owned by immigrants now represent most small businesses in Los Angeles, Miami, and Washington, DC. Across the nation, "immigrants own most gas stations, dry cleaners and grocery stores" (Henderson, 2015). On a national scale, "immigrant-owned companies now generate more than $775 billion in annual revenue and $100 billion in income, employing one out of every 10 workers" (Alsever, 2014, p. 56).

Grimaldi (2005) provides an example of the empowering effects of owning one's own business. Yolanda Langley, a native of the Dominican Republic, operates out of a tiny shop in Providence, Rhode Island. Yolanda believed that people from her country ate too much fat and fried foods and wanted to "teach them how to eat" better and felt she could be a part of this effort. She sells "food supplements and homeopathic medicines such as bee pollen, primrose oil and shark cartilage. Each one is considered a remedy for some malady or physical shortcoming"

> ## Critical Thinking Question 12-3
>
> In what other ways might a community help to develop and promote immigrant owned businesses?

EP 7a;
7c; 7d

(p. 1). Her goal is "to teach our people how to work with the system." She is also a member of the Rhode Island Hispanic American Chamber of Commerce, another source of empowerment as small businesses join together to strengthen their power in the communities they serve. Participation in groups such as this help develop leadership skills that can be used to benefit their businesses, customers/clients, and communities.

In recognition of the importance of immigrant-owned businesses, governmental agencies at all levels are sponsoring workshops and services to enhance the owner's knowledge and skill. They also purchase products or services from the immigrant-owned business, provide consultation, and sometimes help with financing in collaboration with local banks.

Populations-at-Risk in the Macro Environment: Lesbian, Gay, Bisexual, Transgender, and Questioning People

EP 1a; 2;
3; 3b; 5b;
5c; 8b;
8c; 8d

Earlier chapters introduced the concepts of sexual orientation, the expression of gender, and several related terms. We have defined *sexual orientation* as sexual and romantic attraction to persons of one or both genders.

Elze (2006) explains the historical context facing gay, lesbian, bisexual, transgender, and questioning (LGBTQ) people:

> The history of gay, lesbian, bisexual, and transgender people in America is a history of oppression and resistance. Since colonial times, gender-variant people, and people who love and sexually desire those of the same sex, have been imprisoned, executed, witch-hunted, pilloried [placed in a frame with hands and head locked in as a means of public embarrassment], confined in asylums, fired, excommunicated, disinherited, evicted, extorted, entrapped, censored, declared mentally ill, drugged, and subjected to castration, hormone injections, clitoridectomy [surgical removal of the clitoris], hysterectomy [surgical removal of the uterus], ovariectomy [surgical removal of the ovaries], lobotomy [surgical cutting of the nerves connecting the brain's two frontal lobes], psychoanalysis, and aversive therapies such as electro-shock and pharmacologic shock. (p. 43)

Please note that various acronyms are used to refer to this diverse population, depending on the source. LGBTQ refers to lesbian, gay, bisexual, transgender, and questioning or queer (Carroll, 2013; Rosenthal, 2013). The "Q" is a relatively new addition to the acronym, so often citations use LGBT or GLBT. Additionally, sometimes legislation and some issues don't apply to transgender or questioning people, but are pertinent for lesbian and gay people. In these cases, the acronym LGB or GLB might be used.

A **political action organization** is based on the concept of a social action group. It is an organization that raises money privately to influence legislation, elect political candidates, and promote issues of interest to their contributors. Changing legislation and social policy on behalf of LGBTQ people can involve the provision of due and equal rights, the purging of discrimination, and the enhancement of overall well-being.

The National Association of Social Workers *Code of Ethics* states that "Social workers should not practice, condone, facilitate, or collaborate with any form of discrimination on the basis of ... sexual orientation" (NASW, 2008, 4.02). It continues that "social workers should act to prevent and eliminate domination of, exploitation of, and discrimination against any person, group, or class on the basis of ... sexual orientation" (NASW, 2008, 6.04d). It is the ethical obligation of social workers to advocate on the behalf of LGBTQ people so that they have the right to self-determination and equal treatment under the law.

Important Issues for LGBTQ People

Many issues concerning LGBTQ people require attention, four of which are mentioned here (Barusch, 2015; Karger & Stoesz, 2013). They include workplace discrimination and the need for nondiscrimination laws, the recognition of same-sex relationships, family policies for LGBTQ parents, and harassment and violence against LGBTQ people.

Workplace Discrimination and the Need for Nondiscrimination Laws   First, there is a need for nondiscrimination laws. Although debates are currently taking place at the state and local levels, there is no federal legislation prohibiting discrimination against LGBTQ people in employment (Karger & Stoesz, 2013; Tate, 2012). Barusch (2015) reflects:

> In some ways, the history of policies affecting GLBT[Q] Americans parallels the civil rights movement. In both cases government authorities have at times served as agents of oppression; in both cases, the rights of a minority have weighed against the opinions of the majority; and in both cases the courts have played an important and controversial role. (p. 324)

Twenty-one states ban discrimination in employment for lesbian and gay people; 15 of these also ban discrimination concerning gender identity (Tate, 2012). Barusch (2015) explains that in the "states that do not include sexual orientation in their human rights statutes, employment discrimination against GLBT individuals is perfectly legal. Any resident can be denied a job or a promotion or be fired for being gay, lesbian, bisexual, or trans" (p. 332). In addition, while over than 250 counties and municipalities have laws that protect LGBT residents in states that lack such coverage, some states have eliminated, or are trying to eliminate, the right of local governments to protect this population (Ridings & Cohan, 2016).

At the time of this writing, there were 52 recognized anti-LGBT hate groups in the United States (SPLC, 2017). These groups' activities include "criminal acts, marches, rallies, speeches, meetings, leafleting or publishing. According to a US Senate committee, discrimination against LGBTQ people is common" (Tate, 2012). Burns and Kreheley (2011) report the following statistics:

- Of LGBTQ people, 15 to 43 percent have been subject to some type of workplace discrimination due to their sexual orientation or transgender status.
- Of transgender people, 90 percent indicate they have experienced some type of ill treatment or harassment at work due to their gender identity.
- Of LGBTQ people, 8 to 17 percent state they were either denied a job or were fired because of their sexual orientation or transgender status.
- Of LGBTQ people, 10 to 28 percent maintain that they failed to get a promotion or were given a poor work evaluation because of their sexual orientation or gender identity.
- Of LGBTQ people, 7 to 41 percent have suffered verbal or physical maltreatment at work, or experienced vandalism.

Other studies and reports suggest that these numbers are likely underreported (Pizer, Mallory, Sears, & Hunter, 2012).

Although many cities, counties, and companies have nondiscrimination policies, this does not provide LGBTQ people in other settings with adequate protection. It also doesn't allow them the right to legal recourse if discrimination does occur. In lieu of a federal law, political action organizations can work to establish legislation enhancing rights at the state and local levels.

Note that Congress passed and President Barack Obama signed legislation that allows lesbian and gay military personnel to overtly disclose their sexual orientation. This replaced the former "Don't ask, don't tell" policy, where the issue was concealed and was simply not to be discussed. During that policy's 18-year duration, over 14,000 lesbians and gay men left the military, taking their expertise and special abilities with them; it is estimated that this loss of personnel cost the military approximately $53,000 for each person let go (Tate, 2012).

Recognition of Same-Sex Relationships   A second issue critical to LGBTQ people involves the recognition of same-sex relationships, particularly the legalization of same-sex marriage. The federal Defense of Marriage Act (DOMA) identified marriage as an officially authorized union between a man and a woman. Additionally, it allows states to reject marriages performed in other states that allowed same-sex marriages. In 2013, the US Supreme Court overturned the DOMA law as a violation of the fifth amendment to the constitution guaranteeing equal rights. Absence of health and pension benefits for partners is still a problem in many other contexts as well, although this is changing slowly. Still other difficulties involve the lack of decision-making rights when partners are seriously ill and unable to make decisions for themselves, and even the lack of visitation rights when a partner is hospitalized.

A 2016 Gallup Poll revealed that, for the first time, the majority of adults living in the United States (61 percent) support same-sex marriage (Gallup, 2016). This reflects a significant change from the 27 percent of people in favor of same-sex marriage in 1996. However, some clear trends exist that relate to political affiliation and age. Significant numbers of Democrats (79 percent) and political independents (65 percent) support same-sex marriage, but only 40 percent of Republicans do. Younger people age 18 to 29 are more likely to support same-sex marriage (83 percent), whereas adults age 50 and older are less likely to support it (53 percent). Historically, support for LGBT marriage has been higher for the young and lower for older men. The 2016 survey is the first time that support for same-sex marriage was above 50 percent for respondents over age 65 (53 percent).

Family Policies for LGBTQ Parents   Almost 14 percent of households with unmarried male partners contain children, and 26.5 percent of households with unmarried female partners contain them (Krivickas & Lofquist, 2011). Thus, many LGBTQ people have children. Sexual orientation is frequently a factor in family law. One major issue is child custody. Some research shows that about "30 percent of all lesbian and bisexual female parents have been threatened with loss of custody. Fathers, known sperm donors, female co-parents, grandparents and other relatives all have the potential of bringing custody challenges against lesbian mothers" (Cahill, Ellen, & Tobias, 2002, p. 74, cited in Messinger, 2006, p. 441). Other issues often affecting LGBTQ parents include parental and stepparent visitation rights, and eligibility to become foster care parents or to adopt children (Karger & Stoesz, 2013). LGBTQ people may be subject to the whims of judges who may have preconceived notions that bias these judges' views and affect their decisions. Concerning adoption, although laws governing adoption are often modified, at the time of this writing no states forbid adoption to lesbian or gay couples. At the same time, some states unnecessarily complicate the process for those couples, and this will undoubtedly lead to litigation.

Harassment and Violence against LGBTQ People   A fourth area threatening the rights of LGBTQ people involves harassment and violence (Park & Mykhysalyshn, 2016). Even though the Matthew Shepard and James E. Byrd, Jr., Hate Crimes Prevention Act was signed into law in 2009, hate crimes against LGBTQ people continue to increase. The Hate Crimes Prevention Act specifically includes hate crimes involving sexual orientation and gender identity (in addition to other categories, including race and color). "In 2015 there were more transgender homicide victims than in any other year that advocates have recorded" (Human Rights Campaign, 2015, p. 2). Unfortunately, thousands of police and sheriff departments in the United States have never reported a single case of transgender homicide,

Critical Thinking Questions 12-4

EP 8a

What are your personal views concerning workplace discrimination and the need for nondiscrimination laws? Recognition of same-sex relationships? Family policies for LGBTQ parents? Explain.

raising serious questions about the veracity of information reported to the FBI (Cassidy, 2016).

Concerning the act's name, Matthew Shepard, a 21-year-old resident of Wyoming, died in 1998 after being kidnapped, severely beaten, and left outside on a cold night for 18 hours (Matthew Shepard Foundation, 2010). James E. Byrd Jr., a 49-year-old African American, accepted a ride from three White men in East Texas one night also in 1998; he had been walking home from his niece's bridal shower (CNN.com, 1998). The men drove to an isolated area, beat Byrd, tied him to the back of their pickup truck, and dragged him down a rugged road. He was later found dead, shredded and in pieces.

Minorities of color and transgender women are the most likely victims of LGBTQ hate crimes; this may be because they belong to more than one diverse group (including those based on race, color, ethnicity, sexual orientation, gender identity, and gender expression) (Dallara, 2011). These two groups were also the most likely not to report their victimization or receive medical treatment for injuries. Often, hate crimes go unreported.

EP 3b;
5b; 5c;
8c

Empowering LGBTQ People through Political Action Organizations   Political action organizations working on the behalf of LGBTQ people to address these and other issues can function in at least three ways. These include providing direct support to political candidates, educating the public to gain support, and conducting legislative advocacy (Messinger, 2006).

Providing Support to Political Candidates   Political action organizations can identify and support the campaigns of political candidates advocating for LGBTQ rights. Haynes and Mickelson (2003) describe candidate selection:

> Because it is not unusual for a political candidate to slant a position on a particular issue in order to gain the support of specific groups, often it becomes necessary to determine how a politician really stands on issues that may not be of major campaign interest. In the case of incumbents, the best measurement is action already taken. Consequently, to give a clearer picture of the candidate's position on certain issues, PACs often prepare and publicize a record of the candidate's votes on relevant pieces of legislation—sometimes referred to as the "report card." (p. 155)

Questions can be posed. To what extent did the candidate support LGBTQ rights in the past? What is the candidate's verbal stance and/or voting record on such issues as anti-hate legislation and gay marriage?

Critical Thinking Questions 12-5

EP 8a

What do you think are the reasons behind hate crimes against LGBTQ people? How might such violence be prevented? Why do hate crimes often remain unreported?

Because political campaigns cost money, a primary means of supporting political candidates is through financial support. This is often done by forming and working through a **political action committee** (PAC), a group whose purpose is to raise money and provide support for designated political candidates (Haynes & Mickelson, 2003). PACs may be formed within a political action organization or in other organizations pursuing a broader range of goals than exclusively political action. A PAC can participate in any number of fundraising activities, from bake sales to walk-a-thons to direct solicitation for financial support.

Political action organizations can also provide candidates support by endorsing them. The "PAC can endorse the candidate by stating that the membership organization (e.g., NASW [National Association of Social Workers]) recommends that social workers vote for that candidate" (Haynes & Mickelson, 2003, p. 159). Haynes and Mickelson (2003) elaborate:

> Services and support can be offered [by a PAC], including mailing and telephone lists. Candidates are aware that the endorsement alone will not guarantee membership votes, but mailing lists and telephone numbers facilitate the candidate's ability to reach PAC members and to gain their support and labor....
>
> A PAC can recruit and assign volunteers from its membership to assist candidates, thereby increasing the effect of the endorsement. PACE [Political Action for Candidate Endorsement, NASW's political action component] has found this to be most effective because candidates have discovered that social workers have excellent campaign skills. Social workers listen well, are organized, are trained to take a broad perspective, and can work well with a variety of individuals (Wolk, 1981). Some candidates enlist social workers as campaign managers. Also after an election, social workers often are hired as aides to work out constituent problems. (pp. 159–160)

Educating the Public to Gain Support   A political action organization can work to influence public opinion to enlighten citizens about LGBTQ issues and mobilize citizens to vote on LGBTQ people's behalf. Citizens support politicians who, in turn, formulate laws that govern our macro social environment. Social workers can urge voters to critically think about issues of self-determination and expand their perceptions about human rights with respect to LGBTQ people.

To educate effectively, it's first important to define the issues and know the relevant facts. Myths and stereotypes that support prejudice against gay and lesbian people must be identified and disputed. The following facts should be emphasized (Morrow, 2006, p. 4; Crooks & Baur, 2014; Carroll, 2016):

■ Sexual orientation is "an innate orientation," not "a lifestyle choice" (p. 4). Significant research supports a strong biological component in the development of sexual orientation.

■ Using the term **sexual preference** is inappropriate when used to refer to the dynamic of **sexual orientation**. Sexual preference places the attraction to and choice of a sexual partner in the same category as other options in one's life. One person prefers to live in the city, eat prime rib, drive an SUV and watch football instead of baseball on television. These are decisions that are made but are not by any sense immutable. Faced with no football on TV, the person can choose to watch something else. If the restaurant is out of prime rib, a T-bone steak may suffice. When most straight men say they are heterosexual, they don't mean that they *prefer* women over men as sexual partners. They mean that their attraction is to women and that having a man as a sexual partner is not simply another option, like French fries instead of a baked potato. The use of the term *preference* reduces one's innate identity and drive to a simple choice. *Orientation* is a much more accurate description because it acknowledges the individual's innate attraction and nature. While the exact cause of this orientation is still undetermined, substantial evidence suggests that biology and genetics play a significant role (Crooks & Baur, 2014; Carroll, 2016). If preference or choice enters in at all, it is that one accepts or rejects her or his orientation.

- Sexual orientation is a normal facet of human diversity. Chapter 2 established that the expression of gender is a complex concept. Van Wormer, Wells, and Boes (2000) explain that in a homophobic society that has much anxiety about sexuality, "sexual expression is often perceived as dirty, disgusting, and lustful, particularly same-sex sexuality" (p. 89). This reflects the larger society's attitudes and behavior and contributes to the violence that so many GLBTQ people experience.

- GLBTQ people are just as likely to be good parents as heterosexual people (Bos & van Balen, 2008; Bos et al., 2008; Crooks & Baur, 2014). Good parenting skills have no relationship to sexual orientation. LGBTQ parents are not more likely to molest children. In reality, most child sexual abuse is committed by heterosexual men who usually are people trusted by and close to the child (e.g., a family friend, a father, stepfather, or brother) (Carroll, 2016; Rosenthal, 2013). There is no evidence to support several false homophobic stereotypes about gay parents. Children are no more likely than those raised in heterosexual families to become gay or lesbian. Children who have gay parents are just as psychologically healthy as those with heterosexual parents. They are just as socially well-adjusted and experience no greater frequency in behavioral problems than children with heterosexual parents.

- Same-sex couples "develop long-term, committed relationships" just like heterosexual couples do (Morrow, 2006, p. 6). Relationships are complex. Just as heterosexuals, LGBTQ people may enter permanent relationships or may have a series of shorter-term relationships. However, LGBTQ people lack some of the social and legal supports provided to married heterosexuals.

Legislative Advocacy   **Advocacy** is the practice of actively intervening on the behalf of clients so that they get what they need (Kirst-Ashman & Hull, 2018b). **Legislative advocacy** is the process of influencing legislators to support legislation promoting specific goals. **Lobbying** is the practice of seeking to "influence political decisions and public policy through a variety of means" (Kirst-Ashman & Hull, 2018b, p. 444). The expression originated when people seeking to influence law-makers met with them in the lobbies of legislative houses. Political organizational members can lobby legislators or testify before legislative committees to educate decision makers about issues and encourage them to vote in LGBTQ people's best interest. The same principles involved in the earlier discussion concerning educating the public also apply here.

An example of a political action organization activity is establishment of a list-serv or similar system where all members or subscribers can be notified simultaneously about the need to respond to an issue. Before legislative decisions are made, members can alert each other to the issues via the network. Members can then exert immediate pressure on legislative decision makers by writing letters, emailing, or phoning in their pleas advocating for whatever LGBTQ rights issue has current legislative attention.

We've established that empowerment can be pursued in many ways. Highlight 12-2 provides examples of programs empowering LGBTQ people through special social services.

Highlight 12-2

Empowerment of LGBTQ People through Special Social Services

EP 7d; 8

There are many ways social services can respond to the needs of LGBTQ people. Special social services can be developed to lessen oppression and educate the public about the need for gay rights. Mann (1997) identifies projects including a national organization and two community initiatives pursuing these ends on their behalf.

The Bridges Project sponsored by the American Friends Service Committee (AFSC), a Quaker organization, serves as a "national clearinghouse" to provide "information, resources, referrals and assistance to LGBT[Q] and their allies nationwide" (Mann, 1997, p. 96). The project serves to "support the formation of new youth-led organizations; enable mainstream organizations to effectively accept their LGBT[Q] youth; work with adult LGBT[Q] groups to include LGBT[Q] youth as leaders within their organizations; refer individuals and groups to sources that can help answer questions; and link groups working on similar issues" (pp. 96–97).

A second example of how special services can be developed to address issues is the Rural Transportation Program "sponsored by the State of Nevada's Bureau of Disease Control and Intervention Services" (Mann, 1997, p. 98). The program's purpose is to assist HIV-positive people who live in rural areas in transporting themselves to medical or social services appointments in urban areas. The program provides a credit card to eligible service recipients that can be used to pay "for transportation related purchases by the consumer and/or a family member, a friend, or volunteer assisting the consumer"; purchases can include "gas, oil, windshield wiper fluid, anti-freeze, food, water, sodas and juices" (Mann, 1997, p. 99).

A final example of how a community has developed special services to meet lesbian and gay persons' needs is Beyond the Closet, a rural central Oregon organization. Its goals are to educate citizens, advocate for lesbian and gay rights, and provide support where needed (Mann, 1997). The organization has achieved the following accomplishments:

> the organizing of the premiere gay and lesbian lecture series in rural Oregon; the facilitation of a meeting between area clergy and Beyond the Closet spokespersons; . . . and the organization of several events such as a "queer" book sale and film series, concerts by out lesbian performers, and the distribution of radio, television and printed interviews and opinions regarding issues relevant to the LGBT community. (Mann, 1997, pp. 99–100)

Populations-at-Risk in the Macro Environment: Women

EP 2

Lorber (2005) comments on the status of women:

As a **social institution** [an established and valued practice or means of operation in a society resulting in the development of a formalized system to carry out its purpose], gender determines the distribution of power, privileges, and economic resources [emphasis added]. Other major social statuses combine with gender to produce an overall stratification system, but gender privileges men over women in most social groups.

Through parenting, the schools, and the mass media, gendered norms and expectations get built into boys' and girls' sense of self as a certain kind of human being. Other social statuses, such as racial ethnic identification and religion, are similarly socially constructed and reproduced, but gender is so deeply embedded that it is rarely examined or rebelled against. By the time people get to be adults, alternative ways of acting as women and men and arranging work and family life are literally unthinkable. (p. 242)

Many facts support the existence of oppression for women (US Census Bureau, 2016c):

- The median income of women who work full-time is 80 percent of what men earn, a difference of over $10,000.
- Women of color are significantly more disadvantaged than White women. Hispanic women earn less than Black women and both groups earn less than White women. The only group that earned more than White women were Asian females.
- For all races, women earn significantly less than men do at every educational level. The median annual earnings for women with a high school degree is 65.2 percent of what men earn. For women with a bachelor's degree the difference is 67.9 percent of what men earn at that same educational level.
- Women are clustered in low-paying supportive occupations such as clerical workers, teachers, and service workers, whereas men tend to assume higher-paying occupations such as managers, professionals, and construction workers.
- Women earn significantly less than men in the same job category for most categories.

In addition, with respect to poverty levels:

- Women are significantly more likely to be poor than men.
- Women of color are significantly more likely to be poor than White women.

Shaw and Lee (2012) describe similar disparities in terms of household tasks:

Although the amount of housework done by U.S. women has dropped considerably since the 1960s and the amount of housework done by men has increased, women are still doing considerably more housework than men. Married women currently perform about two-thirds of all household labor.... [D]aughters are also more likely to do household work than their brothers with consequences for their leisure and other activities. Couples with higher levels of education tend to have more equitable divisions of household labor. ...

When women marry, unfortunately most gain an average of 14 hours a week of domestic labor, compared with men, who gain an average of 90 minutes. Husbands tend to create more work for wives than they perform....

Finally, when it comes to household work, women seem to be better at multitasking, and, as a result, often under-report the work they do because they are performing multiple tasks at the same time....

[Another major issue] concerns the gender division of household labor. This means that women and men (and girl and boy children) do different kinds of work in the home. Women tend to do the repetitive, ongoing, daily kinds of tasks, and men are more likely to perform the less repetitive or seasonal tasks, especially if these tasks involve the use of tools or machines. Studies show that heterosexual couples are more likely to share cooking and childcare and less likely to share cleaning, the bulk of which is overwhelmingly performed by females (women and girl children). Some tasks are seen as more masculine and some as more feminine.... Researchers find that while women invest almost ten times the work that men do in laundry, five times in cleaning the home, and approximately four times the effort in preparing and cleaning up after meals, men devote between a third and two-thirds more effort in paying bills and are more likely to do repairs and outside chores. The work women are more likely to perform takes more time (between 10 and 20 hours a week), compared with the "masculine" tasks that take between 4 and 7 hours a week.

It is important to note that the "feminine," frequently performed tasks are less optional for families and are also more likely to be thought of as boring by both women and men. (pp. 394–397)

Empowerment for Women in the Macro Environment

Because women are an oppressed population-at-risk, it is social workers' responsibility to work in the macro environment for positive change. Earlier chapters introduced several feminist principles that can be applied to the treatment of women by macro systems. These include use of a gender filter, adoption of a pro-woman perspective, empowerment, consciousness raising, the personal as political, the importance of process, unity in diversity, and validation (see At a Glance 12-2). The important thing is for social workers to be sensitive to women's special circumstances and work on their behalf in the pursuit of social and economic justice. The following section presents a case example for empowering at-risk pregnant women.

Critical Thinking Questions **12-6**

What are the reasons for these differences in income, employment, poverty, and contribution to household work? To what extent do you feel women are oppressed, and why?

At a Glance **12-2**

Feminist Principles Applied to Women in the Macro Social Environment

Using a gender filter: Viewing the world so that women and women's issues become the focus of attention.

A pro-woman perspective: Working on the behalf of equal rights, responsibilities, and opportunities for women.

Empowerment: Promoting the well-being of women by emphasizing and using their strengths.

Consciousness raising: Development of personal awareness and understanding of women's circumstances and reality.

The personal as political: Identification of one's own feelings and conditions, then subsequently relating these to the macro environment and political reality.

The importance of process: *How* things get done being as important as *what* gets done.

Unity in diversity: Appreciation of diversity being as important as unity and harmony.

Validation: The process of accepting a person and a person's actions as justifiable and relevant.

Empowering At-Risk Pregnant Women

**EP 5b;
8b; 8c;
9b**

Prenatal care is critically important for mothers and infants. However, receipt of prenatal care by pregnant mothers varies significantly from state to state (Centers for Disease Control [CDC], 2014; Papalia, Olds, & Feldman, 2009). For instance, one data source indicates that 26.3 percent of pregnant women did not receive any prenatal care during the first trimester (Child Health USA, 2013).

Papalia and colleagues (2009) explain:

Early, high-quality prenatal care, which includes educational, social, and nutritional services, can help prevent maternal or infant death and other birth complications. It can provide first-time mothers with information about pregnancy, childbirth, and infant care. Poor women who get prenatal care benefit by being put in touch with other needed services, and they are more likely to get medical care for their infants after birth. …

Although use of prenatal care has grown, especially among ethnic groups that tend not to receive early care, the women most at risk of bearing low-birth-weight babies— teenage and unmarried women, those with little education, and black and non-Hispanic White women—are still least likely to receive it. (p. 90)

CenteringPregnancy (Austin, 2017) programs are using a group model of prenatal care to both empower and engage pregnant women. Rather than following the traditional model of one-on-one service, the programs bring women into a group where they receive both prenatal care and information. Designed to enhance the outcomes by making it easier to access prenatal care, it involves the women in taking a more significant role in their own care. The model was based on prior research showing that merging social support with prenatal education reduced the risk of low-birth-weight babies and reduced substance abuse on the part of the mothers. Groups of 8 to 12 women are formed based on when their child is due and last for 10 sessions. Topics covered include dealing with stage-related pregnancy issues to helping other children in the family prepare for the new arrival. By reducing isolation and helping the women learn about other community services, the goal is to improve the care the women receive. The program has also been utilized outside of a clinic setting to reach homeless and low-income women while also being of value to women with health complications such as diabetes. Most important, the program shows decreases in premature births, fewer babies born with low weights, and increased use of breastfeeding, while receiving high levels of satisfaction from participants.

Another program designed to empower pregnant women at risk operates in Edmonton, Alberta. The HER program (the Healthy, Empowered and Resilient Pregnancy Program) combines professional staff and peer support to help inner city street-involved women access health and medical services. A nurse and social worker aided by three support staff offer the program in a community service agency. Like the CenteringPregnancy program, the HER effort has achieved positive outcomes. These include the following:

- Helping women to keep and parent their babies
- High frequency of use of program during pregnancy (an average of 29 times)
- Clients using health and social resources previously unavailable
- Lowered rates of substance abuse and risky sexual practices during pregnancy
- Decreased homelessness among participants
- Increased sense of empowerment
- A financial outcome that returns over $8 for every dollar put into the program (Canada FASD Research Network, 2014)
- These outcomes are evidence that the program is working and evaluations like this should be undertaken by anyone pursuing empowerment goals.

Populations-at-Risk in the Macro Environment: Older Adults

EP 2; 2c; 3; 3b; 5b

At each age, people have different needs and experience different conditions. McInnis-Dittrich (2009) explains the significance of generalist practice with older adults:

One of the greatest challenges of the twenty-first century will be the tremendous increase in the number of persons over the age of 65. Due to both the graying of the baby boomer generation (those persons born between 1946 and 1964) and improvements in health and medical care, the sheer numbers of persons entering "the third age" [often referred to as "old age" in an unflattering manner] will be staggering. Social institutions, including the health care system, education, income maintenance and social insurance programs, the workplace, and particularly social services, are bound to be radically transformed. Current and future generations of older adults will undoubtedly forge new approaches to the aging process itself and demand services that reflect positive and productive approaches to this time in their lives. As major providers of service to older adults and their families, social workers need a wide variety of skills and resources to meet these demands. (p. 1)

Generalist practitioners must advocate for the rights of older adults and help to address the negative attitudes they often face. Social workers must also confront their own stereotypes about older adults. McInnis-Dittrich (2009) continues:

> The term *ageism* refers to the prejudices and stereotypes attributed to older persons based solely on their age (Butler, 1989). These stereotypes are usually negative and convey an attitude that older adults are less valuable as human beings, thus justifying inferior or unequal treatment. These attitudes develop early in life as children observe parental, medical, and social attitudes toward older adults. Parents may unintentionally send the message that aging parents and grandparents are a nuisance to care for, demanding, needy, or unpleasant. Even simple comments such as "I hope I never get like Grandma" or "Put me to sleep if I ever get senile," may be interpreted literally by children. Every time parents refer to aches and pains as "I must be getting old," the subtle message becomes clear that aging is destined to be painful and debilitating. (p. 20)

Aging is part of life, with its pros and cons. Each stage of life tends to be characterized by positive and negative experiences. It is the generalist practitioner's job to emphasize "the dignity and worth of the person" of any age; "each person regardless of position in society, has basic human rights, such as freedom, safety, privacy, an adequate standard of living, health care, and education" (CSWE, 2015, EP 3).

Needs of Older Adults

EP 7d; 8

The rational approach to "caring for" older adults is to provide a wide continuum of services to meet their ever-changing needs (Payne, 2012). As people get older, they tend to experience increasing health issues and therefore require more services. Most older adults who need assistance get it from members of their families. However, when this is not available or caregivers are no longer able to provide care, older adults may enter the formal service system where a variety of care options are provided, including:

- **Home care services**—Agencies providing home health care utilize teams of professionals to identify and meet the needs of older adults. The team may include nurses, physicians, and social workers as well as aides. The aides are typically nonprofessionals with training to assist clients with such daily living tasks as bathing, using the bathroom and dressing. Other workers may help clients with shopping, meal preparation, housekeeping, and similar household tasks.
- **Senior centers**—Senior centers are facilities that provide opportunities for older adults to spend time with their peers and engage in educational and/ or physical/relaxational activities as well as social stimulation. Most also provide at least one meal per day. For those needing additional services, the senior centers will provide information and referral services.
- **Congregate and home-delivered meal services**—As noted above, many senior centers also provide congregate meals where participants can get one or more nutritious meals per day. Many retirement communities and similar facilities also offer this service. Home delivered meals are usually provided by nonprofit agencies using funds provided by the federal Older Americans Act.

Delivery of the prepared meals is often done by volunteers and community service groups such as the Kiwanis. The cost of providing meals for senior citizens for a year is about the same cost as one day in a hospital according to Meals on Wheels America (Fottrell, 2017).

- **Adult day services**—As "a setting for older adult care that falls between independent living and skilled nursing care," "adult day health care can provide individually designed programs of medical and social services for frail older adults who need structured care for some portion of the day. . . . These older adults do not need full-time nursing care or even full-time supervision but do require assistance with some of the activities of daily living" (McInnis-Dittrich, 2009, p. 12).

- **Respite services**—Respite services are designed to help achieve two major goals. The first goal is to provide care for older adults at such times as the main caregiver is not available. Perhaps, the respite care will be offered when a caregiver needs to work and the older adult cannot be left home alone. The second goal is to give caregivers for older adults a respite or break from their responsibilities. Most respite care is provided in the home ands last several hours while the caregiver can take time for shopping, relaxing, taking in a movie, or some other activity. Respite care is provided by several categories of people, including home-health aides, nursing personnel, or other companions.

- **Supportive housing**—This is a living arrangement where older adults who can live independently reside in a retirement community. Typically, the community has a minimum age requirement such as 55, and many do not allow children to live in the community. It is a popular arrangement for an increasing proportion of older adults, at least in part because of the array of recreational and social activities provided in the community. The community often includes a clubhouse and swimming pool, and does most of the maintenance activities provided in condominiums.

  One older widow comes to mind. When it became too difficult for her to take care of her single-family home by herself, she moved into an apartment in a retirement community. She was delighted to find out that not only were numerous social activities (e.g., card-playing groups, bingo, and lectures on a wide range of topics by professors from a local university) and opportunities for social interaction (e.g., afternoon "teas," holiday parties, and receptions) available, but the facility also offered weekly church services. As she was no longer driving, for several years she had been forced to depend on friends or relatives to drive her to church when they were available. Now that problem was solved. All she had to do each Sunday was walk down the hall.

- **Continuing retirement communities** provide a continuum of care to older adults. For example, the individual may begin living independently, move to supportive housing when needed, and finally enter a nursing facility when no longer able to care for her needs.

- **Nursing homes**—The nursing home or long-term care facility provides the largest array of care services for older adults. All aspects of the resident's life are managed by the facility and staff. Skilled nursing homes, for example, work with the frail older adults who need full-time care and assistance.

Meals, housekeeping, medical care, and activities are part of the comprehensive services offered.

- **Hospice**—Hospice programs provide end-of-life care to terminally ill people. The intent is to make people as comfortable as possible during their final days. Services may be provided either in a comfortable setting outside the home or in the home.

Strengths-Based Perspectives for Older Adults: Means to Empowerment

EP 7c

The traditional approach to working with "the elderly" focuses on identifying weaknesses and on finding substitutions to make up for what older adults *cannot* do. Even the term *the elderly* conjures up visions of limitations, helplessness, and inability. Following this view, older adults are assessed in terms of their deficits and subsequent needs. Kaye (2005) proposes a very different "strengths-based perspective" to viewing and celebrating older adulthood (p. 8). This outlook emphasizes hope, development, autonomy, activity, and empowerment (Kaye, 2005; Payne, 2012). Kaye (2005) explains:

This perspective embraces growth and capacity, potential yet to be realized, and the continuing aspirations and enhancements of people over time, regardless of their relative age and health. It dwells less on consolidating and coming to terms with past accomplishments or failures, but rather it integrates present-day and future-oriented perspectives....

Social workers ... have a more explicit role to play in a variety of nontraditional settings, including retirement planning, travel and recreational programming, employment training and counseling, volunteer services, self-help programming, exercise programs, and continuing and lifelong learning programs. Such programs emphasize active engagement in community life and societal interaction. Increased social work involvement in these fields of practice will translate into more direct contact with and, ultimately longer-term engagement of active [older adults] ... in the very programs that reinforce and reward productive older adult behavior. ...

A productive aging perspective may also be viewed as having greater relevance to financially secure and physically robust adults. To the contrary, it is believed that a productive aging perspective has universal relevance. All older persons will benefit enormously from a philosophy that promotes choice, opportunity, creativity, and personal development regardless of financial well-being or health status. Regardless of the degree of physical, functional, and emotional health, all persons as they age, are challenged to sustain a high quality of life, set genuine goals for themselves, structure their daily lives meaningfully, and remain engaged in community and family life. It is crucial that we remember that the way active engagement is framed can vary dramatically from one person to the next. Furthermore, the ability to remain productive and vital will be determined by a host of personal factors, including but not limited to attitude, physical and emotional well-being, motivation, education and experience, and changing societal attitudes and expectations. For this reason, work with productive [older adults] ... can and must take place in traditional settings in which a large proportion of geriatric social workers are already employed (e.g., long-term care facilities, adult day care, senior citizen centers, hospices, chronic and acute care hospitals, and in-home programs). In these settings, the capacity of social workers to identify, to reinforce, and to help preserve those dimensions of older adult capacity that reflect a productive aging philosophy is particularly crucial. (pp. 8–10)

Spiritual Communities and Empowerment   LO 12-4

We've established that **spirituality** "includes one's values, beliefs, mission, awareness, subjectivity, experience, sense of purpose and direction, and a kind of striving toward something greater than oneself" (Frame, 2003, p. 3). Chapter 9 addressed the importance of spiritual values and religion for many African Americans and First Nations Peoples. The following two case examples reflect how spiritual communities can empower their members. First, an African American spiritual community serves as a safe haven for its youths. Second, a Diné spiritual and cultural community empowers its senior citizens through the provision of spiritually and culturally sensitive care to nursing home residents.

A Spiritual Community as a Haven for African American Youths

EP 2; 7d; 8

A common theme in the lives of many African Americans involves strong religious beliefs and a close relationship with the church, especially an African American church (Murphy & Dillon, 2015; Dhooper & Moore, 2001; Diller, 2015). Many African American families consider the church to be a part of the extended family, providing similar nurturance and support. Dhooper and Moore (2001) explain:

> The African-American church continues to address not only the religious and spiritual needs of the individual, family, and community, but also their social needs. It serves as a coping and survival mechanism against the effects of racial discrimination and oppression and as a place where African-Americans are able to experience unconditional positive regard. (p. 101)

The following is an example of how social workers can help enhance a community's functioning, in this case, an African American spiritual community in Utah. Social workers can serve as human resources in a wide range of capacities. First, a study is discussed that explores the values and opinions of the spiritual community's members. Subsequently, a project is described that demonstrates how social workers can creatively work with a spiritual community to help meet its needs.

Haight (1999) conducted an ethnographic study targeting African American youths belonging to the First Baptist Church in Salt Lake City, Utah. The church was established over 100 years ago by "'a Baptist Prayer Band,' a group of African-Americans who, excluded from worshipping in the white churches, met in one another's homes" (p. 247). Haight (1999) notes that "African-American Utahns, like African-Americans in other parts of the country, experience racial discrimination in employment, housing, education, and everyday social interactions" (p. 248).

African Americans are a tiny minority in Utah. Additionally, most of the Utah population belongs to the Church of Jesus Christ of Latter-Day Saints, a tightly knit spiritual community that sponsors a wide realm of social and cultural activities for its members.

Extensive interviews with First Baptist Church members revealed a local environmental context for children that was "negligent at best and virulently racist at worst" (Haight, 1999, p. 249). Of special concern was the perceived "negative expectations" of White educators in the public school system (p. 249). In response, First Baptist Church members felt the church's spiritual community provided a safe haven where children could learn about their cultural heritage in a safe, supportive environment. Emphasis was placed on "helping children understand the relevance of, and then apply, biblical concepts to their own lives" (p. 252). Additionally, children were strongly encouraged to participate in ongoing learning activities. One illustration is that children were expected to respond to a series of "call-and-response sequences." Haight gives an example: "When the teacher said that they would no longer be fishermen, but that they would be fishers of —?, the class responded that they would be fishers of men" (p. 253). In this way, each individual was expected to actively participate. The nurturing spiritual community provided children with an environment where they could develop resilience to cope with any rejection, isolation, or discrimination they experienced in the external environment. Church members also placed great importance on positive, supportive relationships between adults and children.

Along with First Baptist Church leaders, social workers initiated and developed "an intervention, informed by knowledge generated through the ethnographic study, to support the development of children's resilience" (Haight, 1999, p. 253). This intervention strategy was the establishment of a "Computer Club" (p. 254). First Baptist Church members "both prioritized educational achievement and identified school as problematic for African-American children" (p. 254). Furthermore, children's computer literacy was perceived as "a specific area of need, and learning more about computers as an opportunity that children and families would embrace" (p. 254). Thus, members felt that enhancing children's competence in using computers was a valuable goal. Although the Computer Club's primary focus was educational computer games, student volunteers from a local university also participated with children in a range of activities, including field trips, parties, picnics, computer-generated art shows, African dance groups, and a gospel choir (p. 254). The activities provided a healthy atmosphere for students and children to enjoy mutual experiences, share ideas, and develop positive relationships.

The workers portrayed in this example first explored the values and strengths of the community and then worked together with community members toward a mutually desirable goal. The process was based on mutual respect and cooperation. Haight (1999) concludes that

> the ability of social workers to develop knowledge of cultural beliefs and practices relevant both to African-American communities in general and to the unique African-American communities in which they are practicing is critical to the development of ethnic-sensitive social work interventions such as the Computer Club. (p. 255)

The Diné (Navajo) Community, Spirituality, and Respect for Older Adult Members

**EP 2; 2b;
5b; 7c; 7d;
8; 8e**

Sue and Sue (2016) reflect on Native Americans' (First Nations Peoples) view of spirituality and life:

> The sacred Native American beliefs concerning spirituality are a truly alien concept to modern Euro-American thinking. The United States has had a long tradition in believing that one's religious beliefs should not enter into scientific or rational decisions (Duran, 2006). Incorporating religion in the rational decision-making process or in the conduct of therapy has generally been seen as unscientific and unprofessional. The schism between religion and science occurred centuries ago and has resulted in a split between science/psychology and religion (Fukuyama & Sevig, 1999). This is reflected in the oft-quoted phrase "separation of Church and State." The separation has become a serious barrier to mainstream psychology's [and medicine's] incorporation of Indigenous forms of healing into mental health [and other health] practice, especially when religion is confused with spirituality. While people may not have a formal religion, indigenous helpers believe that spirituality is an intimate aspect of the cognitive, and affective realms, it only makes passing reference to the spiritual realm of existence. Yet indigenous helpers believe that spirituality transcends time and space, mind and body, and our behaviors, thoughts, and feelings (Lee & Armstrong, 1995; Smith, 2005). (pp. 340–341)

The Diné (Navajo) are a matrifocal tribe where women are considered the core of the family and males are considered less well attached to the household (Stone, 2014). The tribal community traditionally has maintained a rich fabric of spiritual beliefs intertwined with its cultural traditions and values. It is a community because of its intricate interpersonal relationships, sense of identity, and recognition of members' belonging regardless of where they reside. Many Diné live on the Navajo reservation, a large (27,000 square miles) geographical community located in the south-central Colorado Plateau including parts of Arizona, New Mexico, and Utah. Approximately 175,000 Diné live on the reservation.

An ongoing theme in social work practice is the importance of responding to diverse ethnic, cultural, and spiritual values and needs. This example portrays how the Diné community has responded to meet the needs of aging members in ways differing from commonly held European Caucasian traditions. First, values focusing on spiritual beliefs and family centrality are discussed. Subsequently, a Diné community's nursing home's responsiveness to meeting Diné residents' needs is explored.

Traditional Diné older adults, referred to here as "Grandparents," adhere to cultural values that differ from European Caucasian traditions. For one thing, Mercer (1996) explains that

> traditional [Diné] Navajo religion deals with controlling the many supernatural powers in the [Diné] Navajo world. Earth Surface People (living and dead humans) and Holy People (supernatural beings) interact. . . . [Diné] Navajos

abide by prescriptions and proscriptions (taboos) given by the Holy People to maintain harmony with others, nature, and supernatural forces.... The goal of traditional [Diné] Navajo life is to live in harmony and die of old age. If one indulges in excesses, has improper contacts with dangerous powers, or deliberately or accidentally breaks other rules, then disharmony, conflict, evil, sickness of body and mind, misfortune, and disaster result. (pp. 182–183)

Thus, when an imbalance occurs, a person may become sick, which can be attributed to "infection by animals, natural phenomena, or evil spirits such as ghosts (**chindi**) and witches" (Bane, 2016; Mercer, 1996 p. 183). Preventive ceremonies can address the root of the illness, involve the appropriate Holy People, seek to restore harmony, and avoid ill fortune. "As major social and religious events involving entire communities, ceremonies are a major investment of time and resources for the afflicted person, extended family, and clan" (Mercer, 1996, p. 183).

Another primary traditional value in Diné life is the importance placed on the extended family. Referred to as a clan, such families include a much more extensive membership than that of grandparents, parents, and children. The Diné community has a large number of clan-based kinship groups. A related concept is the importance of the **Hogan**, or home, as the center of Diné family life (Williams, 2014). Hogans were built based on spiritual instructions prescribed by tradition and were either male or female. The female hogans were for family living and the male hogans constructed for public ceremonies, meetings with enemies, or treatment of ill members of the tribe. The female hogan was to be a safe environment for the family,, and neither disease nor enemies were welcome there.

Mercer (1996) explored the treatment of senior Diné people, the Grandparents, who reside in the Chinle Nursing Home, a tribally operated, nonprofit agency whose board of directors is composed solely of Diné. She investigated how treatment for Grandparents in the Chinle home differed from typical treatment provided outside of the reservation. She found that, essentially, the Chinle home emphasized the importance of spiritual values and **cultural care**, "the learned and transmitted values and beliefs that enable people to maintain their well-being and health and to deal with illness, disability and death" (Mercer, 1996, p. 186).

Culturally and spiritually, sensitive care is applied in at least six major areas: "communication; clan associations and social structure; personal space, modesty, privacy, and cleanliness; traditional food; dying and death; and cultural rituals" (Mercer, 1996, pp. 186–188).

1. *Communication.* Few Diné Grandparents are fluent in English, so translators are used. Such translation is done with great sensitivity, as often the Diné language has no word that means exactly what an English word does. Additionally, sensitivity is important while listening, as interrupting a speaker is considered extremely rude.
2. *Clan associations and social structure.* Clan associations are very important to Diné people. Upon introduction, Diné traditionally announce their clan membership. Nursing home staff are sensitive to the fact that Grandparents

would often have many visitors from their clan who traveled great distances at significant cost.

3. *Personal space, modesty, privacy, and cleanliness.* The Grandparents value personal space. They often find it difficult and uncomfortable to sleep in the high nursing home beds, having been accustomed to mattresses or sheepskins on the floor. Staff members comply with Grandparents' wishes to sleep where they want and usually find that Grandparents eventually adjust to sleeping in beds.

   Grandparents value modesty and privacy. Therefore, communal showering is a problem. Rather, Grandparents often prefer sweat baths, which they feel cleanse them both physically and spiritually. The nursing home provides saunas to simulate these sweat baths and offers showers to residents twice each week.

   Finally, Grandparents often prefer sleeping in their daytime clothes rather than changing into nightgowns or pajamas. Staff allow Grandparents to sleep in whatever they want. In due time, most come to choose nightclothes.

4. *Traditional food.* Grandparents prefer "grilled mutton [meat of a mature sheep], mutton stew, fry bread, corn, fried potatoes, and coffee" (p. 187). In response, nursing home staff serve lamb three times a month and usually bake fresh bread. Staff also encourage family members to bring foods the Grandparents prefer (that is, those that comply with health-related dietary constraints).

5. *Dying and death.* "Traditional [Diné] Navajo people have many restrictions regarding contact with the dead. They do not talk about death, believing that discussing death may 'bring it to you'" (p. 187). [Diné] families will usually move a dying person to a nearby brush shelter to avoid having death occur in the *hogan.* In the event of a home death, that *hogan* is usually deserted and even demolished.

   Traditionally, people touching a dead body followed specific rituals to avoid taboos. Similarly, most Grandparents and staff want to avoid touching a dead person or a dead person's clothing. Usually, a dying Grandparent is transferred to a hospital so that death will not occur in the nursing home. If a death does occur there, cleansing rituals are performed before other residents inhabit the room.

   Because of their aversion to talking about death, no Grandparents will discuss such issues as living wills or power of attorney. Staff respect this value and do not pressure residents to do so.

6. *Cultural rituals.* In order to hold cultural rituals, a *hogan* was constructed near the Chinle home and is made available for ceremonies and prayers that remain important aspects of Grandparents' lives.

The point here for social workers is the importance of understanding, appreciating, and respecting the values inherent in any spiritual community. Practice should then focus on emphasizing clients' strengths and meeting clients' needs within their own value system.

Populations-at-Risk in the Macro Environment: People with Intellectual and Other Developmental Disabilities LO 12-5

EP 2

Roden is a grocery bagger at the nearby Grocery Supermarket, a locally owned busi-
ness. Roden is 28 years old and lives with his older sister, where he moved after his last
parent died. He has worked at the store for the past 12 years and is popular with cus-
tomers and other employees. Roden was born with a mild intellectual disability (tradi-
tionally referred to as mental retardation) and has a tested IQ of 79. Roden is
unfailingly polite, happy, and willing to help customers by bagging and taking their
groceries out to their car. Employees of the grocery store keep an eye on Roden and
remind him to takes his required lunch. If they did not, he would work all afternoon.

The store environment identified in this vignette provides an empowering organizational environment for Roden. People enjoy his presence, support him, and
include him in daily life of the grocery. He feels like he belongs.

The purpose of social work education is "to promote human and community
well-being . . . Every person regardless of position in society, has fundamental human rights, such as freedom, safety, privacy, an adequate standard of living, health
care, and education" (CSWE, 2015, p. 7). Thus, social workers should "advocate
for human rights," "engage in practices that advance social, economic, and environmental justice," and work "to inform and improve practice, policy, and social
service delivery" (CSWE, 2015, pp. 5, 8).

People with intellectual and other developmental disabilities are populations-
at-risk, as they likely experience more difficulties in daily living, discrimination, and
lack of adequate services to address their disabilities. Therefore, social workers must
maintain sharp awareness of how the macro social environment affects people with
intellectual and other developmental disabilities, their choices, and their behavior
(Rothman, 2003). Communities and organizations in the macro social environment
can serve to promote or deter their optimal well-being. Roden's example shows how an
organization in a community has adapted itself to empower him. Means of empowerment in organizational and community environments for people with intellectual and
other developmental disabilities is the primary theme of the remainder of this chapter.
This topic is given significant attention here because of its importance to practitioners
and because it often receives minimal coverage in other social work textbooks.

Defining Developmental Disabilities

"Developmental disabilities are a group of conditions due to an impairment in
physical, learning, language, or behavior areas. These conditions begin during the
developmental period, may impact day-to-day functioning and usually last throughout a person's lifetime" (CDC, 2016, p. 1). Five attributes characterize people
with developmental disabilities (CDC, 2015; Institute on Community Integration,
2011). First, the disability is both severe and chronic, resulting from some mental or physical impairment. Second, the disability occurs before age 22. Third, the
conditions are likely to be permanent. Fourth, the disability results in substantial
limitations in three or more major life activities such as "self-care, receptive and
expressive language, learning, mobility, self-direction, capacity for independent

living, economic self-sufficiency" (Administration on Intellectual and Developmental Disabilities, 2013). Fifth, a developmental disability demonstrates the need for lifelong supplementary help and services.

Examples of developmental disabilities are intellectual disabilities, cerebral palsy, hearing impairment or deafness, visual impairment or blindness, and autism spectrum disorders (CDC, 2015). Each results in serious implications for living in the macro social environment that will be discussed in the following sections.

Intellectual Disabilities   **Intellectual disabilities (ID)** "are neurodevelopmental disorders that begin in childhood and characterized by intellectual difficulties as well as difficulties in conceptual, social, and practical areas of living." Three criteria must be met before this diagnosis can be given to a person. First, there is deficit in intellectual functioning "reasoning, problem solving, planning, abstract thinking, judgment, academic learning, and learning from experience" (Criterion A).

The second criterion (Criterion B) is that there are deficits in adaptive functioning that significantly hamper conforming to developmental and sociocultural standards for the individual's independence and ability to meet their social responsibilities. The onset of these deficits occurs during childhood (Criterion C) (American Psychiatric Association [APA], 2013, p. 33). Highlight 12-3 discusses the use of terms to refer to this population-at-risk.

The first criterion for intellectual disabilities concerns scoring significantly below average on standard intelligence tests and requires a clinical evaluation. The second criterion involves adaptive functioning, which the APA defines as

> how effectively individuals cope with common life demands and how well they meet the standards of personal independence expected of someone in their particular age group, sociocultural background, and community setting. Adaptive functioning may be influenced by various factors, including education, motivation, personality characteristics, social and vocational opportunities, and the mental disorders and general medical conditions that may coexist with Mental Retardation. Problems in adaptation are more likely to improve with remedial efforts than is the cognitive IQ, which tends to remain a more stable attribute. (APA, 2000, p. 42)

| Highlight **12-3** |

Terms for People with Intellectual Disabilities

Note that the technical medical diagnosis for intellectual disabilities is still *mental retardation.* Historically, legislation has also used this term. However, because of the term *mental retardation*'s negative connotations, a preferred term is *intellectual disabilities* (Friend, 2011). In fall 2010, President Barack Obama signed legislation requiring the term "mental retardation" to be changed to "intellectual disabilities" in federal legislation (Diament, 2010). Depending on the state and location, you may also hear the terms *cognitive disability, cognitive impairment, mental impairment, mental disability,* or *mental handicap* used in place of *intellectual disability* (Friend, 2011, p. 235).

An empowerment perspective focuses on abilities, not on retardation. It is also important to refer to *people* with intellectual disabilities as people before referring to any disability they might have. For example, referring to them as *intellectually, mentally,* or *cognitively challenged* people tends to emphasize the disability because the disability is stated first. Our intent is simply to respect their right to equality and dignity.

Individuals with intellectual disabilities, to some degree, are unable intellectually to grasp concepts and function as well and as quickly as their peers. The exact prevalence of intellectual disability is unknown, partly because some studies do not include cases of mild ID; however, some estimate that this disability affects 2 to 5 percent of the population (Boat & Wu, 2015). "These data suggest that school-age children with intellectual disabilities are possibly underidentified" (Friend, 2011, p. 237).

Cerebral Palsy   **Cerebral palsy** is a disability involving problems in muscular control and coordination resulting from damage to the brain before it has matured, that is, before or during birth. Problems include lack of balance, problems walking, paralysis, weakness, uncontrolled or restricted movements, and psychological impairment, depending on where the brain damage occurred (Friend, 2011; Hallahan et al., 2012). It should be emphasized that people with cerebral palsy may experience only motor impairment, with cognitive ability being unaffected.

Hearing Impairment   **Hearing impairment** "is a general concept indicating a hearing loss that can range from mild to extremely severe" (Friend, 2011; Hallahan et al., 2012). Friend (2011) explains:

> People may describe themselves as being deaf, Deaf, hard of hearing, hearing impaired, or having a hearing disorder. Initially, you might think that deafness would be a simple concept describing a condition that could be diagnosed through administration of a hearing test. However, the psychological, cultural, and educational issues that are unique to individuals who have a hearing loss make it more difficult to define; it is not a simple matter of saying that an individual has a particular percentage of a hearing loss. Examples of considerations include the age of onset of the hearing loss, the cause of the hearing loss, the age at which intervention began, the family response, the hearing status of the family, the presence of additional disabilities, and the type of education program attended. (pp. 331–332)

Highlight 12-4 addresses the significance of the Deaf community and Deaf culture.

Highlight **12-4**

The Significance of the Deaf Community and Deaf Culture

Friend (2011) describes the importance of the Deaf community:

EP 7c

It is … important to recognize use of the term *Deaf* with a capitalized *D*. This term is used to refer to members of the **Deaf community** who embrace **Deaf culture**, a unique subset of American society. … Membership in the Deaf community varies from place to place. Factors often mentioned as important for Deaf culture identity include (1) being deaf; (2) using **American Sign Language (ASL)** as a primary means of communi-

cating, which is a visual-gesturing language that has its own rules of grammar distinct from English; and (3) attending a residential school for the deaf…. However, the fundamental value of Deaf culture is that deafness is not a disability—that it is not a condition that needs to be "fixed." Instead, deafness is viewed as an identity with its own rich history, traditions, and language (Obasi, 2008). The Deaf community often organizes local, regional, state, national, and international events such as conferences, athletic competitions, art shows, plays, and pageants. (p. 333)

Visual Impairment   **Visual impairment** is difficulty in perception compared to the norm that is experienced through sight. Many people have a mild visual impairment correctable by glasses or contact lenses. People of special concern here are those whose vision cannot be corrected and therefore experience significant functional limitations. **Legal blindness** is the condition where a person

> has visual acuity [sharpness of perception] of 20/200 or less in the better eye even with correction (e.g., eyeglasses [or contact lenses]) or has a field of vision so narrow that its widest diameter [extends] … a distance no greater than 20 degrees. The fraction 20/200 means that the person sees at 20 feet what a person with normal vision sees at 200 feet. (Normal visual acuity is thus 20/20.) The inclusion of a narrowed field of vision in the legal definition means that a person may have 20/20 vision in the central field but severely restricted peripheral vision. Legal blindness qualifies a person for certain legal benefits, such as tax advantages and money for special materials. (Hallahan et al., 2012, p. 332)

Autism Spectrum Disorder   **Autism spectrum disorder (ASD)** "is a complex neurological and developmental disorder that begins early in life and affects how a person acts and interacts with others, communicates, and learns. ASD affects the structure and function of the brain and nervous system" (NICHD, 2017). "Different people with autism can have different symptoms," which is why it is called a spectrum disorder. The symptoms of autism include problems communicating and interacting with others and restricted interests and engagement in repetitive behaviors. Other difficulties include "intellectual problems, including problems with reasoning or memory, and language problems, such as learning to speak" (NICHD, 2017). There may also be underlying medical or genetic problems that relate or contribute to autism. ASD can continue to affect people all through their lives.

Prior to May 2013, the Diagnostic and Statistical Manual of Mental Disorders of the American Psychiatric Association identified ASD as a category with four types of autism, referred to as:

- Autism
- Asperger syndrome
- Childhood disintegrative disorder
- Pervasive development disorder not otherwise specified

With the publication of DSM5, these terms are no longer used by health care providers. Rather, those with a diagnosis of ASD are simply identified as having "very mild to very severe" ASD (NICHD, 2017). Note that each person with any of these disabilities is a unique individual with a distinctive blend of strengths, traits, and needs. A person may exhibit serious problems in communication but only mild difficulties with repetitive behavior.

At a Glance **12-3**

Developmental Disabilities

Developmental disability: A condition that is severe and chronic, occurs before age 22, is likely permanent, results in functional limitations in at least three areas, and creates the need for lifelong supplementary help and services.

Intellectual disabilities: A condition where there is "significantly subaverage general intellectual functioning . . . accompanied by significant limitations in adaptive functioning" in at least two areas, and that has an onset occurring before age 18 (APA, 2000, p. 41).

Cerebral palsy: A disability involving problems in muscular control and coordination resulting from damage to the brain before it has matured, that is, before or during birth.

Hearing impairment: A general concept indicating a hearing loss that can range from mild to extremely severe.

Visual impairment: Difficulty in perception compared to the norm that is experienced through sight.

Autism spectrum disorders (ASDs): A group of disorders including autism and conditions having characteristics similar to those of autism that range from very mild to very severe.

Critical Thinking Questions **12-7**

EP 8a

Do you know of anyone who has one of these developmental disabilities? If so, which one? Describe the person's characteristics. What kinds of support does the person need and get? What difficulties, if any, does the person experience? What are the person's strengths, and how can they be used to empower the person?

Treatment of People with Intellectual and Other Developmental Disabilities Yesterday and Today: Quests for Social and Economic Justice LO 12-6

**EP 2; 3;
5b; 9b**

Because of the difficulties experienced by people with developmental disabilities, community support systems and available agency resources are extremely important. How community residents and macro-level decision makers view people with developmental disabilities has tremendous implications concerning the latter's quality of life. To more fully understand the macro social environment's impacts, it is important to show how community attitudes and resulting social policies have changed over recent decades.

Prior to the Late 1960s

Prior to 1970, the emphasis of public policy and treatment in the community was on the individual's pathology or disorder. This was consistent with a medical model that conceptualized "patients" as individuals with a diagnosis and an array of problems. Many people with developmental disabilities were placed in large state or regional institutions where they received custodial care and were kept clean and safe. One of this book's authors first served as an intern at a large state institution providing such care. These times obviously did not foster the current strong professional values of client self-determination and empowerment.

The 1970s and 1980s

The period from 1970 to the early 1980s saw significant changes in how people with developmental disabilities were viewed. Principles becoming important, especially for people with intellectual disabilities, were deinstitutionalization, and planning based on the individual's needs rather than their category.

Persons with intellectual disabilities began to receive care based on a belief in **normalization**. Normalization emphasizes "that every person, even those with the most severe disabilities, should have life conditions and behavioral patterns that are as close as possible to those ordinarily experienced by others in the social and physical environment" (Kirst-Ashman, 2013, p. 352). Prior to the late 1960s, people with developmental disabilities were placed out of sight and mind in obscurely located institutions. During the 1970s and 1980s, however, communities and organizations started viewing such people as clients who had a right to live as normally as possible. Clients now had rights. This approach encouraged the development of community resources that would emphasize the importance of the social environment for an individual's quality of life.

A parallel concept to normalization is **deinstitutionalization**, the process of providing services and care for people within their own communities rather than in institutional settings. Their residences included such facilities as group homes, family care homes, and halfway houses. Sometimes, these facilities are referred to as community-based residential facilities (CBRFs). As explained earlier, this concept assumes that the more people with developmental disabilities can be assimilated into the community and live "normal" lives, the better their quality of life will be.

Although the thought to deinstitutionalize services was good and there were many successes, there were also significant problems. For one thing, clients simply being placed in the community did not necessarily mean integration or acceptance in that community. It also did not mean automatic attitude readjustments on the part of community residents to alter their old stereotypes and unfounded fears about people with developmental disabilities.

Another problem with deinstitutionalization concerned inadequate community resources and services. Institutions were expensive, but so were community-based services. People could get lost and be severed from service provision altogether. Frequently, community-based services offered by a combination of state and local and public and private agencies were fragmented, confusing, and overly complex. Other criticisms of deinstitutionalization included people being discharged too quickly and without adequately planning for post-discharge care.

Individual Program Planning   Social workers, often functioning as case managers, developed *individual programs*, a second principle espoused in the 1970s and 1980s. A **case manager** is a designated person who seeks out services, plans how they might be delivered, coordinates service provision, and monitors progress on the behalf of a client, usually one having ongoing multiple needs (Kirst-Ashman & Hull, 2018b). Such individual programs emphasized people's environments and intervention results that would enhance people's functioning within those environments. Intervention stressed helping people with disabilities develop their maximum potential in the least restrictive environment.

The concept of **least restrictive environment** concerns the encouragement of clients to enjoy as much freedom and make as many decisions for themselves as they can. This concept is related to normalization and deinstitutionalization. People living in the community should be more likely to live "normal" lives and make their own decisions than those living in institutional care. Program evaluation for organizational effectiveness was also stressed.

The Developmental Model   Another important concept during the 1970s and 1980s was that treatment should be based on a **developmental model** that espoused a continuum of service. People received services depending on the intensity and type of their needs. People with developmental disabilities were *clients* whom professionals assessed in terms of their needs. These professionals then determined necessary services, depending on where the clients fell on the developmental continuum of service. You might picture a ruler. If a client was assessed as functioning at the 6.25-inch point, then that client would receive the services appropriate for that exact point. Likewise, a client at the 10-inch point would receive services designated for that level of assessment. Emphasis was not placed on the individual as a unique personality, but rather, on the assessed level of need and the designated services available to address that need.

Often, clients' needs change over time. One assumption was that many clients made progress toward greater independence in a step-by-step process. A client had to master one skill first before attempting a more difficult one. For example, a young woman with a mild intellectual disability might start out living in a group home where she could learn basic housekeeping, cooking, and self-care skills, including shopping and paying bills. She might then move to an apartment complex or boarding house for people with intellectual disabilities. Houseparents or residential caregivers would not be living with her, but they would be available in another apartment to help her with problems or questions. Eventually, the woman might achieve enough self-care mastery to live on her own or with a roommate.

Other clients' needs change over time but require increasing levels of help and assistance. A person with a deteriorating orthopedic problem involving his knees might require increasingly more intensive help as he loses mobility. Depending on his assessed state of need at any point in time, in the 1970s and 1980s he would receive a designated level of service.

The 1990s and Beyond: Consumer Empowerment

**EP 5b;
5c; 7c;
8b**

The 1990s brought a significantly greater emphasis on individual choice and personalized planning for people with developmental disabilities than there was in earlier decades (Raske, 2005; Rothman, 2003). Essentially, such an emphasis laid the foundation for an empowerment approach. Before, people with developmental disabilities were *clients* whom professionals assessed and provided services prescribed for their level of functioning. There was relatively little variation of service provision at the assessed level. Today's perspective reflects three new important concepts—consumers, choice, and innovation.

Clients as Consumers   Today, practitioners should stress a much more individualized approach, characterized by two major principles (Mackelprang & Salsgiver, 2009).

First, "services are driven by client needs, and clients are viewed as consumers with choices" (p. 253). The term **consumer** implies greater power and choice than does the term **client**. Consumers choose their purchases or resource providers within a competitive market rather than having someone else make these choices for them. Second, "service delivery mechanisms allow for innovative provision of supports to help children stay with families, and adults live as independently as possible" (p. 253). Innovation is stressed to develop unique avenues of service provision in response to individual needs.

Emphasis on Choice   One key word here is *choice*. Here the ruler concept explained earlier no longer applies. Rather, clients are encouraged to assess the choices available and decide what supports they want and what goals they wish to pursue.

Mackelprang and Salsgiver (2009) promote the "independent living model":

> Traditional models view people with disabilities as patients and clients. The independent living model views persons with disabilities as individuals, citizens, consumers, and/or participants in service. The roles of professionals … are also different. They may be considered experts in their field; however, that expertise does not translate into control over people's lives (White, Gutierrez, & Seekins, 1996). Instead, they act as consultants and assistants. Their roles are akin to those of financial investment consultants, who educate and sell investment packages to consumers. However, decisions rest with consumers, who decide whether they act on the advice of their consultants. (p. 429)

Consider Bertram, age 44, a quadriplegic whose condition is the result of a congenital spinal cord malformation. Instead of professionals assessing his capabilities and designating where it is best for him to live, he can make that decision himself. With practitioners and other caregiving professionals' input regarding what resources and services are available, Bertram can determine the environment providing him with what he perceives as the highest quality of life. Of course, his choices are influenced by his own capabilities and the resources available. It is impossible for Bertram to live in an apartment alone with no supportive help. His viable choices might include living in a nursing home or a group home for people with severe physical disabilities, staying in an apartment with the necessary supportive attendants, or living with his family whose members would serve as primary caregivers (assuming, of course, that they were willing to do so).

EP 8a

Critical Thinking Questions **12-8**

If you were Bertram, what alternative would you prefer? What do you think your major concerns would be?

EP 8a

Critical Thinking Question **12-9**

If you were Bertram, what choice do you think you would make for yourself and why?

Innovation   A vital word in today's approach toward working with people with developmental disabilities is **innovation**, the initiation, development, and application of new ideas. Innovative service provision may involve a totally unique combination of services depending on what an individual wishes to accomplish. In other words, individuals with a disability define their own future to include the community where they choose to live their lives, doing work they want, learning what they want, and making decisions about such issues as marriage or partnership and children.

For example, Emmaline, age 7, has spina bifida, a "neurological physical disability in which the bones of the spine do not close properly" (Friend, 2011, p. 510). The split may occur at any point along the bones supporting the spinal column; the unprotected spinal nerves may be exposed and damaged, resulting in paralysis below that point (Hallahan et al., 2012). Emmaline has an individualized service plan designed to meet her unique needs. She can live at home with an innovative combination of supports. A motorized wheelchair maximizes her mobility. Family counseling provides her parents with information and help in responding to Emmaline's special needs. A wheelchair-accessible van provides her with transportation to and from school. A teacher's aide assists her with any help she needs in completing school assignments. Designated medical staff help Emmaline and her family meet her special health and surgical needs.

Empowerment of People with Intellectual and Other Developmental Disabilities

The empowerment approach continues to reflect our most current perspective on service provision for people with disabilities (Mackelprang & Salsgiver, 2009; Rothman, 2003). It focuses on what people can do, not what they cannot. Pfeiffer (2005) discusses the misconceptions about disability:

(1) Disability is not a tragedy; (2) disability does not mean dependency; (3) disability does not mean a loss of potential, productivity, social contribution, value, capability, ability, and the like; (4) disability is a natural part of life, everyone's life; and (5) there is as much variation between people with disabilities as between people in general.

In other words, disability does not mean grief, guilt, and bitterness. People with disabilities are not courageous, noble, and brave any more than anyone else. People with disabilities can be very sexual and sensual. People with disabilities can be very good parents. People with disabilities are not poor unless they are unemployed. People with disabilities are not ignorant unless they were segregated from mainstream education and even then many are quite brilliant in spite of so-called special education. People with disabilities do not have to be with "their own kind," whatever that means. (p. 38)

Critical Thinking Questions **12-10**

EP 8a

What are your reactions to these statements about the misconceptions of disability? To what extent do you automatically respond positively or negatively to them? Explain why.

An empowerment model emphasizes a number of practices (Rothman, 2003). First, it helps people with disabilities reach their full potential by endorsing changes in their living conditions to maximize their capacities. Second, empowerment means improving social policies to enhance their well-being and seek social and economic justice. Third, an empowerment approach focuses not on what's "wrong" with a person, but rather on what's right. It emphasizes how a person's strengths can be put to use. Fourth, a social worker adopting an empowerment approach "can help the client to motivate and to see himself or herself as actor, rather than acted upon. Empowerment practice involves the worker in helping the client to act, rather than in acting on his or her behalf" (p. 211).

Rothman (2003) continues by discussing an empowerment approach with respect to people with disabilities as a community:

> The empowerment model for communities is an extension of the empowerment model for individuals and is built upon the same foundations: that human dignity and respect are an essential part of optimal functioning, and that oppression, exclusion, and discrimination undermine self-esteem. On this broader level, empowerment focuses on supporting a feeling of group competence, connectedness, and the group's ability to effect change for the good of all of the members of the group. The skills, abilities, and personal characteristics of each member of the group are used together to promote and achieve the mutually determined goals. (p. 226)

People with developmental disabilities continue to suffer widespread discrimination (Karger & Stoesz, 2013). Focus on Ethics 12-1 describes a case example of discrimination against a person with disabilities and raises questions about the ethics involved in decisions made about her.

Focus on Ethics **12-1**

Case Example: Discrimination against a Person with a Disability   LO 12-7

EP 1

Sandra, a 34-year-old woman with Down syndrome, was denied a heart-lung transplant even though insurance covered the $250,000 necessary for the operation (Whelan, 2014). "Down syndrome is a set of cognitive and physical symptoms that result from having an extra chromosome 21 or an extra piece of that chromosome. It is the most common chromosomal cause of mild to moderate intellectual disabilities. People with Down syndrome also have some distinct physical features, such as a flat-looking face, and they are at risk for a number of other health problems" (NICHD, 2017).

"In 1960, when Sandra was born, Sandra's mother had been told that Sandra would not live past her teens, so she should not bother going to a cardiologist. However, when Sandra turned 25, she went to a cardiologist, that told her if her heart defect had been managed when she was a baby, it would have been relatively simple to correct. Unfortunately, since then her condition had spread to her lungs, making an organ transplant necessary" (Whelan, 2014).

One of the transplant centers said those with Down syndrome are considered "categorically inappropriate," while the other said that her condition made her "unable to follow the complex post-transplantation medical regimen required of her." Judgments of health and judgments of worth became intertwined, and Sandra was stuck between a rock and a hard place.

Sandra and her doctor strongly disagree with these allegations. Sandra "was an independent woman who lived on her own and held various part-time or volunteer jobs, even acting as an advocate for those with disabilities. (Whelan, 2014). Sandra had already assumed responsibility for taking various medications and monitoring her blood pressure every day. Publicity compelled the hospitals to reconsider her plea. Without the surgery Sandra only had a few years to live.

To what extent do you feel that the hospitals' decisions and their rationales were reasonable? To what extent were these decisions fair and ethical? What do you think should or should not have been done? Explain your reasons.

Generalist Social Work Practice with People Who Have Intellectual and Other Developmental Disabilities LO 12-8

EP 1c; 8d

May (2005) comments on how people with disabilities are treated differently than other populations-at-risk:

> Great effort is expended to ensure that everyone understands the value of diversity (read "deviation") in contemporary U.S. Culture. Not so when disability is the issue. Here, the focus is on "restoring" the person who is labeled "disabled" so he or she no longer deviates from normative expectations. There is no systematic effort to identify sources of pride or to instill positive connotations on being "disabled."
>
> The implications for social workers and other intentional helpers are profound and require a "working with" orientation with the … client [who has a disability] versus a "working on" orientation. From this "working with" perspective, the client system is not merely the collection of difficulties or clinical symptomatology, but is one component of an interactive system that may produce impairment. Solutions, then, are not to be found solely in the person with the disability, but in the larger social environment. (p. 84)

Social workers often must use brokering, case management, and advocacy skills to provide effective services. **Brokering** is the linkage of clients (consumers) to needed resources. **Case management** is the process of organizing, coordinating, and maintaining a network of needed services provided by any number of agencies, organizations, or facilities on the behalf of a client with many needs. Obviously, many people with developmental disabilities require an innovative range of services to maximize self-determination and pursue an optimal quality of life. The key here is coordinating and monitoring services so that clients with ongoing or changing needs get these needs met.

Advocacy is "a process of affecting or initiating change either with or on behalf of client groups to:

- *obtain services or resources that would not otherwise be provided*
- *modify or influence policies or practices that adversely affect groups or communities*
- *promote legislation or policies that will result in the provision of requisite resources or service*" (Hepworth, Rooney, Rooney, & Strom-Gottfried, 2017, p. 435).

There is usually no problem when adequate resources and services are available. However, in reality, this is usually not the case. When clients are not getting their needs met, it is the practitioner's responsibility to advocate on their behalf. Resources may require redistribution. Policies may require change and improvement. New services may need development.

One facet of advocacy is helping clients advocate for themselves when they are capable instead of doing everything for them (Mackelsprang & Salsgiver, 2009). This is another form of client empowerment. For example, it might be easy for Kofi, a social worker, to advocate for his client Thanasi, age 38, who has *muscular dystrophy*. There are many different kinds of muscular dystrophy. Symptoms of the most common variety begin in childhood, primary in boys. Other types don't surface until adulthood (Mayo Clinic, 2014).

Thanasi was diagnosed with the disease at age 12. Although Thanasi can take a few steps by herself, it is very difficult for her and she usually uses a motorized wheelchair. Balance is difficult, as she has lost eight of her toes from the disease. She has little strength in her arms and hands and so accomplishes tasks such as writing and eating very slowly. As muscles deteriorate, her voice is weakening, so she tries to do most of her necessary talking earlier in the day when she is stronger. Thanasi is a strong, independent person who prides herself in accomplishing her goals. For example, she has earned a bachelor's degree in accounting and is able to work part-time at her own pace.

Thanasi lives in a group home, where Kofi is the social worker, with other people who have physical disabilities. Thanasi has several issues to address, including some funding glitches and the need for a new wheelchair and other medical equipment. Kofi talks to Thanasi about these needs and eagerly volunteers to make the calls, write the letters, and advocate on her behalf. He is taken aback when Thanasi responds with a dour look on her face and then avoids eye contact with him. He asks her what's wrong. She hesitantly responds that she would much rather do it herself, although she admits she probably needs help negotiating the complicated maze of services. Kofi suddenly grasps the issue like being hit by a two-by-four. He backs off and volunteers to help find out whom she needs to contact and what information she needs to present. Although it will be much slower for her to advocate for herself than for him to do it, the process will empower her. Kofi decides it's best for him to support her in her advocacy efforts instead of performing the primary advocacy role himself.

Avenues of Legislative, Community, and Worker Empowerment   LO 12-9

**EP 3;
5b; 5c**

A positive piece of legislation passed in 1990 and revised in 2010 is of special significance in terms of improving access to resources in the macro social environment (Barusch, 2015; Karger & Stoesz, 2013). The Americans with Disabilities Act of 1990 (ADA) was intended to provide people with physical or mental disabilities access to public spaces and to workplaces by eliminating barriers that prevented them from fully accessing opportunities available to most other citizens. The ADA defines an individual with a disability "as a person who has a physical or mental impairment that substantially limits one or more major life activities, a person who has a history or record of such an impairment, or a person who is perceived by others as having such an impairment. The ADA does not specifically name all of the impairments that are covered" (US Department of Justice, 2017).

> Major life activities include, for example, caring for oneself, performing manual tasks, seeing, hearing, eating, sleeping, walking, lifting, bending, breathing, learning, concentrating, communicating, and working. "A major life activity also includes the operation of a major bodily function, including but not limited to functions of the immune system, normal cell growth, digestive, bowel, bladder, neurological, brain, respiratory, circulatory, endocrine, and reproductive functions. (US Department of Justice, 2009)

The act also forbids discrimination against people with a record of a disability, such as mental illness, heart disease, or cancer, and against people perceived of as having a disability, such as those with a severe facial deformity (US Department of Justice, 2009). About 56.7 million people in the United States have a disability (US Census Bureau, 2017). Despite the benefits of the ADA, the employment rate of persons with a disability is substantially less than those without a disability.

ADA Requirements   ADA provisions help people with disabilities in at least two major ways. First, the ADA prohibits discrimination against people with disabilities in employment, transportation, public accommodation, communications, and governmental activities. The ADA also establishes requirements for telecommunications relay services (US Department of Labor, 2017).

The ADA's second major thrust requires that "workplaces and public facilities provide 'reasonable accommodation' and accessibility for people with disabilities" (Segal, 2013, p. 158). This means that "discriminatory practices, such as environmental and telecommunication barriers, need to be replaced with accessible structures in instances where cost would not be prohibitive" (DePoy & Gilson, 2004, p. 100).

The ADA has changed the way we look at the challenges faced by people with disability from one focused on the individual's health to one focused on social and structural issues. It redefines problems as belonging to the *community*, not people with disabilities living in the community. Instead of trying to determine how best to help a person get around in an office with a wheelchair, the focus is on the accommodations the office needs to make to facilitate access. Thus, the problem is not inherent in the individual but in the failure of the community to plan for the needs of those with a disability.

Jansson (2005) reports on some of the ADA's "remarkable improvements" for people with disabilities:

Elevators and ramps were added to most public buildings. Work accommodations were provided by public and private employers, including use of computer-assisted technologies, flexible work assignments, and special training programs. Lifts were placed in buses, as were reserved seats. Kitchens and bathrooms were redesigned in housing units. (p. 335)

Countering this view, Karger and Stoesz (2013) indicate:

Despite the ADA and other federal laws, discrimination is still widespread against people with disabilities. For instance, most buildings still do not meet the needs of [people with physical disabilities] … in terms of access, exits, restrooms, parking lots, warning systems, and so forth. Many apartment complexes and stores continue to be built without allowing for the needs of people with disabilities. The struggle for full social, political, and economic integration remains an ongoing battle. (p. 85)

Critical Thinking Questions **12-11**

EP 8a

To what extent do you think the ADA has been successful in fighting discrimination against and increasing access for people with disabilities? Do you know anyone with a disability? If so, what is that person's opinion?

Supreme Court Decisions and the ADA   As you know, Supreme Court decisions can shape the application of policy and refine how it's interpreted. Since its passage, challenges to the ADA have produced a substantial body of case law. DiNitto (2011) explains that for some time,

> in the prevailing conservative political climate, rulings were more likely to favor business (defendants) rather than employees (plaintiffs who brought the suits). In a number of cases, the court concluded that individuals whose impairment could be corrected, for example, with medication or eyeglasses, are not truly disabled and therefore are not entitled to disability employments protections [for example, against discrimination]. The outcome was that some people were considered not "disabled enough" to receive protection under the ADA, but they were considered "disabled enough" to be refused a job or fired because an employer felt their physical or mental limitations kept them from safely or effectively fulfilling job requirements. In various cases, courts ruled against individuals who claimed they were disabled due to vision impairments, high blood pressure, carpal tunnel syndrome [a disease characterized by compression of nerves at the wrist, resulting in weakness, pain, or lack of sensation in the hand], liver disease, and stroke. The US Supreme Court supported a strict definition, indicating that a disability must interfere with essential tasks such as brushing one's teeth or washing one's face.... The definition of disability was interpreted so strictly "that hardly anyone could meet it." (pp. 216–217)

In other words, to be given ADA protection, people with a disability had to be unable to function in major aspects of everyday life. This did not necessarily relate to their ability to perform required functions at work. Barusch (2015) provides an example of a case:

> In 2002 the Supreme Court ruled on the case of *Toyota Motor Mfg., Ky. v. Williams.* Ella Williams was employed at a Toyota plant and requested accommodation for carpal tunnel syndrome. She later sued, claiming that she had been denied ADA accommodation. The Supreme Court found that, although her disability did limit her ability to perform some manual tasks, it did not limit her ability to perform major life activities such as household chores, bathing, and brushing her teeth, so she was not eligible for ADA protections. (p. 245)

DiNitto (2011) continues:

> Major changes were made to the ADA in 2008. To return the act to what Congress originally intended, the definition of disability is supposed to be interpreted more broadly than the narrower definition or high standard that was being used. Except for "ordinary eyeglasses and contact lenses," other "mitigating measures" like hearing aids, medication, and prosthetic devices are no longer to be included in determining whether an individual is disabled. The definition of "major life activity" has also been broadened so that more people can now be able to make claims for ADA protection. In addition to self-care, examples of major life activities are "manual tasks, seeing, hearing, eating, sleeping, walking, standing, lifting, bending, speaking, breathing, learning, reading, concentrating, thinking, and communicating" and "major bodily

functions" such as "functions of the immune system, normal cell growth, digestive, bowel, bladder, neurological, brain, respiratory, circulatory, endocrine, and reproductive functions."

The ADA act amendments should make it easier for employees to take action under the third prong of the ADA's definition of disability [that the person is *perceived* by others as having a disability]. Previously, employees had to prove that the employer "regarded" them as having a disability that substantially limited a major life activity. Under the new, broader standard, the language is that the employer "perceived" the individual to have a disability even if a perceived (or actual) disability does not limit a major life activity. (p. 217)

One case of special note is the *L. C. & E. W. v. Olmstead* case decision by the Supreme Court in 1999. Hayashi (2005) explains:

L. C. and E. W. were patients in a state psychiatric hospital in Georgia. They challenged their placement in an institutional setting rather than in a community-based program. The Supreme Court decided that unnecessary institutionalization of individuals with disabilities is discrimination under the ADA, and that the state must provide services in the most integrated setting appropriate to individual clients. (p. 49)

Community Support and Empowerment

Communities and organizations in the macro environment can offer resources and support to people with intellectual and other developmental disabilities in at least two major ways. First, mandated federal and state legislation can provide for programs available to community residents with developmental disabilities. The last sections reviewed two major pieces of federal legislation passed on the behalf of this population. Second, community residents can work together to establish their own innovative resources within the community.

Some examples of how to make progress through legislation, direct community support, and social work advocacy are presented next. The populations-at-risk addressed include people with visual impairments and those with intellectual disabilities.

Legislative Empowerment for People with Visual Impairments LO 12-10

EP 5b

The Rehabilitation Act of 1973 and its 1992 amendments approve reimbursement for some services provided by agencies for people with visual impairment specifically designated to help this population. One requirement of the act is that websites and other government documents be accessible to people with visual impairments.

Other examples of supportive legislation are two 1930s laws that provide special employment opportunities for people who have a visual impairment; the Wagner-O'Day Act (P.L. 75–739) set up sheltered workshops and the Randolph-Sheppard Act (P.L. 74–734) gave those who are blind preference in operating vending facilities in federal buildings. Many of the largest US Post Offices or court-houses would have a newsstand or lunch counter operated by a person with a visual disability. **Sheltered workshops** or **sheltered employment** provide programs "involving work in a safe, closely supervised environment for people who have trouble functioning more independently" (Kirst-Ashman, 2017, p. 50).

Additionally, people who are legally blind, unemployed, and have assets falling below prescribed levels may receive Supplemental Security Income (SSI). SSI is a federal public assistance program that provides a minimum income to poor people who are older adults, have a disability, or are blind. Benefits are provided on the basis of need instead of one's work history.

The 1931 Pratt-Smoot Act (P.L. 71–787) provides an example of legislation making reading material more accessible for people with visual impairment; it established a Library of Congress program that later formed the foundation for regional centers providing Braille and recorded materials to people with visual impairment.

Community Empowerment for People with Visual Impairments

EP 7d; 8

Laws and mandated programs may make some resources available. However, communities themselves can also enhance and make easier the lives of people with visual impairment. Community groups and government units can disseminate information concerning the issues addressed and the strengths inherent in people with visual impairment. These people and their families require relevant knowledge about legislation, available resources, and alternative approaches to completing necessary tasks of daily living (e.g., doing housework, getting places, or accessing information). Communities can sponsor self-help groups where people with visual impairment can come together, discuss issues, provide each other with ideas, and find support. Schools who have students with visual impairment can make it a point to educate parents about services, resources, and aides. Schools can encourage students with visual impairment to participate in sports, recreation, and other extracurricular and educational activities just as children with perfect vision do.

Even such a basic thing as ensuring that public buildings use Braille next to the floor indicator buttons on elevators is very helpful. Esther, a student with a visual impairment, comes to mind. She attended a state university renowned for its support of and services for students with disabilities. Esther felt that the campus focused its attention on serving people with physical disabilities involving mobility and viewed people with visual impairment as less significant. All buildings and classrooms had been readily accessible for as long as anyone could remember. She advocated for years to have Braille information installed in elevators throughout the campus with little response by university administration. After persistent pressure, she finally was able to make her point, and all elevators were furnished with Braille directions.

Empowerment for People with Visual Impairments and Social Work Practice

Social workers can serve as important advocates in their communities and agencies to provide needed services for people with visual impairments. People initially dealing with a visual impairment in themselves or another family member will need time to adjust to the situation and cope with its ramifications. Social workers can help people realize that the long cane (a mobility aid used by individuals with visual impairment who move the cane along the ground before them), a guide dog, human guides, recorded information, adapted computers, and other technological devices (such as reading machines that convert print into spoken words) can help people organize home, work, and social lives in an effective, efficient, although different, manner (Hallahan et al., 2012).

Community Empowerment for People with Intellectual Disabilities

EP 7d; 8

Because people with intellectual disabilities constitute a large proportion of people with developmental disabilities, and because they are likely to use services provided by state agencies, we will spend considerable time discussing them. As with people who have visual impairment, legislation provides some support and programs for people with intellectual disabilities who qualify for such services. Funding for people with intellectual disabilities comes from a range of sources depending on whether individuals fulfill eligibility criteria often related to their income level. For example, SSI may be available to people with intellectual disabilities whose income and assets are low enough to meet established criteria.

Communities can creatively develop resources and programs to integrate people with intellectual disabilities and enhance their quality of life. For instance, one state has a Community Options Program (COP) funded at the state level that "provides assessments, case plans, and community services as an alternative to nursing home placements" (ARC Milwaukee, undated, b, p. 2).

ARCs and Related Resources Can Empower People and Enhance Quality of Life

One excellent example of how a community can use a support system for people with intellectual disabilities is an organization called ARC. Historically known as the Association for Retarded Citizens, ARCs now are established in communities throughout the United States. The following discussion focuses specifically on ARCs. However, the types of services ARCs provide can certainly be sponsored by other organizations and community groups.

Typically funded through a variety of sources, including donations by private citizens, corporations, local service clubs, foundations, and by government service contracts, ARCs provide a wide range of services. They reflect a creative alliance of public services, private contributions, and community groups to provide services for this population-at-risk. Potential services include information and referral service, help lines, noninstitutional residential opportunities, vocational and employment programs, support services, intervention advocacy, volunteer programs, and recreational activities.

Information and Referral Services and Help Lines

An **information and referral service** is a source of information about what community resources and services exist and helps clients connect with the appropriate assistance. A **help line** is an information and referral system based on telephone contact. Persons requiring information about services, laws, or issues related to a specific problem or population, in this case, intellectual disabilities, call a trained professional who connects them with the appropriate resource or provides them with necessary information. Many ARCs develop an extensive computerized system that can quickly identify relevant linkages between questions, needs, information, and resources.

Provision of Noninstitutional Living Opportunities

One type of resource that can help people with a disability maintain maximum independence and self-determination is linkage with noninstitutional living opportunities. As we discussed earlier in the context of deinstitutionalization, the intent is to place people in the least restrictive setting possible. These placements include adult family care homes where clients reside in the home of caregivers who supervise and care for them. Another setting is a group home or community-based residential care facility (CBRF). Residents often are selected on the basis of having similar needs, such as required levels of supervision and support. For example, one CBRF might have residents capable of taking care of personal needs and working at a sheltered workshop. Another CBRF might have clients who require a higher level of supervision, where staff must provide more direct input concerning how they dress, eat, and interact.

Other even more independent, supported living options include living with a roommate or by oneself in an apartment. Some limited supervision and assistance such as help with paying bills or arranging transportation to work is usually needed in these cases.

Vocational and Employment Opportunities

ARCs are also quite creative regarding provision of vocational and employment opportunities. They can assist people in gaining community employment by preparing clients for the expectations of employment, assisting in placement, helping employers restructure jobs to maximize clients' abilities to complete job tasks, and providing job coaching concerning basic work skills (such as getting to work on time and following supervisory instructions).

Individuals may also gain employment in more structured settings such as sheltered workshops. One ARC agency developed an employment program where clients made and finished ceramic gifts for special occasions such as weddings and graduations. Another ARC organization developed a work setting where clients manufactured pillows for a major national airline.

People who are unable to function in more demanding settings may receive "day services"; these aim to "maximize an individual's independent functional level in self-care, physical and emotional growth, mobility and community transportation, socialization, recreation, leisure time, and education and pre-vocational skills" (ARC Milwaukee, undated, a, p. 2).

Other Support Services

Support services can have many facets. Organizations can provide outreach support services to clients in their own homes that involve instruction in daily living skills, budgeting and financial management, transportation, parenting skills, and personal issues including interpersonal interaction, leisure activities, self-esteem, and assertiveness. Respite care programs provide caregiving services to parents or other caregivers of persons with intellectual disabilities. Caregivers can take some time off from responsibilities to give them a break and refresh their efforts. Family services geared to senior caregivers can provide support to aging caregivers who find it increasingly difficult to provide the same level of care they could in the past. For example, because of increasing strength limitations, an aging caregiver might find it much more difficult to assist a person with a severe disability in dressing himself. Family services for older adult caregivers can also provide support during crises, such as a caregiver experiencing her own acute health problems. They can also be used to assist caregivers in long-term planning for and with the person who has the disability. A common concern of aging caregivers is what will happen to the individual with a disability when the caregiver can no longer assume that function.

Support groups are another support mechanism, and they can focus on many different issues. Parent support groups "provide parents with an opportunity to get together and share stories, concerns and achievements with other parents who are experiencing similar circumstances" (ARC, undated, a, p. 2). Support groups for seniors with disabilities can give them opportunities to share concerns, discuss suggestions, and talk about how to maximize their quality of life.

Advocacy

EP 3; 5b; 5c; 8c

Intervention advocacy "is designed to respond to the needs of persons with disabilities and their families when serious problems arise affecting legal rights, safety and health, financial security, or access to community resources" (ARC, undated, c, p. 2). The service system is complicated, and clients along with their families may find it very difficult to negotiate. Advocacy is often necessary to link clients with services they need and deserve. Advocacy is also essential when needed services don't exist. Social workers can provide leadership in advocating for improved policies and service provision, including client access to the services of social work. Practitioners can also collaborate with colleagues to establish policies and services that enhance clients' social and economic well-being.

Using Community Volunteers

There are numerous ways in which volunteers can help ARC programming. These include performing clerical duties and answering the phone, caring for small children while parents attend support groups, serving as a matched "friend" with a person who has a disability to provide support and encouragement, giving support via telephone to persons needing intermittent help, participating in fundraising activities, assisting at supervision of events such as group outings, and helping with household upkeep and maintenance (ARC, undated, c).

Providing Recreational Activities

Recreational activities and functions provide still another means of enhancing the quality of life for people with disabilities. Examples include ongoing athletic programs, support for Special Olympics, and operation of a summer camp where groups of clients of any age group can interact socially, work on crafts, participate in games and plays, learn appreciation for nature, increase leisure skills, and gain confidence in expressing themselves (ARC, undated, c).

Highlight 12-5 provides a case example of how a community supports and fails to support a person with an intellectual disability in some of the areas just discussed.

EP 8a

Critical Thinking Questions **12-12**

Do you know a person with an intellectual disability? If so, to what resources does that person have access? What resources does that person need, but doesn't get? What are the reasons for any unavailability of resources?

Highlight **12-5**

A Case Example: A Community Helps and Hinders Hiroshi, a Person with Intellectual Disabilities

Consider Hiroshi and how the environment both succeeds and fails to support him. Hiroshi, age 64, lives in a Midwestern town of about 8,000 people in a rural farming community. Hiroshi has a mild intellectual disability. He graduated from high school but only because in those days students like him were given "social promotions." *Social promotion* was a practice of passing students on to the next grade regardless of whether they had satisfied all of the necessary courses. He is very proud of the high school ring he purchased at graduation. The macro environment, especially the school system, did not serve him well. Instead of receiving special services and training that might now be available, the system basically ignored him and passed him on through.

A major problem for Hiroshi is his speech. He has difficulty forming words, and he takes considerable time to structure his sentences. His comprehension of verbal communication is good, however, and he has an excellent sense of humor. His difficult speech often fools people who don't know him well into thinking he is much less competent than he really is. Speech therapy may have helped if it had been available when he was young.

Hiroshi works at a sheltered workshop in addition to working six hours per week as a janitor at Bertha's Butter Burgers. Hiroshi has a strong work history. For almost 20 years, he worked at a local tanning factory hauling deer hides from one area to another as they proceeded through the leather-making process. It was gruesome, backbreaking work. The place was doused with various chemicals. When

Hiroshi got home, he was exhausted. At the time, he was living with his father, who cooked for him, did his laundry, and helped him with other daily living tasks.

Work at the tanning factory had not been without its problems. Once, Hiroshi confessed to his relatives a story about another "guy at work" who liked to pick on him. Hiroshi had lots of experience being picked on. The guy liked to draw a knife and tease Hiroshi, pretending to cut him. Once, he made quite a slit in Hiroshi's right hand. Hiroshi's confession involved payback time. One night after work, he slit all the guy's tires. The guy, who was fired shortly thereafter, never did find out who did it.

Hiroshi was a saver. He would wear the same pair of polyester pants for years, until the threads in the seams gave way. Although Hiroshi made little more than minimum wage, he put almost all of it into savings. When the plant closed and he was laid off, he had accumulated over $40,000. Investing with the help of his brother Egbert and a slick certified financial planner brought his assets to almost $200,000 by the time he turned 64. Unfortunately, this prevented him from receiving public assistance and resources because he did not meet various programs' means tests. *Means tests* involve using established criteria to evaluate clients' financial resources and to decide whether they're eligible for service.

When his father died, with Egbert's help, Hiroshi was able to live in and pay rent for his own apartment. He told Egbert he preferred living alone to living with a roommate. One of Hiroshi's strengths was his strong relationship with

continued

Highlight **12-5** *continued*

Egbert and his family, although they lived inconveniently about 185 miles away. Hiroshi didn't see his family as often as he liked since buses were deregulated and federal regulations no longer required companies to sponsor less popular runs. Egbert and his wife were periodically forced to endure a gravely dull three-hour trip through flat farmland to pick Hiroshi up and another three hours to drive him home.

A major strength in Hiroshi's life was his involvement with the local Center for People with Developmental Disabilities, an agency that did not have a means test. In its sheltered workshop, Hiroshi felt productive and established many social contacts. As one of the highest-functioning clients, he achieved significant social status. At the center's periodic social dances, he was quite accomplished and admired. Hiroshi also had a knack for taking pictures and recordings, which he did regularly at the center's events. The center sponsored or cosponsored numerous events, including Special Olympics, bowling tournaments, picnics, and outings to movies in nearby towns. Hiroshi was extremely proud of a Volunteer's Award Plaque he received from the center for all of the conscientious time he spent photographing and recording events.

At the center, he was assigned a case manager, Cornelia, who evaluated his daily living skills. She linked him with a trainer who tried to teach him how to cook. However, Hiroshi didn't like to cook and so ended up subsisting mostly on TV dinners. It might be noted that Egbert, who had superior intelligence, did not "know how" to boil water. He didn't like to cook, either. Cornelia also helped coordinate any other supportive services Hiroshi might need with Egbert and his family.

Although Cornelia and Egbert tried to encourage Hiroshi to manage his own finances and checkbook, this was too difficult for him. Hiroshi didn't like making computations or sending checks, and he typically made significant mistakes.

When mail-ordering gifts for family members, he would always send cash despite the risk of losing it. Egbert finally gave up and determined that it was easier just to keep track of Hiroshi's finances himself than to keep after Hiroshi on a regular basis.

Another major community strength was the support Hiroshi received from his church. He attended services regularly and was involved in a group called The Sunday Evening Club, consisting of adult church members who met every other Sunday for a potluck dinner and a chance to socialize or hear speakers.

Hiroshi's work at Bertha's was helpful in terms of making him feel useful and conserving his savings. However, the six-hour weekly work allocation was minimal. The management could have given him many more hours if they had not viewed him as an inadequate, "retarded" person. The town provided no public transportation, so Hiroshi had to walk to get anywhere, including two miles to work.

In summary, community strengths for Hiroshi include the Center for People with Developmental Disabilities; its sheltered workshop; his case manager, Cornelia, responsible for Hiroshi's care; public recognition by receiving a Volunteer's Award; his spiritual involvement at church; his job at Bertha's; and strong connections with his family despite the fact that they lived so far away. For Hiroshi, weaknesses in the community include the history of inattention to his needs through decades of absent service; the community residents who made fun of him whenever they had the chance; inadequate involvement in his paid work environment; and lack of public transportation. In some ways, Hiroshi's community environment supported and integrated him, thereby enhancing his quality of life. In other ways, lack of community support served to hinder his ability to live the most useful, productive, and happy life possible.

More Examples of Community Integration for People with Intellectual Disabilities

There are several situations in which adults with intellectual disabilities can be mainstreamed[2] and integrated as part of a large urban community.

1. Perry, age 28, thrives at playing games. Perry's neighbor acquainted him with the local Boys Club. He now volunteers there regularly, teaching children games and supervising their activities.

---

2 *Mainstreaming* originally meant moving children with intellectual and other developmental disabilities from special education classes into regular classes. The term may also be applied to moving a person into the group that includes most other people or moving an idea into the mainstream of ideas.

2. Felicita, age 22, spends most weekdays at a day program with other people who have intellectual disabilities. She passes much of her time coloring and watching other residents. She is an exceptionally warm person who will light up with a dazzling smile when spoken to or given any attention. One of the day program staff introduced her to a local daycare center to see if she could help out there.

   At first, the day program staff always accompanied her and provided some supervision. Now she goes to the daycare center by herself several times a week. The children love her and her attention. She always has time to listen to what they have to say and give them a hug when needed. They realize she's different than their other teachers because sometimes they have to help her out in completing activities. They don't care. They love her anyway.

3. Joe, age 68, lives in a group home. He loves to bowl. Julietta, a member of the area's neighborhood association, stopped by one day to see if there was anything the association could do for Joe and the other residents. She found out about Joe's desire to bowl and remembered that a local church had a Thursday night bowling league. She talked to the team members and asked them if they would consider including Joe on their team. They were a bit hesitant, as they took bowling very seriously and played desperately to win. They were even more hesitant when they discovered Joe was not a very good bowler. However, Joe was obviously ecstatic about being on the team. Team members worked out a rotation system where Joe could periodically bowl but his score was omitted from the final total. Joe continued to beam as he proudly wore his Beaver's Bowling Buddies T-shirt.

4. Norma, age 35, is a pleasant, soft-spoken, shy woman who had lived with her senior parents. She and her parents would often shop at a small local drug store and gift shop across the street from their modest home. Myrtle, who owned the store, got to know and like Norma and her family. Myrtle was concerned that Norma rarely got out of the house except for shopping and other errands with her parents. She started taking Norma out for lunch or a movie every other week or so. Although a busy businesswoman, Myrtle enjoys her time with Norma and feels Norma really appreciates it. She harbors some growing fears about what will happen to Norma when her parents die. Myrtle has become part of Norma's natural helping network.

There are many ways that community residents can discover and invent to help people with intellectual disabilities. Help can be given by formal groups such as ARCs or Social Service Departments, or by concerned individuals such as neighbors and fellow church members. The key is concern for the well-being of other community members, sensitivity to their needs, and the willingness to contribute precious energy on the behalf of others in need.

Critical Thinking Questions **12-13**

EP 8a

Of these examples of how to integrate people with intellectual disabilities into the community, which do you feel are most creative, and why? Can you think of any other creative ways to integrate people with intellectual disabilities? If so, describe them.

Chapter Summary

The following summarizes this chapter's content as it relates to the learning objectives presented at the beginning of the chapter. Objectives include the following:

LO 12-1 **Describe how groups, including African Americans, Hispanics, LGBTQ people, women, and older adults, are populations-at-risk.**

Despite major triumphs concerning legal and social racial equality, African Americans still fall markedly behind their White counterparts in most measures of social and economic well-being. The economic and educational picture for the Hispanic (or Latino/Latina) population is much poorer than that for Whites. Values often characterizing Hispanic families include the significance of a common language, the importance of family, personalismo, machismo, and marianismo, and spirituality. Important issues for LGBTQ people include workplace discrimination and the need for nondiscrimination laws, the recognition of same-sex relationships, family policies for LGBTQ parents, and harassment and violence against LGBTQ people. Many social and economic indicators, including income, occupation, and household responsibilities, reflect women's oppression. A continuum of services is available to meet the needs of older adults.

LO 12-2 **Discuss how empowerment can occur in the macro environment for each group.**

Means used to empower African-American grandparents who are primary caregivers for their grandchildren include establishing support groups, training grandparents as group leaders, and undertaking political advocacy. Policy, research, and practice recommendations are made to advance the well-being of these caregivers. Latinas can empower people in their macro environment through community involvement. One case example portrayed Latina mothers who used social action to seek social and economic justice in housing. Latina-owned grocery stores can provide a wide range of empowering services to their communities. Latino and Latina youth can empower their communities by conducting a community assets assessment and putting identified strengths to use in community projects.

Political action organizations can empower LGBTQ people by providing support to political candidates who advocate for LGBTQ rights, educating the public about LGBTQ issues, and providing legislative advocacy through lobbying. LGBTQ people can also be empowered through special social services.

At-risk pregnant women can be empowered through a community program that educates the public regarding issues and provides needed resources.

A new strengths-based empowerment approach toward aging emphasizes hope, development, autonomy, and activity, regardless of personal situation. This is in contrast to the traditional perspective that focused on deficits.

LO 12-3 **Respond to critical thinking questions.**

Critical thinking questions were raised concerning the effects of discrimination on Hispanic people, Latina community empowerment, a community project's enhancement of Latino and Latina youths' self-esteem, your personal views about LGBTQ issues, reasons for violence against LGBTQ people, gender differences concerning economics and household work, what people with developmental disabilities are like, alternative choices for people with physical disabilities, misconceptions about disability, success of the ADA, resources available for a person with intellectual disabilities, and integration of a person with intellectual disabilities into the community.

LO 12-4 **Provide examples of how spiritual communities can empower their members.**

An African American Baptist church in Utah empowered its youths by assisting them in educational pursuits and providing a range of social activities aimed at improving self-confidence and competence. A Diné (Navajo) community empowered its older adults in the Chinle Nursing Home by providing culturally and spiritually sensitive care in a range of areas.

LO 12-5 Discuss intellectual and other developmental disabilities.

Developmental disabilities are severe and chronic, occur before age 22, are likely permanent, result in significant functional difficulties, and create the need for lifelong supplementary services and help. They include intellectual disabilities, cerebral palsy, hearing impairment, visual impairment, and autism spectrum disorders. Intellectual disabilities involve intellectual functioning significantly below normal along with considerable limitations in adaptive behavior, occurring before age 18. It's important to understand the significance of the Deaf community and Deaf culture.

LO 12-6 Identify differences and similarities between the history of how people with developmental disabilities have been treated and current trends.

Prior to the late 1960s, community treatment and public policy emphasized individual pathology. Trends during the 1970s and 1980s included normalization, deinstitutionalization, individual program planning, and the developmental model. Since the 1990s, approaches have focused on clients as consumers, emphasis on choice, innovation, and empowerment.

LO 12-7 Describe ethical issues in diversity and empowerment.

An ethical issue addressed discrimination against a person with disabilities.

LO 12-8 Describe generalist social work practice with people who have developmental disabilities.

Generalist practitioners employ brokering, case management, and advocacy, among other skills, when working with people who have developmental disabilities.

LO 12-9 Summarize avenues of legislative, community, and worker empowerment.

The Americans with Disabilities Act (ADA) provides an example of empowering legislation. Supreme Court debates and decisions have centered on the definition of *disability*.

LO 12-10 Examine the macro environment's potential for empowering people with visual impairment and intellectual disabilities.

Numerous laws emphasize the rights and needs of people with visual impairments. It is social workers' responsibility to advocate in their communities and agencies to provide needed services.

ARCs, information and referral services, noninstitutional living opportunities, vocational and employment opportunities, other support services (such as outreach services and support groups), advocacy, the use of community volunteers, and the provision of recreational activities can empower people with intellectual disabilities in communities.

Looking Ahead

This chapter investigated human diversity, populations-at-risk, and empowerment for these populations in the macro social environment.

The next chapter will explore the macro environment and social justice on a global scale.

Competency Notes

The following identifies where Educational Policy (EP) competencies and component behaviors are discussed in the chapter.

EP 1 (Competency 1)—Demonstrate Ethical and Professional Behavior. *(p. 431, 468):* Ethical questions are posed regarding discrimination against a person with a disability.

EP 1a Make ethical decisions by applying the standards of the NASW *Code of Ethics,* relevant laws and regulations, models for ethical decision-making, ethical conduct of research, and additional codes of ethics as appropriate to context. *(p. 439):* The NASW *Code of Ethics* forbids discrimination on the basis of sexual orientation.

EP 1c Demonstrate professional demeanor in behavior; appearance; and oral, written, and electronic communication. *(p. 430):* Social workers should demonstrate professional demeanor through the appropriate use of language when referring to Hispanic and other populations. *(p. 469):* Professional roles are discussed that involve working with clients who have disabilities.

EP 2 (Competency 2)—Engage Diversity and Difference in Practice. *(p. 425):* African American grandparents who are caregivers for their grandchildren are affected by dimensions of diversity, including race, age, and class. *(p. 426):* The marginalization of grandparent caregivers is related to the intersectionality of multiple factors, including race, age, class, and status as a relative. *(p. 429):* Race, color, ethnicity, and culture are dimensions of diversity. For a number of reasons, Hispanic populations experience oppression. *(p. 434):* Religion and spirituality are important aspects of human diversity. *(p. 439):* Social workers should recognize the extent to which LGBTQ people are oppressed. Sexual orientation and sex are dimensions of diversity. *(p. 447):* Gender is a dimension of diversity. The oppression of women is discussed. *(p. 450):* Practitioners should recognize how society and stereotypes may oppress older adults. *(p. 450):* Age is a dimension of diversity. *(p. 454, 456):* Religion and spirituality, race, and culture are all dimensions of diversity. *(p. 459):* Disability is a dimension of diversity. *(p. 463, 469):* Analyzing historical policies concerning the treatment of people with disabilities increases social workers' understanding of the oppression, alienation, privilege, and power that can affect these populations.

EP 2a Apply and communicate understanding of the importance of diversity and difference in shaping life experiences in practice at the micro, mezzo, and macro levels. *(p. 429):* Social workers should recognize how race, color, ethnicity, and culture shape life experiences for Hispanic people. *(p. 431):* Practitioners should recognize the extent to which cultural values shape life experiences.

EP 2b Present themselves as learners and engage clients and constituencies as experts of their own experiences. *(p. 430):* Social workers should learn from their Hispanic clients what terms and language are appropriate. *(p. 431):* Learning from clients about their cultures and respecting their values is a career-long process. *(p. 456):* Practitioners should learn from their clients about their clients' cultural values. *(p. 456):* The Chinle Nursing Home example demonstrates how professionals, including social workers, should view themselves as learners and learn about cultural needs and expectations from the clients who are residents and their families.

EP 2c Apply self-awareness and self-regulation to manage the influence of personal biases and values in working with diverse clients and constituencies. *(pp. 430–431):* Practitioners should strive for enhanced self-awareness of personal biases to eliminate the influence of such biases in working with Hispanic and other populations. *(p. 450):* Social workers should increase self-awareness about any stereotypes they may harbor to about older adults.

EP 3 (Competency 3)—Advance Human Rights and Social, Economic, and Environmental Justice. *(p. 428):* Grandparent caregivers are often offered far fewer resources and services than other out-of-home care providers. *(p. 429):* Social workers should strive to understand the mechanisms of oppression for Hispanics. *(p. 436):* This case example explores oppression concerning Latina mothers and their rental housing. *(p. 439):* The oppression of LGBTQ people is described. *(p. 450):* Ageism and its oppressive results are recognized. *(p. 463):* Learning about the history of legislation concerning and treatment of people with disabilities enhances practitioners' understanding of oppression and discrimination. *(p. 477):* Past judicial interpretation of the ADA allowed for the oppressive treatment of people with disabilities.

EP 3b Engage in practices that advance social, economic, and environmental justice. *(p. 428):* Practitioners should advocate on the behalf of grandparent caregivers. *(p. 439):* This case scenario depicts how social workers along with their clients can engage in practices that advance social and economic justice, in this case concerning the availability of housing for Latina clients. *(p. 443):* Practitioners are encouraged to advocate for human rights and social and economic justice on behalf of LGBTQ people. This includes becoming active in political action organizations. *(p. 450):* Social workers should advocate on the behalf of older adults. Concepts and practices are discussed that advance social and economic justice for people with disabilities. Practitioners can advocate for improved policies and services that enhance the human rights of people with intellectual disabilities. The ADA's intent is to promote practices that advance social and economic justice for people with disabilities.

EP 4a Use practice experience and theory to inform scientific inquiry and research. *(p. 428):* More social work research needs to be conducted concerning the needs and costs of providing resources to grandparents who are caregivers for grandchildren.

EP 5 (Competency 5)—Engage in Policy Practice. *(p. 426):* Social workers should strive to establish policies and programs that adequately support African American grandparents who are caregivers for their grandchildren. *(p. 436):* This case example depicts how social workers and clients can analyze policies and advocate for practices that advance social well-being. *(p. 439):* Social workers should advocate for policies that advance the social well-being of LGBTQ people. *(p. 443):* One way for social workers to advocate for policies that advance the social well-being of LGBTQ people is to become active in political action organizations. *(p. 449):* A program is described that formulates policies and practices that advance the social well-being of at-risk pregnant women. *(p. 450):* Social workers should advocate for policies that provide appropriate services for, respect the human rights of, and advance the social well-being of older adults. *(p. 456):* The Chinle Nursing Home has formulated organizational policies that advance the social well-being of Diné (Navajo) residents within a culturally sensitive framework. *(p. 463):* Analyzing policies concerning the treatment of people with disabilities can enhance social workers' ability to formulate and advocate for policies that advance social well-being. *(p. 465):* Concepts and policies are discussed that serve to advance the social well-being of people with disabilities. *(p. 470):* The ADA is an example of a policy that advances the social well-being of people with disabilities. *(p. 476):* Policies that advance the well-being of people with visual impairment are discussed. *(p. 477):* Social workers can formulate and advocate for policies that advance the social well-being of people with disabilities.

EP 5c Apply critical thinking to analyze, formulate, and advocate for policies that advance human rights and social, economic, and environmental justice. *(p. 428):* One of the practice suggestions presented here involves advocating for client access to social work services. *(p. 477):* Practitioners can and should advocate for client access to the services of social work.

EP 7a Collect and organize data, and apply critical thinking to interpret information from clients and constituencies. *(p. 439):* This case example portrays how community data can be collected and used.

EP 7c Develop mutually agreed-on intervention goals and objectives based on the critical assessment of strengths, needs, and challenges within clients and constituencies. *(p. 426):* Practitioners in the case example presented here assess and emphasize the strengths of grandparent caregivers in addition to addressing their limitations. *(p. 439):* This case example portrays a method of assessing a community client system's assets and strengths. *(p. 453):*

Social workers should assess and emphasize the strengths of older adults to help empower them. (*p. 456*): Work with Diné (Navajo) people should focus on their numerous strengths. Staff at the Chinle Nursing Home work with residents and their families to develop a mutually agreed-on, culturally sensitive focus on service provision. (*p. 461*): Social workers should assess and emphasize the strengths inherent in the Deaf community. Concepts discussed here emphasize the assessment and use of client strengths.

EP 7d Select appropriate intervention strategies based on the assessment, research knowledge, and values and preferences of clients and constituencies. (*p. 426*): This case example discusses appropriate intervention strategies for grandparents caring for their grandchildren. (*p. 439*): This case example explores how information about a community is used to establish appropriate intervention strategies. (*p. 446*): Creative intervention strategies for working with LGBTQ people are described. (*p. 451*): Social workers can select the appropriate intervention strategies for older adults and link these clients with suitable services. (*p. 454*): This case example reflects the use of appropriate intervention strategies for these African American youths. (*p. 457*): Intervention strategies employed at the Chinle Nursing Home are appropriate because they coincide with cultural values. (*p. 456*): Community intervention strategies are described for people with visual impairment. (*pp. 474–475*): Various community intervention strategies are suggested for people with intellectual disabilities.

EP 8 (Competency 8)—Intervene with Individuals, Families, Groups, Organizations, and Communities (*p. 426*): This case example illustrates how a program can help clients resolve problems. (*p. 446*): This case example reflects how New Bridges sought to achieve its organizational goals. (*p. 451*): Various means of helping clients resolve problems through special social services for LGBTQ people are described. (*p. 454*): This case example reflects how a program can help resolve problems. (*p. 456*): The Chinle Nursing Home initiates practices that are culturally sensitive in

order to achieve effectively its organizational goal of serving clients. (*p. 474*): Social workers can help older clients resolve problems by linking them with the appropriate support and services. Staff at the Chinle Nursing Home employ culturally sensitive strategies to help clients address issues and resolve problems. (*pp. 475–476*): Ways that communities can help people with visual impairments resolve problems are identified. Various community actions are proposed to help people with intellectual disabilities address problems.

EP 8a Critically choose and implement interventions to achieve practice goals and enhance capacities of clients and constituencies. (*pp. 434, 436, 439, 442, 443, 463, 466, 467, 471, 478, 480*): Critical thinking questions are posed.

EP 8b Apply knowledge of human behavior and the social environment, person-in-environment, and other multidisciplinary theoretical frameworks in interventions with clients and constituencies. (*p. 428*): Practitioners should continuously respond to the changing issues and conditions affecting African American grandparents who are caregivers for their grandchildren. (*p. 436*): This case example demonstrates how social workers should discover and attend to changing conditions affecting their clients. (*p. 439*): Social workers should attend to the changing issues and trends affecting LGBTQ people in order to provide relevant services. (*p. 449*): Social workers should continuously attend to changing needs and societal trends, such as at-risk pregnant women's receipt of prenatal care, in order to provide relevant services. (*p. 465*): Social workers should attend to and keep abreast of emerging societal trends regarding the treatment of people with disabilities in order to provide relevant and effective services.

EP 8c Use inter-professional collaboration as appropriate to achieve beneficial practice outcomes. (*p. 428*): Social workers should provide leadership in promoting changes in service delivery and practice on the behalf of African American and other grandparents who provide care for their grandchildren. (*p. 436*): This case example portrays how social workers can collaborate with colleagues and clients to address and change the landlord's oppressive decisions regarding rental policy. *(p. 439)*: Social workers should provide leadership in promoting improvements in service delivery and practice on the behalf of LGBTQ people. *(p. 443)*: Social workers can join and work with political action organizations for effective policy action on the behalf of LGBTQ people. *(p. 449)*: Social workers can collaborate with colleagues and clients for effective policy action by becoming involved in political action organizations. *(p. 477)*: Shared Beginnings reflects a program where professionals collaborate with colleagues and clients to establish effective policies and practices for at–risk pregnant women. Social workers can serve as leaders to develop relevant programs such as Shared Beginnings. Practitioners can collaborate with colleagues for effective policy action on the behalf of people with intellectual disabilities. Practitioners can provide leadership in promoting changes in policy and practice to improve the quality of service provision for people with intellectual disabilities.

EP 8d Negotiate, mediate, and advocate with and on behalf of diverse clients and constituencies. *(pp. 436–439)*: Social workers are responsible for advocating on the behalf of LGBTQ clients. *(p. 469)*: Helping clients with disabilities advocate for themselves is discussed.

EP 8e Facilitate effective transitions and endings that advance mutually agreed-on goals. *(p. 456)*: Staff, including social workers at the Chinle Nursing Home, can help make clients as comfortable as possible and give them as much control as possible as clients prepare for death.

EP 9b Apply knowledge of human behavior and the social environment, person-in-environment, and other multidisciplinary theoretical frameworks in the evaluation of outcomes. *(p. 449)*: The CenteringPregnancy program demonstrated effectiveness using multiple indicators. *(p. 463)*: Modern approaches to managing intellectual disabilities have emphasized the use of program evaluation for organizational effectiveness.

Media Resources

MindTap for Social Work

Go to MindTap® for digital study tools and resources that complement this text and help you be more successful in your course and career. There's an interactive eBook plus videos of client sessions, skill-building activities, quizzes to help you prepare for tests, apps, and more—all in one place. If your instructor didn't assign MindTap, you can find out more about it at CengageBrain .com.

13 | Social Justice and the Global Community

Aaron Huey/National Geographic Creative/Alamy Stock Photo

Social injustice and poverty characterize much of the world. Pictured here are young beggar children in Karachi, Pakistan.

LEARNING OBJECTIVES

After reading this chapter...

13-1 Describe globalization, social justice, and human rights and their significance for international social work practice.

13-2 Describe social issues of poverty, economic justice, global conflict, immigration, and forced migration of people in need.

13-3 Respond to critical thinking questions.

13-4 Describe ethical issues in international social work practice.

13-5 Discuss the theoretical foundations of community development and social development

13-6 Summarize a feminist perspective on global development.

13-7 Define and explain international social work.

13-8 Identify and describe two international social work and social welfare organizations.

13-9 Define *international nongovernmental organizations* and provide examples.

13-10 Discuss social work values and cross-cultural values in global perspective.

13-11 Identify some of the cultural differences existing in organizational contexts.

- *Venezuela seeks United Nations help with medicine shortages[1]*
- *Protestors seek to stop Great Britain from leaving European Union[2]*
- *Yemen suffers 50,000 casualties and disastrous food crisis[3]*
- *European Union leaders celebrate 60th anniversary and pledge unity[4]*
- *Help victims of famine in Africa and Yemen[5]*
- *Muslim group raises 25 thousand dollars in 2 days to help London victims[6]*
- *Russian and the west: 100 years of suspicion[7]*
- *Immigrants in United States prepare for deportation[8]*
- *US and UK ban laptops on flights from Turkey, Middle East, and North Africa[9]*
- *Girl Guides from Canada will no longer come to the U.S.[10]*
- *China lifts ban on Brazilian Meat[11]*
- *Eighteen-year-old Singapore blogger gets asylum in United States[12]*

Each of the above is a headline found either online or in a financial newspaper. What do you think they all have in common? Each, in its own way, refers to the integral way our world is interconnected. Neither we nor citizens in any other country are isolated entities able to do whatever we please. The point is that we live in a global environment that is interconnected in a complex web of social, economic, and political policies.

Brueggemann (2014) paints a disturbing picture of this world:

If we could shrink the earth's population to a village of precisely 100 people, with all the existing human ratios remaining the same there would be:

57 Asians
21 Europeans
14 from the Western Hemisphere, both north and south
8 Africans
52 would be female
48 would be male

---

[1] This is a headline in the May 19, 2009, *Financial Times*, p. 7.

[2] This is the headline of an article by L. Woodchill, dated June 20, 2012, retrieved from http://www.forbes.com/sites/louiswoodhill/2012/06/20/the-greek-election-is-a-warning-for-president-obama/.

[3] This is the headline of an article by D. Esposito, dated April 18, 2012, retrieved from http://www.pennystockdetectives.com/penny-stocks/chinas-record-oil-imports-to-drive-oil-prices.

[4] This is the headline of an article by R. Wolf, dated October 28, 2011, retrieved from http://www.usatoday.com/money/world/story/2011-10-27/eurozone-crisis-deal/50963370/1.

[5] This is a headline in the May 19, 2009, *Financial Times*, p. 2.

[6] This is a headline in the May 19, 2009, *Financial Times*, p. 6.

[7] This is a headline in the May 19, 2009, *Financial Times*, p. 11.

[8] This is the headline of an article by A. Haigh, dated June 22, 2012, retrieved from http://www.bloomberg.com/news/2012-06-23/most-asian-stocks-rise-as-greece-election-tempers-growth-concern.html.

[9] This is the headline of an article by J. Johnson-Freese, dated June 20, 2012, retrieved from http:// www.cnn.com/2012/06/20/opinion/freese-china-space/index.html?hpt.

[10] This is a headline in the May 22, 2009, *Financial Times*, p. 7.

[11] This is the headline of an article by D. Moyo, dated June 27, 2012, retrieved from http://www.nytimes.com/2012/06/28/opinion/beijing-a-boon-for-africa.html?_r=1.

[12] Planned change, as described in Chapter 1, involves engagement, assessment, planning, implementation, evaluation, termination, and follow-up.

70 would be non-White
30 would be White
70 would be non-Christian
30 would be Christian
89 would be heterosexual
11 would [have a same-gender sexual orientation]
6 (all from the United States) would possess 59% of the world's wealth
80 would live in substandard housing
50 would suffer from malnutrition
1 would have a college education
1 would own a computer
70 would be unable to read or write

If you have food in the refrigerator, clothes on your back, a roof overhead, and a place to sleep, you are richer than 75% of the world's people. If you have money in the bank, in your wallet, and spare change in a dish someplace, you are among the top 8% of the world's wealthy. If you woke up this morning with more health than illness, you are more blessed than the million who will not survive this week. If your parents are still alive and still married, you are very rare, even in the United States and Canada. If you have never experienced the danger of battle, the loneliness of imprisonment, the agony of torture, or the pangs of starvation, you are more fortunate than 500 million people in our global society. (p. 469)

This chapter intends to expand your perspective from a local, state, and national one to a perspective that is **international** (involving designated nations) and **global** (involving the whole world). The international macro environment affects every citizen on earth. We will address some of the global issues we all face, explore the concept of social justice, and discuss international social work.

We Live in a Global Macro Environment   LO 13-1

**EP 3a;
5c; 8b**

We have emphasized the importance of social workers understanding their macro environment to practice effectively. We've discussed how social workers practice within organizational environments. Organizations exist in the context of neighborhoods and communities. Communities subsist in a state government environment, subject to state rules, regulations, and laws. Individual states, the District of Columbia, and Puerto Rico, in turn, exist within the national environment of the United States and must function under federal directives. The macro environment doesn't stop there, which is no news flash. The United States is part of a complex global network that is intricately involved with other countries economically, politically, and socially (Finn & Jacobson, 2003). **Globalization** is the "growing economic, political, and social interconnectedness among societies throughout the world" (Mooney et al., 2017).

In other words, it means that what happens in one part of the world directly influences what happens in other parts (Brueggemann, 2014, p. 437).

A friend of mine investing for retirement recently mentioned that in the past he had been very hesitant to invest in international stocks because he felt safer sticking to investments at the national level. He said a stockbroker friend of his told him, "Good luck. Almost everything's involved internationally now. Finding good investments strictly at the national level is almost impossible." Although that might be a bit of an exaggeration, the point is that we live in a global environment with a global economy. Daily, we face fluctuating gasoline prices, the threat of terrorism, and the possibility of global warming (which most claim is due to human activity and carbon dioxide emissions). Isolation is no longer a viable option for your country or for you.

In a global economy, what social and economic forces impact one nation may well result in repercussions in many other nations and social work has a role to play. Hokenstad and Healy (2014) explain:

> Social work can rightfully be considered a human rights profession because one major function of social work nationally and internationally is the promotion and protection of human rights for all and specifically for the most socially and economically vulnerable members of the society.

Of course, social work is just one of many professions and groups that deal with the impact of our mutual interdependence with the rest of the world. While some would argue that the United States should "Put America First," this is a distinctly shortsighted vision. Only the United States and other nations and international organizations have the capacity to address the conflicts and challenges that exist in our world. On a more limited scale, most social workers encounter clients or situations in which the cause of difficulties lies outside the place we call home. Refugees, displaced workers, immigrants escaping poverty and hardship, survivors of abuse, and those seeking a better life comprise a portion of our professional clientele.

Likewise, it is often the policies and practices of governments, corporations, and other organizations that contribute to immigration either by forcing people out of their country of origin or encouraging them to leave their homeland for a better life elsewhere. For example, by selling US corn to Mexico for less than what it costs Mexican corn farmers to produce it, we put 2 million small-scale Mexican farmers out of work and increased illegal migration to the United States (Weisbrot, Lefebvre, & Sammut, 2014). This is an example of what is known as an **iatrogenic effect** because the goal of the North American Free Trade Agreement (NAFTA) was never to put Mexican farmers out of work. It was an unintended consequence of lowering barriers and tariffs to increase trade between the United States, Canada, and Mexico.

Social workers must maintain an international perspective to be effective in their helping roles. National borders no longer serve their original purpose in a global world. The problems that beset people in Syria, Mexico, and the Congo affect all of us in both large and small ways. A decision by a repressive government to eliminate opposing points of view increases the tendency for its citizens to seek freedom elsewhere. The policy of a corporation to move its manufacturing facilities to China results in lost jobs, potential poverty, and mental health challenges here. Lack of work for the young in one country pushes them to seek employment in an adjacent nation. Gangs forced out of one country will seek new locations to ply their trade, forcing the new country to spend resources trying to eradicate problems caused by their unwelcome guests.

**EP 1a;
3b; 5b;
8d**

We have established that social work's mission "is to enhance human well-being and help meet the basic human needs of all people, with particular attention to the needs and empowerment of people who are vulnerable, oppressed, and living in poverty" (NASW, 2008). We have also noted that the National Association of Social Workers (NASW) *Code of Ethics* states that "social workers should advocate for resource allocation procedures that are open and fair. When clients' needs can be met, an allocation procedure should be developed that is non-discriminatory and based on appropriate and consistently applied principles" (NASW, 2008, 3.07b). We have indicated that the *Code* instructs:

> Social workers should promote the general welfare of society, from local to global levels, and the development of people, their communities, and their environments. Social workers should advocate for living conditions conducive to the fulfillment of basic human needs and should promote social, economic, political, and cultural values and institutions that are compatible with the realization of social justice. (NASW, 2008, 6.01)

Three key concepts inherent in these quotes are the terms *global*, *advocate*, and *social justice*. A *global* focus concerns looking beyond your immediate local, state, and even national environment. A basic social work value is the importance of focusing on human rights issues around the world, not just those affecting you in your own backyard. We have defined *advocacy* as the act of speaking up, pushing for change, or pleading the causes of clients and those in need (Hoefer, 2006). Finally, *social justice* is the philosophical perspective that all people have the right to enjoy equal opportunities in economic, political, and social realms. Thus, it is social workers' responsibility to attend to and advocate for social justice on a global basis.

Social justice is one of the six core values identified in the NASW *Code of Ethics* (NASW, 2008). The *Code* explains:

> Social workers pursue social change, particularly with and on behalf of vulnerable and oppressed individuals and groups of people. Social workers' social change efforts are focused primarily on issues of poverty, unemployment, discrimination, and other forms of social injustice. These activities seek to promote sensitivity to and knowledge about oppression and cultural and ethnic diversity. Social workers strive to ensure access to needed information, services, and resources; equality of opportunity; and meaningful participation in decision making for all people. (NASW, 2008, Ethical Principles)

Highlight 13-1 explores another concept critical whenever addressing social justice—global human rights. Subsequent sections will discuss issues concerning global human rights and organizations that strive to attain them.

Global Issues Affect Us All

Developing a global focus means becoming aware of the issues facing the human population in the twenty-first century. From a social work perspective, global problems are everyone's problems. We have established that it is the ethical obligation of social workers to do what they can to help solve them. Out of the multitude of

Highlight 13-1

Global Human Rights

In response to the atrocities of World War II, the General Assembly of the United Nations adopted a Universal Declaration of Human Rights (UDHR) in December 1948 (United Nations [UN], 1948). **Human rights** involve the premise that all people—regardless of race, culture, or national origin—are entitled to basic rights and treatment. Mapp (2014) elaborates:

Within the UNDR, there are three areas of rights:

[1] political and civil rights, [2] social, economic, and cultural rights, and [3] collective rights. Political and civil rights are often referred to as "negative freedoms" as they require a government to refrain from an overuse of its power against individuals. Included in this are rights such as freedom of speech and the right to a fair trial. The second grouping of rights—social, economic, and cultural rights—is referred to as "positive freedoms" as they require a government to act for them to be realized for individuals. They include such rights as medical care, the right to an education, and the right to a fair wage. The last group, collective rights, includes rights for groups of people and includes the rights to religion, peace, and development. (p. 17)

---

social problems that should be addressed, we will arbitrarily choose three to identify here. These are poverty and economic inequality, global conflict, and forced migration of people in need.

Poverty and Economic Inequality · LO 13-2

EP 2; 2a

Poverty is the condition where people lack the money or material goods available to other members of a society. Poverty concerns lack of access to adequate resources. There are a few terms related to poverty. "**Income** refers to the amount of money a person makes in each year. **Wealth** is the total value of that person's assets: real estate and personal property, stocks, bonds, cash, and so forth" (Coleman & Kerbo, 2009, p. 167).

The Complexity of Defining Poverty Poverty is not a perfectly clear-cut concept. **Absolute poverty** "refers to the lack of resources necessary for well-being—most important, food and water, but also housing, sanitation, education, and health care" (Mooney, Knox, & Schacht, 2017, p. 179). **Relative poverty**, on the other hand, "refers to the lack of material and economic resources compared with some other population" (Mooney et al., 2017, p. 179). Leon-Guerrero (2011) reflects:

Our mainstream standard of living defines the "average" American lifestyle. Individuals in this category may be able to afford basic necessities, but they cannot maintain a standard of living comparable to other members of society. Relative poverty emphasizes the inequality of income and the growing gap between the richest and poorest Americans. (p. 40)

In the United States, the Social Security Administration (SSA) established an **official poverty line**, or **poverty threshold**, that was based on data saying families spend about one-third of their income on food. It then multiplied food costs by a factor of three. The official poverty line is an indication of the amount of money required for a family to barely subsist (Mooney et al., 2017). The poverty line has some shortcomings; it does not consider where people live, is based on pretax income, not net income, and ignores family wealth.

In addition, the official poverty threshold has been criticized as underestimating the extent of poverty in the United States. The formula was initiated in 1964, at which time people did spend about one-third of their income on food (Mooney et al., 2017). Although the index is adjusted each year, the amount of money necessary for adequate food is still multiplied by three based on the 1964 formula. Costs of food, however, have not risen nearly as fast as the costs of other necessary costs of living such as housing, fuel, transportation, child care, and health care. It is estimated that families now spend much less than one-third of their income on food, while other costs have risen dramatically (Mooney et al., 2017; Segal, 2013). Establishing the poverty line at three times what a family needs to spend on food simply won't cut it.

The implication is that the poverty line should be adjusted to reflect the much higher costs of living. This would result in a significantly higher official poverty line and significantly more people officially living "in poverty." However, it is highly unlikely that any US president would approve of changing a measure that would appear to produce more poverty under her or his administration. Using the current method, the US Census Bureau indicates that 13.5 percent of the US population lives below the poverty level (US Census Bureau, 2016c).

The Widening Gap in the United States   Another facet of economic inequality in the United States involves the widening gap between the very rich and very poor (Macionis, 2010; Mooney et al., 2017). According to the Pew Research Organization (Fry & Kochhar, 2014), several facts stand out about income inequality:

- "In 2013, the median wealth of the nation's upper-income families ($639,400) was nearly seven times the median income of middle-income families ($96,500)." This was the highest level ever recorded.
- "America's upper-income families have a median net worth that is nearly 70 times that of the country's lower-income families, also the widest wealth gap between these families in 30 years."
- "The data have shown a growing gap in wealth along racial and ethnic lines since the recession ended."
- Middle-income families did not regain their wealth after the recession ended; however, the upper-income families did.
- Middle class household wealth has stagnated over the past 30 years.
- The wealth levels of both "middle- and lower-income families are comparable to where they were in the early 1990s."
- In that same period of no-growth in wealth for lower- and middle-income families, upper-income families' wealth doubled from $318,100 to $639,400.

Other means of comparison are provided by Mooney et al. (2017):

- A person needs just $3,650 (in US dollars) of wealth to be among the wealthiest half of the world's population; $77,000 to be in the top 10 percent; and $798,000 to be among the richest 1 percent worldwide.
- In 2014, the richest 1 percent of adults (ages 20 and older) in the world owned nearly half (48 percent) of global wealth; the richest 10 percent owned 87 percent of global wealth.
- In 2014, the richest 80 people in the world owned as much wealth as the 3.5 billion people at the bottom half of the world's population.

EP 8a

Where do you stand personally in terms of your overall wealth? What factors in your own background have contributed to your current financial status and your potential future financial status?

A vast discrepancy in income is mirrored by compensation received by CEOs and ordinary workers (Mooney et al., 2017). In 2014, CEOs of the top 350 US corporations received an average compensation 303 times the average pay of US workers. In 1965, the ratio was 20 times. Other demographic variables affect a US citizen's potential to be in poverty. For example, females and people of color are significantly more likely to be poor (Lean-Guerrero, 2011; Mooney et al., 2017; US Census Bureau, 2016c). Poverty levels also vary by state. For example, in 2015, 8.4 percent of the population fell below the poverty line in New Hampshire, whereas 18 percent or more did so in Arkansas, Kentucky, New Mexico, and the District of Columbia; over 22 percent of the population fell below the poverty level in Mississippi (US Census Bureau, 2015c).

Focus on Ethics 13-1 raises questions regarding how ethical it is for a government to allow such enormous discrepancies in resources.

Global Poverty   Poverty is defined differently depending on where in the world you are and the measurement criteria used. Mooney and colleagues (2017) describe one measurement approach:

> One billion people—14.5 percent of the world's population—are extremely poor, living on less than $1.25 a day [a threshold set by the World Bank for measuring poverty] (World Bank, 2015). Most of the world's poor—80 percent—live in sub-Saharan Africa or South Asia. [The formal name for the **World Bank** is the International Bank for Reconstruction and Development. Headquartered in Washington, D.C., it has branches around the world that make loans and provide economic consultation to countries that have low per capita incomes and lack resources.]

Another poverty measure is the **Multidimensional Poverty Index** (MPI), developed by the United Nations Development Programme (UNDP) and the Oxford Poverty and Human Development Initiative (UNDP, 2011). The MPI measures

Focus on Ethics **13-1**

Should the Government Allow Such Vast Discrepancies in Wealth?   LO 13-4

EP 1

What do you think are the reasons for the widening gap in wealth in the United States? Is it fair and ethical for the government to allow these discrepancies? Can or should something be done about them (e.g., via taxes, regulation, or increased service provision)? Explain.

multidimensional aspects of poverty, and how they intermingle and overlap. Its indicators measure: (1) living standards (assets, floor, electricity, water, toilet, and cooking fuel); (2) education (children enrolled and years of schooling); and (3) health (child mortality and nutrition). People are considered impoverished if they suffer deprivation in one-third of the indicators. Approximately 1.5 billion people in 109 nations assessed by the MPI, or one-third of these countries' populations, suffered multidimensional poverty.

Still another measure of poverty involves the percentage of people who take in less than the number of daily calories considered necessary to preserve good health; worldwide, more than 10 percent of the Earth's population are considered undernourished by this measure (Mooney et al., 2017). Price **inflation**—an increase in the cost of items and corresponding fall in the purchasing value of money—can further erode the ability to purchase food and other necessities.

Cox and Pawar (2013) summarize:

> Poverty, with its associated problems such as infant mortality, malnutrition, and vulnerability, is commonly regarded as the world's most serious problem. Depending on how poverty is defined and measured, no one would dispute the claim that, at the very least, approximately one in every three of the world's people lives in poverty. This is partly because many people around the globe exist so close to the poverty line that any one of several common occurrences, even at a minor level, will push them into poverty. Such occurrences include economic changes, such as increases in inflation rates, deteriorating trade arrangements, or reductions in a government's subsidies of basic necessities; ecological changes, such as deterioration of the environment or depletion of essential food sources; social conflict within a nation or war between nations; demographic changes through migration or natural increase; and natural disasters that destroy people's homes and livelihoods. (p. 69)

Problems Related to Poverty   Numerous other problems, of course, are related to poverty. If people don't have the resources, they may not be able to get many of the things they need to survive and thrive. These related problems include hunger, homelessness, unsafe water supplies, and lack of health care, among many others, all of which are beyond the scope of this text. They all are serious issues that social workers around the world must address. Focus on Ethics 13-2 speaks to this issue. Highlight 13-2 stresses the significance of global conflict.

Focus on Ethics **13-2**

The Crisis of Global Poverty

What are the reasons for such extreme global poverty? Is it ethical for richer, industrialized nations to allow such conditions to continue?

To what extent is it these wealthier nations' ethical responsibility to address global poverty? What, if anything, can or should be done to help?

EP 1

Highlight **13-2**

Global Conflict

Cox and Pawar (2013) summarize the state of conflict in this and the past century:

A reading of any global history reveals the extremely common inability of social groupings, nations, and empires to live at peace with their neighbors. In pursuit of territory, booty of all kinds, slaves, power, and status, conflict at all levels has been a significant aspect of the human story. The last century witnessed two of the worst wars known to history, and since the end of the Cold War in 1989 the scourge of civil war has intensified alarmingly. In recent times, the world has been experiencing upwards of 30 civil wars at any one time, with very high casualty figures, especially among civilians.

A major goal of the UN [United Nations] is world peace, yet its work and that of national governments and regional associations, along with that of many organizations of civil society, have together failed to do more than perhaps contain many situations. Only when we add together the widespread consequences of conflict on people's personal lives and social contexts, economic conditions, physical infrastructure, and the environment, do we begin to appreciate the enormity of this global problem. Yet because conflict once again has many causes, it seems difficult for the international community to significantly reduce the impact of conflict in the foreseeable future. Finally, it has become clear in recent times that rebuilding a society after conflict is a complex, hugely expensive, and extremely difficult undertaking. (p. 71)

Critical Thinking Questions **13-2**

EP 8a

To what extent do you or did you support the US presence in places like Afghanistan and Iraq? What are your reasons? How would you articulate the US rationale for being there? What are the global consequences for and resulting perceptions about the United States? What are the consequences for the citizens of such war-torn countries?

Immigration Status: Forced Migration of People in Need

EP 1c; 2; 2a

It is estimated that about 50 million people worldwide are displaced from their community of origin, although they would prefer to have remained at home (Cox & Pawar, 2013). Cox and Pawar (2013) explain why:

One inevitable consequence of extreme poverty, widespread social conflict, serious natural disasters, ecological degradation, and low levels of development is that many people are forced to leave their usual place of abode and seek refuge, assistance, or a better future elsewhere. (p. 73)

Immigration involves the permanent movement from one country to another. **Immigration status** is a person's position in terms of legal rights and residency when entering and residing in a country that is not that person's legal country of origin. Social workers are often called upon to work with immigrants, so it's important to understand the terms and issues involved. Potocky-Tripodi (2002) defines many of the important concepts when discussing these populations:

The fundamental distinction between immigrants and refugees is that **immigrants** leave their countries voluntarily (usually in search of better economic opportunities) whereas **refugees** are forced out of their countries because of human rights violations against them.... Refugees are also sometimes referred to, or refer to themselves, as **exiles** or **émigrés**....

Legally, anyone who is not a citizen of the United States is termed an **alien**. Aliens are further classified as immigrants and nonimmigrants, and as documented or undocumented. In this classification, an *immigrant* is a person who has been legally admitted into the United States and granted the privilege to be a permanent resident (a "green card" holder). A **nonimmigrant** is a foreign-born person who is in the United States temporarily, such as a tourist, a student, or a journalist. Nonimmigrants also include temporary or seasonal workers, who come to the United States to work during certain periods of the year and return to their countries during the rest of the year. This typically refers to agricultural laborers.

A **documented alien** is one who has been granted a legal right to be in the United States. This legal right is determined by admissions policy. The admissions policy details many categories of people who are eligible to be legally admitted. It also specifies how many people from each country may be legally admitted into the U.S. each year....

An **undocumented alien** is one who does not have a legal right to be in the United States. These people are also sometimes referred to as **illegal immigrants**. They are also referred to as **deportable aliens**, because if discovered by immigration authorities, they are subject to deportation, or forcible return to their countries of origin. There are two ways in which people become undocumented aliens. One is by entering the U.S. illegally. This means that the person has not received authorization to enter the United States. For example, people who cross the border from Mexico without going through the immigration authorities are undocumented aliens. The second way that people become undocumented aliens is by entering the U.S. legally, but then violating the terms of the visa (the authorization to stay in the U.S.). For example, a tourist may be granted a visa to stay in the United States for a limited period of time.... [Anyone staying longer than the specified time period then] becomes an undocumented alien. (pp. 4–5)

Potocky-Tripodi (2002) continues:

A foreign-born person's legal status can, and usually does, change over time. This is referred to as *adjustment of status*. After one year of residence, a refugee is eligible to become a permanent resident. Permanent residents (including those who were formerly refugees and immigrants) may be eligible to become U. S. citizens after five years of residence.... [Upon attaining] citizenship, they are referred to as **naturalized citizens**. Undocumented aliens may sometimes become eligible to become legal permanent residents. For example, a law passed in 1986 allowed a large number of undocumented aliens to change to legal status. (pp. 8–9)

Many people from other countries may receive or need social services. The data on immigration highlight the situation as of 2017. About 13 percent of people in the United States are foreign born (42 million). Of this population, 18 million are naturalized citizens and another 13 million are documented noncitizens. That leaves a guesstimate of the number of unauthorized immigrants at around 11 million people. This number goes up and down over time as economic conditions in the United States change. During the recession that began in 2008, large numbers of undocumented immigrants left the country because of the loss of jobs here (Heartland Alliance, 2017).

In 2014, immigration from Mexico was about 240,000, while 428,000 new immigrants came from India and China (Henderson, 2016). Altogether, more than one-quarter of all immigrants to the United States are from Mexico, 6 percent are from India, with China and the Philippines each at 5 percent. At about 3 percent are El Salvador, Vietnam, and Cuba, with the Dominican Republic, Korea, and Guatemala following at 2 percent. These 10 countries make up about 58 percent of US immigration in 2015 (Migration Policy Institute, 2017). Contrary to much political rhetoric, about 8.1 million of the 11 million undocumented immigrants who work do pay taxes; more than $11.8 billion in state and local taxes in 2012, despite living here illegally (Institute on Taxation and Economic Policy, 2017).

EP 9d

People with different national origins often find it difficult to integrate themselves into the mainstream culture. This is intensified when the use of different languages is a factor because locating jobs, finding housing, and fitting into a neighborhood or community all require a degree of fluency in the local language. Not being able to fit in can lead to feelings of isolation, stress, and difficulty meeting

At a Glance **13-1**

Immigration Status and Related Terms

Immigration: The permanent movement from one country to another (documented immigrants in the United States hold a "green card").

Immigration status: A person's position in terms of legal rights and residency when entering and residing in a country that is not that person's legal country of origin.

Nonimmigrant: "A foreign-born person who is in the United States temporarily, such as a tourist, a student or a journalist."

Alien: "Legally, anyone who is not a citizen of the United States."

Documented alien: "One who has been granted a legal right to be in the United States."

Illegal immigrant (undocumented alien): "One who does not have a legal right to be in the United States."

Deportable alien: One who is not a US citizen and is subject to deportation upon discovery.

Refugees (exiles or émigrés): People who have been "forced out of their countries because of human rights violations against them."

Adjustment of status: "A foreign-born person's legal status" that can "change over time."

Naturalized citizens: "Permanent residents (including those who were formerly refugees or immigrants)" who become US citizens after five years of residence (upon attaining citizenship). (Potocky-Tripodi, 2002, pp. 4–5, 8–9)

EP 8a

Critical Thinking Question **13-3**

What do you think the US policy should be toward people migrating illegally across the southern border?

the expectations of the new culture. They may have difficulties understanding new behavioral expectations imposed on them, interacting effectively with others in the new culture, and achieving the goals they had sought. These concerns and challenges are the same ones faced by social workers when working in cultures with which they are not familiar. Learning about other cultures, practices, customs, and norms requires that the social worker listen and consider others as the true experts with respect to their own cultures.

Community Development LO 13-5

EP 6

What should be done in response to the turbulence and many issues faced by the global community? How can resources be distributed more equitably and enhanced social justice attained? **Community development** provides one positive avenue to help communities and nations in need. Rivera and Erlich (2001) state:

> Community Development refers to efforts to mobilize people who are directly affected by a community condition (that is, the "victims," the unaffiliated, the unorganized, and the nonparticipating) into groups and organizations to enable them to take action on the social problems and issues that concern them. A typical feature of these efforts is the concern with building new organizations among people who have not been previously organized to take social action on a problem (emphasis amended) (Erlich & Rivera, 1981; Fisher, 1984). (p. 256)

Community development involves helping a designated community of people who share cultural values and experience similar social and economic conditions; goals are to improve living conditions and enhance residents' quality of life in the social environment by using a planned change process (Healy, 2008).[12] Development entails growth, progress, and empowerment of community members through their active involvement. We have defined a *community* as "a number of people who have something in common that connects them in some way and that distinguishes them from others" (Homan, 2016, p. 10). A key feature of a community is the fact that participants share some mutual characteristic. Common features might include shared physical location, identification, interests, culture, or other activities. The following section describes the theoretical functions of community that provide a context for community development. Such theory guides social workers by helping to organize the issues that affect their work as change agents.

Theoretical Functions of Communities

An important theoretical perspective on communities that serves as a foundation for community development involves the functionalist perspective introduced earlier in Chapter 9. Warren (1983), one of the leading early theorists on communities, cited five basic functions that communities should serve:

1. "**Production-distribution-consumption** relates to local participation in the process of producing, distributing, and consuming those goods and services that are a part of daily living and access to which is desirable in the immediate locality" (pp. 28–29). People need access to goods such as food, clothing,

and housing, in addition to services such as police and fire protection. In various communities around the world, this function is seriously obstructed.

2. "**Socialization** involves a process by which society or one of its constituent social units transmits prevailing knowledge, social values, and behavior patterns to its members" (p. 29). People in communities, which may be local or national, are socialized regarding expectations for behavior and "appropriate" values. One primary method of socialization is education, which is sorely lacking in many areas of the world.

3. "**Social control** involves the process through which a group influences the behavior of its members toward conformity with its norms" (p. 29). The first thing that comes to mind might be the government with its branches of police and courts. However, "many other social units, including the family, the school, the church, and the social agency, also play a part" (p. 29).

4. "**Social participation**" concerns the involvement of citizens in social, political, and economic processes. Various social entities provide avenues for social participation, including churches and religious organizations, "businesses, government offices, . . . voluntary and public health and welfare agencies, . . . family and kinship groups, friendship groups, and other less formal groupings" (p. 29). From a global perspective, various local and national communities limit social participation based on gender, or ethnic or religious status. Social participation is often a primary goal in achieving social justice.

5. **Mutual support** involves encouragement, assistance, caring, and cooperation among people in communities (p. 29). "Traditionally, such mutual support, whether in the form of care in time of sickness, exchange of labor, or helping a local family in economic distress, has been performed locally very largely under such primary-group auspices as family and relatives, neighborhood groups, friendship groups, and local religious groups" (p. 29). Today, many mutual support functions, at least in wealthier industrialized nations, have been assumed by public welfare departments, private health and welfare agencies, governmental and commercial insurance companies, and other formalized organizational structures (p. 29).

Community Development Practice

EP 7; 8;
5c; 5, 6;
9d

At least six basic principles characterize practice when undertaking community development. First, community development calls for *community members' active participation* (Healy, 2008; Homan, 2016; Mathie & Cunningham, 2008). Social workers can use their leadership, organizing, problem-solving, planning, and communication skills to encourage community members to work together and

Critical Thinking Questions **13-4**

EP 8a

How does the community in which you live fulfill the five functions mentioned here? If something is lacking, how might community functioning be improved?

achieve community goals. Community members must be integrally involved in each phase of the planned change process from initial assessment through planning and implementation to final evaluation of results. The idea is to enhance community functioning through participation of as broad a range of community members as possible, evaluate the outcomes, and use the information to improve practice effectiveness.

A second principle concerns *establishing common goals*. Tropman (2008) explains:

**EP 5b;
8b; 8c**

> Emphasis is placed on goal selection, prioritization, and goal application. . .. In some instances goal selection will already have occurred. Frequently, the very process of discussion of goal alternatives results, in an almost automatic way, in the clear selection or desirability of one particular goal over others.
>
> On the other hand, there may well be competing interests and competing perspectives with regard to which goal should be selected. The worker needs to continue a process of interaction and encouragement with community members around the process of selecting a goal and prioritizing the efforts needed to get to that goal. (p. 130)

Help in determining goals often involves the worker attending community meetings, working closely with community leaders, raising questions to community groups, suggesting alternatives, providing ongoing encouragement for consensus, and assisting in initial implementation of goals (Tropman, 2008).

A third practice principle involved in community development entails *reaching out to various diverse groups, constituencies, and organizations* within the community (Homan, 2016). It's important to mobilize as many community factions as possible to work together toward community goals. Numbers and solidarity can enhance the power necessary to get and use resources for the community's benefit.

Highlight 13-3

Sustainability on a Global Community Level

EP 8c

Community development can affect communities of any size, ranging from small local communities to nations at the global level. The well-being of the global community has become a pressing concern. Mary (2008) reflects:

The world is changing. Our human activities are clearly becoming global in nature. Our understanding of nature—the infrastructure upon which all humankind rests—is changing as well.... We have reached a point in our understanding of systems at which social welfare must be considered part of a larger global imperative of planetary survival. There is a profound connection between the micro problems that individuals and families manifest (e.g., environmental

pollution, the lack of sustaining and meaningful work, addiction, domestic violence) and the macro problems that local and global communities experience [e.g., rampant poverty, lack of educational infrastructure, widespread unemployment, inadequate food production, political unrest]. (p. 1)

A concept related to global and international development is the concept of sustainability. In the global context, **sustainability** involves "development that meets the current needs of the present generations without jeopardizing the ability of future generations to meet their needs" (Mary, 2008, p. 32). This concept encompasses much more than just economic or community development. In view of concerns about overpopulation and overcrowding, insufficient

continued

Highlight **13-3** *continued*

food and fresh water, global warming, and a host of other issues, sustainability involves the need for citizens of the earth to work together to save themselves and their world (Healy, 2008; Mary, 2008).

An internationally supported document entitled the **Earth Charter** has been developed to define and stress the importance of sustainability on a global basis (Earth Charter Initiative, 2011). After many years of planning, cooperation, and compromise, socially concerned organizations around the world met to create a document with the following intent:

> We must join together to bring forth a sustainable global society founded on respect for nature, universal human rights, economic justice, and a culture of peace. Towards this end, it is imperative that we, the peoples of Earth, declare our responsibility to one another, to the greater community of life, and to future generations. (Earth Charter Initiative, 2011)

The Charter emphasizes four categories of principles necessary to promote "a sustainable way of life by which the conduct of all individuals, organizations, businesses, governments, and transnational institutions is to be guided and assessed"; these include "respect and care for the community of life [with all its diversity]," "ecological integrity," "social and economic justice," and "democracy, nonviolence and peace" (Earth Charter Initiative, 2011). Many of these goals are consistent with social work's quest for social, economic, and environmental justice.

The Charter calls for "a new sense of global interdependence and universal responsibility" where all the citizens of earth "imaginatively develop and apply the vision of a sustainable way of life locally, nationally, regionally,

and globally" (Earth Charter Initiative, 2011). It has been endorsed by thousands of organizations around the globe and has significantly influenced the United Nations Educational, Scientific, and Cultural Organization (UNESCO) (Healy, 2008). It is "now increasingly recognized as a global consensus statement on the meaning of sustainability, the challenge and vision of sustainable development, and the principles by which sustainable development is to be achieved" (Earth Charter Initiative, 2011).

To achieve sustainability, Mary (2008) calls for major shifts in our economic system. For example, she suggests that some military spending could be shifted to the following earth-preserving goals:

Basic Social Goals

- Universal primary education
- Adult literacy
- School lunch programs for the world's 44 poorest countries
- Assistance to preschool children and pregnant women in the world's 44 poorest countries
- Universal basic health care
- Reproductive health and family planning
- Closing the condom gap

Earth Restoration Goals

- Reforesting the Earth
- Protecting topsoil on cropland
- Restoring rangelands
- Stabilizing water tables
- Restoring fisheries
- Protecting biological diversity (pp. 188–189)

A fourth dimension of community development concerns an emphasis on *using community assets* (Hardcastle, Powers, & Wenocur, 2011; Homan, 2016; Mathie & Cunningham, 2008). Strengths provide the foundation for development. "People in communities can organize to drive the development process themselves by identifying and mobilizing existing (but often unrecognized) assets, thereby responding to and creating local economic opportunity" (Mathie & Cunningham, 2008, p. 283).

A fifth community development practice principle involves the *empowerment of community members to help themselves* and become self-reliant (Homan, 2016). The community development process should enhance the self-confidence and competence of community members so that they can maintain the progress they made. The intent is for them to continue to grow and develop, initiating and supporting their own goals without being dependent on external professional leadership. Emphasizing the integral involvement of oppressed and powerless groups in the community is also essential as part of the empowerment process to provide them with access to resources and services.

A sixth principle involved in community development is related to empowering community members to become self-reliant in maintaining the progress they've made. This idea involves the concept of sustainability. In the context of community development, *sustainability* is the condition of having a project, program, or some aspect of community development be sustainable, that is, have access to continued support after it is first initiated. Oftentimes, a project is started with a grant or designated limited funding. When the grant or funding runs out, the project may simply end. Thus, it's important that those undertaking community development think about the future and how whatever progress is made can be maintained over time. Highlight 13-3 explores sustainability on the global community level.

Note that community development must progress within the value structure of the community's people. Values and priorities vary dramatically from one culture or location to another. A subsequent section addresses the issue of cross-cultural value differences.

Examples of Community Development

EP 7d; 8

Midgley and Livermore (2004) provide examples of community development in Africa:

> In many African countries, social workers have mobilized local people to engage in small-scale agricultural activities, construct rural bridges and feeder roads, establish cooperative enterprises [a program owned and run by people receiving its services], and accumulate community assets. These projects have a direct and positive impact on economic development. Community built and owned feeder roads provide easier access to the markets in larger towns and ensure that farmers get their produce to these markets in a timely way. Community development has also been used to assist women to engage more effectively in agricultural activities and microenterprises [such as small businesses] and to become economically independent.
>
> Community development has ... been used to promote social welfare projects that ... contribute to economic development. Throughout Africa, local people have collaborated with both governmental and nongovernmental agencies to build community centers, schools and clinics, sanitary and other public health facilities, and to provide safe drinking water. The use of community development to provide safe drinking water in many rural areas in Africa has been particularly impressive, [and a clear goal of environmental justice]. Many communities that relied on rivers, streams, and marshes were exposed to the hazard of being infected with waterborne diseases. Community participation has been vital in providing access to clean drinking water. Village people have played an important role by providing labor for the construction of wells and channeling clean water to local communities from unpolluted mountain springs. (pp. 124–125)

Sowers and Rowe (2007) provide other examples of community development in Carmelita (Guatemala), Ghana, and Indonesia:

> In Carmelita, the Guatemalan government has established 13 locally managed forest concessions [governmental grants of land for specified use] in the jungle village. The cooperative that works the 130,000-acre concession in the rain forest consists of 56 impoverished families from the jungle village. The concessions are logged in accordance with rules laid down by the Forest Stewardship Council, a nonprofit organization based in Bonn, Germany. Environmental organizations credit the approach with reducing deforestation and protecting watersheds and wetland areas while providing a steady income for local residents (Replogle, n.d.) ....
>
> The Ghana Community School Alliances Project, a community-mobilization initiative funded by USAID, fosters community participation in more than 300 primary schools throughout Ghana to build an environment of mutual respect, responsibility, and action among community members, schools, and education administrators as they work to meet the learning needs of Ghanaian children. [USAID, the United States Agency for International Development, is "the principle US agency to extend assistance to countries recovering from disaster, trying to escape poverty, and engaging in democratic reforms" (USAID, 2009).] In addition, the project trains district-level education managers to use data for decision making at the local level (Educational Development Center, n.d.) ....
>
> In the aftermath of the December 2004 Indian Ocean tsunami that killed more than 200,000 people in Indonesia and neighboring countries, Mercy Corps field managers quickly mobilized local workers to rebuild schools, clean up water systems, and repair commercial fishing boats. [Mercy Corps is a charitable organization founded in 1979 that focuses on relief assistance and "long-term solutions to hunger and poverty" (Mercy Corps, 2009).] Through innovative cash-for-work programs, tsunami survivors earned income to support their families and reclaim their lives (Mercy Corps. n.d.). (p. 220)

Social Development

EP 2; 5b; 5c; 6; 7; 8; 8b; 8c

A term related to community development is social development, initially coined when the British colonial administration began promoting economic development in West Africa in the 1940s. **Social development** is a planned change process on behalf of an entire population that emphasizes economic development based on two principles: first, economic development integrates social and economic policy, and, second, it sponsors investment-oriented social programs "that contribute positively to economic development" (Midgley & Sherraden, 2009, p. 283). At least four concepts are important here.

First, social development is pursued *on behalf of the entire community* and all its residents. It involves comprehensive change that encompasses multiple systems and dimensions within a community.

Second, the definition stresses the *importance of economic development* for communities. Rothman (2008) reflects:

Community economic development ... believes that what distressed communities need most is an upgrade of economic conditions. According to Soifer (2002), this means concentrating on housing development, land development, job creation, and setting up more relevant financial institutions—primarily banks. This is consistent with a U.N. study of intervention results, where experts who were surveyed indicated that project outcomes are better when there is adequate prior planning, including the preparation of supportive organizational and resource [economic] elements. (p. 154)

The third significant concept regarding social development emphasizes the importance of *linkage between social and economic policy*. Midgley and Sherraden (2009) remark:

Integrating economic and social policy is ... key ... This requires the creation of formal arrangements that effectively link economic and social policies and programs. In many countries, governmental organizations concerned with social welfare have few ties to agencies engaged in economic development. The social development perspective seeks ... to ensure that social policy is not [of secondary importance] ... to the economy. Instead, it advocates an integrative approach that regards economic and social policies as two essential elements of a sustainable ... development process. (p. 283)

A fourth major principle characterizing social development is that economic development sponsors *investment-oriented social programs* that are sustainable. Midgley and Sherraden (2009) explain:

Social development proponents believe that economic participation is the primary means by which most people meet their social needs. Unlike the traditional income maintenance and social service approaches [that some view as a "drain on the economy" (Gamble & Hoff, 2005, p. 170)], the social development perspective seeks to shift the emphasis from consumption-based and maintenance-oriented services [for example, Food Stamps and public assistance] to social programs that contribute directly to economic development[,] ... enhance economic participation[,] and contribute to growth . . .

[S]ocial development advocates do not merely urge social welfare clients to become economically productive; they argue that adequate investments should be made to ensure that people have the skills, knowledge, resources, opportunities, incentives, and subsidies to participate effectively in the productive economy. Of course, this principle applies not only to the consumers of welfare services but also to the population as a whole. Social development advocates require that government regulations, subsidies, and supports be provided to all to ensure that economic participation results in adequate living wages, access to universal health care, full educational opportunities, affordable housing, and the other dimensions of a decent and satisfying living standard. (pp. 282–283)

Wetzel (2004) provides an example where economic development in the social development process had a successful impact on social conditions:

EP 7d; 8; 8e

> Probably the world's most successful economic development program is the Grameen Bank of Dhaka, Bangladesh, founded in 1976 by Muhammad Yunus, an economist who was making loans for commercial banks. (Grameen means "rural" or "village" in English.) Yunus was appalled by the living conditions of people in rural Bangladesh, the second poorest nation in the world. He was struck especially by the severe situation of women who are in a particularly precarious position when they are abandoned or divorced. They have no means of livelihood, and their families will not allow them to return to their homes. Consequently, the self-esteem of these women is as impoverished as their economic. . . . [resources]. Banks would not grant them loans without collateral guarantees, so Yunus decided to become a personal benefactor to the region for micro-enterprises for low-income women. His credit union was opened to men as well, but 77 percent of the loans continue to be granted to women. Their payback rate has proven to be even better than their male counterparts. Because people without . . . [economic resources] seldom have access to credit, the Grameen model requires the group members themselves to become the collateral, promising to pay any outstanding debt that is not paid by the grantee [any individual who does not repay the loan]. It has seldom been necessary to do so. (pp. 108–109)

Consequently, the Grameen model has been used successfully in developing and industrialized countries to help impoverished people (Rosenberg, 2000). Success has been attributed to three aspects—an emphasis on enhanced "self-esteem," "group support," and "collaboration in reaching . . . goals" (Wetzel, 2004, p. 109). [In 2006, the bank and its founder shared the Nobel Prize for Peace.]

Highlight 13-4 describes a feminist perspective on global development that can be used both in community and social development.

Highlight 13-4

A Feminist Perspective on Global Development   LO 13-6

EP 2; 5b; 5c; 6; 7; 7d; 8; 8c

Community development can emphasize improving the status of and conditions for women. Ferree (2012) suggests that focusing on gender can serve at least three purposes. First, women can be encouraged to participate in political activities on their own behalf. Second, such a gender-oriented perspective can "empower women to challenge limitations on their roles and lives" (p. 294). Third, a focus on gender can "create networks among women that enhance their ability to recognize existing gender relations as oppressive and in need of change" (pp. 294–295). Such perspectives can boost confidence and, in turn, result in an increased sense of self-worth.

Wetzel (1995) discusses the importance of women's mental health on a global level as a necessity to maintain their optimal well-being. She cites several standards based on feminist principles that should govern the development of programs for women around the world. For each she provides an international example. Although programs may vary, they should address the improvement of women's self-concepts, increasing their ability to act assertively on their own behalves, and enhance supportive relationships.

Standard 1. "Raising consciousness regarding gender roles and the importance and worth of every female" (p. 181). Work that is traditionally "women's work" should be respected and appreciated as work just as traditional

continued

Highlight **13-4** *continued*

"men's work" (work outside of the home) is respected. The rights and emotional well-being of women deserve respect.

Filomena Tomaira Pacsi, a women's social action group in Peru, provides an example. The issue addressed the plight of the wives of rural miners who were traditionally belittled and abused by their spouses. *Filomena* consisted of a group of urban women from Lima who worked with these rural women "to reduce their feeling of isolation (negative alone-ness), enhance their solidarity (positive connectedness), encourage social action, and increase their self-perception and sense of worth by recognizing how important their roles are to their husbands, children, and communities" (p. 182). Wetzel (1995) elaborates:

> The urban women of *Filomena* joined with these ru-ral women to raise their consciousness and change their lives. When the mines were being closed without notice, the rural women encouraged their husbands and families to make sacrifice marches hundreds of miles to the city. With the help of *Filomena*, the women of Lima began to realize how important they were to the mining struggle. The rural women took charge of the marches, feeding their families in community kitchens and providing educa-tion for their children along the way. The women also took responsibility for health care, surveying the needs of children and arranging for mobile health units staffed by paramedics. . . .
>
> The presence of the urban women of *Filomena*, in the words of the rural women of the mines, brought them "tremendous joy, sweeping them off their feet." The solidarity and spirit of the two groups of women spread to the rural women's husbands, who stopped being violent toward their wives and showed them newfound respect. Respect for the rural women's roles was enhanced by bonding among the women and the recognition of their organizational expertise. It was the women who taught their husbands to advocate for better working conditions rather than to settle for their poor circumstances. The women opened their husbands' eyes to the responsibilities of companies and the rights of human beings in their employ. (p. 182)

Standard 2. "*Forming interdisciplinary professional part-nerships with poor women and training indigenous* [those originating in the community] *trainers to serve their own communities*" (p. 182). It's important for professionals from various backgrounds to work together with poor women to train them. These poor women then, in turn, can return to and help their own communities by providing training for the women there.

The Women in Development Consortium of Thailand was a program co-sponsored by three Thai universities in conjunction with York University in Canada. The project, called "Train the Trainers," was undertaken by "Friends of Women, an interdisciplinary group of professional women and a few men who [were] . . . kindred spirits. These women and men [were] . . . devoted to working in partnership with low-income female factory workers who [were] . . . exploited. Using a nonhierarchical participative group approach, the professional facilitators train[ed] selected leaders from the factory, who in turn train[ed] the other female factory work-ers, hence, the Train the Trainer program title."

The training included five parts. First, the participants' feelings of isolation were addressed and their connected-ness as a potentially supportive group emphasized. Most participants originated in rural areas and traveled to work in the relatively better economic urban environment. The second part of training involved health concerns in an industrial setting including "chronic exhaustion from dev-astating working conditions" (p. 182). The third training segment addressed participants' individual economic is-sues such as "personal incomes and expenses, analyzing their situations in the context of their poor status" (p. 182). Feminist labor lawyers and educators led the fourth phase, where labor laws and rights were discussed. Collective bargaining and lobbying in the political arena were also explained. The fifth training unit concerned a "synthesis" of all that participants had learned. Connections between personal and social problems and economic and politi-cal concerns were clearly identified, and the necessity of working individually and collectively for social change was emphasized (p. 183). The process resulted in participants' enhanced self-esteem and vision concerning what they might be able to achieve. Participants could then return to their factory environments and share what they learned with other workers.

Standard 3. "*Teaching women that both personal devel-opment and action, as well as collective social development and action, are essential if their lives are to change for the better*" (p. 186). We have identified feminist principles that stress how consciousness raising, an enhanced perception of one's life circumstances, and an increased understand-ing of self are extremely important for women. We have also

continued

Highlight **13-4**   *continued*

emphasized that, according to feminist theories, the personal is political. Personal development is fine, but it must coincide with political and social action. Only then can conditions be improved and social justice be attained for all women.

An example of a program adopting this standard is *Stree Mukti Sanghatana*, a group that uses street theater to raise consciousness and advocate for women's rights in Mumbai, India. Dramatic performances, entertainment, and other visual media such as posters serve as conduits to convey information and identify issues. Examples of performances include *No Dowry, Please* and *We Will Smash the Prison*.

Critical Thinking Questions **13-5**

EP 8a

To what extent do you agree with the three feminist principles concerning global development discussed in Highlight 13-4? How valuable did the principles seem in implementing the three programmatic examples?

International Social Work   LO 13-7

EP 1c; 3; 3a; 3b; 5; 5c; 8b; 8c

International social work is "international professional action and the capacity for international action by the social work profession and its members. International social work has four dimensions: internationally related domestic practice and advocacy, professional exchange, international practice, and international policy development and advocacy" (Healy, 2008, p. 10). International social work involves adopting a global focus, whether working in one's own country or in an international context. It also means establishing the global goal of firmly establishing social work as a respected profession around the world (Cox & Pawar, 2013). The following content elaborates on the four dimensions inherent in international social work:

1. *Internationally related domestic practice and advocacy.* The first dimension inherent in the definition of international social work concerns advocating for domestic policy that supports international social justice. It also means educating others about international issues to solicit their support on behalf of global social justice. This is true for social workers practicing primarily in the United States, Canada, Puerto Rico, the Caribbean, and anywhere else in the world.

   One way of practicing international social work in one's own country includes international adoption. International adoptions are those in which children are brought from other countries and placed for adoption in the United States. Another way of practicing international social work here is working with immigrants, refugees, and with agencies serving those individuals and families.

2. *Professional exchange.* The second dimension of international social work involves developing international arrangements and structures to encourage travel among countries and communication among professional colleagues.

Various international social work and related organizations are discussed later in the chapter. These organizations sponsor conferences and serve as clearinghouses for information and ideas concerning global issues. Other positive avenues of professional exchange include international field internships sponsored by social work programs, volunteer activities in international helping organizations, and international social work faculty exchange programs.

Turner (2001) provides an example of a professional exchange concerning Robert Wiles, who was a graduate student at the University of Calgary (Turner, 2001). He entered a three-month practicum where he was involved in "the development of the practicum component of the Associate Degree in Social Work at the University College of Belize" (p. 5). He emphasized:

"My experience in Belize was outstanding," …. [stated] Robert. "Certainly, the opportunity to work within another country was an incredible privilege, but being and living there was an intense learning experience. Beyond the classroom and university setting, interacting and learning about another culture was the most beautiful part of the experience." (p. 5)

3. *International practice.* Practicing in other countries can involve a wide range of social work activities, including participating in community development activities, working directly with individuals, families, and groups, assuming management positions, and assisting in policy development. Ways of getting your foot in the door for international social work positions include volunteering for or getting a job in a global social welfare organization such as CARE (a humanitarian organization dedicated to combating global poverty) or Save the Children (a humanitarian organization committed to helping children in need around the world and improving their potential for a better quality of life) (Brueggemann, 2014). Examples of potential paid positions include project director, proposal writer, area director, child protection officer, shelter coordinator, program director, education specialist, program specialist, regional HIV/AIDS director, technical advisor, program officer, case management specialist, training manager, global challenge coordinator, community campaigns and organization manager, advocacy and policy advisor, and campaigner (CARE, 2016; Oxfam, 2017).

Note that it's important to be prepared to face and overcome possible hurdles when practicing in other countries. These include potential resistance on the part of indigenous citizens; funding shortages; lower salaries; different certification, licensing, and credentialing regulations; and language barriers (Turner, 2001).

Highlight 13-5 illustrates a case example in international social work practice.

4. *International policy development and advocacy.* International social work involves supporting positive policy development and advocacy in the pursuit of global social justice. An aspect of international social work includes joining and actively working for global organizations just as one would a national organization. These organizations often encompass groups of people

dedicated to housing and hunger, social and environmental justice, peace, and gender issues, among others. Supporting global organizations seeking positive humanitarian policy changes such as the United Nations is another facet of this dimension.

Be alert to subtle and not so subtle opposition to some global organizations. Groups, businesses, corporations, and other bodies whose interests are threatened by socially conscious organizations will try to stop or at least hamper the efforts of these helpers. For example, President's Trump's first budget proposal called for eliminating or cutting payments to several international organizations whose goal is to help undeveloped parts of the world, including The United Nation's Green Climate Fund, the World Bank, and for US programs aiding international development such as the African Development Foundation, US Trade and Development Agency, and the McGovern-Dole International Food for Education program, among others. Distrust of bodies like the UN is also evident in strange places such as La Verkin, Utah, which, in 2001, declared itself a "UN Free Zone," prohibited its citizens from the flying of the UN flag or housing UN troops, and proposed requiring anyone who did business with the UN to post a sign indicating this. Fortunately, a later vote overturned this odd law. About the same time, another Utah city, Virgin, considered adopting a similar ordinance but settled for one requiring each home to have a firearm instead (WorldNetDaily.com, 2003).

Highlight 13-5

International Social Work: A Case Example in Mauritius

EP 7d; 8

Healy (2008) presents an example of social work practice in Mauritius, an island country in the Indian Ocean. She notes that it is facing staggering changes as it makes the transition from an agricultural to an industrial society; skilled jobs are replacing unskilled, and family structures are being transformed from extended to nuclear.

Most Mauritian social workers are employed by public agencies such as Social Security and probation departments. Note that "no single case is typical of social work in a country" (p. 213). However, the case of "Jean," a 4-year-old boy with a serious intellectual disability, is depicted here "because it illustrates Mauritian social work in transition, recognizing child development needs, yet hampered by incomplete service development and lack of resources" (p. 213).

The Case

Healy (2008) describes the case:

Jean is a 4-year-old boy who lives with his father, 7-year-old sister, and grandmother in a three-room corrugated iron-sheet house. The parents are separated, and mother lives elsewhere. The case was reported to the Child Development Unit of the Ministry of Women, Family Welfare and Child Development by a medical worker in the hospital. A caseworker (a social worker whose practice primarily focuses on work with individuals and families) visited and found that Jean, mentally retarded, was being "grossly neglected." The house was filthy; according to the grandmother, the father is an alcoholic, and she said she is too old to care for such a child who needs constant care. The caseworker discovered that Jean could not speak. He made noises and followed the caseworker everywhere, touching him frequently. The child seemed to the worker to be deprived of affection. Making a second visit, the caseworker interviewed the father. The father said he had no objection to the child being placed in a home. Mother was summoned to the office, but she refused to take Jean.

The caseworker tried to admit Jean to an institution but could not find a vacancy in a place equipped to care for handicapped children.

continued

Highlight **13-5** *continued*

Soon thereafter, Jean was left tied to a bed, unfed and unattended. He became ill and was admitted to a hospital. During his 2-month stay, no relative visited him. Discharge planning was challenging, as no placement could be found. The caseworker attempted to admit Jean to the Shelter for Women and Children in distress, a temporary shelter. However, the agency refused him admission, as they claimed they were not equipped to cope with Jean's multiple needs. The caseworker took the case to the Ministry's Permanent Secretary and to the magistrate [a judicial administrative official] to get an order to admit Jean to the shelter. Now, he is waiting while SOS Children's Village determines whether it will admit him for longer term care (Boodajee, 1997). (p. 214)

Commentary

Healy (2008) reflects:

The case such as Jean's could occur in many societies. It illustrates the functions of the social worker in investigation, efforts at family intervention, referral, and finally case advocacy to secure needed services for the client. It points out the need for further advocacy for service development to ensure that the needs of children with disabilities can be addressed. The case also illustrates the transition being experienced in Mauritian social work. Rather than focusing on child survival, the caseworker is focusing on child protection. As more appropriate services can be developed, child development will increase in importance. (pp. 213–214)

The NASW has also become "a member of InterAction, a large alliance of US-based international development and humanitarian nongovernmental organizations" (NASW, 2005, p. 1). Being a member of NASW indirectly supports InterAction's humanitarian efforts.

International Social Work Organizations LO 13-8

**EP 3b;
4c; 5b;
5c; 8b;
8c**

We've discussed organizations and communities in various contexts. When addressing the global community, it's important to understand how international organizations function within it. International social work organizations that actively engage social workers around the globe include the International Federation of Social Workers (IFSW) and the International Association of Schools of Social Work (IASSW). Two other international organizations that have values closely related to social work are the International Council on Social Welfare (ICSW) and the International Consortium for Social Development (ICSD) (Brueggeman, 2006).

International Federation of Social Workers (IFSW) Established in 1956, the IFSW "is a global organisation striving for social justice, human rights and social development through the promotion of social work, best practice models and the facilitation of international cooperation" (IFSW, 2017). The IFSW focuses on promoting social work to achieve social development, advocating for social justice on a global basis and facilitates international cooperation. It works with other organizations such as the United Nations Economic and Social Council, The UN Children's Fund, the World Health Organization, and the UN offices for Refugees and Human Rights.

The IFSW consists of five regions—Africa, Asia and the Pacific, Europe, Latin America and the Caribbean, and North America. It publishes a monthly newsletter for members. The IFSW also sponsors regional and global conferences to teach skills, train educators to teach in various areas related to social justice, and provide a forum for the discussion and development of ideas for addressing critical global issues.

The attainment of human rights on a global basis is central to the IFSW's mission. The IFSW campaigns for human rights by publishing statements on various human rights issues. It seeks to increase the social work profession's awareness about these issues and the profession's commitment to address them. The IFSW stresses that the pursuit of human rights is central to the social work profession, and is heavily involved in opposing human rights violations. The IFSW's home website is http://www.ifsw.org.

International Association of Schools of Social Work (IASSW)   The IASSW is a "worldwide association of schools of social work, other tertiary level social work educational programmes, and social work educators. The IASSW promotes the development of social work education throughout the world, develops standards to enhance [the] quality of social work education, encourages international exchange, provides forums for sharing social work research and scholarship, and promotes human rights and social development through policy and advocacy activities" (IASSW, 2017). It also serves as a consultant to the United Nations.

The IASSW is based on humanitarian values and the quest for social justice on the behalf of oppressed populations. It holds a biennial conference for social work educators, publishes a member newsletter, provides representation at the United Nations, co-sponsors with the IFSW and the ICSW (discussed in the next section) the journal *International Social Work*, sponsors various committees and task forces, and funds "small cross-national projects in social work education" (IASSW, 2017). (The IASSW's home website is http://www.iassw-aiets.org.)

International Council on Social Welfare (ICSW)   Established in 1928, the ICSW is an international nongovernmental organization whose membership includes local and national organizations in more than 70 countries (ICSW, 2017a). (Highlight 13.6 describes international nongovernment organizations.) The ICSW's membership consists of "tens of thousands of community organisations that work directly with people in poverty, hardship or distress" (ICSW, 2017b). The ICSW collects relevant information and dispenses it to various community groups, governments, and other organizations; provides training and support for members and other organizations; assists in policy development; sponsors global and regional meetings; publishes papers and reports on issues; and advocates for oppressed populations (ICSW, 2017c). Its website is http://www.icsw.org.

Highlight 13-6

International Nongovernmental Organizations   LO 13-9

EP 3; 3a; 3b; 5c; 8d

International nongovernment organizations (INGO) are nonprofit agencies whose purpose is to address designated social problems and issues (Cox & Pawar, 2013). It is usually funded privately through such sources as donations and grants. INGOs' activities at the international level include advocating for human rights, assisting in economic development, providing education to citizens, helping people address crises, monitoring governments' treatment of their citizens, and consulting with local and national governments. Examples of goals include helping refugees relocate and aiding in reconstruction after a crisis such as a hurricane, earthquake, or war (Cox & Pawar, 2013). One of the oldest, most famous

continued

Highlight 13-6 *continued*

INGOs is the *International Red Cross*, originating in 1863 (Cox & Pawar, 2013). The Red Cross and Red Crescent are dedicated to alleviating human suffering, promoting public health and helping when disaster strikes. However, "many Christian humanitarian organizations, Jewish welfare agencies, and the American Medical Association were founded even earlier" (Belgbeder, 1991; Cox & Pawar, 2013, p. 85).

Amnesty International (AI) is another example of an INGO (Brueggemann, 2014). It "is a global movement of more than 7 million people in over 150 countries and territories who campaign to end abuses of human rights, ... [and] lobby governments and other powerful groups such as companies" (AI, 2017). The organization also provides legal resources to those who are victims of human rights abuses.

Examples of AI's campaigns involve taking action to:

- Prevent homelessness among 1000 Roma families being evicted from their homes
- Stop violence against women

- Defend the rights and dignity of those trapped in poverty
- Abolish the death penalty
- Oppose torture, disappearances, and imprisonment without charge
- Combat terror with justice
- Protect civilians caught in military conflicts
- Free prisoners of conscience
- Protect the rights of refugees and migrants
- Regulate the global arms race (AI, 2017)

One issue being addressed at the time of this writing is the effort to protect civilians from being attacked by armed groups in places such as Syria, Yemen, and Libya, as well as abuse of civilians by government security forces in Congo, Tunisia, Myanmar, and Ukraine, to name just a few. To illustrate the horrible conditions that these organizations confront, consider that in Syria alone, half of the population needs food, water, shelter, and health care, and 4.9 million Syrians are now refugees outside their own country (AI, 2017).

Focus on Ethics 13-3 discusses international codes of ethics. **LO 13-10**

Focus on Ethics **13-3**

International Social Work: Codes of Ethics

EP 1a

Although the NASW *Code of Ethics* is the primary code followed by social workers in the United States, note that other ethical codes also are available in other nations and on an international basis. Consider, for example, the Association of Canadian Social Workers (CASW) Code of Ethics, accessible at http://www.casw-acts.ca/en/Code-of-Ethics.

The IFSW and IASSW have developed an *Ethics in Social Work, Statement of Principles* that may be applied when addressing *international* (involving two or more nations) or *global* (involving the entire world) ethical issues. Often, these issues concern human rights. The document, concurrently supported by both organizations, consists of the following five parts:

1. *Preface*
2. *Definition of social work*
3. *International conventions* (that refer to various organizations' specific statements of human rights)

4. *Principles*
5. *Professional conduct* (IASSW, 2012b; IFSW, 2012c)

The "principles" in the *Ethics in Social Work, Statement of Principles* include "human rights and human dignity" and "social justice." The former indicates how "social work is based on respect for the inherent worth and dignity of all people, and the rights that follow from this. Social workers should uphold and defend each person's physical, psychological, emotional and spiritual integrity and well-being." It continues that "social workers have a responsibility to promote social justice, in relation to society generally, and in relation to the people with whom they work"; this involves "challenging negative discrimination," "recognizing diversity," "distributing resources equitably," "challenging unjust policies and practices," and "working in solidarity" (i.e., social workers as a group have the responsibility to confront social injustice).

Social Work and Cross-Cultural Values in Global Perspective

EP 2; 2c

"Social work practice does not follow the same patterns in all parts of the world. The form of social work that develops in any society is shaped by the prevailing social, economic, and cultural forces" (Doel & Shardlow, 1996; Sowers & Rowe, 2007, pp. 29–30). Therefore, it's of critical importance to view and understand community development within the context of the society where it's happening.

Sowers and Rowe (2007) maintain that "social work has been profoundly influenced by Western thought, values, and views" (p. 30; Sacco, 1996). They continue:

> Arising from the dominant Western cultural point of view, human needs are based on the assumption that each individual needs a decent standard of living, education, housing, medical care, and social services, and that the provision of universal services would lead to the elimination of poverty, the advancement of underprivileged groups, and the narrowing of gaps in income, education, and employment (Barretta-Herman, 1994). (p. 30)

Verschelden (1993, pp. 766–767) proposes the following as fundamental global social work values that transcend cultural and national differences:

1. Primary importance of the individual
2. Respect and appreciation for differences
3. Commitment to social justice and the well-being of all in society
4. Willingness to persist despite frustration

Some research indicates that the last three are generally held by social workers around the globe; however, the first is addressed quite differently depending on the culture (Rowe, Hanley, Moreno, & Mould, 2000; Sowers & Rowe, 2007). Social workers must respond to the diverse cultural values of the societies in which they work. The ways in which individuals expect to be treated and the ways they prioritize their values vary from one culture to another. Highlight 13-7 identifies some cultural differences that must be considered when undertaking community development.

Highlight **13-7**

Cultural Differences in an Organizational Context   LO 13-11

EP 3

Dubrin (2007) cites four cultural differences in the context of working with and within large organizations. These also are significant when working effectively with organizations in the community and with community citizens. It's essential to establish goals with community residents that fit well with their own value systems. It's also crucial for people commencing community development to be aware of their own value orientations so as not to impose them on people in the community.

Individualism *versus* Collectivism

Individualism is "a mental set in which people see themselves first as individuals and believe that their own interests take priority." At the other end of the spectrum, "**collectivism** is a feeling that the group and society receive top priority .... Highly individualistic cultures include the United States, Canada, Great Britain, Australia, and the Netherlands. Japan, Taiwan, Mexico, Greece, and Hong Kong are among the countries that strongly value collectivism" (Dubrin, 2007, p. 386).

continued

Highlight 13-7 *continued*

Sowers and Rowe (2007) comment concerning differences in how individual importance is perceived:

> For instance, within the African context, traditional African thinking understands human nature and human flourishing as a network of life forces that emanate from God and end in God, who is the source of all life forces. For many Africans, personhood is attainable only in community and the single most important concept within African traditional life is the inclusion of all into the community.

Van Wormer (2006) reflects on the value of collectivism for First Nations Peoples:

> The sense of interconnectedness is a staple of traditional indigenous culture. The First Nations people in North America rely on the metaphor of the Medicine Wheel, which exemplifies the wholeness of all life. The Medicine Wheel teaches about the cycle of life, a cycle that encompasses infancy through old age, the seasons, and four directions of human growth—the emotional, mental, physical, and spiritual. This is not a linear system; all the parts are interconnected. American Indian teachings are traditionally presented as narratives and shared within a talking circle.... [V]alues are: a strong emphasis on *being*, not doing, and cooperation over competition; a group emphasis; working only to meet one's needs; nonmaterialism; ... and living in harmony with nature. The theme of these values is social interconnectedness. (p. 57)

Sowers and Rowe (2007) conclude that "working out an understanding of human beings and personal development that incorporates cultural conceptions and beliefs is critical to effective social work practice, particularly in a global context" (p. 30).

Materialism *versus Concern for Others* (Dubrin, 2007 p. 386).

Materialism is the value that material things and money are extremely important, much more so than humanitarian or spiritual pursuits. There is also a tendency to emphasize, "Me, Me, Me" rather than focus on other people's needs and issues. In contrast, *concern for others* refers to genuine, active concern for other people's well-being and a focus on the importance of interpersonal relationships. As Dubrin notes, "Materialistic countries include Japan, Austria, and Italy. The United States is considered to be moderately materialistic ... Scandinavian nations all emphasize caring as a national value" (p. 386).

Formality *versus* Informality

According to Dubrin, "A country that values **formality** attaches considerable importance to tradition, ceremony, social rules, and rank. At the other extreme, **informality** refers to a casual attitude toward tradition, ceremony, social rules, and rank." Dubrin states that people in Latin American countries "highly value formality, such as lavish public receptions and processions. Americans, Canadians, and Scandinavians are much more informal" (p. 386).

Urgent Time Orientation *versus* Casual Time Orientation

Dubrin notes:

> [I]ndividuals and nations attach different importance to time. People with an **urgent time orientation** perceive time as a scarce resource and tend to be impatient. People with a **casual time orientation** view time as an unlimited and unending resource and tend to be patient. Americans are noted for their urgent time orientation. They frequently impose deadlines and are eager to get started doing business. Asians and Middle Easterners, in contrast, are [much more] patient. (p. 387)

EP 8a

Critical Thinking Question 13-6

How would you describe yourself concerning these four global social work value dimensions, and why?

What You Can Do on the Behalf of Global Social Justice

EP 1; 2b; 8c

There are at least six things that you can do to address and enhance social justice on a global basis. First, vote for political candidates who appreciate the importance of global cooperation to address human rights issues and solve social ills (Verschelden, 1993). Second, you can continue to become more knowledgeable about global issues and educate others including legislators about the issues' significance (Verschelden, 1993). Third, you can become politically involved yourself by actively participating in political debate and working to support political candidates. You might even decide to run for office yourself. Fourth, you can join organizations, several of which were mentioned earlier, that seek to help needy and hurting people around the world. Fifth, you can volunteer your time to support the work of international helping organizations. Sixth, you can become a macro practice social worker participating in community development in the international context.

Chapter Summary

The following summarizes this chapter's content as it relates to the learning objectives presented at the beginning of the chapter. Objectives include the following:

LO 13-1 Describe globalization, social justice, and human rights and their significance for international social work practice.

We live in a global environment with multiple interconnections. *Globalization* is the "growing economic, political, and social interconnectedness among societies throughout the world" (Mooney et al., 2017). The concepts *global*, *advocate*, and *social justice* are critical aspects of social work's global perspective.

Social justice is the philosophical perspective that all people have the right to enjoy equal opportunities in economic, political, and social realms.

Human rights involve the premise that all people—regardless of race, culture, or national origin—are entitled to basic rights and treatment. Developing a global focus means becoming aware of the issues facing the human population in the twenty-first century. From a social work perspective, global problems are everyone's problems.

LO 13-2 Describe social issues of poverty, economic justice, global conflict, immigration, and forced migration of people in need.

Poverty is the lack of money or material goods available to other members of a society. The gap between rich and poor is widening in the United States, which raises serious questions concerning economic justice. Global poverty is a major problem with numerous consequences related to it. Global conflict is rampant, with the goal of peace being very difficult to attain.

Immigration status is a person's position in term of legal rights and residency when entering and residing in a country that is not that person's legal country of origin. Millions of people worldwide are involuntarily displaced from their country of origin. Related terms include legal and illegal immigrants, nonimmigrants, refugees, documented and undocumented aliens, deportable aliens, adjustment of status, and naturalized citizens.

LO 13-3 Respond to critical thinking questions.

In this chapter, critical thinking questions addressed personal views on financial status, support of the US military presence in various other countries, illegal immigration, community functioning, feminist principles concerning global development, and agreement with proposed global social work values.

LO 13-4 Describe ethical issues in international social work practice.

Ethical issues focused on the gap between the rich and the poor in the United States, reasons and responsibility for global poverty, and international codes of ethics.

In summary, this chapter explored the macro environment and social justice on a global scale. The intent is to help you develop a perspective that extends far beyond that of your immediate environment—school, work, neighborhood, city or town, and even state and country.

LO 13-5 Discuss the theoretical foundations of community development and social development.

"Community development refers to efforts to mobilize people who are directly affected by a community condition into groups and organizations to enable them to take action on the social problems and issues that concern them" (Rivera & Erlich, 2001, p. 256). Important concepts in the conceptualization of community development are production-distribution-consumption, socialization, social control, social participation, and mutual support. Community development practice is based on six basic practice principles: community members' active participation; establishing common goals; reaching out to various diverse groups, constituencies, and organizations; using community assets; empowerment of community members to help themselves; and sustainability. Sustainability in a global community context involves meeting current needs without jeopardizing the well-being of future generations. Examples of community development in Africa, Guatemala, and Indonesia are provided.

Social development, a concept related to community development, is a planned change process on the behalf of an entire population that emphasizes economic development based on two principles; first, economic development integrates social and economic policy, and, second, it sponsors investment-oriented social programs "that contribute positively to economic development" (Midgley & Sherraden, 2009, p. 283). A case example is the Grameen Bank of Dhaka, Bangladesh.

LO 13-6 Summarize a feminist perspective on global development.

A feminist perspective on global development involves "raising consciousness regarding gender roles and the importance and worth of every female"; "forming interdisciplinary professional partnerships with poor women and training indigenous trainers to serve their own communities"; and "teaching women that both personal development and action, as well as collective social development and action, are essential if their lives are to change for the better" (Wetzel, 1995, pp. 181–186).

LO 13-7 Define and explain international social work.

International social work is "international professional practice and the capacity for international action by the social work profession and its members" (Healy, 2008, p. 10). It involves advocacy on an international level, interaction and cooperation among professionals, and international policy practice. A case example of social work in Mauritius is provided.

LO 13-8 Identify and describe two international social work and social welfare organizations.

International social work and social welfare organizations include the International Federation of Social Workers (IFSW), the International Association of Schools of Social Work (IASSW), and the International Council on Social Welfare (ICSW). Although each focuses on its own goals, these generally include the pursuit of social justice and the international exchange of ideas to improve the human condition.

LO 13-9 Define *international nongovernmental organizations* and provide examples.

International nongovernment organizations are nonprofit agencies whose purpose is to address designated social problems and issues. Examples include the International Red Cross and Amnesty International (AI). A current concern addressed by

AI is homelessness of the Roma and the end of un-lawful detention of citizens by several countries.

LO 13-10 Discuss social work values and cross-cultural values in global perspective.

Social workers must be sensitive to the major differences in cultural values around the world. The IFSW and IASSW have developed an *Ethics in Social Work, Statement of Principles* that may be applied when addressing international or global ethical issues.

LO 13-11 Identify some of the cultural differences existing in organizational contexts.

Cultural differences in an organizational context include "individualism versus collectivism," "materialism versus concern for others," "formality versus informality," and "urgent time orientation versus casual time orientation" (Dubrin, 2007, pp. 386–387).

Competency Notes

The following identifies where Educational Policy (EP) competencies and component behaviors are discussed in the chapter.

EP 1 (Competency 1)—Demonstrate Ethical and Professional Behavior. *(p. 494):* Ethical questions are posed concerning whether government should allow vast discrepancies in wealth among those in its population. *(p. 495):* Ethical questions are raised concerning the reasons for extreme global poverty and whose responsibility it is to help. *(p. 516):* Learning about global and political issues is a career-long process.

EP 1a Make ethical decisions by applying the standards of the NASW *Code of Ethics,* relevant laws and regulations, models for ethical decision-making, ethical conduct of research, and additional codes of ethics as appropriate to context. *(p. 491):* The NASW *Code of Ethics* directs social workers to advocate on the behalf of people who are vulnerable and in need. *(p. 513):* The IFSW/ IASSW *Ethics in Social Work, Statement of Principles* is summarized.

EP 1c Demonstrate professional demeanor in behavior; appearance; and oral, written, and electronic communication. *(p. 496):* Social workers should demonstrate professional demeanor in communication by understanding and using appropriate terminology when referring to immigration status. *(p. 508):* Potential professional roles in international social work are identified.

EP 2 (Competency 2)—Engage Diversity and Difference in Practice. *(p. 492):* Practitioners should recognize the extent to which poverty and economic inequality may oppress, marginalize, or alienate people. Poverty is discussed. *(p. 496):* Immigration status is a dimension of diversity. Depending on their immigration status, people may be subject to marginalization alienation, privilege, or increased power. *(p. 504):* The social development model addresses social and economic marginalization and alienation. *(p. 506):* Gender is a dimension of diversity. *(p. 513):* Social workers should recognize the extent to which various cultures' values may result in oppression or the acquisition of power.

EP 2a Apply and communicate understanding of the importance of diversity and difference in shaping life experiences in practice at the micro, mezzo, and macro levels. *(p. 492):* Poverty on a global basis has dramatic effects on life experiences. *(p. 496):* Immigration status shapes life experiences.

EP 2b Present themselves as learners and engage clients and constituencies as experts of their own experiences. *(p. 516):* These concerns and challenges are the same ones faced by social workers when working in cultures with which they are not familiar. Learning about other cultures, practices, customs, and norms requires that the social worker listen and consider others as the true experts with respect to their own cultures.

EP 2c Apply self-awareness and self-regulation to manage the influence of personal biases and values in working with diverse clients and constituencies. *(p. 514)*: Practitioners must work hard at gaining self-awareness regarding any biases they may have concerning values evident in other cultures.

EP 3 (Competency 3)—Advance Human Rights and Social, Economic, and Environmental Justice *(p. 508)*: Social workers should be knowledgeable about global interconnections of oppression and other issues. *(p. 512)*: International social work focuses on the global interconnections of oppression. International social work addresses the worldwide forms and mechanisms of oppression. *(pp. 514–515)*: NGOs recognize and investigate oppression and discrimination concerning the global interconnections of oppression and they work to promote human rights. NGOs. Social workers should understand how cultural differences in organizations affect people's conditions and performance.

EP 3a Apply their understanding of social, economic, and environmental justice to advocate for human rights at the individual and system levels. *(p. 489)*: We have emphasized the importance of social workers understanding their macro environment to practice effectively. *(p. 508)*: The first dimension inherent in the definition of international social work concerns advocating for domestic policy that supports international social justice. *(p. 512)*: INGOs' activities at the international level include advocating for human rights, assisting in economic development, providing education to citizens, helping people address crises, monitoring governments' treatment of their citizens, and consulting with local and national governments.

EP 3b Engage in practices that advance social, economic, and environmental justice. *(p. 491)*: Generalist practitioners should advocate for human rights and social and economic justice. *(p. 508)*: International social work focuses on advocating for human rights and social and economic justice. *(p. 511)*: International social work

organizations advocate for human rights and social and economic justice. *(p. 512)*: NGOs advocate for human rights and social and economic justice.

EP 4c Use and translate research evidence to inform and improve practice, policy, and service delivery. *(p. 511)*: International social work organizations provide mechanisms for sharing research to inform practice.

EP 5 (Competency 5)—Engage in Policy Practice. *(pp. 508)*: **International social work** is "international professional action and the capacity for international action by the social work profession and its members. International social work has four dimensions: internationally related domestic practice and advocacy, professional exchange, international practice, and international policy development and advocacy" (Healy, 2008, p. 10).

EP 5b Assess how social welfare and economic policies impact the delivery of and access to social services. *(p. 491)*: Social workers should advocate for policies that advance social and economic well-being on a global basis. *(p. 501)*: Community development practice promotes policies that advance community well-being. *(p. 504)*: Social development practice promotes policies that advance community well-being. *(p. 506)*: Case examples demonstrate a feminist analysis and formulation of policies and practices that enhance women's well-being. *(p. 511)*: International social work involves analyzing, formulating, and advocating for policies that advance social well-being on an international and global basis. International social work organizations advocate for policies that advance social well-being.

EP 5c Apply critical thinking to analyze, formulate, and advocate for policies that advance human rights and social, economic, and environmental justice. *(p. 489)*: Community development practice involves strategies that advance social and economic justice. *(p. 500)*: Social development practice involves strategies that advance social and economic justice. *(p. 504)*: Case examples depict practices that advance social and economic justice for women. *(p. 506)*: Practitioners involved in international social work engage in practices that advance social and economic justice on international and global levels. *(p. 508):* International social work organizations advocate for client access to the services of social work. *(p. 511):* NGOs engage in practices that advance social and economic justice. *(p. 512):* Social workers can engage in practices that advance social and economic justice on a global level.

EP 6 (Competency 6)—Engage with Individuals, Families, Groups, Organizations, and Communities.

(p. 498): Generalist practitioners should be knowledgeable about communities and practice with communities, such as community development. *(p. 500):* The community development practice theoretical framework guides the processes of engagement, assessment, intervention, and evaluation in order to enhance community capacities. *(p. 504):* The social development conceptual framework is explained as it applies to development in the global context. It involves assessment, intervention, and evaluation. *(p. 506):* A feminist theoretical framework is used to guide the macro intervention process.

EP 7 Assess Individuals, Families, Groups, Organizations, and Communities.

(p. 500): The community development practice model is discussed and analyzed. *(p. 504):* The social development model is discussed and analyzed. *(p. 506):* A feminist model on global development is discussed.

EP 7d Select appropriate intervention strategies based on the assessment, research knowledge, and values and preferences of clients and constituencies.

(p. 503): Case examples reflect appropriate community development strategies. *(p. 506):* This case example depicts an appropriate social development strategy. *(p. 506):* Case examples portray appropriate intervention strategies using a feminist perspective. *(p. 510):* The case example in Mauritius demonstrates appropriate intervention strategies providing an international perspective.

EP 8 (Competency 8)—Intervene with Individuals, Families, Groups, Organizations, and Communities.

(p. 500): Community development practice requires the appraisal and integration of multiple sources of knowledge and analyzed. *(p. 503):* Case examples portray how community development practice can help communities solve problems. *(p. 504):* This case example reflects how social development can help abandoned and divorced women in Bangladesh solve problems and support themselves. *(p. 506):* Case examples depict how clients can be helped to solve problems. *(pp. 506, 510):* These case examples provide an international perspective regarding how a social worker can help clients solve problems.

EP 8a Critically choose and implement interventions to achieve practice goals and enhance capacities of clients and constituencies.

(pp. 494, 496, 498, 500, 508, 515): Critical thinking questions are posed.

EP 8b Apply knowledge of human behavior and the social environment, person-in-environment, and other multidisciplinary theoretical frameworks in interventions with clients and constituencies.

(p. 489): Generalist practitioners should keep abreast of global issues concerning social justice and potential advocacy to provide relevant services. *(p. 501):* Community development practice involves continuous appraisal of societal trends in order to provide relevant services. *(p. 504):* Social development practice involves continuous appraisal of societal trends in order to provide relevant services. *(p. 508):* International social work requires continuous appraisal of emerging societal trends and technological developments in order to provide relevant services. *(p. 511):* International social work organizations share information and continuously appraise changing locales, populations, technological developments, and emerging societal trends to promote improved service delivery.

EP 8c Use inter-professional collaboration as appropriate to achieve beneficial practice outcomes.

(p. 501): Community development practice involves collaboration with colleagues and clients for effective policy action. Social workers can provide leadership in promoting sustainable changes in community development service delivery and practice. *(p. 501):* Social workers can provide

leadership in promoting sustainable, effective services in communities. *(p. 504):* Social development practice involves collaboration with colleagues and clients for effective policy action. *(p. 506):* The feminist perspective emphasizes collaboration with colleagues and clients. *(p. 508):* International social work provides opportunities for practitioners to promote sustainable changes in service delivery to improve quality. *(p. 511):* International social work organizations provide opportunities for social workers to become leaders in providing improved service delivery. *(p. 516):* Social workers can provide leadership in promoting improved changes in service availability and practice in global contexts.

EP 8d Negotiate, mediate, and advocate with and on behalf of diverse clients and constituencies. *(p. 491):* Social workers should advocate on behalf of clients in the global community. *(p. 512):* A major goal of international social work is to advocate for clients and other people in need.

EP 8e Facilitate effective transitions and endings that advance mutually agreed-on goals *(p. 506):* This case example portrays a social development strategy to prevent the alienation of abandoned and divorced women in Bangladesh.

EP 9b Apply knowledge of human behavior and the social environment, person-in-environment, and other multidisciplinary theoretical frameworks in the evaluation of outcomes. *(p. 500):* In community development practice, the idea is to enhance community functioning through participation of as broad a range of community members as possible, evaluate the outcomes, and use the information to improve practice effectiveness.

Media Resources

MindTap for Social Work

Go to MindTap® for digital study tools and resources that complement this text and help you be more successful in your course and career. There's an interactive eBook plus videos of client sessions, skill-building activities, quizzes to help you prepare for tests, apps, and more—all in one place. If your instructor didn't assign MindTap, you can find out more about it at CengageBrain .com.

References

Abramovitz, M. (2010). Ideological perspectives and conflicts. In J. Blau (Ed., with M. Abramovitz), *The dynamics of social welfare policy* (3rd ed., pp. 131–188). New York: Oxford.

Administration on Intellectual and Developmental Disabilities. (2013). *The Developmental disabilities assistance and bill of rights act of 2000.* Retrieved from https://acl.gov/Programs/AIDD/DDA_BOR_ACT_2000/p2_tI_subtitleA.aspx.

African American History. (2017). *Desire housing project, New Orleans, Louisiana (1956-2001).* Retrieved from http://www.blackpast.org/aah/desire-housing-project-new-orleans-louisiana-1956-2001.

Alberti, R., & Emmons, M. (2017). *Your perfect right: Assertiveness and equality in your life and relationships* (10th ed.). Atascadero, CA: Impact.

Albrecht, K. (1988). *At America's service.* New York: Warner Books.

Aldag, R. J., & Kuzuhara, L. W. (2005). *Mastering management skills.* Mason, OH: South-Western.

Alsever, J. (2014). Immigrants: America's job creator. *Fortune, 169*(8), 55–56.

Alter, C. F. (2009). Building community partnerships and networks. In R. J. Patti (Ed.), *The handbook of human services management* (2nd ed., pp. 435–454). Thousand Oaks, CA: Sage.

American Psychiatric Association (APA). (2000). *Diagnostic and statistical manual of mental disorders: Text revision. DSM-IV-TR* (4th ed.). Washington, DC: Author.

American Red Cross. (2017). *Partnering to build ready neighborhoods.* Retrieved from http://www.redcross.org/local/california/northern-california-coastal/local-programs-services/ready-neighborhoods.

Amnesty International. (AI). *Who we are.* Retrieved from https://www.amnesty.org/en/who-we-are/.

Anderson, K. M. (2016). Assessing strengths. In D. Saleebey. *The Strengths Perspective in Social Work Practice* (6th ed.). Upper Saddle River, NJ: Pearson Education.

Anderson, R. E., Carter, I., & Lowe, G. R. (1999). *Human behavior in the social environment: A social systems approach* (5th ed.). New York: Aldine De Gruyter.

Andrews, J. O., Felton, G., Wewers, M. E., & Health, J. (2004). Use of community health workers in research with ethnic minority women. *Journal of Nursing Scholarship, 36,* 358–365.

Appleby, G. A., & Anastas, J. W. (1998). *Not just a passing phase: Social work with gay, lesbian, and bisexual people.* New York: Columbia University Press.

ARC Milwaukee. (undated, c). *Services profile.* Milwaukee, WI: Author.

Arredondo, P., & Perez, P. (2003). Counseling paradigms and Latina/o Americans: Contemporary considerations. In F. D. Harper & J. McFadden (Eds.), *Culture and counseling: New approaches* (pp. 115–132). Boston: Allyn & Bacon.

Asian Americans for Civil Rights and Equality (AACRE). (2017). About. Retrieved from http://aacre.org/about/

Austin, D. (2017). *CenteringPregnancy: A group model for prenatal care to empower and engage women— Led by UCSF Certified Nurse Midwives.* Retrieved from https://obgyn.ucsf.edu/midwifery/centeringpregnancy-group-model-prenatal-care-empower-and-engage-women-%E2%80%93-led-ucsf-certified

Austin, D. M. (2002). *Human services management: Organizational leadership in social work practice.* New York: Columbia.

Axelrod, N. R. (2005). Board leadership and development. In R. D. Herman (Ed.), *The Jossey-Bass handbook of nonprofit leadership and management* (2nd ed., pp. 131–152).

Ayner, S. R. (2013). An afrocentric approach to working with African American Families. In E. P. Congress & M. J. Gonzalez (Eds.). *Multicultural perspectives in social work practice with families* (3rd ed., pp. 129–140). New York: Springer.

Bane, T. (2016). *Encyclopedia of spirits and ghosts in world mythology.* Jefferson, NC: McFarland & Company.

Barbuto, J. E. Jr., & Wheeler, D. W. (2005). *Becoming a servant leader: Do you have what it takes?* Lincoln, NE: University of Nebraska-Lincoln Extension, Institute of Agriculture and Natural Resources, A-15 General.

Barrera, T.L., Szafranski, D.D., Ratcliff, C.G., Garnaat, S.L., & Norton, P.J. (2016). An experimental comparison of techniques: Cognitive defusion, cognitive restructuring, and in-vivo exposure for social anxiety. *Behavioural and Cognitive Psychotherapy, 44*(2), 249–254.

Barretta-Herman, A. (1994). Revisioning the community as provider: Restructuring New Zealand's social services. *International social work,* 37(1), 7–21.

Barusch, A. S. (2015). *Foundations of social policy: Social justice in human perspective* (5th ed.). Stamford, CT: Cengage Learning.

Belgrave, F. Z., & Allison, K. W. (2014). *African American psychology: From Africa to America* (3rd ed.). Thousand Oaks, CA: Sage.

Belkin-Martinez, D. (2010). "Solidaridad y justicia": Latinas, community organizing, and empowerment. In R. Furman & N. Negi (Eds.), *Social work practice with Latinos: Key issues and emerging themes* (pp. 282–291). Chicago: Lyceum.

Biegel, D. E., Shore, B. K., & Gordon, E. (1984). *Building support networks for the elderly.* Beverly Hills: Sage.

Bernard, J. (1973). *The sociology of community.* Glenview, IL.: Scott, Foresman.

Bertram, A. G., Sears, K., Burr, B., Fuller, J., & Green, K. (2016). Building communities: College preparation education for grandparents raising grandchildren. *Journal of intergenerational relationships,* 14(1), 17–26.

Beutler, B. (2016). Minutes. *New Republic,* Retrieved from https://newrepublic.com/minutes/136603 /donald-trump-will-turn-ignorant-generals-hes -smarter-destroy-isis-bigly

Boat, T. F., & Wu, J. T. (2015). *Mental disorders and disabilities among low-income children.* Washington, DC: National Academies Press.

Boodajee, K. Y. (1997). *A critical appraisal of the functioning of the Child Development Unit of the Ministry of Women, Family Welfare and Child Development with reference to case studies showing strengths and weaknesses of the unit.* Social Work Diploma Project, University of Mauritius, Reduit.

Bos, H., & van Balen, F. (2008). Children in planned lesbian families; Stigmatization, psychological adjustment and protective factors. *Culture, Health and Sexuality, 10,* 221–236.

Bos, H., van Balen, F., Gartrell, N. Peyser, H., & Sanfort, T. (2008). Children in planned lesbian families: A cross-cultural comparison between the United States and the Netherlands. *American Journal of Orthopsychiatry, 78,* 211–219.

Brammer, R. (2012). *Diversity in counseling* (2nd ed.). Belmont, CA: Brooks/Cole.

Brave Heart, M. Y. H. (2001). Lakota—Native people's spirituality. In M. Van Hook, B. Hugen, & M. Aguilar (Eds.), *Spirituality within religious traditions in social work practice* (pp. 18–33). Belmont, CA: Brooks-Cole.

Beigbeder, Y. (1991). *The role and status of international humanitarian volunteers and organisations.* Dordrecht, the Netherlands: Martinus Nijhoff.

Brennan Center for Justice. (2016). Restricting the Vote. Retrieved from https://www.brennancenter.org /issues/restricting-vote

Breton, M. (2004). An empowerment perspective. In C. D. Garvin, L. M. Gutierrez, & M. J. Galinsky (Eds.), *Handbook of social work with groups* (pp. 58–75). New York: Guilford.

Bricker-Jenkins, M., & Netting, F. E. (2009). Feminist issues and practices in social work. In A. R. Roberts (Ed.), *Social workers' desk reference* (2nd ed., pp. 277–283). New York: Oxford.

Brody, R., & Nair, M. (2014). *Effectively managing human service organizations* (4th ed.). Thousand Oaks, CA: Sage.

Brueggemann, W. G. (2014). *The practice of macro social work* (4th ed.). Belmont, CA: Brooks/Cole.

Burbank, M. D., Hunter, R., & Gutiérrez, L.A. (2012). Redefining the lines of expertise: Educational pathways through communities together advocacy project. *Journal of community engagement and scholarship,* 5(1), 33–43.

Burghardt, S. (2014). *Macro practice in social work for the 21st century* (2nd ed.). Thousand Oaks, CA: Sage.

Burk, M. (2012). Power plays: Six ways the male corporate elite keeps women out. In S. M. Shaw & J. Lee (Eds.), *Women's voices, feminist visions: Classic and contemporary readings* (5th ed., pp. 436–438). New York: McGraw-Hill.

Burns, C., & Kreheley, C. (2011). Gay and transgender people face high rates of workplace discrimination and harassment. Retrieved from http://www .americanprogress.org/ issues/2011/06/workplace _discrimination.html

Business Insider (2017). *10 Reasons why the US health care system is the envy of the world.* Retrieved from http://www.businessinsider.com/10-reasons -why-the-us-health-care-system-is-the-envy-of-the -world-2010-3#1-most-preemptive-cancer-screening-1

Butler, R. N. (1989). Dispelling Ageism: The Cross -cutting Intervention. *Annals of the American Academy of Political and Social Science* 503: 138–147.

Cahill, S., Ellen, M., & Tobias, S. (2002). *Family policy: Issues affecting gay, lesbian, bisexual, and transgendered families.* New York: National Gay and Lesbian Task Force Policy Institute.

Canada FASD Research Network. (2014). Impact evaluation of the Healthy, Empowered and

Resilient (H.E.R.) Pregnancy Program in Edmonton, Alberta. *Girls, Women, Alcohol, and Pregnancy.* Retrieved from https://fasdprevention.wordpress .com/2014/02/07/impact-evaluation-of-the-healthy -empowered-and-resilient-h-e-r-pregnancy-program -in-edmonton-alberta/

Canda, E. R., & Furman, L. D. (2010). *Spiritual diversity in social work practice: The heart of healing* (2nd ed.). New York: Oxford.

CARE. (2016). *CARE.* Retrieved from http://www.care.org

Carlton-LaNey, I., Murty, S., & Morris, L. C. (2005). Rural community practice: Organizing, planning, and development. In M. Weil (Ed.), *The handbook of community practice* (pp. 402–417). Thousand Oaks, CA: Sage.

Carr, E. S. (2004). Accessing resources, transforming systems: Group work with poor and homeless people. In C. D. Garvin, L. M. Gutierrez, & M. J. Galinsky (Eds.), *Handbook of social work with groups* (pp. 360–383). New York: Guilford.

Carroll, C., Bates, M., & Johnson, C. (2004). *Group leadership: Strategies for group counseling leaders* (4th ed.). Denver: Love.

Carroll, J. L. (2013). *Sexuality now: Embracing diversity* (4th ed.). Belmont, CA: Wadsworth.

Carroll, J. L. (2016). *Sexuality now: Embracing diversity* (5th ed.). Boston: Cengage Learning.

Casey, E. A., Brown, R., Rowan, D., Howard, A. C., & Taylor, K. (2010). Violence and Latino communities. In R. Furman & N. Negi (Eds.), *Social work practice with Latinos: Key issues and emerging themes* (pp. 145–157). Chicago: Lyceum.

Cassidy, C. A. (2016). *AP: Patchy reporting undercuts national hate crimes count.* Retrieved from http://bigstory .ap.org/article/8247a1d2f76b4baea2a121186d edf768/ap-patchy-reporting-undercuts-national-hate -crimes-count

Cassidy, C., & Kreitner, R. (2010). *Supervision: Setting people up for success.* Mason, OH: South-Western.

Center on Budget and Policy Priorities. (2016). *TANF Cash benefits have fallen by more than 20 percent in most states and continue to erode.* Retrieved from http://www.cbpp.org/research/family-income -support/tanf-cash-benefits-have-fallen-by-more-than -20-percent-in-most-states

Center on Budget and Policy Priorities. (2015). *Policy Basics: An introduction to TANF.* Retrieved from http://www .cbpp.org/research/policy-basics-an-introduction-to-tanf

Centers for Disease Control (CDC). (2014). *Routine Prenatal care visits by provider specialty in the United States, 2009–2010.* Retrieved from https://www.cdc.gov/nchs/data/databriefs/db145 .htm#x2013;2010%3C/a%3E

Centers for Disease Control (CDC). (2015). Key Findings: Trends in the prevalence of developmental disabilities in U.S. Children, 1997-2008. Retrieved from https://www.cdc.gov/ncbddd/developmentaldis abilities/features/birthdefects-dd-keyfindings.html

Centers for Disease Control (CDC). (2016). *Facts about developmental disabilities.* Retrieved from https://www .cdc.gov/ncbddd/developmentaldisabilities/facts.html

Center for Youth and Family Solutions. (2017). *Mission.* Retrieved from https://www.facebook.com/TCYFS/info

Chamberlain, A. (2016). *Demystifying the Gender Pay Gap. Glassdoor, March 2016,* retrieved from http:// nymag.com/thecut/2016/03/media-has-one-of-the -biggest-gender-wage-gaps.html

Child Health USA. (2013). *Prenatal Care Utilization.* Retrieved from https://mchb.hrsa.gov/chusa13/health -services-utilization/p/prenatal-care-utilization.html

Champoux, J. E. (2006). *Organizational behavior: Integrating individuals, groups and organizations* (3rd ed.). Mason, OH: South-Western.

Chang, Y., Schneider, J.K., & Sessanna, L. (2011). Decisional conflict among Chinese family caregivers regarding nursing home placement of older adults with dementia. *Journal of Aging Studies, 25*(4), 436–444.

Choudhuri, D. D., Santiago-Rivera, A. L., & Garrett, M. T. (2012). *Counseling & diversity.* Belmont, CA: Brooks/Cole.

Coleman, J. W., & Kerbo, H. R. (2009). *Social problems* (10th ed.). New York: Vango.

Community Tool Box. (2016). *Identifying community assets and resources.* Retrieved from http://ctb.ku.edu/en /table-of-contents/assessment/assessing-community -needs-and-resources/identify-community-assets /main

Commonwealth Fund. (2015). *U.S. health care from a global perspective.* Retrieved from http://www.com monwealthfund.org/publications/issue-briefs/2015 /oct/us-health-care-from-a-global-perspective

Compton, B. R., Galaway, B., & Cournoyer, B. R. (2005). *Social work processes* (7th ed.). Belmont, CA: Brooks/Cole.

Congressional Research Service. (2016). *Trends in child care spending from the CCDF and TANF.* Retrieved from www.fas.org/sgp/crs/misc/R44528.pdf

Corey, G. (2016). *Theory & practice of group counseling* (9th ed.). Boston: Cengage.

Corey, G., Corey, M. S., Corey, C., & Callanan, P. (2015). *Issues and ethics in the helping professions* (9th ed.). Stanford, CT: Cengage Learning.

Corey, M. S., Corey, G., & Corey, C. (2014). *Groups: Process and practice* (9th ed.). Belmont, CA: Brooks/Cole.

Cormier, S., & Hackney. H. (2008). *Counseling strategies and interventions* (8th ed.). Boston: Allyn & Bacon.

Corporation for National & Community Service. (2009b). Retrieved from http://www .americorps.gov /about/programs.vista.asp

Council on Social Work Education (CSWE). (2015). *Educational policy and accreditation standards (EPAS)*. Alexandria, VA: Author.

Cournoyer, B. (2017). *The social work skills workbook* (8th ed.). Boston: Cengage Learning.

Cox, C. B. (2002). Empowering African American custodial grandparents. *Social Work, 47*(1), 45–54.

Cox, D., & Pawar, M. (2013). *International social work: Issues, strategies, and programs* (2nd ed.). Thousand Oaks, CA: Sage.

Cromartie, J. (2013). *How is rural America changing?* Retrieved from http://www.census.gov/newsroom/cspan /rural_america/20130524_rural_america_slides.pdf

Crooks, R., & Baur, K. (2014). *Our sexuality* (12th ed.). Belmont, CA: Wadsworth.

Daft, R. L. (2016a). *Management* (12th ed.). Boston: Cengage Learning.

Daft, R. L. (2016b). *Organization theory and design* (12th ed.). Boston: Cengage Learning.

Daft, R. L., & Marcic, D. (2017). *Understanding management* (10th ed.). Boston: Cengage Learning.

Daley, M. R., & Avant, F. L. (2004). Rural social work. In T. L. Scales & C. L. Streeter (Eds.), *Rural social work: Building and sustaining community assets* (pp. 34–42). Belmont, CA: Brooks/Cole.

Dallara, A. (2011). Research shows increase in hate crimes against LGBT people. Retrieved from http:// www.glaad.org/2011/07/14/ research-shows-increase-in-hatecrimes-against-lgbt-people/

Davis, L. E., Wallace, J. M., Jr., & Shanks, T. R. W. (2008). African Americans: Overview. In T. Mizrahi & L. E. Davis (Eds.), *Encyclopedia of social work* (Vol. 1, pp. 65–75). Washington, DC: NASW Press.

Day, P. (2009). *A new history of social welfare* (6th ed.). Boston: Allyn & Bacon.

Delgado, M. (2000). *Community social work practice in an urban context: The potential of a capacity -enhancement perspective*. New York: Oxford.

Delgado, M. (2007). *Social work with Latinos: A culture assets paradigm*. New York: Oxford.

DePoy, E., & Gilson, S. F. (2004). *Rethinking disability: Principles for professional and social change*. Belmont, CA: Brooks/Cole.

Dew, K., Scott, A., & Kirkman, A. (2016). *Social, Political and Cultural Dimensions of Health*. Switzerland: Springer.

DeYoung, K., & Miller, G. (2016). Key figures purged from Trump transition team. *Washington Post* (November 15, 2016). Retrieved from *https:// www.washingtonpost.com/...transition-team/.../ ed4e2a36-ab6b-11e6...*

Dhooper, S. S. (2012). *Social work in health care: Its past and future* (2nd ed.). Thousand Oaks, CA: Sage.

Dhooper, S. S., & Moore, S. E. (2001). *Social work practice with culturally diverse people*. Thousand Oaks, CA: Sage.

Diament, M. (2010). Obama signs bill replacing "mental retardation" with "intellectual disability." Retrieved from http://www.disabilityscoop .com/2010/10/05/obama-signsrosas-law/10547/

Diaz, M. L. (2010). A tale of two groups: Culturally sensitive group therapy for Latinos. In R. Furman & N. Negi (Eds.), *Social work practice with Latinos: Key issues and emerging themes* (pp. 247–261). Chicago: Lyceum.

Diller, J. V. (2015). *Cultural diversity: A primer for the human services* (5th ed.). Stamford, CT: Cengage Learning.

DiNitto, D. M. (2011). *Social welfare: Politics and public policy* (7th ed.). Boston: Allyn & Bacon.

DiNitto, D. M., & Johnson, D. H. (2012). *Essentials of social welfare: Politics and public policy*. Upper Saddle River, NJ: Pearson.

Doel, M., & Shardlow, S. (1996). Introduction to the context of practice learning: An overview of key themes. In M. Doel & S. Shardlow (Eds.), *Social work in a changing world: An international perspective on practice learning*. Brookfield, VT: Arena Ashgate.

Dolgoff, R. (2005). *An introduction to supervisory practice in human services*. Boston: Allyn & Bacon.

Dolgoff, R., & Feldstein, D. (2013). *Understanding social welfare: A search for social justice* (9th ed.). Upper Saddle River, NJ: Pearson.

Dolgoff, R., Loewenberg, F. M., & Harrington, D. (2012). *Ethical decisions in social work practice* (9th ed.). Belmont, CA: Brooks/ Cole.

Donald Trump/Immigration. (2016). Retrieved from https:// www.google.com/search?q=trump+on+immigration &ie=utf-8&oe=utf-8#eob=m.0cqt90//short

Downs, A. (1981). *Neighborhoods and urban development*. Washington, DC: The Brookings Institution.

Downs, S. W., Moore, E., & McFadden, E. J. (2009). *Child welfare and family services: Policies and practice* (8th ed.). Boston: Allyn & Bacon.

Draper, C., & Freedman, D. (2010, October–December). Review and analysis of the benefits, purposes, and motivations associated with community gardening in the United States. *Journal of Community Practice, 18*(4), 458–492.

Dubrin, A. (2007). *Fundamentals of organizational behavior* (4th ed.). Mason, OH: South-Western.

Dubrin, A. J. (2012). *Essentials of management* (9th ed.). Mason, OH: South-Western.

Dubrin, A. J. (2016). *Leadership: Research findings, practice, and skills* (8th ed.). Boston: Cengage Learning.

Dudley, J. R. (2016). *Spirituality matters in social work: Connecting spirituality, religion, and practice.* New York: Routledge.

Dufrene, D. D., & Lehman, C. M. (2011). *Building high-performance teams* (4th ed.). Mason, OH: South-Western.

Dumler, M. P., & Skinner, S. J. (2008). *A primer for management* (2nd ed.). Mason, OH: South-Western.

Durkheim, E. (1947). *Division of labor in society.* Glencoe, IL: Free Press.

Dworkin, S. H. (2000). Individual therapy with lesbian, gay, and bisexual clients. In R. M. Perez, K. A. DeBord, & K. J. Bieschke (Eds.), *Handbook of counseling and psychotherapy with lesbian, gay, and bisexual clients* (pp. 157–181). Washington, DC: American Psychological Association.

Earth Charter Initiative. (2011). *The Earth Charter.* Retrieved from http://www.earthcharterinaction.org/content/pages/Read-the-Charter.html#top

Egan, G. (2014). *The skilled helper: A problem-management and opportunity-development approach to helping* (9th ed.). Belmont, CA: Brooks/Cole.

Engelhardt, B. J. (1997). Group work with lesbians. In G. L. Greif & P. H. Ephross (Eds.), *Group work with populations at risk* (pp. 278–291). New York: Oxford University Press.

Ephross, P. H., & Vassil, T. V. (2004). Group work with working groups. In C. D. Garvin, L. M. Gutierrez, & M. J. Galinsky (Eds.), *Handbook of social work with groups* (pp. 400–414). New York: Guilford.

Erhlich, J. L., & Rivera, F. G. (1981). Community organization and community development. In N. Gilbert & H. Specht (Eds.), *Handbook of the social services* (pp. 472–489). Englewood Cliffs, NJ: Prentice Hall.

Etzioni, A. (1964). *Modern organizations.* Englewood Cliffs, NJ: Prentice-Hall.

Ewalt, P. L., & Mokuau, N. (1996). Self-determination from a Pacific perspective. In P. L. Ewalt, E. M. Freeman, A. E. Fortune, D. L. Poole, & S. L. Witkin (Eds.), *Multicultural issues in social work: Practice and research* (pp. 255–268). Washington, DC: NASW Press.

Farley, R. (2017). Fact check: Trump claims massive voter fraud; here's the truth. Retrieved from http://www.usatoday.com/story/news/politics/2017/01/26/fact-check-trumps-bogus-voter-fraud-claims-revisited/97080242/

Fellin, P. (2001a). *The community and the social worker* (3rd ed.). Belmont, CA: Brooks/Cole.

Fellin, P. (2001b). Understanding American communities. In J. Rothman, J. L. Erlich, & J. E. Tropman (Eds.), *Strategies of community organization* (3rd ed., pp. 118–132). Itasca, IL: F. E. Peacock.

Ferree, M. M. (2012). Globalization and feminism: Opportunities and obstacles for activism in the global arena. In D. S. Eitzen & M. B. Zinn (Eds.), *Globalization: The transformation of social worlds* (3rd ed., pp. 291–302). Belmont, CA: Wadsworth.

FindLaw. (2016). *Sexual Orientation Discrimination in the Workplace.* Retrieved from http://employment.findlaw.com/employment-discrimination/sexual-orientation-discrimination-in-the-workplace.html

Finn, J. L., & Jacobson, M. (2003). *Just practice: A social justice approach to social work.* Peosta, IA: Eddie Bowers.

Finn, J. L., & Jacobson. M. (2008). *Just practice: A social justice approach to social work* (2nd ed.). Chicago: Lyceum.

Fisher, R. (1984, Summer). Community organization in historical perspective: A typology. *The Huston Review*, 8.

Fisher, R., & Burghardt, S. (2008). Social advocacy: The persistence and prospects of social action. In J. Rothman, J. L. Erlich, & J. E. Tropman (Eds.), *Strategies of community intervention* (7th ed., pp. 315–332). Peosta, IA: Eddie Bowers.

Flewelling, R.L., & Hanley, S.M. (2016). Assessing community coalition capacity and its association with underage drinking prevention effectiveness in the context of the SPF SIG. *Prevention Science, 17*(7), 830–840.

Fottrell, Q. (2017). This is how much it costs Meals on Wheels to feed one elderly person for a year. *Market Watch* (March 18, 2017). Retrieved from http://www.marketwatch.com/story/this-is-how-much-it-costs-meals-on-wheels-to-feed-one-elderly-person-for-a-year-2017-03-16

Frame, M. W. (2003). *Integrating religion and spirituality into counseling: A comprehensive approach.* Belmont, CA: Brooks/Cole.

Friend, M. (2011). *Special education: Contemporary perspectives for school professionals* (3rd ed.). Upper Saddle River, NJ: Pearson.

Fry, R., & Kochhar, R. (2014). *America's wealth gap between middle-income and upper-income families is widest on record*. Pew Research Center. Retrieved from http://www.pewresearch.org/fact-tank/2014/12/17/wealth-gap-upper-middle-income/

Fukuyama, M. A., & Sevig, T. D. (1999). *Integrating spirituality into multicultural counseling*. Thousand Oaks, CA: Sage.

Furman, R., Negi, N. J., Iwamoto, D. K., Rowan, D., Shukraft, A., & Gragg, J. (2009). Social work practice with Latinos: Key issues for social workers. *Social work*, 54(2), 167–174.

Gallup. (2016). *Record-high 61% of Americans support same-sex marriages*. Retrieved from http://www.gallup.com/poll/191645/americans-support-gay-marriage-remains-high.aspx?g_source=gay+marriage&g_medium=search&g_campaign=tiles

Gamble, D. N., & Hoff, M. D. (2005). Sustainable community development. In M. Weil (Ed.), *The handbook of community practice* (pp. 169–188). Thousand Oaks, CA: Sage.

Gambrill, E. (2000). The role of critical thinking in evidence-based social work. In P. Allen-Meares & C. Garvin (Eds.), *The handbook of social work direct practice* (pp. 43–64). Thousand Oaks, CA: Sage.

Gambrill, E., & Gibbs, L. (2009). *Critical thinking for helping professionals: A skills-based workbook* (3rd ed.). New York: Oxford.

Gambrill, E. (2013). *Social Work Practice*. New York: Oxford.

Gardella, L. G., & Haynes, K. S. (2004). *A dream and a plan: A woman's path to leadership in human services*. Washington, DC: NASW Press.

Gardner, M., & Brooks-Gunn, J. (2009). Adolescents' exposure to community violence: Are neighborhood youth organizations protective? *Journal of Community Psychology*, 37(4), 505–525.

Garvin, C. D. (1987). Group theory and research. In T. Mizrahi & L. E. Davis (Eds.), *Encyclopedia of social work* (Vol. 1, pp. 683–696). Washington, DC: NASW Press.

Garvin, C. D., & Cox, F. M. (1995). A history of community organizing since the Civil War with special reference to oppressed communities. In J. Rothman, J. L. Erlich, & J. E. Tropman (Eds.), *Strategies of community intervention* (pp. 64–99). Itasca, IL: Peacock.

Gibelman, M., & Furman, R. (2013). *Navigating human service organizations* (3rd ed.). Chicago: Lyceum.

Ginsberg, L. (1995). Concepts of new management. In L. Ginsberg & P. R. Keys (Eds.), *New management in human services* (2nd ed., pp. 1–37). Washington, DC: NASW Press.

Ginsberg, L. H. (2005). Introduction: The overall context of rural practice. In L. H. Ginsberg (Ed.), *Social work in rural communities* (4th ed., pp. 1–14). Alexandria, VA: Council on Social Work Education.

Gitterman, A. (2014). *Handbook of social work practice with vulnerable and resilient populations*. New York: Columbia.

GlenMaye, L. (2003). Empowerment of women. In L. M. Gutierrez, R. J. Parsons, & E.O. Cox (Eds.), *Empowerment in social work practice: A sourcebook* (pp. 2–51). Mason, OH: Cengage.

Goldenberg, H., & Goldenberg, I. (2002). *Counseling today's families* (4th ed.). Belmont, CA: Brooks/ Cole.

Gotterer, R. (2001). The spiritual dimension in clinical social work practice: A client perspective. *Families in Society*, 82(2), 187–193.

Grandparents Raising Grandchildren of Massachusetts. (2017). *Greetings Grandparents and Relatives Raising Grandchildren*. Retrieved from http://www.massgrg.com/index.php

Green, J. W. (1999). *Cultural awareness in the human services: A multiethnic approach* (3rd ed.). Boston: Allyn & Bacon.

Griffin, R. W. (2016). *Fundamentals of management* (8th ed.). Boston: Cengage Learning.

Griffin, R. W., & Moorhead, G. (2014). *Organizational behavior: Managing people and organizations* (11th ed.). Mason, OH: South-Western.

Grimaldi, P. (2005). *Latino small business owners banking on unity for empowerment*. Providence Journal, September 4, 2005.

Grogan-Kaylor, A., Woolley, M., Mowbray, C., Reischl, T. M., Gilster, M., Karb, R., MacFarlane, P., … (2006). Predictors of neighborhood satisfaction. *Journal of community practice*, 14(4), 27–50.

Gryn, T. (2016). *The foreign-born by urban-rural status of counties: 2011–2015*. Retrieved from http://www.census.gov/newsroom/blogs/random-samplings/2016/12/the_foreign-bornby.html

Gruskin, E. P. (1999). *Treating lesbians and bisexual women: Challenges and strategies for health professionals*. Thousand Oaks, CA: Sage.

Gutheil, I. A., & Congress, E. (2002). Resiliency in older people: A paradigm for practice. In R. R. Green (Ed.), *Resiliency: An integrated approach to practice, policy, and research* (pp. 40–52). Washington, DC: NASW Press.

Gutierrez, L. M. (2001). Working with women of color: An empowerment perspective. In J. Rothman, J. L. Erlich,

& J. E. Tropman (Eds.), *Strategies of community intervention* (6th ed., pp. 209–217). Itasca, IL: Peacock.

Gutierrez, L. M., & Lewis, E. A. (1999). *Empowering women of color*. New York: Columbia.

Gwynne, S. C. (1998, March 9). Miracle in New Orleans. *Time*, 74.

Haag, M. (2017). Steve King says civilization can't be restored with somebody else's babies. *New York Times*, March 12, 2017. Retrieved from https://www.nytimes.com/2017/03/12/us/steve-king-white-nationalism-racism.html

Habitat for Humanity International. (2012). *Habitat for Humanity International mission statement and principles*. Retrieved from http://www.habitat.org/how/mission_statement.aspx

Haight, W. L. (1999). "Gathering the spirit" at First Baptist Church: Spirituality as a protective factor in the lives of African American children. In P. L. Ewalt, E. M. Freeman, A. E. Fortune, D. L. Poole, & S. L. Witkin (Eds.), *Multicultural issues in social work: Practice and research* (pp. 245–255). Washington, DC: NASW Press.

Hallahan, D. P., Kauffman, J. M., & Pullen, P. C. (2012). *Exceptional learners: An introduction to special education* (12th ed.). Upper Saddle River, NJ: Pearson.

Hannam, J. (2012). *Feminism*. Harlow, England: Pearson.

Halley, A. A., Kopp, J., & Austin, M. J. (1998). *Delivering human services: A learning approach to practice* (4th ed.). New York: Longman.

Hardcastle, D. A., with Powers, P. R., & Wenocur, S. (2011). *Community practice* (3rd ed.). New York: Oxford.

Hardina, D. (2004). Guidelines for ethical practice in community organization. *Social Work*, 29(4), 595–604.

Hartford Institute for Religion Research. (2017). *A quick question: How does faith exist in social services?* Retrieved from http://hirr.hartsem.edu/research/quick_question16.html

Hartwig, K. A., & Mason, M. (2016). Community gardens for refugee and immigrant communities as a means of health promotion. *Journal of community health*, 41(6), 1153–1159.

Harvey, A. R. (2011). Group work with African-American youth in the criminal justice system: A culturally competent model. In G. L. Grief & P. H. Ephross (Eds.), *Group work with populations at risk* (3rd ed., pp. 264–282). New York: Oxford.

Hasenfeld, Y. (2009). Human services administration and organizational theory. In R. J. Patti (Ed.), *The handbook of human services management* (2nd ed., pp. 53–80). Thousand Oaks, CA: Sage.

Hawdon, J., & Ryan, J. (2011). Neighborhood organizations and resident assistance to police. *Sociological forum*, 26(4), 897–920.

Hayashi, R. (2005). The environment of disability today: A nursing home is not a home. In G. E. May & M. B. Raske (Eds.), *Ending disability discrimination: Strategies for social workers* (pp. 45–70). Boston: Allyn & Bacon.

Haynes, K. S., & Mickelson, J. S. (2003). *Affecting change: Social workers in the political arena* (5th ed.). Boston: Allyn & Bacon.

Hayslip, Jr., B., & Garner, A. (2015). Social support and grandparent caregiver health: One-year longitudinal findings for grandparents raising their grandchildren. *Journals of Gerontology: Series B*, 70(5), 804–812.

Healy, K. (2005). *Social work theories in context: Creating frameworks for practice*. New York: Palgrave.

Healy, L. M. (2008). *International social work: Professional action in an interdependent world* (2nd ed.). New York: Oxford.

Heartland Alliance. (2017). *Immigrants—Fact sheet*. Retrieved from *www.heartlandalliance.org/GetInformed/Immigrants*

Helgeson, S., & Schneider, D. (2015). Authentic community-based youth engagement: Lessons from across the nation and through the lens of violence prevention. *National Civic Review*, 104(3), 16–23.

Hellriegel, D., & Slocum, J. W., Jr. (2011). *Organizational behavior* (13th ed.). Mason, OH: South-Western Cengage Learning.

Henderson, T. (2016). Here's where most immigrants are coming from (and it's not Mexico). *The Fiscal Times*. Retrieved from http://www.thefiscaltimes.com/2016/03/09/Heres-Where-Most-Immigrants-Are-Coming-and-Its-Not-Mexico

Henslin, J. M. (2011). *Social problems: A down-to-earth approach* (10th ed.). Boston: Allyn & Bacon.

Hepworth, D. H., Rooney, R. H., Rooney, G. D., & Strom-Gottfried, K. (2017). *Direct social work practice: Theory and skills* (10th ed.). Boston: Cengage Learning.

Herrell, R. K. (1992). The symbolic strategies of Chicago's gay and lesbian pride parade. In G. Herdt (Ed.), *Gay culture in America: Essays from the field* (pp. 225–252). Boston: Beacon Press.

Hill, C. W., & Jones, G. R. (2013). *Strategic management: An integrated approach* (10th ed.). Mason, OH: South-Western.

Hinton, M. (2017). Murals making a difference. *School Library Journal, 63*(2), (p. 12).

Ho, M. K., Rasheed, J. M., & Rasheed, M. N. (2004). *Family therapy with ethnic minorities* (2nd ed.). Thousand Oaks, CA: Sage.

Hodgson, P. (2015). Top CEOs make more than 300 times the average worker. *Fortune*, Retrieved from http://fortune.com/2015/06/22/ceo-vs-worker-pay/

Hoefer, R. (2006). *Advocacy practice for social justice.* Chicago: Lyceum.

Hogan, M. (2013). *Four skills of cultural diversity competence: A process for understanding and practice.* Belmont, CA: Brooks/ Cole.

Hokenstad, M. C., Healy, L.M., & Segal, U. A. (2013). *Teaching Human Rights.* Alexandria, VA: Council on Social Work Education.

Hokenstad, M. C., & Midgley, J. (1997). Realities of global interdependence: Challenges for social work in a new century. In M. C. Hokenstad & J. Midgley (Eds.), *Issues in international social work: Global challenges for a new century* (pp. 1–10). Washington, DC: NASW Press.

Homan, M. S. (2016). *Promoting community change: Making it happen in the real world* (6th ed.). Belmont, CA: Brooks/Cole.

Hugen, B. (2001). Spirituality and religion in social work practice: A conceptual model. In M. Van Hook, B. Hugen, & M. Aguilar (Eds.), *Spirituality within religious traditions in social work practice* (pp. 1–17). Belmont, CA: Brooks-Cole.

Human Rights Campaign. (2015). *Addressing Anti-Transgender Violence.* Retrieved from https://www.nytimes.com/interactive/2016/06/16/us/hate-crimes-against-lgbt.html?_r=0

Hunter, S., & Hickerson, J. C. (2003). *Affirmative practice: Understanding and working with lesbian, gay, bisexual, and transgender persons.* Washington, DC: NASW Press.

Institute on Community Integration. (2011). About developmental disabilities. Retrieved from http:// ici.umn.edu/welcome/definition.html

Institute on Taxation and Economic Policy. (2017). *Undocumented immigrants' state & local tax contributions.* Retrieved from http://www.itep.org/immigration/

International Association of Schools of Social Work (IASSW). (2017). Retrieved from https://www.iassw-aiets.org/about-iassw/

International Council on Social Welfare (ICSW). (2017a). *Home.* Retrieved from http://www.icsw.org/index.php

International Council on Social Welfare (ICSW). (2017b). *Our members.* Retrieved from http://www.icsw.org/index.php/members

International Council on Social Welfare (ICSW). (2017c). *What we do.* Retrieved from http://www.icsw.org/index.php/about-icsw/what-we-do

International Federation of Social Workers (IFSW). (2017). *What we do.* Retrieved from http://ifsw.org/what-we-do/

Ivey, A. E., & Ivey, M. B. (2016). *Essentials of intentional interviewing: Counseling in a multicultural world* (3rd ed.). Boston: Cengage Learning.

Ivey, A. E., Ivey, M. B., & Zalaquett, C. P. (2014). *International interviewing and counseling: Facilitating client development in a multicultural society* (7th ed.). Belmont, CA: Brooks/Cole.

Jacobs, E. E., Schimmel, C. J., Masson, R. L., & Harvill, R. L. (2016). *Group counseling: Strategies and skills* (8th ed.). Boston: Cengage Learning.

Jang, H., & Tang, F. (2016). Effects of social support and volunteering on depression among grandparents raising grandchildren. *International journal of aging and human development, 83*(4), 491–507.

Jansson, B. S. (2005). *The reluctant welfare state: American social welfare policies: past, present, and future* (5th ed.). Belmont, CA: Brooks/Cole.

Jansson, B. S. (2014). *Becoming an effective policy advocate: From policy practice to social justice* (7th ed.). Belmont, CA: Brooks/Cole.

Johnson, B. J., & Halegoua, G. R. (2015). Can social media save a neighborhood organization? *Planning, practice and research, 30*(3), 248–269.

Johnson, D. W., & Johnson, F. P. (2012). *Joining together: Group theory and group skills* (11th ed.). Essex, England: Pearson.

Johnson, L. C., & Yanca, S. J. (2010). *Social work practice: A generalist approach* (10th ed.). Upper Saddle River, NJ: Pearson.

Kadushin, A. (1968). Games people play in supervision. *Social work, 13*(3), 23–32.

Kadushin, A., & Harkness, D. (2014). *Supervision in social work* (5th ed.). New York: Columbia.

Karenga, M. (2000). Making the past meaningful: Kwanzaa and the concept of Sankofa. In S. L. Abels (Ed.), *Spirituality in social work practice: Narratives for professional helping* (pp. 51–67). Denver, CO: Love.

Karenga M. (2012). *Nguzo Saba: The seven principles.* Retrieved from http://www.officialkwanzaawebsite.org/NguzoSaba.shtml

Karger, H. J., & Stoesz, D. (2013). *American social welfare policy: A pluralist approach* (Brief edition). Boston: Allyn & Bacon.

Kaye, L. W. (2005). A social work practice perspective on productive aging. In L. W. Kaye (Ed.), *Perspectives on productive aging: Social work with the new aged*. Washington, DC: NASW Press.

Kendall, D. (2013). *Social problems in a diverse society* (6th ed.). Upper Saddle River, NJ: Pearson.

Kenyon, P. (1999). *What would you do? An ethical case workbook for human service professionals*. Belmont, CA: Brooks/Cole.

Kettner, P. M., Moroney, R. M., & Martin, L. L. (2017). *Designing and managing programs: An effectiveness-based approach* (5th ed.). Thousand Oaks, CA: Sage.

Kirk, G., & Okazawa-Rey, M. (2007). *Women's lives: Multicultural perspectives* (4th ed.). Boston: McGraw-Hill.

Kirk, G., & Okazawa-Rey, M. (2010). *Women's lives: Multicultural perspectives* (5th ed.). Boston: McGraw-Hill.

Kirk, G., & Okazawa-Rey, M. (2012). *Women's lives: Multicultural perspectives* (6th ed.). Boston: McGraw-Hill.

Kirst-Ashman, K. K. (2017). *Introduction to social work & social welfare* (5th ed.). Belmont, CA: Brooks/Cole.

Kirst-Ashman, K. K., & Hull, G. H., Jr. (2018a). *Generalist practice with organizations and communities* (7th ed.). Boston: Cengage Learning.

Kirst-Ashman, K. K., & Hull, G. H., Jr. (2018b). *Understanding generalist practice* (8th ed.). Boston: Cengage Learning.

Knopf, R. (1979). *Surviving the BS (bureaucratic system)*. Wilmington, NC: Mandala Press.

Krivickas, K. M., & Lofquist, D. (2011). *Demographics of same-sex couple households with children*. Retrieved from http://www.census.gov/hhes/samesex/files/Krivickas-Lofquist% 20PAA%202011.pdf

Kubisch, A. C., Auspos, P., Brown, P., Chaskin, R., Fullbright-Anderson, K., & Hamilton, R. (2008). Strengthening the connections between communities and external resources. In J. DeFilippis & S. Saegert (Eds.), *The community development reader* (pp. 319–326). New York: Routledge.

Lauffer, A. (2011). *Understanding your social agency* (3rd ed.). Thousand Oaks, CA: Sage.

Laughlin, L. (2016). *Beyond the farm: Rural industry workers in America*. Retrieved from http://www.census.gov/newsroom/blogs/random-samplings/2016/12/beyond_the_farm_rur.html

Lawrence, J. (2008). *"Community organizer" slams attract support for Obama*. Retrieved from http:// www.usatoday.com/news/politics/ election2008/2008-09-04-community_N.htm

Lee, C. C., & Armstrong, K. L. (1995). Indigenous models of mental health intervention: Lessons from traditional healers. In J. G. Ponterotto, J. M. Cases, L. A. Suzuki, & C. M. Alexander (Eds.), *Handbook of multicultural counseling* (pp. 441–456). Thousand Oaks, CA: Sage.

Lehman, C. M., & DuFrene, D. D. (2017). *BCOM* (9th ed.). Boston: Cengage Learning.

Leigh, J. W., & Green, J. W. (1982). The structure of the Black community: The knowledge base for social services. In J. W. Green (Ed.), *Cultural awareness in the human services* (pp. 106–107). Englewood Cliffs, NJ: Prentice Hall.

Leonard, E. C., Jr. (2010). *Supervision: Concepts and practices of management* (11th ed.). Mason, OH: South-Western.

Leonard, E. C., Jr., & Trusty, K.A. (2016). *Supervision: Concepts and practices of management* (13th ed.). Boston: Cengage Learning.

Leong, F. T. L., Lee, S. H., & Chang, D. (2008). Counseling Asian Americans. In P. B. Pedersen, J. G. Draguns, W. J. Lonner, & J. E. Trimble (Eds.), *Counseling across cultures* (6th ed., pp. 113–128). Thousand Oaks, CA: Sage.

Leon-Guerrero, A. (2011). *Social problems: Community, policy, and social action* (3rd ed.). Thousand Oaks, CA: Sage.

Levine, E. S., & Padilla, A. M. (1980). *Crossing cultures in therapy: Pluralistic counseling for the Hispanic*. Bellmont, DA: Wadworth.

Lewin, K. (1951). *Field theory in social science*. New York: Harper & Row.

Lewis, J. A., Lewis, M. D., Daniels, J. A., & D'Andrea, M. J. (2011). *Community counseling: A multicultural-social justice perspective* (4th ed.). Belmont, CA: Brooks/Cole.

Lewis, J. A., Packard, T. R., & Lewis, M. D. (2012). *Management of human service programs* (5th ed.). Belmont, CA: Brooks/Cole.

Line, C. M. (2005). Social work in a rural school district. In L. M. Grobman (Ed.), *Days in the lives of social workers: 54 professionals tell "real-life" stories from social work practice* (3rd ed., pp. 105–109). Harrisburg, PA: White Hat Communications.

Lohmann, R. A., & Lohmann, N. (2005). Introduction. In N. Lohmann & R. A. Lohmann (Eds.), *Rural social work practice* (pp. xi–xxvii). New York: Columbia.

Long, C. R., & Curry, M. A. (1998). Living in two worlds: Native American women and prenatal care. *Health Care for Women International, 19*(3), 205–215.

Longres, J. F. (2008). Diversity in community life. In J. Rothman, J. L. Erlich, & J. E. Tropman (Eds.), *Strategies of community intervention* (7th ed., pp. 77–106). Peosta, IA: Eddie Bowers.

Lorber, J. (2005). *Gender inequality: Feminist theories and politics* (3rd ed.). Los Angeles: Roxbury.

Lum, D. (2005). *Cultural competence, practice stages, and client systems: A case study approach*. Belmont, CA: Brooks/Cole.

Lum, D. (2011). *Culturally competent practice: A framework for understanding diverse groups and justice issues* (4th ed.). Belmont, CA: Brooks/Cole.

Lussier, R. N. (2012). *Management fundamentals: Concepts, applications, skill development* (5th ed.). Mason, OH: South-Western.

Lussier, R. N., & Achua, C. F. (2016). *Leadership: Theory, application, & skill development* (6th ed.). Boston: Cengage Learning.

Lynch, J. P. (2012). *Corrections in the United States*. Washington, DC: Retrieved from https://www.census.gov/newsroom/cspan/incarceration/20120504_incarceration_bjs-slides.pdf

Macionis, J. J. (2010). *Social problems* (4th ed.). Upper Saddle River, NJ: Prentice-Hall.

Mackelprang, R. W., & Salsgiver, R. O. (2009). *Disability: A diversity model approach in human service practice* (2nd ed.). Chicago: Lyceum.

Mackie, P. F., Zammitt, K., & Alvarez, M. (2016). *Practicing rural social work*. Chicago: Lyceum.

Magaña, S., & Ybarra, M. (2010). Family and community as strengths in the Latino community. In R. Furman & N. Negi (Eds.), *Social work practice with Latinos: Key issues and emerging themes* (pp. 69–84). Chicago: Lyceum.

Mann, W. M. (1997). Portraits of social services programs for rural sexual minorities. *Journal of Gay and Lesbian social Services, 7*(3), 95–103.

Mapp, S. C. (2014). *Human rights and social justice in a global perspective*. New York: Oxford University Press.

Martin, J. L. (2003, July). What is field theory? *The American Journal of Sociology, 109*(1), 1–50. Retrieved from http://infotrac.thomsonlearning.com

Mary, N. L. (2008). *Social work in a sustainable world*. Chicago: Lyceum.

Massat, C. R., Constable, R., McDonald, S., & Flynn, J. P. (2009). *School social work: Practice, policy and research* (7th ed.). Chicago: Lyceum.

Matthew Shepard Foundation. (2010). Our story. Retrieved from http:// www.matthewshepard.org/our-story

Mathie, A., & Cunninghan, G. (2008). From clients to citizens: Asset-based community development as a strategy for community-driven development. In J. Rothman, J. L. Erlich, & J. E. Tropman (Eds.), *Strategies of community intervention* (7th ed., pp. 282–298). Peosta, IA: Eddie Bowers.

May, G. E. (2005). Changing the future of disability: The disability discrimination model. In G. E. May & M. B. Raske (Eds.), *Ending disability discrimination: Strategies for social workers* (pp. 82–98). Boston: Allyn & Bacon.

Mayo Clinic. (2014). *Muscular dystrophy. Diseases and Conditions*. Retrieved from http://www.mayoclinic.org/diseases-conditions/muscular-dystrophy/basics/definition/con-20021240

McInnis-Dittrich, K. (2009). *Social work with elders: A biopsychosocial approach to assessment and intervention* (3rd ed.). Boston: Allyn & Bacon.

McKnight, J., & Block, P. (2010). *The abundant community: Awakening the power of families and neighborhoods*. San Francisco: Berrett-Koehler.

McLaughlin, L. A., & Braun, K. L. (1999). Asian and Pacific Islander cultural values: Considerations for health care decision-making. In P. L. Ewalt, E. M. Freeman, A. E. Fortune, D. L. Poole, & S. L. Witkin (Eds.), *Multicultural issues in social work: Practice and research* (pp. 321–336). Washington, DC: NASW Press.

McSpirit, S., Faltraco, L., & Bailey, C. (2012). *Confronting ecological crisis in Appalachia and the South: University and community partnerships*. Lexington, KY: University Press of Kentucky.

McWhirter, J. J., McWhirter, B. T., McWhirter, E. H., & McWhirter, R. J. (2013). *At Risk Youth*. Belmont, CA: Brooks/Cole.

Médecins Sans Frontières (MSF)/ Doctors Without Borders. (2016). *International Activity Report 2015* (2nd ed.). Retrieved from http://www.msf.org/en/article/msf-international-activity-report-2015

Médecins Sans Frontières (MSF)/ Doctors Without Borders. (2017). *MSF History*. Retrieved from http://www.msf.org/en/msf-history

Medicaid.gov. (2017). *Managed Care*. Retrieved from https://www.medicaid.gov/medicaid/managed-care/index.html

Medline Plus. (2017). *Managed care*. Retrieved from https://medlineplus.gov/managedcare.html

Megivern, D. M., McMillen, J. C., Proctor, E., Striley, C. L., Cabassa, L. J., & Munson, M. R. (2007). Quality of care: Expanding the social work dialogue. *Social Work, 52*(2), 115–124.

Mercer, S. O. (1996, March). Navajo elderly people in a reservation nursing home: Admission predictors and culture care practices. *Social work, 41*(2), 181–189.

Merritt, C. D., & Collins, T. (2008). The place of rural community development in urban society. In J. DeFilippis & S. Saegert (Eds.), *The community development reader* (pp. 148–156). New York: Routledge.

Merton, R. K. (1968). *Social theory and social structure* (enlarged ed.). New York: Free Press.

Messinger, L. (2004). Comprehensive community initiatives: A rural perspective. *Social work, 49*(4), 535–546.

Messinger, L. (2006). Social welfare policy and advocacy. In D. F. Morrow & L. Messinger (Eds.), *Sexual orientation & gender expression in social work practice: Working with gay, lesbian, bisexual, & transgender people* (pp. 427–459). New York: Columbia University Press.

Midgley, J., & Livermore, M. (2004). Social development: Lessons from the global south. In M. C. Hokenstad & J. Midgley (Eds.), *Lessons from abroad: Adapting international social welfare innovations* (pp. 117–135). Washington, DC: NASW Press.

Midgley, J., & Sherraden, M. (2009). The social development perspective in social policy. In J. Midgley & M. Livermore (Eds.), *The handbook of social policy* (2nd ed., pp. 279–294). Thousand Oaks, CA: Sage.

Miller, J., & Garran, A. M. (2008). *Racism in the United States: Implications for the helping professions.* Belmont, CA: Brooks/ Cole.

Milligan, S. E. (2008). Community building. In T. Mizrahi & L. E. Davis (Eds.), *Encyclopedia of social work* (Vol. 1, pp. 371–375). Washington, DC: NASW Press.

Miltenberger, R. G. (2015). *Behavior modification: Principles & procedures* (6th ed.). Boston: Cengage.

Migration Policy Institute. (2017). *Frequently requested statistics on immigrants and immigration in the United States.* Author. Retrieved from http://www.migrationpolicy.org/article/frequently-requested-statistics-immigrants-and-immigration-united-states

Moberg, D. (2007, April 27). *Obama's community roots.* Retrieved from http://www.thenation.com/doc/20070416/moberg/

Money, J. (1987). Sin, sickness, or status: Homosexual gender identity and psychoneuroendocrinology. *American psychologist, 42,* 384–394.

Mooney, L. A., Knox, D., & Schacht, C. (2017). *Understanding social problems* (9th ed.). Stamford, CT: Cengage Learning.

Morrow, D. F. (2006). Sexual orientation and gender identity expression. In D. F. Morrow & L. Messinger (Eds.), *Sexual orientation & gender expression in social work practice: Working with gay, lesbian, bisexual, & transgender people* (pp. 3–17). New York: Columbia University Press.

Murphy, B. C., & Dillon, C. (2015). *Interviewing in action in a multicultural world* (5th ed.), Stamford, CT: Cengage Learning.

Murphy, Y., Hunt, V., Zajicek, A. M., Norris, A. N., & Hamilton, L. (2009). *Incorporating intersectionality in social work practice, research, policy, and education.* Washington, DC: NASW Press.

Murray, S. (1992). Components of gay community in San Francisco. In G. Herdt (Ed.), *Gay culture in America* (pp. 107–146). Boston: Beacon Press.

Myers, M. (2015). Three trends affecting managed care. *Managed Healthcare Executive.* Retrieved from http://managedhealthcareexecutive.modernmedicine.com/managed-healthcare-executive/news/three-trends-affecting-managed-care

Napholz, L. (2000). Balancing multiple roles among a group of urban midlife American Indian working women. *Health Care for Women International, 21*(4), 255–266.

National Association of Social Workers. (2008). *NASW code of ethics.* Washington, DC: Author.

National Association of Social Workers. (2012). *Social work speaks: National Association of Social Workers policy statements 2012–2014.* Washington, DC: NASW Press.

NASW Center for Workplace Studies & Social Work Practice. (2011). *Social work salaries by gender: Occupational profile.* Retrieved from http://workforce.socialworkers.org/studies/profiles/ Gender.pdf

National Institute of Child Health and Human Development (NICHD). (2017). *About Autism.* Retrieved from https://www.nichd.nih.gov/health/topics/autism/conditioninfo/Pages/default.aspx

National Institute of Mental Health. (2017). *Post-Traumatic Stress Disorder.* Retrieved from https://www.nimh.nih.gov/health/topics/post-traumatic-stress-disorder-ptsd/index.shtml

Negroni-Rodriguez, L. K., & Morales, J. (2001). Individual and family assessment skills with Latino/Hispanic Americans. In R. Fong & S. Furuto (Eds.), *Culturally competent practice: Skills, interventions, and evaluations* (pp. 132–146). Boston: Allyn & Bacon.

Neighborhood House of Milwaukee, Inc. (2017a). *Mission and vision statements.* Retrieved from https://www.neighborhoodhousemke.org/about/annual-report/

Neighborhood House of Milwaukee, Inc. (2017b). *Outdoor/environmental education.* Retrieved from https://www.neighborhoodhousemke.org/programs/nature-programs/

Nelson, D. L., & Quick, J. C. (2015). *ORGB4* (4th ed.). Stamford, CT: Cengage Learning.

Netting, F. E., Kettner, P. M., McMurtry, S. L., & Thomas, M. L. (2012). *Social work macro practice* (5th ed.). Boston: Pearson.

Netting, F. E., Kettner, P. M., McMurtry, S. L., & Thomas, M. L. (2017). *Social work macro practice* (6th ed.). Boston: Pearson.

Neuliep, J. W. (2015). *Intercultural communication: A contextual approach* (6th ed.). Thousand Oaks, CA: Sage.

Norman, E. (2000). Introduction: The strengths perspective and resilience enhancement—A natural partnership. In E. Norman (Ed.), *Resiliency enhancement: Putting the strengths perspective into social work practice* (pp. 1–16). New York: Columbia.

Norton, A. R., & Abbot, M. J. (2016). The efficacy of imagery rescripting compared to cognitive restructuring for social anxiety. *Journal of Anxiety Disorders, 40,* 18–28.

Northouse, P. G. (2016). Leadership: *Theory and practice* (7th ed.). Thousand Oaks, CA: Sage.

Northouse, P. G. (2015a). *Introduction to leadership: Concepts and practice* (2nd ed.). Thousand Oaks, CA: Sage.

Northouse, P. G. (2015b). *Leadership: Theory and practice* (6th ed.). Thousand Oaks, CA: Sage.

Obama, B. (1990). Why organize? Problems and promise in the inner city. *Illinois Issues.* Retrieved from http://www.edwoj.com/Alinsky/AlinskyObamaChapter1990.htm

Obasi, C. (2008). Seeing the Deaf in "Deafness." *Journal of deaf studies and deaf education, 13,* 140–147.

O'Connor, M. K., & Netting, F. E. (2009). *Organization practice: A guide to understanding human service organizations* (2nd ed.). Hoboken, NJ: Wiley.

Ohio Office for Children and Families. (2013). *Ohio Child and Family Services Review Program Improvement Plan.* Columbus, Ohio: Author.

Ohmer, M. L., Meadowcroft, P., Freed, K., & Lewis, E. (2009, October–December). Community gardening and community development: Individual, social and community benefits of a community conservation program. *Journal of community practice, 17*(4), 377–399.

Oxfam. (2017). *Oxfam.* Retrieved from https://www.oxfamamerica.org/explore/about-oxfam/careers/available-positions/?p=jobs

Paniagua, F. A. (2014). *Assessing and treating culturally diverse clients: A practical guide* (4th ed.). Thousand Oaks, CA: Sage.

Papalia, D. E., Olds, S. W., & Feldman, R. D. (2009). *Human development* (11th ed.). New York: McGraw-Hill.

Park, H., & Mykhyalyshyn, I. (2016). L.G.B.T. people are more likely to be targets of hate crimes than any other minority group. *New York Times, June 16, 2016.*

Parsons, R. J. (2008). Empowerment practice. In T. Mizrahi & L. E. Davis (Eds.), *Encyclopedia of social work* (Vol. 2, pp. 123–126). Washington, DC: NASW Press.

Parsons, T. (1951). *The social system.* New York: Free Press.

Patient Advocate Foundation. (2017). *Glossary of managed care definitions.* Retrieved from http://www.patientadvocate.org/index.php?p=384

Payne, M. (2014). *Modern social work theory* (4th ed.). Chicago: Lyceum.

Payne, M. (2012). *Citizenship social work with older people.* Chicago: Lyceum.

Perez-Koenig, R. (2000). The Unitas extended family circle: Developing resiliency in Hispanic youngsters. In E. Norman (Ed.), *Resiliency enhancement: Putting the strengths perspective into social work practice* (pp. 143–153). New York: Columbia.

Petrocelli, A. M. (2012). *Prejudice to pride: Moving from homophobia to acceptance.* Washington, DC: NASW Press.

Pew Hispanic Center. (2012). When labels don't fit: Hispanics and their views of identity. Retrieved from http://www.pewhispanic.org/2012/04/04/when-labels-dont-fithispanics-and-their-views-ofidentity/

Pfeiffer, D. (2005). The conceptualization of disability. In G. E. May & M. B. Raske (Eds.), *Ending disability discrimination: Strategies for social workers* (pp. 25–44). Boston: Allyn & Bacon.

Phillips, J. M., & Gully, S. M. (2014). *Organizational behavior: Tools for success* (2nd ed.). Mason, OH: South-Western.

Phillips, N. K., & Straussner, S. L. A. (2002). *Urban social work: An introduction to policy and practice in the cities.* Boston: Allyn & Bacon.

Pincus, A., & Minahan, A. (1973). *Social work practice: Model and method.* Itasca, IL: Peacock.

Pittenger, S. L., Huit, T. Z., & Hansen, D. J. (2016). Applying ecological systems theory to sexual revictimization of youth: A review with implications for research and practice. *Aggression & Violent Behavior, 26,* 35–45.

Pizer, J., Mallory, C., Sears, B., & Hunter, N. (2012). Evidence of persistent and pervasive workplace discrimination against LGBT people: The need for federal legislation prohibiting discrimination and providing for equal employment benefits. *Loyola Law Review, 45*(3), 715–780.

Poole, D. L. (2005). Rural community-building strategies. In N. Lohmnann & R. A. Lohmann (Eds.), *Rural social work practice* (pp. 124–143). New York: Columbia.

Poole, D. L., & More, S. (2004). The use of asset-based community development to increase rural youth participation in higher education. In T. L. Scales & C. L. Streeter (Eds.), *Rural social work: Building and sustaining community assets* (pp. 147–159). Belmont, CA: Brooks/Cole.

Pope, C. (2011). *No, BP won't make it right.* Retrieved from http://www.huffingtonpost.com/carl-pope/nobp-wont-make-it-right_b_828245.html

Potocky-Tripodi. M. (2002). *Best practices for social work with refugees & immigrants.* New York: Columbia.

Poulin, J. (2010). *Strengths-based generalist practice: A collaborative approach* (3rd ed.). Belmont, CA: Brooks/Cole.

Powell, G. N., & Graves, L. M. (2003). *Women and men in management* (3rd ed.). Thousand Oaks, CA: Sage.

Powell, G. N. (2011). *Women and men in management* (4th ed.). Thousand Oaks, CA: Sage

Price, J. (2016). Informed shared decision-making in planning for the end of life. *British Journal of Nursing. 25*(7), 378–383.

Provence, M. M., Rochlen, A. B., Chester, M. R., & Smith, E. R. (2014). "just one of the boys": A qualitative study of gay men's experiences in mixed sexual orientation men's groups. *Psychology of men and masculinity, 15*(4), 427–436.

Puglia, B., & House, R. M. (2006). Group work: Gay, lesbian, and bisexual clients. In D. Capuzi, D. R. Gross, & M. D. Stauffer (Eds.), *Introduction to group work* (4th ed., pp. 515–547). Denver: Love.

Quinn, R. (2016). WVSU seeking to help more grandfamilies. (*Charleston Gazette, 12/19/2016*). Retrieved from http://www.wvgazettemail.com/news-education/20161218/wvsu-seeking-to-help-more-grandfamilies

Race, P. R. (2008, January). Evidence-based practice moves ahead. *NASW News,* 4.

Raske, M. (2005). The disability discrimination model in social work practice. In G. E. May & M. B. Raske (Eds.), *Ending disability discrimination: Strategies for social workers* (pp. 99–112). Boston: Allyn & Bacon.

Reichert, E. (2006). *Understanding human rights: An exercise book.* Thousand Oaks, CA: Sage.

Reiman, J., & Leighton, P. (2010). *The rich get richer and the poor get prison* (9th ed.). Boston: Allyn & Bacon.

Reina, A. S., Lohman, B. J., & Maldonado, M. M. (2014). "He said they'd deport me": Factors influencing domestic violence help seeking practices among Latina immigrants. *Journal of Interpersonal Violence, 29,* 593–615.

Renuka, R. (2007). Immigrants: The unsung heroes of the U.S. Economy. *U.S. News & World Report, 142*(7).

Rhynes, L., Hayslip, B., Caballero, D., & Ingman, S. (2013). The beneficial effects of senior center attendance on grandparents raising grandchildren. *Journal of Intergenerational Relationships, 11,* 162–175.

Rhynes, L., & Ingman, S. (2013). The beneficial effects of senior center attendance on grandparents raising grandchildren. *Journal of Intergenerational Relationships, 11*(2), 162–175.

Ridings, A., & Cohan, E. (2016). Helping state and local officials advocate for LGBT communities. *American Progress.* Retrieved from https://www.americanprogress.org/issues/lgbt/news/2016/06/08/138830/helping-state-and-local-officials-advocate-for-lgbt-communities/

Rivera, F. G., & Erlich, J. L. (2001). Organizing with people of color. In J. Rothman, J. L. Erlich, & J. E. Tropman (Eds.), *Strategies of community intervention* (pp. 254–269). Itasca, IL: Peacock.

Rivera, G. (2010). Art as a source of strength in the Latino community. In R. Furman & N. Negi (Eds.), *Social work practice with Latinos: Key issues and emerging themes* (pp. 102–126). Chicago: Lyceum.

Robert, H. M. (2016). *Robert's Rules of Order.* Carlisle, MA: Applewood Books.

Robbins, S. P., Chatterjee, P., & Canda, E. R. (2012). *Contemporary human behavior theory: A critical perspective for social work* (3rd ed.). Boston: Allyn & Bacon.

Rosenberg, T. (2000, October 26). Looking at poverty, seeing untapped riches. *New York Times,* p. A34.

Rosenthal, M. J. (2012). *Maryland gay marriage law: New poll shows voters narrowly favor repeal.* Retrieved from http://www.huffingtonpost.com/2012/03/28/ maryland-voters-favor-gaymarriage-repeal_n_1385685.html

Rosenthal, M. S. (2013). *Human sexuality: From cells to society.* Belmont, CA: Wadsworth.

Rothman, J. (2001). Approaches to community intervention. In J. Rothman, J. L. Erlich, & J. E. Tropman (Eds.), *Strategies of community intervention* (pp. 27– 64). Itasca, IL: Peacock.

Rothman, J. (2007). Multi modes of intervention at the macro level. *Journal of community practice*, *15*(4), 11–40.

Rothman, J. (2008). Multi modes of community intervention. In J. Rothman, J. L. Erlich, & J. E. Tropman (Eds.), *Strategies of community intervention* (7th ed., pp. 141–170). Peosta, IA: Eddie Bowers.

Rothman, J. C. (2003). *Social work practice across disability*. Boston: Allyn & Bacon.

Rowe, W., Hanley, J., Moreno, E. R., & Mould, J. (2000). Voices of social work practice: International reflections on the effects of globalization. *Canadian social work*, *2*(1), 65–87.

Rubin, A. (2008). *Practitioner's guide to using research for evidence-based practice*. Hoboken, NJ: Wiley.

Rubin, H. J., & Rubin, I. S. (2008). *Community organizing and development* (4th ed.). Boston: Allyn & Bacon.

Rural Health Information Hub (RHIhub). (2017). Human services to support rural health. Retrieved from https://www.ruralhealthinfo.org/topics/rural-human-services

Ruscio, J. (2006). *Critical thinking in psychology* (2nd ed.). Belmont, CA: Wadsworth.

Sacco, T. (1996). Towards an inclusive paradigm for social work. In M. Doel & S. Shardlow (Eds.), *Social work in a changing world: An international perspective on practice learning*. Brookfield, VT: Arena Ashgate.

Saleebey, D. (2006). *The strengths perspective in social work practice* (3rd ed.). Boston: Allyn & Bacon.

Saleebey, D. (2013). *The strengths perspective in social work practice* (6th ed.). Boston: Allyn & Bacon.

Sanchez, T. W., & Jones, S. (2010). The diversity and commonalities of Latinos in the United States. In R. Furman & N. Negi (Eds.), *Social work practice with Latinos: Key issues and emerging themes* (pp. 31–44). Chicago: Lyceum.

Santiago-Rivera, A. L., Arredondo, P., & Gallardo-Cooper, M. (2002). *Counseling Latinos and la familia: A practical guide*. Thousand Oaks, CA: Sage.

Saulnier, C. F. (1997). Alcohol problems and marginalization: Social group work with lesbians. *Social Work with Groups*, *20*, 37–59.

Schmid, H. (2009). Agency-environment relations. In R. J. Patti (Ed.), *The handbook of human services management* (2nd ed., pp. 411–433). Thousand Oaks, CA: Sage.

Schriver, J. M. (2011). *Human behavior and the social environment: Shifting paradigms in essential knowledge for social work practice* (5th ed.). Boston: Allyn & Bacon.

Scott, G., Keckley, P., & Copeland, B. (2013). *The future of health care insurance: What's ahead?* Deloitte University Press. Retrieved from https://dupress.deloitte.com/dup-us-en/deloitte-review/issue-13/the-future-of-health-care-insurance-whats-ahead.html

Segal, E. A. (2013). *Social welfare policy and social programs: A values perspective* (3rd ed.). Belmont, CA: Brooks/Cole.

Senge, P. (2006). *The fifth discipline: The art and practice of learning organizations*. New York: Doubleday/Currency.

Serrata, J. V., Hernandez-Martinez, M., & Macias, R.L. (2016). Self-empowerment of immigrant Latina survivors of domestic violence: A Promotora model of community leadership. *Hispanic Health Care International*, *14*(1), 37–46.

Shaw, S. M., & Lee, J. (2012). *Women's voices/Feminist visions: Classic and contemporary readings* (5th ed.). New York: McGraw-Hill.

Sheafor, B. W., & Horejsi, C. J. (2012). *Techniques and guidelines for social work practice* (9th ed.). Boston: Allyn & Bacon.

Sheafor, B. W., & Horejsi, C. J. (2015). *Techniques and guidelines for social work practice* (10th ed.). Boston: Allyn & Bacon.

Shobe, M., & Coffman, M. J. (2010). Barriers to health care utilization among Latinos in the United States. In R. Furman & N. Negi (Eds.), *Social work practice with Latinos: Key issues and emerging themes* (pp. 127–144). Chicago: Lyceum.

Shorkey, C., Garcia, E., & Windsor, L. (2010). Spirituality as a strength in the Latino community. In R. Furman & N. Negi (Eds.), *Social work practice with Latinos: Key issues and emerging themes* (pp. 85–101). Chicago: Lyceum.

Siegel, L. M., Attkisson, C. C., & Carson, L. G. (2001). Need identification and program planning in the community context. In J. E. Tropman, J. L. Erlich, & J. Rothman (Eds.), *Tactics & techniques of community intervention* (4th ed., pp. 105–129). Itasca, IL: F. E. Peacock.

Skelton, R., & Miller, V. (2016). *The Environmental Justice Movement*. NDRC. Retrieved from https://www.nrdc.org/stories/environmental-justice-movement

Slattery, J. M. (2004). *Counseling diverse clients: Bringing context into therapy*. Belmont, CA: Brooks/Cole.

Smith, D. P. (2005). The sweat lodge as psychotherapy. In R. Moodley & W. West (Eds.), *Integrating traditional healing practices into counseling and psychotherapy* (pp. 196–209). Thousand Oaks, CA: Sage.

Soifer, S. (2002). Principles and practices of community economic development. In A. R. Roberts &

G. J. Greene (Eds.), *Social workers' desk reference* (pp. 557–562).

Solomon, B. B. (2002). Social work practice with African Americans. In A. R. Morales & B. W. Sheafor (Eds.), *The many faces of social work clients* (pp. 295–315). Boston: Allyn & Bacon.

Sowers, K. M., & Rowe, W. S. (2007). *Social work practice & social justice: From local to global perspectives.* Belmont, CA: Brooks/ Cole.

Southern Poverty Law Center (SPLC). (2017). *Hate Map.* Retrieved from https://www.splcenter.org /hate-map

Squires, D. A. (2012). Explaining high health care spending in the United States: An international comparison of supply, utilization, prices and quality. *Issues in International Health Policy.* Retrieved at www.commonwealthfund.org.

Staples, L. H. (2004). Social action groups. In C. D. Garvin, L. M. Gutierrez, & M. J. Galinsky (Eds.), *Handbook of social work with groups* (pp. 344–359). New York: Guilford.

Stauffer, M. D., Pehrsson, D. E., & Briggs, C. A. (2010). Groups in mental health settings. In D. Capuzi, D. R. Gross, & M. D. Stauffer (Eds.), *Introduction to group work* (5th ed., pp. 373–404). Denver: Love.

Steinberg, A., & Almeida, C. (2015). Opening the door: How community organizations address the youth unemployment crisis. *Jobs for the Future.* June, pp. 1–30.

Stone, L. (2014). *Kinship and Gender.* Boulder, CO: Westview Press.

Sue, D. W., Rasheed, M. N., & Rasheed, J. M. (2016). *Multicultural social work practice.* Hoboken, NJ: Wiley.

Sue, D. W., & Sue, D. (2016). *Counseling the culturally diverse: Theory and practice* (7th ed.). Hoboken, NJ: Wiley.

Summers, N. (2009). *Fundamentals of case management practice: Skills for the human services* (3rd ed.). Belmont, CA: Brooks/Cole.

Swinomish Tribal Mental Health Project. (2002). *A gathering of wisdoms, tribal mental health: A cultural perspective.* LaConner, WA: Swinomish Tribal Community.

Sundel, M., & Sundel, S. S. (2005). *Behavior change in the human services: Behavioral and cognitive principles and applications* (5th ed.). Thousand Oaks, CA: Sage.

Tangenberg, K. M. (2005). Faith-based human services initiatives: Considerations for social work practice and theory. *Social Work,* 50 (3), 197–206.

Tate, C. (2012, June 11). *Federal ban on job bias still eludes gay rights groups.* Retrieved from http://www .kansascity .com/2012/06/11/3652764/federal-ban -on-job-bias-still.html

Toseland, R. W., & Rivas, R. F. (2008). Task groups: Specialized methods. In J. Rothman, J. L. Erlich, & J. E. Tropman (Eds.), *Strategies of community intervention* (7th ed., pp. 27–60). Peosta, IA: Eddie Bowers.

Toseland, R. W., & Rivas, R. F. (2012). *An introduction to group work practice* (7th ed.). Boston: Allyn & Bacon.

Toseland, R. W., & Rivas, R. F. (2017). *An introduction to group work practice* (8th ed.). Boston: Pearson.

Tracy, E. M. (2002). Working with and strengthening social networks. In A. R. Roberts & G. J. Greene (Eds.), *Social workers' desk reference* (pp. 402–405). New York: Oxford.

Tropman, J. (2008). Phases of helping. In J. Rothman, J. L. Erlich, & J. E. Tropman (Eds.), *Strategies of community intervention* (7th ed., pp. 127–140). Peosta, IA: Eddie Bowers.

Tucker, C. M., Daly, K. D., & Herman, K. C. (2010). Customized multicultural health counseling: Bridging the gap between mental and physical health for racial and ethnic minorities. In J. G. Ponterotto, J. M. Casas, L. A. Suzuki, & C. M. Alexander (Eds.), *Handbook of multicultural counseling* (3rd ed., pp. 505–513). Thousand Oaks, CA: Sage.

Tully, C.T. (2001). *Lesbians, gays, and the empowerment perspective.* New York: Columbia University Press.

Turner, G. (2001, Winter). The puzzling world of international social work careers. *The new social worker,* 4–7.

Unitas Therapeutic Community. (2016). *Serving children and families in the South Bronx for four decades.* Retrieved from http://www.unitastc.com/documents /UnitasBrochure2007.pdf

United Nations (UN). (1948). *Universal declaration of human rights.* Adopted December 10, 1948. GA Res. 217 AIII (Un Doc. A/810). Retrieved from http:// www.un.org/ Overview/rights.html

United Nations Development Programme (UNDP). (2011). *Multidimensional poverty index (MPI).* Retrieved from http://hdr .undp.org/en/statistics/mpi/

Unze, D. (2011). Facebook helps spark movements. Retrieved from http:// www.usatoday.com/news/nation /2010-03-25-facebook_N.htm

US Bureau of Labor Statistics. (2017). Highlights of women's earning in 2016. Retrieved from https://www .bls.gov/opub/ted/2017/womens-median-earnings -82-percent-of-mens-in-2016.htm

US Census Bureau. (2009). Profile America facts for features: Grandparents' day 2009. Retrieved from http://www.census.gov/ newsroom/releases/archives/facts_for_features_special_editions/ cb09-ff16.html

US Census Bureau. (2012). *The American Indian and Alaska Native Population: 2010*. Retrieved from http://www.census.gov/search-results.html?q=indian+reservations&page=1&stateGeo=none&searchtype=web

US Census Bureau. (2013). *Metropolitan and Micropolitan statistical areas of the United States and Puerto Rico*. Retrieved from http://www.census.gov/population/metro/data/maps.html

US Census Bureau. (2017a). *Metropolitan and Micropolitan Statistical Areas Main*. Retrieved from http://www.census.gov/population/metro/

US Census Bureau. (2017b). *Working veterans*. Retrieved from https://www.census.gov/library/visualizations/2017/comm/cb17-15_veterans.html

US Census Bureau. (2016a). *Black (African-American) History Month: February 2016*. Retrieved from https://www.census.gov/newsroom/facts-for-features/2016/cb16-ff01.html

US Census Bureau. (2016b). *New census data show differences between urban and rural populations*. Retrieved from http://www.census.gov/newsroom/press-releases/2016/cb16-210.html

US Census Bureau. (2016c). *Income and poverty in the United States: 2015*. Washington, DC: US Government Printing Office.

US Census Bureau. (2016d). *Grandparents living with children*. Retrieved from https://www.census.gov/content/census/en/library/visualizations/2016/comm/cb16-ff17_grandparents/jcr:content/map.detailitem.600.medium.jpg/1473457700919.jpg

US Census Bureau. (2016e). *FFF: Hispanic Heritage Month, 2016*. Retrieved from https://www.census.gov/newsroom/facts-for-features/2016/cb16-ff16.html

US Census Bureau. (2015a). *Quick facts United States*. Retrieved from https://www.census.gov/quickfacts/table/PST045216/00

US Census Bureau. (2015b). Hispanic or Latino origin by specific region. *2011–2015 American community survey*. Washington DC: Author.

US Census Bureau. (2015c). State and County Estimates for 2015. *Small Area Income and Poverty Estimates*. Retrieved from https://www.census.gov/did/www/saipe/data/statecounty/data/2015.html

US Department of Justice. (2009). *Americans with Disabilities Act of 2009 as amended*. Retrieved from https://www.ada.gov/pubs/adastatute08.htm?txtlnkusaolp00000619#12101note

US Department of Justice. (2017). *A guide to disability rights laws*. Retrieved from https://www.ada.gov/cguide.htm#anchor62335

US Department of Labor. (2016). *Earnings*. Retrieved from https://www.dol.gov/wb/stats/earnings_2014.htm#Ratios

US Department of Labor. (2015a). *Hispanic women in the labor force*. Washington, DC: US Government Printing Office.

US Department of Labor. (2015b). Women of Working Age. Retrieved from https://www.dol.gov/wb/stats/latest_annual_data.htm#labor

US Department of Labor. (2017). *Americans with Disability Act*. Retrieved from https://www.dol.gov/general/topic/disability/ada

United Way. (2017). *United Way Worldwide*. Retrieved from https://www.unitedway.org/

Urban Institute. (2012). *Facilitating postsecondary education and training for TANF recipients*. Retrieved from https://www.acf.hhs.gov/opre/resource/facilitating-postsecondary-education-and-training-for-tanf-recipients

van Soest, D., & Garcia, B. (2003). *Diversity education for social justice: Mastering teaching skills*. Alexandria, VA: Council on Social Work Education.

van Wormer, K. (2006). *Introduction to social welfare and social work: The U.S. in global perspective*. Belmont, CA: Brooks/Cole.

van Wormer, K., Well, J., & Boes, M. (2000). *Social work with lesbians, gays, and bisexuals: A strengths perspective*. Boston: Allyn & Bacon.

Vecchio, R. P. (2006). *Organizational behavior* (6th ed.). Mason, OH: South-Western.

Verschelden, C. (1993). Social work values and pacifism: Opposition to war as a professional responsibility. *Social Work, 38*(6), 765–769.

Vietnam-culture.com. (2017). *Vietnamese cultural values*. Retrieved from http://www.vietnam-culture.com/articles-57-6/Social-relationships.aspx

Walsh, J. (2013). *Theories for direct social work practice* (3rd ed.). Stamford, CT: Cengage Learning.

Walsh, K. T. (2007, August 26). *On the streets of Chicago, a candidate comes of age*. Retrieved from http:// www.usnews.com/usnews/news/ articles/070826/3obama_print.htm

Warren, E. (1977). The functional diversity of urban neighborhood. *Urban Affairs Quarterly, 13*(2), 151–179.

Warren, R. (1983). A community model. In R. M. Kramer & H. Specht (Eds.), *Readings in community organization practice* (pp. 28–36). Englewood Cliffs, NJ: Prentice-Hall.

Warren, R., & Warren, D. I. (1977). *The neighborhood organizers handbook*. South Bend: University of Notre Dame Press.

Watkins, T. R. (2004). Natural helping networks: Assets for rural communities. In T. L. Scales & C. L.

Streeter (Eds.), *Rural social work: Building and sustaining community assets* (pp. 65–76). Belmont, CA: Brooks/Cole.

Weaver, H. N. (2005). *Explorations in cultural competence: Journeys to the four directions*. Belmont, CA: Brooks/Cole.

Weinbach, R. W., & Taylor, L. M. (2015). *The social worker as manager: A practical guide to success* (7th ed.). Boston: Allyn & Bacon.

Weisbrot, M., Lefebvre, S., & Sammut, J. (2014). Did NAFTA Help Mexico? An Assessment After 20 years. *Center for Economic and Policy Research*. Washington DC: Center for Economic and Policy Research.

Wetzel, J. W. (1995). Global feminist zeitgeist practice. In N. Van Den Bergh (Ed.), *Feminist practice in the 21st century* (pp. 175–192). Washington, DC: NASW Press.

Wetzel, J. W. (2004). Mental health lessons from abroad. In M. C. Hokenstad & J. Midgley (Eds.), *Lessons from abroad: Adapting international social welfare innovations* (pp. 93–116). Washington, DC: NASW Press.

Wheelan, S. A. (1999). *Creating effective teams: A guide for members and leaders*. Thousand Oaks, CA: Sage.

Whelan, L. (2014). Allocating organs to those with Down syndrome: Compliance as a scapegoat. *The Bioethics Project*. Retrieved from http://blogs.kentplace.org/bioethicsproject/2014/02/10/allocating-organs-syndrome-compliance-scapegoat/

White, G. W., Gutierrez, R. T., & Seekins, T. (1996). Preventing and managing secondary conditions: A proposed role for independent living centers. *Journal of rehabilitation, 62*(3), 14–22.

Whitley, D., & Fuller-Thomson, E. (2017). African-American Solo Grandparents Raising Grandchildren: A representative profile of their health status. *Journal of Community Health, 42*(2), 312–323.

Wilkerson, P. A., & Davis, D. J. (2011). Grandparents in kindred care: Help or hindrance to family preservation? *Journal of family strengths, 2*(1). Retrieved from http://digitalcommons.library.tmc.edu/

Williams, C. (2016a). *MGMT8* (8th ed.). Boston: Cengage Learning.

Williams, C. (2016b). *Effective management* (7th ed.). Boston: Cengage Learning.

Williams, C. L. (1995). *Still a man's world: Men who do women's work*. Berkeley: University of California Press.

Wood, G. G., & Tully, C. T. (2006). *The structural approach to direct practice in social work: A social constructionist perspective* (3rd ed.). New York: Columbia.

Wolk, J.L. (1981). Are social workers politically active? *Social Work, 26*, 283–288.

Woodside, M., & McClam, T. (2014). *An introduction to human services* (8th ed.). Belmont, CA: Brooks/Cole.

World Bank. (2015). *Annual Report 2015*. Retrieved from *https://openknowledge.worldbank.org/handle/10986/22550*

World Economic Forum. (2015). *Which countries will be most affected by rising sea levels?* Retrieved from https://www.weforum.org/agenda/2015/11/which-countries-will-be-most-affected-by-rising-sea-levels/

WorldNewsDaily.com. (2003). *Utah town to become U.N.-free zone*. Retrieved from http://www.wnd.com/2003/05/18820/

Worland, G. (2016). City's oldest community center marks 100 years: Neighborhood has welcomed the world to Madison for a century. *Wisconsin State Journal, 01/17/2016*, A1.

Wyatt, S. (2009). The brotherhood: Empowering adolescent African-American males toward excellence. *Professional School Counseling, 12*(6), 463–470.

Yalom, I. D., & Leszcz, M. (2005). *The theory and practice of group psychotherapy* (5th ed.). New York: Basic Books.

Yan, M. C. (2004). Bridging the fragmented community: Revitalizing settlement houses in the global era. *Journal of community practice, 12*(1/2), 51–69.

YMCA. (2006a). Welcome to the YMCA. Retrieved from http:// www.ymca.net

YWCA. (2006b). Eliminating racism, Empowering women. Retrieved from http://www.ywca.org

Zarya, V. (2016). The percentage of female CEOs in the Fortune 500 drops to 4%. *Fortune 500*. Retrieved from http://fortune.com/2016/06/06/women-ceos-fortune-500-2016/

Zimmerman, G. M., Welsh, B. C., & Posick, C. (2015). Investigating the role of neighborhood youth organizations in preventing adolescent violent offending: Evidence from Chicago. *Journal of Quantitative Criminology, 31*, 565–593.

Glossary

Absolute poverty refers to the lack of resources necessary for well-being—most important, food and water, but also housing, sanitation, education, and health care.

Acclaim Enthusiastic public praise.

Accreditation is an official body's formal recognition that some organization has met all the standards required by the accrediting body.

Accountability is the worker's and the profession's responsibility to clients and the community to work effectively and achieve the goals that have been established.

Acculturation, the adjustment and adaptation of the individual from the culture of origin to the dominant culture.

Action system includes those people who agree to and will work together to attain a proposed macro change.

Active listening is paying full attention to the speaker, listening to understand and involves asking questions, using paraphrasing to test for accuracy, nodding to show interest, and maintaining appropriate eye contact.

Activity systems are clusters of work activities performed by designated units or departments within an organization.

Adaptation A system's capacity to adjust to surrounding environmental conditions through an ongoing process of change.

Administrative groups Various clusters of supervisors and managers organized to maintain and improve agency functioning.

Administrative theory of management is a concept from Henri Fayol who proposed five basic functions that management should fulfill. These included planning, organizing, command, coordination, and control.

Adult day services provide care for older adults who fall between independent living and skilled nursing care, and can provide programs of medical and social services for those who need structured care for some part of the day.

Advance directive is a person's formally recognized statement signed before witnesses that gives instructions for what medical alternatives should be pursued if the person becomes incapable of making such choices.

Advocacy is the act of stepping forward on behalf of the client system in order to promote fair and equitable treatment or gain needed resources.

Advocate is one who steps forward and speaks out on behalf of the client system to promote fair and equitable treatment or gain needed resources.

Affirmative action is the extensive array of policies and other efforts to correct historical imbalances in opportunities based on race and sex in work and educational settings.

Afrocentricity is a worldview focused on the culture, experiences, and history of individuals with black African ancestry.

Agenda is a list of topics to be covered at a meeting. Agenda items are usually one to a few words that alert committee members to discussion and decision topics.

Agenda-controlled is a leadership style in which the leader maintains strict order by using Robert's Rules of Order or some other structured form for running a meeting.

Aggressive communication is communication that engenders bold and dominating verbal and nonverbal behavior whereby a speaker presses his or her point of view as taking precedence above all other perspectives. An aggressive speaker considers only his or her views important and devalues what the receiver says.

Alien is anyone who is not legally a citizen of the United States.

Alienation is when a person or group does not feel a part of the larger group in a society.

American Disabilities Act (ADA) is a law designed to improve services to and remove barriers from individuals with various disabilities.

American Sign Language (ASL) is a primary means of communicating for some people with hearing impairments. It is a visual-gesturing language that has its own rules of grammar distinct from English.

Analyst/Evaluator One who determines the effectiveness of a program or agency for an organization or community.

Anomic neighborhood is one that is dysfunctional and provides little social support for residents.

Anomie is a sociological term that means a state of normlessness. It occurs when norms are weak or in conflict, leading to alienation and social instability.

Assertive communication includes verbal and non-verbal behavior that permits a speaker to get points across clearly and straightforwardly. Assertive speakers take into consideration both their own values and the values of whoever is receiving their message.

Assertiveness can be thought of as a continuum where communication and behavior can range from nonassertive to assertive to aggressive.

Assets are potential persons, groups, and resources in a community that can help it grow and prosper.

Asset mapping is an assessment of a community that emphasizes that its strengths, capabilities, and assets instead of the community's problems and weaknesses.

Assuming a pro-woman perspective is the perspective that women's diverse histories, conditions, developmental patterns, and strengths are shaped and subjugated under conditions of oppression but can be reshaped through collective work to achieve justice in relationships.

Attention is the process of noticing or becoming aware of particular stimuli.

Authoritarian leaders take control of group functioning and make decisions with little or no input from other group members.

Autism spectrum disorder (ASD) is a complex neurological and developmental disorder beginning early in life and affecting how a person acts and interacts with others, communicates, and learns. ASD affects the structure and function of the brain and nervous system.

Backstabbing is a behavior where you pretend to be nice but all the while are planning someone's demise.

Behavioral rehearsal is the act of practicing a new behavior, interaction, or manner of communication in a group setting.

Board of directors is an administrative group authorized to formulate the organization's mission, objectives, and policies, in addition to overseeing the organization's ongoing activities.

Bodegas are small grocery stores that serve as resource centers for the Hispanic community.

Botanicas are small stores located in Latino communities selling such products as Spanish-language books, records, and herbs.

Boundaries are the borders or margins that separate one system or group from other groups or from the external environment and help give it an identity.

Bourgeoisie is Marx's term for the wealthy who he believed owned the factories and businesses, and ran the government.

Broker is a social work role that links the macro client system with community resources and services such as financial, legal, educational, psychological, recreational, or health oriented.

Brokering is the linkage of clients (consumers) to needed resources.

Bulimia nervosa is a condition occurring primarily in females that is characterized by uncontrolled overeating followed by purging activities such as self-initiated vomiting and the use of diuretics, as well as excessive guilt and shame over the compulsive behavior.

Bureaucracy encompasses formal administrative structure with clearly defined boundaries, units or functions, and hierarchical relationships among the functions.

Capacity building is the ability to increase the leadership and organizational skills of local people for the purpose of strengthening their own organizations and networking capacities.

Capitalism is an economic system in which businesses are privately owned by people called **capitalists** who operate them for profit.

Capitation is a system managed care plans use to pay physicians or hospitals, in which the providers receive a fixed, predetermined sum of money to care for plan members.

Case management is the process of organizing, coordinating, and maintaining a network of needed services provided by any number of agencies, organizations, or facilities on behalf of a client with many needs.

Case manager is a social work role in which the case manager who seeks out services, plans how they might be delivered, coordinates service provision, and monitors progress on behalf of a client, usually one having ongoing multiple needs

Casual time orientation   is the perspective of people who view time as an unlimited and unending resource and tend to be patient.

Cerebral palsy   is a disability resulting from damage to the brain before, during, or shortly after birth resulting in problems with muscular coordination and speech.

Change agent system   is the individual who initiates the macro change process.

Change   is a transition or transformation from one condition or state to another. Change can be either rapid or slow, radical or conservative, evolutionary or revolutionary.

Channels of communication   are complex systems of communication whereby staff members convey and receive information.

Chindi   are ghosts in the Diné (Navajo) tribe.

Citizen participation   is the dynamic, voluntary involvement of community members to address issues and concerns affecting their community including social policies, laws, and programs.

Clarification   is making certain that what a person or group member says is understood, often this is done by asking a question about a statement.

Client system   is any individual, family, group, organization, or community that will ultimately benefit from social work intervention.

Climate of trust and openness   is a desirable goal in organizations that helps each person feel comfortable communicating honestly with each other.

Club sociales   serve as recreational settings as well as helping to link patrons to other community resources.

Coaching   is guidance from a practitioner provided to help a person or group member acquire new behaviors.

Coalitions   are alliances of individuals, groups, and organizations with similar goals that become more influential and powerful when united.

Code of Ethics   is the set of standards that guide an organization in its involvement with individuals, groups, organizations, and communities. The NASW *Code of Ethics* is the standard for social workers in the United States.

Code-switching   refers to the use of Spanish and English in the same sentence and is usually employed to emphasize a point with a particular English or Spanish word.

Coercive power   is the capability of dispensing punishments or negative reinforcement to influence other members' behavior.

Cognition   is the process of thinking.

Cognitive restructuring   is the process of identifying and evaluating one's cognitions, understanding the negative behavioral impact of certain thoughts, and learning to replace these cognitions with more realistic and adaptive thoughts.

Cognitive-behavioral theory   is a combination of components of learning theory and cognitive theory. Behavioral theory (also known as behavioral therapy) involves the practical application of learning theory principles to changing behavior. Cognitive theory emphasizes people's ability to make rational decisions and alter their behavior.

Cohesion   is the collective sum of forces affecting individuals that encourage them to remain group members.

Collectivism   *characterizes* groups and society where people are part of a cohesive entity in which they receive protection in exchange for demonstrating loyalty to the group. In collectivist societies, the society has more importance than the individual.

Committee   is a group of persons given the authority and responsibility to consider, research, act on, and report on a topic or issue.

Communication   is the exchange of information.

Community   is a number of people who have something in common that connects them in some way and distinguishes them from others.

Community building   involves the process of enhancing a community's strengths by linking community residents, organizations in the community, and external resources to tackle community problems and work together toward positive change.

Community built   means that a project is undertaken with the support and under the direction of a community neighborhood.

Community capacity development   focuses on empowering people with the knowledge and skills to work together to overcome a problem they are experiencing.

Community development   refers to efforts to mobilize people who are directly affected by a community condition into groups and organizations to enable them to take action on the social problems and issues that concern them.

Community neighborhood   is a neighborhood that includes at least 30 square blocks in area.

Compadrazco   is a Latino word for godparenting.

Compadres   are godparents. Godparents often serve as substitute parents.

Competence is the capacity to handle life challenges or to get assistance from others when needed.

Competition concerns the condition where community members struggle for control over various aspects of their environment.

Comprehensive community initiative *(CCI)* is a strategy that uses coalitions of public and private agencies, religious organizations, neighborhood groups, community leaders, and individuals to work together on neighborhood councils, task forces, planning committees, and advisory boards to identify needs in the community and develop and implement a comprehensive plan for multisystem change.

Conceptual framework is a collection of organized hypotheses, ideas, and concepts intended to describe and explain some observable occurrence, event, trend, or fact. Other terms for conceptual framework are **theoretical perspective** and theory.

Confidentiality the principle that workers should not share information provided by or about a client unless they have the client's explicit permission to do so.

Conflict is a clash or struggle between opposing forces or interests.

Conflict theories are based on the assumption that groups in society are engaged in a continuous power struggle for control of scarce resources.

Confrontation is a face-to-face encounter where people come together with opposing opinions, perspectives, or ideas to scrutinize or compare them.

Congregate and home-delivered meal services provide meals to participants either in a central location or in the person's home, where participants can get one or more nutritious meals per day.

Consciousness raising is the process of developing personal awareness and understanding of the cultural, personal, economic, and political conditions that mold people's reality. It is also the process of enhancing people's awareness of themselves, or others, or of issues in the social environment.

Consensus is the extent to which group members concur about group goals and other aspects of group interaction.

Consultation is the process of seeking out and receiving expert help from an individual, group, or organization to resolve an identified problem or address a designated issue.

Consumer is a term for those receiving services that implies greater power and choice than does the term client.

Contingency means that things depend on other things.

Contingency theory maintains that each element involved in an organization depends on other elements; therefore, there is no one perfect way to accomplish tasks or goals.

Continuing retirement communities provide a continuum of care to older adults.

Continuous improvement is an ongoing commitment to increase product and service quality by constantly assessing and improving the processes and procedures used to create those products and services.

Contracts are agreements between two people, organizations, or bodies that specify that one will provide certain services in exchange for payments from the other.

Contrast error involves placing too much emphasis on how a job candidate compares with other candidates in the pool of those who applied.

Coordinator is a social work role that brings people involved in various systems together and organizes their performance.

Coping is an adaptation to stress that people use to reduce the stressor in some manner.

Corporate violence can be defined as actual harm and/or risk of harm inflicted on consumers, workers, and the general public as a result of decisions by corporate executives or managers.

Costs include negative experiences, the expenditure of time and energy required to maintain a relationship, or the loss of rewards because of making ineffective choices. What an individual offers another in an exchange—whether energy, time, or resources—is referred to as a "cost."

Critical thinking is making a judgment about the truth inherent in a statement or the process by which we analyze an issue to formulate a conclusion.

Cultural care is a type of health care in which cultural values and beliefs enable people to maintain their well-being and health and to deal with illness, disability, and death.

Curanderismo, among Mexican Americans and other Central and South Americans, is the practice of curing physical, emotional, and folk illnesses.

Curanderos/as are healers who use a range of treatments, such as herbal remedies, inhalation, sweating, massage, incantations, and **limpieza** (a ritual cleansing).

Customer satisfaction is the condition where an organization's services meet or exceed customer expectations.

Deaf community encompasses those who embrace **deaf culture**, a unique subset of American society.

Defense mechanisms are any unconscious attempt to adjust to conditions such as anxiety, frustration, or guilt that are painful to experience.

Deinstitutionalization is the process of providing services and care for people within their own communities rather than in institutional settings.

Delegate council is a group of representatives from a series of agencies or units within a single agency.

Democratic leaders maximize member input and participation.

Demographics are characteristics of communities that include population size, composition, density, heterogeneity, and similar items.

Density is the ratio of people living within a particular physical area or space.

Determination is the desire to get the job done and includes characteristics such as initiative, persistence, dominance, and drive.

Developmental disabilities are a group of conditions due to an impairment in physical, learning, language, or behavior areas. These conditions begin during the developmental period, may impact day-to-day functioning, and usually last throughout a person's lifetime.

Developmental model *is one that espouses* a continuum of service in which people receive services based on the intensity and type of their needs.

Differentiation is a system's tendency to move from a simpler to a more complex existence.

Diffuse neighborhoods offer residents a strong sense of neighborhood identification but relatively little social interaction.

Dignidad is Latino word for a sense of inner dignity and Latinos frequently expect others to show respect (**respeto**) for that dignidad.

Discretion is the opportunity to make independent judgments and decisions concerning what one says or does.

Discrimination is the act of treating people differently based on their membership in some group rather than on their individual merit.

Distortion represents a wide range of messages that a sender may use between the extremes of lying and complete honesty.

Distributive justice refers to people's perceptions of the fairness with which rewards and other valued outcomes are distributed within the organization.

Diversity is strength is the feminist principle that stresses unity and harmony, on the one hand, and appreciation of diverse characteristics on the other.

Documented alien is one who has been granted a legal right to be in the United States. This legal right is determined by admissions policy.

Dual or **multiple relationships** occur when professionals assume two or more roles (professional and personal) at the same time or sequentially with a client such as counseling a person while also employing them. Such relationships are considered unethical by most helping professions.

Earth Charter is an international agreement that was developed to define and stress the importance of sustainability on a global basis.

Economic forces are the resources that are available, how they are distributed, and how they are spent.

Economic justice is the distribution of resources in a fair and equitable manner.

Ecosystems theory (ecological systems theory) serves as a conceptual framework to help social workers comprehend people's interaction with various systems in the macro social environment.

Educational group is a group that primarily provides information to participants.

Educator is a social worker role involving giving information and teaching skills to other systems.

Ego is the rational component of the mind that evaluates consequences and determines courses of action in a logical manner.

Emotional intelligence (EI) is the ability to do such things as understand one's feelings, have empathy for others, and regulate one's emotions to enhance one's quality of life.

Empathy is the interpersonal practice not only of *being in tune* with how another person feels but also *conveying* to that person that you understand how he or she feels.

Empowerment has several related meanings including the process of increasing personal, interpersonal, or political power so that individuals can take action to improve their lives; power sharing, the delegation of power or authority to subordinates in an organization; and the process where women come together concerning a common cause and promote human liberation. Feminist *empowerment* involves women coming together around a common cause and promoting human rights and liberation.

Enabler is a social work role that provides support, encouragement, and suggestions to members of a macro client system so that the system may complete tasks or solve problems more easily and successfully.

Energy is the natural power of active involvement between people and their environments.

Entropy is the natural tendency of a system to progress toward disorganization, depletion, and death.

Environmental justice is a state of being in which all people are treated fairly in the establishment and enforcement of environmental policies and laws.

Equifinality is the notion that there are many different means to achieve the same end.

Espiritismo, among Puerto Ricans, is the belief in spirits. Everyone is believed to have spirits of protection, and these can be increased by performing good deeds and decreasing evil.

Espiritistas are spiritist healers who communicate with spirits and can be incarnated by them.

Ethics concern principles that specify what is good and what is bad.

Ethical dilemmas problematic situations where one must make a difficult choice among two or more alternatives where ethical standards conflict.

Evaluator is a social worker role involved in determining the extent to which a program or agency is effective.

Expert power is power based on established authority or expertise in a particular domain.

Extended neighborhood is larger than an immediate neighborhood and might include several square blocks.

Face-saving is behavior that attempts to avoid being accountable for the full consequences of one's negative behavior, decisions, and performance.

Facilitator is a social work role in which the worker guides a group experience.

Familismo is the significance placed on relationships within the nuclear and extended family, including aunts, uncles, cousins, and grandparents, as well as close friends.

Field theory, initially developed by Kurt Lewin (1951), views a group as an entity moving through its immediate environment in pursuit of its goals.

Feedback is a special form of input by which a system receives information about that system's own performance.

Filial piety is a devotion to and compliance with parental and familial authority, to the point of sacrificing individual desires and ambitions.

First-impression error happens when, for whatever reason, an interviewer formulates an initial impression based on the perceptions of some variables and then refuses to change that impression.

Flexibility is the ability to adjust to changing environments or situations.

Focus groups are groups of 8 to 10 people who come together to discuss a topic in depth.

Formal groups tend to have structured representation in membership, including delegate councils, committees composed of elected representatives, and task forces appointed by administration.

Formality is a characteristic of countries that attach considerable importance to tradition, ceremony, social rules, and rank.

Formal motions in parliamentary procedure are proposed actions that a group is asked to support.

Foster care is the physical supervision and care of children in an alternative family context when the biological parents or legal guardians are unable to care for these children.

Foundations are organizations that collect private funds and distribute them for a variety of purposes.

Free form is a leadership style in which no leader emerges and group members feel free to contribute at will.

Functionalist theories emphasize a community's purpose or *function* and how that community can continue working to attain that purpose. A community must operate well enough to maintain its population, such as having enough food and other resources available.

Fundraising is the process of soliciting and raising financial resources through any of a variety of means.

Gatekeeping is the required authorization by a designated primary care physician to make all decisions about such things as tests, treatments, and the services of specialists.

Gender is the cluster of psychological, behavioral, social, cultural, physical, and emotional traits commonly linked with being a male or female.

Gender roles are culturally defined behaviors that are seen as appropriate for males and females.

Generalist practice is the application of an extensive and diverse knowledge base, professional values, and a wide range of skills to promote human well-being for individuals, families, groups, organizations, and communities.

Gentrification is the process in which more affluent people move into an area and rehabilitate its buildings to enjoy the advantages, activities, and services that available in an urban setting.

Global means involving the whole world.

Globalization is the growing economic, political, and social interconnectedness among societies throughout the world.

Goal attainment comprises what is supposed to happen through the intervention process.

Goal-directed organizations exist for some specified purpose.

Goal displacement is the substitution of a legitimate goal with another goal which the organization was not developed to address, for which resources were not allocated and which it is not known to serve.

Grant is a sum of money given to individuals or organizations to perform work in their areas of expertise.

Group is at least two individuals gathered together because of some common bond, to meet members' social and emotional needs, or to fulfill some mutual purpose.

Group activities are the happenings and actions conducted in a group.

Group cohesion is the extent to which group members feel that they belong in a group and desire to continue being members.

Group cohesiveness is the extent to which group members feel close to each other or connected as group members.

Group-directed leadership is leadership approaches that allow group members to have greater control over what happens in the group.

Growth group refers to a group aimed at expanding self-awareness, increasing potential, and maximizing optimal health and well-being of its members.

Habitats are the specific settings in which we live and work.

Halo effect is the condition where one positive or negative characteristic dominates the way that person is viewed by others.

Harmony is the practice in some cultures of getting along peacefully and not causing trouble for the family

Health maintenance organizations (HMOs) are group plans requiring monthly premiums in which participants choose a primary care physician who coordinates care; such care is usually only paid for if provided within the service network and emphasizes preventive care.

Hearing impairment is a general concept indicating a hearing loss that can range from mild to extremely severe.

Help line is an information and referral system based on telephone contact.

Hermaphrodite is a person born with both fully formed ovaries and testes.

Heterogeneity refers to the extent to which community members have diverse characteristics.

Hispanic and ***Latino****(a)* have generally been used to refer to people originating in countries in which Spanish is spoken.

Hogan, or home, is at the center of Navajo family life.

Home care services are provided by agencies that utilize teams of professionals to identify and meet the needs of older adults.

Hot seat is a leadership technique in which the leader maintains control by directing all attention to one group member (in the hot seat) while the other members watch.

Homeostasis is the tendency for a system to seek to maintain a relatively stable, constant state of balance.

Housing assistance are federal government programs that provide rental subsidies or vouchers to assist with rent, mortgage payments, and low-rent public housing, or block grants to state and local governments for developing affordable housing.

Hospice is a nonhospital facility where people having terminal illnesses can die as comfortably as possible with the best quality of life possible.

Human diversity refers to the vast array of differences among human beings, including such factors as gender, ethnicity, values, culture, spiritual/religious beliefs, sexual orientation, and both mental and physical health.

Human relations movement viewed organizations as cooperative systems and treats workers' orientations, values, and feelings as important parts of organizational dynamics and performance.

Human resources are the knowledge and abilities characterizing some people that can be used to enhance other people's quality of life.

Human rights is a concept and belief that all people, regardless of race, culture, or national origin, are entitled to basic rights and treatment.

Humility is a personal condition involving modesty and lack of arrogance.

Iatrogenic effect is an unintended and unanticipated outcome of an otherwise positive action.

Id is the primitive force operating in the unconscious arena of the brain that represents basic primitive drives such as hunger, sex, and self-preservation. It is also a place where a wizard may be found.

Immediate neighborhood is one consisting of a limited number of family units and lodgings located in a relatively small area.

Immigrants are those who leave their countries voluntarily (usually in search of better economic opportunities). The term is also used to describe a person who has been legally admitted into the United States and granted the privilege to be a permanent resident (a "green card" holder).

Immigration involves the permanent movement from one country to another.

Immigration status is a person's position in terms of legal rights and residency when entering and residing in a country that is not that person's legal country of origin.

Impact in communication is what the receivers actually comprehend.

Impact objectives specify outcomes to be achieved because of program activities. They detail the return expected on the organization's investment of time, personnel, and resources.

Importance of process is the perspective that *how* things get done is just as important as *what* gets done.

Income refers to the amount of money a person makes each year.

Indigenous worker is a community member who either volunteers or is employed to assist professionals.

Individualism is a mental set in which people see themselves first as individuals and believe that their own interests take priority.

Inflation is a general increase in prices and a corresponding fall in the purchasing value of money.

Influence is a form of power.

Informal groups are groups where participants come together simply because of mutual interests.

Informality refers to the attitudes of a country that has a casual outlook toward tradition, ceremony, social rules, and rank.

Informational justice is the perceived fairness of information used to arrive at decisions.

Information and referral service is a source of information about what community resources and services exist and helps clients connect with the appropriate assistance.

Informed consent in medical settings requires that physicians and health care staff inform an individual patient about his or her diagnosis, prognosis, and alternatives for treatment.

Ingratiation is the act of seeking acceptance and support through deliberate efforts that aren't totally honest. They include unmeant flattery, support of others' opinions you don't agree with, running errands you really don't want to do, or laughing heartily at jokes you really don't think are all that funny.

Initiator is the person or persons who call attention to an issue.

Innovation is the initiation, development, and application of new ideas and pioneering service provision for persons with developmental disabilities that may involve a totally unique combination of services depending on what an individual wishes to accomplish.

Input is the energy, information, or communication flow received by other systems.

In-service training program is a program provided by an employing agency, usually conducted by a supervisor or an outside expert, designed to help agency staff improve their effectiveness or better understand agency functioning.

Insight is an understanding of one's motivations, emotions, behaviors, and issues, and is often a primary goal of the group process.

Institutional social services are those provided by major public service systems that administer such benefits as financial assistance, housing programs, health care, or education.

Integral neighborhoods are those manifesting high levels of all three conditions: interpersonal interaction, residents' identification with the neighborhood, and social connectedness with other systems outside of the neighborhood.

Integrator/coordinator One who oversees the process of assembling different elements to form a cohesive whole, product, or process (e.g., a new agency policy) and subsequently watches over its functioning to ensure it's effective.

Integration is the process of assembling diverse groups of people, including different races, into a cohesive whole, whereby group members fit and work together.

Integrity is the solid adherence to moral and ethical principles.

Intellectual disabilities (ID) are neurodevelopmental disorders that begin in childhood and are characterized by intellectual difficulties as well as difficulties in conceptual, social, and practical areas of living.

Intelligence is cognitive ability to think critically, to solve problems, and to make decisions.

Intent is the information that the sender is trying to communicate.

Interactionists focus on how we use language, words, and symbols to create and maintain our social reality. This microlevel perspective highlights what we take for granted: the expectations, rules, and norms that we learn and practice without even noticing.

Interactions are the reciprocal behaviors and communications engaged in by group members.

Interest groups are formed because of common goals or pursuits.

Interface is the point where two systems (including individuals, families, groups, organizations, or communities) come into contact with each other, interact, or communicate.

International is a term describing the involvement of more than one nation.

International nongovernment organizations (INGO) are nonprofit agencies whose purpose is to address designated social problems and issues. It is usually funded privately through such sources as donations and grants.

International social work is international professional action and the capacity for international action by the social work profession and its members. International social work has four dimensions: internationally related domestic practice and advocacy, professional exchange, international practice, and international policy development and advocacy.

Interpersonal conflict is a controversy that occurs whenever two of more people involved in some relationship have incompatible or contradictory needs, expectations, desires, or goals.

Interpersonal interaction is the result of verbal and nonverbal communication, expressed emotions and attitudes, and behavior between or among persons.

Interpersonal justice is the degree of fairness people see in how they are treated by others in their organization.

Interpretation is the process of attaching meaning to new knowledge.

Intersectionality involves the idea that people are complex and can belong to multiple, overlapping diverse groups.

Intersex a person born has some combination of physical characteristics common to both sexes.

Intimidation is the use of threatening behavior to make other people feel like something bad might happen to them if they don't do what you want them to.

Invasion is the tendency of each new group of people coming into an area to force existing groups out.

Key informants is another needs assessment technique in which interviews are held with select community members who have extensive knowledge and understanding of the community's needs and issues.

Kin caregiving or kinship care is the provision of caregiving out of the child's home by relatives, including grandparents.

Kwanzaa is an African and Pan-African holiday celebration of family, community, and culture that takes place between December 26 and January 1st each year.

Labeling theory, developed from symbolic interactionism, indicates that no behavior is inherently bad. Rather, society determines which behaviors it considers deviant and labels them as such. Thus, when an individual is labeled as "being mentally ill" or a "criminal," these labels reposition that person from being thought of as normal to being considered deviant.

Laissez-faire leaders   assume a laid-back, nondirectional approach where the group is left to function or struggle on its own.

Latent functions   are the unintended consequences of an activity or social process that are hidden and remain unacknowledged by participants.

Leader-directed leadership   is a leadership approach that involves greater structure and control imposed by the leader.

Leadership   is the act of exerting influence on other group members to direct their behavior, activities, attitudes, or interaction.

Learning organization   is one that works to facilitate the lifelong learning and personal development of all of its employees while continually transforming itself to respond to changing demands and needs.

Learning theory   is a theoretical orientation that explains the social environment in terms of behavior, its preceding events, and its subsequent consequences.

Least restrictive environment   is the goal to have clients live where they want, enjoy maximum freedom, and make as many decisions for themselves as they can.

Legal blindness   is the condition where a person has visual acuity (sharpness of perception) of 20/200 or less in the better eye even with correction (e.g., eyeglasses or contact lenses) or has a field of vision so narrow that its widest diameter is a distance no greater than 20 degrees.

Legislative advocacy   is the process of influencing legislators to support legislation promoting specific goals.

Legitimate power   is power that one has attained because of one's position and vested authority.

Legitimacy   is having appropriate legal status and justification for existence.

Legitimation   is the condition where the external environment provides an agency with the appropriate status or authorization to perform agency functions and pursue agency goals.

LGBTQ   is an acronym that refers to lesbian women, gay men, bisexuals, transgenders, and questioning individuals.

Liberal feminism   grew out of liberalism, a theory in which women are considered equal to men and, therefore, should have equal rights.

Lines of authority   concern the specific administrative and supervisory responsibilities of supervisors involving their supervisees.

Lobbying   is the practice of seeking to influence political decisions and public policy through a variety of means.

Locality development   is an approach to community change that emphasizes broad community participation to identify goals and pursue activities to achieve them.

Machiavellianism   is a tendency to manipulate others for personal gain. Such people thrive on gaining power for power's sake.

Machismo   is a man's obligation to demonstrate strength, masculinity, dominance, and provide for and protect his family

Macro client systems   include communities, organizations, and larger groups of clientele with similar issues and problems.

Macro social environment   extends beyond the individual's interaction with immediate friends, relatives, and other individuals. It encompasses all aspects of society.

Macro system   is any system larger than a small group.

Managed care   is a health care delivery system organized to manage cost, utilization, and quality, including decisions about the need for tests, procedures, and treatments provided by health care staff.

Management   is the attainment of organizational goals in an effective and efficient manner through planning, organizing, leading, and controlling organizational resources.

Manager   in social work is one who assumes some level of administrative responsibility for a social services agency or other organizational system.

Manifest functions   are intended and recognized consequences of an activity or social process. A manifest function of education, for example, is to provide students with knowledge, skills, and cultural values.

Mapping assets   is an assessment of a community that emphasizes that community's strengths, capabilities, and assets instead of the community's problems and weaknesses.

Marginalization   is the condition of having less power and being viewed as less important than others in the society because of belonging to some group or having some characteristic (e.g., being poor).

Marianismo   is the counterpart role to machismo for Latinas, which places a high value on virginity, purity, and sacrifice for family and children.

Materialism   is the value that material things and money are extremely important, much more so than humanitarian or spiritual pursuits.

Maypole is a communication style in which the leader (e.g., a social worker) remains at the center of the group, controlling the members and paying attention to everyone separately.

Mediator is a social work role that involves solving arguments or disagreements among and between individuals (micro systems), groups (mezzo systems), organizations, or communities (both macro systems).

Metropolitan is a term used to describe communities with at least 50,000 people.

Metropolitan statistical areas are locales that have at least one urbanized area of 50,000 or more inhabitants.

Mezzo system refers to any small group.

Micropolitan statistical areas are locales with an urban core of at least 10,000 but less than 50,000 population.

Micro system is an individual.

Minority refers to groups that have limited access to power even when they represent a numerical majority.

Mission statement is a declaration of the organization's purpose that establishes broad and relatively permanent parameters within which goals are developed and specific programs designed.

Mobilizer is a social work role involving identifying and convening community people and resources and making them responsive to unmet community needs.

Modeling is the learning of behavior by observing another individual engaging in that behavior.

Multidimensional Poverty Index (MPI), developed by the United Nations Development Programme (UNDP) and the Oxford Poverty and Human Development Initiative, measures multidimensional aspects of poverty, and how they intermingle and overlap. Its indicators measure: (1) living standards (assets, floor, electricity, water, toilet, and cooking fuel), (2) education (children enrolled and years of schooling), and (3) health (child mortality and nutrition).

Multidisciplinary teams are those that include representatives from a variety of fields and with a range of backgrounds.

Muscular dystrophy This condition is a group of diseases that cause progressive weakness and loss of muscle mass. In muscular dystrophy, abnormal genes (mutations) interfere with the production of proteins needed to form healthy muscle.

Mutual aid is the act of providing support, feedback, and information within a group context.

Mutual support is encouragement, assistance, caring, and cooperation among people in communities.

Natural helpers are ordinary citizens whom other community residents consider as people with good listening and problem solving skills.

Natural helping networks are informal support systems or social networks of people willing to help out their friends and neighbors.

Naturalized citizen is an immigrant or refugee who has obtained citizenship.

Need identification describes health and social service requirements in a geographic or social area.

Needs assessment is an evaluation process aimed at estimating the relative importance of a community's needs.

Negative entropy is the process of a system toward growth and development. It is the opposite of entropy.

Negative feedback a form of input where a system receives information about shortcomings in its own performance. The system can choose to correct any deviations or mistakes and return to a more homeostatic state.

Negative functions, or dysfunctions, are the undesirable consequences of an activity or social process that inhibit a society's ability to adapt or adjust.

Negative reinforcement is the removal of a negative or aversive event or consequence that serves to increase the frequency of a behavior.

Negotiator is a social work role in which the worker is an intermediary who acts to settle disputes and/or resolve disagreements. However, unlike mediators, negotiators clearly take the side of one of the parties involved.

Neighborhood center is a community-based agency that advocates for community residents and works with them to provide a wide array of services to meet their needs; it is funded primarily through government agencies, but also through some grants and the United Way.

Neighborhood is a geographical/residential area in which people share similar values, lifestyles, and housing types, and exhibit a sense of cohesion.

Neighborhood watch organizations are voluntary groups of neighborhood residents who help each other by keeping a careful eye on each other's property for potential damaging criminal activity, and report any suspicious incidents to each other and police.

Niche is a specific social position that a person holds within the habitat's social structure. An individual's niche can be positive and supportive, or negative and isolating.

NIMBY (Not in my backyard) is the term used to describe when a neighborhood or community responds negatively to proposals to locate group homes, homeless shelters, or half-way houses in their area.

Nominal group technique is another way of assessing community needs in which group members are gathered and asked to silently write down the needs that exist in their community. This is followed up by discussion and ultimately prioritizing the list as the group reaches a consensus.

Nonassertive communication is communication from speakers who devalue themselves completely. They feel the other person and what that person thinks are much more important than their own thoughts.

Nongeographical communities provide an arena for forming relationships where a person can receive support, encouragement, praise, and information. They include professional communities, spiritual, ethnic communities and people of color and communities based on sexual orientation, among others.

Nonimmigrant is a foreign-born person who is in the United States temporarily, such as a tourist, a student or a journalist. Nonimmigrants also include temporary, or seasonal workers, who come to the United States to work during certain periods of the year and return to their countries during the rest of the year.

Noninterference is the concept that people should be able to make their own decisions without meddling from others.

Nonverbal communication is any means by which information is conveyed other than through spoken or written words.

Nonprofit social agencies are run to accomplish some service provision goal, not to make financial profit for private owners. They usually provide some type of personal social services.

Normalization is a goal in which every person, even those with the most severe disabilities, has life conditions and behavioral patterns that are as close as possible to those ordinarily experienced by others in the social and physical environment.

Norming is a stage in group development where group members reach consensus about the members' roles and appropriate group norms. It is also described as the stabilization and working phase of a group.

Norms are the collective rules and expectations held by group members regarding how they should behave in the group. They may be written or unwritten.

Nursing homes or long-term care facilities provide the largest array of care services for older adults.

Objectives are smaller, behaviorally specific sub-goals that serve as stepping stones on the way to accomplishing the main goal.

Official poverty line, or **poverty threshold,** was designed by the Social Security Administration to identify the amount of money required for a family to barely subsist.

Operant conditioning is the changing of behavior by giving reinforcements that occur immediately following the behavior.

Operational objectives convey the intent to improve the general operation of the organization.

Oppression is putting extreme limitations and constraints on some person, group, or larger system.

Organizations are structured groups of people who come together to work toward some mutual goal and perform established work activities that are divided among various units.

Organizational behavior "is the study of human behavior in the workplace, the interaction between people and the organization, and the organization itself. . . . The major goals of organizational behavior are to explain, predict, and control behavior" (Dubrin, 2007, p. 2).

Organizational culture is the set of key values, beliefs, understandings, and norms shared by members of an organization.

Organizational goals are goal statements of expected outcomes dealing with the problem that the program is attempting to prevent, eradicate, or ameliorate.

Organizational justice involves the perceptions of people in an organization regarding fairness; organizational justice can be divided into four types—distributive, procedural, interpersonal, and informational justice.

Organizational politics are attempts by individuals to influence the behavior of others as a means to protect their self-interests, meet their own needs, and advance their own goals.

Organizational structure is the set of formal tasks assigned to individuals; formal reporting relationships including lines of authority, decision responsibility, number of hierarchical levels, and span of manager's control; and the design of systems to ensure effective co-ordination of employees across departments.

Organizational theories   are ways to conceptualize and understand how organizations function by identifying specific concepts and explaining how these concepts relate to each other.

Output   is what happens to input after it's gone through and been processed by some system.

Paraprofessional   is a person with specialized skills and training who assists a professional in conducting his or her work.

Parkinson's disease   is a chronic, progressive disorder that may produce tremors in various part of the body, muscular rigidity, slowed movement, and balance and coordination impairments.

Parliamentary procedure   is a highly structured technique designed to make decisions and conduct business.

Parochial neighborhood   is one high on interaction and identification but low on community connections.

Parole officers   supervise criminal offenders who have been released on the likelihood of good behavior; the officers' goal is to avert future criminal activity.

Passive-aggressiveness   is another form of aggressiveness, where an individual is aggressive, but only secretly or covertly so.

Path-goal theory   is an organizational/leadership theory that states that leaders can increase subordinate satisfaction and performance by clarifying and clearing the paths to goals and by increasing the number and kinds of rewards available for goal attainment.

Pattern maintenance   is what a group does when it adheres to its basic processes and procedures.

Perception   is the process by which individuals attend to, organize, interpret, and retain information from their environments.

Performing   is a phase of the group where the focus is on completing tasks.

Personal as political   is the view that individual and collective pain and problems of living always have a cultural and/or political dimension.

Person-in-environment fit   is the extent to which a person or group has the resources to survive and flourish within the environment.

Personal empowerment   is when people feel they can directly control what's happening in their own lives.

Personalismo   is a Latino attitude that recognizes the worth and dignity of others based simply on their humanity.

Personal social services   address more individualized needs involving interpersonal relationships and people's ability to function within their immediate environments.

Planned change   is a seven-step process of developing and implementing a strategy; the goal of which is to improve or alter a behavior pattern, condition, or situation so that it enhances the well-being of the client.

Point-of-service (POS)   are health plans that allow participants to choose between an HMO and PPO each time health services are needed (MedlinePlus, 2017).

Policy advocacy   is "policy practice that aims to help relatively powerless groups, such as women, children, poor people, African Americans, Asian Americans, Latinos, Native Americans, gay men and lesbians, and people with disabilities improve their resources and opportunities" (Jansson, 2012, p. 1).

Political forces   are the current governmental structures, the laws to which people are subject, and the overall distribution of power among the population.

Policy advocacy   aims to help groups with little or no power to enhance and improve their lives through the creation or revision of social policies.

Policy practice   entails efforts to change policies in legislative, agency, and community settings by establishing new policies, improving existing ones, or defeating the policy initiatives of other people (Jansson, 2014).

Political action organization   is an organization that raises money privately to influence legislation, elect political candidates, and promote issues of interest to their contributors. Also known as a **political action committee** (PAC).

Political diagnosis   is an assessment of the location of power in an organization and the type of political behavior that is likely to happen identifying "politically active individuals and coalitions in the organization, the amount of power they have, and the likely ways they will use their power."

Political-economy theory   emphasizes how organizations must adapt to their external environments, stressing the effects of resources and power.

Political power   is the ability to influence entities that make decisions concerning the organization's ability to function.

Population size   is the total number of persons living in a designated community or geographical area.

Populations-at-risk are populations or groups of people who share some identifiable characteristic that places them at greater risk of social and economic deprivation and oppression than the general mainstream of society.

Positive feedback is the informational input a system receives about what it is doing correctly in order to maintain itself and thrive.

Positive functions are purposeful dynamics that serve to sustain people in the community context.

Positive reinforcement is the positive event or consequences that follow a behavior and act to strengthen or increase the likelihood that the behavior will be repeated in the future.

Postmodern feminism stresses women's experiences in cultural and historical contexts to account for differences among women based on socio-cultural attributes. Gender is viewed as a continuum rather than two separate states.

Posttraumatic stress disorder (PTSD) is a disorder that develops in some people who have experienced a shocking, scary, or dangerous event

Poverty line or poverty threshold is the minimal annual cash income level established by the federal government, which is based on family size, that determines whether people are living in poverty.

Poverty is the lack of money or material goods available to other members of a society.

Power is the potential or actual ability to move people on a chosen course to produce an effect or achieve some goal.

Power from is power that protects us from the power of others. May also be called **resistance**.

Power over is power used to make another person act in a certain way; it may be called **dominance.**

Power to is power that gives others the means to act more freely themselves; it is sometimes called *empowerment.*

Preferred provider organizations (PPOs) are groups of hospitals and health care providers who have contracted with a managed care plan to provide services to plan members in exchange for negotiated fees and co-payments made by the member.

Primary settings are those agencies or organizations where social work is the main or primary profession employed.

Private social agencies are privately owned and run by people not directly employed by some level of government.

Privilege describes the special rights or benefits enjoyed because of elevated social, political, or economic status.

Problem solving refers to the steps followed to resolve some difficulty.

Procedural justice involves people's perceptions of the fairness of an organization's procedures and processes as well as how the organization carries out tasks and achieves goals

Product objectives are designed to provide a tangible outcome to benefit a target population or a community.

Production-distribution-consumption relates to local participation in producing, distributing, and consuming those goods and services that are a part of daily living and access to which is desirable in the immediate locality.

Projection is the tendency for people to see their own traits in other people.

Proletariat is a Marxist term for workers who live in poverty and earn low wages, and whom the bourgeoisie exploit for profit.

Proprietary, or **for-profit, social agencies** provide some designated social services, often quite like those provided by private social agencies, but with the goal of making a profit for its owners.

Protection is a dimension of resiliency that concerns those factors that moderate against the threat from risk.

Pro-woman perspective is concerned with such things as the experiences, development, resiliency, strengths, and histories of women.

Psychoanalytic theory emphasizes the impact of early life experiences on current feelings and behavior.

Psychosomatic disorders are physical symptoms caused by emotional problems.

Public forum is a data gathering method in which an open event is held where all community residents are invited and encouraged to attend. Any community member may serve as a significant source of information.

Punishment is the presentation of an aversive event or the removal of a positive reinforcer that results in a decrease in frequency or elimination of a behavior.

Purchase-of-service involves a financial agreement or contract where one agency, often a public agency, agrees to purchase services from another agency.

Relatedness is the ability to connect to other people, groups, or organizations.

Quality assurance is a technique used to assess "organizational processes and systems" (as opposed to organizational outcomes or goals) to make certain these processes and systems meet expected standards.

Quality circle is a group of 6 to 12 volunteer employees who meet regularly to discuss and solve problems affecting the quality of their work.

Radical feminism views women as an oppressed class and emphasizes how male domination influences every area of society.

Referent power a type of power held by a person because of other group members' respect and high esteem for that individual.

Refugees is a term used to describe people who are forced out of their countries because of human rights violations against them. Refugees are also sometimes referred to, or refer to themselves, as **exiles** or **émigrés**.

Reinforcement is a procedure or consequence that increases the frequency of the behavior immediately preceding it.

Relationship is the dynamic interpersonal connection between and among group members.

Relationship management is the ability to work well with others, which is dependent on the other Emotional Intelligence components.

Relationship-related leadership is a leadership approach that stresses the importance of interaction, communication, cooperation, and group members' satisfaction.

Relative poverty refers to the lack of material and economic resources compared with some other population.

Religion is a set of beliefs and practices of an organized religious institution. It is important to note that *religion* is one form of spirituality.

Rephrasing is stating what another person says, but using different words than those used by that person.

Research-informed practice is a term in social work to describe the use of practice approaches and interventions that research has determined are effective.

Resiliency is the ability of any size system, including a community, to recover from adversity and resume functioning even when suffering serious trouble, confusion, or hardship.

Respite services are designed to help achieve two major goals. The first goal is to provide care for older adults at such times as the main caregiver is not available. The second is to give caregivers for older adults a respite or break from their responsibilities.

Respondent conditioning refers to the elicitation of behavior in response to a specific stimulus.

Retention is the process of remembering interpreted information. Retention affects what we recall and commit to memory after we have perceived something.

Reward power is a form of power based on the ability of a person to provide positive reinforcement or rewards to others.

Rewards are the pleasures, fulfillment, enjoyment, and other positive emotions a person experiences when involved in a relationship.

Risk is a dimension of resiliency that involves stressful events or environmental conditions that affect individuals' ability to protect or defend themselves.

Robert's Rules of Order is a book about parliamentary procedure that provide guidance for running meetings with highly structured techniques such as motions and voting procedures.

Role is a culturally expected behavior pattern for a person having a specified status or being involved in a designated social relationship.

Round robin is a communication style in which the leader maintains control but each group member takes turns speaking.

Rural communities are communities that have traditionally been characterized as having 2,500 residents or less.

Santeria, among Cuban Americans, are practices that combine African deities with Catholic saints.

Santeroslas are priests who function as healers, diviners, and directors of rituals.

Scientific management is a concept introduced by Frederick W. Taylor characterized by standardized and planned tasks and cooperation between workers and management.

Secondary settings are agencies or organizations characterized by the presence of a variety of professional staff in addition to social workers.

Segregation, the opposite of integration, is separating a group of people based on race, class, ethnic group, or other characteristic from the general population in society. The term is also used to describe the detachment or isolation of some group having certain common characteristics, such as race, ethnicity, or religion, through social pressure, restrictive laws, or personal choice.

Self-awareness is the ability to perceive one's own emotions and how they affect one's behavior.

Self-concept   refers to a person's overall positive or negative feelings about him- or herself.

Self-confidence   is a description of the personal condition of having a positive self-concept and the belief in one's ability to get things accomplished.

Self-determination   is every person's right to make his or her own decisions.

Self-direction   involves people's feeling or belief that they have a degree of control over their lives and hold themselves accountable for their own behaviors.

Self-disclosure   is the sharing of personal feelings and information with others.

Self-esteem   involves the degree to which individuals feel they are inherently worthwhile and important.

Self-management   refers to the ability to control troublesome emotions both in oneself and in others.

Self-promotion   is the act of describing oneself in an unwarranted and overly positive manner.

Senior centers   are facilities that provide opportunities for older adults to spend time with their peers and engage in educational and/or physical/relaxational activities as well as social stimulation.

Sentiments   describe the emotions and reactions manifested by group members.

Servant leadership   is a leadership style based on simultaneously meeting the needs and goals of employees while meeting the goals of the organization. Servant leaders lead from positions of moral influence, not power, and are very follower-centered.

Service objectives   are the organization's tally of activities provided or services rendered. Some-times these are referred to as **activity or process objectives**.

Settlement houses   were historically operated in communities and run in part by client groups, and they emphasized social reform rather than relief or assistance. They worked to improve housing conditions, organized protests, offered job training and labor searches, supported organized labor, worked against child labor, and fought against corrupt politicians.

Sexual orientation   is an inherent sexual and romantic attraction to persons of one or both genders. Using the term **sexual preference** is an inappropriate term for this.

Sheltered workshops or sheltered employment   provide programs involving work in a safe, closely supervised environment for people who have trouble functioning more independently.

Similarity error   happens when interviewers place too much importance on the similarities and differences between themselves and the interviewees.

Sociability   is the tendency to search out others and form congenial social relationships.

Social action   is coordinated effort to advocate for change in a social institution to benefit a specific population (e.g., homeless people), solve a social problem, enhance people's well-being, or correct unfairness (e.g., racism).

Social action group   is a group formed to engage in some planned change effort to shift power and resources to modify or improve aspects of the macro social, economic or physical environment.

Social advocacy   is the application of pressure upon people and institutions that are the cause of a problem or stand in the way of its solution.

Social agency, or social services agency,   is an organization providing social services that typically employs a range of professionals, including social workers, office staff, paraprofessionals (persons trained to assist professionals), and sometimes volunteers.

Social awareness   is the ability to understand others.

Social class   is the ranking of people in society based on their wealth, power, and family background. Indicators of social class usually include job type, educational level, amount of income, and typical lifestyle.

Social control   is the process through which a group influences the behavior of its members toward conformity with its norms.

Social development   is a planned change process on behalf of an entire population that emphasizes economic development that integrates social and economic policy, and sponsors investment-oriented social programs that contribute positively to economic development.

Social disorganization   is the breakdown of social structure, so that its various parts no longer work together as smoothly as they should.

Social empowerment   is the condition in the social environment where people have access to opportunities and resources to make personal choices and maintain some control over their environment.

Social environment   is the sum total of social and cultural conditions, circumstances, and human interactions that encompass human beings.

Social entities   are organizations made up of people, with all their strengths and failings.

Social exchange at its most basic level refers to interpersonal interaction, which involves both rewards and costs. Social exchange theory suggests that individual group members continue in the group because they receive social rewards for group membership.

Social exchange theory is an approach that stresses the importance of the individual within the group context. It views the group as the place where social exchange takes place.

Socialist feminism grew out of Marxist economic theories and is concerned with economic aspects of women's lives.

Social forces are values and beliefs held by people in the social environment that are strong enough to influence their activities, including how government is structured or restricted.

Social indicators is another means of assessing a community's needs. It involves gathering information such as demographic characteristics, health and education statistics, socioeconomic variables, employment patterns, and family patterns.

Social institution is an established and valued practice or means of operation in a society resulting in the development of a formalized system to carry out its purpose. Examples of social institutions are families, the military, religion, education, social welfare systems, and government.

Socialization is a process by which society or a constituent social unit transmits prevailing knowledge, values, and behavior patterns to its members.

Socialization group is a group that helps participants improve members' interpersonal behavior, communication, and social skills so that they might better fit into their social environment.

Socialization is the process by which a group or society conveys its knowledge, values, beliefs, and expectations to its members.

Social justice is the philosophical perspective that all people have the right to enjoy equal opportunities in economic, political, and social realms.

Social participation is the involvement of citizens in social, political, and economic processes.

Social planning involves "a technical process of problem-solving with regard to substantive social problems, such as delinquency, housing, and mental health."

Social (positive) reinforcement by a group leader or other group members in the form of praise, approval,

support, and attention can also be powerful in changing cognition and behavior.

Social problems are conditions in a society that many people believe should be changed.

Social services include the work that social work practitioners and other helping professionals perform in organizations for the benefit of clients.

Social support network is a term used to describe individuals or groups who share a connection with others and who provide support to one another in times of need.

Social-psychological theories emphasize the importance of how community members feel about themselves and how they interact with others.

Social welfare in the broadest sense is the entire system of services, benefits, and programs designed to help people sustain themselves and their families.

Spirituality concerns people's values, beliefs, mission, awareness, subjectivity, experience, sense of purpose and direction, and a kind of striving toward something greater than oneself. It also encompasses a search for purpose and meaning in life, a sense of being connected with self, others, and the universe, and an ability to transcend our immediate experience to something larger known by many to be a Higher Power beyond human power.

Staff development group is a group formed to improve, update, and refine workers' skills, the goal being improved services to clients.

Status is the relative rank assigned to members within the group.

Stepping-stone is a type of neighborhood characterized by the temporary nature of residents.

Stereotype is a fixed mental picture of a member of some specified group based on some attribute or attributes that reflect an overly simplified view of that group, without consideration or appreciation of individual differences.

Storming is a phase in a group where conflict occurs, a characteristic that applies to both the beginning phase of a group and the assessment stage.

Stress is the resulting physiological and/or emotional tension produced by a stressor that affects a person's internal balance.

Stressor is any situation or event that places a demand on the individual resulting in some degree of physiological and/or emotional tension, in other words, stress.

Structural theories   look at how communities are organized, how components relate to each other and usually take into account a political perspective, geographical organization, and the power structure.

Subsystem   a subsystem is any subordinate or secondary systems within the group system.

Succession   is the replacement of the original occupants of a community or neighborhood by new groups.

Superego   in psychodynamic theory is the conscience, which decides what actions and behaviors are right and wrong.

Supervision   is the process by which a designated supervisor watches over and evaluates a worker's performance, directs and coordinates activities, and provides feedback. The supervisor has multiple functions including administrative, educational, and problem solving.

Supplication   is behavior that suggests the need for help even though help is not really needed.

Support group   is a group of participants with common issues or problems who meet on an ongoing basis to cope with stress, give each other suggestions, provide encouragement, convey information, and furnish emotional support.

Supportive housing   is a living arrangement where older adults who can live independently reside in a retirement community.

Sustainability   in a global community context involves meeting current needs without jeopardizing the well-being of future generations.

Symbolic interactionist theories   emphasize using a microlevel analysis of how people act toward one another and how they make sense of their lives. The symbolic interactionist perspective views society as the sum of the interactions of individuals and groups.

System   is a set of related elements that are orderly, interrelated, and a functional whole.

Target of change (or *target system*)   the system that social workers need to change or influence in order to accomplish goals.

Target system   is the system that social workers must change or influence in order to accomplish their goals.

Task force   is a team or committee, often made up of representatives from different units within an organizational or community context, who come together on a temporary basis to serve some designated purpose or achieve a particular goal.

Task groups   are collections of people that apply the principles of group dynamics to solve problems, develop innovative ideas, formulate plans, and achieve goals within the context of an organization or a community. Also called **work group**.

Task-related leadership   is a style of leadership hat focus more on adherence to procedures and goal accomplishment.

Team   is a group of two or more people gathered together to work collaboratively and interdependently with each other to pursue a designated purpose.

Theory X and Theory Y   Theory X reflects aspects of classical scientific management in its focus on hierarchical structure, providing a contrasting approach to Theory Y, which focuses on human relations.

Therapy group   is a group that helps members with serious psychological and emotional problems change their behavior.

Third-party payments   are reimbursements to service providers from government agencies or insurance companies.

Time orientation   is a reference to whether individuals and nations attach importance to time. Some see time as a scarce resource and limited while others see it as unlimited and unending. A time orientation may be seen as a continuum with an urgent time orientation on one end and a casual time orientation on the other.

Total quality management (TQM)   is an approach to management with three core principles: focus on customer needs and satisfaction; continuous improvement in service or product; and teamwork.

Transgenderism, or *transgender identity,*   including "people whose appearance and/or behaviors do not conform to traditional gender roles" (Crooks & Baur, 2014, p. 129).

Transitory neighborhoods   resemble steppingstone neighborhoods in terms of the transitory nature of residents. However, residents in such neighborhoods have much less access to resources and are probably not moving up in the world.

Treatment conference   is a group that meets to establish, monitor, and coordinate service plans on the behalf of a client system.

Treatment groups   help individuals solve personal problems, change unwanted behaviors, cope with stress, and improve group members' quality of life.

Trust   is confidence in another individual's intentions, motives and sincerity of that person's word.

Trustworthiness   is a personal characteristic that inspires confidence and belief by others in one's honesty and dependability.

Undocumented alien   is one who does not have a legal right to be in the United States. These people are also sometimes referred to as **illegal immigrants.** They are also referred to as **deportable aliens**, because if discovered by immigration authorities, they are subject to deportation, or forcible return to their countries of origin.

United Way   is an international alliance of 1,800 local organizations that raises funds for allocation to various social service organizations and other projects; goals include enhancing education, attaining financial stability, and promoting healthy lives.

Unity in diversity (diversity is strength)   is the view that aspects of diversity should be appreciated as strengths and used to establish unity.

Urban   communities are usually composed of many smaller neighborhoods, communities, and even smaller cities enveloping a central nucleus of social, business, and political activity.

Urban social work   is practice within the context of heavily populated communities, with their vast array of social problems, exceptional diversity, and potential range of resources.

Urgent time orientation   applies to people who perceive time as a scarce resource and tend to be impatient.

Using a gender filter   is viewing the world with women and their issues becoming the focus of attention.

Utilization management   is the term used to describe situations when a health provider must receive approval from a utilization manager who assesses whether the care is medically necessary and appropriate to the patient's needs.

Valences   are forces that push one toward or pull one away from involvement and participation.

Validation   is the process of accepting a person and a person's actions as justifiable and relevant.

Values   involve what you do and do not consider important.

Virtual team   is a small group of people who conduct almost all of their collaborative work by electronic communication rather than in face-to-face meetings.

Visual impairment   is difficulty in perception compared to the norm that is experienced through sight.

Wealth   is the total value of that person's assets: real estate and personal property, stocks, bonds, cash, and so forth.

World Bank   is the short name for the International Bank for Reconstruction and Development. Headquartered in Washington, D.C. It has branches around the world that make loans and provides consultation to countries that have low per capita incomes and lack resources.

Name Index

Subject Index

Physical therapy, 125n3
Pilloried, 439
Planned change process, 28, 29, 136, 337
Planned Parenthood agencies, 2n1
"Planning and policy practice", 36
Planning step, 29
Point-of-service (POS), 195
Policies and power, 349
Policy advocacy, 37
Policy Change for Human Well-Being, 428
Policy practice, 36
Political action committee (PAC), 443, 444
Political Action for Candidate Endorsement
 (PACE), 444
Political action organization, 440
 empowering LGBTQ people by, 443
Political advocacy, 481
Political and civil rights, 492
Political behavior, 234
Political capacity model, 412
Political diagnosis, 236
Political forces, 10, 11
Political ideology, 50
Political network, 237
Political perspective, 311
Political power, 158
Political-economy theory, 150, 158–159
Politics
 in communities, 359
 in organizations, 231–234
Popularity fallacy, 34
Population, trends in rural areas, 331–332
Population size, 329, 362
Populations-at-risk, 62
Positive connectedness, 507
Positive feedback, 15, 163
Positive forces, 72
"Positive freedoms", 492
Positive functions, 313, 315
Positive reinforcement, 75
Positive social functions, 313–314
Positive transaction, 18
Positive verbal communication, 91
Postmodern feminism, 86
Posttraumatic stress disorder (PTSD), 286
Potential ability, 349
Poverty, 62, 63, 429, 491–495
 crisis of global poverty, 495
 definition of, 492–493
 global, 494–495
 problems related to, 495

and social injustice, 63
 widening gap in United States, 493–494
Poverty line/threshold, 190, 492
Power, 62, 72, 83–84, 98–99, 159, 231, 269, 315, 316,
 318, 355
 in formal structure, 210
 leadership and, 100
 people and power in communities, 349–352
 sources in groups, 98
 types, 231–232
 of youth, 352–353
Power from, 98
Power over, 98
Power structure, 311–312
Power to, 98
Power-oriented managers, 234
Practice settings, ethical responsibilities in, 45
Practice-based research, 34
Practice-informed research, 34
Pratt-Smoot Act, 474
Preferred provider organization (PPO), 195
Prenatal care, 449
Price inflation, 495
Pride, work, 261
Primary settings, 171
Private social agencies, 148
Privilege, 62
Pro-woman perspective, 86, 449
Problem solving, 29
Problematic behavior, 77
Procedural justice, 235
Process, 88–89
 objectives, 175
 supersedes progress, 180
 vagueness of, 256–257
Producer cooperatives, 376
Product objectives, 176
Production-distribution-consumption function,
 499–500
Professional communities, 324–325
Professional ethics, 43
 application of, 43–44
Professional identity and professional roles, 391
Professional skill, 124
Professional values, 43
 adherence to, 43–44
Professionals, ethical responsibilities to, 46–47
Projection, 218
Proletariat, 316, 318
Promoting group functioning, 106
Promotora approach, 435